AMPHIBIOUS WARFARE 1000-1700

1 : 10 - 45
2 : 50 - 67
4 : 357 - 413
   233 - 242

Imama Quli Khan's soldiers fighting the Portuguese at Ormuz (MS in British Library)

AMPHIBIOUS WARFARE 1000-1700

Commerce, State Formation and European Expansion

EDITED BY

D.J.B. TRIM AND MARK CHARLES FISSEL

BRILL

LEIDEN · BOSTON

2011

This book is printed on acid-free paper.

Library of Congress Control Number: 2006275543

This paperback was originally published in hardback under ISBN 978 90 04 13244 3 as volume 34 in the series *History of Warfare*.

ISBN 978 90 04 20594 9

To Jodi
and
Wendy
with love

CONTENTS

PREFACE AND ACKNOWLEDGEMENTS

The essays that follow were assembled because of the editors' mutual belief that amphibious operations were of profound importance in the medieval and early-modern world because they affected both attempts at projecting power and the commercial intercourse on which state development was founded. These essays investigate such matters as European expansion, commerce and absolutism, as well as the conduct of military operations, so that the volume engages with issues which are usually considered by specialists in economic history, political science, international relations, and global studies/world history. The theme of combined operations as practised by European powers provides a natural unifying *motif* but the danger with a volume that touches bases with so many issues is that its contents will be too disparate. In the case of *Amphibious Warfare*, however, all the contributors are not only aware of each other's topics, but have read synopses and/or complete drafts of the essays others are producing. In addition, the majority have gathered twice in informal conferences—the first at Harris Manchester College, Oxford, the second at Newbold College in Berkshire—at which the general theme and the issues to be raised have been discussed, along with how best to treat these in their personal contributions. We are greatly obliged to those contributors who attended these meetings.

We are additionally grateful to the contributors for providing such stimulating essays (generally in timely fashion); for their cheerful cooperation over a prolonged period in working to refine and enhance their contributions; for helping with the creation of an impressive collection of maps; and for providing striking (and mostly previously unpublished) illustrations. We single out from our resolute band only one: the late R. B. (Bruce) Wernham, whose final work of scholarship appears here. The pioneering work of this indefatigable archival historian has greatly inspired both editors. He trained Mark Fissel's dissertation supervisor, T. G. Barnes, and delivered the Una's Lectures at Berkeley in 1978, which provided occasion for Fissel to make his acquaintance. David Trim visited Bruce in his Hampshire home several times in the years immediately preceding his passing, during which they discussed, *inter alia*, themes that appear in this book. Trim is working with Patrick Williams of the University of Portsmouth on editing a *festschrift* in Wernham's memory.[1]

We have greatly appreciated the encouragement and practical support of Julian Deahl and Marcella Mulder at Brill, especially when the volume became significantly overdue as a result of David Trim's ongoing debilitating illness. We thank Lynne Miles-Morillo for her work as copy editor; J. P. M. van der Avert for his help in preparing the map of Scandinavia and the Sound; and Matthew Jennings and Randle Berlin for their invaluable assistance with all the maps. We are greatly obliged to Ralph Waller, Principal of Harris Manchester College Oxford and Andrea Luxton, formerly Principal of Newbold College, for their generous provision of hospitality for the meetings of contributors in 1997 and 2001. Mark Fissel, John Guilmartin and John Stapleton participated in a session on amphibious warfare in the early-modern world at the Society for Military History conference in Charleston, S.C., February 2005, together with Mark H. Danley and John A. Lynn, whose contributions were much appreciated.

Material from the papers of Admiral Sir Bertram Ramsay, held in the Churchill Archives Centre, Churchill College, Cambridge, is quoted by kind permission of Major General Charles Ramsay. Map 12 is reprinted from John F. Guilmartin, Jr, *Gunpowder and Galleys* (Cambridge: 1974), p. 182, by kind permission of the author and the Syndics of Cambridge University Press. Maps 1, 9 and 10 have been adapted from maps 4 and 8 in R. B. Wernham, *After the Armada* (Oxford: 1984) and maps 5 and 6 in his *The Return of the Armadas* (Oxford: 1994), with the permission of the author and Oxford University Press. We are grateful to several institutions for kind permission to reproduce as illustrations material to which they hold copyright, as follows: the British Library, the frontispiece and figures 5, 10–12 and 20; the Patrimonio Nacional (Spain), figures 6 and 7; Biblioteca Nacional, Madrid, figure 8; The National Archives (UK), figure 9; Hargrett Rare Book and Manuscript Library, University of Georgia Libraries, figures 15 and 16: the Bibliothèque Nationale de France, figures 17 and 19; and Universiteitsbibliotheek Leiden (Leiden University Library), figures 21–26 and 28.

---

[1] For a memoir of Prof. Wernham see G. W. Bernard, 'Richard Bruce Wernham (1906–1999)', *Proceeding of the British Academy*, 124 (2004), 375–96.

Additionally, Mark Fissel would like to thank a gallant band of historians who have welcomed him into their scholarly Sherwood Forest: Wayne Mixon, Wendy Turner, "Cowboy Mike" Searles, Hubert P. van Tuyll van Serooskerken, Christopher Murphy, and Michael Bishku. David Trim thanks Lynda Baildam and other staff at the Newbold Library, who maintain consistently high standards of friendly and helpful service in the face of constant pressures; the staff at Duke Humphrey's at the Bodleian Library, for their courteous assistance; and the School of History at the University of Reading, which arranged access, through the University Library, to on-line collections of primary and secondary sources that were essential to completion of chapters 1, 11 and 12. He is also deeply grateful to Mark Fissel, for his labours in preparing the maps and illustrations, which went beyond what might be expected of even an assiduous co-editor, and for his affirming support during chronic illness.

Finally, the editors count themselves fortunate in that they married historians. They therefore ask their long-suffering wives, Jodi Lynn Noles Fissel and Winifred Blair Johnson Trim to accept the dedication of this book with love and gratitude.

MCF
DJBT
Augusta, Ga. and Reading, Berks.
May 2005

LIST OF MAPS*

1. Europe, Eastern Atlantic and the Azores (adapted from R. B. Wernham, *After the Armada: Elizabethan England and the Struggle for Western Europe 1588–1595* (Oxford: 1984), p. 234; and idem, *The Return of the Armadas: The Last Years of the Elizabethan War against Spain 1595–1603* (Oxford: 1994), p. 170; both © Oxford University Press)
2. Western Mediterranean 1000–1700
3. The Eastern Mediterranean and the Black Sea, 1000–1700
4. The Narrow Seas and their Littoral: the English Channel, Bristol Channel, part of the North Sea (modern coastlines)
5. Scandinavia and The Sound 1360–1700
6. Holland and Zealand in the Sixteenth Century
7. Indian Ocean 1500–1700
8. The Baltic, 1360–1700
9. Western Atlantic and the Caribbean; inset of Puerto Rico and San Juan (adapted from R. B. Wernham, *After the Armada*, p. 234, and idem, *The Return of the Armadas*, p. 250; both © Oxford University Press).
10. Brittany and its environs (1590–1700) (adapted from R. B. Wernham, *After the Armada*, p. 400; © Oxford University Press)
11. Ireland 1550–1690
12. The Siege of Malta, 1565 (reproduced from J. F. Guilmartin, Jr, *Gunpowder and Galleys: Changing Technology and Mediterranean Warfare at Sea in the Sixteenth Century* (Cambridge: 1974), p. 182; © Cambridge University Press)

---

* Maps 1–11 are on pp. xxv–xxxv. Map 12 is on p. 148.

LIST OF ILLUSTRATIONS*

Frontispiece. 'Imama Quli Khan's soldiers fighting the Portuguese at Ormuz' (MS in British Library).

1. Christian III's attack on Copenhagen, 1536 (woodcut from Hermann Hamelmann *Oldenburgisch Chronicon, das ist, Beschreibung der löblichen vhralten Grafen zu Oldenburg vnd Delmenhorst* [Oldenburg: 1599]).
2. The fleet of Pedro Álvares Cabral, 1500 (from *Memória das Armadas* [*c.* 1568], Academia das Ciéncias de Lisboa).
3. Portuguese ships entering the Bab El-Mandeb (from the *Roteiro . . . do Mar Roxo*, by Dom João de Castro, MS in University of Coimbra Library).
4. A Portuguese *nau do alto bordo* (carrack) (detail from 'The Fall of Icarus' [*c.* 1555], by Pieter Brueghel, Musées Royaux des Beaux-Arts de Belgique, Brussels).
5. Portuguese *naus* before al-Suk, Socotra. 'Tavoa da aguada do Xeque' (from the *Roteiro . . . do Mar Roxo*, by Dom João de Castro, MS in British Library).
6. The Spanish landing in the Azores, 1583, fresco from the *Sala de Batallas*, El Escorial Palace (Patrimonio Nacional, Madrid).
7. As previous: detail of landing craft.
8. Spanish troop barges towed by longboats upon river in Low Countries, *c.* 1580s (Biblioteca Nacional, Madrid, MS Res 210/272).
9. The waterways of Northern Ireland in the late Elizabethan-early Stuart period (The National Archives, Kew, MPF 312, f. 276).
10. English troops crossing the River Erne, 10 October 1592 (British Library, Cottonian MS, Augustus I/ii, f. 38).
11. Siege of Enniskillen castle, February 1594, panorama (British Library, Cottonian MS Augustus I/ii, f. 39).
12. As previous: detail of three amphibious assault craft.
13. The passage of the Dutch army across the Scheldt, 21 June 1600 (plate in Jan Janszoon Orlers, *Den Nassauschen Lauren-crans* (Leyden: 1610), between pp. 148–9).

---

* The illustrations can be found between pages 420 and 421.

LIST OF CONTRIBUTORS

Matthew Bennett, a Fellow of the Royal Historical Society, is Senior Lecturer at the Royal Military Academy Sandhurst. In addition to many papers on medieval and military history, he is also the author of *Agincourt, 1415* (George Philip, 1991), *Campaigns of the Norman Conquest* (Osprey, 2001) and *Castles and Crusaders: Medieval Frontier Warfare* (Cassell, forthcoming), and co-edited *The Cambridge Illustrated Atlas of Warfare: The Middle Ages, 732–1487* (Cambridge University Press, 1996) and *The Hutchinson Dictionary of Ancient and Medieval Warfare* (Helicon, 1998).

Mark Charles Fissel has held professorships in history at universities in the United States, been a Fulbright Senior Lecturer in Istanbul, Turkey, the Dean of Harris Manchester College, Oxford, and currently teaches at the historic Augusta Arsenal (Georgia, USA). His publications include *War and Government in Britain, 1598–1650* (Manchester University Press, 1991), *The Bishops' Wars: Charles I's Campaigns against Scotland, 1638–1640* (Cambridge University Press, 1994) and *English Warfare, 1511–1642* (Routledge, 2001). Professor Fissel is a Fellow of the Royal Historical Society.

Jan Glete is Professor of History at Stockholm University, Sweden. He has published several studies of nineteenth- and twentieth-century Swedish industrial and financial history, as well as studies of Swedish naval and military history from the sixteenth to the twentieth centuries. In English he has published *Navies and Nations: Warships, Navies and State Building in Europe and America, 1500–1860* (Almqvist & Wiksell, 1993), *Warfare at Sea, 1500–1650: Maritime Conflicts and the Transformation of Europe* (Routledge, 2000) and *War and the State in Early Modern Europe: Spain, the Dutch Republic and Sweden as Fiscal-Military States, 1500–1660* (Routledge, 2002).

John F. Guilmartin, Jr, is professor of military history at The Ohio State University. He served in the United States Air Force from 1962 and was twice decorated before retiring as a Lieutenant Colonel in 1983. In addition to publications on air power and on modern conflicts, he is the author of *Gunpowder and Galleys: Changing Technology and Mediterranean Warfare at Sea in the Sixteenth Century* (Cambridge University Press, 1974; 2nd edition, Naval Institute Press, 2003) and *Galleons and Galleys: Gunpowder and the Changing Face of Warfare at Sea, 1300–1650* (Cassell, 2002).

MALYN NEWITT is Charles Boxer Professor of History in the Department of Portuguese and Brazilian Studies at King's College London. A Fellow of the Royal Historical Society, he is a distinguished historian of Portugal and its former colonies. His books include *Portugal in Africa: The Last Hundred Years* (Hurst, 1981), *The Comoro Islands* (Westview Press, 1984), *The First Portuguese Colonial Empire* (University of Exeter, 1985), *A History of Mozambique* (Hurst/Indiana University Press, 1995), *East Africa* (Ashgate, 2002), and *A History of Portuguese Overseas Expansion 1400–1668* (Routledge, 2004).

GUY ROWLANDS, a Fellow of the Royal Historical Society and at the time of writing Lecturer in History at Newnham College, Cambridge, is now Lecturer in Modern History at the University of St Andrews. He is the author of a dozen articles and chapters on early-modern French and military history, and of *The Dynastic State and the Army under Louis XIV: Royal Service and Private Interest, 1661–1701* (Cambridge University Press, 2002), which won the Royal Historical Society's Gladstone Prize in 2003.

LOUIS SICKING is Lecturer in History at the University of Leiden. His publications include *Zeemacht en onmacht. Maritieme politiek in de Nederlanden, 1488–1558* (Bataafsche Leeuw, 1998), *Neptune and the Netherlands: State, Economy and War at Sea in the Renaissance* (Brill, 2004), *Across the North Sea: Maritime Relations and Migration between the Netherlands and Norway* (Verloren, 2004), and over twenty papers on the history of the Netherlands, of European expansion, and maritime history.

JOHN M. STAPLETON, JR, presently Assistant Professor of History at the United States Military Academy, West Point, is the author of a Ph.D. thesis, 'Forging a Coalition Army: William III, the Grand Alliance, and the Confederate Army in the Spanish Netherlands, 1688–1697' (The Ohio State University, 2003).

D. J. B. TRIM is Lecturer in History at Newbold College and Visiting Research Fellow at the University of Reading. He has published widely on early modern history, including, as editor, *The Chivalric Ethos and the Development of Military Professionalism* (Brill, 2003) and *Cross,*

Crown and Community: Religion, Government and Culture in Early-Modern England (Peter Lang, 2004), and is a Fellow of the Royal Historical Society.

R. B. WERNHAM was Professor of Modern History at the University of Oxford from 1951 until his retirement in 1972, Editor of Foreign Calendars for the Public Record Office from 1932 until his death in 1999, and a Fellow of the British Academy. His publications include *England under Elizabeth* (Longmans, 1932), *Before the Armada: The Growth of English Foreign Policy, 1485–1588* (Jonathan Cape, 1966), *The Making of Elizabethan Foreign Policy* (University of California Press, 1980), *After the Armada* (Oxford University Press, 1984), *The Expedition of Sir John Norris and Sir Francis Drake to Spain and Portugal, 1589* (Navy Records Society, 1988), *The Return of the Armadas* (Oxford University Press, 1994); and eleven volumes of calendars and lists and analysis of records in the National Archives (U.K.).

ABBREVIATIONS

ARA Nationaal Archief [Netherlands] (formerly Algemeen Rijksar-
     chief), Den Haag
BL   British Library, London
BNF Bibliothèque Nationale de France, Paris
CAC Churchill Archives Centre, Churchill College, Cambridge
CSP *Calendar of State Papers*
HL   Huntington Library, San Marino, California
HMC Historical Manuscripts Commission [U.K.]
L&A *List and Analysis of State Papers, Foreign Series, Elizabeth I, Preserved
     in the Public Record Office*, ed. R. B. Wernham, 7 vols. (London:
     1964–2000)
MS(S) Manuscript(s)
OBL University of Oxford, Bodleian Library
PRO National Archives [U.K.] (formerly Public Record Office),
     Kew, London
SP   State Papers

These are abbreviations used in two or more chapters; abbreviations
of primary source material that are unique to one chapter are listed
at the start of the respective bibliographies.

MAPS

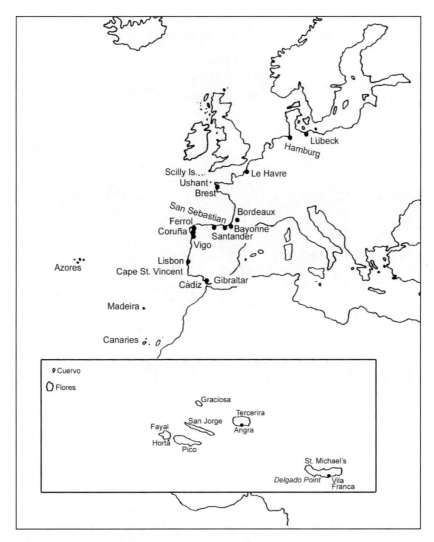

Map 1. Europe, Eastern Atlantic and the Azores (adapted from R. B. Wernham, *After the Armada: Elizabethan England and the Struggle for Western Europe 1588–1595* (Oxford: 1984), p. 234 and idem, *The Return of the Armadas: The Last Years of the Elizabethan War against Spain 1595–1603* (Oxford: 1994), p. 170; both © Oxford University Press)

Map 2. Western Mediterranean 1000–1700

The Eastern Mediterranean
and the Black Sea, 1000-1700

Map 3. The Eastern Mediterranean and the Black Sea, 1000–1700

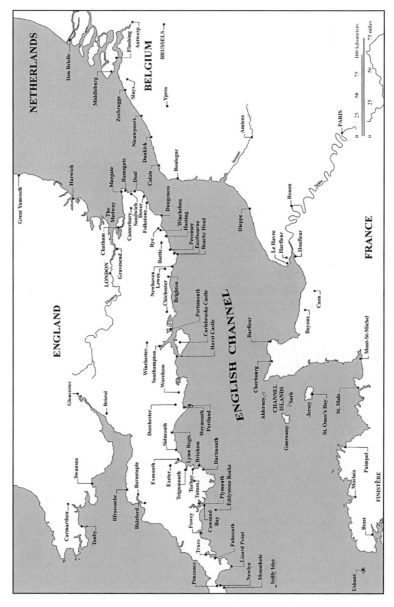

Map 4. The Narrow Seas and their Littoral: the English Channel, Bristol Channel, part of the North Sea (modern coastlines)

Map 5. Scandinavia and The Sound 1360–1700

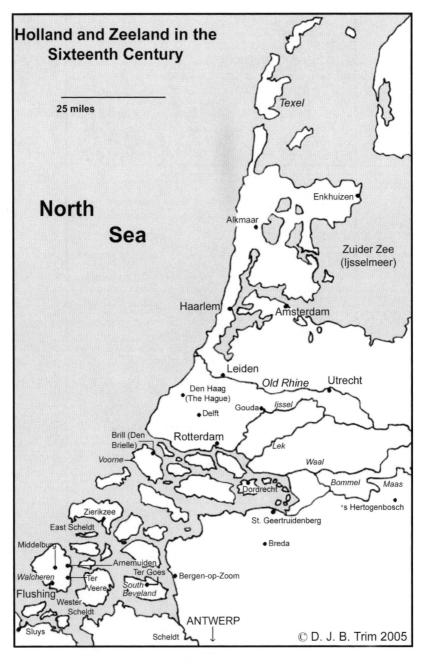

Map 6. Holland and Zealand in the Sixteenth Century

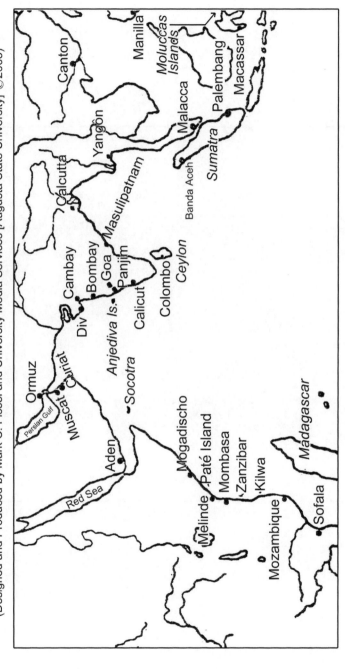

Map 7. Indian Ocean 1500–1700

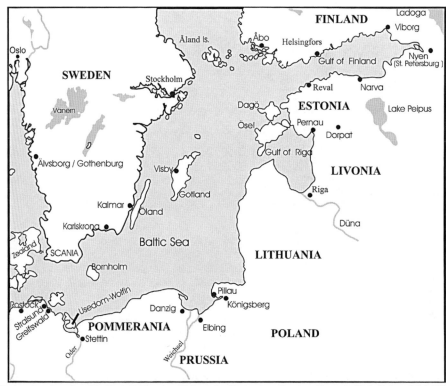

Designed and produced by Mark C. Fissel and Information Technology Services (Augusta State University) © 2005

Map 8. The Baltic, 1360–1700

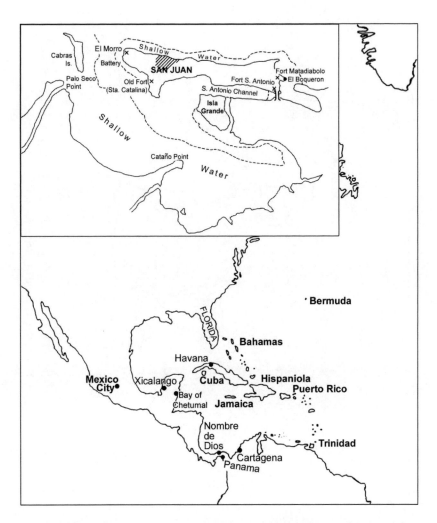

Map 9. Western Atlantic and the Caribbean; inset of Puerto Rico and San Juan (adapted from R. B. Wernham, *After the Armada*, p. 234, and idem, *The Return of the Armadas*, p. 250; both © Oxford University Press)

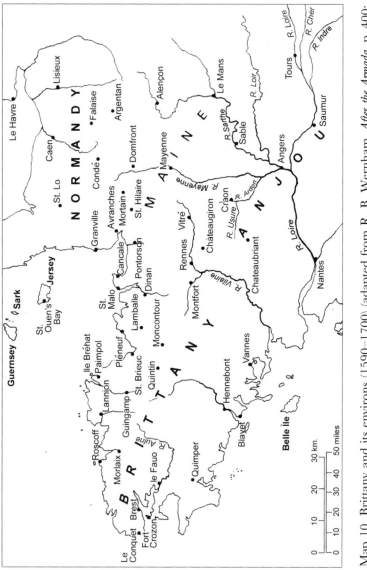

Map 10. Brittany and its environs (1590–1700) (adapted from R. B. Wernham, *After the Armada*, p. 400; © Oxford University Press)

Ireland
1550-1690

North Atlantic Ocean

Lough Foyle

Londonderry
Culmore
Coleraine
River Foyle
ANTRIM
TYRONE
Carrickfergus
Bangor Bay
Lough Neagh
ULSTER
Donegal
Lough Derg
Belfast
Assaroe Abbey
Ballyshannon
Dungannon
Erne
Donegal Bay
River Erne
Lower Lough Erne
Enniskillen Castle
DOWN
Strangford Lough
Blackwater Fort
Belleek Castle
Strangford
MONAGHAN
The Yellow Ford
FERMANAGH
Monaghan
Sligo
Upper Lough Erne
ARMAGH
Lough Gill
Newry
Lough Conn
Moyry Pass
Carlingford Lough
Carlingford
Dundalk
CONNAUGHT
The Boyne
Castle Necallye
(Hag's Castle)
Oldbridge
Lough Mask
Boyne
Drogheda
Lough Corrib
Lough Ree
Irish Sea
Trim
Galway
Dublin Castle
THE PALE
Lough Derg
Clonoan Castle
LEINSTER
Limerick Castle
KERRY   MUNSTER
Smerwick
Ross Castle
Lakes of Killarney
St.George's Channel
Castle Dunboy
Conjectural route of St. George Carew in 1602
Cork
Beara Peninsula
Dursey
Bandon Bridge
Kinsale
Bantry Bay

Legend
✗ Battles / Sieges
▦ Castles
● Towns
COUNTIES MARKED IN CAPITALS
PROVINCES MARKED IN CAPITALS & ITALICISED

Designed and produced by Mark C. Fissel and Information Technology Services (Augusta State University) © 2005

Map 11. Ireland 1550–1690

AMPHIBIOUS WARFARE, 1000–1700:
CONCEPTS AND CONTEXTS*

D. J. B. Trim and Mark Charles Fissel

This volume examines the organisation, conduct and purpose of medieval and early-modern amphibious warfare. That is, it examines a form of warfare which usually takes place on coasts, whether of continents or islands, but which sometimes takes place on inland waterways—a form of warfare in which land-based and waterborne forces cooperate, whether against a similar conjunction of forces, or against a solely land- or water-based enemy. Between 1000 and 1700 AD, amphibious (or 'combined' or 'joint') operations[1] were conducted with ever increasing frequency and sophistication—especially (though not only) by the nascent nation-states of Christendom; the ability to undertake such operations was an important quality for embryonic military establishments; and attempts to carry them out shaped the pattern of many conflicts. Yet amphibious operations in this period have largely been ignored by scholars, or considered as purely military or naval, rather than combined, operations. This is unfortunate, because medieval and early-modern amphibious warfare has characteristics that are inherently interesting for students of the art of war, while it also played a profound role in wider developments in this period.

The re-emergence in Europe after *c.* 1000 of international commerce and the creation of financial institutions and credit networks that came with it, benefited monarchies and city-states through higher

---

* The editors thank Matthew Bennett, Robert Frost, Malyn Newitt, Louis Sicking, John Stapleton, Jr., and Paul Van Dyke for their enlightening contributions to discussions about amphibious warfare, which greatly helped in the formulation of this introduction. However, responsibility for concepts and ideas, and any errors of fact or judgment, rests only on our shoulders.
[1] In American (and, in World War II, Allied) usage, 'joint' refers to inter-service and 'combined' to inter-allied organizations or operations, but in British usage, inter-service operations have typically been 'combined operations': Murray & Millett (2000), 579–80; Gatchel (1996), 8–9. We have preferred the latter usage.

tax revenues and greater facility for state borrowing. The desire of
kings and merchant princes to secure the trade routes from which
financial power derived, which really meant securing the ports through
which trade flowed, ensured that warfare became increasingly amphibious by necessity, even as the greater financial resources and maritime infrastructure available made amphibious operations an attractive
new option in making war.

By *c.* 1700, the coalescence of semi-independent territories into
centralized nation-states, begun in the eleventh century, was finally
concluded; but in many cases this was a recent development and
the fruit of war, including amphibious operations. The great conflicts
between imperial nation-states still lay in the future. The two centuries of religious warfare that had fractured Latin Christendom and
caused conflict 'in Africa, America and Asia as well as in many parts
of Europe' were over[2]—but the concurrent discoveries from the 1490s
on meant there was no prospect of a return to the relatively closed
world of the Middle Ages. European nations had laid greedy eyes
on the rest of the world, but it was only just becoming apparent
that further expansion across the globe was to be the prerogative of
France and Great Britain, with Portugal, Spain, the Ottoman Turks
and the Netherlands only just clinging on to what they had, Denmark
and Sweden confined to Europe, and Scotland and Venice subsumed
within greater states. There had been technological and organisational developments that laid the foundations for later industrialization, but industrialization was yet to occur.[3]

In the eighteenth century, the great empires of France and Great
Britain would wage amphibious wars that dwarfed all that had gone
before, while Sweden, the Dutch Republic and the Ottoman and
Russian Empires would also consistently maintain and use amphibious forces. The industrial revolution would bring about the age of
'gunboat diplomacy'.[4] But the amphibious operations of the eighteenth century and after are well known. The earlier period, however, from the eleventh century when amphibious warfare became
a practicable—and favoured—tool of governments (as opposed to
raiding bands), to the end of the seventeenth century, is less well

---

[2] Parker (1979), 189; Thompson (1985), 262.
[3] Duplessis (1997).
[4] Preston & Major (1967); Cable (1994).

known. As we will see, however, how amphibious warfare was practised in the eighteenth century owed much to the conduct of combined operations in the earlier era of transition from relatively
primitive, albeit ambitious, monarchies into multi-continental empires.
It was in these transitional seven centuries that European states were
forged and then forged the means by which eventually they would
dominate the globe—and in both processes amphibious warfare was
pivotal.

This was because amphibious warfare was important in both warfare and commerce: this interconnectedness is one of the main themes
of this volume. That amphibious operations influenced naval warfare is obvious (indeed, amphibious warfare is often categorized as
a branch of sea warfare),[5] but the lack of a clear distinction between
early modern land warfare and naval operations demands better
definition of, and a closer look at, combined operations. In addition,
historical scholarship has yet to recognise the potential of amphibious warfare—a potential that arose out of necessity. Cooperation on
land and water was almost essential in the period 1000–1700, because
socio-geographical considerations ensured that commerce and conflict
alike took place in coastal and riverine waters almost as often as on
land. Medieval and early-modern roads were few and poor in quality, while even ocean-going ships were often small enough (and thus
with sufficiently shallow draught) to penetrate far inland via rivers.
As a result, merchandise and *matériel* alike were despatched by sea
and river wherever possible; artillery trains, in particular, were virtually dependent on waterborne transport.[6] In consequence, if waterborne and ground forces could be combined in *offensive*, as well as
logistical, operations there was huge potential to damage a hostile
state's military-naval infrastructure or indeed its entire economy; this
potential, too, was greater than was afforded by either purely maritime or terrestrial operations. Combining different forces in different
elements to good effect was to prove immensely difficult, but where
it could be done it was to the benefit of those who did so. Amphibious
capacity, though, did not come cheap and the nature of late-medieval
and early-modern government was such that combined operations

---

[5] Below, p. 31.
[6] See e.g. Braudel (1972), 1:103–5, 208, 217–20, 276, 279–84, 578–9; Cunliffe
(2001), 331–6, 542; and below: Glete, ch. 5, p. 125 and Trim, ch. 11, *passim*.

could often be mounted only as partly commercial ventures.[7] Then, too, attempts to protect or expand trade, because it was so often water-borne, often required amphibious capabilities, so that combined operations and commercial policies became intertwined; amphibious warfare was a necessary component of mercantilism.

In sum, as the essays in this volume collectively demonstrate, when states could wage amphibious warfare effectively, they gained an edge over their rivals, both because of the dimension that was added to their war-making ability, and because of the opportunity to spread the prohibitive costs of war and/or to increase revenues. The ability to combine maritime and land forces for conquest, and for the propagation and protection of religion and commerce, was one of the primary means for the development and expansion of European states. In turn, amphibious warfare became the quintessential warfare of European imperialism. Sea power was required to deliver and sustain land power to and in the (West) European peripheries of the Mediterranean and the Baltic as well as Africa and the East and West Indies. Commerce not only followed, but precipitated conflict, for trade based on sea power (the prime medium of European expansion) required ports, which had to be obtained and retained, while the possibilities of plunder were sometimes enough to initiate military action by more developed states, which typically involved combined operations. The colonies acquired by European powers were generally littoral in nature and thus required a combination of land and sea force to protect them. The skills of amphibious warfare that the European powers inflicted on the rest of the world had, however, been learned and honed in intra-European conflicts, which often reflected Western ideological preoccupations.

This volume thus has a primarily military-historical focus—the conduct of amphibious warfare—but this, in turn, has important secondary implications of concern to a wide constituency. The contributors are aware of and sensitive to these implications and their essays illuminate, even when not explicitly engaging with, issues of economy, industry, ideology, and power.

That said, the chapters in this volume *are* primarily essays in military history and especially in the history of warfare. They focus on tactics, operational art, strategy, and logistics; they take into account

---

[7] See 'Conclusion', below, pp. 422–7.

developments in military and naval institutions and technology; and they illuminate both current debates about amphibious-operational praxis and wider debates in military historiography. In particular they shed light on the 'military revolution' thesis, the chief advocate of which has been Geoffrey Parker, that developments in military technology and operational art in early-modern Western Europe were significant enough to be classed as revolutionary, and were chiefly responsible for European domination of the globe. Certainly amphibious warfare played a heretofore unrecognized role, whether for good or ill, in what has been termed the 'rise of the West' (or 'ascendancy of Western Eurasia').[8] Whether developments in the practice of amphibious operations also constituted an example of revolutionary innovation will become part of the military revolution debate. The contributors to this volume do not have a uniform view of that debate and most do not specifically address it in their essays here; however, in practice their essays tend to support Parker more than his critics, of whom the most notable is Jeremy Black.[9] Black identifies 'multi-centred [military] developments' across the globe instead of 'one pattern of military development' spreading across and then from Western Europe—but amphibious warfare, as a consciously-chosen and sophisticated mode of warfare, emerges in this volume as having been developed in and disseminated from Europe (for the Ottomans were, in this period, genuinely a European power), though the volume supports Black's argument that the margins of Europe, too, were important sites of military-naval development.[10]

As noted above, however, the volume also looks beyond purely military history. The essays that follow consider the influence of amphibious warfare on commercial development, state formation and European expansion—matters that are intrinsically long-term in nature and therefore need to be analysed in as great geographic breadth as possible, and within a broad chronological framework, so as to allow for proper comparison and contrast. What follows, therefore, are a range of different types of studies, not only chronologically, but also geographically and thematically.

---

[8] Parker (1988; 1996; 1999); Thompson (1999).

[9] The key contributions to the military revolution debate up to the mid-1990s are in Rogers, ed., (1995); the latest important statements are Black (2003) and Parker (2003). See also Black (1999) and (2002); and Parker (1996; 1999), esp. 'Afterword'.

[10] Cf. Black (2002), 1–2.

The chapters are a mix of long-term overviews, strategic surveys, thematic analyses and operational case-studies, based on original research in Belgian, British, Danish, Dutch, French, Irish, Spanish and Swedish archives, and on syntheses of the most important secondary studies. They are likewise diverse in their geographical coverage, embracing the Baltic, Mediterranean and North Seas, and the Atlantic and Indian Oceans, as well as the rivers and lakes that constitute the continents' intestines. And every century in the period is covered in at least one chapter. Furthermore, the span of years covered in each chapter overlap (with two exceptions), sometimes in summary, sometimes in detail, so that the volume as a whole covers every decade in the whole of the period 1050–1700, though not all events in those years, save for the 1260s–1350s and the 1380s–1480s. There are a cluster of essays on the second half of the sixteenth century and on the mid- to late-seventeenth century, but this reflects the fact that these periods saw crucial developments in the art of amphibious warfare. Ottoman practice of combined operations is not examined from the Turkish point of view; however, it is encountered from Portuguese, Spanish and French perspectives. More seriously, there are no specific studies of amphibious warfare in the Far East, whether by Europeans or Asians. This does not reflect any feeling, of either the editors or contributors, that the practice of amphibious warfare other than by Western Europeans was unimportant.[11]

However, the main focus of *these* studies of medieval and early modern amphibious operations is Europe, partly because, as already noted, we see them as having played an important role in European developments that had global implications. Also, we do not claim this volume as the last word on medieval or early modern amphibious warfare. Rather, it is intended to open up new ground—we hope that other scholars will adopt the lens of amphibious warfare to examine developments in commerce, colonisation and state-building not only in Europe, but also in the Americas, Africa and Asia, whether by Europeans or indigenous peoples.

---

[11] Ch. 11 does consider Asian examples as part of a wider thematic study. This volume was originally to have included a study of Dutch operations in Indonesia and the Philippines in the early 17th century but changes in the author's personal circumstances made delivery of his contribution impossible.

Having outlined the main themes of the volume, this introductory essay goes on to define and conceptualise amphibious warfare—a subject that has been too infrequently subject to theoretical analysis. It then situates our conceptual model of amphibious warfare in the general context of the overall history of amphibious warfare and the particular context of amphibious warfare in the period 1000–1700, as revealed in the essays that follow hereinafter. Conclusions are drawn separately, in the last chapter.

Current Concepts of Amphibious Warfare

The history of amphibious warfare is apparently well served, with numerous published books and papers for a wide variety of readerships: academic, practitioner and general. Yet there is no easy answer to the question, 'What is "Amphibious Warfare"?' The simplest answer—that it is a form of warfare revolving around amphibious operations—is no answer at all, because it begs the question: 'What is an "amphibious (or "combined" or "joint" or "expeditionary") operation"?' There is no simple answer to this question, either, because these terms have been and continue to be used for a wide variety of actions.[12] They can denote or refer to:

i) landings that are not opposed, but are intended to pre-empt hostile actions, or to reinforce friendly forces;
ii) assault landings with only an immediate purpose, whether the infliction of damage (be it physical or moral), or the acquisition of *matériel* or intelligence—essentially raids and never meant to be other than ephemeral;
iii) assault landings that, while more than raids, are precursors to short-lived occupations, *not* to full-fledged invasions—i.e. attempts either at conquest (whether of nation or region), or counter-conquest ('liberation');
iv) the whole expedition which delivers landings of any of the first three types (inclusive of planning, rehearsal, embarkation, transport and landings);

---

[12] Both 'expeditionary operation' (and the alternative term for amphibious warfare to which it gives rise, 'expeditionary warfare') are recent innovations: used e.g. by Guthrie (2001); Stevens (forthcoming); and in Till, ed. (2001), 94, and the website of the Office of the Chief of Naval Operations [US] 'Expeditionary Warfare Division' (which is responsible for more than amphibious operations): URL http://www.exwar.org/. On the various use of 'combined' or 'joint', see fn. 1.

   v) the assault landings that are sometimes (but not always) the first
      act of an invasion; or, though less frequently,
  vi) actual invasions, inclusive of all aspects (including not just the land-
      ings but also the land campaign that follows them); or
  vii) defensive operations conducted against a landing (whatever its type).

Either the landings or the subsequent occupying force (if any, and
whether short-lived or an invasion army):

  a) may require naval support, whether in terms of gunfire or simply
     the carriage of men, munitions and/or provisions; or
  b) may be at least in intention self-sufficient; or alternatively again
  c) may be in support of what are otherwise essentially naval raids,
     briefly seizing headlands or batteries to allow fleets to do their
     work.

Shore-based defensive operations against landings may also utilize
naval (or other waterborne) forces.

Furthermore, the word 'amphibious' is used to characterize not
only specific operations and types of operations, but also a type of
strategy (sometimes labelled 'expeditionary strategy' but often lumped
in with 'maritime strategy'), or approach to war. Such usage can
conflict with the more common, operationally focused, usage.

None of this is meant to imply that any of the usages outlined
above are incorrect, but it does show how far from straightforward
must be the answer to the apparently simple question 'What is
amphibious warfare?' It has rightly been observed that the 'whole
business [. . .] is famously ambiguous' when it comes to 'definitions'.[13]

There are in fact serious problems with the historiography of
amphibious warfare, despite the bounty of publications composing
that historiography. It is distorted by significant chronological and
thematic biases, while in addition it has been inadequately theo-
rized—this is not a matter of mere academic interest, because the
result is terminological fuzziness that is ultimately confusing. In consequence, before summarising how the essays in this volume contribute to the history of combined operations, commercial development,
state formation and European expansion, it is necessary to consider
how the history of amphibious warfare has been written, and the
manifold forms 'amphibious operations' can take.

---

[13] Till (1997), 11.

Historiography

Most studies of amphibious warfare consider the nineteenth century and after—and they are heavily skewed to the 'after'. It is natural enough that the great majority examine the great amphibious campaigns of the two World Wars; but if one ignores technical studies of the remarkable methods of delivery developed and manufactured by the Allies, journalistic narratives, or simple memoirs and reminisces, there is still an over-concentration on the World Wars.[14] Even general histories of amphibious warfare and works that consider it in a broad context tend to ignore combined operations from before the industrial revolution; when earlier examples *are* examined they are rarely from earlier than the eighteenth century.

For example, although the U.S. Marine Corps has a history of combined operations going back into the first half of the nineteenth century, amphibious doctrine for World War II was formulated on the basis of operations only from the half a century that preceded it (save for a handful of exercises involving Civil War scenarios)— and modern historical studies of the Corps tend to have similar chronological restrictions.[15] In the early 1900s a retired British Royal Marine general who attempted to stimulate interest in 'amphibious wars' took for the first of his historical case studies the Chilean war of 1891.[16] A 1964 history of amphibious operations aimed at the general market begins with Julius Cæsar's invasion of Britain in 55BC—but then leaps forward to the Seven Years' War (1756–1763) and, after covering the next century and a half in only a further two chapters, devotes eight more to the twentieth century.[17] A more recent popular book on amphibious warfare considers four case studies: the first is the celebrated operation against Quebec in 1759 during the Seven Years' War; the other three are from 1915, 1950 and 1982.[18] Academic studies are similar. One notable early practitioner,

---

[14] Cf. Isely and Crowl (1951), v. Maund (1949) unusually combines analysis of hardware with memoir and a degree of operational analysis, but lacks historical perspective.

[15] Isely and Crowl (1951), 4–5, 17, 20–2, 27, 29, 33–43; Schaffer (1972), 46; O'Connor (1974). There was greater interest in 18th- and 19th-cent. examples of American amphibious warfare immediately after World War II: *e.g.*, Ainsworth (1945), Moran (1945) and Shaw (1953).

[16] Aston (1911; 1920).

[17] Whitehouse (1964).

[18] Foster (1995)—reprinted in 1998 as a 'military classic'.

despite an avowed concern to learn 'the lessons of history' from five case studies of *Amphibious Warfare and Combined Operations*, drew four of these from the twentieth century—plus Quebec.[19] Another retired practitioner, in a recent study of *Maritime Strategy and Continental Wars*, takes all his historical examples of amphibious operations (and of 'maritime strategy' more generally) from the nineteenth and twentieth centuries.[20] He does briefly examine the (substantial) influence on maritime strategy of the late-Victorian and Edwardian historian, Sir Julian Corbett, but although Corbett was *inter alia* an influential historian of Drake and his successors, considers only his writings on the Royal Navy in the mid-eighteenth century and after.[21] Even studies of twentieth-century amphibious warfare that claim to establish historical context often do so with less than a paragraph devoted to the medieval and early-modern periods.[22] Dedicated studies of pre-industrial amphibious warfare are still in the minority. They ignore the Middle Ages and deal only with the later early-modern period, mostly examining the combined operations mounted (particularly by the British Royal Navy) during the eighteenth-century conflicts between European empires and in the Napoleonic Wars.[23] That there are studies of amphibious warfare in classical antiquity[24] only highlights that from then until AD 1700 is a black hole for the historiography of amphibious warfare.[25]

---

[19] Keyes (1943), 7 *et passim*.

[20] Menon (1998), ch. 5.

[21] Ibid., 31–2; cf. Till (1997), 5–6. For Corbett's influence, on both naval history and strategy (including use of amphibious operations), see the notes and bibliography of Wernham, ch. 7, below; Harding (1989), 37–8; Harding (1991), 170, 191, 197; and Strachan (1994), 418–20.

[22] E.g., Speller (2001A), 2; Till, ed. (2001), 94; cf. Gatchel (1996), 5. Richmond (1941) likewise passed quickly over Elizabethan amphibious warfare before concentrating on the 19th and 20th centuries.

[23] Harding (1989); and (1991); Middleton (1993); Smelser (1955); Syrett (1973); Moran (1945); Shaw (1953); Duffy (1987); Burne (1939); Barker (2000); Cooper (1997); Ainsworth (1945); and the works discussed by Black (2000), 170–1, 175–6.

[24] E.g., Belfiglio (1998), (1999) and (2001); Stephenson, ed. (2003), 113–19, 227–33; Pinder (2004). This does not include studies of classical naval warfare, which frequently had an amphibious dimension.

[25] Waley (1954) is, and Stevens (forthcoming) will be, notable exceptions; and the amphibious features of 16th-cent. Mediterranean naval warfare are stressed by Guilmartin (1974), 51, 56–7, 81, 107, 178–9, 218, 273, as part of a more general study: one article, one thesis and parts of one book on 700 years. Similarly, the branch of the US Navy responsible for amphibious warfare, in a catalogue of examples of 'Early Amphibious Warfare', 490 BC–1798 AD, lists three from classical antiquity, three from medieval Japan, but only two from medieval Europe and none in Europe from 1066 to 1705: see http://www.exwar.org/Htm/8000.htm.

This historiography does not only suffer from chronological imbal-
ance. As Richard Harding points out, amphibious warfare is of excep-
tional interest to Britons and Americans: 'combined operations have
had a particular fascination for public and politicians in the English-
speaking world.'[26] Amphibious operations were something of a spe-
cialty with the Royal Navy, simply because, as an island, Britain had
to land troops from the sea in order to intervene in other people's
countries, and because, since its security depended on naval strength,
it was prepared to attack other countries' navies in harbour, or the
docks and logistic infrastructure that supported them. Although the
United States is not an island, by achieving continental domination
its strategic situation became effectively insular. Then, in the Second
World War, the Anglo-American alliance could only defeat Germany,
Italy and Japan by conducting landings on opposed shores and thereafter supporting armies by maritime commerce. Since then, the
United Kingdom and the United States have continued to have an
interest in using combined operations to 'project power', while America
has made use of combined capability in a new variant of gunboat
diplomacy. Then, too, combined operations have often had a roman-
tic and heroic air: from Sir Francis Drake at Cadiz to the US Marines
at Tarawa, Saipan and Iwo Jima, select groups of courageous (British
and American) men have conducted raids or heroic assaults against
overwhelming odds, to prick the prideful bubbles of tyrants (perceived or real), from Philip II of Spain to Napoleon to Hitler and
Tojo and lay the foundations for ultimate victory. This is at any
rate what emerges from movies, pulp fiction and popular histories.
Professional historians may disdain such media, but the attractive-
ness of the subject is still there. Certainly Anglophone scholars have
focused on amphibious warfare to a greater extent than scholars
writing in other languages.[27] The literature of amphibious warfare is
mostly in English and mostly, too, about operations carried out by
the English-speaking peoples.

---

[26] See Harding (1989), 35–36 at 35.

[27] A notable exception is Merglen (1968), but his work was intended partly as a
rebuke to the French military establishment for ignoring amphibious operations:
ibid., 12, 202. Although Menon is Indian, his book (1998) is in English and reflects
mostly on the Anglo-American inheritance. Alvarez (1999), 83–97, examines a 20th-
cent. Spanish amphibious operation but his subject matter is unusual—and he writes
in English. It should be noted that the Soviet armed forces had, while the Russian
armed forces still have, a doctrine for amphibious operations: Till (1997), 11.

In sum, amphibious warfare is effectively understood as being something carried out by English, British or American forces; it is, moreover, typically understood in the context of the Seven Years' War, the Napoleonic Wars, the Crimean War, the First and Second World Wars, and of some 'small wars' in the second half of the twentieth century.[28] Brief nods to Julius Cæsar, the Saxons, Vikings and Normans (all, of course, invaders of the British Isles), and the Elizabethan sea dogs and their combats with Spain, do not change the fact that amphibious warfare is practically defined in very limited historical terms.

Moreover, general histories of warfare in the period 1000–1700 do not fill the gap, for they analyse amphibious warfare little or not at all, even when considering areas like the Low Countries, the Baltic, or Ireland where combined operations were an integral part of warfare. The 'unfashionable'-ness of military history in the Netherlands has resulted in a dearth of studies of the conduct of war during the Dutch Revolt (1568–1648);[29] it is not surprising, then, that amphibious operations, whether by the Dutch or the Spanish, are a non-subject. In contrast, the wars of early-modern Scandinavian and Baltic states are better treated by scholarship.[30] Yet even the most recent overview pays little attention to the amphibious aspects of strategy, logistics and tactics in the Baltic, despite the predominant interest of its author in states and their ability to wage wars—a perspective from which amphibious wars are very interesting, because, as will be seen, they are especially challenging in strategic planning, command and co-operation between various parts of the armed forces.[31] Likewise, the military history of early modern Ireland is well treated by scholarship but it has failed to address the amphibious dimension that was, as chapter 8 reveals, of pivotal importance in the military incorporation of Ireland into Britain.[32]

There are thus significant omissions in the historiography of coastal operations and amphibious warfare. It is entirely reasonable that

---

[28] Even Belfiglio (2001) examines Roman amphibious operations within the framework of US military doctrine.
[29] Zwitzer (1991), 9–13 at 9, and 240; Trim (2003), 276–8, 282–3.
[30] For overviews see Oakley (1987) and (1992) and Frost (2000).
[31] Cf. Frost (2000). We are indebted to Jan Glete for discussion of these issues.
[32] E.g., a recent overview has thematic chapters on different types of warfare, some of them excellent, but none on amphibious warfare: Lenihan, ed. (2001).

there should be a focus on the twentieth century, given that in it amphibious operations were of unprecedented scale, complexity and importance. However the implication of current literature is that combined operations were beyond the means of medieval and early-modern states, not to mention best carried out by the armies, navies and marines of Britain, its empire, and the United States of America. There is a great need for analysis of amphibious operations in the Middle Ages and the earlier early-modern epoch, because these centuries were pivotal in the history of state formation, the development of industries and global trade, and European expansion. The essays in this volume are collectively a first step to correcting the existing imbalances in the historiography of amphibious warfare. They highlight the importance for medieval and early-modern states of amphibious operations; they additionally point to the frequency and relative proficiency therein of Danish, Dutch, French, Portuguese, Spanish, Swedish and Turkish, as well as English, military and naval establishments, without hiding the difficulties that all experienced in waging the most complex form of warfare.

Definition—Some Preliminary Remarks

The activity described by the term 'amphibious warfare' and its cognates is, as we have already observed, ambiguous; as a result, it is difficult to define. This reflects, in part, its nature. The reality of operations in which water-borne and ground forces cooperate is that such collaboration can take a multitude of forms. Because it is a multiplex form of warfare, amphibious warfare is inherently inexact and susceptible to different interpretations, with theoretical definitions potentially difficult to apply in practice to actual events.[33] As the editors and contributors to this volume discovered in several dialogues, a clear concept of amphibious warfare is rather like the animal amphibians: slippery and hard to pin down.

Amphibious warfare, however, is terminologically and conceptually fuzzy partly because scholars have been too quick to accept that the task of definition is impossible. Even if a precise definition *is* impossible to achieve, a practicable definition may be within reach

---

[33] As Till (1997), 11, notes, the term amphibious warfare 'does not lend itself to exact definition'.

and a working definition is still desirable. Certainly one was essential for this volume, to guide editors and contributors as to what should or should not be included. The definition we adopted[34] sets the parameters for this volume's contents, but it will also, we trust, prove helpful to students of amphibious warfare regardless of period, by providing, together with the general discussion that accompanies it, a starting point for new and more rigorous conceptualisations of amphibious warfare.

There has been insufficient theorization of amphibious warfare.[35] It is usually defined implicitly, rather than explicitly. Overt attempts at definition are few, brief, and frequently over-reliant on uncritical applications of recent or current US or British military doctrine. Most authors simply assume that their subject is clearly understood, requiring no delineation; although they take for granted that it is obvious what amphibious, or combined-ops, or expeditionary, warfare *is*, they actually apply or understand the term(s) in different ways. Even if most readers of works on the subject probably do have a generally recognisable concept in their mind when encountering such terms, it is not always the same concept; because authors do not explicitly delimit their subject, meanings multiply and confusion arises. Hence, when the term 'amphibious' is used in the context of warfare, it will conjure up certain images and ideas in the minds of readers as to what type of combat or campaign is involved—but these can vary widely (as our tabulation on pp. 7–8 of the different operations that are described as 'amphibious' makes plain). Equally, as our discussion of historiography reveals, 'amphibious' warfare will also be implicitly assumed by many readers to take place only in certain periods of history and to involve only certain nationalities (or even particular corps). Thus, it is by no means obvious what amphibious warfare is.[36] At present, amphibious warfare is *not* undefined— it is defined badly.

Recognising this fact, several contributors to this volume devote more or less space to defining their understanding of amphibious

---

[34] On p. 1 above and p. 27, below.
[35] *Pace* Richmond (1941); O'Connor (1974), 97; Harding (1991), 1–2; and Till (1997), 11—in each case the theoretical discussion is very brief.
[36] As Sir Betram Ramsay (World War II's greatest practitioner of amphibious warfare) pointed out, even to many naval and army officers, 'the words "Combined Operations" probably convey little meaning': CAC, RMSY 8/22, f. [1].

warfare.[37] The discussion of definition that follows here differs in some respects from theirs, but the multifaceted nature of amphibious warfare is such that a definitional section will often be desirable in an essay on the subject, to clarify what types of amphibious warfare a scholar is considering and how s/he sees their work fitting into broader conceptual frameworks.[38] Our definition amplifies, more than it corrects, those of our contributors, while it also forms part of a more general theoretical conceptualization of amphibious warfare than space permitted any of them.

In the next part of this essay, we explain the grounds for our definition, based on a range of historical amphibious operations. Its main purpose is to enable clearer and comparative understanding of the essays that follow, but we hope that our interpretative framework will benefit the study of amphibious warfare in general, whether by historians, or military or naval professionals.

What is Amphibious Warfare? Describing and Defining the Subject

In defining amphibious warfare we recognise that, because it has always effectively been defined in terms of 'what looks and feels like an amphibious operation' (both to authors and readers), any definitional schema must make sense in light of existing prejudices and presumptions about amphibious warfare, as well as standard definitions of sea and land warfare. In the following discussion, we therefore draw not only on the medieval and early-modern combined operations that are the focus of this volume, but also on operations from other periods that may be better known to many readers. Because the roots of our definition lie, as they must do, in what is already generally accepted as amphibious, it is descriptive as much as prescriptive.

There are two obvious starting points in answering the question, 'What is amphibious warfare?' First is the meaning of 'amphibious'

---

[37] Bennett, ch. 2 (p. 51); Sicking, ch. 3 (p. 69); and Glete, ch. 5 (p. 123); and Stapleton, ch. 10, which is the most detailed (pp. 317–23). But NB that other contributors knew that the editors would address the issue of definition in this Introduction.

[38] Guilmartin, ch. 6, does not define amphibious warfare, but makes explicit 'the highly specialized and essentially amphibious form of warfare . . . in question' in his essay (p. 149); Stapleton, while relating his definition to current 'taxonomies' of warfare, notes that he is discussing amphibious warfare as practiced 'in the latter seventeenth century' (pp. 4–5).

itself, which clearly is all-important. The word 'amphibious' is defined by lexicographers as 'of or relating to or suited [or adapted] *for both land and water*'.[39] Second are the terms oft-used as alternatives for amphibious operations: combined or joint operations; or 'conjunct operations', carried out by 'conjunct expeditions', in the language of eighteenth-century British theorists and Prime Ministers (not least William Pitt), whose proclivity for them made amphibious war seem a characteristically 'British way of warfare' to historians and subsequent national leaders alike.[40] It was, of course, the army and navy that were being combined, joined, or conjoined.

Amphibious warfare, then, requires a conjuncture. That much is plain. But it involves the conjuncture of two further conjunctures or combinations: firstly, in its site; secondly in its composition. The first combination is of the physical elements in which operations take place; the second of different types of organisation and institution—and, furthermore, involves cooperation, not *just* conjuncture. These two combinations are *integral* to amphibious warfare; but in addition we suggest that *inherent* in amphibious warfare is a third conjuncture: of different types of strategic potential. Amphibious operations can be employed to further both land-based and sea-based strategies. Different specific operations will, although joint or combined, have a specific 'maritime or continental tilt'.[41] But as a *type* of operation, amphibious operations can go either way.[42]

---

[39] Oxford Dictionary (1996); *Merriam-Webster's Collegiate Dictionary*, from *Encyclopædia Britannica Standard Edition 2004 CD-ROM*. Copyright © 1994–2003 Merriam-Webster, Inc. Emphasis supplied. Early-modern usage implied an intermediate or even indeterminate status, but in the military context from the 1690s it was used to indicate soldiers with maritime skills: PRO, SP 105/54, f. 109, 7/17 July 1695; Stapleton, ch. 10, below, p. 323.

[40] See Molyneaux (1759); Keyes (1943), 7–8; Harding (1989), 37–8; Till (1997), 6–9; Harding (1991), 195–6; Middleton (1993), 74; Liddell Hart (1932); Strachan (1994); for Winston Churchill's fondness in World War II for amphibious 'descents', often explicitly on the basis of 18th-cent. precedents, see Murray & Millett (2000), 218–19, 299, 381; and Barnett (1991), *passim*. Cf. the choice of the recently retired Chief of the [UK] Defence Staff, General Sir Charles Guthrie, of the term 'New British Way in Warfare' for the post-Cold War British defence approach, which is 'about expeditionary operations': Guthrie (2001) (italics supplied). On the concept of a 'British way of warfare', see below, p. 31.

[41] Gray (1995–6), 36 n. 20.

[42] This is an important point, given that amphibious operations are generally perceived as quintessentially maritime—this is discussed below, pp. 30–32.

Conjuncture in Site

The most obvious conjuncture necessary in amphibious warfare is the geophysical one, which probably will be generally presumed to be the conjuncture of land and sea. An amphibious operation, in that case, would be an operation that takes place at 'the sea-land interface', or a 'sea-ground task force operation', to use the latest jargon.[43] Certainly it is in these terms that amphibious warfare has generally been understood. Thus, in twentieth-century British and US military doctrine an amphibious operation has variously been the landing of troops on an enemy coast line, a landing or embarkation involving the integration of sea and land forces, and the launching onto land, from the sea, of 'naval and landing forces'.[44] Standard reference works define amphibious warfare, or operations, in almost identical terms.[45] Those contributors to this volume who define amphibious warfare all do so similarly, in terms of the projection, by landings or bombardments, of power from sea onto land.[46]

What, however, of inland waterways? Many famous examples of operations on or across rivers have clearly been instances of specifically naval or land warfare (and treated as such in the respective historiographies).[47] However, from the first three centuries AD, when Rome maintained fleets on the Rhine and Danube Rivers that cooperated with the Legions,[48] to the later twentieth century, when the US Army, Navy and Coast Guard jointly operated a 'brown water' fleet on the rivers and canals of South Vietnam,[49] there have been numerous river-based actions in which army, navy and/or marines (or their forerunners) combined. Were these amphibious? Given the prevailing

---

[43] Belfliglio (1999), 20 and (2001), title; Naval Studies Board (2000), 14. 'Land-sea interface' is probably more common in the sciences.

[44] Bittner (1991), 351; Speller (2001A), 1; O'Connor (1974), 97; Belfiglio (1999), 15; Till (1997), 11. As for 'combined operations', Sir Bertram Ramsay, when lecturing Allied officers on the subject in 1944, characterized them as the landing of troops by 'seaborne expeditions': CAC, RMSY 8/22, f. [1] *et passim*.

[45] Encyclopædia Britannica (2003); Oxford Dictionary (1996).

[46] See fn. 37.

[47] E.g., Chakravarti (1930), 654–7; Lenihan, ed. (2001), 158–9, 164, 173. Stephenson, ed. (2003), 51–70, 161–2. The same is true of battles on lakes; e.g., the Battle of Lake Champlain is typically treated simply as an episode in the history of the US Navy.

[48] Connolly (1988), 273.

[49] We are indebted to Bill Wells for guidance about the complex organisation of US forces for operations on inshore and inland waterways in the Vietnam War.

tendency to characterise 'amphibious' as something situated at the sea-land interface, perhaps riverine operations should be classed as a discrete form of warfare, distinct from, rather than a part of, amphibious warfare?

In practice, however, operations on inland waterways are included as amphibious by historians often enough that they must be regarded as constituent of amphibious warfare in any definition thereof. General surveys of the subject typically refer (albeit only in passing) to the Vikings, the crews of whose longships had only to beach their vessels and disembark to become devastatingly effective ground forces; but this was not only true on coastlines and an integral part of the Viking practice of warfare was deep penetration of target kingdoms via rivers.[50] Wolfe's capture of Quebec in 1759 is, as already noted, the starting point for many histories of amphibious warfare. The evacuation of George Washington's army from New York, across the Hudson River in 1776; Washington's celebrated Trenton campaign in the winter of 1776–7 (with its crossing and re-crossing of the Delaware River); the British use of rivers to outmanoeuvre Washington and capture Philadelphia in 1777; the British landings in the Patuxent and Potomac Rivers in 1814, and the brief campaign that followed and resulted in the capture and burning of Washington, D.C.: all are regarded as amphibious.[51] Because of the importance of riverine operations in the American Civil War, with cooperation between 'river navies' and armies essential in several campaigns, the Civil War has been declared 'among the greatest amphibious wars in history'.[52] In 1944, the campaign by Canadian and British forces to clear the banks of the Scheldt estuary (essential for the use of the port of Antwerp, which in turn was vital if supply was to be maintained to Allied armies in Europe) included operations that standard histories term amphibious, including one launched not from, but towards the North Sea, from inland.[53] Equally,

---

[50] See, e.g., Bennett, ch. 2, below, p. 52; and the Anglo-Saxon Chronicle entries for AD 851, 860, 867, 871, 872, 875–6, 879–87, 892–6, 914, 994, 997–9, 1004, 1006, 1009–1010, 1013, and indeed 1066: *ASC* (1982), 89, 92–3, 96–9, 102, 106–7, 111, 116, 145, 147, 149–51, 157, 194.

[51] E.g., by the US Navy's expeditionary warfare division: http://www.exwar.org /Htm/8000.htm, 'History of Amphibious Warfare'; and Billias (1960) ch. 1.

[52] *Military Affairs* (1954).

[53] Murray & Millett (2000), 437–8, 443, 458–9. See also below, ch. 11, pp. 385, 386.

although (as noted above) Matthew Bennett, Louis Sicking, Jan Glete and John Stapleton in this volume define amphibious operations in sea-focused language, each actually treats actions on rivers as amphibious.

The riverine operations in question are mostly, to be precise, estuarine or deltaic ones, as was also the case with the actions around New York, Philadelphia, Washington, D.C. and Antwerp. Thus they might still be regarded as 'operations . . . against coastal targets', which is how Stapleton defines amphibious operations, or of 'littoral warfare', which Glete recognizes as one of two types of amphibious warfare.[54] However, Glete in practice includes inland waterways in his 'littoral' category, which he explicitly contrasts with oceanic-based amphibious operations, while Bennett highlights the ability of some medieval expeditions 'to penetrate deep inland' via rivers, and includes operations in swamps.[55] All this reflects geographic reality. Ports are often far up estuaries (like Antwerp—or, even more so, Quebec).[56] Even today there are many river-ports lying well inland that can be reached by ocean-going vessels; in the period before 1700, when ships were smaller with shallower draught, the range of ports navigable from the sea was even greater. Furthermore, as essays in this volume make clear, the sea blurs into estuaries, shallows, marshlands, lagoons, 'sea loughs' and rivers without clear dividing lines.[57] Thus, to define operations launched from the sea as being of a separate type of war to those launched from or across inland waterways is to impose an artificial distinction, especially because, reflecting geographic reality, operations begun from saltwater have often organically and easily extended to include activity on freshwater. This was especially common in the ancient, medieval and early modern periods, The authority of pre-industrial era admiralty officials, charged with regulating maritime affairs and gathering ocean-going fleets, often extended not only to the high sea and river mouths, but also to 'lakes natural or artificial, and rivers'.[58] To define amphibious

---

[54] Below, pp. 318, 123.
[55] Below, pp. 52–3. And Newitt, ch. 4, who does not delimit amphibious warfare, includes both operations launched from the sea and those carried out on rivers: below, pp. 112, 118.
[56] On ports, see below, p. 429–32; and Trim, in ch. 11, p. 384.
[57] See in particular chs. 8 and 11.
[58] Chakravarti (1930), 648; and see also, e.g., Sicking (2004), ch. 2, for the

warfare as something directed against coasts one must extend the
meaning of 'coastal' to include the shores of all the rivers that flow
into the sea and their tributaries and associated lakes, as far as those
rivers can be navigated (and not only from the sea). This is already
done, to some extent. The nominal status of the Great Lakes as the
USA's 'fourth coast' (so that Chicago, though almost a thousand
miles inland is legally 'an arm of the sea'),[59] shows how broad is the
spectrum of waters on which so-called 'coastal' or 'littoral' operations might be conducted. But this pushes the definition of 'the land-
sea interface' beyond what most of us find credible.

By its very nature, then, amphibious warfare cannot be defined
as war that takes place only at the cusp of land and sea. It makes
more sense simply not to bring the sea into a definition of amphibious warfare. What all operations typically included in the literature
of amphibious warfare *do* have in common, however, is that they
take place (in the words of the title of one history) 'at the water's
edge', regardless of whether the water in question is oceans and seas
or rivers and lakes.[60]

That is, amphibious operations combine not land and sea, but
earth and water—two of the four elements recognised in medieval and
early-modern natural philosophy. When artillery and, in twentieth-
century cases, airpower, are added, three or all four elements may
be involved, since fire and air are encompassed as well. The nature
of modern land and sea warfare is such, however, that each naturally involve the conjunction of earth, fire and air, and of water, fire
and air, respectively. However, warfare that involves the conjunction or combination of earth *and* water, of land *and* sea, is a distinctive form: only it requires land-based *and* water-borne capability—
and cooperation. And chapters two and three will remind us that it
can take place without firepower, much less air power. This distinctive form of warfare is amphibious warfare.

It is characterized, though, not only by the physical elements in
which it takes place—its *site*—but also by the types of force applied,

---

authority of early-modern admiralties over cities whose access to the sea was only
via rivers.

[59] The Chicago Yacht Club used the fourth coast status as grounds for a successful legal challenge to allow it to enter a contestant in the 1987 America's Cup,
which is limited to yacht clubs 'on an arm of the sea': see http://www.ultimate-
sail.com/Library/Documents/.

[60] Gatchel (1996).

or groups taking part—its *organisation*. The ability to operate in earth and water that defines an amphibian animal does not alone define an amphibious or combined operation, because numerous combats and campaigns have taken place that involved a conjuncture of earth and water, but are clearly examples of land or sea warfare and universally regarded as such.

Many land battles have taken place in which rivers were crossed, and the configuration of lakes and rivers has been sufficiently influential or decisive in the conduct or outcome of many others for them to be said to have involved a conjuncture of earth and water. However, to take the examples of the Battles of the Granicus, the Jaxartes, the Trebbia and Lake Trasimene (334, 329, 218 and 217 BC), the crossing of the Berezina (1812) and Operation Market Garden (1944), all clearly are land battles, not amphibious actions, and treated as such in all histories.[61] Equally, since 'through most of history, warships have been tactically and strategically dependent on the land', many naval battles have been fought within sight of the shore—and the configuration of the shore played an important part in the tactics or results of battles, from Salamis in 480 BC, through Malta (1283), the Nile (1798) and Mobile Bay (1864), to Pearl Harbor in 1941.[62] All these clearly are naval, not amphibious, battles and have their place in naval historiography.

In all these cases, one *type* of unit was involved or one *type* of force applied, so that there was only a geophysical conjuncture. Thus, while the conjuncture of land and sea is too limiting as a definition, a definition involving *only* the conjunction of earth and water is too broad; too much would be incorporated. Amphibious operations entail a second conjuncture—in the composition of at least one of the forces involved.[63]

Compositional Conjuncture and Cooperation

This conjuncture can often be expressed as one of different organisations (or types of organisation), including subordinate but distinct

---

[61] If Market Garden was 'combined' it is because of the integral involvement of airborne troops.

[62] Stephenson, ed. (2003), 227; see Guilmartin (1974), 56–7, 96.

[63] As Harding notes: it is helpful 'to define amphibious operations, not just by their objectives, but by the composition of forces involved as well': (1991), 1.

establishments within one over-arching organisation. Further, *cooperation* is surely implicit in the idea of a combined operation. Thus, an amphibious operation is not one in which land and sea power (or military and naval force) confront each other; they have to combine not in the operation as a whole, but on *one side*, which necessarily entails cooperation. For example, bombardments by ships of hostile positions or populations on shore are not in and of themselves amphibious operations (though, as suggested below, they may form part of an amphibious strategy), because the water-based and land-based forces are placed in opposition, rather than conjunction—there is a collision, rather than a combination. Thus, an amphibious operation involves not only a conjuncture in how a force is composed, but also cooperation between the different components of that force. Cooperation need not be efficient or competent—history indicates that often it will be neither; but good intentions will suffice.[64]

The typical presumption about compositional conjuncture would probably be that what is combined is armies and navies. However, to define amphibious warfare as 'a form of warfare that demands the services of both the navy and the army to be effective' does not work. The remit is too broad: as Professor Harding observes, by such a definition the First World War can, from a British standpoint, be classified as an amphibious war, since the British Expeditionary Force was 'dependent upon the Royal Navy for securing the supply lines across the channel to Britain'.[65] In addition, however, the existence of distinct armies and navies with separate responsibility for land and sea warfare is a relatively recent innovation in much of the world—while in any case, even since their advent, amphibious operations have at times been mounted by units drawn solely from armies or navies. It is necessary, then, to speak in terms of a conjuncture of (and cooperation between) different types of organisation, rather than simply of armies and navies.

Certainly in medieval and early-modern Europe (as in the classical world, in which galleys invariably landed at night), the distinc-

---

[64] *Pace* Richmond (1941) (quoted by Harding (1991), 1–2; and Bennett, below, p. 51); and Bittner (1991), 345–7, who define amphibious operations as well-planned with clear objectives. This may reflect a desire to influence future good practice; it does not reflect the historical record.

[65] Harding (1991), 1.

tion between 'ground forces' and naval forces did not exist in the modern sense: in eleventh-century England the same term was used for a military force 'operating on land *or* sea'. Five and six centuries later, there was still no 'sharp division between land and sea forces', especially in areas dominated by galley warfare.[66] This was, firstly, because medieval and early early-modern states had not so much navies as 'maritime potential'—permanently maintained ships in government pay were few or non-existent, and so hierarchies and permanent structures were limited or also non-existent. Fleets were mustered by mobilising merchant and other private ships from coastal towns. Only with the early sixteenth-century introduction of cannon fired through gun-ports did a clear distinction begin to emerge between merchantmen and military ships, necessitating separate, permanent establishments of the latter; only in the late seventeenth century did such heavily armed, 'line-of-battleships', emerge that use of merchantmen in combat finally became extinct.[67] Only thereafter were large fleets along with the requisite infrastructure and administrations permanently maintained. Even then separate 'Ordnance' establishments remained responsible in many European states for providing cannon and their associated munitions to both armies and navies until the late eighteenth century.

Secondly, ships invariably carried soldiers, which were an integral part of 'war at sea' from ancient until early-modern times, because naval battles generally took the form of combats between rival boarding parties. Even in classical antiquity, when ramming was a common battle tactic, it never superseded use of troops for boarding. In the Middle Ages, as Louis Sicking observes, 'troops were part of the fighting equipment' of ships in the way that cannon were to be from the sixteenth century onwards (albeit only from the seventeenth century did cannon *supplant* soldiers).[68] Equally, sailors could easily be

---

[66] Bennett, in ch. 2, below, pp. 51–2 (emphasis supplied); Mallett & Hale (1984), 217; Guilmartin (1974), 77, 96, 107.

[67] See Braudel (1972), 1:636; Guilmartin (1974), 3, 40, 58–9; Sicking (2001), *passim*; idem, below, ch. 3, pp. 71, 94; Anderson (1988), 26–7. NB: 'line-of-battleships' is the term used in chs. 5 and 9; the more common contemporary term was 'ship of the line', used in chs. 8 and 10.

[68] Connolly (1988), 265, 267, 271–3; Sicking, ch. 3, below, pp. 71, 94–5; Guilmartin (1974), 40, 62, 72–3, 114, 118, 138.

soldiers—and this was true even after the division of war into naval and military. Nineteenth-century 'gunboat diplomacy' worked not only because Western ships could rain down destructive fire on cities that, because less technologically advanced, lacked the defensive works which could deter all but the strongest fleets from engaging in duels with shore defences;[69] but also because Western ships could additionally put ashore landing parties to project power very effectively on land. For example, the French fleet that overran Hawaii in 1849 did not need to fire its guns; as a British consular official observed, it put ashore 'an armed force which took military possession of the fort, the government offices, and the custom house', spiked the fort's guns, and poured the gunpowder into the harbour. Commodore Matthew Perry's squadron of four ships sent the Japanese capital 'of Edo into an uproar' in 1853, partly because of the threat his ships posed to maritime trade, but partly because the Japanese, who were well aware of Perry's Marines, knew that their coastal defences could not withstand landings supported by bombardment.[70] And Marines typically comprised only an important part, rather than the whole of landing parties: from sixteenth- and seventeenth-century Barbary corsairs and seventeenth-century Dutch privateers to nineteenth-century European whalers and merchantmen, it was never only naval ships that could engage with foes ashore by use of short-term landing parties.[71] Sailors could be converted into temporary soldiers for raiding purposes, as easily as soldiers became sailors for the purpose of boarding enemy ships to engage in a medieval or sixteenth-century naval battle.

The creation of Marine units subject to naval authorities only meant that Navies had an even greater potential to carry out amphibious operations without recourse to Armies. Contrariwise, when Armies have maintained riverboat forces, for combat as well as transport,

---

[69] See Turnbull (1982), 158, and Bliss (2003), 21–2, 28, for the success obtained by the threat of bombardment of Nagasaki (1808) and Honolulu (1842 and 1845), in each case by just one 'modern' warship; and Turnbull (1982), 172, for the collapse of the Shogunate, in the face of a fleet anchored off Yokohama and then the actual bombardment of Kagoshima (1863). See in general Hagan (1973); and Preston & Major (1967).

[70] PRO, FO 881/179: memo, instances of coercive measures since 1830, 15 June 1850; Bliss (2003), 2; Turnbull (1982), 158–59.

[71] E.g., Barnby (1970); Guilmartin (1974), 77, 112; BNF, MS Néerlandais 17: log of the *Haerlem*, 3 May–17 Nov. 1628; Bliss (2003), 8–9, 16.

as in Burma during World War II, the jungles of South Vietnam,[72] and southern Iraq in 2003, they have had the potential to undertake amphibious operations with no or little reference to Navies.

Thus, a definition of an amphibious operation as one involving the cooperation of 'army' and 'navy' will not work, especially when dealing with history prior to *c.* 1700. In many amphibious operations, however, there was a clear organisational conjuncture in force-composition. Most obviously, this may be indeed army and navy, especially in the eighteenth century and after. In addition, however, in medieval Europe, clear administrative distinctions between soldiers and mariners (whether sailors or oarsmen) emerged. Fleets were largely provided by coastal towns or, increasingly, by admiralty boards. The soldiers that served on the ships in those fleets, however, were frequently provided by different hierarchies; and they were regularly paid at different rates to, and are generally distinguished in official records from, mariners. For most of this period, the soldiers were integral to the conduct of sea battles, but, even when employed to row landing boats or galleys, they were clearly distinct from the mariners, albeit operationally and sometimes organisationally part of navies.[73] This did not change with the introduction of specifically 'Marine' units, raised by Admiralties or Navy Boards.[74] Clear distinctions were still maintained between ships' crew on the one hand, even though the latter now manned ships' guns as well as sails and oars, and soldiers on the other hand, whether serving in separate units of marine infantry and artillery, or on shipboard.[75] When these soldiers were deployed for amphibious operations, then, an organisational conjuncture took place, since the soldiers formed a discrete sub-set within navies. This was, of course, even truer of Marines, while when riverine operations are carried out by army units, they are generally discrete units, often composed of specialists.

Against this, however, in Greek warfare, the soldiers carried by galleys were distinct from the oarsmen and sailors only in equipment,

---

[72] Made famous (or infamous) by the film *Apocalypse Now* (1979).

[73] See below, chs. 2–7. See also, e.g., Teensma, ed. (1999), 1:40, 81–4, 107n., 2:18.

[74] Below, chs. 9 and 10.

[75] This was for security (*i.e.*, to guard against mutiny by crews) as well as operational reasons.

not in organisational origins, or command hierarchies.[76] Also, as already noted, ships did not have to carry detachments of soldiers or marines to undertake amphibious assaults. In a sense, amphibious threat is inherent in naval power, even if it is only a limited amphibious threat, confined to raids and short-lived occupations. Nevertheless, although boarding involves hand-to-hand combat, it, ramming and bombardment can all be distinguished as aspects of *naval* force. All take place *on water* and can take place without any reference to land. When ships deploy their crews against land, they are deploying *military* force. Thus, even when amphibious warfare does not involve an amalgamation of different organisations, institutions, hierarchies or bureaucracies, it does involve the conjunction of different types of *force*. This distinction between types of force, as opposed to types of forces, is a difficult one to delineate, however— certainly military tactics sometimes adapt amphibious practice, so that, as at the Erne and Blackwater Rivers in Ireland in the 1590s, river crossings by ground troops can look very like amphibious assaults.[77] And of course 'naval force' looked very much like military force (displaced to decks from soil) for much of its history. It is difficult to find clear criteria for defining different types of force; combinations of forces from different organisations, or sub-organisations, are easier to identify and therefore this is what we use in defining amphibious warfare.

A final point needs to be made in this connection: namely that, as noted earlier, amphibious warfare involves conjunctures in venue *and* composition. Army and navy can combine in one element—this is *not* amphibious warfare. We have already seen how soldiers were an integral, but distinct, part of naval forces, even when amphibious operations were not envisaged—their role in ship combats was strictly naval. Similarly, 'naval brigades' of sailors serving on land in many British colonial wars of the late nineteenth century and US Marines fighting in land campaigns in World War I, Korea and Vietnam had all effectively become ground troops. The forces in which they served combined different organisations, but not different types of force. Bluejackets manning Gatling guns in the Sudan or 4.7–inch guns in South Africa were, almost literally, fish out of water.

---

[76] Connolly (1988), 262–5.
[77] Fissel, ch. 8, below, pp. 237–8.

It is when soldiers and sailors (to put it crudely) cooperate in two elements, rather than one, that amphibious warfare occurs.

Amphibious Warfare is . . . Definition and Theoretical Model

Amphibious warfare thus entails a double conjuncture, involving (1) cooperation of organisations or sub-organisations that are organisationally or institutionally land-focused with organisations or sub-organisations that are organisationally or institutionally sea-, river- or lake-focused, which (2) takes place in activities that take place both on land and in the water. This can be summarised as: involving the cooperation of land-based and water-based (or waterborne) forces. A true amphibian is an animal that lives on *both* land *and* the water. Units that function both on land and sea are rare, but even if the units involved in operations do not themselves *combine* land and sea capabilities, if those operations entail *cooperation* between both ground troops and waterborne units, acting in their primary function, then they are amphibious, for they involve an amalgamation of different elements and different types of force.

Hence our definition of amphibious warfare: *A form of warfare in which land-based and waterborne forces cooperate, on at least one side, whether against a similar conjunction of forces, or against a solely land or water-based enemy.* This definition can, however, work at different levels; there is tactical, operational, strategical, and grand-strategical amphibious warfare.[78] This amplification is important, because some types of combat or operation, while not amphibious at one level, may be at another.

Conceptualising Amphibious Warfare

At the TACTICAL level, the conjunction or cooperation of ground forces and waterborne forces occurs *in combat*—as, for example, in

---

[78] Our understanding of these terms draws on Murray & Millett (2000), 583–91. The contrast between levels of amphibious warfare is also discussed by Sicking, ch. 3, Glete, ch. 5 and Stapleton, ch. 10, all of whose views accord with that presented here; Sicking and Glete deal summarily with the strategic and operational levels (albeit their terminology varies) while Stapleton emphasises tactics. See below, pp. 69–70, 123, 318–20.

the celebrated British raid on St Nazaire in 1942; the Crusader attack at Constantinople in 1203, described in chapter two, in which knights rode straight from their transports onto the shore and into combat; or the English attack on Enniskillen Castle in 1594, described in chapter 8.[79] A fair proportion of historical 'combined operations' have taken place at the tactical, rather than operational, level. The 'amphibious raids' and 'amphibious reconnaissances' of current US amphibious doctrine take place at the tactical level;[80] so do assault landings and contested river-crossings; bombardments in support of all of these or of ground forces;[81] defences against all the above; and many (though not all) evacuations. Whereas at the tactical level the enemy is present and engaged, at higher levels the enemy may be actual or potential.

OPERATIONAL-level amphibious warfare can be distinguished from tactical because the cooperation of land- and water-based forces occurs *both* in combat *and also* immediately before and/or after it; or, alternatively, when no amphibious combat occurs, or combat takes place *solely* in land or on water, the OPERATION is still clearly amphibious when the nature of the objective necessitates coopera- tion in different elements. Thus, although the British intervention in Kuwait in 1961, when a specialist Royal Navy task force landed Royal Marines and later army troops to pre-empt Iraqi invasion, was not tactically amphibious (for the landings were not opposed), the forces were intended to go into combat, conceivably shortly after landing, required maritime logistical support, and could only be trans- ported there by the navy.[82]

An amphibious STRATEGY is a general *plan* for the deployment and employment of armed forces in which cooperation and conjuncture at the operational level is essential; however, this may take place *either* in amphibious operations, *or* in a combination of land and mar- itime operations. Intent is intrinsic to strategy, as well as practice, so that an amphibious strategy may envisage combined operations which may, however, never eventuate. This was the case with the intended Habsburg expedition to the Baltic in 1536, preparations

---

[79] Below, pp. 56, 236–7.
[80] E.g., Belfiglio (1999), 15.
[81] See 'Conclusion', below, pp. 442–4.
[82] Speller (1984), 89.

for which reached an advanced stage before cancellation and the planned offensive by an Anglo-Dutch 'fleet of defence' against Spanish interests in Asia, in 1620–22, which envisaged amphibious operations but in the end only carried out naval ones. Both, however, were aspects of an amphibious strategy.[83]

Amphibious operations may not even be required at the GRAND STRATEGIC level. This describes an *approach* to war that entails activity on both land and sea, in pursuance of aims chiefly determined neither by maritime considerations nor by territorial ambitions.[84] It is what many commentators would term a 'maritime' (as opposed to a 'continental') strategy, but there are historical examples of grand strategy whose goals were neither predominantly maritime nor predominantly territorial but still required cooperation on land and sea. They are examples of an amphibious GRAND STRATEGY.

Amphibious warfare thus does not consist *only* of amphibious operations, inasmuch as cooperation in two elements may, at the strategic or grand strategic levels, be achieved via the combination of operations conducted purely by ground forces or naval forces: so that a maritime or military operation may form part of an amphibious strategy. Equally, some actions at the tactical level may be incorporated into amphibious operations or strategies.

For instance, the mere transportation of a military force on ships or boats (whether at sea or on rivers or canals) is neither tactically nor operationally amphibious. Although ground and naval forces are acting jointly, they do so in only one element—water. Land- and water-based forces are in juxtaposition, rather than conjunction, which only occurs if the troops' destination is (or is potentially) defended by hostile forces; otherwise their landing is a simple debarkation, which is an integral part of voyaging—only if the landing will or may take place against opposition does it require joint planning, at least (and possibly joint execution). Thus, 'the transport of troops and equipment over water' is not in and of itself an amphibious operation, which, in the words of a former Royal Marine Commandant-General, is more than 'the movement of troops from A to B'.[85]

---

[83] See Sicking, ch. 3, below; Van Dyke (1997).

[84] As it will usually be at the trans-continental level, it will transcend inland waterways, so we use 'sea' here advisedly.

[85] Bittner (1991), 345; M. Garrod, 'Amphibious Warfare: Why?', *Journal of the Royal United Services Institute*, 113 (1988): 26, quoted in Bittner (1991), 346–7 at 347.

However, as Glete argues in chapter 5, 'movements of armies across the sea' are a strategic form of amphibious warfare, as opposed to the tactical form. Thus, while transportation of troops, whether across a sea, bay, lake, river or canal, to a friendly shore is *not* an amphibious/combined *operation*, it can be a component in warfare that is strategically or grand-strategically amphibious. Examples include the frequent passage of English armies to France in the fourteenth through sixteenth centuries, and to Ireland in the sixteenth and seventeenth centuries; the conveying of Spanish armies to Naples in the 1490s; and the transportation of the Earl of Leicester's army to the Netherlands in 1585–86—in contrast to which, attempts to transport troops to Antwerp in 1584 and Sluys in 1587 involved passing enemy defences that were both water- and land-based and so were amphibious operations.

To take another case, naval forces today, in the world of aircraft carriers and sea-based land attack missiles can very effectively 'project power' onto the shore, without the use of land forces.[86] This was less true in the world of the broadside armed man-of-war, simply because of range, but bombardments by warships were commonplace.[87] Attacks of this kind when in support of landings or ground forces, form part of amphibious operations; when not, they are naval, tactically or operationally (depending on size and complexity), but can still be examples of amphibious warfare, because they can form important aspects of an amphibious *strategy*. Likewise, logistical support by a fleet or squadron (whether from salt or freshwater) to ground forces in the immediate aftermath of a landing is regarded as an aspect of operational-level amphibious warfare. When it is provided more long-term, as by the fleets coasting alongside the English army in Scotland in 1547, the Dutch army in Flanders in 1600, or the Allied army in southern France in the Nine Years' War, it transcends an amphibious operation—but constitutes an important (or essential) part of an amphibious strategy or grand strategy.

It must be emphasised that what we term 'grand strategic amphibious warfare' is not the same as 'maritime strategy', despite similarities. Amphibious warfare is too often seen simply as the projection

---

[86] As Speller (2001), 84, points out.
[87] And are also discussed in the conclusions: below, pp. 442–4.

of power 'from the sea' onto land—too often conceptualized as only an adjunct of naval/sea power or 'maritime power projection', or an aspect of 'maritime strategy'.[88] The first presumption is erroneous because, as we have seen, amphibious warfare can be waged inland. As for the second set of presumptions, their roots lie firstly in Sir Julian Corbett's influential Edwardian identification both of a distinctly British 'maritime strategy' and its importance in creating the eighteenth-century British Empire, and secondly in Basil Liddell Hart's arguably even more influential inter-war misappropriation of Corbett. Reacting to the slaughter on the Western Front, Liddell Hart ignored (unlike Corbett) the important role played by the armies of Britain's Continental allies. He over-stressed Britain's use of its 'natural' naval strength for 'sea-borne expeditions against the . . . vulnerable extremities' of its enemies, which he interpreted as 'a distinctively British practice of war, based on experience, and proved for three centuries of success'—using this, in turn, to support his claim that a 'strategy of indirect approach' (which in practice revolved around amphibious operations) could achieve victory over a Continental power without the bloodshed of a head-on confrontation with its armies (as in World War I).[89]

To be sure, a precondition for undertaking coastal landings is some degree of sea power and many amphibious operations have indeed been exercises in the projection of maritime, naval or sea, power, or been undertaken in furtherance of a maritime strategy. However, to conceptualize amphibious warfare *only* in such terms takes too limited a view. Amphibious warfare involves more than strength on sea; moreover, it is not only a component in strategies that army professionals tend to regard as circumlocutions, whether Liddell Hart's 'indirect approach', or the 1980s US strategy of peripheral horizontal escalation.[90] Williamson Murray and Allan Millett

---

[88] E.g., Corbett (1911); Mearsheimer (1986), 24–27; Brooks (1986), 65, 71, 82; Evans (1990); Alexander & Bartlett (1995); Gray (1995–6), 33, 36 n. 19; Gatchel (1996), 9; Menon (1998); Till, ed. (2001), ch. 4; and Stapleton, below, ch. 10. Also cf. Aston (1920), Richmond (1941) and Maund (1949)—though not using these terms, this patently was their concept.

[89] Corbett (1911 etc.) and see fn. 21, above; Liddell Hart (1932), quoted as part of a detailed critique by Strachan (1994), 417–23 at 417; Liddell Hart (1929; 1941).

[90] For the latter, see Mearsheimer (1986); Brooks (1986); and Alexander & Bartlett (1995).

rightly (but unusually) insist that amphibious operations may be actions to seize 'continental entrant[s]', in which case instead of being harassments of a continental enemy, or examples in maritime or indirect strategy, they may be precursors to a full-scale land campaign.[91] The Allies in World War II eventually rejected a 'maritime strategy' (or possibly an amphibious grand strategy!) of occupations only of (mostly littoral) so-called weaker areas around fringes of Nazi power (i.e., what some recent maritime strategists might term its perimeter or peripheries); yet the necessary first step in their strategy of confronting and defeating Nazi forces in France and Germany was the greatest combined operation in history.

None of this is to deny the importance or relevance of maritime strategies and naval power projection in many situations. But amphibious operations can also be an adjunct to land warfare and an aspect of Continental strategies—or of amphibious grand strategies.

Contextualising Amphibious Warfare

The four different categories may overlap or may be, to an extent, mutually exclusive. They are probably best understood by reference to actual examples. We therefore summarily examine a range of well-known historical examples of amphibious warfare to provide further historical context for the theoretical concepts outlined above.

The Norman invasion of England in 1066 was not amphibious *tactically*, because the landing was unopposed. Indeed, a contested landing was never envisaged: William the Conqueror's fleet was always intended only to transport his army, so that the invasion from the point of embarkation to the point of disembarkation was a naval, or rather (as William lacked a *fighting* navy), a maritime, triumph— of ships over (an arm of) the sea. However, the Norman invasion was an amphibious *operation* because, though it had a strictly military objective, maritime capability had also to be used to attain that objective, and the troops had to be supplied from the sea in the immediate aftermath of the landing. For these reasons, Matthew Bennett includes it chapter 2 as one of the examples of medieval amphibious warfare.[92]

---

[91] Murray & Millett (2000), 588.
[92] Below, pp. 52–3.

The English determination to keep Calais and its Pale, even after the loss of the rest of France in the 1450s, owed a great deal to pride, but somewhat to the awareness, dating back at least to the fifteenth century, that Calais, with Dover, controlled 'the narowe see' between the Continent and England and were thus England's bulwark against invasion.[93] Maintenance of a land presence in France thus owed something to naval strategic concerns. However, the defence of the pale of Calais of course depended not only on its military garrison but also on support from the nascent Royal Navy (when Calais fell it was partly because contrary winds prevented it being reinforced). It thus was the fruit of an amphibious grand strategical view. In the 1590s, England maintained an army in Brittany essentially to prevent the Breton ports becoming bases for a Spanish armada. Ground forces were maintained abroad, then, and waged land battles, to further naval strategic concerns; however, they had to be maintained logistically, and were supported tactically in sieges, by naval forces, so that the campaign in Brittany was also an amphibious *strategy*, occasionally involving amphibious *operations*.[94]

The long war between the Habsburg Spanish and Ottoman Turkish empires in the sixteenth century, marked by celebrated actions such as the sieges of Tunis (1535) and Malta (1565) and the Battle of Lepanto (1571), provides an example of a conflict dominated by amphibious grand strategy on both sides. John F. Guilmartin's observations on Spain are equally true of the Ottomans: 'strategic combinations did not separate cleanly into land and sea categories. Even where the primary commitment of military forces was on land, movement and sustenance by sea played a major role in almost every case'. Operations, too, 'were amphibious in character, revolving around the use of war galleys to transport land forces to their objectives and to support them there.'[95]

In the Seven Years' War, 'Britain's control of the seas allowed her to choose to fight in land theatres which could be sustained by the navy, campaigns limited in method and in geographical extent, but unlimited in their objectives.'[96] British grand strategy has thus

---

[93] Anon. (1436), 2 *et passim*; Runyan (1993), 92–3.
[94] Operations in Brittany are discussed by Wernham and Fissel, chs. 7 and 8.
[95] Guilmartin (1993), 116; see also idem (1974), 56–7, 81, 107, 218; and ch. 6, below.
[96] Strachan (1994), 418, citing Corbett (1911).

typically been perceived as maritime and provided the historical ammunition for Corbett's and Liddell Hart's claims for maritime strategy. To be sure, British war plans revolved around sea power—both what it necessitated and the opportunities it offered. Britain's approach to war at this time involved deploying Britain's armies against strategically key points on the enemy's perimeter (rather than against the enemy's main armies in Europe), making use of naval superiority; so it was certainly not a continental strategy. However, it was not a maritime strategy either, because the approach was not only conceived as a way to secure greater control of key waterways, or of destroying enemy sea power—these were the means, not the ends. And other means included land campaigns by British armies in India and the North American interior (as well as campaigning with allies in Europe). The ends included acquisition of continental as well as insular territory (and for what it could yield, as well as for strategic maritime advantage) with the expansion of Britain's land empire a major war aim. British grand strategy under Pitt the Elder is thus best conceptualised as amphibious, rather than maritime.

General Wolfe's celebrated campaign that culminated in the capture of Quebec in 1759 was amphibious *strategically*, because only through cooperation and combination could Quebec be taken: naval transport was necessary to deliver the combined force and to command inland waterways but ground forces had to carry out fighting on land. The campaign in its preliminary stages involved *tactical* amphibious warfare—the army and fleet together made assault landings, and ground forces then made attacks supported by naval bombardment. Because of the role of cooperation before and after, the campaign was also amphibious *operationally*. Indeed, although in the campaign's final operation the army was landed unopposed (albeit on a potentially hostile shore) and though the final victory on the Plains of Abraham that clinched the fall of Quebec was purely a land battle, with no intervention from waterborne forces, the operation as a whole was amphibious, because the army was transported into the enemy's vicinity prior to combat by the navy: the nature of the objective of the operation necessitated cooperation of land- and water-based forces.[97] This gives a good example of how even

---

[97] This summary draws on Keyes (1943), 9–16; Whitehouse (1964), 49–58; and Syrett (1972), 270–2.

an action that is not amphibious in the immediate tactical sense may nevertheless be amphibious in other senses.

British grand strategy during the French Revolutionary Wars can reasonably be termed 'maritime' rather than amphibious—the British did not seek territorial acquisition, and when British troops fought on the Continent they did so in land campaigns conducted in areas or regions from which British sea power might be threatened, or in amphibious campaigns such as that in North Holland in 1799. The expedition to Copenhagen in 1801, which culminated in the famous battle at which Nelson used his blind eye as an excuse to ignore a signal to break off action and won the day, was always naval. Shore-based artillery was part of the Danish defence, but no British troops were sent, other than the small contingents of marines on board ships (whose purpose was as much naval as amphibious: they participated as sharpshooters in naval battles and helped keep order among the crew) and there was never any intention of making a landing. Thus, only naval force was applied, so there was no conjuncture or cooperation—only the collision of land and sea.

In the Napoleonic Wars, however, British pursued an amphibious grand strategy. As in the Seven Years' War, British war plans were founded on maximising (and preserving) British mastery of the sea. However, land campaigns were aimed at creating a continental military confrontation, as well as at securing littoral goals that had naval strategic importance. Naval strategy motivated attacks on Copenhagen in 1807 and Rochefort and Walcheren in 1809, intended to destroy France's potential and actual naval strength and to capture the chief potential base for an invasion of Britain. However, whereas the destruction by fireships of much of a French fleet at Rochefort was a purely naval venture, land forces were an essential ingredient in the expeditions to Copenhagen and Walcheren; thus the attacks on these two resulted from amphibious, not naval, strategy. Wellington's great victories in Portugal and Spain were clearly military operations and largely served a military strategy, but they depended on constant naval logistical support, and thus clearly reflect an amphibious grand strategy.

The British military effort in the Crimean War was in pursuance of a maritime grand strategy. The main aim was to neutralise Russian sea power in the Black Sea; however, this required the capture of the large port-city of Sebastapol, which in turn necessitated the cooperation of both ground and naval forces on both land and sea to succeed. Thus, British strategy on the Crimean peninsula was amphibious. It involved one large-scale amphibious operation, in the siege of Sebastapol. There was no combination of forces in actual combat, although a putative combined assault on the city was prevented only when the Russians sealed up the harbour with scuttled vessels. However, because Sebastapol was a port, cooperation of land-based and seaborne forces was necessary for its capture; the fleet was vital for the transmission of reinforcements and supplies, and evacuation of wounded and thus took an active part in the operation logistically, if not tactically; and contingents of sailors were landed to help man the siege lines. Thus, the siege of Sebastapol was *operationally* amphibious, as well as being part, together with purely military and naval operations, of an amphibious *strategy*.

The subsequent operations in the Sea of Azov, against Kerch and other ports, were also in pursuance of an amphibious strategy—for, since its goals were to destroy the transport that might be used to convey enemy supplies to Sebastapol *and* as much of those supplies as possible, achievement of those goals had to be obtained on both sea and land. This necessitated not only sweeps by men-of-war at sea, but strikes on ports and the littoral. The campaign in the Sea of Azov involved naval actions by the fleet, designed to sweep the enemy from the sea; sea movements of both ground and naval forces; and a series of assault landings, some of which were followed by limited land actions, with the troops debarked (and re-embarked) by smaller vessels, which, operating inshore, also acted as artillery support.[98] In short, it was *strategically, operationally* and *tactically* amphibious.

The bombardment of the Turkish forts at Gallipoli in 1915 by Anglo-French fleets was not an instance of amphibious warfare.[99] It was a straight contest between land forces on the one side, and sea forces on the other and, because the bombardment was originally intended to clear the Dardanelles without landings, nor was this naval operation part of an amphibious strategy. In contrast, the Allied landings on the Gallipoli peninsular, which followed, were amphibious both *operationally* and *tactically*, with naval forces landing ground

---

[98] Merrill (1956), esp. 17, 22–26.
[99] As one Royal Marine stressed soon afterwards: Aston (1920), xiv.

forces, against opposition, in order to capture objectives which, while land-based, controlled a waterway.

The Allied landings in Normandy on D-Day were obviously amphibious, the greatest in the history of warfare, but while tactically and operationally amphibious, in grand strategical terms they were not, for their purpose was to deliver armies to Europe in order to pursue a continental strategy. Indeed, much of the tension between the British and Americans in World War II was due to the perceived British preference for the amphibious grand strategy pursued through 1942–3, as opposed to the continental strategy favoured by the Americans and adopted by the Allies in 1944. That 'every major offensive launched by the United States during World War II was initiated by an amphibious assault'[100] reflected the isolation of the North American continent from the main theatres of war, rather than US grand strategy. Grand strategy against Japan, in contrast, was maritime or amphibious throughout.

Amphibious Warfare 1000–1700

Applying the Model

How does the model of amphibious warfare that has just been outlined relate to the essays in this volume? They not only treat what might be termed obvious amphibious warfare—that is, engagements at the tactical level—but also amphibious operations and strategies. However, this volume's chief concern is with actual cooperation between land-based and waterborne forces. For this reason, when contributors deal with strategically amphibious warfare, they generally examine purely naval or military operations in less detail than the combined operations that formed part of amphibious strategies. In grand-strategical amphibious warfare, actual cooperation of land and sea forces in the two elements often may not occur. It is necessary, when constructing a theoretical model of amphibious warfare, to recognise that land and sea operations may fit into strategies or grand strategies which are amphibious in conception, but the history of

---

[100] Whitehouse (1964), 12.

these operations is best dealt with in specialist studies of land warfare, sea warfare, or strategy. Thus the grand-strategical level *per se*
is only explicitly considered in this volume in chapters five and ten,
both of which are still operationally focused; other chapters consider
particular amphibious operations that formed part of such grand
strategies.[101]

In all the actions and campaigns treated in this volume, ground
and waterborne forces cooperated both on land and in water. The
logistics, organisation, and what might be called *mentalité* of amphibious warfare are all extremely important and are considered in several chapters, but the main focus of the essays that follow is the
actual *practice* of late-medieval and early early-modern amphibious
warfare at the tactical and operational level.

This balance reflects the nature of medieval and early-modern
amphibious warfare, as opposed to twentieth-century combined operations, in which 'the preliminaries' have been deemed more important than 'execution of ... the operation'.[102] This is not to suggest
that administrative issues were unimportant during the eleventh-to-
eighteenth centuries. Then as now, amphibious operations were more
complex than operations only on land or sea. As in warfare in general in this period, however, the forces involved in amphibious operations, though large by the standards of what had gone before, were
still limited enough that personal brilliance could sometimes overcome institutional weaknesses.

What emerges clearly from the mix of studies that follow is that
states had to overcome immense organisational, logistical and cultural challenges even before an amphibious force was despatched.
These difficulties were far greater than those faced after *c.* 1700,
when combining military and naval forces in a particular space and
time still proved tricky, but the existence of standing armies and
navies provided an institutional basis for mounting amphibious expeditions and the principles of amphibious tactics had largely been

---

[101] Guilmartin in ch. 6 examines an operation within a war in which, as we suggested above, both sides pursued an amphibious grand strategy. English grand strategy in the Elizabethan war with Spain (Wernham, ch. 7) arguably was amphibious,
too. In contrast, Portuguese expansion in the Indian Ocean and its littoral in the
sixteenth century (Newitt, ch. 3) resulted from what is probably best characterized
as a maritime grand strategy.

[102] CAC, RMSY 8/22: lecture on combined operations, [1944], rubric 'Conclusion'.

established already, by the pioneers analysed in this volume. Earlier generations faced administrative and conceptual problems of the most fundamental sort just to equip, man and supply expeditions appropriately; if these problems were not overcome then proficiency at amphibious tactics and operational art might be for naught. On the other hand, even a well-founded amphibious expedition might not succeed if its strategic purpose was unclear and certainly would not succeed if its personnel could not conduct combined operations and combats capably. That amphibious expeditions sometimes succeeded, in the face of substantial logistical limitations, suggests that tactical and operational facility was, at this stage in the history of amphibious warfare, more important than administrative expertise—but when the latter was taken for granted, disaster frequently followed.

It is important to emphasise, however, that amphibious warfare was about more than organising and deploying offensive action. A number of essays in this volume consider defensive, as well as offensive, combats and operations. This is an important corrective to the generic assumption in studies of amphibious warfare that it is offensive in nature.[103] To be sure, the majority of essays in this volume are written from the attacker's perspective; and one of the major arguments of the volume as a whole is that the particular advantages (of flexibility, manoeuvrability and application of firepower) which amphibious operations offered to the offensive meant that it played a key role in the commercial and territorial expansion of European states, especially outside Europe.[104] Nevertheless, defensive amphibious capability was also important, especially in conflicts with states that also deployed amphibious power; indeed, as combined operations became more common, princes and states began to make conscious preparations to defend against amphibious assault. Guilmartin explores the interplay of amphibious attack, defence and counter-attack, and important

---

[103] E.g. in Merrill (1956), 27; Whitehouse (1964), 16 *et passim*; Merglen (1968); Bittner (1991), 347, 357 *et seq.*; Belfiglio (1999), 20; and even in the titles of Maund (1949); Bartlett (1983); Foster (1995); Alexander (1997); and Belfiglio (2001). For notable exceptions, see Keyes (1943), 16–17 and Gatchel (1996); and NB that, while both the US Marine Corps and Royal Marines (pre-World War II) conceived amphibious warfare as essentially offensive, they also recognized the need for defending against it: Isely and Crowl (1951), 23; Ulbrich (1999); and Bittner (1991), 349, 353–6.

[104] See below, pp. 445–8.

points about defence against amphibious operations are also made by Wernham, Stapleton and Trim.[105]

Overview of Volume

Latin Christendom first launched an offensive against the Moslem world during the era of the Crusades, which as well being wars for religion have been identified as the first instance of the European colonising impulse (chapter 2). With the waning of the Middle Ages and the first voyages of the age of discovery, Western states began attempts to find and to dominate new markets, first on the Continent's borderlands, then further afield (chapters 3 and 4). Amphibious expeditions were revealed to have excellent potential for profit-making and hence amphibious war began to be a continuation of commerce by other means.

The Reformation and coinciding resurgence of Islam in Europe, led to a renewal of religious war, this time within Europe, both between Protestants and Catholics and between Christendom and the Ottoman Empire. It was during this period that Europeans began to build on developments in both military and naval technology to master the techniques of combined operations, although total proficiency remained elusive. Amphibious warfare proved a valuable addition to the state's armoury, both in conflict with confessional and commercial rivals and in increasing state power at home. (Chapters 5, 6, 7, 8 and 11.)

Confessional conflict was also a factor in European expansion to Asia and the Americas, but materialistic considerations were more significant. From the mid-seventeenth century, amphibious warfare was again primarily a tool for commercial and political power projection, but also played an important part in the wars by which Europe's great powers resolved their relative status *vis-à-vis* each other and the rest of the world. By the end of the seventeenth century, the centralised governments of Europe's leading states had already developed relatively sophisticated amphibious tactics and had an increasingly good track record of successfully carrying out amphibious operations, albeit this remained a challenge for another two centuries at least. (Chapters 5, 8, 9, 10 and 11.) European proficiency

---

[105] Below, chs. 6; and 7, 10 and 11.

stood its imperial powers in good stead as they began a second surge of global expansion in the eighteenth century.

CHAPTER TWO is an overview of the history of amphibious warfare from the eleventh to the thirteenth centuries, beginning in the northern seas, but focused mostly on the Mediterranean and the practice of amphibious warfare by the Crusaders. Matthew Bennett examines tactical and operational amphibious warfare, exploring how amphibious warfare was actually carried out in combat and on campaign. He shows that forces launched from the sea could be decisive against fortresses, even before the advent of cannon-armed warships and that ingenuity could overcome the problems later generations solved with advanced technology. Complex combined operations were *not* beyond the capacity of medieval forces, but experienced and expert personnel were vital—and rare.

CHAPTER THREE examines amphibious warfare at the operational and strategical levels, and explores, too, its financing and organisation. Louis Sicking looks at three case-studies of amphibious warfare in the northern seas: two actual campaigns and one planned operation. The two campaigns occurred in the fourteenth century and pitched the cities of the Hanseatic League, allied to German princes and the king of Sweden, against the king of Denmark, with the king of Norway first Denmark's enemy and then its ally. The planned operation was a sixteenth-century attack by an amphibious expedition sent from Holland against the Danish foes of the Netherlands' Habsburg rulers.

In the first two episodes, the territorial princes allied to 'the Hansa' had an essentially military strategy, in which the purpose of naval forces was to deliver and then support armies that would dismember the Danish kingdom in a land campaign. In contrast, the Hanseatic cities initially had an essentially maritime strategy; their reason for going to war was to preserve trade and commercial advantages, and because the war was about commerce, sea-power was to be used to project power onto the land only to capture such towns, fortresses and islands as could allow safe passage to friendly shipping. The divergent strategic foci helped to distract the coalition partners to disastrous effect in the first instance, but in the second the Hansa ensured a focus on an amphibious strategy and obtained a great victory, despite having committed slightly smaller amphibious forces. The third case study reveals the difficulties that could be experienced in mounting amphibious operations, especially in a country lacking strong naval (as opposed to maritime) institutions: marrying centralised military forces to largely private-enterprise naval forces proved extremely difficult.

CHAPTER FOUR is a large-scale case-study of Portuguese amphibious warfare in the Indian Ocean. The Portuguese relied almost exclusively on combined operations throughout the sixteenth century, but Malyn Newitt concentrates here on the crucial first years after their arrival in the Indian Ocean, from 1500 to 1520, examining the tactical and operational system developed by the Portuguese and the organisation of forces on which the system depended. He provides a useful corrective to recent revisionist attempts to downplay the importance of Portuguese military strength in acquiring their empire.[106] The Portuguese mastered amphibious warfare to a remarkable degree and thereby obtained an empire that would have been otherwise beyond such a small nation. But amphibious warfare still required considerable resources and was thus most effectively deployed, at least initially, by the crown. However, because amphibious warfare was so expensive, profit was all-important; thus, commercial imperatives and private interests dictated where, when and how combined operations were undertaken. Ultimately, amphibious strength on the oceans did not strengthen the Portuguese state.

CHAPTER FIVE is an overview of amphibious warfare in the Baltic from the mid-sixteenth century to the end of the seventeenth century. Jan Glete mixes narrative and thematic analysis and concentrates on amphibious operations waged by Denmark-Norway and Sweden, whether against each other, or other Baltic rivals, touching on strategy, tactics, operational art, command and control, supply, state institutions, and geographical considerations. He shows that the attainment by Sweden and Denmark-Norway of the ability to carry out 'complex military operations' ahead of their neighbours gave them a vital advantage in conflict in the Baltic region and identifies '[m]ajor amphibious operations [as] a sign of a maturing state formation process'.[107] The Scandinavian countries seem to have showed unusually little interest in the economic potential of amphibious operations, but it must be borne in mind that in general 'trade through [the Baltic Sea] formed an important element in its conflicts.'[108]

---

[106] Cf. Morillo (1995), 78.

[107] Below, p. 146.

[108] Oakley (1987), 52; the only example of an economically motivated amphibious operation, by Sweden against Poland, is at p. 134.

CHAPTER SIX is a case-study of one pivotal amphibious campaign: the siege of Malta in 1565. This, as John Guilmartin has previously suggested, in his classic study, *Gunpowder and Galleys*, 'represented the apex of sixteenth-century amphibious warfare' at least in the Mediterranean, involving cooperative action between a rich variety of land- and water-based forces.[109] Examining this key moment in the long amphibious war between the Spanish Monarchy and the Sublime Porte, Guilmartin's narrative focuses on the actual practice of amphibious combat, especially at the tactical level, but also touches on organisation, and highlights the importance of proficiency in operational art by 'senior commanders and their staffs'.

The next two chapters both consider amphibious warfare waged by and in early-modern England and Britain.

CHAPTER SEVEN is a narrative of English combined operations undertaken during the Elizabethan war with Spain, in the Atlantic and against Spanish-controlled Atlantic ports. The late R. B. Wernham examines amphibious warfare mainly at the strategical and operational levels, although he includes snapshots of tactical practice; he also explores organisation and finance, revealing the complex processes required to mount the expeditions made famous by their association with Sir Francis Drake. His focus is on amphibious warfare as economic warfare, both by the state and by individuals. As with the Portuguese in the Indian Ocean, amphibious operations were often for-profit enterprises, but commercial imperatives clashed with the crown's war aims. Wernham shows that though collaboration between the state and military entrepreneurs was often necessary, it was only when the state had the whip hand that strategic objectives were met.

In CHAPTER EIGHT, Mark Fissel's focus is on amphibious warfare as projection of state power. In contrast to chapter seven, his essay is a thematic analysis, not a narrative; it deals with tactical and operational amphibious warfare; its subject area is mostly the seas around and waterways within the British Isles; and its chronological span is much longer. It includes the Irish Nine Years' War, 1594–1603 (also called Tyrone's rebellion), which must be distinguished from the European Nine Years' War, 1688–1697 (also known as the War of the Grand Alliance), which is the subject of John Stapleton's essay.[110]

---

[109] Guilmartin (1974), 178–9 at 178.
[110] We borrow the terminology of Pádraig Lenihan in terming these two conflicts the Irish and European Nine Years' Wars: Lenihan (2001), 377.

Fissel emphasises that the English amphibious practice actually flourished, not with the celebrated 'sea dogs' like Drake, but with officers carrying out operations on Ireland's rivers and lakes, and with the seventeenth-century Republican admiral, Robert Blake; 'the immaturity of the English state and the practical complexities of combined operations prevented amphibious warfare from reaching [its] full potential'.[111]

Two chapters follow on the role of amphibious warfare in great power conflicts in late seventeenth-century Europe.

CHAPTER NINE analyses the management and conduct of amphibious warfare by France in the Mediterranean, from the first amphibious campaign launched by Louis XIV in 1664, to the end of the European Nine Years' War in 1697. Guy Rowlands' highlights logistical, institutional and administrative aspects of amphibious warfare, with some consideration of operational practice. This chapter is the most detailed consideration in the volume of how amphibious warfare was supplied and administered, and it reveals the vital difference that permanent military and naval establishments could make for preparing amphibious expeditionary forces, especially when, as in France, institutional structures for amphibious operations were created alongside standing armies and navies. The contrast between the relatively polished and efficient amphibious machine created under the Sun King and the far more haphazard conduct of combined operations by the Portuguese, Habsburgs (outside the Mediterranean) and English a century or so before could not be more marked. Rowlands thus also offers an important revisionist corrective to current historiographical assumptions that the French never took amphibious warfare seriously and were always behind their British rivals.

CHAPTER TEN is a survey of the practice of amphibious warfare by the British and Dutch allies during the Nine Years' War (1689–97) around Ireland, and in the English Channel and Mediterranean Sea. Analysis of Allied strategy and grand strategy is studded with more detailed consideration of tactical and operational practice, including an innovative emphasis on the role of naval bombardments. In contrast, then, to the preceding study of the general French management of amphibious war, John Stapleton concentrates on the Allied

---

[111] Below, p. 257.

conduct of amphibious operations. Again, the impact of the creation of permanent military and naval establishments is evident—late seventeenth-century practice was a far cry from the fumbling of the Dutch in the 1530s or the mixed bag of English practice under the last Tudor, early Stuarts, and Republic. In consequence, amphibious operations promised much; however, because, as Stapleton argues, of a lack of strategic focus (and hence of clear objectives), they never fully delivered on that promise.

CHAPTER ELEVEN is wholly thematic, concentrating on amphibious warfare as waged in inshore and inland waters across the period and across the world. D. J. B. Trim examines operations that, while launched from the sea against land, required substantial combined fighting thereafter on inshore or inland waterways to achieve their objectives; or operations that took place essentially or entirely inland, even if with some input from forces brought from the seas. He sketches out the main characteristics of these two different, but related (and little-studied) forms of amphibious operation. This chapter thus deals with amphibious warfare mostly at the tactical and operational levels, although it makes some points about strategy. It also considers amphibious warfare from the perspective of geography, revealing how it influenced strategy and the conduct of amphibious operations; and it, too, highlights the frequency with which targets of amphibious operations reflect commercial and economic, rather than purely strategic or operational, exigencies.

These essays do not do justice to the whole sweep of amphibious operations, tactics, strategies and grand strategies from the dawn of the eleventh century to the end of the seventeenth century. However, they bring to light a rich variety of evidence about the organisation, conduct and purpose of medieval and early modern amphibious warfare. If the essays impel historians and practitioners of amphibious warfare to include these seven centuries in comparative analysis of their subject, then this volume will have served its purpose.

Bibliography

Archival Sources

BNF   MSS Néerlandais.
CAC   RMSY Ramsay Papers.
PRO   SP 105 SP Foreign, Archives of British Legations, 1568–1871.
        FO 881 Foreign Office, Confidential Prints and Reports, 1827–1914.

Published Primary Sources

ASC (1982) *The Anglo-Saxon Chronicles*, trans. and ed. A. Savage (London: 1982; Book Club Associates edn, 1983).
Anon. (1436) *'The Libelle of Englyshe Polycye.' A Poem on the Use of Sea-Power 1436*, ed. G. Warner (Oxford: 1926).
Molyneux T. M. (1759) *Conjunct Expeditions: or Expeditions that have been carried on jointly by the fleet and army, with a Commentary on a Littoral War*, 2 vols (London: 1759).
Teensma B., ed. (1999) *Dutch-Brazil, 1, Two Unpublished Manuscripts about the Dutch Conquest (1624) and the Iberian Recovery (1625) of Salvador da Bahia in Brazil, 2, A Forgotten Letter Written by Martim Correia de Sá* (Rio de Janeiro: 1999).

Published Secondary Sources

Ainsworth W. L. (1945) 'An Amphibious Operation that Failed: The Battle of New Orleans', *Proceedings of the United States Naval Institute* 71 (1945) 193–201.
Alexander J. H. (1997) *Storm Landings: Epic Amphibious Battles in the Central Pacific* (Anapolis, Md.: 1997).
Alexander J. H. and Bartlett M. L. (1995) *Sea Soldiers in the Cold War: Amphibious Warfare, 1945–1991* (Annapolis, Md.: 1995).
Alvarez J. E. (1999) 'Between Gallipoli and D-Day: Alhucemas, 1925', *Journal of Military History* 63 (1999) 75–98.
Anderson M. S. (1988) *War and Society in Europe of the Old Regime* (London: 1988).
Aston G. (1911; 1920) *Letters on Amphibious Wars* (London: 1911; 2nd edn, London: 1920).
Barker T. M. (2000) 'A Debacle of the Peninsular War: The British-Led Amphibious Assault against Fort Fuengirola 14–15 October 1810', *Journal of Military History*, 64 (2000) 9–52.
Barnby H. (1970) 'The Algerian Attack on Baltimore 1631', *The Mariner's Mirror* 56 (1970) 27–31.
Barnett C. (2000) *Engage the Enemy More Closely: The Royal Navy in the Second World War* (London: 1991; paperback edn, London: 2000).
Bartlett M. L. (1983), ed. *Assault from the Sea. Essays on the History of Amphibious Warfare* (Anapolis, Md.: 1983).
Belfiglio V. J. (1998) 'Roman Amphibious Operations Against Britain in 55 B.C.', *Military and Naval History Journal* no. 7 (March 1998) 3–13.
——. (1999) 'The Roman Amphibious Raid Against Britain in 54 B.C.', *Military and Naval History Journal* no. 9 (April 1999) 15–21.
——. (2001) *A Study of Ancient Roman Amphibious and Offensive Sea-Ground Task Force Operations* (Lewiston, N.Y.: 2001).
Billias G. A. (1960) *General John Glover and his Marblehead Mariners* (New York: 1960).
Bittner D. F. (1991) 'Britannia's Sheathed Sword: The Royal Marines and Amphibious Warfare in the Interwar Years—A Passive Response', *Journal of Military History* 55 (1991) 345–364.

Black J. (1999) 'Introduction' to *European Warfare 1483–1815*, ed. *idem* (Basingstoke and New York: 1999).
——. (2000) 'Britain as a Military Power, 1688–1815', *Journal of Military History* 64 (2000) 159–77.
——. (2002) *European Warfare, 1494–1660* (London and New York: 2002).
——. (2003) 'On Diversity and Military History', in 'Military Revolutions: A Forum', *Historically Speaking* 4:4 (April 2003) 7–9.
Braudel F. (1972) *The Mediterranean and the Mediterranean World in the Age of Philip II*, 2 vols, trans. S. Reynolds (New York, Evanston, San Francisco and London: 1972; as *La Méditerranée at le monde méditerranéen à l'Époque de Philippe II*, Paris: 1966).
Brooks L. F. (1986) 'Naval Power and National Security: The Case for the Maritime Strategy', *International Security* 11:2 (Autumn 1986) 58–88.
Burne A. H. (1939) 'An Amphibious Campaign—North Holland, 1799', *Army Quarterly* 39 (1939–40) no. 1, 103–23.
Cable J. (1994) *Gunboat Diplomacy 1919–1991: Political Applications of Limited Naval Force* (3rd edn, Basingstoke: 1994).
Chakravarti P. C. (1930) 'Naval Warfare in Ancient India', *Indian Historical Quarterly* 4 (1930) 645–64.
Connolly P. *Greece and Rome at War* (London: 1988), app. 1, 'War at Sea'.
Cooper R. G. S. (1997) 'Amphibious Options in Colonial India: Anglo-Portuguese Intrigue in Goa, 1799', in *New Interpretations in Naval History: Selected Papers from the Twelfth Naval History Symposium held at the United States Naval Academy, 26–27 October 1995*, ed. W. B. Cogar (Anapolis, Md.: 1997) 95–113.
Corbett J. (1911, etc.) *Some Principles of Maritime Strategy* (London: 1911; new edn, 1918; repr., London: 1972, 1988; New York: 1972).
Cunliffe B. W. (2001) *Facing the Ocean: The Atlantic and its Peoples 8000 BC–AD 1500* (Oxford: 2001).
Duffy M. (1987) *Soldiers, Sugar and Seapower: The British Expeditions to the West Indies and the War against Revolutionary France* (Oxford: 1987).
Duplessis R. S. (1997) *Transitions to Capitalism in Early Modern Europe* (Cambridge: 1997).
Encyclopædia Britannica (2003) 'Amphibious Warfare', in *Encyclopædia Britannica Standard Edition 2004 CD-ROM.* Copyright © 1994–2003 Encyclopædia Britannica, Inc. May 30, 2003.
Evans M. H. H. (1990) *Amphibious Operations: The Projection of Sea Power Ashore*, foreword by J. Thompson (London: 1990).
Foster S. (1995; 1998) *Hit the Beach! Amphibious Warfare from the Plains of Abraham to San Carlos Water* (London: 1995; repr., London: 1998).
Frost R. I. (2000) *The Northern Wars: War, State and Society in Northeastern Europe, 1558–1721* (Harlow: 2000).
Gatchel T. L. (1996) *At the Water's Edge: Defending against the Modern Amphibious Assault* (Anapolis, Md.: 1996).
Gray C. (1995–6) 'On Strategic Performance', *Joint Forces Quarterly* no. 10 (1995–96) 30–6.
Guilmartin J. F. Jr (1974) *Gunpowder and Galleys: Changing Technology and Mediterranean Warfare at Sea in the Sixteenth Century* (Cambridge: 1974).
——. (1993) 'The Logistics of Warfare at Sea in the Sixteenth Century: The Spanish Perspective' in Lynn, ed. (1993) 109–36.
Guthrie C. (2001) 'The New British Way in Warfare', *Liddell Hart Centre for Military Archives Lecture* (2001) http://www.kcl.ac.uk/lhcma/info/lec01.htm.
Hagan K. J. (1973) *American Gunboat Diplomacy and the Old Navy, 1877–1889* (Westport, Conn.: 1973).

Harding R. (1989) 'Sailors and Gentlemen of Parade: Some Professional and Technical Problems Concerning the Conduct of Combined Operations in the Eighteenth Century', *Historical Journal* 32 (1989) 35–55.

——. (1991) *Amphibious Warfare in the Eighteenth Century. The British Expedition to the West Indies 1740–1742*, Royal Historical Society Studies in History 62 (Woodbridge, Suffolk, and Rochester, N.Y.: 1991).

Isely J. A. and Crowl P. A. (1951) *The U. S. Marines and Amphibious War: Its Theory, and Its Practice in the Pacific* (Princeton and London: 1951).

Keyes R., Lord (1943) *Amphibious Warfare and Combined Operations; The Lees Knowles Lectures, 1943* (2nd edn, Cambridge: 1943).

Lenihan P., ed. (2001) *Conquest and Resistance. War in Seventeenth-century Ireland*, History of Warfare 3 (Leiden: 2001).

Liddell Hart B. (1929) *The Decisive Wars of History: A Study in Strategy* (London: 1929)

——. (1932) *The British Way in Warfare* (London: 1932; revd edns, 1935, 1942).

——. (1941) *The Strategy of Indirect Approach*, revd edn of idem (1929) (London: [1941]; new enlarged edn., intro. E. E. Dorman-Smith, 1946).

Lynn J. A., ed. (1993) *Feeding Mars: Logistics in Western Warfare from the Middle Ages to the Present*, Mershon Center Series on International Security and Foreign Policy, History, and Warfare (Boulder Col. & San Francisco: 1993).

Mallett M. E. and Hale J. R. (1984) *The Military Organization of a Renaissance State: Venice c. 1400 to 1617* (Cambridge: 1984).

Maund L. E. H. (1949) *Assault from the Sea* (London: 1949).

Mearsheimer J. J. (1986) 'A Strategic Misstep: The Maritime Strategy and Deterrence in Europe', *International Security* 11:2 (Autumn 1986) 3–57.

Menon R. (1998) *Maritime Strategy and Continental Wars*, Naval Policy and History 3. (Ilford, Essex: 1998).

Merglen A. (1968), trans. K. Morgan. *Surprise Warfare: Subversive, Airborne and Amphibious Operations* (London: 1968; published as *La guerre de l'inattendu*, Paris: 1966).

Merill J. M. (1956) 'British-French Amphibious Operations in the Sea of Azov, 1855', *Military Affairs* 20 (1956) 16–27.

Middleton R. (1993) 'The British Coastal Expeditions to France, 1757–1758', *Journal of the Society for Army Historical Research* 71 (1993) 74–92.

Military Affairs (1954) 'River Navies in the Civil War', *Military Affairs* 18 (1954): 29–32.

Moran C. (1945) 'D'Estaing, an Early Exponent of Amphibious Warfare', *Military Affairs* 9 (1945) 314–32.

Morillo S. (1995) 'Guns and Government: A Comparative Study of Europe and Japan', *Journal of World History* 6 (1995) 75–106.

Murray W. and Millett A. R. (2000) *A War to be Won: Fighting the Second World War* (Cambridge, Mass. and London: 2000).

Naval Studies Board (2000) *2000 Assessment of the Office of Naval Research's Marine Corps Science and Technology Program* (Washington, D.C.: 2000) [available at www.nap.edu/openbook/0309071380/html/14.html].

Oakley S. (1987) 'War in the Baltic, 1550–1790', in *The Origins of War in Early Modern Europe*, ed. J. Black (Edinburgh: 1987) 52–71.

——. (1992) *War and Peace in the Baltic 1560–1790* (London and New York: 1992).

O'Connor R. G. (1974) 'The U.S. Marines in the 20th Century: Amphibious Warfare and Doctrinal Debates', *Military Affairs* 38:3 (Oct. 1974) 97–103.

Oxford Dictionary (1996) *Oxford English Reference Dictionary* 2nd edn (1996).

Parker G. (1979) *Spain and the Netherlands, 1559–1659* (London: 1979).

——. (1988) *The Military Revolution: Military Innovation and the Rise of the West, 1500–1800. The Lees Knowles Lectures 1984, given at Trinity College, Cambridge* (Cambridge: 1988).

——. (1996) Ibid., 2nd edn (Cambridge: 1996).

——. (1999) *Ed. cit.*, revised reprint (Cambridge: 1999).

——. (2003) 'Military Revolutions, Past and Present', in 'Military Revolutions: A Forum', *Historically Speaking* 4:4 (April 2003) 2–7.
Preston A. and Major J. (1967) *Send a Gunboat! A Study of the Gunboat and its Role in British Policy, 1854–1904* (London: 1967).
Richmond H. (1941) *Amphibious Warfare in British History*, Historical Association Pamphlet 119 (Exeter: 1941).
Rogers C., ed. (1995) *The Military Revolution Debate: Readings on the Military Transformation of Early Modern Europe* (Boulder, Co.: 1995).
Runyan T. J. (1993) 'Naval Logistics in the Late Middle Ages: The Example of the Hundred Years War', in Lynn, ed. (1993) 79–100.
Schaffer R. (1972) 'The 1940 Small Wars Manual and the "Lessons of History"', *Military Affairs* 36:2 (Apr. 1972) 46–51.
Shaw H. I. Jr (1953) 'Penobscot Assault—1779', *Military Affairs* 17 (1953) 83–94.
Sicking L. (2001) 'Charles V: Master of the Sea?', in *Carlos V, Europeísmo y universalidad*, ed. J. Castellano and F. González, vol. 2, *La organización del poder* (Madrid: [2001]) 553–73.
——. (2004) *Neptune and the Netherlands: State, Economy, and War at Sea in the Renaissance*, History of Warfare 23 (Leiden: 2004).
Smelser M. (1955) *The Campaign for the Spice Islands, 1759: A Study of Amphibious Warfare*, foreword by S. E. Morrison (Chapel Hill, N.C.: 1955).
Speller I. (2001A) *The Role of Amphibious Warfare in British Defence Policy, 1945–56* (Basingstoke and New York: 2001).
——. (2001B) 'The Role of Amphibious Warfare in British Defence Policy, 1945–2000', in Till (2001) 84–94.
Strachan H. (1994) 'The British Way in Warfare,' in *The Oxford Illustrated History of the British Army*, ed. D. Chandler and I. Beckett (Oxford and New York: 1994) 417–34.
Stephenson M., ed. (2003) *Battlegrounds: Geography and the History of Warfare* (Washington, D.C.: [2003]).
Syrett D. (1973) 'The Methodology of British Amphibious Operations during the Seven Years' and American Wars', *The Mariner's Mirror* 58 (1973) 269–80.
Thompson I. A. A. (1985) 'The European Crisis of the 1590s: The Impact of War' in *The European Crisis of the 1590s: Essays in Comparative History*, ed. P. Clark (London: 1985) 261–84.
Thompson W. R. (1999) 'The Military Superiority Thesis and the Ascendancy of Western Eurasia in the World System', *Journal of World History* 10 (1999) 143–78.
Till G. (1997) 'Amphibious Warfare and the British', in *Amphibious Operations*, Strategic and Combat Studies Institute Occasional Paper 31 (Camberley: 1997).
Till G., ed. (2001) *Seapower at the Millennium* (Stroud: 2001).
Trim D. J. B. (1999) 'The Context of War and Violence in Sixteenth-Century English Society', *Journal of Early Modern History* 3 (1999) 233–55.
——. (2003) 'Army, Society and Military Professionalism in the Netherlands during the Eighty Years' War', in *The Chivalric Ethos and the Development of Military Professionalism*, ed. idem, History of Warfare 11 (Leiden: 2003) 269–89.
Turnbull S. (1982) *The Book of the Samurai: The Warrior Class of Japan* (Greenwich, Conn.: 1982).
Ulbrich D. J. (1999) 'Clarifying the Origins and Strategic Mission of the US Marine Corps Defense Battalion, 1898–1941', *War and Society* 17:2 (Oct. 1999) 81–109.
Waley D. P. (1954) '"Combined Operations" in Sicily, A.D. 1060–78', *Papers of the British School at Rome* 12 (1954) 118–25.
Whitehouse A. (1964) *Amphibious Operations* (2nd edn; London: 1964).
Zwitzer H. L. (1991) *De Militie van den Staat: Het leger van de Republiek der Verenigde Nederlanden* (Amsterdam: 1991).

Unpublished Secondary Sources

Bliss B. (2003) 'The Paulet Affair of 1843: A Turning Point in the Use of Coercive Force in Anglo-Hawaiian Relations during the Years 1825–1854?' (MA diss., King's College London, 2003).

Pinder D. (2004) 'The Claudian Invasion of Britain' (paper read at the British Commission for Military History Summer Conference 2004).

Stevens M. A. (forthcoming) 'Power Projection: Maritime and Expeditionary Warfare, 1557–1587' (PhD thesis, University of Exeter, forthcoming).

Van Dyke P. (1997) 'Maritime Rivalry in Early Modern Trade: The Anglo-Dutch Fleet of Defence, 1620–1622' (paper read at Harris Manchester College, Oxford, June 1997).

AMPHIBIOUS OPERATIONS FROM THE NORMAN CONQUEST TO THE CRUSADES OF ST LOUIS
c. 1050–*c.* 1250

Matthew Bennett

'The term "Amphibious Warfare" was adopted a few years ago to indicate a form of strategy of which the characteristic was the descent of sea-borne armies upon the coasts and ports of an enemy.'

So Admiral Sir Herbert Richmond, Master of Downing College, Cambridge began his brief article on 'Amphibious Warfare in British History', published for The Historical Association early in the Second World War. He went to describe such operations as part of an 'active defence', for: 'Passive defence produces no positive results, exerts no pressure upon the enemy, gives no hope to an ally.' Citing examples of amphibious warfare beginning in the reign of Elizabeth I up to the Napoleonic wars and then resuming with the disastrous Dardanelles campaign of the First World War, he stresses the limited nature of such operations. For Richmond, while 'the Seven Years War, the war of the American Revolution and the Russian War of 1854–55 could be called "amphibious wars" . . .' he restricts his definition to 'those expeditions sent over sea with certain definite and limited objectives.' What is interesting is that he does *not* mention medieval examples, including the one most likely to come to the mind of anyone writing in the British Isles: the Norman Conquest. The Admiral was writing in 1941, though, which may explain his reluctance to consider a conquest coming from northern France. But his narrow approach does not do justice to the "amphibious wars" of the eleventh to thirteenth centuries to which I wish to draw attention in this essay.[1]

For it is possible to analyse amphibious operations in some detail, at a period when there was not the same differentiation between armies and navies as later. In Pre-Conquest England the word for a military force—*here*—was then further defined as operating on land

---

[1] Richmond (1941).

or sea. In the ninth and tenth century Scandinavians were renowned for their ability not just to sail across the North Sea and all around the coasts of northern Europe, but also to penetrate deep inland with their longships. Using this strategy they conquered England in 1016 after a decade of warfare.[2] It is with their descendants in northern France that this investigation of amphibious warfare begins. We possess no accurate figures for the size of duke William of Normandy's forces in 1066.[3] Luckily the Bayeux Tapestry has left us with a visual record of a military campaign unparalleled between Trajan's Column and Charles V's tapestries recording his attack on Tunis.[4] Unfortunately, its illustrations often seem naive to us (although they doubtless conveyed a great deal more information to contemporaries). William the Bastard transported several hundred horses across the Channel in open, longship-style shipping. Some commentators have doubted this, seeking to identify the transfer of Mediterranean technology to northern waters in order to make it possible; but I consider this to be an unnecessary interpretation.[5]

The Tapestry shows the horses in the vessels like chess-piece knights, set in grinning pairs. This can be understood as two horses standing athwart the vessel, quite possibly in stalls. The disembarkation looks a little strange perhaps, as it shows the animals leaping out of the ship. But the scene also shows the sailors pulling on the mast to bring one gunwale down to the shore, quite a feasible activity in such a shallow draught vessel. Since horses cannot step over an obstacle in the same way as humans, they must jump. A Danish experiment conducted in the 1960s proves this to be practical.[6] We can only rely on the pro-Norman chroniclers who assure us of the success of the crossing and disembarkation, which took place in the

---

    [2] See Hooper (1989), 203–13.
    [3] Numbers of the fleet given vary considerably, from the 3,000 of the contemporary chronicler William of Jumiéges, to the perhaps spurious detail of 776, in the Ship List of (apparently) 1067–72, or to the supposed eye-witness account recorded a century later by the poet Wace, of 676. All these numbers are probably far too high and give us no idea of how many warriors and their horses which were transported. See Brown (1969), 149–51 for a discussion of numbers.
    [4] Wilson (1985).
    [5] Bachrach (1985), 505–31. Recent research has emphasised the role of the broader, deeper *knarr* in the Viking expansion, and it may that William used this type of vessel as horse transports. See Gardiner (1996), esp. chs. 5, 7, & 8 on Norse vessels and modern reconstructions.
    [6] Wilson (1985), plates 40–44; comments on disembarking horses, 227.

shallow, marshy waters of what was Pevensey Bay. Also, the Normans were fortunate in not having a contested landing, which would almost certainly have rendered their techniques inadequate.

The Norman Conquest did not end in 1066, as is often supposed. English opposition continued until 1071. William's campaign against the famous rebel Hereward, who fortified the island abbey of Ely in the Fens, was also a combined operation. His fleet blockaded Ely from the East, while land forces constructed a causeway and a siege castle at the west end of the island, to throttle the opposition. In 1072, King William mounted an offensive against Malcolm Canmore, King of Scots and supporter Edgar, claimant to the English throne. We have few details, but it is clear that a land force, supported by a fleet, advanced beyond Forth and forced the Peace of Abernathy.[7]

There were others Normans, though, land-grabbing in far-off Italy, who had already engineered amphibious landings. In 1061, Robert d'Hauteville, called 'Guiscard' (i.e., the Wily), and his brother Roger had transported a known number of knights and their horses across the narrow but perilous Straits of Messina. They were launching an attack from their base in southern Italy upon Muslim-controlled Sicily. They crossed at night (as William was to do) with 270 horses in 13 ships, then the ships returned to pick up another 140 mounts. The first historian to identify this, Daniel Waley, published a piece on these 'Combined Operations' in 1954 (reflecting his own involvement in the 1943 Sicily landings).[8] It is now possible to add some ideas on the type of vessels used. This is a result of the innovative work of Dr John Pryor, who is both an academic and a practical sailor.[9]

As he points out, there is plenty of evidence for the Byzantines moving horses by sea during the mid-tenth century reconquest era. The Byzantine fleets included horse-transports with twelve animals per vessel and chroniclers record them being unloaded, already mounted, straight on to the beaches. In the late twelfth century specialised vessels were capable of carrying forty horses per ship.[10] So

---

[7] See Whitelock (1961), annals for 1070–72 at 150–55. These could be seen as 'combined operations' rather than amphibious ones, but for the purposes of this paper the distinction will not be pressed.

[8] Waley (1954).

[9] Pryor (1992), (1984).

[10] See below, n. 16.

the Norman transports of 1060, supposedly carrying about twenty
horses each, fit well into this continuum of steadily increasing capacity. There may be some doubt as to whether the Normans had access
to the specialised type of vessel necessary. Waley believed that they
were kept in a central pool at Constantinople, but this is only a
guess, and it is also possible that they were available throughout the
Byzantine provinces. Certainly the new Norman rulers of southern
Italy had inherited the traditional naval service of the ports of the
Byzantine Catepanate. It may be significant that the usual name for
the horse transport in the region was *tarida*—an Arabic name—since
the Islamic powers contributed greatly to naval development in the
Mediterranean. The Crusaders called such vessels *huissiers* (in Old
French), because they had a door in them.[11]

Jean, sire de Joinville, biographer of Louis IX (St Louis) provides
a description of such a transport in 1248:

> we went aboard our ships in Marseilles in the month of August. On
> the day we embarked on the ships, the door of the ship was opened
> and all the horses we wanted to take overseas were put inside. And
> then the door was closed and well-caulked, just as when a cask is sub-
> merged, because, once the ship is on the high seas, the entire door is
> in the water.[12]

What did a *tarida* look like? We must wait until the late thirteenth
century for an accurate description, taken by Pryor from the now
largely destroyed Angevin archives in Naples. The crucial design feature was a square stern with two stem-posts, which enabled there to
be a door, or ramp, lowered and raised between them. With a third,
central stem-post there could be two doors. The advantage of these
vessels was that they could be backed onto the beaches using their
oars, providing a roll-on-roll-off facility reminiscent of a modern land-
ing-craft. A manuscript of Peter of Eboli's Sicilian chronicle gives a
contemporary version of how this looked.[13] Now, it is likely that
Joinville's description is, in fact, of a roundship, rather than a *tarida*.
Detailed records survive of St Louis' contracts with Italian maritime
republics for his Tunis Crusade two decades later (1270) giving
specifications for large roundships. They may have carried 70–100

---

[11] Waley (1954), 120. See also Bennett (1992).
[12] Joinville (1963), 196.
[13] Pryor, (1984) reproduces this illustration 11.

horses on two decks, although they had the disadvantage that they could not be unloaded ship-to-shore like the *tarida*. They required quays, which were in short supply even in the 13th century Mediterranean.[14]

There can be no doubt that horse transports existed; but can we take our chronicles on trust that knights were able to ride off them straight into battle? We have several descriptions of just this. A source for the Norman attack on Durazzo in 1081, states that:

> The ships numbered 150 and the soldiers, all-told, came to 30,000, each carrying 200 men with armour and horses. The expedition was equipped thus because they would probably meet the enemy in full armour and on the beaches.[15]

These numbers are certainly excessive, based on the complement of a fully-manned fighting ship, and the author, Anna Komnene, was writing in the 1140s. Just how practicable was such a manoeuvre? Certainly an account of Richard the Lionheart's invasion of Cyprus in 1191 would seem to cast doubt on it. We know that Richard had contracted for the supply of fourteen vessels (called *busses* by an English chronicler) from Marseilles. Each was capable of carrying 40 horses, 40 squires and 40 foot-soldiers, giving a potential mounted force of 560 knights—a very large number by twelfth century standards.[16] When Richard landed on Cyprus on 5 May this was done under cover of darkness, because, according to the poet Ambroise:

> The king gave the word to disembark/All the horses, after dark . . . The horses then were exercised,/For they were all benumbed and sore and stiff from the whole month before/Which they had spent upon the seas,/Unable to lie down at ease./With this small rest, for all their plight/Was to merit more by right,/At morn straightway mounted the king.[17]

So the next day Richard led his men to rout the Greeks in a cavalry charge. This all sounds rather more practical than leaping off the boats and into battle, and also squares with what we know about operations in Sicily in 1061 and England in 1066 (even if the vessels

---

[14] For the importance of harbour facilities see: Bennett (1992), 50 n. 29 & 55 n. 63.

[15] Komnene (1969), I, xvi, 69.

[16] Gillingham (1989), citing Roger of Howden's account, 147.

[17] Ambroise (1941), 88–89, ll. 1: 565–66; 1: 570–77.

were very different).[18] Yet, Fourth Crusader Robert de Clari does describe a ship-to-shore attack at Constantinople in 1203:

> As soon as they reached the shore, the knights came out from the transports on their horses, for the transports were made in such a way that there was a door that could be opened and a bridge thrust out by which the knights could ride out onto land, already mounted.[19]

This seems to be unequivocal evidence of this capability. There is the proviso that the genre of de Clari's vernacular history, linked closely to contemporary prose romances, might tend to fantasy. Yet, if such an operation were possible, then the situation at Constantinople, where the horses were transported only across the Golden Horn, seems most credible.

The first section of this paper has presented an interpretation of amphibious landings. I have concentrated on the delivery of that medieval weapons system—the knight—to perform his mounted charge. But more often medieval warfare was dominated by dour sieges—not glorious gallops—whatever the myth of chivalry might suggest. And it was in sieges that naval forces proved to be particularly important, especially on Crusade.[20]

Up to the mid-twelfth century naval forces were usually employed for blockade purposes. This may have been the intention of the Norman attacks on Durazzo in 1081 and 1108. We cannot be sure because on both occasions the Norman fleet was outmatched by that of their opponents. In 1081, Emperor Alexius' Venetian allies brought a fleet of far superior vessels to attack Guiscard's ships. Apparently they were taller and equipped with 'fighting tops'. That is to say, they winched ships' boats to the tops of their masts and filled them with marines equipped with crossbows with which they could rake

---

[18] It is also worth mentioning that horses are unlikely to be able to leap off a platform and into battle. See, for example, the famous scene from the movie 'Butch Cassidy and the Sundance Kid' (1969) where the 'Hole in the Wall Gang' are surprised by a posse galloping out of a stationary train which they were about to rob. This *coup de cinéma* could only be achieved by having a ramp on the other side of the truck for the horses to gallop up.

[19] Clari (136), 42. Pryor (1984) discusses the likelihood of the disembarkation, 22, 24. Bennett, (1992) discusses both the importance of good harbour facilities and the implications of the lack of quays in the Mediterranean of the period, 50 n. 29, 55 n. 63.

[20] For the debunking of the myth of the military supremacy of cavalry in the medieval period see Bennett (1998), 304–16.

the enemy decks. They also threw bombs designed to smash through the fragile bottoms of the Norman boats. These were 'very thick pieces of wood cut into lengths of not more than a cubit (forearm length); into these they hammered sharp nails.'[21] Now, the Normans had apparently constructed wooden towers covered with hides on their ships when they set out from Italy, but these had been destroyed in a storm which also seriously damaged their fleet. Anna Komnena also mentions that their ships were protected by 'every type of war-like machine', which may have been intended to mean siege weapons.[22] Whatever the case, there are no accounts of ships being used in an assault role against the coastal fortifications of Syria when these were being captured from the Muslims in the first half of the twelfth century. This is the case even for the Venetian crusade of 1128. The first reference that I have found to ships being used in a direct support role of an attack on seaside walls is at Lisbon in 1147. A combined North Sea fleet including Anglo-Normans, Flemings and Germans besieged the city for almost four months. An early attempt at taking the city by assault involved attacking the walls from the sea. Eight ships, lashed, together in pairs, attempted to lower bridges on top of the walls but were driven off by the defenders.[23] Just how this was being attempted is not made clear until the sources associated with the Fourth Crusade and the conquests of Constantinople in 1203 and 1204.

In 1187, Saladin inflicted a crushing defeat on Latin forces at the battle of Hattin. This was swiftly followed by the recapture of Jerusalem and almost all the coastal towns by his forces. Only Tyre held out and it was from Tyre, in August 1189, that King Guy led a small army to besiege Acre. This well-fortified city was the key to reconstructing a Christian power-base in the Holy Land. An epic siege followed, during which Crusader forces were constantly increased by new arrivals from overseas. But little could be achieved against Acre's formidable land walls. What is more, Saladin arrived with large forces to besiege the besiegers from the landward side. Also, his Egyptian fleet was able to supply the city. Essentially the situation

---

[21] Komnene (1969), IV, ii, 138.
[22] Komnene (1969), III, xii, 132.
[23] See Bennett (2001), 71–89, citing Edgington (1986); the passage is on 338 where the 'VII' ships of the text is a mistake for 'VIII'.

was a stalemate until the arrival of new forces under the kings of
England and France in the Spring of 1191. Again, the assaults by
mining and battery were on the land walls. Two huge trebuchets
were constructed to hurl rocks at the towers and walls of the
fortifications. The crucial difference was made by the naval blockade it now became possible to establish. The only use of a vessel in
an offensive capacity was the attempt of 24 September 1190 to send
a fireship against the Tower of the Flies, which controlled one end
of the chain across Acre harbour. This failed. But the blockade combined with increasingly fierce assaults drove the defenders to desperation, despite the pleas of Saladin to his commander in the city.
Acre surrendered on 12 July, only one month after the establishment of a watertight blockade. The city was held by the Christians
for another hundred years. It formed a bridgehead for the recovery
of the entire coast from Tripoli south to Ascalon on the borders of
Egypt.[24]

Although Richard the Lionheart failed to take Jerusalem, the Holy
City was recovered in 1228 by the western emperor Frederick II. It
was lost again as a result of an influx of Khwarismians in 1244 that
upset the whole balance of power in the Middle East. The Khwarismians in turn were fleeing from the Mongols, who also became a
powerful player in war and politics for the rest of the century. This
was the background of the Western response to losing Jerusalem
again: St Louis' crusade of 1248–54, which involved a long campaign in Egypt. But before we look at that I want to go back to
two earlier crusades: the attack on Constantinople in 1203–4 and a
prior Egyptian crusade of 1218–21.

In 1198, Pope Innocent III announced a crusade to the Holy
Land. The many French crusaders were led by Theobald of Cham-
pagne, whose Marshal, Geoffrey de Villehardouin, wrote a detailed

---

[24] Although not entirely in keeping with the main theme of this chapter it seems
wrong to ignore a heroic episode involving Richard. In late July 1192, when the
king was apparently intending to leave the Holy Land, Saladin closely besieged
Jaffa. Its defenders managed to win a few days respite in case of relief, but the city
was stormed. At the very last moment Richard appeared off-shore with a small
force. Not hesitating, despite the turmoil evident in Jaffa, Richard stripped off his
leg armour, and, with a handful of knights (and only three horses), supported by
the spears and crossbows of his foot soldiers, drove off the enemy in confusion.
This incident, worthy of a Hollywood epic, is clearly amphibious warfare at its most
personal. See Nicholson (1997), 349–58; Ambroise (1941), ll. 10: 807–11: 266.

account of the expedition. Obviously, this was from the point of view of one of the leaders. We also have another valuable account written by an ordinary crusader, Robert de Clari, (whom some historians consider to have been a knight).[25] Villehardouin was one of the ambassadors to Venice to arrange the supply of a fleet. He was expecting to take 4,500 knights and their horses, 9,000 squires and 20,000 ordinary footmen. He and his colleagues negotiated with the Doge for the provision of ships to take a force of this size. Unfortunately for the crusaders, only half this number actually turned up at Venice in 1203, and they found themselves obliged to the Venetians. So, in repayment they agreed to fight in Venetian campaigns. This led the crusaders to attack fellow Christians. First they attacked Zara on the Dalmatian coast and then, in support of a Byzantine imperial claimant, Constantinople itself. I shall leave out the political implications of all this for now and concentrate on the significance of naval assault in the first capture of the best fortified city in the Mediterranean world.[26]

The significance of crusader naval superiority became apparent in their first, opposed, landing. Having established their camp at Scutari on the Asian side, the crusaders' first objective was to seize the Galata Tower and remove the chain across the Golden Horn which it protected. When they attacked on 5 July 1203, the troop transports, towed in by galleys, were preceded by vessels full of missilemen: crossbows and archers. Their task was to drive the defenders away from the beachhead, enabling the fighting men to scramble ashore. This they achieved, and Villehardouin describes the knights leaping into the sea up to their waists, fully-armed, while: 'The sailors now began to open the doors at the sides of the transports and lead out the horses. The knights mounted quickly, . . . and drew up in good order.'[27] Obviously this contradicts Clari's statement cited earlier. It may be that this version is to be preferred; but it suggests that the ships must have been brought up against some kind of quay to enable the doors 'in the side of the ships' to have been utilised. Once formed-up, with the mounted knights supported by dismounted

---

[25] See Villehardouin (1963), 33. For Clari see note 15, above.
[26] See Queller (1978) for an excellent and detailed account of the crusade, esp. chs. 8 and 11 from which much of the following description of the siege is drawn.
[27] Villehardouin (1963), 67.

sergeants and missile-men, the crusaders quickly drove off the Greek
defenders on the shore. During the night, the Greeks in the Galata
Tower launched several damaging sallies. When they attempted to
repeat their success the following day, they over-reached themselves.
The crusaders beat off the attacks and, in pursuing the defenders
closely, were able to break in through the gates and seize the tower.
All that remained was to break the chain across the Golden Horn.
In order to do this the largest ship in the crusader fleet, the *Eagle*,
which had its prow reinforced by iron, was sailed at full speed against
it. As a result, the entire Byzantine fleet sheltering behind the chain
were either destroyed or fell into crusader hands.[28] Given that the
crusaders already controlled the Galata suburb, and so presumably
had access to that end of the chain, it may be that this spectacular
demonstration was intended to prove the superiority of Latin vessels
to the watching Greek populace.

We have already seen that the Italian maritime republics, and
Venice in particular, were in the forefront of developing naval archi-
tecture. Once inside the Golden Horn, it must have become apparent to Constantinople's defenders that the Venetian roundships were
tall enough to overtop Constantinople's fortifications. In addition, the
city's walls were much weaker there than on the landward side. On
land the Franks constructed a camp opposite the palace of Blachernae,
which also constituted a weak point, and bombarded it with their
siege engines. The Crusaders' combined assault was to be aimed at
the north-eastern corner of the city. The attack was launched on
July 17. The Franks used a ram to batter the walls while their assault
troops attacked with scaling ladders. They got two ladders into position and even a few men onto the walls, but after fierce fighting
they were driven off.

Meanwhile, the Venetians attacked by sea. Their ships were
equipped with 'flying bridges', that is to say bridges of planks apparently wide enough for three men, suspended from the mast tops so
that they could be swung on top of the walls. These were constructed
of ships' yards and given leather and canvas covering to protect the
attackers from missiles and Greek Fire. Robert de Clari, who provides this description, gives measurements of bridges 30 *toises* long

---

[28] Queller (1978), 97–98.

and 40 *toises* above the ground.[29] Since a *toise* is equivalent to a fathom (i.e. six feet) these measurements must be seen as very exaggerated, at least by a factor of two. The assault was conducted with siege ladders as well, and a ram made a breach in the wall. The flying bridges when fixed to the tops of towers fed large numbers of attackers onto the walls. The defenders fled and the Venetians seized 25–30 towers around the Petrion (about a quarter of the entire wall). This was a dramatic achievement, made possible by the presence of the large ships and the innovation of the flying bridges, and contrasts strongly with the Franks' failure on the landward side. The significance of this success cannot be exaggerated. The supposedly impregnable walls of Constantinople had been breached largely as a result of superior western technology. In fact, the city did not fall immediately, because the emperor Alexius was able to fight a drawn battle against the Franks outside the land-walls. This had two repercussions. The first was that the Venetians had to withdraw from their foothold. But secondly, once Alexius withdrew into the city again, he lost the support of its citizens and was forced to flee. This enabled the crusaders to negotiate with the defenders and install their candidate on the throne.

As a result of truly Byzantine politics the Crusaders found themselves needing to assault the city again nine months later. On this occasion the French leaders agreed to combine with the Venetians in attacking across the Golden Horn. Three types of vessel were arranged alternately in line: the galleys which carried dismounted troops; the horse transports with the knights aboard (these were to disembark at the foot of the walls); and the other transports equipped with flying bridges. The Byzantine response had also taken account of the events in the previous year. Timber fortifications had been constructed to raise the height of the towers and to create additional towers along the walls. Outside the wall a double ditch was dug to impede the movement the siege engines. In fact, these precautions, combined with a south wind which prevented many ships from getting close into the walls, proved sufficient to defeat an assault on April 8. The galleys and horse transports landed their troops and siege engines, but only five ships could get their flying bridges close

---

[29] Clari (1936), 70–1.

enough to a tower and none could get a secure fixing. After severe
fighting the Crusaders withdrew, leaving much of their equipment
behind.

They did not give up, however, and were ready for another assault
by 12 April. Forty of the large roundships were tied together in pairs
to concentrate greater numbers against an individual tower on the
walls. Also, the ships were protected by leather and vines against
Greek stone-throwers. Some of the Venetian vessels were equipped
with Greek fire, but the wooden hoardings topping the walls had
also been protected with hides to prevent them from burning. Also,
only four or five of the largest ships were tall enough to swing their
flying bridges onto the heightened towers. The *Paradise* and the *Pilgrim*,
a pair of vessels tied together and aided by a north wind which
drove them up against the walls, did manage eventually to land several men on a tower. The bridge was secured but then had to be
cut free as the turbulence of the wind and sea threatened to destroy
it. This foothold was exploited from the base of the walls with scaling ladders. The key to this success was the technological advantage
of employing the large Venetian roundships as floating siege towers.
Great acts of personal bravery were necessary as well. The crucial
breakthrough was made at a walled-up postern gate, where, as Robert
de Clari records, his brother Aleaumes, a cleric, led the way through
a small hole to drive back the defenders. A group led by Peter of
Amiens, a giant of a man, with ten knights including de Clari and
60 sergeants, entered the breach and defended it against counter-
attack. Then he instructed his sergeants to break down a nearby
gate and the crusaders gained free access to the city.[30]

The two final examples of amphibious operations to be examined
took place in the Nile Delta. In fact, they were more in the nature
of combined operations, because although ships played a vital role
in the initial attacks, the campaigns were much longer and involved
extensive activity on land. Egypt, rich in both men and money and
base for the largest Muslim fleet in the Levant, was clearly a crucial player in the strategic game of preserving the Holy Land in
Christian times. The kings of Jerusalem and their crusading allies
had been campaigning against Egypt since the mid-twelfth century.
After the loss of Jerusalem in 1187 it became the greatest focus of

---

[30] Clari (1936), 97–98, for his personal account.

crusader operations. After his failure to recapture Jerusalem in
1191–92, Richard the Lionheart indicated that control of Egypt was
crucial to the recovery and protection of the Holy Land. So the
Fifth Crusade was directed at taking Cairo and thus the country.
But in order to reach Cairo it was necessary to force the defences
of the Nile Delta, principally the fortified town of Damietta.[31]

Damietta stood on the right bank of the Nile, some three miles
south of its mouth. One tower of the city contained one end of the
chain which stretched across the river and was secured to a tower
on the far side. The chain had been reconstructed by Saladin and
could be protected by a bridge of boats. The eyewitness account of
Oliver of Paderborn describes three walls surrounding the city, each
higher than the other. The middle wall had 28 towers and there
was a moat between this and the outer wall, apparently wide enough
to accommodate vessels.[32] Lake Manzalah lay behind the city, making it effectively an island fortress. In May 1218, the crusaders set
up camp on the left bank of the river and began their attack on
the chain-tower, in order to gain access upriver. But it was difficult
to reach the tower with ships as the water was too shallow. Artillery
bombardment also proved inadequate so on 23 June there was a
general assault. Some 70–80 ships attacked the city and especially
the chain-tower, but without success. On 1 July several ships carrying towers and ladders were sent against the chain-tower. One ship
attacking here suffered the disaster of its mast breaking under the
weight of armoured knights, who fell into the river. Another ship
anchored in midstream in order to deliver a barrage of missiles from
crossbows or siege engines, which caused heavy casualties in the city
and on the bridge of boats until it was driven off by the defenders'
use of Greek Fire.

So the chronicler Oliver devised a floating siege tower which could
be constructed upon two ships tied together. As we have seen, this
technique may have been used since the mid-twelfth century, although
he claims it as an innovation. It was built by the Frisians and consisted of four masts erected on the two ships then bound together
with beams and ropes. At the top of the masts they constructed a
fort covered with hides against artillery stones and Greek Fire. Out

---

[31] See Powell (1986) for a model study of a crusading army in operation.
[32] Oliver of Paderborn (1971), 94–95.

from the platform stretched a ladder 30 feet beyond the prows of the ships to provide access to the chain tower. Another bridge was constructed at a lower level, probably from the forecastle.[33] An attack was launched on 24 August, despite difficult conditions as the Nile was in flood. The siege tower was bombarded by stone-throwers and as it drew closer it was doused in oil and set on fire. The flying bridge fell into the river, taking with it the assault troops, but the attackers managed to get the ladder in place and get men on top of the tower. The defenders retired below and set the upper storey alight, but the crusaders hung on. They also attacked the tower's door from the lower level. Despairing, the tower's garrison leapt into the river or surrendered. The fall of the tower did not immediately bring about the capture of the bridge of boats or indeed the fall of the city. The campaign dragged on and Damietta had to be starved into submission, which took until November 1219.

Furthermore the advance on Cairo did not take place for another eighteen months, due to other concerns pressed upon the leaders of the crusader states. The campaign was a stalemate: the crusaders remained secure in their camp while the sultan turned his attention to attacking Syria. Even when the offensive recommenced only about one-third of the army took part. Advancing to Mansourah, supported by '630' ships, the Crusaders were guilty of a poor appreciation of the situation. They had failed to recognise that they could be cut off by land and water by the sultan's forces. This is what happened. Al-Kamil sent ships into the Nile down the al-Mallah canal and sank four ships across the river to block retreat. When the crusaders did try to pull back, harassed by Muslim archery and attack, they fell into disorder. The Egyptians opened the sluices and flooded the river banks. Eventually, after suffering heavy losses and huddling into an indefensible position, the crusaders bargained their freedom for the city of Damietta that had cost them so much effort and blood to capture.[34]

An analysis of why the crusade failed should centre on the disparate nature of the forces which composed it and its divided com-

---

[33] Ibid., 64–65. In ch. 12, Oliver describes the construction of his floating siege tower in detail. He claims that his work was original, being seemingly unaware of the Venetian exploits at Constantinople barely two decades earlier.

[34] See Hooper and Bennett (1996), 111–13 for a more detailed description of the campaign and maps illustrating its course.

mand. Perhaps a centrally directed crusade could succeed where a loose conglomeration of commands had failed?

Louis IX set out for Egypt in August 1248. His was such an expedition: well-planned, centrally directed and funded by the richest kingdom in Europe. He had constructed the fortress-city of Aigues Morte as a base for the crusade.[35] Genoa had provided him with a large and well-equipped fleet of the most modern vessels. The fleet sailed to Cyprus, arriving in September. The crusaders then overwintered on the island. Jean de Joinville details the huge quantities of supplies prepared to support the expedition: barrels of wine stored-up over the preceding two years in piles the size of barns and mounds of grain which looked like small hills.[36] This was to support an army of 2,500 knights and 10–12,000 foot-soldiers, large by expeditionary standards. The king took his time and made sure everything was ready before making the relatively short journey south to Egypt. The crusaders landed on June 4 outside Damietta, which had resisted for so long in 1218–19. Yet only two days later it was in their hands, its defenders having withdrawn because they could elicit no message of support from their sultan. Yet Louis did not order an immediate attack upon Cairo; he waited until the Nile floods had subsided. It was not until October that the advance resumed against the strategically-placed town of Mansourah. The army marched along the left bank of the river, while the fleet transported the supplies and siege engines. Progress was delayed because of the many feeder streams and canals running into the Nile that the land forces had to traverse; but this was not necessarily a problem for the crusaders. While they kept together and maintained a satisfactory level of supply and lines of communications, they posed a substantial threat to the Egyptians. Arriving outside Mansourah on 21 December, the crusaders made camp between two branches of the river. Only a canal stood between them and the town.

The siege began with thorough preparations. First, under the protection of covering sheds, the engineers began the construction of a causeway. The defenders' response was to dig out the far side as fast as the attackers advanced. They also bombarded the crusaders with Greek Fire. In Joinville's famous description:

---

[35] For the construction of Aigues Mortes and its significance in supporting Louis' crusades see Labarge (1968), 102–03 & 234–38.

[36] Joinville (1963), 197.

This is what Greek Fire was like: it came straight at you as big as a vinegar barrel, with a tail of fire behind as long as a big lance. It made such a noise as it came that it seemed like the thunder of heaven; it looked like a dragon flying through the air. It gave so intense a light that in the camp you could see as clearly as by daylight in the great mass of flame which illuminated everything.[37]

The causeway had obviously failed as a means of crossing the canal, so Louis set his men to find a ford to cross the obstacle and outflank Mansourah. This was achieved in early February when a renegade Muslim informed the crusaders of a route across. So an attack was launched on the 8th. The initial dispositions were thoroughly professional, with a predetermined order of march. The king and his brothers led the vanguard while the duke of Burgundy commanded the rearguard in the crusader camp. The plan was to force a bridgehead, sending archers and crossbowmen over a pontoon bridge to provide covering fire for the knights. The Egyptians were taken completely by surprise. The vanguard caught them still sleeping and destroyed the artillery which had caused the crusaders so many problems earlier. Unfortunately, Robert of Artois (the king's brother), despite the advice of the Templar Master, led a rash charge into the town. With their formation broken as the knights filtered through the narrow streets, and lacking the support of the missile-men, the count and his cavalry were massacred. A few escaped, their retreat covered by bowmen and the counter-charges of the remaining knights; but the crusaders had snatched defeat from the jaws of victory. The invaders were now on the defensive as Egyptian forces grew under the leadership of Turanshah, the new sultan, who arrived with reinforcements at the end of February. The besiegers became the besieged within the cramped and unhealthy conditions of the canal bridgehead.

Inevitably, disease struck the crusaders. Many began to suffer from dysentery, even King Louis himself. Increasingly heavy attacks over Easter forced him to recognise that retreat was inevitable. On April 5, with the sick and wounded loaded onto ships, it began. Louis, who insisted on accompanying the land forces despite the fact that he could not sit his horse properly, contributed to making the march even slower. Also, because no-one had thought to break down the pontoon bridge to cover the retreat, the Egyptians were able to

---

[37] Joinville (1963), 216, (translation slightly adapted).

harass the already weakened crusaders. The crusader fleet was also attacked by Egyptian galleys, many vessels being captured. The fate of most of the wounded they carried was to be slaughtered, although those like Joinville, who could afford a ransom, were spared. The following day Louis instructed a general surrender. In a repeat of the end of the Fifth Crusade thirty years earlier, the king negotiated the release of the survivors. The situation became very fraught when, on 1 May, Turanshah was assassinated by his Mamluks, who raised up one of their number, Qutuz, as the new sultan. Eventually, upon promise of the return of Damietta and a huge sum of money, the crusaders were allowed to travel to Acre. Louis spent another two years in the Holy Land, restoring its fortifications; but his combined operation had proved a disaster.

In conclusion, it might appear from the last two examples that the kind of campaigns described in Egypt were beyond the capacity of medieval forces. I would argue that this was far from the case. It was possible, as we have seen, to manage both amphibious and combined siege operations successfully. Crucial to this was the presence of expertise: especially engineers and seamen. Such men could devise and employ superior technology against defensive fortifications, which normally had an advantage in this period. The danger was when the land forces became separated from naval support. Then it was easy for a campaign to bog down, or for the army to become isolated and cut off from supplies. But this is true of any period of military history.

Bibliography

Primary Sources

Ambroise (2003) *The History of the Holy War: Ambroise's Estoire de la Guerre Sainte*, ed. M. Ailes and M. Barber, 2 vols. (Woodbridge, Suffolk: 2003).
—— (1941) *The Crusade of Richard the Lionheart by Ambroise*, trans. M. J. Hubert, ed. J. J. La Monte (New York: 1941).
Anna Komnene (1969) *The Alexiad of Anna Comnena*, trans. E. R. A. Sewter (London: 1969).
Clari R. de (1936) *The Conquest of Constantinople*, trans. E. H. McNeal (New York: 1936).
Joinville J. de (1963) *Life of St Louis*, in: *Joinville and Villehardouin: Chronicles of the Crusades*, trans. M. R. B. Shaw (London: 1963) 163–353.
Nicholson, H. J. (1997) *Chronicle of the Third Crusade: a translation of the Itinerarium Peregrinorum et Gestis Regis Ricardi*, Crusade Texts in Translation 3 (Aldershot: 1997)
Oliver of Paderborn (1971) *The Capture of Damietta*, trans. J. J. Gavigan in *Christian Society and the Crusades 1198–1229*, ed. E. Peters (Philadelphia: 1971) 49–139.

Villehardouin G. de (1963) *The Conquest of Constantinople in: Joinville and Villehardouin: Chronicles of the Crusades*, trans. M. R. B. Shaw (London: 1963) 29–160.

Whitelock, D., ed. (1961) *The Anglo-Saxon Chronicle* (Norwich: 1961).

Wilson, D. (1985) *The Bayeaux Tapestry* (London: 1985).

Secondary Sources

Bachrach, B. (1985) 'On the Origins of William the Conqueror's Horse Transports', *Technology and Culture* 26 (1985) 505–31.

Bennett, M. (1992) 'Norman Naval Activity in the Mediterranean *c.* 1050–1108', *Anglo-Norman Studies* 15 (1993) 41–58.

——. (1998) 'The Myth of the Supremacy of Knightly Cavalry' in *Papers of the 1996 Harlaxton Conference* ed. M. Strickland (Stamford, Lincolnshire: 1998) 304–16.

——. (2001) 'Military aspects of the siege of Lisbon, 1147', *The Second Crusade*, ed. J. Phillips and M. Hoch (Manchester: 2001) 71–89.

Brown, R.A. (1969) *Normans and the Norman Conquest* (London: 1969).

Edgington, S. B. (1986) 'The Lisbon Letter of the Second Crusade', *Bulletin of the Institute of Historical Research* 70 (1986) 328–39.

Gardiner, R. ed. (1994) *Cogs, Caravels and Galleys: the sailing ship 1000–1650* (London: 1994).

——. (1996) *The Earliest Ships: the evolution of boats into ships* (London, 1996)

Gillingham, J. B. (1989) *Richard the Lionheart*, 2nd edn (London: 1989).

Labarge, M. W. (1968) *Saint Louis* (London: 1968).

Hooper, N. (1989) 'Some observations on the Navy in Late Anglo-Saxon England', *Studies in Medieval History presented to R. Allen Brown* ed. C. Harper-Bill, C. Holdsworth and J. L. Nelson (Woodbridge: 1989) 203–13.

Hooper, N. and Bennett, M. (1996) *Cambridge Atlas of Warfare: the Middle Ages 768–1485*, (Cambridge: 1996).

Powell, J. M. (1986) *Anatomy of a Crusade 1213–1221* (Philadephia: 1986).

Pryor, John H. (1984) 'Transportation of horses during the era of the Crusades, eighth century to 1285, Part I: to *c.* 1285, *Mariners' Mirror* 70 (1984) 9–27.

——. (1992) *Geography, technology, and war: Studies in the maritime history of the Mediterranrean, 649–1571* (Cambridge: 1992).

Queller, D. (1978) *The Fourth Crusade* (Leicester: 1978).

Richmond, Admiral Sir H. (1941) *Amphibious Warfare in British History*, Historical Association Pamphlet 119 (Exeter: 1941).

Waley, D. P. (1954) "Combined Operations" in Sicily, A.D. 1060–78', *Papers of the British School at Rome* 12 (1954) 118–25.

AMPHIBIOUS WARFARE IN THE BALTIC: THE HANSA, HOLLAND AND THE HABSBURGS (FOURTEENTH–SIXTEENTH CENTURIES)

Louis Sicking[1]

Introduction

This essay considers amphibious operations during the later Middle Ages and in the early modern era—operations carried out by joint expeditions consisting of ships with landing-forces on board that had the aim of occupying from the sea a territory of the enemy. Their aims were both strategic and tactical. A distinction must be made between smaller and greater landings. Smaller landings consisted merely of plundering and damaging enemy islands and coastal towns and had a more or less tactical character. Greater landings, aiming in particular at the occupation of important towns or islands and the taking of fortresses significant for the strategic control of the nearby sea or waterways, played a decisive role in wars and were above all strategic in purpose. This article will focus on three greater landings which are most relevant to the study of amphibious warfare in general and in Denmark in particular.

The first two amphibious operations were undertaken during the so-called first and second wars of the Hansa, or Hanseatic League, against King Valdemar IV of Denmark (r. 1338/40–1375), which took place in 1361–1362 and 1367–1370 respectively. The wars aimed at stopping and countering Valdemar's expansionist policy and the Hanseatic League was part of a larger coalition in which several German and Scandinavian princes participated. The two landings organized by the Hansa, one during each of these wars, are

[1] The author thanks Dr Jan Bill from the National Museum in Copenhagen for his comments and Dr David Trim for his help with English; but of course the author bears full responsibility for the text. The research for this essay was made possible by fellowships from the Netherlands Organisation for Scientific Research (NWO), and the Royal Netherlands Academy of Arts and Sciences (KNAW).

notably early and great amphibious operations in the North European history of warfare.[2]

The third amphibious operation to be treated in this essay never took place. It was cancelled just before the whole enterprise was supposed to have started. Amphibious invasions were in fact 'frequently . . . cancelled or not even attempted',[3] but the preceding decision-making process is nevertheless important for the understanding of the motivation for amphibious warfare in this period. The Habsburg government in the Netherlands envisaged this amphibious operation in 1536 during the Danish wars of succession (1523–1544). During these years, the House of Habsburg and the county of Holland, as well as a group of Hansa members—the so-called Wendish towns, which acted mainly at the initiative of Lübeck—tried to take advantage of Denmark's internal strife for their own interests. Attention will not be limited to the planned expedition of 1536. Other operations and plans for operations to the Baltic during the Danish wars of succession will also be considered.

The aim of this essay is to investigate the importance of the above-mentioned amphibious enterprises in the rivalries of the involved parties in Denmark and the Baltic. The way in which political or dynastic and economic interests influenced the decision-making process concerning maritime strategy and tactics will be the central theme. This is why the amphibious operations will be treated within their broader political and economic context. The wars against Valdemar will be the subject of the first part of this essay. Then attention will be focused on foreign intervention during the Danish wars of succession of the sixteenth century. Finally a comparison will be made between the amphibious interventions of the Hansa in the fourteenth century and the planned amphibious operation of the Habsburgs in 1536.

General Comments

It must be noted that the amphibious operations against Valdemar took place before the introduction of heavy artillery on board ships;

---

[2] Fritze and Krause (1989), 221–2; revised edition which is referred to here: Fritze and Krause (1997), 34–5.

[3] Ch. 5, below, p. 123.

fleets functioned in the first place as fighting platforms for troops in sea combat, and as the means by which belligerents tried to carry war to enemy territory. The preparation for the landing in Copenhagen by the Habsburg government of the Netherlands took place a few decades after the invention of the gun port, which was at the centre of a revolution in naval warfare. Gun ports made possible the introduction of heavy artillery below decks so that the enemy could be fought without boarding.[4] Guns could thus be a substitute for armed men at sea. Whereas in the Middle Ages the fighting power of a navy carrying an invading army was the army itself, in the sixteenth century an invading army could no longer transform its manpower into an efficient armed force at sea. With infantry becoming the dominant force in armies and with the reduced importance of armies at sea, armies and navies became separate organizations. The presence of troops on board, which had been crucial for all naval warfare during the Middle Ages, was no longer necessary for war at sea; their place was now on transports or in amphibious operations. Thus, whereas in the Middle Ages all naval warfare could in principle become amphibious warfare, since troops were part of the fighting equipment, from the sixteenth century onwards amphibious operations became a more or less separate form of warfare in which navies and armies had to cooperate.

Amphibious operations became much more risky because if the defenders were strong at sea, then even if their army was weaker they could now try to defeat the invader at sea, where the latter's stronger army could not act. The Spanish Armada of 1588 against England offers a most dramatic example of this. With gun-armed ships the sea had become an excellent site for stopping or delaying an invading army. The chances of a successful landing were thus reduced. At the same time, warships with guns on board acquired the ability to attack targets onshore. The mobile firepower carried by ships was more dangerous for medieval fortifications, which were highly vulnerable to gunfire, than heavy and immobile land-based guns were against ships. As cities and coastal areas became more vulnerable to sea borne guns, gun-armed navies also became more important in the defence of such areas.[5] All this increased the risks

---

[4] Parker (1996), 83–4, 90.
[5] Glete (2000), 33.

and dangers of an amphibious operation, which now required a
gun-armed naval fleet to protect the transport fleet of an infantry
army.

The Hansa and Denmark

The great shoals of herring that swarmed along the south coast of
Scania each year had long attracted large numbers of fishermen,
merchants and craftsmen during the season. Most of the fishermen
were Danes, whereas the merchants and craftsmen came from the
Wendish towns of the Baltic coast. Others sailed from the North
Sea coast and the Zuiderzee, from Hamburg and Bremen, Kampen
and Zwolle and many other towns, weighing anchor for the most
part off the Skanör peninsula.[6] The Baltic merchants usually took
quarters in Falsterbo. On both Scanian peninsulas the merchants
from various towns built *Vitten*, settlements that contained accommodation for the merchants and craftsmen, rooms for business and
storage, and in most cases a church or chapel. Although a Danish
bailiff supervised them and collected levies in the king's name, each
town appointed its own bailiff to manage the settlement and administer justice. In the course of the fourteenth century commerce
intensified. Not only fish but also cloth, canvas, salt, grain, beer,
iron, wax, skins and other goods were traded. Great trade fairs came
into being, at which German merchants exchanged these goods with
colleagues from the Netherlands, England and Scandinavia.[7]

King Valdemar IV tried to reassert control over the Danish realm
after a collapse of royal authority under his predecessor, and he
aimed to get a larger share of the income from the markets. He
regarded the written privileges enjoyed by the Hansa merchants in
Scania as infringing upon his financial interests and judicial authority. In 1360 and 1361 Valdemar conquered the Scania peninsula
and took the town of Visby on the island of Gotland. This altered
the balance of power in Northern Europe, with economic consequences for the Hanseatic towns. New taxes and tolls made catch-

---

[6] The most recent study covering amongst others the Scania herring fishery and
trade is Jahnke (2000).
[7] Schildhauer (1985), 44–5.

ing and selling herring more expensive and stunted the markets at Skanör and Falsterbo in their growth. Besides, with the bloody capture of Visby, the King of the Danes had waged war against one of the oldest members of the Hansa. Threatened by further limitation of their freedom to trade and irritated by the attack on one of their most venerable members, the Hanseatic League decided to retaliate with military force.[8]

The Hanseatic cities lacked the power to control extensive territories. They were, however, important centres of seafaring and shipbuilding and possessed the financial means to turn their trading fleets into war fleets. At the *Hansetag* in Greifswald in 1361, representatives of the Hanseatic towns agreed to break off all trade with Denmark forthwith and mobilize an armed force. The war was financed by means of the *Pfundzoll*, a levy raised in every Hansa port. Four *pfennigs* for every pound in value was collected for each ship and each load transported from a town. A strong anti-Danish coalition was formed at the initiative of the Hansa. Hanseatic diplomacy managed to win over King Magnus II of Sweden (1319–1364) and his son Håkon VI (1355–1380), King of Norway, as well as the Duke of Schleswig and the Count of Holstein to support the coalition. The Grandmaster of the Teutonic Order promised financial aid.[9]

The war aims of the various partners differed considerably. The Hanseatic League aimed in the first place at confirmation and enhancement of its trading privileges, such as free trade in Denmark and confirmation of the special position of the Hansa merchants in Scania. The princely allies aimed at a general undermining and weakening of the Danish kingdom by pillaging Danish territory. Various factors unfavourably influenced the Hanseatic plans for the start of hostilities. The most important weapon of Hanseatic policy in times of crisis—a trade blockade—failed to work, since the towns on the Zuiderzee continued to trade with Denmark.[10] Furthermore, the Swedish and Norwegian kings turned out to be very neglectful allies. Originally the war against Denmark should have started at

---

[8] Jahnke (2000), 52–3; Olesen (2003), 717.
[9] Fritze and Krause (1997), 81–2; Seifert (1997), 46; Schildhauer (1985), 45.
[10] For a detailed analysis of the scarce information on the position of the towns on the Zuiderzee, especially Kampen, see Seifert (1997), 49–52. See also Henn (1994), 39–56 and Weststrate (2003), 13–40.

11 November 1361 but the messengers sent by the towns to the kings
in order to get ratification of the treaties in which the joint attack
was agreed had not yet returned on 19 November. As a consequence,
the military enterprise was postponed until the following spring.[11]

The original plan of the Hansa was offensive in nature and aimed
at Copenhagen, the centre of royal power. The Hanseatic towns
may have wanted to strike the king at the centre of his power in
order to force him to negotiations on their trading privileges in
Scania. Control over Copenhagen may have been advantageous for
the Hanseatic towns because of its strategic location near Scania.
But the allied Nordic kings had urged the towns to direct their
actions against the Helsingborg fortress, where the kings promised
to send their forces as soon as possible to assist the towns. The towns
did indeed follow the royal request. At the end of April 1362, between
Rügen and Hiddensee, 27 cogs and another 25 small craft with some
3,000 armed men aboard set sail through the Sound to Helsingborg
(see appendix 1). When the allies did not appear, the commander
of the Hanseatic fleet, Johann Wittenborg of Lübeck, decided to
carry out the original plan to attack Copenhagen. This was done
successfully, and to avenge Visby the Danish capital as well as the
fortress was severely plundered. After this light siege the fleet went
back to Helsingborg. Since the Swedes and the Norwegians still did
not appear, Wittenborg decided to take the fortress on his own. For
twelve weeks Wittenborg and his troops lay before the key to the
Sound but the fortress was more than a match for the Hanseatic
attacks with large catapults, day and night. The Hanseatics were not
strong enough to besiege on the land and maintain strength at sea
at the same time. In fact Wittenborg needed more landing forces
than he had. As a consequence he left only a small group of men,
including a contingent of 40 men from Kiel on board the ships. The
Danes took advantage of this weakness and attacked the almost unde-
fended Hanseatic ships at anchor. The Hansa was easily defeated
by Valdemar's fleet, which captured 12 large cogs full of weapons
and victuals. The Danish fleet, now master of the Sound, made reinforcement of the expedition from the Hansa towns impossible. This
must have been around the middle of July. It is not known how the

---

[11] Fritze and Krause (1997), 82.

remaining troops returned home: it may have become possible through a truce that Valdemar was prepared to sign with the towns in 1363.[12]

The failure of the amphibious attack before Helsingborg caused the failure of the whole enterprise. Later the towns themselves described their defeat in the worst terms. They had been struck by "very great, irreplaceable and immeasurable ruin and misfortune during which they had been crushed and imprisoned and had suffered endless damage by the loss of ships, goods and other things and by the extortion of money and ransom for the prisoners." Of course it was in the interests of the towns not to underestimate their damages within the context of negotiations with the Danes. But even in the discussions between the towns it becomes clear that their losses had been severe. The number of dead and wounded is impossible to estimate but at least the number of prisoners gives an indication of the size of the defeat. The 40 men from Kiel, 125 Rostockers, two or three captains of cogs, and 54 heavily armed men and bowmen had been imprisoned. At least 36 Lübeckers were taken prisoners although there must have been many more of them since the Lübeckers calculated that the Hanseatic towns had to pay 40,000 marks ransom in total. In the beginning of 1364 there were still 116 people from the Wendish towns in Danish prisons.[13] Wittenborg paid for his failure with his life. He was executed in the market place in Lübeck. The commander may have been irresponsible by attacking on his own but it was not his fault that the Swedes and the Norwegians never turned up.

After his victory, Valdemar IV went onto the diplomatic offensive. He had sealed an alliance with Sweden and Norway by wedding his daughter Margarete to the Norwegian King Håkon VI. Valdemar's idea was to create a rift between his motley enemies. He tried to foster disunity among the Hanseatic towns. The towns of the Zuiderzee, which had never broken off relations with Denmark throughout the war, received substantial privileges in his dominions. Valdemar also attempted to split the Prussian towns from their Wendish allies. Somewhat complacent after his successes, the Danish king embarked on a journey to several countries of Europe. Meanwhile, there was a sudden turn in the political situation when the Swedish nobles

---

[12] *HR* (1870), 195; Schäfer (1879), 311–13, 315–16; Fritze and Krause (1997), 84.
[13] Schäfer (1879), 313–14.

deposed their King Magnus in February 1364, inviting Albrecht of
Mecklenburg (1364–1389) to ascend the throne of Sweden. There
was a programme behind the coup: resumption of the war against
Denmark, which now faced a coalition between Sweden, Mecklenburg
and Holstein. The Danish king was forced, for the time being at
least, to conclude a peace treaty with the Hanseatic towns, and this
was signed in Wordinborg in 1364.[14]

Despite the peace treaty, the merchants of the Hansa kept up a
constant stream of complaints about the arbitrary treatment to which
they were subjected on Danish soil. Reprisals, bullying and violence
were not confined to the Wendish merchants. It was also meted out
to traders from Prussia and the Zuiderzee, so that the various fac-
tions of Hanseatic towns were drawn together and demanded vigorous measures to temper the Danish king. Lübeck and the other
Wendish towns, with the defeat against Valdemar still fresh in their
minds, did not take the initiative. This time it came from the Prussian
towns and those Hanseatic towns around the Zuiderzee.[15]

In November 1367, representatives from more than 50 towns—
from Dorpat in Estonia to Utrecht in the Netherlands—met for a
Hansetag in Cologne and established the Cologne Confederation.[16]
That so many representatives came from such distant regions to take
part in a Hanseatic conference was almost without parallel. The
Cologne Confederation was a milestone in the development of the
Hanseatic League. Previous cooperation had been built primarily on
economic links, but the need for a *political* alliance amongst the towns
was now particularly evident in order to counter the Danes. Henceforth more solid forms of organization between the towns can be
observed.

This was partly reflected in the status and procedures of the
Hansetag. The Hansa achieved a common approach among its sub-
scribers, even if not every town accepted the will of the majority,
for there were varying degrees of dependence and different local
interests with which to contend. Hamburg, Bremen, and a number
of inland towns, for example, attempted to extricate themselves from
their responsibilities. Nevertheless the provisions of the Cologne

---

[14] Götze (1970), 91; Schildhauer (1985), 46.
[15] Seifert (1997), 53.
[16] For a complete overview of the participants: Seifert (1997), 76–7.

Confederation resembled those of Greifswald a few years earlier; the injuries done by Valdemar and the Norwegian King Håkon to the merchants meant the towns had to take action, and promised each other mutual support. The most important decision taken in Cologne was for an attack on Valdemar in the spring of 1368. This meant a levy of the *Pfundzoll* to finance the war, and the assignment of the contingents of ships and troops to be sent by participating groups of towns (see appendix 2). Furthermore, sanctions were provided for against those members who did not fulfil their obligations or who acted against the decisions taken by the Confederation. Shipping through the Sound was only tolerated for armed trading vessels protected by a war fleet. During the winter further agreements were made concerning the date for the formation of the fleet, its commander and the pursuit of war goals.[17]

The Cologne Confederation established the basis of a whole system of allied relations, created at the initiative of the Wendish towns, in which the new King of Sweden, Albrecht von Mecklenburg, various German princes, and several Danish noblemen participated. Furthermore, the emperor Charles IV, the pope, the kings of England and Poland, and twenty-nine German princes were informed of Danish acts of violence against ships and goods belonging to the Hansa merchants. In this way the diplomatic isolation of Valdemar intended by the system of alliances against Denmark and Norway was to be completed. Again, however, although the great coalition built was doubtless desirable from a diplomatic perspective, it meant that making war would be more difficult, because the interests of the allied partners varied. Whereas the towns cared first of all for the extension of their commercial privileges in Scania, whether it were Danish or Swedish, and for a free passage through the Sound, the allied princes aimed at dividing Denmark amongst them. This proposed partitioning could never be in the interest of the Hanseatic towns, which never expressed any desire to win territory at Denmark's expense in the treaties concluded with the princes. One point, however, the towns did support: the weakening of Denmark—the fortress of Copenhagen had to be demolished. This was clearly defined as a war goal in order to secure the passage through the Sound as well

---

[17] Götze (1970), 108–109; Olesen (2003), 718; Fritze and Krause (1997), 85–6.

as the Scania fishing grounds. It must have been this military objective that justified the amphibious operation realised by the towns.[18]

According to plan, on 9 April 1368 ships from the Wendish and the Prussian towns rendezvoused together at the narrows between Rügen island and Pommern. The fleet of 17 greater and 20 smaller ships, well equipped with about 2,000 men, cavalry and artillery, was a considerable force for its time. The towns had sent over a third more troops than they had originally promised to. The fleet sailed for the Sound in April with Copenhagen as its first objective. On 2 May the city was taken and razed; the harbour was blocked by sinking ships at the entrance. The fortress surrendered 16 June and, instead of being demolished, was used by the Hanseatic League as a base for further actions. Subsequently the allied forces captured Helsingör, which commanded the western side of the northern entrance to the Sound.

In the meantime a squadron formed by the towns around the Zuiderzee, possibly supported by some Wendish ships, attacked various places along the southern coast of Norway as far south as Marstrand, where the fortress, monastery and church were burnt to the ground. In the Sound the squadrons from the Baltic towns and those from around the Zuiderzee were to combine in order to escort a convoy of merchant ships. According to the instructions for the captains of the merchant ships, they had to obey the military commanders. During the passage of the Sound they had to stay with the warships; only thereafter were they allowed to continue on their own. The responsible towns had guaranteed the arming of the merchant ships so that they would be able to defend themselves. By the end of June 1368 Hanseatic forces controlled the Sound so that the maritime trade to Scania could take place without hindrance or risk; on 25 July, King Albrecht of Sweden granted sweeping privileges to several Hansa towns.[19]

In Scania, Hanseatic and Swedish forces combined to fight the Danes. In July the allies conquered Malmö, Falsterbo, Skanör, Trelleborg, Lund, Ystad and Simrishamm. The Hansa towns were also involved in the occupation of the islands Möen, Langeland and

---

[18] Götze (1970), 109–14; Fritze and Krause (1997), 86–7; Jahnke (2000), 55.
[19] Schäfer (1879), 476–81; Götze (1970), 115–16.

Falster, which unquestionably strengthened their position in the western Baltic Sea. Confronted by such overpowering superiority on the part of the Hansa and the princes, King Valdemar left his kingdom to seek support. Worse was to come when King Håkon VI of Norway was obliged to seek a truce from the Hanseatic towns after their destructive attacks on the Norwegian coast. Now that the Danish king had lost his only ally, and the friends he believed he had among the German princes had turned their backs on him, his position was hopeless. Denmark's defeat was inevitable. During the winter of 1368/9, a part of the war fleet remained in the Sound to secure a blockade while allied troops remained in Denmark. The main Hanseatic forces under the command of the Lübeck burgomaster, Bruno Warendorp, together with those of Henry, Duke of Mecklenburg, besieged the fortress of Helsingborg, which eventually capitulated.

Whereas Valdemar's efforts to obtain support had failed completely, the Danish Council tried to make the best of a bad bargain and started negotiations with the Hanseatic League towns in an attempt to split the allies. In this way a partition of Denmark as envisioned by the German princes might be avoided. The peace negotiations opened on 30 November 1369 in Stralsund.[20] The Captain of the Realm, Henning von Putbus, the Archbishop of Lund and the bishops of Odense and Roskilde represented the Danish side, while twenty-three Hansa towns sent representatives. The towns were interested exclusively in securing their trading interests. As a result, the towns and their citizens were accorded complete freedom to trade in Denmark and Scania in return for the traditional levy. The Hansa town bailiffs could continue to administer justice in the Scanian *Vitten*, and no Hanseatic burgher was to be tried before a Danish court. Once more, numerous details concerning trade and fishing in Danish waters and the practice of German craftsmen in Scania were resolved to the advantage of the Hanseatic towns. A second treaty provided a guarantee for the first and obtained compensation for damage by stipulating that the four fortresses on the Sound, Skanör, Falsterbo, Malmö and Helsingborg, were to be conceded to the towns for fifteen years, along with two thirds of their

---

[20] Götze (1970), 117–19.

income, and that the election of the next Danish king would not be valid without Hanseatic approval. The King of Denmark, who returned to his country in 1371 after an absence of four years, was required "if he wishes to keep his kingdom" to ratify these treaties with the seal of the realm.

In the war that ended with the Peace of Stralsund in May 1370 the Hansa had been able to maintain and extend its dominant position in Northern Europe. The Hansa had proved its capabilities in warfare to the princely powers. The main operations during both the first and the second wars against Valdemar were amphibious. They belong among the most remarkable great early amphibious operations in the maritime history of Northern Europe. While the first war was lost, the second war was won despite Hansa amphibious forces that were smaller than during the first conflict (compare appendices 1 and 2). This was due mainly to the broader and more integrated coalition of the second war, but also to a more focused approach in the second war, in which the Hanseatic League achieved domination over the sea-lanes as a preparation for landings. The League also showed its ability to deploy troops landed on the enemy's territory to best ability and secure victory in the land actions. Besides safeguarding commerce through the Sound, the maritime transport of troops, artillery and horses during war conditions to the place of action was a remarkable achievement. Without the support of the princes, however, the second war against Valdemar might have ended like the first one.

The Peace of Stralsund in 1370 has entered the history books not merely as a significant victory for the Hansa, but, indeed, as one of the most important victories by the German bourgeoisie over the princely powers. The Hanseatic towns, with the help of the princes, had scored a military success at the expense of the Danish king, but at the same time the terms of the treaty were proof of their political victory over the princes and over the princes' thirst for annexation. The League's policy was, as ever, essentially a trading policy, and their diplomatic activities were designed to realize the merchants' business interests. The Hansa only resorted to military expeditions if all else failed. The Peace of Stralsund empowered the merchants to exploit their privileged position throughout Denmark and Norway and in Scania. For the merchants of the Hansa, this was the most important aspect of the Peace of Stralsund, which was the foundation underlying their overwhelming economic power in the entire region of the North and Baltic Seas.[21]

The House of Habsburg, Holland and Denmark

During the 1520s and 1530s Denmark was engulfed in wars of succession in which both Lübeck and Holland intervened in order to gain control over the Sound. In 1522 and 1523 the Wendish towns led by Lübeck supported the Danish nobility and clergy against King Christian II (r. 1513–1523) who, in consequence, fled to the Netherlands. As a result, Lübeck closed the Sound as well as the Great and Small Belt on both sides of the Danish island Fyn to Dutch shipping.[22] The rumour of the arrival of a merchant fleet from Holland escorted by twelve warships caused Lübeck and the new Danish king, Frederick of Holstein (r. 1523–1533), to negotiate with Holland for a commercial treaty. Denmark and Lübeck accepted a request for free passage through the Sound for all Netherlandish ships but only once Holland agreed to withhold its support from Christian II. The treaty was signed in 1524.[23]

The exiled Danish king, however, tried everything he could to regain his crown. At first the Holy Roman Emperor Charles V, sovereign lord of the Netherlands, and the Dutch cities refused any assistance to Christian, but the pillaging of Christian's troops in the Netherlands and more importantly the fear that the king would close the Sound to Dutch ships once he recovered the throne changed the mind of the States of Holland. On 24 October 1531, Christian II left the harbour of Medemblik with at least twelve ships and 7,000 men on board and sailed for Norway. He had promised free passage through the Sound for Dutch ships if his undertaking were successful—but it was not. In August 1532 the ex-king fell into the hands

---

[21] Schildhauer (1985), 47–8; Dollinger (1970), 148–62; Jahnke (2000), 56; Olesen (2003), 719.

[22] The word 'Dutch' is used here as an adjective for Holland and its inhabitants. The word 'Netherlandish' is used as an adjective when referring to the Netherlands as a whole.

[23] Tracy (1990), 107 assumed that such a fleet actually did sail, but this is incorrect. Häpke (1914), 101, 110–15; Nübel (1972), 135; Schäfer (1913), vol. 5.

of his opponent Frederic of Holstein and was imprisoned for four-teen years.[24]

Lübeck regarded the supply of ships from Holland for Christian's expedition as a *casus belli*. Thus, in 1532 Lübeck warships crossed the Baltic and the North Seas and captured a number of Dutch ships. Lübeck's aggression coupled with the fear of a closure of the Sound caused the mercantile cities of Holland to take measures to guarantee their seafaring trade in the Baltic. In May 1532 Amsterdam proposed to fit out forty warships for a mission to Lübeck to block-ade the city from the sea. The costs would be equally divided between the Habsburg government and the merchants of Holland, who were even prepared to pay for the whole fleet if the government were unwilling to share in the costs. This plan illustrates the importance of the Baltic trade to Holland's merchants. Charles V and his sister Mary of Hungary, regent of the Netherlands (1531–1555), agreed to Holland's plan. They believed that the common interests of the Netherlands were at stake, since numerous provinces suffered from the stagnation of the grain trade that was a direct consequence of Lübeck's aggression. It is likely that the threat of the war fleet moved Lübeck to negotiations and in July 1532 the Netherlands, Lübeck and the other Wendish cities, Denmark, and Sweden renewed the commercial treaty of 1524.[25]

As has been mentioned, shortly after the conclusion of the treaty, Christian II was imprisoned by Frederick of Holstein. Stirred up by Lübeck, Frederick was no longer content with Holland's promise not to support the ex-king; he demanded 300,000 guilders compensation from Holland for damages done by Christian in Denmark and Norway. The regent turned down the claim for indemnity and stressed that war with Holland would mean war with the emperor, the Nether-lands and Spain.[26] Lübeck, however, was now determined to con-tinue its quarrel with Holland, even when the city was no longer

[24] Häpke (1913), 10, 16; Gorter-Van Royen (1995), 210–12. Bregnsbo's state-ment that a serious attempt to reinstall Christian II on the Danish throne was never undertaken is incorrect. Bregnsbo (2002), 666. The attempt of 1531 was very seri-ous, although it failed. Details concerning the imprisonment of Christian II in: IJssel de Schepper (Zwolle 1870), 214–17, 361–2, 364–5.
[25] Häpke (1913), 27–37, 40–2, 56–7, 69–70; Tracy (1990), 108–9.
[26] Häpke (1913), 70, 77, 80, 93; Gorter-Van Royen (1995), 214–15; IJssel de Schepper (1870), 224–5; Ter Gouw (1884), 223–5.

sure of Danish support, following the death of Frederick in April 1533. Lübeck's preparations for naval action forced the Hollanders to reconsider Amsterdam's fleet plan of the previous year. From April to August, the States of Holland negotiated over the fitting out and financing of warships. Should the naval expedition be perceived as a Dutch offensive, the cities of Holland feared that, in retaliation, the enemy would give their competitors (in the Netherlands' provinces of Flanders and Zeeland) preferential commercial concessions. Therefore, the States of Holland wanted their war against Lübeck to be given imperial sanction, rather than being left as a provincial matter. The Habsburg government paid 30,000 *ponden* and appointed a Fleming, Gerard van Meckeren, as commander of the fleet, which was nominally a Habsburg fleet. In fact, however, the whole expedition was a Holland enterprise. The fleet consisted of twenty-one ships, all of which were fitted out in Holland, while the States of Holland granted a subsidy of 50,000 *ponden* for it.[27]

Historians do not agree whether the expedition of 1533 was a success or a failure.[28] This can only be assessed by comparison of the instructions Van Meckeren received with the actual movements of the fleet. Unfortunately his instructions have not been preserved. According to a contemporary chronicle (the *Historie van Hollant*), the *stadhouder* (or governor) of Holland, Anthony de Lalaing, told Van Meckeren that he was to punish Lübeck by capturing ships and goods from the city.[29] The fleet left in September and operated from Helsingör, from where it kept the Sound under Dutch control and captured several Hanseatic ships. Though Van Meckeren wanted to sail to Lübeck, the exhaustion of his victuals and the approaching winter forced him to return to the Netherlands in November.[30]

Whatever Van Meckeren's instructions might have been, it is clear that his enterprise was an offensive one. It was directed against

---

[27] Häpke (1913), 84, 89, 91; Van der Goes and Van der Goes (1791), 385, 399–400, 405–7; Tracy (1990), 109–10, 253, n. 65; Ter Gouw (1884), 226–7.

[28] De Meij (1976), 307–37, 322 and Gorter-Van Royen (1995), 215. According to ter Gouw (1884), 228, however, the Amsterdammers were very disappointed over the result of the expedition.

[29] Tracy (1990), 110–11; Ter Gouw (1884), 228.

[30] The return-journey did not pass without problems. Three ships were captured by Gelderlanders (not yet part of the Netherlands), two ships were lost in a storm in which others had to drop their heavy artillery so as to survive: ter Gouw (1884), 231. Account of the fleet of 1533, ARA The Hague, C Ch. Ac., no. 4991, ff. 211r–218v.

Lübeck and intended to insure free passage through the Sound. If
the goal of the fleet was to punish Lübeck, the results of the expedition must be judged limited, since the costs of the fleet were enormous, while the damages done to Lübeck ships were small by
comparison. It is also possible, however, that the expedition was
mounted to bring Lübeck to the negotiation table, as in 1532. In
that case the Habsburg government had an interest in more restrained
action, which would leave the door open for diplomatic approaches.
In October 1533 Mary of Hungary signed a peace treaty with the
Danish Council and Frederick's son, Christian, who was to become
the new King of Denmark. In exchange for the normal toll, the
treaty guaranteed free passage through the Sound for Netherlandish
ships. As a result of mediation by Hamburg, the States of Holland
and Lübeck concluded a truce the following year—Lübeck was probably moved to participate in the negotiations by the maritime threat
and diplomatic isolation.[31] The despatch of the war fleet of 1533
made it clear to all parties that Holland was prepared for military
action when its Baltic trade was at stake.

The death of Frederick of Holstein resulted in new competition
for the Danish throne, with consequent dangers for all seafaring
traffic through the Sound. The nobility in the Danish Council supported the candidacy of Frederick's son, Christian of Holstein.[32] He
also obtained the endorsement of Amsterdam, not only because he
had played a role in the peace treaty of 1533, but also because the
city had contacts with his entourage. Another candidate was Count
Christopher of Oldenburg, who pretended to represent the interests
of his imprisoned cousin, Christian II. Christopher was supported by
Lübeck, which, by trying to put its own claimant on the throne,
tried to gain hegemony over the Sound and, thereby, over the entire
Baltic Sea. The city's truce with Holland was only meant to avoid
a war on two fronts. In the succession struggle that followed, the
so-called Count's War (*Grafenfehde*) (1534–1536), Christopher gained
control of Copenhagen; Christian of Holstein, who in August 1534
had been chosen King of Denmark as Christian III (r. 1534–1558)
by a majority in the Danish Council, took possession of Jutland (the
Danish mainland).

---

[31] Häpke (1913), 136–138; Ter Gouw (1884), 232–4; Fritze and Krause (1997),
163–4; Tracy (1990), 111; Gorter-Van Royen (1995), 216.
[32] Since Christian was Lutheran he was unacceptable to the clergy in the council.

In accordance with the commercial interests of the Netherlands, the regent Mary of Hungary tried to befriend both parties. She hoped to secure free passage of the Sound for all Netherlandish shipping, regardless of who might win the Danish throne. The ambitious dynastic plans of Emperor Charles V, however, forced the regent to embark on a new course. The emperor wanted Frederick of the Palatinate (1482–1554) to marry Dorothy, a daughter of Christian II. On the basis of this marriage Frederick would become another claimant to the throne of Denmark. Charles and his brother Ferdinand of Austria had agreed to this in concert, since they could very well use a strong ally in the German empire. Moreover, Habsburg influence in Scandinavia would enhance if Frederick ascended the Danish throne. In that case, free passage through the Sound for Netherlandish ships would also be guaranteed. In spite of objections raised with Charles V by Mary of Hungary, the emperor went through with his plan; Frederick of the Palatinate and Dorothy of Denmark married in May 1535.[33]

In the meantime Christian III had conquered Travemünde, thereby hindering Lübeck's access to the sea. There then followed the fall of Jurgen Wullenwever, the protestant leader of the Lübeck patricians, who had wanted to restore the high-days of the Hansa by excluding Dutch competition and by bringing the Sound under Hansa control. Charles V restored the power of Lübeck's catholic patricians and the Hansa withdrew from Danish succession war. By the peace concluded on 14 February 1536, Lübeck recognized Christian III as King of Denmark and gave up all support to Christian's enemies. Lübeck's fate was sealed. The city's role in the Sound was over.[34] If the emperor had abandoned his dynastic ambitions and recognized Christian III as King of Denmark, nothing would have stood in the way of peaceful relations between the Netherlands and Denmark.

---

[33] Gorter-van Royen (1995), 215–19; Tracy (1990), 111. I do not share the opinion of Bregnsbo (2002), 661 who claims that Charles V gave priority to the commercial interests of the Netherlands in the Baltic over his dynastic ambitions in Scandinavia. On the contrary, until the Peace of Speyer (concluded 1544), Charles was willing to sacrifice Netherlandish commercial interests for his dynastic policy in Scandinavia. The regents of the Netherlands, Margaret of Austria and Mary of Hungary, were much more keen to defend the Baltic interests of the Netherlands. However, Bregnsbo fails to distinguish between the different attitudes of these members of the house of Habsburg.

[34] Van Tielhof (1995), 119; Fritze and Krause (1997), 169.

Instead the emperor accepted an offer from Christopher of Oldenburg. After Lübeck had denied its support to him, the count declared that he held Copenhagen for Frederick of the Palatinate and that he expected help from the Habsburgs. At the end of February 1536, the central government of the Netherlands in Brussels launched an expedition to relieve Copenhagen. A war fleet to be equipped in the Netherlands was to take the troops of the Count Palatine to the Danish capital; and an embassy sent by Mary of Hungary to the besieged city informed Count Christopher of the military succour he was to receive.[35]

At first, the regent tried to move the States of Holland to equip the fleet. In the name of the emperor, she stated that it was in the interest of Holland's trade that Copenhagen be 'liberated' and that Frederick of the Palatine come to power in Denmark. In that case Dutch ships would have free passage through the Sound permanently. If the Hollanders did not support the fleet project, the Duke of Holstein—the Habsburgs refused to recognize him as Christian III—would remain on the Danish throne and, Mary predicted, would arrest Dutch ships in the Sound as compensation for his costs of war. The States of Holland, however, took a different view. After long deliberations, which took the greater part of April, they rejected the plan. They observed, wisely, that it was easy to become embroiled in a war, but that it was difficult to get out of it. The States wanted to avoid the war becoming an exclusively Dutch war. Precisely then, Holland risked exclusion from seafaring trade through the Sound. Moreover, the province would be unable to defend itself against the duchy of Guelders, because its valuable and scarce artillery would be needed for the ships. The *stadholder* and the first councillor of the Court of Holland, Gerrit van Assendelft, both still tried to convince the Dutch towns. They pointed out that the interdiction of seafaring to the Baltic, which had been proclaimed in the beginning of March in view of the Danish war situation, did not only apply to the Hollanders but to all Netherlanders. Holland just happened to have more seagoing vessels than all other counties combined. The ships for the expedition to Copenhagen could afterwards continue

---

[35] Van der Goes and Van der Goes (1791), 467–8; Häpke (1913), 296–7, 301, n. 2.

their trip for the benefit of the Baltic trade. All this however was of no avail—the States of Holland persisted in their refusal.[36]

Mary of Hungary nevertheless determined to proceed with the expedition. Initially she appealed to Anthony of Lalaing, *stadholder* of Holland and Zeeland, to collect the necessary ships. The *stadholder* had himself pressed for the mounting of an expedition because Holland's seafaring trade and thus the whole province was in danger. Since he had been responsible for equipping the fleet of 1533 he claimed to dispose of the necessary experience for the organisation of the fleet to Copenhagen. This was why the regent thought him the most capable person for the task, the more so because Lalaing had never accepted that the Admiral of the Netherlands— or anyone else—could lead an expedition concerning Holland's shipping. Lalaing had told the regent that leadership of equipping the fleet belonged to his competence as stadholder.[37] This justification for his authority has to be considered in connection with his resentment of the office of Admiral of the Netherlands, whose authority in Holland the regional authorities refused to recognize.[38] In any event, the *stadholder* did not acquit himself well in his task. He pretended to be ill and claimed not to be able to raise the necessary loans for chartering ships with the money the regent had sent him.[39] For such financial transactions the influence of the States of Holland was indispensable.[40] On 19 May 1536, Mary wrote to Charles V about the unsatisfactory situation involving Lalaing and the next day the Admiral, Adolph of Burgundy, Lord of Veere, was charged with the leadership of the expedition to Copenhagen in the name of the emperor.[41]

Veere received his instructions jointly with Cornelis de Schepper and Gotschalk Ericksen. De Schepper or Scepperus had taken up office in service of the emperor in 1526 at the recommendation of

---

[36] Häpke (1913), 304–5; Van der Goes and Van der Goes (1791), 470–86. The interdiction of seafaring to the Baltic dated from 3 March 1536. Lameere (1902), 520; Tracy (1990), 111–12; Gorter-Van Royen (1995), 221.

[37] Häpke (1913), 310–311. Generally provincial governors tried to maximise their authority as much as possible. Rosenfeld (1959), 2–64.

[38] See Sicking (2004), 105–21.

[39] Häpke (1913), 310–11; Lanz (1845), 639; Henne (1858–1860), 139; Gorter-Van Royen (1995), 222.

[40] Tracy (1990), 123.

[41] Häpke (1913), 310–11; Pinchart (1865), 238. Account of ships and crew of the fleet of 1536, ARA Brussels, Ch. Ac., no. 26104, f. 1r. Henne (1858–1860), 151–2.

the regent. Ericksen, who was also called Erici, followed De Schepper's example. They had been chancellor and vice-chancellor respectively of the Danish king Christian II, and thus must have had a good knowledge of Danish affairs. Both had been sent to the Baltic before as envoys.[42] Their role was to advise the admiral, who was to command the fleet in person. The instructions, dated 1 September 1536, contained directives that were both political and military. The political goal of the expedition was to restore the succession of Christian II in favour of Frederick and Dorothy; Christian II was only to be set free after his assurance that he would abdicate his throne to his daughter. The most important task of the fleet was to convey the troops of Frederick of the Palatinate to Copenhagen, but if a hostile fleet were encountered it was to be attacked without mercy. The forces of the Count Palatine, which were under the command of his brother Wolfgang, together with Netherlandish troops under the command of Reinoud of Brederode, would have to secure Copenhagen as well as other towns and places in Denmark. The fleet's company was to help the landing forces with their task without putting the fleet at risk.[43]

Although the extant sources do not contain further details of either the military actions that were to be pursued or the amphibious landing itself, Gerard van Meckeren, commander of the fleet that went to the Baltic in 1533, presented detailed advice for the 1536 expedition and this has survived. He had once visited Copenhagen, which was a well-fortified town [plate 1], in size comparable to his own town St Winoksbergen (present day Bergues in France). He thought it could well be possible to approach the fortress of Copenhagen without problems if the enemy were only present on land. Everything would depend on the wind, which determined how the water in the Sound behaved, as the movement of the tides there was of minor importance. He also thought that Christian III would not be able to equip a fleet as large as the Habsburgs' would be: that is, a fleet carrying at least 4,000 soldiers. He was furthermore of the opinion

---

[42] On De Schepper: Van Ditzhuyzen (1981), 41; *BNB*, 712; IJssel de Schepper (1870), 39–40; Häpke (1913), 151, 163, 291; Sicking (2004), passim.

[43] Instruction (minute), (July 1536), ARA Brussels, Aud., no. 1659/3^E, ff. 1–4, printed by Häpke (1913), 319–22. Commission and letter of articles (1 Sept. 1536), Copulaatboek VI, ZA, Ch. Ac. A., no. 457, ff. 26r–34v.

that the ships of Holland were not as fit for war as ships from Biscay or elsewhere, since the former were only built for carrying merchandise, not for defence. He thought that with three or four galleys and calm weather it would be easy to capture all Baltic ships in the vicinity. He may have considered that a combination of sailing ships and galleys was an attractive one for carrying out a landing, a strategy more than once attempted by France.[44] Concerning equipping the ships, he advised that this should not be done in Holland for two reasons. On the one hand the ships had to be equipped in both Amsterdam and Enkhuizen, which was inefficient. On the other hand the ships could only be fully equipped when anchored outside the harbours, across the shallow known as Pampus. This caused extra transport costs. Van Meckeren knew what he was talking about since he had experienced this in 1533.[45]

The preparations for the expedition had hardly begun when Holland faced the risk of an attack on its own territory. At the beginning of May, Meinert van Ham, acting under orders of the Duke of Guelders (at this time an ally of Christian III), passed with 3,000 men through Overijssel to Groningen. He occupied Appingedam and threatened to attack Holland if the expeditionary force left for Copenhagen. Only after Mary had promised to use other resources to expel Meinert and his troops did the States of Holland reluctantly agree to the use of ships from Holland for the escorting fleet. They demanded, however, that the costs be borne by the emperor and that the ships be equipped in Zeeland. In that province, so the States claimed, many great ships from abroad were available that could better be fitted out for war than in Holland; moreover, it was cheaper to charter ships in Zeeland than in Holland, where most ships were already loaded. Unloading the ships would incur extra costs. In this manner, Holland wished to give colour to the story that it was not involved in the campaign against Christian III. Finally, the States

---

[44] On the importance of galleys for naval warfare in the sixteenth century see for example Guilmartin (2002), 118–25. Even in Northern waters galleys were considered of strategical and tactical importance. They were able to carry out amphibious operations independently of the wind. Glete (2000), 120, 139–44.

[45] Häpke (1913), 308–9. The ships were 'leggende over 't Pamphuys over 't Vlaeck in 't Vlie ende elders in de Zuyderzee'. For the costs of transport of victuals and artillery between the harbours and the ships in 1533: Account of the fleet of 1533, ARA The Hague, C. Ch. Ac., no. 4991, ff. 148r–154r.

insisted that Adolph of Burgundy fulfil his task not in his quality as Admiral, but on the basis of a special commission for the occasion. No precedent dangerous to Holland's claims to exemption from the admiral's authority could thus be established.[46] This demand had already been fulfilled since Adolph had received special instructions; in the eyes of the Hollanders the admiral was no more than a temporary commander of the fleet. What emerges is the extent to which the early-modern state, even under so powerful a monarch as Charles V (albeit transmitted through a regent) had to negotiate with, and overcome, regional authorities and mercantile interests in order to mount a powerful amphibious campaign.

In June 1536 Adolph of Burgundy assembled at Veere an impressive fleet of 45 Spanish, Portugese and Netherlandish ships. (For the composition of the fleet, which may have counted a 46th ship, perhaps a galley from Italy, see appendix 3.) The cost of chartering these ships was estimated at about 16,000 guilders per month (see appendix 4); 3,000 seamen and 4,500 soldiers would make up the fleet's company. The number of men indicated probably does not include the military force of Frederick of the Palatinate. It had proved very difficult to bring these troops to Zeeland. They had first had to engage in a campaign with Meinert van Ham, after Anthony of Lalaing and Maximilian of Egmond, Count of Buren, had refused allow Mary to commit their own troops. After a successful battle near Heiligerlee under the command of the Frisian stadholder George Schenck van Tautenburg, the troops of the Count Palatine marched on to Harlingen to cross the Zuiderzee. Then they marched to Dordrecht and from there, again by boat, they were transported to Zeeland. The admiral also encountered many difficulties collecting the necessary artillery. Various Dutch towns were afraid of an attack by the Duke of Guelders and refused to put their artillery at the admiral's disposal. The equipping of the fleet lasted from the middle of June till the beginning of September. The total costs reached more than 191,000 guilders.

All pains, however, were of no avail. On 29 July, before the expedition was ready to sail, Copenhagen fell. The amphibious operation that was to have been the culmination of Habsburg interference

---

[46] Häpke (1913), 312; Van der Goes and Van der Goes (1791), 491–96 (24 May 1536); Tracy (1990), 112–13.

in Denmark became moot. The States of Holland immediately realised that there was no point in dispatching the fleet; Mary of Hungary, however, only decided in September not to send the expedition forth, as she did not want to be accused of reneging on her promise of help to Copenhagen. In March 1537 she sent in her resignation, though it was not accepted. She was not, however, to be blamed for the failure of a plan that she had never supported. It was not her sin either of commission or ommission, but rather Holland's particularism, the impotence of the admiral and the institution of the admiralty, and the emperor's illusions of seating Frederick on the Danish throne, which were to blame for the failure of 1536.[47]

Emperor Charles V stood by his refusal to recognize Christian of Holstein as King of Denmark and adhered to the dynastic policy that aimed at procuring the Danish throne for Frederick of the Palatinate. Consequently diplomatic relations between the Netherlands and Denmark remained problematic. In 1541 Christian joined the anti-Habsburg opposition in Europe by concluding an alliance with Francis I of France, the chief enemy of the Habsburg monarchy. In 1542 and 1543 the Sound and the Belt were once again closed to Netherlandish shipping.[48] The city of Amsterdam's plan to use violence to force the Sound had no chance of being executed since the provinces of the Netherlands were themselves now in danger.[49] The French attacked in the south, the Gelderlanders in the east, while the Danes were in position with a fleet of their own off the Netherlandish coast. Finally in 1544 at Speyer a peace treaty was concluded; the emperor recognized Christian III as king of Denmark and free passage through the Sound was guaranteed.[50] Between 1544 and start of the so-called Seven Years' War between Denmark and

---

[47] Accounts of the warfleet of 1536, ARA Brussels, Ch. Ac., no. 26104, ff. 5r–20r; no. 26105, f. 132v; Tracy (1990), 112–13; Häpke (1913), 323–4.

[48] This is explicit proof that Bregnsbo's statement that Charles gave priority to the commercial interests of the Netherlands is incorrect: Bregnsbo (2002), 661. In fact, by not recognizing Christian III as King of Denmark the emperor endangered the truce concluded between the Netherlands and Denmark on 3 May 1537. Häpke (1914), 227–8, 332–7. For a full analysis of Habsburg and Netherlandish policies and interests in the Baltic and their intertwinement during the first half of the sixteenth century see Sicking (2004), 207–41.

[49] Häpke (1913), 405–6.

[50] Häpke (1913), 370–74, 380–82, 414–17, 419–21; Gorter-Van Royen (1995), 224–5.

Sweden in 1563, Holland's Baltic trade prospered because the Sound remained open.[51] But the Dutch were prepared if necessary to pursue their traditional strategy of using violence to secure their trading interests. In 1565 when fighting in the Seven Years' War forced the closure of the Sound, the States of Holland considered that ". . . the closure of the Sound is a bad consequence . . . the damage caused by it costs more . . . than a small war would cost".[52] From this statement it is clear that in taking decisions concerning military actions, costs and benefits were weighed. In contrast with the Hanseatic League in the fourteenth century, however, Holland did not consider amphibious warfare necessary to safeguard its commercial interests. A 'small war' certainly did not include amphibious operations, which, from the logistical and strategical perspectives, were among the most difficult and most risky undertakings in the early modern period.

Comparison and conclusion

What can be learned from a comparison between the amphibious operations of the Hansa in the fourteenth century and the Copenhagen landing planned by the Habsburgs in 1536? The first and most striking difference concerns the fact that the Hansa both in 1362 and in 1368 concluded coalitions with several German and Scandinavian princes, whereas the Habsburgs did not succeed in involving the county of Holland in their plan. This is the more striking since Holland formed part of the Habsburg territories, whereas the Hanseatic towns had much looser links with the princes that participated in the coalitions against Valdemar. This means that the link between the sovereign and its subjects was not decisive for joint military action, at least not in the cases treated here. The existence or absence of common interests may have played a role, but one has to be aware that interests of allies did not necessarily have to coincide for joint military action.

In the case of the wars against Valdemar it is clear that the princes had territorial ambitions that could only be realised by conquest. A

---

[51] Van Tielhof (1995), 119–20. But in 1557 it was necessary to take measures to defend the seafaring trade to the Baltic against the French: Sicking (2004), 280–85.
[52] Häpke (1923), 133.

landing in Copenhagen would threaten the King of Denmark at the heart of his kingdom. This would encourage the disintegration of the kingdom and thus make a conquest easier to realise. Now the Hansa, as has been shown, had no interest in the division of Denmark by the allied princes, and economic interests prevailed in their strategy. How then could economic interests justify amphibious attacks on Danish territory and fortresses? By attacking Copenhagen the Hanseatic towns first of all wanted to force Valdemar to respect their trading privileges. The fact that Copenhagen was located near the Scania peninsula and the Scania fishing grounds, which were vital to most of the Hanseatic towns participating in the coalition against Valdemar, was probably also important. As sovereign of Scania, Valdemar could not only limit Hanseatic privileges on the peninsula; from his power base in Copenhagen he could enforce the measures he took against the Hansa merchants. Here not the interests but the military goals of both the Hanseatic towns and the princes coincided. Both parties believed their respective interests would be served by a joint amphibious enterprise. That both the Hansa and the princes tried to form as broad a coalition as possible partly reflects their recognition that amphibious operations belong to the most complicated and risky military actions conceivable. The necessity of coalition warfare became clear during the first war against Valdemar when the amphibious attacks failed because the princes did not turn up. It was only when all parties kept their promises that the amphibious enterprise could be accomplished. The fact that the towns concluded a separate peace with Valdemar shows clearly that their interests were indeed distinct from those of the princes.

The battle for the Danish throne led in 1534 to an opposition of interests between the Habsburg dynasty and Holland's merchants. For more than a decade, Charles V pursued the unrealistic goal of installing Frederick of the Palatinate upon the Danish throne. Habsburg support for the Count Palatine culminated with the equipping of the expedition of 1536 with the intent of an amphibious attack on Copenhagen. The regent of the Netherlands, Mary of Hungary, who preferred good diplomatic relations with both royal pretenders to the complexities of combined operations conflict, supported the expedition against her will. Since Holland refused to participate in the expedition it became a purely imperial expedition financed by the emperor and equipped by the Admiral, based in Zeeland. With the exception of the years 1531–1533, when both the Habsburg authorities in the Netherlands and the county of Holland found common purpose in a joint expedition against Lübeck, the imperial ambitions of Denmark directly endangered Holland's Baltic trade. Although the Habsburg authorities tried to convince the Dutch cities that an attack on Copenhagen would be in their own interest, the States of Holland were of a different opinion. In their view a costly and above all hazardous amphibious undertaking was of no advantage of them. Their sole aim in Denmark was to secure a free passage for their ships taking grain from the Eastern Baltic harbours either through the Sound or through the Great and Small Belt. In contrast with the Hanseatic towns they had no direct interest at stake in Denmark or any nearby region and therefore an amphibious attack was not necessary. In case of a closure of the Sound or a threat of this, as in 1533, the Hollanders considered a purely naval operation more cost-effective than an amphibious one.

There were more differences between amphibious warfare in the 1360s and the 1530s that must be considered. Whereas in the 1360s troops were needed for any naval warfare, with the introduction of heavy artillery on board after the start of the sixteenth century, naval operations could be carried out without troops. Since the costs for naval warfare were dominated by pay and victuals[53] a war fleet with troops on board was much more expensive than a war fleet without troops.[54] If one accepts that an analysis of costs and benefits lay at the basis of all commercial activity, including military intervention for commercial ends, then it is no surprise that when it became possible to undertake naval operations without troops these were preferred by the merchants whose interests were limited to safeguarding vital sea links. This was the option chosen by Holland in 1533. Before the introduction of heavy artillery on board such an option was non-existent and thus not relevant for the Hanseatic towns in the 1360s: an amphibious attack was their only naval option to put Valdemar under pressure.

Since medieval war at sea was not much more than combat between troops on board ships all naval warfare could potentially become amphibious. In fact, naval warfare during the Middle Ages was often reduced to the transportation of troops to hostile territory,

---

[53] Brulez (1978), 386–406, 392; Sicking (2004), 367–9. See also appendix 4.
[54] Assuming that the costs of armament were equal for both fleets.

which technically is nothing less than an amphibious operation.[55] After the gunpowder revolution, land and naval warfare became more distinct. As a consequence amphibious warfare became a specific kind of warfare, which had to be chosen beforehand and which needed careful planning. The difference between naval warfare before and just after the naval revolution should at the same time, however, be somewhat relativized, in that the introduction of gun-armed ships did not immediately lead to the disappearance of troops as integral parts of ships' companies. In fact, at least up to *c.* 1560, the strength of contending fleets was still reckoned in terms of armed men and large ships with many soldiers were still regarded as important. As late as 1588 the Spaniards had not yet abandoned this approach to warfare at sea. Moreover, the ability of sailing warships and temporarily armed merchantmen to reach decisive areas of action was far from certain. As long as sailing ships had little ability to sail close to the wind, amphibious operations with sailing ships could not be carried out independently from the wind.[56] As for the planned operation of 1536, the great distance between the Netherlands and Copenhagen made an amphibious operation carried out by sailing ships extremely hazardous. This was no consolation for Mary of Hungary, who considered giving up the regency of the Netherlands after the preparations that had consumed so much time and money proved to be for nothing when Copenhagen fell before the fleet could leave the harbour.

Appendix 1. The composition of the Hanseatic fleet of 1362

Towns	Cogs	Boats	Men
Lübeck	6	6	600
Hamburg	2	–	200
Rostock, Wismar	6	6	600
Strasund, Greifswald	6	6	600
Kolberg, Stettin, Anklam	6	6	600
Bremen	1	–	100
Kiel	–	1	40
Total	27	25	2740

Source: Fritze and Krause (1997), 83.

---

[55] Compare Introduction, above, pp. 29–30.
[56] Glete (2000), 143–4; Martin and Parker (1988), 22.

Appendix 2. The composition of the Hanseatic fleet of 1368

Towns	Cogs	Boats	Men
Lübeck	3	–	300
Rostock	2	–	150
Stralsund	2	–	200
Wismar	1	20	100
Stettin	1	–	80
Greifswald	1	–	60
Kolberg	1	–	40
Prussian towns	5	–	500
Hamburg	1	–	100
Zuiderzee towns	1	–	100
Zeeland	2	–	200
Kampen	1	2	150
Total	21	22	1980

Source: Fritze and Krause (1997), 87.

Appendix 3. The composition of the warfleet equiped in the
Netherlands in 1536

Name ship	Name shipmaster	Size of the ship In *brouage**	Men (soldiers excluded)
Netherlandish ships			
De Pelikaan	Claes Waernu	2400	113
Samson	Pieter Geerbrantsz, Enkhuizen	2400	112
	Hans Balsser	2000	152
	Kersten Jonge	2000	140
De Salvator	Albert Frederyckxz	1900	105
	Lijbert Harincx	1875	74
	Hendrik Rooclaeys	1850	104
	Pieter Symonsz Maeckscoon	1825	98
De Christoffel	Roucke van Amsterdam	1825	90
De Blauwhulk	Clays Jacobsz, Enkhuizen	1800	109
Zeewolf	Geert Geertbrantsz, Enkhuizen	1725	97
	Claes Illebrantz Spronck	1600	91
	Geert Woutersz	1550	97
	Jacob Visscher	1425	78
Sint Jan van Edam	Jan Gribber	1375	76
	Jan Reiniersz van Edam	1375	83
	Pauwels Recx	1350	87

Table (*cont.*)

Name ship	Name shipmaster	Size of the ship In *brouage**	Men (soldiers excluded)
De Ham	Willem Hooft	1350	77
De Margriet	Lambert Claysse	1300	71
	Jan Jacopsz van Hoorn	1225	71
't Hof van Vrieslandt	Frederyck	1175	90
't Galjoen van Hoorn	Geert Jacopz	1175	80
	Wolffaert Jansz van Hoorn	1150	76
De Adolf van Rotterdam	Geert Jansz Moeyer	1100	77
De Admiraal van Sluis	Job Jansz	1000	77
	Tolgraaf	800	43
	Pedro de Balasco	700	44
	Claeys Volckaertsz	400	41
Boeier van Enkhuizen		350	48
't Haenken		200	25
Loodsmansboot van Amsterdam		100	23
Loodsmansboot van Sluis		100	6
Seinschip		100	9
Spanish ships		In *vaten**	
	Johan de Sainttourche Montelliano	250	82
	Johan de Scalante	238	83
	Ochoa de Capitillo	230	91
	Johan de Vassaury	225	84
	Pedro Salazar	225	90
	Domingo de Gamboa	190	77
Portuguese ships		*vaten**	
	Antonio Louys	196	70
	Alfonso Louys	175	69
	Aluro Eaunes	145	123
	Francisco Eaunes	135	60
	Bartolomeo Rodrigo	75	44
	Pedro Carindo	60	44
Italian ship		*vaten*	
Alfonchiael van Ferrara	Ludovico de Scaldo	300	109
Total	46 ships	9,527.33 *vaten*	3,590 men

Source: ARA Brussels, Ch. Ac., Acquits, no. 5207.
* Contemporary measures of capacity: 1 *vat* equals 6 *brouage*.

Appendix 4. Estimated and actual costs for the expedition to Copenhagen in 1536

	Estimated price per unit or person and per month, unless otherwise indicated	Estimated cost (per month)	Total actual expenditure
Rent ships			
41 ships: 10,600 *vaten* (*tonnelades*)	30 s per *vat* (*tonnelade*)	15,900 lb	33,465 lb
Total rent ships		**15,900 lb**	**33,465 lb**
Pay			
1,000 officers (captains, pilotes, skippers, quartermasters, cannoneers, cooks etc.)		9,498 lb 18 s	
1,950 sailors	3 guilders 12 s	7,020 lb	
4,500 soldiers	3 Philippus guilders	16,875 lb	
'Double pay' of 4,500		4,500 lb	
Coronel of the solders with ten halberdiers, and servants; provost with four halberdiers and three sergeants, an *escouteté* with a *huissier* and a notary; marshal of quarters		1,000 lb	
Total pay		**38,894 lb**	**45,961 lb**
Victuals for 7,500 persons	2 s per person per day	22,500 lb	47,823 lb
Total victuals		**22,500 lb**	**47,823 lb**
Total per month		77,293 lb 18 s	
Total for 3 months		231,881 lb 14 s	127,249 lb
Extra ordinary costs			
Artillery, munition etc.			
300 tuns powder	48 guilders per tonnel	14,400 lb	
Iron balls		1,076 lb 13 s 4 d	
6,600 Stone balls	5 s per ball	1,650 lb	
Lead balls		150 lb	
1200 livres Lead on roll	3 guilders 12 s per 100 livres	43 lb 4 s	
Iron		180 lb	
Balls		3,175 lb	
Lead		207 lb 10 s	
Lead on roll and iron		293 lb 11 s	
120 salted skins	36 s per skin [sic]	259 lb 4 s	

Appendix 4 *(cont.)*

	Estimated price per unit or person and per month, unless otherwise indicated	Estimated cost (per month)	Total actual expenditure
12 sheep skins	5 g.	13 lb 2 s	
144 axes	3 s. per axe	21 lb 12 s	
Leather for the pomps, sacs for powder, hammers, (pump) handles etc.		300 lb	
2,200 half pikes	8 guilders for 100	176 lb	
5.400 spears and lances	5 lb for 100	270 lb	
876 harquebuses *a queue*	30 s per harquebus	1,314 lb	
Total artillery, munition etc.		**24,020 lb 4 s**	**34,567 lb**
Carpentry, various activities, transports etc.		4,000 lb	
Other costs			**9,375 lb**
Total extra ordinary costs		28,020 lb 4 s	63,942 lb
Total (ordinary costs for 3 months and extra ordinary costs)		**259,301 lb 18s** *sic*	**191.191 lb**

Note: 1 lb (pound) = 20 s (shillings) = 240 d (pennies). 1 Pound of 40 *groten* corresponds with 1 (karolus) guilder.

The descriptions in the first two collumns only relate to the estimated cost, except those printed in bold. Therefore when comparing the numbers of the last two collumns one should bear in mind that the latter do not necessarily correspond with the estimated number of ships, officers etc. and comprise a period longer than one month, that is the whole period of the preparation of the expedition. The costs for the admiral, the vice-admiral and Duke Wolfgang and their respective entourages were not included in the estimated costs. The costs for the flags, estimated at 500 lb, were not included either.

Source: ARA Brussels, Aud., no. 1627; Ch. Ac., nos. 26104–26106.

Sources and Bibliography

Archival Sources

ARA Brussels   Algemeen Rijksarchief Brussels
                  Aud.   Archives of the Council of State and *Audience*
                  Ch. Ac.   Archives of the Chamber of Accounts

ARA The Hague   Nationaal archief (former Algemeen Rijksarchief) The Hague
                          C. Ch. Ac. Archives of the Count's Chamber of Accounts
ZA   Zeeuws Archief Middelburg
                          Ch. Ac. A. Archives of the Chamber of Accounts A

Printed Primary Sources

HR   *Die Recesse und andere Akten der Hansetage von 1256–1430*, 1 (Leipzig: 1870).
ROPB   *Recueil des ordonnances des Pays-Bas*, 2nd series, *1506–1700*, 3, ed. J. Lameere *et al.* (Brussels: 1902).
Goes, A. van der, and A. van der Goes (1791). *Holland onder de regeering van keizer Karel den Vijfden, bij den overdragt der Nederlanden aan, en geduurende het bestier van, zijnen zoon koning Philips den Tweeden of verzameling van alle de notulen, propositien, resolutien en andere besognes, in de dagvaarden bij de vergadering van de Staaten dier provincie gehouden, genomen en gedaan door A. van der Goes* . . . I/2 (Amsterdam: 1791).
Häpke, R. (1923), ed. *Niederländische Akten und Urkunden zur Geschichte der Hanse und zur Deutschen Seegeschichte*, I, *1531–1557* (München and Leipzig: 1913); 2, *1558–1669* (Lübeck: 1923).
Lanz, K. (1845), ed. *Correspondenz des Kaisers Karl V*, 2 (Leipzig: 1845).
Schäfer, D., (1913), ed. *Hanserecesse von 1477–1530. Dritte Abtheilung*, 9 (Leipzig: 1913).

Secondary Works

BNB   *Biographie nationale publiée par l'académie royale des sciences, des lettres et des beaux-arts de Belgique*, 5 (Brussels: 1876).
Bregnsbo, M. (2002) 'Karl V und Dänemark', in A. Kohler, B. Haider and C. Ottner (eds), *Karl V. 1500–1558 Neue Perspektiven seiner Herrschaft in Europa und Übersee* (Vienna: 2002) 655–666.
Brulez, W. (1978) 'Het gewicht van de oorlog in de nieuwe tijden. Enkele aspecten', *Tijdschrift voor geschiedenis*, 91 (1978) 386–406.
Ditzhuyzen, R. E. van (1981) 'Cornelius Duplicius de Schepper (Scepperus), lid van de Raad van State 1538–1555', in: *Raad van State 450 jaar* (The Hague: 1981) 37–47.
Dollinger, Ph. (1970) 'Die Bedeutung des Stralsunder Friedens in der Geschichte der Hanse', *Hansische Geschichtsblätter* 88 (1970) 148–162.
Fritze, K., and G. Krause (1989) *Seekriege der Hanse* (Berlin: 1989).
—— (1997) *Seekriege der Hanse. Das erste Kapitel deutscher Seekriegsgeschichte* (Berlin: 1997).
Glete, J. (2000) *Warfare at sea, 1500–1650. Maritime conflicts and the transformation of Europe* (London and New York: 2000).
Gorter-Van Royen, L. V. G. (1995) *Maria van Hongarije regentes der Nederlanden. Een politieke analyse op basis van haar regentschapsordonnanties en haar correspondentie met Karel V* (Hilversum: 1995).
Gouw, J. ter (1884), *Geschiedenis van Amsterdam*, 4 (Amsterdam: 1884).
Götze, J. (1970) 'Von Greifswald bis Stralsund. Die Auseinandersetzungen der deutschen Seestädte und ihrer Verbündeten mit König Valdemar von Dänemark 1361–1370', *Hansische Geschichtsblätter* 88 (1970) 83–122.
Guilmartin, J. F. (2002) *Galleons and galleys* (London: 2002).
Häpke, R. (1914) *Die Regierung Karls V. und der europäische Norden. Veröffentlichungen zur Geschichte der Freien und Hansestadt Lübeck* 3 (Lübeck: 1914).
Henn, V. (1994) '". . . De alle tyd wedderartigen suederseeschen stedere". Zur Integration des Niederrheinisch-Ostniederländischen Raumes in die Hanse', *Hansische Geschichtsblätter* 112 (1994) 39–56.

Henne, A. (1858–1860) *Histoire du règne de Charles-Quint en Belgique* VI (Paris etc.: 1858–1860).

IJssel de Schepper, G. A. (1870) *Lotgevallen van Christiern II en Isabella van Oostenrijk, koning en koningin van Denemarken; voornamelijk gedurende hunne ballingschap in de Nederlanden,* (Zwolle: 1870).

Jahnke, C. (2000) *Das Silber des Meeres. Fang und Vertrieb von Ostseehering zwischen Norwegen und Italien (12.–16. Jahrhundert),* Quellen und Darstellungen zur hansischen Geschichte, 49 (Cologne, Weimar and Vienna: 2000).

Martin, C., and G. Parker (1988) *The Spanish Armada* (London etc.: 1988).

Meij, J. C. A. de (1976) 'Oorlogsvaart, kaapvaart en zeeroof', in G. Asaert, J. van Beylen and H. P. H. Jansen eds., *Maritieme Geschiedenis der Nederlanden* I (Bussum: 1976) 307–337.

Nübel, O. (1972) *Pompejus Occo, 1483 bis 1537. Fuggerfaktor in Amsterdam* (Tübingen: 1972).

Olesen, J. E. (2003) 'Inter-Scandinavian relations' in K. Helle ed., *The Cambridge history of Scandinavia* I Prehistory to 1520 (Cambridge: 2003) 710–770.

Parker, G. (1996) *The Military Revolution. Military Innovation and the Rise of the West 1500–1800* (second edn, Cambridge etc.: 1996).

Pinchart, A. (1865) *Inventaire des archives des Chambres de Comptes, précédé d'une notice historique,* 4 (Brussels: 1865).

Rosenfeld, P. (1959) 'The provincial governors in the Low Countries from the minority of Charles V to the Revolt', *Standen en Landen,* 17 (1959) 2–64.

Schäfer, D. (1879) *Die Hansestädte und König Valdemar von Danemark. Hansische Geschichte bis 1376* (Jena: 1879).

Schildhauer, J. (1985) *The Hansa. History and culture* (Leipzig: 1985).

Seifert, D. (1997) *Kompagnons und Konkurrenten. Holland und die Hanse im späten Mittelalter.* Quellen und Darstellungen zur Hansischen Geschichte, 43 (Cologne, Weimar, Vienna: 1997).

Sicking, L. (2004) *Neptune and the Netherlands. State, economy, and war at sea in the Renaissance* (Leiden and Boston: 2004).

Tielhof, M., van (1995) *De Hollandse graanhandel, 1470–1570. Koren op de Amsterdamse molen* (The Hague: 1995).

Tracy, J. D. (1990) *Holland under Habsburg Rule, 1506–1566. The formation of a body politic* (Berkeley, Los Angeles and Oxford: 1990).

Weststrate, J. (2003) 'Abgrenzung durch Aufname. Zur Eingliederung der Süderseeischen Städte in die Hanse, ca. 1360–1450', *Hansische Geschichtsblätter* 121 (2003) 13–40.

PORTUGUESE AMPHIBIOUS WARFARE IN THE EAST IN THE SIXTEENTH CENTURY (1500–1520)

Malyn Newitt

Portuguese Arrival in the East and the Development of Armed Conflict

Vasco da Gama entered the Indian Ocean with a fleet of three ships in 1498. Between that date and the 1520s Portuguese ships explored the Indian Ocean and Indonesia, travelling as far as Canton, and established a formal imperial structure with its centre of government on the west coast of India. Until the last quarter of the sixteenth century, this empire was wholly based on sea-power and Portuguese military might was almost invariably exercised by means of amphibious operations. Detailed accounts of the wars they waged, their conquests and punitive raids during this period show clearly the potential as well as the limitations of this form of warfare. This chapter focuses on the period up to the death of Afonso de Albuquerque in 1515. It begins by explaining why the arrival of the Portuguese in the East involved them in violent conflict, describes the strategy and tactics used by Portuguese sea-borne forces, and looks at the structure of maritime power that amphibious warfare was able to create.

Vasco da Gama's first voyage to the East was largely peaceful. But the second Portuguese voyage, made in 1500 by a fleet under Pedro Alvares Cabral [figure 2], began a pattern of conflict that was to continue and intensify as the century progressed. Most historians have held that this violent confrontation set a precedent for future European contacts with the East and, by implication, have considered that it could have been avoided had the Portuguese been less ideologically predisposed to use force. In a recent work on the Portuguese in eastern Africa, M. N. Pearson has written, "we can question whether the whole basis of Portuguese policy was fatally flawed . . . one could argue that they would have done better to trade on the east African coast, and indeed the whole Indian Ocean, on a basis of equality with all the other traders there . . . peaceful competition would have meant no vast expense on fleets, soldiers and forts."[1] In other words the Portuguese (and subsequently the English and Dutch) had a choice, and deliberately chose the use of force rather than peaceful co-existence.

The origin of this conflict was seen by sixteenth century writers to have been the traditional hostility of the Muslims and the Portuguese, born of religious hatred and rooted in the conflicts in the Iberian Peninsula, in North Africa and more recently in the expansion of Turkish power in the Mediterranean. According to this interpretation, Muslims and Portuguese were so deeply suspicious of each other's intentions that the simplest contact between them could lead to misinterpretation, to hostage taking, reprisals and more widespread violence. There is certainly some truth in this, and Álvaro Velho's account of the first voyage of Vasco da Gama shows clearly how simple misunderstanding became translated by the Portuguese suspicion of Muslims into evidence of conspiracies which in turn provided the occasion for pre-emptive violence.[2] Fear fed on suspicion, and reprisals and counter-reprisals spiralled out of control as the Portuguese, conscious of their vulnerable position as tiny isolated bands thousands of miles from home, adopted the tactic of striking first and of intimidating their supposed enemies by indulging in atrocities—mutilation being a particular hallmark of their dealings with Muslims who fell into their hands.

However, there were other causes of this quick descent into violence, and when these were not present Portuguese and Muslims could get on well enough with each other and act as allies and friends. First, the Portuguese had much more implacable enemies than local Muslim traders, namely the Venetians who feared that they would lose their near monopoly of the trade in spices to Europe. It was not just paranoia that led the Portuguese to believe that they were facing a great conspiracy, for at every opportunity Venetian agents intrigued against them and financed any Asiatic ruler willing to take up arms to oppose them.

However, more important even than the hostility of the Venetians was the precarious nature of Portugal's presence in the East. The Portuguese ships that made the lengthy sea voyage from Europe were few in number and arrived storm battered, with sick and

---

[1] Pearson (1998), 140.
[2] Velho (1898).

depleted crews. Portugal's presence in the East often consisted only of a few hundred men aboard a handful of ships without any place to refit, recuperate or replenish their supplies. Indeed the early fleets, including the first fleet commanded by da Gama, had to take supply vessels with them. The vulnerability of the Portuguese fed their sense of insecurity and in turn encouraged those with whom they had dealings to drive hard bargains.

The situation of the Portuguese was made worse by the fact that they were in a poor position to trade. They were not able to supply the Indian Ocean market with the goods it required and had to rely on supplies of silver brought from Europe. Peaceful commerce, therefore, proved next to impossible for people who not only had local enemies and were perceived to be weak and vulnerable, but who in addition did not have the commodities that the market demanded.

Some of the violence shown by Cabral and Vasco da Gama during the early voyages to the East can be explained quite simply in terms of their immediate needs. They believed they had to protect themselves against potential enemies, by pre-emptive strikes if necessary, and they had to force their way into local markets and demand that traders sell to them. Moreover they had to obtain pilots and supplies for their fleets. However, after the initial voyages the growing violence of the Portuguese became rooted much more deeply in the structural requirements of their eastern enterprise.

First, the Portuguese needed to acquire safe heavens in the Indian Ocean, bases where their ships could be laid up for repair, where crews could recover their health, and where supplies could be taken on board. Such bases would also allow some ships to stay in the Indian Ocean instead of all vessels having to make the precarious voyage to and from Europe every year. At first, the Portuguese tried to find coastal allies whose ports they could use. The Sultans of Melinde on the east coast of Africa, for example, early struck up an alliance which was to last throughout the century. The Rajas of Cochin and Cannanore in western India also soon became firm allies, but in both cases the alliances were motivated by the existence of powerful local rivals against whom the ruler needed protection. These alliances did not give the Portuguese the long-term security or the resources they required, and a decision was made to secure bases under Portugal's own control. In 1505 Anjediva off the coast of western India and Socotra off the coast of Aden were chosen as

possible sites, occupied and fortified [figure 5]; but it was soon found
to be impracticable to establish bases on remote islands where there
existed no local economy to support the needs of the fleets.

Meanwhile ships continued to arrive in the East with pressing
needs that had to be met. The fleets had to have supplies and the
royal factors needed trade goods to be able to buy in the spice markets of western India. In these circumstances the Portuguese captains saw no alternative to supporting their enterprise by force. Three
courses of action were adopted.

First, the Portuguese fleet commanders began to take the law into
their own hands and to plunder captured ships or vulnerable coastal
settlements to obtain much needed supplies. Afonso de Albuquerque's
cruise along the Arabian coast in 1507 has to be seen in this light.
When he took over command of the fleet from Tristan da Cunha
in August 1507 he found "there were only fifteen days' supplies on
board the fleet." He called together his captains and pilots and discussed with them the route the fleet should take so that it should
be "best supplied with supplies, for there was great need of them."
They decided to sail along the Arabian coast towards Muscat and
Ormuz.[3] The first haul was a fleet of thirty or forty fishing boats
which the Portuguese burnt—not, however, without first taking "the
ships' boats with masts and sails." Proceeding to Curiat, Albuquerque
captured the town and remained there "until the supplies had been
collected, for there was great need of them . . . And as soon as the
supplies were collected, and as much spoil as they could carry away,
he ordered the place to be set on fire." At Muscat it was a similar
story. Having taken the city, Albuquerque authorized his men to
sack it, first ordering his captains "that each one must take care to
collect into his ship as large a quantity of provisions as possible."
As by this time the fleet's water barrels had disintegrated, an order
was issued to remove water containers from the houses and if these
were too large to go through hatches into the holds of the ships,
they were to be stored full of water on deck. When this was completed, he "ordered them to fit out the ships with masts, yards, and
shrouds."[4] After the second capture of Goa, we are told that "Albu-

[3] Albuquerque (1774/1875–84), 1:57, 58.
[4] Ibid., 1:62, 71, 80–1.

querque began to make his fleet ready, with the intention of not passing the winter in Goa, because of the dearth of supplies therein, and because there was not enough money to pay his men . . . Duarte de Mello was appointed chief captain of the sea with four ships and three galleys under orders to cruise along the coast and provide the city with whatever was required."[5] It was not just towns that were plundered but ships as well. We are told that while three of Albuquerque's ships "were in the latitude of Magadoxo, they captured a ship of Cambaya, laden with clothing, and having stripped her of all she carried, they set her on fire. Afonso de Albuquerque was highly delighted at the arrival of Diogo de Melo and Martim Coelho, and divided with them the spoils of the prize ship."[6]

Second, the Portuguese decided to levy tribute on coastal states and cities—the tribute to take the form of food supplies, material to repair the ships, money, or trade goods. Finally, the Portuguese Crown decided to capture and occupy a series of major towns around the Indian Ocean to serve as permanent bases for the fleets and centers for commerce.

As this policy evolved, so the justification for it became more elaborate. Initially plunder was justified in terms of the traditions of religious conflict—as Pero d'Anhaia was instructed to tell the Muslims he plundered in Sofala, "we do so by reason of their being enemies of our holy faith and because we wage war continually upon them"[7]— but the Portuguese soon established a firmer juridical base for their actions. The Crown advanced the idea that it was sovereign of the Indian Ocean, the legitimate ruler of the sea and had the right to levy taxes, take tribute from, and to insist on passports for, all those crossing the royal domain. This claim, of course, could be upheld by force.

However, the royal factors still needed bullion and trade goods with which to purchase spices. At first the Portuguese resolved this problem through plunder. Ships were captured and stripped of their cargoes, while coastal towns were attacked and plundered of the cotton cloth and other goods needed for trade. Hans Mayr, who wrote an uninhibited account of Almeida's sack of Mombasa, described the

---

[5] Ibid., 3:43.
[6] Ibid., 1:202.
[7] *DPMCA*, 1:181.

process. "Then everyone started to plunder the town and to search the houses, forcing open the doors with axes and iron bars. There was a large quantity of cotton cloth for Sofala in the town, for the whole coast gets its cotton cloth from here. So the Grand-captain got a good share of the trade of Sofala for himself."[8]

In spite of successes like this, the Portuguese also realized that they themselves needed to become active participants in the regional trade of the Indian Ocean to obtain the locally made goods that could be traded for spices in western India. This encouraged them to target important trading cities whose capture would not only provide the naval bases needed by the fleets but would also give the Portuguese a dominant position in local trade. Once Albuquerque succeeded Almeida as governor in 1509, he proceeded to establish bases at Ormuz, Malacca and Goa, all three substantial cities with large populations and extensive trading networks. Capturing port-cities, however, would not in itself solve the problem of being able to trade successfully in eastern markets. The military victories had to be underpinned by the establishment of royal monopolies which would confine the trade in certain key commodities to the Portuguese royal factories. Imperial policy thus came to form a strategic whole.

This grand strategy was first set out in the instructions prepared for the first viceroy, Dom Francisco de Almeida, who was sent to the east in 1505.[9] Sofala and Kilwa were captured by Almeida's fleet to act as bases on the East African coast and at the same time to establish the monopoly of the gold trade which, if secured, would put Portugal in a dominant position in Indian Ocean trade. Kilwa and Sofala were relatively small towns and there was some debate among the Portuguese about the wisdom of capturing and occupying major cities to use as bases. One school of thought, represented by the viceroy Almeida, held that Portuguese would be best to limit itself to the exercise of sea-power and concentrate on securing the annual pepper cargoes. Against this a faction led by Albuquerque believed that without a firm territorial base the maritime enterprise could not be sustained. The disagreement between these two fac-

---

[8] Hans Mayr's account can be found in *DPMCA*, 1:518–541. This extract has been taken from Freeman-Grenville, ed. (1962), 110.

[9] 'Instructions to the captain-major D. Francisco de Almeida, Lisbon, 5 March 1505', *DPMCA*, 1:157–262.

tions led in 1507 to a mutiny by three of the captains under Albuquerque's command, who left his fleet and sailed to India to lodge an official deposition stating that "the chief captain ought not to take upon himself to build a fortress, for it is very little to the interest of the king and loss of his material, and risk of the men and artillery remaining in it."[10]

In 1510 Albuquerque, who had succeeded Almeida as governor the previous year, captured Goa and turned it into the principal Portuguese base in western India. However, Goa was also the centre of the horse trade between Arabia and India and Albuquerque coupled the seizure of the city with the establishment of a monopoly in this lucrative regional commerce. Other bases were targeted for their commercial as well as their strategic importance—Ormuz was captured in 1515 to control access to the Gulf, and Malacca was taken in 1511 to control the sea routes to Indonesia. Later the Portuguese were to add other important bases: Muscat on the Arabian coast, Colombo in Ceylon, Diu in the all important cloth-producing region of Cambay in north-western India, and Tenate in the distant Moluccas from which the Portuguese sought to control the trade in cloves. These towns were to be at the same time bases for the Portuguese fleets, centres for trade and the exercise of the royal monopolies, but also sites for the administration of the king of Portugal's dominion over the seas, where passes (cartazes) could be obtained and customs duties paid.[11] All these towns had substantial populations that paid taxes to Portugal and could provide the artisans and seamen needed to sustain the empire.

Not all the Portuguese enterprises were successful. Calicut was never brought under Portuguese control; Aden was targeted in 1513, but the Portuguese failed to capture it; Kilwa, although captured and fortified in 1505, was deserted by the gold traders and was abandoned by the Portuguese in 1513 in favour of Mozambique Island, where the ship repair facilities and protected anchorage soon led to the establishment of an important naval base, strategically placed at the narrowest part of the Mozambique Channel.

In this way the violent impact of the Portuguese resulted from the weakness and vulnerability of their position and from their

---

[10] Albuquerque (1774/1875–84), 1:207.
[11] For an account of the Portuguese commercial system in the east see Pearson (1976).

determination to overcome these disadvantages in a direct and systematic way. However, none of these activities, not the plundering
of ships and towns, nor the levying of tribute, nor the capture of
major cities could have been achieved, had not the Portuguese developed their capacity for waging amphibious warfare.

Military and Naval Capacity of the Portuguese

The Castilian war bands that enlisted for the *entradas* in Central and
South America were for the most part made up of amateur adventurers who equipped themselves as well as they could and learned
the art of warfare as they went. For them horses proved a decisive
weapon in campaigns which were almost all carried out on land.
Ships played almost no part in the Spanish conquests, the exception
being the brigantines built by Cortes for the siege of Tenochtitlan.

For the Portuguese it was a different story. Portuguese military
power lay in their ships and they could not hope to sustain campaigns on land against large well-armed Asiatic armies. However,
sea power alone would not achieve all their objectives and in particular would not give them control of their key targets like Malacca
and Ormuz. Nevertheless, the judicious combination of sea power
with small, easily deployed and heavily armed land forces brought
them a remarkable degree of success.

The Portuguese fleets that sailed to the East, at least in the early
days, were manned by professional sailors and soldiers who enlisted
in the royal service and who were, in theory, paid a salary, For
example, on Vasco da Gama's second voyage in 1502, soldiers were
paid three cruzados a month plus one cruzado for their maintenance
ashore. In addition they were allowed to ship two quintals of pepper every eighteenth months.[12] The fortresses that were established
were also manned by professional soldiers commanded by royal
officers and were subject to detailed regulations (*regimentos*) that directed
how every activity of the fort was to be organized.[13] With the appointment of the first viceroy in 1505, the Portuguese Crown tried to

---

[12] Correa (1869), 282; lists of those who were paid *moradias* (pensions) by the
Crown are given in *DPMCA*, 1:76–85.
[13] 'Regulations for Sofala', *DPMCA*, 6:304–424.

institute a level of direct royal government in the East unusual for any government in Europe at the time to attempt.

The ships the Portuguese sailed to the East were either *caravels* or *naus*.[14] The *naus* were large three-masted vessels, built like barges with a tall central mast and high castles constructed at each end. Vasco da Gama's *naus* carried six guns on the deck, two on the poop, two guns which fired forwards and eight falconets.[15] The larger *naus* carried considerable numbers of passengers and crew and up to fifty cannon. Some of these were of small calibre and could be mounted in the front of a ship' boat, but the *naus* also carried a number of great guns which could be mounted broadside, turning the ship into a floating battery. During long ocean voyages these guns were stowed below, a custom the Portuguese continued into the seventeenth century.[16]

The *caravelas* were light, lateen-rigged ships carrying small crews. On the whole they were not suitable for making the long voyage from Portugal and were sometimes built or assembled in the East. For example, on his second voyage Vasco da Gama took with him the cut timbers for a caravel which his men assembled in twelve days during their stop at Mozambique Island,[17] while Albuquerque had an oared galley with fourteen banks of oars—a *fusta*—built for him in Socotra for his second expedition to Ormuz. The Portuguese noted that the seamen of the Indian Ocean employed both oar and sail and themselves began to make increasing use of oared vessels built for them in the East. However, in the Indian Ocean these vessels, small as they were, carried guns. When Vasco da Gama attacked the Calicut fleet in 1503, the caravels are described as carrying 30 men, four heavy guns (two on each side) six falconets and twelve smaller swivel guns. The *naus* drew too much water to be used in rivers or in shallow coastal areas, so the Portuguese often employed local boats like the large ocean going dhows, (*zambukos*), or galleys for inshore work. They also made much use of smaller craft, ships boats which could be hoist on board, local canoes (*almadias*) or river boats.

---

[14] For depictions of Portuguese ships in general, see figures 2–5. For the *nau*, in particular, NB fig. 4.

[15] Correa (1869), 286.

[16] Ibid., 367–68.

[17] Ibid., 281.

All representations of the Portuguese fleets show that they were made up of both large and small vessels and the written accounts of the campaigns demonstrate how important the smaller boats were in the amphibious operations. (See plates 2–5.) Two examples can serve to illustrate this. Albuquerque's attack on Goa in 1510 depended on the presence of galleys and other small boats. While the *naus* remained outside the bar the galleys were sent up river filled with armed men to attack the fortresses and anchorages, and eventually to receive the surrender of the city. Before his abortive attack on Aden in 1513 Albuquerque's fleet had lost all its small boats in a storm and the governor had to capture locally made flat-bottomed barges before his troops could be landed.[18]

All Portuguese ships were heavily armed with artillery both for their own use and for the defence of the fortresses that they built. Almeida's fleet of 1505, for example, carried 646 firearms of all kinds ranging from iron and bronze cannon, some designed to fire stone shot, to hand held firearms. Only 27 of these are categorized as *bombardas grossas* but in the early sixteenth century this type of gun could be up to 20 feet long and fire a 90 lball 468 were *berços*, small guns that were fired from a forked prop, and 80 were *espingardas*, hand held firearms. In addition 349 firearms were sent out for the fortress of Sofala. These included 5 *esperas* which fired shot between 12 and 20 lbs, 8 *bombardas grossas* and one *serpentina*, which was also a piece of heavy artillery. The inventory of the fleet's artillery lists fifteen different types of gun in all.[19]

It has sometimes been questioned whether the guns on the Portuguese ships played a decisive role in the amphibious warfare of the period.[20] Although the circumstances of each occasion have to be considered separately, virtually every action involved the Portuguese opening fire with their great ships guns and numerous accounts testify to the range, firepower and terrifying effect of this artillery—even though the damage inflicted was often not as serious as might have been imagined. Two incidents illustrate the range of effectiveness that firearms could have in the early sixteenth century.

[18] Albuquerque (1774/1875–84), 2:100 and 4:6, 10.
[19] 'List of Artillery', *DPMCA*, 1:137–42. For discussions of types of guns see Lewis (1961).
[20] Scammell (1980).

On his first visit to Ormuz in 1507 Albuquerque attacked the fleet he found there sinking two large ships, one of them supposedly of six hundred tons, with only two cannon shot.[21] On the other hand, da Gama, during his first visit to Mozambique Island in 1498, bombarded the palisades which had been erected in front of a village on the mainland for three hours and only succeeded in killing two people.[22]

Frequently the artillery was used to create an effect, to overawe the population and to assist the work of diplomacy. A case in point was Albuquerque's arrival at Malacca in 1511. Reaching the port in the evening, he sailed into the harbour "with all his fleet decked with flags, and the men sounding their trumpets, and ordered them to salute the city with all the artillery. The king of Malacca's response was to ask what was the object of so great fleet [and] whether he came for war or for peace."[23]

The Portuguese ships all carried a complement of soldiers. Soldiers were officially registered in the Crown's service and were liable to serve for a period of five to ten years. At the end of this period a soldier could petition to become a *casado*, or married man, and could establish himself in trade or some civilian occupation, or seek permission to return to Portugal. During the unfavourable monsoons the soldiers would often be unemployed, and the custom grew up for them to be retained by the leading noblemen and captains. They fed at the expense of their patron, often acted as his bodyguard and were ready to enlist under his command once the campaigning season came round. In this way the notion of entering the service of a leading *fidalgo* came to replace that of serving the Crown. As Crown power waned it was replaced by the system of patronage exercised by the rich and powerful.

In addition to soldiers and crews, the ships and the fortresses also had slaves and convicts. Slaves would be obtained to supplement the crews of Indiamen, to act as interpreters, and to be employed in a variety of capacities around the fortresses. The convicts (*degredados*) were brought out with the fleets to be sent ashore on dangerous missions.

---

[21] Albuquerque (1774/1875–84), 1:114.
[22] Velho (1898), 30.
[23] Albuquerque (1774/1875–84), 3:66.

The muster rolls record the skills and ranks of the soldiers employed in the fleets—in Almeida's fleet of 1505 there were pilots, masters, armed seamen, men-at-arms, seamen, gunners, musketeers and cross-bowmen. Rank was clearly marked with different rates of pay and, most significant of all, a different tariff in the share of plunder, for the taking and distribution of plunder was institutionalized. Almeida's instructions (*regimento*) were quite explicit on this matter: "although there should be no shares in the prizes you make . . . since everyone receives wages, we are nevertheless pleased to do them grace and to have it done in this manner" . . . and the *regimento* sets out how the distribution should be done. When a ship was captured or a town taken, the booty was collected together and divided into shares. A fifth was set aside for the Crown, another fifth for the commander of the fleet and the rest was then divided into shares down to the simplest sailor, with six shares being reserved for the building of the monastery at Belem.[24] It is clear that the rewards of plunder far outstripped the meagre and tardy pay that the men nominally received. Albuquerque also allowed his men to plunder any town or city they captured, though his son and biographer emphasizes that the governor was aware of the indiscipline and chaos that could result and always tried to secure the military position before allowing the sack to commence. An example of this occurred after the second capture of Goa in 1510, about which he writes specifically that "after having commanded the captains to take up their positions and guard the fortress [he] gave permission to the soldiers to sack the city, and free right to everything they took."[25] Inevitably also disputes over the distribution of plunder could turn into major grievances and we are told that one reason for the mutiny of three of Albuquerque's captains was "to go to Portugal to petition Manuel for the shares of booty which they were owed and which Albuquerque had not paid them."[26]

Much of the amphibious action undertaken by the Portuguese was therefore designed to obtain plunder, and it was this plunder that sustained the fleets, the trading factories and the morale of the men.[27]

---

[24] 'Instructions to the captain-major D. Francisco de Almeida, Lisbon, 5 March 1505', *DPMCA*, 1:251.

[25] Albuquerque (1774/1875–84), 3:16.

[26] Ibid., 1:206.

[27] For example Albuquerque (1774/1875–84), 1:199 reads 'in order to please the

Portuguese Campaigns in the East

If strategic considerations pointed inexorably towards amphibious operations, these could only be successful if the tactics adopted were such as to bring military success. The Portuguese were aware that their numbers were hopelessly small when compared with the huge armies of Asia and that the principal military advantage they possessed lay in their ships. Unlike the Spanish in the New World, they were seldom tempted far from the sea and almost never embarked on major campaigns on land. The few land expeditions undertaken proved how wise this basic strategy was. The invasion of Ethiopia under Dom Cristovão da Gama in 1541 may have ended in a victory but it was a victory which cost the commander his life and which brought no gains to the Portuguese. Francisco Barreto's invasion of east-central Africa in 1569 proved a fiasco, the commander and most of his army being wiped out by disease. It was only when the Portuguese decided to use local troops and to fight in a manner to which these troops were accustomed that land campaigns began to be successful, for example in Ceylon or in eastern Africa in the early seventeenth century—ironically at the very time that Portuguese naval power was on the wane.

Most of the early Portuguese conquests were, therefore, achieved by amphibious actions, and the Portuguese commanders knew that they could only operate effectively from their ships. Amphibious operations could range from raids carried out by single ships and their crews or descents made on some coastal settlement by a handful of men using local craft, to campaigns involving a whole fleet of *naus* and supporting vessels with thousands of men on board.

In these campaigns the *naus* served a variety of functions. Albuquerque regularly used his flagship for councils of war, for receiving emissaries during negotiations, or as a point of assembly before an attack. However, first and foremost the *naus* were the supply base, barracks and refuge for the soldiers. They carried the arms, food supplies and materiel that enabled the Portuguese forces to move faster and be better equipped than most land armies of the period. The use of large *naus* went a long way towards solving the logistical

---

people still more he [Albuquerque] gave them all a share in the contents of the ship which they had taken on their way'.

problems that beset so many land armies of the time. Moreover, the great ships were very secure. Apart from the storms and other navigational hazards, they proved to be invulnerable to attack by the lightly armed ships or small coastal craft of Asiatic and Africans peoples. Many Portuguese actions involved long waits lying offshore while negotiations took place with rulers of coastal towns. The ships would here be used in support of diplomacy. Rulers or other dignitaries would be invited on board, hostages or prisoners could be kept securely, the ships could be used to overawe or impress. Sometimes the ships were decked out in flags and banners and salvoes of artillery might be fired without hostile intent but to make a statement of the firepower of the fleet and to further the progress of diplomacy.

As military action came nearer, the *naus* would be manoeuvered into a position where they could fire at targets on shore with the *bombardas grossas*. If they could get close enough the ships' guns could start fires, demolish fortifications, or disperse bodies of armed men gathered to oppose a landing. At Calicut in 1502 Vasco da Gama brought his whole fleet in shore and bombarded the city all day till night and only ceased because apparently the ships were being damaged by the recoil of the cannon.[28] In 1505 Almeida found that Mombasa had mounted cannon to protect the entrance to the harbor. His ship's artillery was able to set fire to the gunpowder store.[29] Preparing to attack Muscat in 1507, Albuquerque ordered his ships in shore to bombard the city, taking the precaution of making them cast an anchor to the rear to stop them drifting onto the beach. When his ships were not able to demolish the fortifications immediately opposite, he was able to move along the shore to find a more vulnerable target.[30] At Ormuz Albuquerque used his ships to bombard the fortress, protecting them on the landward side by anchoring a row of local boats between them and the shore.[31]

Sometimes the ships' guns would be landed for better effect. On capturing Calayate in 1507 Albuquerque decided to hold it for a few days while his men plundered the town. To do this effectively he "sent down to the ship for four cannon and placed them upon

---

[28] Correa (1869), 331.
[29] Hans Mayr in *DPMCA*, 1:108.
[30] Albuquerque (1774/1875–84), 1:76.
[31] Ibid., 1:174.

the walls, and began to fire upon the [Arabs]."[32] On his return from cruising in the Red Sea in 1513 Albuquerque decided to attack Aden for a second time. His men occupied a small island in the harbor and "set up a big gun on the principal tower, and from that point began to fire on the city, throwing down a great part of the houses."[33]

The *naus* could also be used to sink enemy shipping at anchor. A famous action took place in the harbour of Ormuz in 1507. Prior to the battle Albuquerque ordered his captains to attach their ships to the enemy vessels with ropes and grapnels. Unable to escape, the ships were then pounded at point blank range with artillery. To finish the action Albuquerque's men launched their small boats to board the enemy ships and destroy them. A similar tactic was used by Albuquerque in attacking a large Javanese ship off Malacca, which was alleged to be of 600 tons. Here, however, the enemy responded by setting fire to their own ship once the Portuguese were firmly attached to it with grapnels.[34] Another effective use of the ships was to move soldiers rapidly to new fronts as required so that a town could be attacked from many points at once. In 1505 Almeida's fleet attacked Mombasa and we are told that "Dom Francisco [de Almeida] appeared to be preparing to make the attack on the front of the town, where Dom Lourenço was, by placing there the largest ships and sending only the small ones to the place where he hoped to land."[35] At Curiat in 1507 Albuquerque attacked the fort by landing one contingent on a small island facing the fort and then "went along the river to disembark at the other part . . . and with all his people went on his way softly."[36]

One great advantage of sea power was the capacity it gave the Portuguese to take their enemies by surprise. There were numerous occasions when an armed Portuguese fleet appeared unexpectedly before a town and was able to take full advantage of the unpreparedness of the enemy. Almeida's instructions specify how this element of surprise was to be used to get possession of Sofala. "You shall first be towed into the entrance of Sofala taking good land-marks and with your long boats ahead, and thus you shall go along the

[32] Ibid., 1:218.
[33] Ibid., 4:56.
[34] Ibid., 3:64.
[35] Almeida in *DPMCA*, 1:99.
[36] Albuquerque (1774/1875–84), 1:70.

river of Sofala so peacefully and leisurely that it might seem you are but trading ships such as have called there before . . . And using this pretence you shall leap ashore there from your long boats and using such care and dexterity as you may, you shall forthwith take all the Moorish merchants who may be there from foreign parts and all the gold and merchandise you find upon them."[37]

Sea power also enabled the Portuguese to concentrate their often limited forces, move them swiftly to where they were needed, and come to the rescue of garrisons under attack from the land. The Portuguese found that by limiting themselves to amphibious operations they could keep their forces better supplied and be more mobile than the land armies of their enemies.

However, the great ships had their limitations. The main disadvantage, particularly in the East, was the difficulty of providing the fleet with water, a factor which often came to dominate the strategy of a campaign. Albuquerque's whole Arabian campaign of 1507, with the abortive attempt to seize Ormuz, hinged around the difficulty of providing the fleet with water. Another disadvantage lay in the very size of the *naus*, and they got larger as the century wore on. For example, many of the East African settlements were almost unapproachable by large ships, and it was the shallow seas and sandy estuaries around Sofala that explain why the town never developed as a major Portuguese port and was replaced by Mozambique. The *naus* found that even Mozambique had a difficult entrance, as had Mombasa, and ships frequently ran aground trying to get into harbour.

Not only could the great ships not navigate easily inshore, they also could not sail effectively in enclosed waters such as those of the Red Sea or the Gulf. If the Portuguese found themselves in a situation where their ships had limited room to manoeuvre, they could be very vulnerable, as Albuquerque found at Goa. After the first capture of the city, he brought his *naus* across the bar into the river, only to find they could not put to sea again because of the unfavourable weather conditions. They had to lie within range of the Turkish artillery that bombarded them from forts at Panjim.[38] Although generally able to withstand bad weather conditions, the size of the *naus* could sometimes be a liability in strong winds. Like a high sided

---

[37] Almeida in *DPMCA*, 1:181.
[38] Albuquerque (1774/1973), 1: pt. 2, 205.

lorry, the *naus* could catch the wind and become unmanageable. Caught in a storm off Socotra, Albuquerque had to order the high stem castle of one of his *naus* to be dismantled, an order which so outraged the captain that he resigned his office.[39]

The Portuguese amphibious campaigns, therefore, needed smaller craft if they were to be effective, and much of the fighting took place from these smaller boats. In engagements on the water the Portuguese would not wait to be attacked in their *naus* but loaded soldiers into smaller boats and went to meet their attackers. The small boats often carried a gun in the prow and the men would be armed with cross-bows and muskets which caused havoc before the enemy craft reached them.

Small boat actions were common. In 1503 Vasco da Gama entered the Indian port of Marabia with his fleet, which had been damaged in a storm. While the ships were being repaired, the caravels patrolled out at sea and captured a large merchant ship from Calicut. Vasco da Gama had the ship systematically plundered, and when the Muslims on board tried to resist he went with some of the small boats to sink her with their guns.[40] Landing troops, of course, had to be undertaken in small boats. Ruy Lourenço Ravasco anchored off Zanzibar in 1506. He sent a small boat full of men to attempt a landing but encountered a crowd of armed men gathered on the beach. When he was in range, Ruy Lourenço opened fire with the boat's gun causing widespread loss of life among the crowd. An exactly similar tactic was used by Tristan da Cunha at Angoja. The local soldiers gathered on the beach to prevent a landing but Cunha ordered "the bombardiers to fire at them with the small cannons that were in the boats. And the Moors, when they saw they were harassed by the shot, deserted the beach."[41] However, landing troops from small boats was sometimes hazardous, as Albuquerque found at Aden when his landing craft grounded a cross-bow shot from the beach and his men had to wade ashore.[42]

Portuguese tactics usually included negotiation under pressure, attack and capture of shipping in the port, and finally assault, which was usually mounted at two or more different places. If the assault

---

[39] Albuquerque (1774/1875–84), 1:204.
[40] Correa (1869), 315.
[41] Albuquerque (1774/1875–84), 1:36.
[42] Ibid., 4:16.

failed, the men could return to their ships; if it was successful the
captives and booty could be brought away from the beaches with
ease and the Portuguese could withdraw before a counter-attack
could be launched.

A classic amphibious action that illustrates many of the features
of Portuguese warfare of this period was Albuquerque's capture and
plunder of Calayate off the coast of Arabia in 1507. Albuquerque's
plan was to make a surprise descent on the town with the *naus*.
However, the wind dropped and his ships could not make land that
day. Instead he sent an oared *fusta* to reconnoitre and then dispatched an ultimatum asking the ruler of the town to come on board
the flagship. When this was refused Albuquerque embarked his men
in small boats to make a landing at two separate points. As they
approached land the Portuguese "began to fire their guns, which
they carried in their boats, to scatter the Moors who were stationed
on the beach and when they found themselves harassed by our
artillery, they fled away." Albuquerque then entered the city and
secured the gates and installed cannon from the ships on the walls.
"When the city had been disposed in this order he gave permission
to all the remaining men to sack it; and after it had been sacked
he ordered Francisco de Tavora to cause all those men to transport
all the provisions and clothes they had seized to the ships." As the
Portuguese were retreating with the spoils the Arabs attacked them,
with the result that the evacuation had to wait till the following day,
when Albuquerque burnt the city as well as 27 ships in the harbour, ending the attack by cutting off the ears and noses of all the
prisoner he had taken.[43]

Amphibious operations are notoriously difficult, as the study of
warfare from the Roman invasions to the Normandy landings makes
abundantly clear. Few countries have relied so exclusively on amphibious warfare or enjoyed such success as the Portuguese of the early
sixteenth century. This type of warfare enabled one of the smallest
and poorest states in Europe to become a military power and to
achieve military objectives in a way that would have been incon-
ceivable had the Portuguese limited themselves to conventional land
warfare or had they tried simply to use their ships to effect blockades. For twenty years the Portuguese employed their particular

---

[43] Ibid., 1:217, 219–221.

brand of amphibious warfare in the East. No Asiatic power had warships which could match their fire-power and ocean-going capability, and for the most part the Portuguese resisted the temptation of being lured far from their ships where they could be overwhelmed by more numerous forces.

Failures there were, notably at Calicut, or at Aden in 1513 when victory was thwarted by the collapse of the scaling ladders, but by the 1520s Portuguese power in the Indian Ocean was well established. Their system of fortified naval bases enabled them to impose a large measure of control over the trade of the western Indian Ocean and to confront and defeat a determined effort by the Turks to wrest the command of the seas from them, first by besieging Diu in 1538 and subsequently by launching a galley fleet in the Red Sea and Gulf. Their sea-power, meanwhile, enabled them to relieve garrisons besieged from the land and rapidly to concentrate their limited resources in such a way as to achieve maximum military effectiveness.

Bibliography

Printed Primary Sources

DPMCA *Documents on the Portuguese in Mozambique and Central Africa, 1497–1840*, vols 1, *1497–1506* and 6, *1519–1537* (Lisbon: 1962–).

Albuquerque A. de (1774/1875) *The Commentaries of the Great Afonso Dalboquerque, Second Viceroy of India . . . from the Portuguese Edition of 1774*, trans. and ed. W. de G. Birch, 4 vols., Hakluyt Society, 53, 55, 62, 69 (London: 1875–84).

——. (1774/1973) *Comentários de Afonso de Albuquerque*, ed. J. Veríssimo Serrão, 2 vols. (Lisbon: 1973).

Correa G. (1869) *The Three Voyages of Vasco da Gama, and his Vice-Royalty. From the Lendas da India of G. Correa*, ed. and trans. H. E. J. Stanley, Hakluyt Society, 42 (London: 1869).

Velho A. (1898) *A Journal of the First Voyage of Vasco da Gama, 1497–99*, ed. and trans. E. G. Ravenstein, Hakluyt Society, 99 (London: 1898).

Secondary Sources

Freeman-Grenville G. S. P., ed. (1962) *The East African Coast: Select Documents from the First to the Nineteenth Century* (Oxford: 1962).

Lewis M. (1961) *Armada Guns* (London: 1961).

Pearson M. N. (1976) *Merchants and Rulers in Gujerat: The Response to the Portuguese in the Sixteenth Century* (Berkeley, Calif., and London: 1976).

——. (1998) *Port Cities and Intruders: the Swahili Coast, India, and Portugal in the Early Modern Era* (Baltimore and London: 1998).

Scammell G. V. (1980) 'Indigenous Assistance in the Establishment of Portuguese Power in Asia in the sixteenth Century', *Modern Asian Studies* 14 (1980) 1–11.

AMPHIBIOUS WARFARE IN THE BALTIC, 1550–1700*

Jan Glete

1. *The Baltic: An amphibious theatre of war*

Amphibious warfare is essentially of two types: strategic movement of armies across the sea and co-operation between armies and navies in littoral warfare. The first type is characterised by the concentration of an army on a transport fleet protected by a fleet of warships. Such operations are limited in time, but may involve major parts of the armed forces of a state. The organisation of such forces often presents administrative and logistical challenges, and invasions are frequently cancelled or not even attempted due to their complicated nature and the risk of serious losses if the operation fails. Routine co-operation between armies and navies along coasts, in archipelagos, as well as on rivers and lakes are more common. Naval forces send troops ashore in the enemy's flank and rear, provide fire support and logistical service to forces on land, and fight enemy naval forces which provide similar support to their army.

When armed force was organised on a temporary basis, amphibious warfare was in one respect less complicated than later. With temporary armed forces, decision makers focused their interest on the operation at hand and shaped the force and its command structure to suit it. During the sixteenth and seventeenth centuries, armies and navies became permanent and articulated organisations for operations on land and at sea. Their doctrines, formations, tactics and weapon systems were tailored to such operations. Amphibious warfare had to be organised as combined operations, based on co-operation between two bureaucratic organisations with separate hierarchical lines of command and professionalism and prestige connected with either warfare on land or at sea. Combined operations therefore became complex operations, as there were usually no integrated

* The research for this paper has received support from the Bank of Sweden Tercentenary Foundation.

organisations with specialised professional skills connected with amphibious capability.

Naval and military operations in the Baltic have often been amphibious in the sense that the sea lines of communications are essential
for warfare on land.[1] The amphibious nature of warfare in this area
has often been forgotten or misunderstood because most of the literature is divided into military or naval history and so underesti-
mates interaction between operations on land and at sea.[2] A decisive
battle at sea might result in an amphibious invasion of a strategically important territory if an army were available to exploit the
opportunity. Control of the sea gave protection from invasions and
a capability to project power to enemy littoral areas. Sea lines of
communication were often decisive for army operations. Battle fleet
operations in the Baltic aimed at controlling trade and logistical supply routes, enforcing and breaking blockades, and increasing the freedom of operation for the army, either by relieving it of defensive
tasks along the coasts or securing the sea for strategic movements
of army forces.

In theory, this makes all battle fleet operations interesting in an
analysis of amphibious warfare. This chapter is, however, limited to
operations where armies and navies actually co-operated tactically in
actions against enemy forces. From the mid-sixteenth century until
1700 such operations were mainly the results of either Swedish
offensive warfare and imperial expansion in the eastern and southern Baltic or of Danish-Swedish contests over territories and political supremacy in northern Europe. The Swedish expansion in the
east and south met little resistance from enemy naval forces while
Swedish-Danish wars were fought between two powers with major
fleets. Consequently, the amphibious operations were different in
character and are treated in two separate sections of this chapter.

Warfare and strategy in the Baltic by their very nature had to be
amphibious, as the sea lines of communication in many decisive

---

[1] Baltic strategic conditions: Glete (1994), esp. 11–18. Surveys of Baltic warfare
in English: Rystad (1994); Lockhart, (1996), which however must be read with cau-
tion in its discussion of naval warfare; and Frost (2000), which has little to say
about naval and amphibious warfare. Naval warfare until 1650: Glete (2000B),
112–30. Anderson (1910/69) lacks analysis and is dated, but it is more reliable than
later works in English.

[2] Glete (1999).

regions were important for the effective concentration of superior military strength. This is most striking when lines of military operation stretched across the sea, although shipping was also usually superior to road transports for logistical support of operations on land. Army units could be landed and maintained on enemy territory by a power which controlled the sea. If necessary they could be evacuated by sea. Important cities—capitals, bases and trading ports—were most easily accessible from the sea if they were to be attacked by an army. Transport by water was especially important for the heavy siege artillery which was necessary for the conquest of a fortified place.

Sea lines could thus be used for power projection, but they were also important for defensive operations. Any large-scale concentration of armed forces in an area, whether for offence or defence, had to be supplied from outside areas, since few areas in the Baltic were affluent enough to feed such concentrations of men for extended periods. Large parts of Sweden, Finland and Norway were covered by deep forests or were so mountainous that major army forces could not operate there without supply from the sea. An army had to be placed at one end of a maritime line of communications controlled by a friendly navy if it were to be efficiently supplied with reinforcements, food and munitions.[3]

The Baltic also has unusual geographic conditions for combined operations. Several important areas were neither suitable for seagoing fleets nor for conventionally operating armies. Coastal areas with shallow water, many islands and narrow passages are common, especially on Sweden's and Finland's Baltic coasts. Danish coasts are usually accessible for sailing ships but also sheltered and suitable for operations with small craft. The coasts along the southern and eastern parts of the Baltic Sea are open and have several good harbours but important areas—the innermost parts of the Gulf of Finland, the Oder and Vistula estuaries and the coast of western Pomerania—are shallow and the Prussian and Pomeranian coast are partly covered with islands or sandbanks. Sailing ships with deep draught might blockade these areas, but for amphibious operations special shallow-draught vessels were required. Major rivers—the Neva, Narova, Düna

---

[3] Kuvaja (1999).

(Daugava, Dvina), Vistula and Oder—were also important, as they
provided an attacker with convenient routes for transports of troops,
artillery and provisions to inland areas of operation. Similarly, the
great lakes in Sweden and Finland and on the border between
Finland, Estonia and Russia (Ladoga, Peipus) might be important
for combined operations and army logistics.

These geographically varied littoral regions created problems and
opportunities for amphibious operations. Because many strategically
important areas were not suitable for large sailing warships with large
carrying capacity and heavy artillery, nor for conventionally trained
infantry and cavalry, shallow-draught ships and oared craft which
combined mobility in confined water with firepower and capacity to
carry soldiers were useful or necessary. Oared warships were in practice also landing craft. Development of such vessels continued in the
Baltic in the eighteenth century when other powers had lost interest.[4]
Armed forces that were able to combine maritime and military skills,
mobile firepower from ships, the ability to assault defended coasts
and provide army forces with seaborne supplies had the best chance
of achieving a decisive concentration of forces at the right place and
at the right moment.

2. Swedish empire-building and amphibious warfare, 1550–1660

Amphibious warfare during Sweden's expansion in the Eastern and
Southern Baltic were practically the same as combined operations
by the Swedish army and navy. Russia, Poland-Lithuania and the
Habsburgs had either no naval forces at all or only small forces.
These were unable to interfere with major Swedish amphibious operations and they lacked offensive capabilities. The fact that the Swedish
Vasa monarchy from the 1520s had created both a permanent army
and a permanent navy was a major advantage which the continental states with far larger populations were unable to challenge before
the Russians did that with a navy of their own in the eighteenth
century. By channelling scarce resources to organised sea power, the
smallest of the contending powers, Sweden, gained strategic and tactical advantages as well as political leverage in the Baltic. It could

---

[4] Glete (1992).

control sea lines of communication, keep enemies without navies at a distance and attack enemy territory from the sea in flanking operations or in the rear.[5]

Combined operations are, however, also complex operations. To combine army and navy forces in the same operation requires careful planning and preparations, an effective joint command structure, suitable vessels and a cadre of experienced leaders with the ability and self-confidence to improvise and take unconventional decisions in uncertain and unusual circumstances. Sweden's development of both land and sea forces did not bring about immediate success in offensive combined operations, in spite of the lack of resistance at sea in the east. Such operations required more skill than basic ability to operate ships, army units and heavy guns.

The major confrontation in the eastern Baltic in the latter half of the sixteenth century was between Sweden and Russia. These powers were traditionally in conflict about the ill-defined border between Finland and Russia. From the late 1550s they also claimed shares of the territories in the Eastern Baltic which were ruled by the disintegrating Teutonic Order. Operations were concentrated in areas around the Gulf of Finland, Ladoga—the largest lake in Europe—and the Neva, a broad river navigable by shallow-draught vessels. The most important fortified places in this area were accessible from the sea: the mercantile cities Viborg, Reval (Tallinn) and Narva, as well as the strategically important Nyen (present-day St Petersburg) and Nöteborg (Schlisselburg, Petrokrepost) on the western and eastern end of Neva.[6] The regional Russian centres Kexholm on the western shore of Ladoga and Pskov on the lake Peipus, connected with the sea by the river Narova, could also be reached by naval forces.

Offensive operations were therefore possible to undertake as combined operations, and oared warships could transport and land large number of soldiers if these served as oarsmen. Large numbers of men could, however, not live for long periods on such open vessels in the Nordic climate and a combined operation with oared warships required camps on land, just as an army on march would if

---

[5] The Swedish navy: Glete (1976–1977). The army: Barkman (1937), Viljanti (1957).

[6] Viborg was Swedish and Nyen and Nöteborg were Russian. Narva was taken by Russia from the Teutonic Order in 1558 while Reval and the surrounding territories placed themselves under Swedish protection in 1561.

the soldiers were to remain in good health. The number of soldiers required for major operations was also too large for the available shipping in mid-sixteenth century Sweden. Large combined operations were therefore normally undertaken with army forces divided between ships and land. Sweden had from the 1540s both a growing galley fleet and a permanent force of peasant soldiers (a kind of royal militia) who could also serve as oarsmen on galleys. The galleys connected three new parts of the Vasa dynasty's armed forces, the navy, the army and the heavy artillery, into operative units with amphibious capacity. The ability to use this new system efficiently depended mainly on organisation and planning.

In the spring of 1555 the Swedish king Gustav I realised that the situation along the Finnish-Russian border had become unusually tense. He decided to move a part of his armed forces eastward. During the summer he transferred about 4,000 soldiers, around 20 galleys and numerous other vessels from central Sweden to the Gulf of Finland. In August Gustav decided to make a surprise attack with the force he had gathered. He ordered most of his galleys and other light vessels together with the soldiers assembled at Viborg to attack Russia along the Neva with the aim of taking Nöteborg and controlling Russian trade. If that were successful they should attack the fortresses at Kexholm and Kopore in order to secure the Kexholm province and Ingria for Sweden. Gustav probably hoped that a rapid Swedish success would induce the Teutonic Order, still in control of the Eastern Baltic, to join him in an alliance against Russia.

This operation was undertaken starting around 8 September 1555 and involved at most 4,000 soldiers and an unknown number of ships, probably most of the galleys. The major part of the army seems to have marched on land while the fleet carried provisions and artillery. After about two weeks of siege it was clear that Nöteborg was stronger than expected and that the Russians gathered a strong relief army in the area. The Swedish forces began to retreat on 29 September. During this, the fleet was twice attacked by land forces which were beaten back by soldiers and artillery sent ashore from the ships. Swedish losses in this operation were small, but as a surprise attack in order to gain easy conquests with mobile forces it was a failure. The war which followed was mainly fought on land. It ended in 1557 with no changes of the border.[7]

---

[7] Viljanti (1957), vol. 2, 421–50.

War between Russia and Sweden started again in 1570 after a period when both powers had been allied against Poland. It lasted for 25 years, although with periods of truces (1583–89, 1593–95).[8] The army forces engaged in actual warfare were only for short periods larger than 10,000 soldiers on each side, mainly due to logistical difficulties. Russia was often on the offensive but, in spite of the length of the war and its proximity to a gulf, river and lake area this state never developed naval forces. Such forces were technologically and organisationally complex and apparently beyond what the Russian state could achieve in this period. Sweden's attempts to use its naval superiority for combined operations were on the other hand far from successful. During 1571 and 1572 king Johan III, who as a young Duke of Finland had observed the operations during his father's war with Russia in 1555–57, planned to repeat the attack against Nöteborg or at least to occupy the Neva estuary. Nothing was achieved, partly because the troops were ready only in the autumn in both years and partly because his brother Duke Karl (IX) influenced operations with plans to conquer territories in Livonia instead. In the spring of 1573 Johan issued instructions for a combined army and navy attack against Narva. This time the local resources in Estonia were too exhausted to support the Swedish army and the fleet could only enforce a blockade of Narva. During the spring of 1574 Johan ordered a new attack on Narva with naval forces which also were to bring in troops from Finland. Again only a blockade could be achieved. In September 1574, when Sweden's resources for offensive warfare were exhausted, the fleet and a small army force made a desperate attempt to take Narva. It failed and the operation ended with some ravaging of the Russian coast.

In 1577 Sweden was able to resume offensive operations. Narva was again the first aim of these, but again co-ordination between naval and army forces failed. The fleet was able to take a fortress at the estuary of the river Narova but attempts to sail upriver to Narva failed due to gunfire. The army never arrived. During 1579 two more Swedish attempts to take Narva failed. In July, a fleet with an army force sailed upriver to Narva and began to assault the fortifications. After some initial successes it was found that essential materials to start a formal siege were lacking and the fleet retired.

---

[8] The text is based on Zettersten (1890), 430–68 and Barkman (1938–39), 271–323. The political and economic background: Attman (1979).

As usual the main army had logistical difficulties in concentrating and when it was ready in late August the king ordered it to attack Russian Novgorod. The army commander regarded that operation as impossible but hoped to attack Narva instead. He asked the admiral commanding the fleet in the Gulf of Finland to bring in the necessary siege artillery. The admiral, who had hoped to lead the operation himself, said no and the army had to retire.

From 1580 a more successful Swedish offensive started under the leadership of Pontus de la Gardie. In 1580 the army took Kexholm, making it possible for the navy to form a flotilla for operations on Ladoga. In 1581 de la Gardie was given command over both the army and the fleet operating in the Gulf of Finland. For a decade, major Swedish operations in this area had been handicapped because the navy and the army were never ready at the same time and because war-ravaged Estonia was too poor to support a major army for an extended period of operations. Part of the army had to live in Finland in order to use the logistical resources there, making strikes across the Gulf of Finland at decisive places and times that required close army-navy co-operation. De la Gardie could now use his combined forces in a systematic way. The fleet brought troops, provisions and artillery from Finland to Narva at the same time as the army in Estonia was ready to attack Narva. This concentrated force was able to take Narva in an operation lasting from August 26 to September 6. After that, three more Russian fortresses in Ingria fell within five weeks and Russia was cut off from the Baltic Sea. A Swedish attempt to take Nöteborg in 1582 with an army supported by the Ladoga flotilla failed, however.

Swedish amphibious operations during the 1570s had been carried out by sailing warships, as the galley fleet had largely been abolished during the 1560s when war with Denmark-Norway and Lübeck made it necessary to concentrate efforts on the sailing fleet. From 1583 to 1589 a truce was in force between Sweden and Russia and Johan III used this period to restructure his navy. The number of sailing warships was reduced and around 30 galleys were built. Even if most of these were smaller than normal Mediterranean galleys this force was one of the largest of its kind in Europe and could transport 3,000 to 4,000 soldiers. Johan obviously had warfare in the Gulf of Finland and rivers and lakes in mind, as galleys could operate in shallow and confined waters, bring heavy artillery close to shores and land troops. These were the types of operations the navy had attempted to undertake since 1571, and it must have become obvious that sailing warships were less than ideal.[9]

Technically, Sweden was therefore well prepared for amphibious offensives when war with Russia started anew in 1590. But in actual warfare from 1590 to 1593 little happened. Swedish lake flotillas were active on Ladoga and Peipus but the galley fleet in the Gulf of Finland was occupied with routine sea control and logistical duties rather than offensive tasks. In 1590, Russia launched an offensive and retook Ingria. Swedish counteroffensives during 1591 were directed against the large city Novgorod in the interior, not against littoral areas accessible from the Gulf. This inefficient use of the galley fleet is not discussed in the literature about the war and the authors are unaware of the restructuring of the navy. The cause for this misuse of the new asset is probably to be found in the high command. King Johan's health was in decline—he died in 1592—and his brother Duke Karl and military leaders from the aristocracy were in conflict. In this situation, decision making and strategic planning deteriorated and no complex operations could be undertaken. Peace was concluded in 1595. Sweden retained Narva as the main conquest from the long war with Russia.

This was the result of the only successful offensive combined operation during the war, that of 1581. Otherwise Sweden had not been able to launch amphibious assaults with decisive effects. The problems were lack of a consistent amphibious doctrine, lack of unified command, insufficient planning of complex operations and, in the 1570s, lack of suitable oared warships. From the Russian point of view, the Swedish fleet was an efficient obstacle against offensive amphibious operations, while the Swedish ability to launch offensive operations from the sea may have tied Russian forces to defensive positions—no strategic study based on Russian sources is available. During the next Swedish-Russian war (1609–17) Swedish offensives were more successful and resulted in the conquest of Ingria and the Kexholm province. In that war, small armed vessels were important for logistics and transport on Ladoga, Narova, Peipus and even on the river Volchov, which connects Novgorod with Ladoga. These

---

[9] Johan III's creation of a galley fleet has not been observed earlier and his usually ambitious naval policy has been misunderstood and not placed in its political context. I intend to treat this in a forthcoming study.

activities were, however, hardly combined operations, as the army dominated them.[10]

From 1600, Sweden began its expansion southwards in the Baltic from Estonia.[11] The background was a split in the Vasa dynasty. Johan III's son Sigismund had been elected king of Poland-Lithuania in 1587 and was usually absent from his hereditary Swedish kingdom. His uncle Duke Karl (IX), who ruled in his absence, revolted and took control of Sweden during a civil war from 1597 to 1599.[12] From 1600, Karl continued this with an offensive into Polish-controlled Livonia with the aim of reaching the river Düna and the great trading city Riga at its estuary. The main Swedish army operations during these years were launched from Estonia, a rather small logistical base for a major army. The navy became heavily engaged in troop transportation, logistical support and blockade.

Tactical co-operation between the Swedish army and navy mainly took place during repeated attempts to gain control over Riga, or at least the Düna estuary with the fortified town Dünamünde. In June 1601 an attempt by the navy to land an army force at the estuary ended in an army mutiny. In August 1601 the main Swedish and Polish armies both operated close to Riga. Karl failed to find a method to take tactical advantage of the fact that his navy controlled the Düna estuary, and his army had to retreat. In 1605 an attempt was made to attack Riga both from land and the sea, and 4,000 soldiers were landed by the fleet. This ended with the battle of Kirkholm, where the Swedish field army was almost annihilated by the Polish and the fleet had to evacuate the remnants. In 1609 another Swedish attempt at combined operations was made in the Düna estuary, but without lasting results.

During a decade of Polish-Swedish warfare, Sweden had committed considerable field armies, often of 10,000 to 15,000 men, and a major part of her large navy to a war in Livonia. No territory had been permanently occupied and the army had proved inferior to the Polish. Control of the sea gave Sweden strategic advantages—

---

[10] Generalstaben (1936), vol. 1, 360, 380, 385, 479, 504–5, 514, Marinstaben (1937), 122–30.

[11] The war 1600–10: Zettersten (1890), 44–68; Barkman (1938–1939), 439–552.

[12] In this war movements of troops between Sweden, Finland, Estonia and Poland were important. As the conditions during a civil war are special they are not treated in this article. Karl waited until 1604 to proclaim himself king of Sweden.

the Poles were unable to attack Sweden and Riga was frequently blockaded—but her armed forces had showed only limited tactical ability to combine ships, firepower and infantry in littoral warfare. Even the ability to use the large navy strategically for launching major military operations in the rear of an enemy without a navy was deficient. During the 1610s, Karl IX's son Gustav II Adolf (r. 1611–32) began to reform his army and navy in order to make them suitable for offensive warfare. His reforms of the army are famous and much discussed in the international literature, but it has been little appreciated that he also was able to develop his army and navy for successful strategic and tactical combined operations. The wars he had in sight in the Baltic were amphibious in character and successful combined operations were decisive for Swedish ability to gain control over the Baltic.[13]

The first important combined operation took place in June and July 1617 against the fortified coastal towns Dünamünde and Pernau in Polish Livonia. It was based on surprise and collaboration with a high-ranking Polish commander. Only around 2,500 soldiers, 10 major and 20 minor warships took part and only Pernau could be kept after the Polish counterattack but it was at least a partial success with a limited force. Gustav Adolf's rapid expansion and reorganisation of his army made it possible to plan a great amphibious expedition in 1621. Nine infantry regiments and ten cavalry companies (around 11,000 soldiers) and a large siege train were transported to Riga with the main fleet: 25 major and 17 minor warships and 106 hired merchantmen. The expeditionary corps had first been gathered in a camp outside Stockholm, where the new regiments had been trained to give them coherence. During the passage the major warships and some transports were divided into nine squadrons, each carrying one regiment. The fleet sailed from Stockholm on 24 July under the command of the king, but due to an unusually long summer gale, it did not reach the Düna until 3 August. Further troops arrived from Finland and Estonia. During the siege of Riga the fleet and the army co-operated in various operations on the Düna. Riga, a city far larger than Stockholm at that time, surrendered on 15 September.

---

[13] Roberts (1953–58).

The Riga operation was the largest combined operation undertaken in the Baltic up to then and it started a decade of major
Swedish power projection operations based on the new ability of the
army and navy to co-operate both strategically and tactically. Part
of the explanation may be a unified command, as Gustav II Adolf
personally led all major combined operations. In order to ensure
tactical versatility, numerous galleys and shallow-draught transport
vessels were built. The galleys, of which about 35 were built in the
first half of the 1620s, were smaller than the sixteenth century galleys and they had no heavy guns. Instead they could be armed with
two short guns of large calibre which could fire grapeshot against
infantry at short range. They were typical of Gustav Adolf's ambition to provide his infantry with efficient tactical fire support from
mobile guns. Essentially the galleys were landing craft with fire support capability.[14] The small vessels were useful for support of the
army operations which during 1621–22 and 1625 brought Livonia
under Swedish control. These operations often followed the Düna
and other rivers where armed vessels gave tactical advantages.[15]

The next major Swedish combined operation was directed against
Prussia and the Vistula estuary. The intention was to gain control
over the economically very important Polish grain exports and blockade the nascent Polish fleet. An army of around 14,000 men left
Stockholm on 23 June 1626 and arrived off Pillau two days later.
Three thousand soldiers from Finland were delayed by lack of equipment and arrived two months later. The main force consisted of 30
sailing warships, 24 galleys, 6 shallow-draught naval transports and
81 hired transports. Its arrival in Prussia was a surprise, so the army
rapidly took control of lightly defended towns and fortified strategic
positions while the navy's light units penetrated the Vistula delta
where they helped the army to build pontoon bridges. After the initial phase the Polish resistance markedly increased. From 1626 to
1629 Sweden and Poland concentrated their resources for intense
campaigns in Prussia. It turned out to be a war of attrition fought
in an economically sensitive part of the Polish realm. On the Swedish
side the campaign retained much of its amphibious character, involv-

---

[14] Glete (2000A).
[15] Generalstaben (1936), vol. 2, 56–132, Marinstaben (1937), 137–46.

ing major parts of the navy. Most light vessels were permanently based in Prussia, even during winters.[16]

During 1628 the great war in Germany spread to the Baltic Sea. The Imperial and Catholic army, which had defeated the Danish and Protestant armies and occupied Jutland, attempted to organise an improvised fleet of merchantmen from the North German cities in order to invade the Danish isles. These Protestant cities declined to co-operate and Stralsund even resisted the Emperor with armed force. Danish and Swedish troops and warships were sent to defend that city and a large-scale siege operation against it failed. The Danish fleet made attacks against enemy positions on land and, under the command of king Christian IV, 6,000 Danish soldiers were landed on the islands Usedom and Wollin in the Oder estuary. These amphibious activities and the threat of a possible Danish-Swedish alliance made the Emperor willing to conclude peace with Denmark in 1629.[17] Sweden and Poland concluded a truce in the same year which left Sweden in control of Livonia, part of Prussia and the right to levy toll on Polish exports.

This released the Swedish army and navy for a possible intervention in the German War. The possibility of making Stralsund, already under Swedish control, into the main bridgehead for the invasion was not seriously considered. The most suitable area for a major amphibious operation was western Pomerania close to the Oder estuary. The Oder was an important line of communication for a penetration of Germany and geographical conditions in its estuary were similar to those in Prussia to which the Swedish forces were accustomed. The coast was covered by islands which could be sealed off from land by naval forces and used as a defended bridgehead. The enemy forces in northern Germany (Pomerania, Mecklenburg and Brandenburg) had a (nominal) strength of more than 50,000 men of which around 9,000 were in the area where Gustav Adolf intended to land. It was necessary to land with a considerable force and build up strength in the bridgehead by faster concentration of resources by sea than the enemy could achieve on land.

By June 1630 an invasion army of 38,112 soldiers had been organised—34,354 were left as a defensive force in Sweden and the

---

[16] Generalstaben (1936), vol. 2, 236–301, Marinstaben (1937), 159–98.
[17] Probst (1996), 173–84.

occupied territories in Livonia and Prussia. The force which was gathered on the main fleet under the direct command of Gustav Adolf was 13,641 soldiers. This fleet consisted of 25 major warships and around 75 small units and transports. It was ready to sail at the end of May but winds were unfavourable and it arrived at the island of Usedom only on 25 June. The landing took place at Peenemünde on the northern end of the island during the last days of June and in the following months additional forces arrived from Sweden, Finland and Prussia. Already by 10 July, 20,000 soldiers had been landed and at the beginning of September around 29,000 Swedish soldiers were in Pomerania. The army was by then strong enough to start offensive operations against the Imperial and Catholic forces. The last and most important of Gustav Adolf's combined operations and one of the largest ever undertaken in early modern Europe had been concluded.[18]

Swedish offensive warfare from 1621 to 1630 had thus been predominantly amphibious in character. Strategically, it meant that Gustav Adolf could choose areas of operation that suited his political intentions and military resources. Riga and the Düna line proved superior to Estonia for the conquest of Livonia; Prussian and Polish grain exports provided Sweden with income and were important enough for the Polish nobility to force them to mobilise major resources for expensive counter-offensives. Sweden's ability to remain in Prussia—at a heavy cost in soldiers' lives—made the Polish nobility impatient with their Swedish king Sigismund and his dynastic quarrels and he was forced to sign a truce with his cousin Gustav Adolf and accept territorial losses. The ability to land and concentrate a large army on the open coast of Germany made it possible to intervene in the German War without any German ally.

Tactically, these operations were based on long and often frustrating Swedish experiences of amphibious warfare. The navy had developed suitable ships and a long experience of troop transport, the army knew the conditions on board ships and how to land large forces and quickly gather the soldiers back into coherent fighting units. Co-operation between light naval craft and army units had become routine and often worked well without much prior preparation. Logistically, the Swedish army and navy administration had

---

[18] Generalstaben (1936), vol. 3, esp. 340–48, 380–444, Marinstaben (1937), 206–21.

learnt how large forces (close to 20,000 men including the crews of the ship) should be concentrated at Stockholm during the spring and be ready to sail with enough provisions to feed the troops during the early phase of the landing.

Before the 1610s, this had often proved impossible even with smaller forces and amphibious operations had been cancelled or delayed until late summer when the operational season was close to an end. The challenging administrative task was to concentrate a large number of ships (expensive to keep in service), conscripted Swedish soldiers (likely to desert), foreign mercenaries (unwilling to fight when not regularly paid) and provisions for a large force in the months of May and June, when agriculturally poor Sweden often had little food left. The army and navy had then to sail across the Baltic as a coherent force able carry out offensive operations immediately after landing. Combined operations were complex operations which required military and naval skills as well as support from the state's administrative apparatus if they should succeed. They were only possible for advanced fiscal-military states and are thus a sign of effective state formation.

There were no more major Swedish amphibious landings in the Eastern and Southern Baltic after 1630. Instead, troops could be sent to territories already controlled by Sweden. This was the case in the German war up to 1648; when Sweden attacked Poland in 1655, the fleet also landed an army in Pomerania and continued to Prussia for a blockade. A landing in Prussia, as in 1626, had been considered, but the new Swedish provinces in Germany were easier to use as bridgeheads for power projection.[19] The risks and complications of a large-scale landing on a hostile coast were if possible avoided. In the long run, however, Sweden forgot much of the unconventional amphibious ability it had learnt during the conquest of the empire and the response to Russian archipelago and galley warfare in the early eighteenth century was slow and hesitant.

3. *Amphibious warfare in Danish-Swedish wars, 1563–1700*

Early modern Denmark-Norway and Sweden (with Finland) consisted of territories intersected by seas. It was necessary to keep control of

---

[19] Askgaard (1974), 28–30.

these waters if the different parts of the states should not be isolated
and rendered incapable of supporting each other in wartime. Denmark-
Norway was especially vulnerable as this state consisted of a peninsula (Jutland), several islands, the southern part of the Scandinavian
peninsula (until 1658) and a mountainous northern territory, Norway,
where the sea provided the main line of communication. If the sea
was controlled by enemy naval forces, these territories were isolated.
The navy would be immobilised, as the seamen were spread around
the country while the warships were in Copenhagen. The army might
be mobilised but not concentrated. If it was concentrated in one
area the enemy might strike in another to which the army could
not be transferred. More than any other state in Europe, Denmark-
Norway was dependent on her navy for survival. For Sweden, ability to launch amphibious assaults on the Danish isles became a prime
concern for military and naval decision-makers.

The creation of a Swedish Baltic empire up to 1660 gave Sweden
similar defence problems. The maritime character of this empire and
the importance of amphibious capability for its defence is often underestimated, in spite of that it became obvious both in the war of
1675–79 and in the decade after the Swedish defeat at Poltava (1709)
when the war continued in the Baltic until 1721. The provinces in
the Eastern Baltic (Estonia, Livonia, Ösel), northern Germany (Pomerania, Wismar, Bremen-Verden) and Gotland were connected with
central Sweden by the sea. The former Danish province Scania was
vulnerable to Danish assaults across the Sound and, as it was separated from Sweden by forests, logistical supply of a large Swedish
army in this area had also partly to be seaborne. Attacks from one
or more continental powers, allied to Denmark with its battle fleet,
might be fatal for this empire. Active Swedish defence had to be
based on co-operation between the army and navy, where the navy
had to act as a "fire brigade" to bring in army reinforcements and
supplies to threatened territories and fortresses and counter attempts
to invade an isolated part of the empire from the sea. The transfer
of the main naval base from Stockholm to the newly founded city
Karlskrona in southern Sweden during the 1680s was a part of a
strategy of amphibiously oriented control of an empire which from
a Swedish point of view was largely maritime in character.

Late medieval wars between Sweden and Denmark (sometimes
also involving the great maritime city Lübeck) had often been amphibious in character. Stockholm and Copenhagen had repeatedly been
attacked from the sea. These operations had however been limited

in scale and in various ways connected with civil wars and political alliances across the borders of these two countries which up to the 1520s formally were in a union. Amphibious operations in the medieval Baltic could not conquer territories if they met determined resistance, but they might give rulers leverage in bargaining with local elites about political control. Such operations were also easier in an age when warships primarily carried infantry and could use this both to defeat the enemy fleet and as an amphibious force. Furthermore, before the age of gunpowder, it was also easy for a fleet to penetrate the Stockholm archipelago and the Sound and use these sheltered areas as a base. The development of heavy guns and gun carrying warships made this simple form of amphibious warfare less viable. A fleet must be able to defeat an enemy fleet with firepower before an amphibious landing could take place. At the same time, armies grew rapidly in size, thus making an amphibious assault against a decisive area even more difficult. Finally and most important in the Nordic case, states grew more centralised and coherent and more difficult to conquer by negotiations with local elites.[20]

The first "modern" war between Sweden and Denmark-Norway was fought from 1563 to 1570 with Lübeck and Poland-Lithuania as Danish allies. It was dominated by intense campaigns on both land and sea, but compared to earlier Baltic wars it was remarkably void of amphibious operations. The fact that both sides had well-organised gun-armed navies made it difficult to achieve the undisputed supremacy at sea which normally is a precondition for a major amphibious operation. The Danes had already by 1560 realised that it was unrealistic to penetrate the Stockholm archipelago, while Swedish offensive war plans aimed at conquest of Danish and Norwegian territories bordering Swedish territories, not a seaborne attack on Copenhagen from the Baltic Sea. Only a victorious Swedish army campaign in Scania might have opened the possibility of moving the army across the Sound to Zealand. During 1565 and especially from 1566—after large Danish-Lubeckian losses of warships in a gale—the Swedish fleet had the superiority which might have made it possible to enter the Sound but no attack was attempted. Such an attack would not have increased control of the sea lines of communication which was her navy's strategic aim in this war. There was no Swedish army available for an attack in the Sound region,

---

[20] Glete (2003).

the strategic, political and economic centre of Danish power. Late in the war, Sweden launched amphibious attacks on the Danish-controlled islands Ösel (1568) and Gotland (1570), but these were limited in scale.[21]

The next Danish-Swedish war (1611–13) was the result of Swedish provocations and king Karl IX's over-confidence in Danish unwillingness to fight. The Danish king Christian IV (r. 1588–1648) was an unusually naval-mined ruler who was determined to use his navy for offensive strikes. The amphibious elements in these were strong. The war started with Christian's surprise attack on the important Swedish fortress town Kalmar with major forces from land and sea. The town fell after a siege in the summer of 1611, eliminating a part of the Swedish fleet based there. In the spring of the next year, the Danes rapidly concentrated around 10,000 men against Sweden's only port in the west, Älvsborg (Gothenburg), which also fell after a three-week siege in May. Christian IV and a large part of the army (figures are lacking) came to Älvsborg by sea, and the success must partly have resulted from Swedish difficulty in predicting this amphibious force's target. No relief army arrived at Älvsborg in time. These were the two major Danish victories in the war and they were both based on efficient co-operation between the army and navy under Christian's personal command. A final attempt by the king to attack the main Swedish fleet in the Stockholm archipelago in August and September 1612 had no effect, as it proved impossible to force the fortifications with the fleet. No attempt was made to eliminate the forts by amphibious means. Christian probably regarded it as impossible to bring up enough troops for an action close to the Swedish capital. His aristocratic council did not allow him to continue the war when a limited victory was secured, and the Swedes preferred to concentrate on their wars with Russia and Poland.[22]

Christian IV's successful combined operations at Kalmar and Älvsborg may well have inspired Gustav II Adolf when he soon afterwards developed his armed forces for similar operations in a larger scale. When Sweden and Denmark-Norway came close to war in 1624, the power relationship had changed in a decade. During a temporary truce with Poland, Sweden could concentrate her armed forces

---

[21] Jensen (1982), Barkman, (1938–1939), 48–270, Barfod (1995).
[22] Generalstaben (1936), vol. 1, Marinstaben (1937), 63–122, Probst (1996), 107–22.

in a mobilisation against Denmark-Norway. With an army of 38,500 soldiers and a fully mobilised navy, Sweden could put much pressure on Christian IV, who only had a small army and a partially mobilised navy. It is significant that Gustav Adolf during the height of the crisis in late June was on board his main fleet: 28 major and 6 minor warships, 23 small galleys (actually amphibious craft) and 13 hired merchantmen. The fleet and 13,700 soldiers were held in readiness in the Stockholm area while 8 more major warships and 2,700 soldiers were at Älvsborg. As Gustav Adolf obviously intended to lead the main operation himself, his intention must have been to confront Christian with the threat of an amphibious attack of the type he had successfully launched against Riga three years earlier. The Sound region and Copenhagen were the most probable targets for such an operation. Christian had to make concessions.[23]

It is of course uncertain how a Swedish amphibious attack would have developed. Weather conditions might have delayed it, giving the Danish fleet more time for mobilisation, and even a smaller Danish fleet might have been able to fight if the Swedish warships had acted as troop-carriers with reduced armament. The events of summer 1624 reveal that the power relationship between the two Nordic states had changed in Sweden's favour, but less dramatically than is often supposed in the literature. Sweden had normally had larger armed forces than Denmark-Norway for almost a century, but these had usually been partly engaged in wars in the eastern Baltic and so were unavailable for action against the western neighbour. Sweden had already in the sixteenth century been able to fight two-front wars of attrition. It was only in the next century that the state was able to *win* wars against more than one enemy at the same time. What had changed dramatically was that Sweden in 1621 had proven its ability to launch a major amphibious assault straight into enemy territory. For Denmark, with its highly maritime geography and small peace-time army, this new Swedish ability was a serious threat.

In late 1643, Sweden deliberately attacked Denmark-Norway at a time when Swedish forces were deeply engaged in the German War.[24] In fact, the Swedish field-army in Germany was a pre-condition for

---

[23] Tandrup (1979), 265–360, Generalstaben (1936), vol. 2, 157–65, Marinstaben (1937), 152–54.
[24] General: Probst (1996), 227–56, Försvarsstaben (1944).

the attack as it could occupy Jutland. Swedish home army forces invaded Norway and Denmark across the borders. The plan was that the Swedish fleet, strengthened with hired merchantmen from the Netherlands, should defeat the Danish fleet, and that the war should then be brought to an end with a combined operation against the Danish isles and Copenhagen. The importance of even a quantitatively inferior fleet for defence against seaborne invasion became obvious in the summer of 1644 when the Danes were able to bring the Swedish offensive to a halt by fleet operations in their home waters, including a battle that ended with a draw. However, in October 1644 the Danes lost control of the straits in a battle where a considerable part of their fleet was captured by superior Swedish forces. The battle of Femern was the result of strategic surprise; the Danish admirals may have decided to fight against heavy odds in the belief that they faced an invasion fleet. Actually, the main Swedish army in Germany had left for a campaign in Bohemia. Nonetheless, in 1645, Christian IV had to accept substantial territorial losses because of the obvious threat that Sweden sooner or later might combine her large army with her now much superior navy in a decisive amphibious attack.

In 1657 Denmark-Norway declared war on Sweden, already at war with Poland and Russia.[25] Unexpectedly, Sweden's main army marched from Poland to Jutland and defeated the Danish main army, but at sea the Danes again defended themselves successfully with a smaller fleet in an indecisive battle with the Swedish fleet in September 1657. It seemed as if the two pre-conditions for a successful combined operation, superiority at sea and on land at the same time would elude the Swedes. However, in early 1658 the Swedish army used a cold winter for a march across the ice from Jutland, first to Funen and from that island to Zealand, where Copenhagen was exposed to attack. The Nordic climate had provided Sweden with an unusual type of amphibious capability and Denmark-Norway had to cede several provinces to Sweden, including Scania on the eastern side of the Sound.

Half a year after this, the Swedish king Karl X Gustav (r. 1654–60) decided to annihilate the Danish state in a surprise attack. Ostensibly preparing to transfer troops to the war against Poland and Brandenburg, he sailed from Kiel on August 6 and landed at Korsör on

---

[25] General: Askgaard (1974).

Zealand the following day with 4,000 infantry and 1,200 cavalry. Zealand was quickly sealed from the rest of Denmark-Norway by the Swedish fleet and more troops were landed in order to take Copenhagen.[26] The Danish capital and possibly Denmark-Norway itself was rescued by a Dutch fleet with provisions and soldiers in the autumn of 1658. Next spring, the Swedish fleet (which had spent the winter in Landskrona at the Sound) got an early start on its operations and in late April Karl Gustav could land part of his army on the islands Falster and Lolland where it could get much needed supplies.

During 1659 the Swedish, Dutch and Danish-Norwegian (and for a time the English) fleets operated around the Danish isles without any decisive results. A planned allied invasion of Funen in the summer was cancelled after a successful Swedish naval attack on a Dutch-Danish squadron and transport fleet. By October the allies decided to make a determined attempt to retake the island. Sixty-two hundred Danish and Dutch soldiers were shipped to the island by a predominantly Dutch fleet under admiral Michiel de Ruyter while 5,000 allied soldiers (Danes, Dutch, Poles, Brandenburgers) were to attack from Jutland. An attempt by de Ruyter's force to make a surprise landing at the fortress town Nyborg failed but on 31 October the army was landed north of the town. In the following weeks the force from Jutland was transferred to Funen. The Swedes had only 5,500 soldiers on the island and they could not be reinforced when the enemy fleet controlled the sea. They were defeated in a battle on 14 November and Funen was liberated.[27]

Peace was concluded the next year after the sudden death of the bellicose Swedish king. The two Danish-Swedish wars of 1657–60 had as a whole been large-scale combined operations taking place on territories dependent on the sea lines of communications. The rather limited size of the actual landings are partly misleading as most operations were decided by the ability to move soldiers and munitions across water. Operations in 1658 and 1659 showed that landings could be organised rapidly and that amphibious warfare had become a well-established routine in the Baltic.

The next Danish-Swedish war of 1675–79 saw three major landings; as usual in Baltic wars, most army and navy operations were closely intertwined.[28] The war was caused by the European alliance

[26] Bergman (1965).
[27] Tersmeden (1965).
[28] General: Askgaard & Stade (1983), Barfod (1977).

system in which Sweden was allied with France while Denmark and Brandenburg-Prussia joined with the Dutch Republic. The aim of the Danish war efforts was to retake the provinces east of the Sound lost in the earlier war, while Brandenburg wished to take Pomerania. In early 1676 the Danish army and navy began to prepare for a major joint operation across the Sound. When the Danish-Dutch fleet defeated the Swedish fleet at Öland on 1 June this operation could rapidly be carried out. Fourteen thousand soldiers were landed at Råå, south of Helsingborg, from 29 June [figure 18]. There were several possible places to land in Scania and two days before the fleet had made a feint landing with 2,000 men at Ystad in the southeast. The Swedish army was consequently spread around the province and could offer no resistance at Råå.[29]

After initial successes the Danish army was defeated in the battle of Lund in December 1676, but control of the southern Baltic Sea made it possible for the Danes to operate in Scania until the end of the war. Control of the sea for the rest of the war was ensured by a Danish victory at sea at Köge Bay on 1 July 1677. The Danes tried to exploit it by a landing on Rügen in September with more than 7,000 soldiers under the command of King Christian V. This force was defeated by the Swedish army in Pomerania in January 1678, but in September the Brandenburgers organised a landing with 350 transports and 15,000 soldiers on Rügen under the protection of the Danish fleet. This quickly sealed the fate of the Swedes in Pomerania, as the army had only Stralsund left and needed Rügen as a supply base. The war ended in 1679, however, with only minimal losses of territory for Sweden when her ally France threatened to intervene against Denmark and Brandenburg.

After more than twenty years of well-armed peace, war started once again in the Baltic in 1700. Three traditional Swedish enemies had formed a secret alliance. Russia and Poland-Saxony (united under the same ruler) attacked Narva and Riga respectively, while Denmark attacked Sweden's ally Holstein-Gottorp. The latter state was, however, protected by several powers, including England and the Dutch Republic. Sweden mobilised 38 battleships and the two maritime powers sent 10 English and 13 Dutch battleships while Denmark only could send 29 battleships to sea. The three allied fleets con-

---

[29] Cohrt (1983).

centrated in the Sound in July and blockaded the Danish fleet in Copenhagen. The Danes had expected that their allies should keep Sweden occupied in the east and their own field army was on Jutland, leaving only 4,500 soldiers to defend Zealand and Copenhagen. Sweden had however concentrated 16,000 soldiers in Scania; with command of the Sound these could now be used for an amphibious operation. In a first wave, 4,900 men landed on 4 August at Humlebaek , south of Helsingör, under the command of Karl XII (r. 1697–1718). The water was deep enough for Swedish battleships to provide close fire support.[30] Within two weeks, more than 10,000 soldiers had been transferred across the Sound and, as the allied fleet made it impossible to transfer Danish troops from Jutland to Zealand, the Danes signed a peace treaty on August 18. Karl XII would have liked to try to take Copenhagen but the Anglo-Dutch fleet declined to support such an operation. The Swedish army and navy moved to the east in counterattacks against the other enemies. The Great Northern War had started and with it a new epoch of amphibious operations in the Baltic.[31]

Combined operations in Danish-Swedish wars always depended on one side gaining a decisive advantage in battle fleet strength. This could be achieved in various ways: by strategic surprise as in 1611, 1624, 1644 and 1658; by alliances as in 1659, 1676 and 1700; or by a decisive victory in combat between the main fleets as in 1677. There also had to be an army ready to exploit the opportunity, as there were in 1611–12, 1624, 1658, 1659, 1676–78 and 1700 but not in 1644–45. It did not need to be very large if the fleet could seal off a territory defended by an inferior force or if the ability to make landings at many places kept the enemy guessing and forced him to spread his army. There was not much need for oared craft or special vessels in the Danish straits and amphibious warfare was carried out using conventional sailing warships and hired merchantmen, usually rather small local vessels that could enter small ports or anchor close to coasts. The maturing Nordic states could in the seventeenth century organise resource mobilisations and solve command problems for large joint operations without much delay, and develop effective tactics and doctrines. It was enemy activity rather than inherent military, naval or administrative weaknesses which foiled such operations.

---

[30] See illustrations, nos 29 and 30.
[31] Generalstaben (1918), 245–97, Barfod (1997), 117–26.

4. *State formation and complex warfare*

The main theme in this chapter has been that early modern amphibious warfare was an unusually complex form of warfare. In order to be successful it required an efficient army and an efficient navy, effective co-ordination of these two armed forces, and an advanced state with administrative structures of sufficient strength to concentrate men, ships, munitions and provisions into a coherent force within a limited time. Major amphibious operations are therefore a sign of a maturing state formation process. The presence of Danish and Swedish kings as personal commanders of most major combined operations shows that such operations were important and that the ruler's unique capacity as political leader and commander-in-chief of both the army and the navy was regarded as essential for success.

In a wider context, this conclusion emphasises that the transformation of early modern European warfare which Anglo-Saxon scholars often discuss as the "Military Revolution" was an integrated part of a larger state formation process. During the sixteenth and seventeenth centuries, European states became, in a gradual and uneven process, able to achieve more complex military operations. This was based on political, technical, tactical and administrative innovations where the growth of fiscal and military power structures—a tax state and permanent armies and navies—was of crucial importance. Russia, Poland-Lithuania, the Habsburgs and Prussia-Brandenburg had all potentially larger resources than Sweden and Denmark-Norway but, until Russia and Prussia had matured as states, it was the two Nordic powers which fought sophisticated wars in the Baltic. Their amphibious activities are important parts of these wars and deserve more attention than they have usually received.[32]

Bibliography

Secondary Sources

Anderson, R. (1910/69) *Naval Wars in the Baltic, 1522–1850* (London: 1910, 1969).
Askgaard, F. (1974) *Kampen om Östersjön på Carl X Gustafs tid* (Stockholm: 1974).
Askgaard, F. and Stade, F. (1983) *Kampen om Skåne* (Copenhagen: 1983).

---

[32] European state formation and permanent armies and navies: Glete (2002), Glete (1993).

Attman, A. (1979) *The struggle for Baltic markets: Powers in conflict, 1558–1618* (Gothenburg: 1979).
Barfod, J. H. (1977) *Niels Juel: A Danish admiral of the 17th century* (Copenhagen: 1977).
——, (1995) *Christian 3.s flåde* (Copenhagen: 1995).
——, (1997) *Niels Juels flåde* (Copenhagen: 1997).
Barkman, B. C. (1937) *Kungl. Svea Livgardes historia* 1 (Stockholm: 1937).
——, (1938–1939) *Kungl. Svea Livgardes historia* 2 (Stockholm: 1938–39).
Bergman, E. (1965) 'Carl X Gustaf och flottan 1657–1658', in A. Stade (ed.), *Carl X Gustaf och Danmark* (Stockholm: 1965).
Cohrt, P. T. (1983) 'Landgangen ved Rå', in Askgaard and Stade (1983) 113–22.
Försvarsstaben (1944) *Slaget vid Femern 13/10 1644* (Gothenburg: 1944).
Frost, R. (2000) *The Northern Wars: War, state and society in northeastern Europe, 1558–1721* (Harlow: 2000).
Generalstaben (1918) *Karl XII på slagfältet* 2 (Stockholm: 1918).
—— (1936) *Sveriges krig 1611–1632* 1–3 (Stockholm: 1936).
Glete, J. (1976–1977) 'Svenska örlogsfartyg 1521–1560: Flottans uppbyggnad under ett tekniskt brytningsskede', *Forum navale*, 30 (1976) 5–74; 31 (1977) 23–119.
——, (1992) 'The oared warship', in Gardiner, R. ed., *The line of battle: The sailing warship, 1650–1840* (London: 1992), 98–105.
——, (1993) *Navies and nations: Warships, navies and state building in Europe and America, 1500–1860*, 2 vols (Stockholm: 1993).
——, (1994) 'Bridge and bulwark: The Swedish navy and the Baltic, 1500–1809', in Rystad (1994).
——, (1999) 'Östersjön som maritimt operationsområde—ett historiskt perspektiv', *Tidskrift i Sjöväsendet*, 1999, 272–80.
——, (2000A) 'Vasatidens galärflottor', in Norman, H. ed., *Skärgårdsflottan: Uppbyggnad, militär användning och förankring i det svenska samhället 1700–1824* (Lund: 2000), 37–49.
——, (2000B) *Warfare at sea, 1500–1650: Maritime conflicts and the transformation of Europe* (London: 2000), 112–30.
——, (2002) *War and the state in early modern Europe: Spain, the Dutch Republic and Sweden as fiscal–military states, 1500–1660* (London: 2001).
——, (2003) 'Naval power and control of the seas in the Baltic in the 16th century', in J. B. Hattendorf and W. R. Unger, eds, *War at sea in the Middle Ages and the Renaissance* (Woodbridge: 2003).
Jensen, F. P. (1982) *Danmarks konflikt med Sverige* (Copenhagen: 1982).
Kuvaja, C. (1999) *Försörjning av en ockupationsarmé: Den ryska arméns underhållssystem i Finland, 1713–1721* (Åbo: 1999).
Lockhart, P. D. (1996) *Denmark in the Thirty Years' War: King Christian IV and the decline of the Oldenburg state* (Selinsgrove: 1996)
Marinstaben (1937) *Sveriges sjökrig 1611–1632* (Stockholm: 1937).
Probst, N. M. (1996) *Christian 4.s flåde* (Copenhagen: 1996).
Roberts, M. (1953–58) *Gustavus Adolphus: A history of Sweden, 1611–1632*, 2 vols (London: 1953–58).
Rystad, G. et al., eds. (1994) *In quest of trade and security: The Baltic in power politics, 1500–1990, vol. I: 1500–1890* (Lund: 1994).
Tandrup, L. (1979) *Mot triumf eller tragedie* 2 (Aarhus: 1979).
Tersmeden, L. (1965) 'Strategisk defensiv: Carl X Gustaf, Philip av Sulzbach och slaget om Fyn hösten 1659', in Stade (1965) 363–98.
Viljanti, A. (1957) *Gustav Vasas ryska krig, 1554–1557*, 2 vols (Stockholm: 1957).
Zettersten, A. (1890) *Svenska flottans historia, 1522–1634* (Stockholm: 1890).

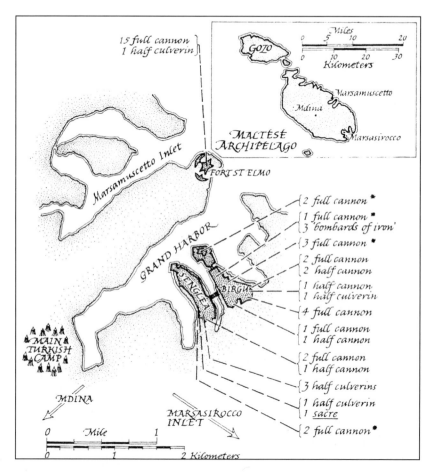

Map 12. The Siege of Malta, 1565 (reproduced from J. F. Guilmartin, Jr, *Gunpowder and Galleys: Changing Technology and Mediterranean Warfare at Sea in the Sixteenth Century* (Cambridge: 1974), p. 182; © Cambridge University Press)

THE SIEGE OF MALTA, 1565

John F. Guilmartin, Jr.

The Great Siege of Malta of 1565 was a major turning point in the struggle between the Spanish Habsburgs and Ottoman Turks for domination of the Mediterranean, a struggle that was itself a central part of a broader conflict with global stakes waged as far afield as the Indonesian archipelago, the Iranian plateau, the Indian Ocean, North Africa, and France, with subsidiary conflicts fought out in the British Isles and Italy.[1] It was also a classic example of the prosecution of a highly specialized and essentially amphibious form of warfare. In 1565, the form of warfare in question, the Mediterranean system of warfare at sea based on the cannon-armed war galley and its symbiotic relationship with the fortified port city, was near its apogee as an instrument of policy. That fact gave the siege of 1565 greater strategic importance than would otherwise have been the case, a consideration that has been overlooked in previous accounts and constitutes an underlying theme in the following analysis.

In addition, the Great Siege of 1565 is of interest as a limiting case of amphibious positional warfare during the Mediterranean system's period of dominance. The Great Siege was rivalled or surpassed in the scale of resources mobilized by Süleyman I's 1522 siege of Rhodes, by Charles V's 1535 Tunis expedition, by his 1541 Algiers expedition, by the Ottoman invasion force that took Cyprus in 1570, by Don Juan of Austria's fleet that took Tunis in 1573, and by the Ottoman expedition that retook the place the following year.[2] It was matched in ferocity and surpassed in length, just under

---

[1] Guilmartin (2002), 126–151, for an overview; for the Ottoman perspective, Hess (1973).

[2] The Ottoman fleet that attacked Malta in May of 1565 had 130 galleys, 8 heavy galleys, 11 large sailing ships, three smaller ones, and 18 galiots. The fleet that Süleyman sent against Rhodes in 1522 is said to have numbered 600 vessels, half of them galleys: Olesa Muñido (1968), 2:1116. Charles V's 1535 Tunis expedition mustered 84 galleys, 30 galiots and nearly 100 sailing vessels, about half of them of some size; and Charles attacked Algiers in 1541 with a force of 65 galleys and some 450 other vessels: Olesa Muñido (1968), 2:363–4. The Ottoman fleet

four months, by the 1522 siege of Rhodes (six months) and the 1570–71 siege of Famagusta (eleven months). But in none of these campaigns were the elements of amphibious siege craft used so fully. Both sides stretched their material and human resources to the limit. Muslims and Christians alike displayed impressive technical virtuosity and tactical skill. Virtually everything that could be tried was tried: destruction of walls by battery, and at uncommonly long ranges; land assault; amphibious assault in small boats; mining; countermining; sapping under cover of artillery, small arms and arrow fire; mobile siege towers; defensive sorties by both cavalry and infantry; incendiary devices of all descriptions; the use of swimmers to clear away underwater obstacles to amphibious assault—opposed in the water by armed swimmers.

Our analysis is complicated by the fact that amphibious warfare is inherently more complex, more prone to uncertainty and ambiguity and more difficult to understand than warfare on land, at sea, or in the air. That reality is in part explainable in terms of the inherently greater complexity of movement along the boundary separating two distinct mediums or performance regimes than within a uniform medium or regime. The hydrodynamics of surface vessels are substantially more complex than those of submarines, for example, and the aerodynamics of transonic flight are far more complex than subsonic or supersonic aerodynamics. A comparison of our amphibious case study with its closest equivalent ashore in time and strategic consequences, the 1529 siege of Vienna, both sustains the analogy and reinforces our sense of the importance of the Great Siege of 1565.

With full wisdom of hindsight, Vienna marked the limits of Ottoman conquest in Central Europe. The reasons begin with geography and the structure of the Ottoman state. An imperial host based on Constantinople could go no further than Vienna in a single campaigning season and still have sufficient strength to accomplish anything of note, nor could one winter over at the objective in more

---

that attacked Cyprus in 1570 had 160 galleys, 60 galiots and *fustas*, 43 *fragatas*, 8 heavy galleys and 40 specialized horse transports plus 7 large sailing vessels and 38 smaller ones: Olesa Muñido (1968), 2:1119. Don Juan's fleet that sailed against Tunis in 1573 numbered 104 galleys, 44 sailing vessels and 59 small craft; the Turkish fleet under Uluch Ali that retook Tunis had 280 galleys, 15 heavy galleys, 15 galiots and 19 sailing vessels: Anderson (1952), 5, 56.

than token strength without serious economic repercussions. At root, this was because the largest striking element of the Sultan's army consisted of *timariot sipahis*, armoured horse archers supported by non-hereditary grants of *timar* land awarded in return for military service.[3] This arrangement was extraordinarily efficient fiscally, in that the *timar* holder supported himself (and his retinue in the case of large *timar* grants) directly from agricultural taxes levied on the enfeoffed peasants for whom he was responsible and for whom he provided local governance and security. It follows that the *timariots* could not be kept in the field over the winter and though a subsequent campaigning season without compromising tax revenues and the rural order and prosperity essential to the health of the Ottoman state.[4] This was done on occasion, but only rarely and under extreme circumstances. Moreover, by the 1530s Habsburg armies, benefiting from the lessons of the Wars of Italy, could take the measure of the Turks in the open field, a factor that reinforced the effects of geographic constraints. Sultan Süleyman I's failure to confront the Habsburg forces before Vienna in 1532 provides eloquent if indirect proof.[5] By contrast, Ottoman potential for expansion in the Mediterranean was less tightly bound by geographic, institutional and operational constraints.

To be sure, geography imposed limits on Ottoman expansion by sea. Indeed, the temporal limits of the maritime campaigning season were more restrictive and the penalties of exceeding them more Draconian. Armies that pressed an unsuccessful siege too late into

---

[3] Imperial Ottoman armies consisted of three basic elements: the salaried *kapu kulu* troops of the imperial household; the *timariot sipahis*; and unsalaried irregular light troops, both mounted and dismounted. The *kapu kulu* troops consisted of the Janissaries and their attached drovers and cart artillery; the *sipahis* of the Imperial Guard; and the bombardiers or siege artillerists. The irregular light troops rivaled or exceeded both the *kapu kulu* elements and the *timariot sipahis* in number, but were useful only for raiding and skirmishing and as raw manpower in sieges. *Timariot sipahis* were the primary maneuver and mounted shock element.

[4] The *timar* holder not only had a direct stake in the security and prosperity of the villagers under him, but the wherewithal to protect them from bandits, enforce justice, and so on.

[5] Oman (1937), 678–82. The key development was Spanish infantry formations that effectively combined the firepower of gunpowder shoulder arms with the shock power of massed pikes. These were the first formations of dismounted combatants capable of resisting first-class cavalry, including horse archers, on level terrain. They appeared in nascent form in the 1510s. By the mid-1520s, they were fully developed and were imitated by, among others, German *Landsknechts*.

the autumn were commonly decimated by disease and exposure, as
befell the Turks retreating from Vienna in 1529 and the Hapsburg
army recoiling from Metz in 1553.[6] By contrast, galley fleets that
sailed too late or dallied too long at their objective could be all but
obliterated and often were: the destruction of Charles V's fleet before
Algiers in October 1541 is the most spectacular example, but by no
means the only one. But while seasonal limits had to be respected,
they did not impose limits of distance and direction as stringent as
those on land. This was for two reasons, one generally applicable
and the other peculiar to the Ottomans. First, sea transport was—
and is—inherently more efficient than land transport, permitting the
carriage of larger forces and heavier loads over greater distances.
Exploiting this reality, sixteenth century Mediterranean naval logis-
ticians, particularly Ottoman and Spanish, had achieved a mastery
of their trade not matched by their counterparts on land for another
century.[7] Moreover, the westward advance of Ottoman armies was
heavily dependent upon the maintenance of a military highway proceeding from Constantinople through Edirne to Belgrade and thence
north along the Danube. The Danube itself connected the highway
with the Ottoman logistical base along the Black Sea, providing the
means for transporting loads too heavy or bulky for land transport.
But while the military highway and the Danube conferred major
logistical advantages, they channelled the Ottoman advance. Ottoman
fleets were less constrained in distance and not at all in direction.
Second, the power and efficiency of Ottoman arms on land were
tied to the presence of the sultan.

The reasons were straightforward. The core of an imperial army,
the Janissaries and their supporting drovers and cart artillery, the
sipahis of the imperial guard, and the siege artillerists, were salaried
kapu kulu troops, many of them *ghulams*, personal slaves of the sultan over whom he alone had full authority. While *timariot sipahis*
comprised the army's largest striking element, their effectiveness
depended on the presence of *kapu kulu* elements.[8] From the begin-

---

[6] For the seasonal limits on Ottoman land campaigns and the disastrous 1529
retreat from Vienna: Murphey (1999), 20–24, 68–70. For the Habsburg retreat from
Metz: Duffy (1979), 51–53.

[7] Guilmartin (1993), 109–136; Lynn (1993), 103–107, esp. 104; and 137–159.

[8] In the field, the *timariot sipahis* deployed in two wings, flanking a center manned
by the Janissaries fighting from behind their barricaded carts with the support of

ning, Ottoman expansion on land depended on the personal leadership of capable and aggressive sultans, and when Süleyman I (1520–66) ceased to take the field after 1552 the efficiency of the Imperial Army began a steady process of deterioration.[9] A measure of imperial power transferred to the grand viziers who henceforth commanded imperial hosts, but they could never enjoy a ruling sultan's full authority. By contrast, Ottoman fleets were habitually commanded by the *Kapudan Pasha*, the high admiral, and were less dependent upon *ghulams* for their tactical effectiveness. The critical command relationship was that of the *Kapudan Pasha* and his squadron commanders over the captains of the galleys that comprised the heart of the fleet. That relationship was never compromised, for the need of squadron discipline to galley warfare was clearly understood by all. Moreover, while the sultan's absence from Constantinople carried with it serious penalties in administrative control and efficiency, that of the *Kapudan Pasha* from his office and holdings was substantially less important.[10] The fact that a significant part of Ottoman strength at sea consisted of North African galleys commanded by men who controlled their own logistical bases, but respected the same command arrangements, reinforced this tendency.

Finally, while *timariot sipahis* and Janissaries served at sea, they were but two elements of tactical power among many. A major difference between land and sea was the importance of war galleys' heavy forward-firing ordnance, ordnance that in the aggregate produced far more firepower than any contemporary army deployed on land. A single twenty-four bank ordinary galley *circa* 1565, rowed by 144 to 192 men and fully manned for a major engagement with 100–150 fighting men plus 50 or so mariners, gunners and *oficiales* (technical specialists), would have mounted a main centreline bow gun firing

---

the cart artillery and backed by the *ghulam sipahis* of the Imperial Guard. In the days of the Ottoman Empire's greatest effectiveness, the sultan commanded personally from his post in the center. At sieges, the *sipahis* ordinarily served as a covering force, though they took part in assaults as well.

[9] At the insistence of his newly-appointed Grand Vizier, Sokullu Mehmet Pasha, Süleyman took the field for a final time in 1566, but was in poor health and died on campaign: Oman (1937), 718–19, 718, n. 1. Suggestively, Sokullu Mehmet was appointed Grand Vizier during or immediately after the Siege of Malta.

[10] From Khaireddin Barbarossa's incumbency (1533–46) onward the *Kapudan Pasha* was a member of the divan, the imperial council, but was subordinate to the Grand Vizier in rank: Cassola (1985), 73.

a thirty to fifty pound ball, flanked by a pair of twelve to nine pounders and perhaps an additional pair of six pounders. A squadron of ten such vessels would have deployed more and heavier artillery than any contemporary field army.

Moreover, galley fleets could transport siege trains of impressive power. The train that the Turkish fleet brought to Malta in 1565, 'two large basilisks and sixty double cannon of battery with 40,000 *quintals* [some 2,028 short tons] of powder and 70,000 iron balls',[11] disposed of more raw destructive power than the largest siege trains on land until the age of railroads and rifled artillery. The two basilisks fired balls of 200 and 150 pounds, respectively, while double cannon of battery typically fired 60–70 pound balls.[12] By comparison, the siege train of Louis XIV of France in 1690 consisted of ten 33-pounders, thirty-six 24-pounders, four 16-pounders, twelve 8-inch mortars and eight stone-throwing pieces, supplied with some 500 short tons of gunpowder.[13]

Just what proportion of a Mediterranean galley fleet's tactical power derived from its heavy, forward-firing ordnance; what proportion from individual missile weapons; what proportion from edged weapons of shock combat; and what proportion from the shock effect of its galleys' spurs on enemy hulls and crews is beyond precise calculation and varied with the tactical circumstances. What is clear is that gunpowder played a more central role at sea than on land, helping to preserve for a time the viability of Ottoman expansion by sea. Simply put, while the Turks had begun to fall behind their western foes in the effective use of gunpowder weapons in field oper-

---

[11] MNM, CN, iv, *documento* [hereafter dto] 19: Don Juan Páez de Castro, 'Rélacion del sitio que puso el Turco á la Ysla de Malta, y del Socorro que introdujo D[n] Garcia de Toledo, por el qual levantó el Campo del enemigo, y se libertó la Ysla. . . . Año 1565'. When I first wrote on this subject, I believed Páez de Castro to have been present during the Great Siege. Anthony Luttrell, then of the Royal University of Malta, apprised me of his doubts on this score in an exchange of correspondence in 1975. While not excluding the possibility that Páez de Castro was present, I am now inclined to agree with Luttrell that he was more likely a member of Don Garcia's staff, or perhaps of Philip II's suite. Either way, Páez de Castro was militarily competent and remarkably well-informed.

[12] Collado (1592), fol. 9, 32, for the size of double cannon of battery and for the weight of projectile fired by the two basilisks used at Malta. Prescott (1904), 3:179, says that the Turks' 'breaching artillery' consisted of sixty-three guns, the smallest of which fired a 56 pound ball.

[13] Lynn (1997), 509.

ations by the 1530s, they were every bit as successful in harnessing the power of gunpowder ordnance to galley warfare. As we will see, they were also every bit as successful in applying gunpowder ordnance to siege warfare.

At this point, a word is in order on the capabilities and limitations of cannon-armed war galleys, the backbone of Mediterranean war fleets from the 1510s until the 1580s. These were not constant, but changed with time. The tactical and operational characteristics of war galleys—meant here to encompass lesser oared fighting craft armed with a main centreline bow gun[14]—derived from two sources: the reliance on human muscle for speed and manoeuvre in combat and the reliance on heavy, forward-firing, ordnance for tactical power. To maximize speed under oars, the war galley's dominant tactical characteristic, galleys had long, slender hulls with shallow draft and low freeboard. A long, slender hull with shallow draft maximized the number of oarsmen as a function of displacement, providing more propulsive energy per unit mass while low freeboard increased the oarsmen's mechanical efficiency. Such hulls, however, are notoriously inefficient in terms of stowage space as a function of displacement. The war galley's large crew made them even less efficient in terms of stowage space per crew member.[15] This placed severe constraints on the galley's radius of action, the principal limiting factor being water. The combination of limited stowage and high water consumption, particularly by the *ciurma*, the oarsmen,[16] meant that

---

[14] The term galley applied both to a particular type of oared fighting ship, the ordinary galley, and to smaller related vessels. These were, in descending order of size, the galiot, *fusta*, *bergantín*, and *fragata*. Of these, the galley, galiot and *fusta* had main centreline bow guns. Ordinary galleys had at least eighteen banks of oars, pulled by six oarsmen to the bank and three to the bench, three by three in contemporary terminology. Galiots had the same number of rowing banks but were rowed two by two. *Fustas* were shorter, having no more than fifteen banks of oars; they were rowed partly three by three and partly two by two. *Bergantínes* were smaller, with ten to fifteen banks of oars pulled two by two. *Fragatas* were smaller still, with fewer than ten rowing banks and a single oarsman per bench. Olesa Muñido (1968), 1:236–41.

[15] This is mostly a matter of geometry. A spherical container is the ultimate in efficiency in that its ratio of internal volume to surface area and mass is greater than that of any other shape. Hulls that most closely approximate a sphere, short, tubby hulls that sit deep in the water, have more stowage space per unit of mass than longer hulls with finer lines. In addition, since the size of internal frames, knees, and so on, is more or less constant, these structural elements occupy a greater proportion of the available space in a long, slender, hull.

[16] I have used the contemporary Italian term *ciurma*, plural *ciurmi*, since there is

a war galley's water supplies lasted without replenishing for two weeks at most.[17]

The general adoption of heavy main centreline ordnance in the 1510s, flanked by smaller forward-firing deck-mounted pieces, complicated matters by increasing the mass of the vessel and placing additional demands on stowage, with powder and shot now competing for space with water, biscuit, wine, preserved fish and meat, and fresh provisions. In principle, the increase in mass should have meant a deterioration in performance under oars, but the added mass at the bow forced a redesign of galleys' hulls with fuller lines forward and a tapering stern. The resultant fish-like shape was clearly more efficient hydrodynamically than what had gone before, for there was no immediate increase in the size of galleys or their *ciurmi* nor is there any evidence of deteriorating performance.[18] Most significantly from the strategic standpoint, there is no evidence of a decline in the radius of action of galley fleets and squadrons for another four to five decades.

Then, beginning in the 1550s, inflation and rising wages combined to force a fundamental change in the way in which galleys were rowed. There is little doubt that economic factors impelled the change, for it was undertaken first in the western Mediterranean where the inflationary spiral hit first and hardest. Unable to afford free oarsmen's wages, the Spanish turned to servile oarsmen between 1552 and 1560 with immediate repercussions in rowing efficiency.[19]

---

no English equivalent and since the Spanish *chusma* and Ottoman *utchurmé* (Olesa Muñido (1968), 2:1152), are clearly Italian loan words.

[17] Guilmartin (1974), 62–63. Pryor (1988), 76–80, estimates that a mid-sixteenth century war galley could carry three weeks water supply based on my estimate of a half gallon per man per day as the minimum requirement and the stowage figures given for Khaireddin Barbarossa's fleet in the 1539 Castelnuovo campaign by Kahlifeh (1831), 67. This estimate is based on minimum individual consumption and total exhaustion of water supplies, something a competent captain would hazard only in the most extreme circumstances. Two weeks is a realistic and representative figure.

[18] For a summation of this hypothesis, Guilmartin (2002), 114–121. Medieval galleys had slab-sided hulls with roughly equal taper at bow and stern and could not have supported the weight of ordnance that we know sixteenth century galleys to have carried: e.g. Whitwell and Johnson (1926), 142–196.

[19] The June 1552 *Asiento* of Don Bernaldino de Mendoza, Captain General of the Galleys of Spain, a document spelling out the number of galleys for which he was responsible and their rowing arrangements, makes it clear that all of his galleys were rowed three by three; MNM, Colección Sanz de Barutell (Simancas),

Hitherto, galleys were rowed according to the system *ala sensile* with three men to a bench, each pulling an individual oar. That arrangement represented an optimum in efficiency, but it demanded skilled oarsmen which, in practical terms, meant free oarsmen. The problem was solved by replacing the three individual oars with a single large oar, but the resultant system, called *a scaloccio* for the ladder-like appearance of hand grips attached to the oar, was less efficient and a fourth oarsman per bench had to be added. That required larger hulls with greater displacement, and that in turn required more oarsmen still if dash speed were to be maintained, an essential condition of survival in combat. The result was a modest increase in the hull size of ordinary galleys accompanied by a disproportionate increase in the size of the *ciurma*. A fully manned ordinary galley of twenty-four rowing banks *a scaloccio* was propelled by 192 oarsmen in contrast to 144 for a twenty-four bank galley *alla sensile*.

The *a scaloccio* system's drawbacks were a reduction in radius of action and increased consumption of provisions. In addition to reduced labour costs, its principal advantage was flexibility, both operationally and in terms of design. The rowing benches did not need to be fully manned and frequently weren't, relaxing the constraints imposed by oarsman availability. In addition, the new system permitted the construction of larger galleys than hitherto with five, six and even seven men to an oar. These could carry larger fighting complements and more and heavier artillery with the obvious tactical advantages that these bestowed. The *capitanas*—flagships—of Piali Pasha and Mustafa Pasha, the commanders of the Ottoman force that besieged Malta in 1565, reflected the trend toward increased size with thirty-five banks and six oarsmen per bench (420 oarsmen) and twenty-seven banks and five oarsmen per bench (270 oarsmen), respectively.[20] These two vessels were extreme examples of lantern galleys, exceptionally heavily armed galleys so called for their elaborate triple stern lanterns that were the symbol of command authority *par excellence*. While lantern galleys were few in number—they numbered only

---

artículo 5, *dto* 29, fos 113–23. Venetian sources indicate that by 1556 his squadron had gone over to the new system, rowing four by four *a galocha*, that is with a single large oar to the bench, with the *capitana* and three other galleys rowed five by five; Tenenti (1962), 34.

[20] MNM, CN 4, dto 19, fos 224–29: Páez de Castro, 'Relación'.

eleven percent of Christian galleys and nine percent of Muslim galleys at Lepanto in 1571[21]—they served as the tactical backbone of
galley fleets and squadrons. While essential tactically, they were costly
to operate.

To sum up, adoption of the *a scaloccio* rowing system in conjunction with slave and convict *ciurmi* served as an effective cost con-
tainment mechanism over the short term, but made it possible, and
therefore necessary, to build larger galleys. The result was a reiter-
ative feedback mechanism whereby galleys were made progressively
larger and more powerful for reasons of tactical survival, leading
inevitably to further reductions in radius of action. Moreover, increases
in the size of galleys and galley fleets and—the pivotal factor—the
crews needed to operate and fight them, overwhelmed the fiscal
advantages of servile *ciurmi* over the long term. A further contributory factor to the decline in the strategic utility of galley fleets was
a gradual increase in the amount of available bronze artillery. As
with dash speed under oars, competitive firepower was an essential
concomitant of tactical survival, and as more guns became available, war galleys were armed more heavily.[22] The galley fleet's principal strategic utility was the reduction of fortified port cities, but to
succeed strategically it had to survive tactically, and for that heavy-
forward firing ordnance was essential. That, of course, meant more
weight and more weight entailed more oarsmen with the consequences already noted. By 1565, the process was largely restricted
to a small number of lantern galleys and exceptionally powerful *capitanas*, but that was to change.

The process varied on a regional basis, taking hold first in Spain
and moving progressively eastward. The Spanish had gone over
almost entirely to servile *ciurmi* by 1560, followed by Genoa, Spain's
lesser Italian dependencies, and the Papal States, while Venice continued to use the *alla sensile* system with free, salaried oarsmen until
Lepanto. Through the 1560s Ottoman galleys were propelled by a

---

[21] Guilmartin (1974), 237–238, 238 n. 1, for the Christian order of battle and
232, 243–44, for the numbers of lantern galleys on both sides. The number of galleys at Lepanto varies slightly depending on the source; my best estimate is 219
Christian galleys and 230 Muslim of which 25 and 21, respectively, were lantern
galleys. See Cayetano (1853), cited in Olesa Muñido (1968), 1:371.
[22] For the argument that the amount of bronze ordnance increased gradually
over the course of the sixteenth century, Guilmartin (1974), 180–81.

mixture of Greek mercenaries; *ʿAzab* light infantry; conscripted Muslim villagers, particularly for major expeditions; and a small but gradually increasing proportion of Christian slaves.[23] The North African Muslim principalities made extensive use of slave oarsmen, a reflection of their small populations, but negated some of their disadvantages by using large numbers of galiots, lighter and easier to row than ordinary galleys and ideally suited for the amphibious raids that were their *raison d'être*.

Having addressed the changing performance, tactical power, and operating costs of the war galley we turn to galley fleets. A mid-sixteenth-century galley fleet based in Constantinople could go no farther than Tunis with the strength needed to mount a protracted siege of a competently defended port city with first-class fortifications. For an Ottoman fleet to winter over at its objective would have imposed an insupportable logistic burden. It would also have left the fleet exposed to decimation by exposure and disease or the possibility of a sudden descent by the Spanish with the galleys pulled ashore and out of commission. The first of these risks could be reduced by staying on with reduced forces, as was done at Rhodes in the winter of 1521–22 and at Famagusta on Cyprus in the winter of 1570–71; but both of these places were deep in the eastern Mediterranean.

All worthwhile targets in the western Mediterranean were within easy reach of Spanish bases and the second risk was therefore too great. The Turks could carry a siege of Rhodes or Famagusta through the winter, but not a siege of Tunis or Puerto Mahon. Malta was a borderline case, or so the evidence suggests. The option of wintering at a friendly port in the western Mediterranean and striking the following spring was feasible, but was dependent on French assistance, for Algiers and the lesser Muslim port cities of the North African coast lacked the resources needed to support a major expedition. These considerations ruled out a descent on the Andalusian coast. If the Spanish Moriscos were to be succoured and their sympathies turned to military advantage, it would have to be through

---

[23] In 1556, of the Ottoman fleet of 42 galleys and 5 *fustas*, only three galleys were rowed by slave *ciurmi*. The *capitana* and the lantern galleys of two prominent subordinate commanders were rowed by Muslim soldiers, presumably *ʿAzabs*, and the rest by salaried Greek oarsmen: Olesa Muñido (1968), 2:1152–54.

the prolonged attrition of *ghazi* warfare, the 'little war' of raid and counter-raid, not a decisive blow struck by a single campaign.[24] That would require a base from which Ottoman raiders could strike at the coasts of Spain in support of the North African Muslims. If, however, such a base were directly accessible to Spanish land power the cost of holding it—if it could be held at all—would be excessive.

At this point, a few words about Ottoman strategic objectives are in order. Traditional interpretations hold that the Ottomans were motivated above all by the desire—indeed, the religious obligation— to expand the *darülislam*, the abode of those who abide by the will of Allah, at the expense of the *darülharb*, the abode of unbelievers (literally the abode of war). In fact, this is an oversimplification; Ottoman strategic ends and means varied according to the circumstances.[25] The Ottomans had, however, achieved their legitimacy, their power and a measure of prosperity through aggressive expansion at the expense of Christendom and took seriously their role as the standard-bearers of Islam. Even before their absorption of the Egyptian Mamluk Sultanate in 1517, the Ottomans had forwarded arms, technical experts and commanders to assist the Mamluks in their effort to halt Portuguese expansion in the Indian Ocean. Victory over the Mamluks, the Ottomans' last Muslim rival in the west, reinforced their commitment to the struggle against Christendom. So did the acceptance of Ottoman legitimacy by the most prominent and dynamic North African Muslim leaders. By contrast, the Ottomans' wars against their Muslim rivals in the east, notably the Shii Safavid Persians, were defensive and had comparatively limited objectives. Indicative of that strategy, Ottoman fleets based in Constantinople ventured deep into the western Mediterranean in the 1540s and '50s, facilitated at times by the on-again, off-again, alliance between Sultan Süleyman I and Francis I of France.

The Great Siege of Malta had its origins in Emperor Charles V's 1524 offer to give the Knights of St. John Malta the Maltese Archipelago and the fortress of Tripoli as replacements for their lost

---

[24] *Ghazi*, from the Arabic root word *ghazwat*, raid, denotes a raider for the faith, one whose life is committed to the continuous struggle between Islam and the world of the unbelievers, particularly Christendom.

[25] Murphey (1999), 1–3.

base of Rhodes. The Knights, struck by the archipelago's remoteness and lack of natural resources, at first declined his offer, hoping for something better and lobbying hard for Syracuse on Sicily.[26] Malta's Grand Harbour was, however, an ideal base for the Knights' corsairing raids and in 1530 the Knights accepted. The difficulty was that Malta's fortifications, constructed before the age of gunpowder, were obsolete. Specifically, the defences of Birgu; Fort St. Angelo, the detached work protecting Birgu's seaward side; and Senglea were vulnerable to plunging fire from higher terrain to the south and—particularly—from the Sceberras peninsula separating the Grand Harbour from Marsamuscetto Inlet (See Map 12). The long-term solution was to build a fortified city atop Sceberras, but the ground was rocky and the peninsula lacked reliable water supplies. Considerable time and money would be required and the Knights were initially reluctant to invest heavily in what they hoped would be a temporary base.

No doubt cognizant of Ottoman embroilment in Hungary and with Persia—an imperial army under Sultan Süleyman took Baghdad in 1533–34—the Knights temporized. In 1537, Süleyman's projected invasion of Italy came a cropper before the Venetian fortifications of Corfu, but Khaireddin Barbarossa's defeat of a combined Habsburg-Venetian fleet at Prevesa the next autumn split the Spanish-Papal-Venetian alliance, leading to a separate Venetian-Ottoman peace in 1540. It is surely less than coincidence that the Knights undertook major improvements the following year, modernizing Birgu's defences and reinforcing Fort St. Angelo with an artillery tower built high enough neutralize the elevation advantage of Sceberras.[27]

The intermittent alliance between Francis I of France and Süleyman (Süleyman's 1537 campaign was planned as part of a joint Franco-Turkish invasion of Italy, though Francis failed to keep his end of the bargain) had no doubt influenced the Knights by suggesting an Ottoman focus on objectives removed from the central Mediterranean. But the alliance was re-activated in the wake of Charles V's disastrous failure before Algiers in 1541 and Barbarossa's fleet laid over in Toulon during the winter of 1542–43 after ravaging the western Mediterranean. Turkish fleets ranged far afield, and in July 1551

---

[26] Blouet (1987), 46.
[27] Ibid., 49–50.

raided the Maltese Archipelago en route to a successful siege of Tripoli.

The 1551 raid was a wake-up call for the Knights of St. John. Strategically, it deprived them of their only other base, focusing their attention on Malta. Tactically, it provided stark evidence of the vulnerability of their position. Though the Turks made no attempt to take Birgu, Senglea or Malta's capital of Mdina, they were able to enter Marsamuscetto Inlet unopposed and disembark at leisure. This was plainly unacceptable, and the next year saw the construction of a modern, *trace italienne* fortress on the tip of the Sceberras peninsula. The fortress, named Fort St. Elmo, suffered from the disadvantage of being dominated by the heights to the southwest, but that was ameliorated by the fact that it was built on solid rock and was separated from the body of the peninsula by a low draw. The place would be all but proof against mining, and any assault force would have to traverse an open space of 300 to 350 yards under the fort's guns.[28] Finally, the Knights constructed a first-class defensive work, Fort St. Michael, at the base of Senglea. Malta was now secure from casual attack.

There matters stayed until 1559–1560 when the strategic calculus underwent fundamental change. In 1559, France, exhausted and perceiving the futility of her Italian adventure, concluded the treaty of Cateau Cambrésis with Spain, recognizing Spanish hegemony over Italy. That released Habsburg resources to be used elsewhere, and to Philip II of Spain, Emperor since Charles' abdication in 1555, the time seemed ripe to go over to the attack.

A strike at Muslim corsairing bases on the North African coast, the 1560 imperial expedition was strategically defensive in nature, an accurate gauge of the relative balance of Habsburg and Ottoman power. The expedition was commanded by Philip's Captain General of the Sea, Gian Andrea Doria, great-nephew of the great Andrea Doria. After extended temporizing and debate over the expedition's objectives, Doria landed an invasion force on the island of Djerba on 7 March and ordered construction of a fort. Work was well under way when the imperial force was surprised on 11 May by a fleet under the Ottoman *Kapudan Pasha*, Piali Pasha, that had sailed from Constantinople on receipt of news of the Christian offensive. The

---

[28] Ibid., 55–56.

result was disaster. Of the 50–55 Christian galleys in Doria's fleet, between 28 and 30 were captured or sunk.[29] The Christian garrison put up a stout defence, but with no hope of relief succumbed after an eighty-one day siege.[30]

The loss at Djerba was not so much in hulls and ordnance, but in skilled manpower, particularly among sailor-arquebusiers and *oficiales*, the skilled technicians who made a war galley work: captains, sailing masters, pilots, sergeants-at-arms, masters of the *ciurma*, coopers, carpenters, boatswains, gunners, barber-surgeons and chaplains. These represented a serious loss, and one that could not be quickly made good, for their skills were the products of a lifetime of preparation and service. The same was true of the sailor-arquebusiers, men recruited from coastal villages who were accustomed to the sea and who handled the rigging and sails. They also formed the bulk of the galley's fighting force and were useful for raiding and skirmishing ashore as well as combat afloat.[31] These men could not be replaced at all, and the Spanish were forced for the first time to embark regular infantry on their galleys, our source says specifically 'after Djerba', with serious problems of efficiency and discipline—'great confusion and much disorder'—resulting.[32]

Djerba presented the Turks with a window of opportunity. The Spanish fleet was crippled, giving the Turks had as free a hand in the Mediterranean as they were ever likely to enjoy. Time, however, was critical and the opportunity diminished with each passing year, for the Spanish loss was in quality and experience rather than raw numbers. Each year of successful campaigning by the Habsburg galley force lessened the danger for Spain. The reality of the opportunity that Djerba offered the Turks was not lost on the Spanish or the Knights of St. John. While each passing year made the Spanish better able to defend their coasts and possessions, each year also saw the Ottomans in a better position to exploit their advantage.

Reports of preparations for a major Ottoman thrust into the western Mediterranean began to circulate soon after Djerba and became

---

[29] Guilmartin (1974), 130.

[30] For the Djerba campaign, Guilmartin (1974), 123–134, and Önalp (1996), 135–174.

[31] Guilmartin (1974), 130–33.

[32] This is from a contemporary analysis of the various *asientos* under which the Galleys of Naples operated from 1552 to 1569, in MNM, Colección Sanz de Barutell (Simancas), *artículo* 4, vol. 2, dto. 311, fo. 382ff.

progressively more compelling.[33] By the summer of 1564 it was apparent that the blow must fall the next year. The warning sent to Philip II by Don Garcia de Toledo, Captain General of the Sea for the Mediterranean, did not even bother to explain the particular need for urgency in that year above all others.[34]

That the Ottoman blow would fall in 1565 was taken for granted; the question was where? The circumstances pointed to Malta, close enough to the Ottoman bases to be attacked with force, yet far enough west for raiders based there to do the Spanish real harm. Its small extent and the scarcity of good beaches insured that getting a relieving force ashore would be no easy task. All of these factors must have been dealt with at length in the deliberations of the Divan. We know that they were presented in roughly this form to Philip II by Don Garcia de Toledo.

Here a word on organization and command relationships is in order, for they would play a significant role in determining Malta's fate. In principle, Ottoman arrangements were superior. The *Kapudan Pasha* had full control of his logistical and manpower base, commanding the imperial dockyards in Constantinople and presiding over a centralized logistical system. In addition, the *Kapudan Pasha* was assigned extensive holdings in the Morea and the Greek Islands. A significant proportion of his fighting manpower consisted of *timar* holders from those regions and many Turkish sailors and oarsmen were their dependents. Biscuit, the hard-baked bread that provided the bulk of a galley crews' nutrition, was supplied by bakeries under the *Kapudan Pasha's* control.[35] Moreover, Piali Pasha, *Kapudan Pasha* since 1555, was a skilled tactician and competent commander.

Sultans traditionally delegated full operational authority to the *Kapudan Pasha*, but in 1565 unity of command was compromised by the appointment of a separate commander of ground forces, Mustafa Pasha. Although Piali controlled naval matters Mustafa exercised overall command.[36]

Spanish command relationships were characteristically decentralized, with the Captain General of the Sea commanding forces afloat

---

[33] Blouet (1987), 51–52.
[34] MNM, CN xii, dto. 79, fol. 292ff.
[35] Olesa-Muñido (1968), 2:1140–43, for a useful summary of the scope of the *Kapudan Pasha's* authority.
[36] Prescott (1904), 3:178.

and the Viceroy of Sicily controlling the Captain General's main source of manpower and supplies. Dockyards and arsenals were independent commands and biscuit was provided by a network of private contractors.[37] Although a dependency of the Spanish monarchy, Malta was effectively under the sovereign authority of the Knights of St John and ruled by the Grand Master of the Order. That post had been occupied since 1557 by Jean Parisot de la Valette, an able and energetic commander and an inspirational leader. Keenly aware of his dependence on the Captain General for support and on Sicily for provisions, Valette had no control over either. Compounding matters, Philip II was a micro-manager who habitually involved himself in his subordinates' affairs.

The incumbent Captain General, Don Garcia de Toledo, was an experienced galley commander, a skilled tactician and an able strategist. In May of 1564, he moved to simplify his command relationships by petitioning Philip to appoint him Viceroy of Sicily in addition to his captain generalcy. Tellingly, he pressed his case by citing the efficiency of Ottoman command arrangements, particularly the *Kapudan Pasha's* control of his logistical and manpower base.[38] Uncharacteristically, Philip granted his request.

The Spanish galley force, in the midst of its post-Djerba build-up, was weak and unreliable. Spain had a single trump card—the infantry of the *tercios* and their mercenary German and Italian comrades in arms. Spanish reserves of trained soldiers had been dented at Djerba but, unlike those of sailor-arquebusiers and *oficiales*, not all but eliminated. It was a card that would have to be played carefully in light of the weakness of the naval instrument upon which it depended for transport and timing would be critical.

Thrown in too soon, a Spanish relieving force might be caught at sea by a fresh and numerically superior Turkish fleet. But if Don Garcia waited until the bulk of Ottoman manpower, guns, and munitions had been expended in the inexorable attrition of a hard-pressed siege, the relief might arrive after its object had fallen. His first problem, therefore, was to insure that whatever place the Turks attacked could hold out long enough to wear the Ottoman forces down to

---

[37] Guilmartin (1993), 109–36, esp. 124–29.
[38] MNM, CN xii, dto. 78, fo. 289: 'Discurso que hizo Dn Garcia de Toledo para representar a S. M. sobre las ventajas que resultarian a su Real Servicio de juntarse el Cargo del Reyno de Sicilia con el de la Mar'.

the point that relief could be introduced. This was a game that required sound understanding of a wide range of variables, strong leadership and exquisite timing. Don Garcia de Toledo possessed all three. So, as we shall see, did Jean Parisot de la Valette.

In light of our posited scarcity of good bronze ordnance, the quantity and quality of artillery used in the Great Siege, about which we are fortunate in knowing a good deal, assumes considerable significance. Of particular interest is the provision of defensive artillery. Taken from an account of the siege written shortly afterward by one Don Juan Páez de Castro, the following list is probably very nearly inclusive:[39]

> Cannon mounted in the defence of Birgu and Senglea (See Map 12):
> 17 full cannon (probably 40–50 pounders)
> 5 half cannon (probably 20–30 pounders)
> 5 half culverins (probably 9 pounders, give or take a little)
> 1 *sacre* (probably about a 6 pounder)
> 3 *lombardas de hierro* (wrought-iron bombards)
>
> Cannon mounted in Fort St Elmo:
> 15 full cannon
> 1 half culverin

Bearing in mind that the Knights of St John of Malta were well-funded and skilled practitioners of the art of positional warfare—as they had demonstrated at Rhodes in 1522—we may assume that any lack of artillery reflected in the above list was the result of non availability rather than penury or ignorance. Indeed, there is no indication that the amount of artillery available to the defence fell short of expectations. Francisco Balbi di Correggio, a participant whose account of the siege was published a few years later, tells us that the Grand Master had 'plenty of artillery' through he was somewhat short of powder.[40] In terms of the expectations among his comrades-in-arms, Balbi was undoubtedly correct.

It is clear, however, that Valette could—and no doubt would—have usefully employed many more cannon had they been available.

---

[39] MNM, CN iv, dto 19: Páez de Castro, *Relación*.

[40] Balbi (1568), 61. Balbi, an ordinary arquebusier in the garrison of Senglea, gives a long and generally accurate, but technically uninformed and occasionally confusing account. For the conduct of the siege I have depended primarily on Balbi and Páez de Castro, cited above, supplemented by Cassola (1985). Prescott (1904),

The weight of artillery that would ideally have been sited in the defence is shown by the fact that nearly half of the full cannon available were assigned to Fort St Elmo (See Map 12). It was there that La Valette believed—correctly—that the first blow would fall. St Elmo would have to extract from the Turks the maximum expenditure in blood, powder and time if the main positions of Senglea and Birgu were to survive. St Elmo was therefore armed as it should have been; Birgu and Senglea were armed as best they could be with what was left over. The disparity is striking and strongly suggests that good heavy ordnance was in short supply.

We should also note the predominance of full cannon in Páez de Castro's list. Faced with limited financial resources and a need for scarce and expensive artillery, the Knights of St John had put their money where it would do the most good, largely ignoring smaller and less powerful pieces. A shortage is also suggested by the presence of three wrought-iron bombards, thoroughly obsolete by 1565 and probably a half century old.

The Ottoman siege train was, as we have seen, more powerful, though not overwhelmingly so in number of guns. Repeating Páez de Castro's figures, the Turks deployed two enormous basilisks and 60 double cannon of battery, numbers that are in line with other accounts, amply provided with powder and shot. Balbi di Correggio tells us that the Ottomans brought to Malta a huge 100 pound siege gun weighing 18,000 pounds (this gun and its ammunition comprised the entire load of a single galley), two eighty pounders weighing 13,000 pounds each, four 60 pounders weighing 11,000 pounds each and a 'large cannon which fired stone shot.' Balbi's first and last pieces were surely Páez de Castro's basilisks.[41] These monsters were plainly intended for knocking down walls by direct battery and so far as we know were used in precisely that role. Páez de Castro, for

---

3:171–272, provides a useful account, drawing on Balbi, Spanish sources and historians of the Order of St John. The discussion of the siege in Braudel (1966), 2:319–29, though general, is sound. Until the appearance of my account, (1974), 176–93, Braudel was unique in defending Don Garcia de Toledo against his detractors. Bradford (1961), is useful in reflecting the bitter (and in my view unfair) accusations that Don Garcia was needlessly dilatory in launching the relief expedition.

[41] Balbi (1568), 31–7. Balbi calls all cannon of great size 'basilisks'. To Páez de Castro and the sources cited in Prescott (1904), 3:179, a basilisk was an exceptionally large, powerful, long-barreled piece, whether designed to fire stone or cast iron projectiles.

example, tells us that two basilisks were emplaced hard up against the south-west corner of Birgu in the final stages of the siege when Christian powder supplies were running low and counterbattery fire was rarely employed.

The balance in manpower was far more one-sided. The Ottoman fleet of some 130 galleys, 18 galiots, 8 *maonas* (heavy galleys), 11 large sailing vessels and three smaller ones left Constantinople in February with around 30,000 fighting men, including as many as 9,000 *timariot sipahis* and 6,000 Janissaries.[42] This total was swelled by some 600 men under the Governor of Alexandria who arrived with 4 galleys on 27 May, by a contingent of 2,500 North Africans under the renowned corsair leader Turgut Re'is who arrived at Malta with 43 galleys, 2 galiots and a siege train on 2 June, and an Algerian contingent of 2,500 (including as many as 500 Janissaries) in 7 galleys and 20 galiots which arrived on 12 July. The Muslim force thus ultimately included, or so the defenders believed, some 36,000 fighting men, well over half of them Janissaries, *sipahis*, or experienced *'azabs* (marine light infantry), *akınjıs* (light cavalry), and *lewends* (light infantry). To this, we must add the fleet's oarsmen, both free and slave, who could be used as sappers and laborers. Even if the number is exaggerated and the combatants numbered no more than 20,000, the proportionate strengths of the various categories are no doubt accurate and it is clear that the Turks enjoyed a huge advantage in numbers of experienced combatants.[43]

The garrison of Malta, by contrast, numbered no more than 2,500 professional fighting men, including 500 Knights and two companies of Spanish infantry of 200 men each, bolstered by 700 or so mercenary oarsmen and armed Greek and Italian residents of Malta plus 5,000–6,000 Maltese of whom perhaps 1,000 were armed.[44]

---

[42] Balbi (1568), 36: his detailed breakdown gives 9,000 *sipahis* who were probably *timariots* (as opposed to salaried *sipahis* of the Porte), most if not all of them archers, and 6,000 Janissaries, 'all musketeers'. Páez de Castro's estimate of 4,500 Janissaries is still impressive. Balbi's 9,000 'adventurers' and 6,000 'corsairs and adventurers' were probably *'azabs* and *lewends*.

[43] Blouet (1987), 64–65, considers it doubtful that the Turks could have transported 30,000 fighting men from Constantinople to Malta and estimates the total number of trained soldiers at 20,000.

[44] Though their breakdowns vary, Balbi, Páez de Castro, and Prescott's sources

After making several stops in the Greek islands to embark additional men and supplies, the Ottoman fleet arrived off Malta early in the evening of 18 May and anchored for the night in a bay on the island's northwest coast. Their arrival came only six days after that of a company of 200 Spanish arquebusiers, earmarked by Don Garcia for the garrison of Fort St Elmo. The next day the Turks, barred from Marsamuscetto by St Elmo's guns, proceeded to Marsasirocco bay on the Malta's southeastern tip. A horseshoe bay with a six and a half mile coastline, Marsasirocco was ideal for disembarkation, permitting the Turks to deploy their entire force while giving the Christians no place to make a stand. It also provided good shelter from the summer winds. Conversely, it was three and a half miles as the crow flies from the main Christian positions and at least half again that far by road. Everything needed for the prosecution of the siege would have to be moved cross country, mostly by human muscle since Malta was anything but a rich source of dray animals. Moreover, the very length of shoreline that facilitated disembarkation made Marsasirocco a poor defensive position. Pulled up against the shore, the Muslim galleys would be vulnerable to a sudden descent by a well-equipped galley force, for an aggressor could strike with locally overwhelming force. While superior numbers provided reasonable security for the moment, the Turks mounted shore batteries as insurance.[45]

Valette offered only token opposition to the Turkish landing: some skirmishing to demonstrate seriousness of purpose. Then the Christians pulled back to their fortifications to await the onslaught. As insurance, Valette concentrated what little cavalry he had in the citadel of Mdina.

Christian chroniclers report a debate among the Muslim commanders concerning their initial objective. How reliable and well-informed their sources were is open to doubt, but there is probably something to the reports, for the conduct of the siege does not suggest the confident implementation of a coherent plan. Be that as it may, the Muslims decided on Fort St Elmo and began wrestling

---

are in general agreement regarding the strength of the garrison. Blouet (1987), 52, gives a total of about 9,000.

[45] Blouet, *Malta*, 53–55. Blouet is a geographer, and his assessments of matters of wind, weather, and terrain are particularly insightful.

their guns and munitions overland from Marsasirocco. By 22 May they were hard at work on Sceberras, digging emplacements for a ten gun battery 'about 600 paces [460 yards]' from St Elmo's ditch,[46] considerably farther than the range considered optimal for battery, 80 to 150 paces (60 to 150 yards).[47] The Turks' decision to emplace their battery so far back was driven partly by topography and partly by respect for St Elmo's guns, most of which were emplaced to defend against land attack.[48]

Most accounts of the siege hold that the decision to attack Fort St Elmo before Birgu and Senglea was a mistake since Marsasirocco would have served as well for an anchorage as Marsamuscetto.[49] This view is based on a misunderstanding of the logistical difficulties involved in supporting large-scale siege operations a considerable distance overland from a floating logistical base. Simply moving heavy guns cross country posed significant challenges and it seems likely that the largest and most powerful guns were held back for the attack on the central position. Significantly, our Christian sources report basilisks in action only against the central position and only after the fall of St Elmo. In addition, with fleet and army widely separated, the Turks had to leave sizeable forces behind to guard the ships. Acceptable early on, such a situation would rapidly have become untenable as more and more men were employed in digging saps and mining, as casualties mounted, and as dray animals were consumed as food. Committing oarsmen to hauling supplies and digging siege parallels would have entailed a permanent loss of mobility to the fleet, not a temporary deficit that could quickly be made good. Likewise, using the Muslim galleys' main centreline guns in battery against the Christian fortifications (as was done against St Elmo on several occasions, notably to cover the assault of 16 June)

---

[46] Balbi (1568), 61; Prescott (1904), 3:182.

[47] Collado (1592), 53–4 (*Tratado* 3, *Capitulo* XXXIII), puts it as follows: 'The distance of the battery [from the wall] will depend upon the circumstances of the [best] site which you can find near the fortress; but the best and most proper distance (if you can do it) is 80 paces from the wall. A distance of 100 paces would be excellent and 150 very good. A distance of 200 paces is not so good and 300 is, without a doubt, too far.' Assuming that Collado was using the *passo comun* of Castile, about 2.29 feet, 80 paces is about 60 yards, 100 paces 70 yards, 150 paces 100 yards, 200 paces 150 yards and 300 paces 230 yards.

[48] Prescott (1904), 3:178.

[49] Bradford (1961), 71–2, presents this argument.

would have been more difficult. Finally, we know that the water supply in the vicinity of Marsasirocco was inadequate for the entire Turkish fleet—galleys were sent to get water at the Bays of St Paul and Salinas to the west of Marsamuscetto less than two weeks after arrival.[50]

On 25 May—remarkably soon given the distance the guns had to be moved and the difficult terrain—the battery on Sceberras opened fire on St Elmo.[51] The defenders responded four days later with a sortie that caught the Turks by surprise, taking the forward trenches and creating panic before the Muslims regained their composure and mounted a counter attack. The over-extended Christians pulled back in disorder, and in the confusion the Turks gained a lodgement in the counterscarp which they managed to fortify. Several days later, the Turks seized St Elmo's ravelin by *coup de main* and, encouraged by this success, tried to take the main position by escalade. The Muslims attacked with *élan*, but had neglected to fill in the ditch and their ladders proved too short. The ensuing slaughter was made worse by the garrison's use of novel pyrotechnics, large hoops covered with fabric soaked in incendiary chemicals, to which the Muslims' robes proved vulnerable. The Turks licked their wounds and reverted to battery; the Christians reinforced and replenished by small boats sent under cover of darkness.

Turgut Re'is' arrival on 2 June comprised a turning point, for he brought not only a useful increment of men and firepower, but his formidable expertise. He promptly emplaced a battery of four culverins on the point facing St Elmo across the mouth of Marsamuscetto. Shortly thereafter, the Turks erected heavier batteries on the tip of the peninsula north east of Birgu and on the point facing St Elmo across the mouth of the Grand Harbour. Shooting at ranges of 500 to 1,300 yards, these batteries brought effective fire on St Elmo, a rare example of long range battery. On 5 June, with St Elmo's masonry crumbling, breaches appearing in the walls and the inside of the fort covered by snipers firing from the ravelin, the garrison concluded that the place was indefensible. They petitioned Valette to let them withdraw, arguing that their honour had been satisfied.

---

[50] Balbi (1568), 61.
[51] For the siege of Fort St Elmo, I have relied upon MNM, CN iv, dto 19: Páez de Castro, 'Relación'; Blouet (1987), 56–60; and Prescott (1904), 3:182–214.

Considerations of chivalric honour aside, they were right: by any rational calculation the place *was* indefensible.

Displaying subtle leadership and a keen awareness of St Elmo's importance in equal measure, Valette shamed the garrison into fighting on. Surviving accounts emphasize his appeal to the Knights' honour, but we must remember that they were a minority, never more than 150 of a garrison that numbered 800 at full strength.

By the 15th, the Turks had created a practicable breach in St Elmo's land wall and launched a major assault at dawn the following day, bringing galleys around to batter the fort by sea. The assault columns, Janissaries prominent among them, were engaged by Fort St Angelo's guns at the remarkable range of some 1,300 yards (unsurprisingly, the initial volley was too close for comfort, killing eight defenders), and sustained serious loss. With exemplary fortitude, they pressed on and were driven back only after hours of close combat.

Meanwhile, the Turks—our sources say at Turgut Re'is' insistence—decided belatedly to extend their siege lines down to the water's edge and emplace a battery to seal St Elmo off from reinforcement. The work was completed by the 19th despite heavy casualties from Christian artillery, for the ground was hard and devoid of cover. Among the casualties was Turgut Re'is, mortally wounded by a stone fragment thrown up by a cannonball, a major loss for the attackers. With St Elmo sealed off, the Turks still needed two major assaults and four days to capture the place. St Elmo held out for thirty-five days, falling on 23 June after three weeks of intensive bombardment and four major assaults, some two and a half weeks after it should have fallen by any reasonable calculation.

The defence cost the Christians some 1,500 men, 123 of them Knights. According to Christian sources, it cost the Turks 6,000 men and 18,000 rounds of artillery ammunition.[52] More important than the number of Turks slain was the fact that a disproportionate number of them were among the most skilled and highly motivated of the besiegers, janissaries and *sipahis* who would play a much less prominent role in subsequent operations. More important still was the time expended. Mustafa Pasha's supplies of powder and shot were adequate. He would get reinforcements. He could, and would,

---

[52] Balbi (1568), 91.

inspire his men to acts of great bravery and fortitude. He could not reclaim the two and a half weeks.

Robbed of time, fighting manpower and resources by St Elmo, the Ottomans quickly brought their fleet around to Marsamuscetto and shifted their main batteries to face the land walls of Birgu and Senglea. Almost simultaneously, Don Garcia dispatched a hand-picked relief force of some 700 men, Spanish infantry and 50 Knights, in his four best galleys. Delayed *en route* by a storm, it came ashore on Malta's north coast during the night of 3–4 July and, in a remarkable feat of arms, managed to slip through the Turkish lines and into Birgu. In this the Christians were aided by the Turks' failure to complete lines of circumvallation around Birgu and Senglea.

The Ottomans at first concentrated their attention on Senglea. Though the land walls, bolstered by the bastions and artillery of Fort St Michael, were more than adequate in their intact state, the defences on Senglea's south west flank along French Creek were weak and the shore adjacent to them gradual and smooth, an obvious invitation to amphibious assault. Serious bombardment of Senglea began on 3 July, concentrating on the south-west corner of the land walls and on the defences along the creek. The Turkish intentions were obvious to the defenders—boats, some of them fairly large, were dragged overland from Marsamuscetto to the head of the Grand Harbour opposite the main Muslim camp—and underwater obstacles, stakes connected with chains and the like, were planted in the shallows. On 15 July Muslim swimmers attempted to clear these away, but were repelled in the water by armed Maltese under cover of arquebus fire.

On 15 July, with Muslim artillery firing at a range of less than 400 yards having leveled the defences along French Creek in places, a major assault was launched, spearheaded by the Algerian contingent which had arrived only three days before and covered by a simultaneous land assault on Fort St Michael.

The main force of the attack was broken by the underwater obstacles which stopped the Muslim boats short of the beach and snared the robes of the fighting men. Nevertheless the fighting along French Creek was severe, lasting some five hours with perhaps 3,000 attackers involved. At the peak of the assault ten boats carrying about 1,000 men, seeing their predecessors entangled in the underwater obstacles, shifted their attack to the low-lying tip of Senglea, hoping to land unopposed with the Christian reserves committed elsewhere—

as in fact they were. Instead, they were taken in flank by a battery firing from a water level platform beneath the tip of Fort St Angelo. Firing at a range of about 300 yards, the Christian guns killed hundreds of Muslims outright with their first volley and sank nine of the ten boats, drowning most of the survivors.[53] The result was a bloody debacle. The Muslim survivors in French Creek retreated to their boats in disorder, pursued by the garrison.

The next day the Muslims shifted their attention to the land defences, opening a violent frontal bombardment of Fort St Michael. Mining against Birgu and Senglea had begun by 17 July, though it was never very effective because of the hard soil. Trenches were advanced under cover of an increasingly intense cannonade and heavy musket fire that kept the defenders' heads down and their guns out of action. An attempted surprise attack on Fort St Michael was beaten back on the 18th. The Turkish batteries continued their work.

Then, at noon on 1 August following an extended bombardment that heavily damaged the walls, the Turks launched a mass assault and succeeded in making lodgements in several places. They were beaten back with great difficulty after five hours of intense fighting, much of it hand-to-hand. Apparently encouraged by indications that Christian manpower reserves were running thin—the Muslim artillery had established nearly total fire superiority at this point—Mustafa Pasha tried again on the 7th.

Hoping to catch La Valette without reserves, the Muslim attack began all along the line at dawn, concentrating on Fort St Michael and the south-west corner of the land wall of Birgu where the ditch was almost completely filled with rubble brought down by Turkish cannonballs. Here the Muslims gained a sizeable foothold and planted a number of standards along the wall. La Valette himself led the counterattack with his last reserves and the battle hung in the balance for nearly nine hours.

Then, as the Muslims had victory within their grasp, the unexpected happened. Dom Pedro de Mezquita, governor of Mdina, had closely monitored the progress of the siege. His tiny force had harassed

---

[53] This incident is mentioned both by Balbi and Páez de Castro. Balbi (1568), 115, colours his account, stating that this force was specially chosen from among non-swimmers to insure against retreat.

Muslim foraging parties from the start, and the previous week had repelled a half-hearted attack on Mdina. This was their moment. Mezquita launched his handful of horsemen and arquebusiers, surely no more than 100 of each, against the Ottoman base camp, stripped of able-bodied men for the assault. Shouting 'victory and relief' they piled into the Muslim camp slashing the wounded, cutting down tents, and burning everything they could lay hands on. The timing was perfect. When one more supreme effort might have overcome Christian resistance, terrified survivors from the camp came streaming into the siege lines and broke the Muslim resolve. Whether on Mustafa Pasha's orders or as an unplanned reflex, the assault troops, half convinced that a relief force was between them and their fleet, pulled back from the walls. The threat was never again to be so severe—though that was hardly apparent to the hard-pressed defenders.

The siege settled down to a deadly game of sniping, sapping, mining and countermining. Showing considerable skill, Ottoman sappers worked their trenches in closer and closer to the south-west corner of Birgu and the half ruined 'spur' of Fort St Michael under a protective hail of musketry and artillery fire. With their powder supplies running low, the defenders responded with artifice, at one point cutting a surprise gunport low in the wall of Birgu to enfilade a particularly menacing Turkish trench. On 20 August Mustafa Pasha launched a major assault against Fort St Michael—and led it in person despite his advanced age, a sign of demoralization among the Muslim shock troops. The next day saw another violent assault spearheaded by the few remaining Janissaries and—according to Balbi—ʿazabs and laborers dressed in the clothing of fallen Janissaries to exaggerate their numbers and demoralize the defenders.

The 24th brought a cold north wind, bringing rain that extinguished the arquebusiers' slow matches, a harbinger of the campaigning season's end. The defenders broke out crossbows to discourage an assault in the rain with cold steel. The next day, a relief force of some 10,000 men embarked in sixty galleys under Don Garcia de Toledo sailed from Syracuse on Sicily's west coast, only to be dispersed by a storm several days later and driven back.[54] The better part of a week was required for reorganization, repairs and replenishment.

---

[54] MNM, CN iv, dto 19, fos 242–44: Páez de Castro, 'Relación'; Blouet (1987), 64.

On the 27th the Turks pushed a siege tower—a throwback to the twelfth century—against Fort St Michael only to have it destroyed by a masked cannon firing through a newly-cut gunport low in the wall. That the Turks could even attempt such a manoeuvre shows the completeness of Muslim fire superiority.

Though much of the fire had gone out of their bellies, the besiegers were still dangerous, while the defenders, although close to the end of their physical and logistical tethers, could see the end in sight. They launched sorties into the Muslim trenches and threw bread and cheese into the sap heads to persuade the Turks that Christian food supplies were ample. The Turks launched assaults on the 28th and again on the 30th. On 1 September, they tried another moveable siege tower—no doubt constructed of wood from galleys that could no longer be manned—its upper story filled with Janissary arquebusiers to clear the walls of defenders, only to have it burnt and destroyed.

Given the exhausted state of the garrison and their depleted powder reserves, another month would surely have brought victory. But, as Mustafa Pasha and Piali Pasha surely knew, Don Garcia de Toledo would give them considerably less than that. Piali's fleet, its best fighting manpower and much of its motive power ground into raw meat and dust, was barely a match for a Spanish fleet that it could have handled with ease a month and a half earlier.

The Turks resorted to mining through the rubble brought down by their cannonballs in an attempt to blast their way into the Christian defences, but to no avail. The heart had gone out of the Muslims and on 4 September the Janissaries had to go into the trenches to beat the sappers to force them to their work.

While this was transpiring, the relief force had completed repairs and put back to sea. On 6 September, it landed at Mellieha Bay on Malta's northwestern tip. Don Garcia's force disembarked with remarkable efficiency, getting their ordnance, provender and munitions ashore in an hour and a half.[55] Don Garcia departed for Sicily the next morning, sailing close enough to land to be seen from the Walls of Fort St Angelo and exchange cannon salutes with the defenders.[56] A Muslim galiot shortly entered Marsamuscetto, confirming

---

[55] MNM, CN iv, dto 19, fos 247–49: Páez de Castro, 'Relación'.
[56] Prescott (1904), 3:248.

the news that the Christian fleet's presence implied: relief was at hand. Working methodically, the Ottomans pulled out their ordnance and embarked the next day. No doubt at Mustafa's urging, Piali disembarked the bulk of the Muslim army at St Paul's bay with the intention of intercepting the relief force short of its objective. Whoever was behind the decision had sorely underestimated the power and efficiency of good imperial infantry, or perhaps overestimated the effectiveness and morale of his own men. The Turks broke at the first encounter and had to be re-embarked under cover of the galleys' bow ordnance. The great siege was over.

The rhythms of Mediterranean warfare at sea combined with Turkish losses to preclude an Ottoman thrust of comparable magnitude for several years. In 1570 when it came, it was aimed at Cyprus, a target much closer to home. Though we cannot say with certainty, among the reasons for the scaling down in strategic aims was surely the Ottoman galley fleet's reduced radius of action, the product of more numerous, larger, and more heavily armed galleys. The Great Siege of 1565 was the last great effort of a organization in transition. By the 1570s, or so I believe, a similar effort would not have been possible, partly for the reason just posited and partly because the Knights of St John had greatly strengthened their fortifications aided by the increased availability of good heavy ordnance.

What lessons can we draw from our study? The competence and ability of senior leaders and the way in which command relationships channelled them played a major role on both sides. The complexity and uncertainty inherent to amphibious operations lent particular importance to these factors and magnified their effects, both positive and negative. The division of authority between Mustafa and Piali clearly helped rob the Muslim effort of a clear operational focus, a lack of focus that was reflected in flawed decisions and errors of omission. The failure to take Mdina early on had serious repercussions. Though the approaches to Mdina were difficult, it was an old place with an inadequate garrison. Moreover, Malta's profusion of stone walls left cavalry essentially road bound, and the avenues by which the garrison could sortie could easily have been blocked. The 7 August attack by Dom Mezquita's force on the Ottoman camp that caused the Muslim assault force to pull back at the moment of victory was the price the Turks paid for their indolence. It would have been simple, albeit costly, for the Turks to have cut Fort St Elmo off from resupply early on; failure to do so was perhaps their single most costly error. The failure to complete lines of investment around Birgu and Senglea expeditiously comes a close second. The first Christian relief force would have had a difficult time cutting its way through even the sketchiest of defensive lines, and its defeat would have been as profoundly depressing to the defenders as its success was uplifting.

Conversely, Don Garcia and Valette kept their focus squarely on the strategic objective: keeping Malta in Christian hands. But that seemingly simple objective presupposed a host of competing operational priorities. Valette had to husband his reserves of powder, manpower and—a pivotal factor in sieges often overlooked by armchair strategists—morale, playing them off against one another and what little space he had to trade for time. Don Garcia had to preserve his fragile naval—in fact, amphibious—instrument, but as a means to an end. For them both, and for Don Garcia in particular, there was no safe way out: they had to accept risk; they had to take chances. Both did so with uncommon intelligence informed by rare tactical perspicacity. Both understood just how important Fort St Elmo was and both arrived at that understanding well in advance of the crisis. The fort's provision of heavy ordnance is evidence of Valette's foresight. The earmarked company of Spanish arquebusiers, delivered just in the nick of time, is evidence of Don Garcia's. Moreover, although the Knights of St John would later impugn Don Garcia's competence, pillorying him for his supposed dilatoriness, the two cooperated effectively. They were in intermittent contact throughout the siege, and although conclusive evidence has not survived we can be sure that the timing of the first relief was prompted not so much by Valette's impassioned pleas as by his assessment of the garrison's circumstances in the wake of St Elmo's impending fall. The operation entailed a level of risk and uncertainty that a commander of Don Garcia's experience and competence would have accepted only in the direst of circumstances.

At a lower level organizationally, there is little to choose between Muslim and Christian combatants in bravery, tenacity and skill. Though the desperation common to trapped and highly motivated defenders may have given the Christians a slight edge at times, the willingness of elite Muslim troops to persist in bloody assaults and in the unglamorous work of advancing saps under fire was impressive. While their direction from above may have faltered—with the notable exception of operations under Turgut Re'is' direction—the troops' execution was exemplary. Both sides' skill in operating on the water's edge between galley and land was remarkable, a point we are apt to miss because of the matter-of-fact way in which it is treated by the sources. The gunners on both sides exhibited remarkable standards of competence.

All of this points to perhaps the most basic lesson of all to emerge from the Great Siege: that in amphibious operations success is highly—perhaps uniquely—dependent on the skill, competence and foresight of senior commanders and their staffs.

Bibliography

Archives

MNM   Museo Naval, Madrid
          CN Colección Navarrete
             Colección Sanz de Barutell (Simancas)

Primary Works

Balbi di Correggio F. (1568) *The Siege of Malta 1565* (London: 1565; second edn, Barcelona: 1568).

Collado L. (1592) *Platica Manual de Artilleria* (Milan: 1592; first published as *Practica Manuale di Artigliera*; Venice: 1586).

Secondary Works

Anderson C. (1952) *Naval Wars in the Levant: 1559–1853* (Princeton: 1952).

Blouet B. (1987) *The Story of Malta*, 3rd revised edn (Malta: 1987).

Bradford E. (1961) *The Great Siege* (London: 1961).

Braudel F. (1966) *La Méditerranée et le Monde Méditerranéen a l'Époque de Philippe II*, 2 vols (Paris: 1966).

Cassola A. (1985) with Îdris Bostan and Thomas Scheben. *The 1565 Ottoman Malta Campaign Register* (Valetta, Malta: 1985).

Cayetano R. (1853) *Historia del Combate Naval de Lepanto* (Madrid: 1853).

Duffy C. (1979) *Siege Warfare: The Fortress in the Early Modern World, 1494–1660* (London: 1979).

Guilmartin J. F. (2002) *Galleons and Galleys* (London: 2002).

——. (1993) 'The Logistics of Warfare at Sea in the Sixteenth Century: The Spanish Perspective', in John A. Lynn, ed., *Feeding Mars: Logistics in Western Warfare from the Middle Ages to the Present* (Boulder, Colorado: 1993).

——. (1974) *Gunpowder and Galleys: Changing Technology and Mediterranean Warfare at Sea in the Sixteenth Century* (Cambridge: 1974).

Hess A. C. (1973) 'The Ottoman Conquest of Egypt and the Beginning of the Sixteenth-Century World War', *International Journal of Middle East Studies* 4 (1973).

Kahlifeh H. (1831) *The Maritime Wars of the Turks*, trans. J. Mitchell (London: 1831).

Lynn J. A. (1997) *Giant of the Grand Siècle: The French Army, 1610–1715* (Cambridge: 1997).

——. (1993) 'Early Modern Introduction', and 'Food, Funds, and Fortresses: Resource Mobilization and Positional Warfare in the Campaigns of Louis XIV', in idem, ed., *Feeding Mars: Logistics in Western Warfare from the Middle Ages to the Present* (Boulder, Colo.: 1993) 103–7 and 137–59.

Murphey R. (1999) *Ottoman Warfare, 1500–1700* (Brunswick, New Jersey: 1999).

Olesa Muñido F.-F. (1968) *La Organización Naval de los Estados Mediterraneos, y en Especial de España durante los Siglos XVI y XVII*, 2 vols (Madrid: 1968).

Oman C. (1937) *A History of the Art of War in the Sixteenth Century* (London: 1937).

Önalp C. (1996) 'La Expedición Española Contra la Isla de Gelves en 1560', *Osmanli Tarihi Araştirma ve Uygulama Merkezi Dergisi*, 7 (1996) 135–174.

Prescott W. H. (1904) *History of the Reign of Philip the Second* (Philadelphia: 1904).

Pryor J. H. (1988) *Geography, Technology and War: Studies In the Maritime History of the Mediterranean, 649–1571* (Cambridge: 1988).

Tenenti A. (1962) *Cristoforo da Canal: la Marine Vénitienne avant Lépante* (Paris: 1962).

Whitwell R. J. and C. J. (1926) 'The "Newcastle" Galley, A.D. 1294', *Archaeologia Aeliana*, 4th series, 2 (1926), 142–96.

AMPHIBIOUS OPERATIONS AND THE ELIZABETHAN ASSAULT ON SPAIN'S ATLANTIC ECONOMY 1585–1598

†R. B. Wernham

The Elizabethan war against Spain was first and foremost a land war, fought out in the Netherlands, northern France, and latterly in Ireland. It was fought to keep alive a nascent Dutch republic struggling to shake off Spanish rule and a French monarchy enfeebled by Spanish-fostered civil war. It was fought to avert a Spanish domination of western Europe; but an integral part of the war effort was a conscious assault on Spain's dominions in the New World, and the Atlantic ports in Europe though which Spain's vital Atlantic trade, which largely funded the Habsburg Monarchy's wars, was conducted.

Such a transoceanic and multi-theatre war put an enormous strain upon England's very limited resources. During its first ten years, £100,000 went in aid to the Dutch and over £300,000 in helping Henry IV of France, this from the government's ordinary revenue of not a great deal more than £250,000 a year, supplemented by parliamentary grants of somewhat over £900,000 (£287,000 of that during the last two years) and by savings of £299,000 accumulated before 1585.[1] Almost inevitably, therefore, one of the principal aims of English naval operations was to supplement the Queen's income by plundering the Spaniards.[2] To have captured a treasure fleet, bringing home from America to Spain over £3,000,000 (at its value

---

Professor Wernham died in the spring of 1999, after completion of the first draft of this chapter and after having discussed changes with the editors but before most of those changes had actually been implemented; in consequence this has been done by the editors, who feel privileged to publish the last essay of a very distinguished scholar, especially as it brings together his chief scholarly interests—Elizabethan England's foreign and military policy, and maritime history.

[1] Wernham (1984), 564–67.

[2] Walsingham wrote to Leicester on 9 July 1586 that upon the success of Drake's voyage 'in very truth dependeth the life and death of the cause': Bruce, ed. (1844), 341.

in English money of the time),[3] would have solved the Queen's financial problems many times over, while merely to interrupt the flow of treasure would do much to handicap the preparation of Spain's armadas and to hamstring Spain's main army in the Netherlands. Even to capture one treasure ship or one East Indian carrack might bring not far short of the equivalent of a year's ordinary revenue for Elizabeth. But the more immediately practicable way of enriching both the Queen and her subjects appeared to be by sacking or ransoming Spanish seaports and settlements in both the New World and the Old. For that, soldiers were needed as well as ships and mariners, and most English amphibious operations had such plundering as a principal purpose.

Now, so long as Spain had an ocean-going fleet in being, Elizabeth was naturally reluctant to send more than half a dozen or so of the twenty, rising by fifteen to just over thirty, warships of her royal navy far from home waters—on the two occasions when she did take the risk (in 1596 and 1597) only the weather saved England from invasion. Moreover, Elizabethan England had no standing army. There were doubts about the legality of pressing men for service outside the country, particularly men from the trained bands, and levies for the Netherlands and France suffered a good deal from desertion, even occasional mutinies. On the other hand, for privateering with a share in the booty, there were always investors and volunteers, from merchants in the great London companies, to farm workers in rural Hampshire.[4]

Naturally, therefore, amphibious operations for the acquisition of plunder tended to be left largely to private enterprise with an element of state investment added. They were for the most part continuations and extensions of the privateering or piracy of pre-war days, with the Queen now contributing a few of her ships as part of the cost. Sir Francis Drake's 1585–6 expedition set the pattern.[5]

---

[3] Wright, ed. (1951), xxxii n. 4.

[4] In 1571, during the first quarrel with Spain, farmers and constables along the Hampshire coast were already complaining that they could not be certain of any servant they had, for those servants said openly, 'why should they serve for five nobles or forty shillings a year and might well make their share at sea within one week four or five pounds': PRO, SP Domestic, lxxi, no. 57.

[5] Hakluyt (1927), 7:73–109; Corbett, ed. (1898), 1–96; Wright, ed. (1951), 12–240; Jameson (1934), 14–31; de Castellanos (1921). The chief secondary works are Corbett (1899), 2:1–59; Williamson (1938), 278–89; and especially Andrews, (1967), chap. 6.

Elizabeth still hoped to stay at peace with Philip II of Spain despite giving him the ultimate provocation by despatching 7,000 English troops officially to support his Netherlands rebels. So she gave Drake commission only to make a demonstration on the Spanish coast to secure the release of English merchant ships arrested there after bringing corn to alleviate a crop failure. If he exceeded that commission, well, 'the gentleman careth not if I should disavow him.' Nevertheless, she contributed £10,000, with two other warships, the 600-ton *Elizabeth Bonaventure* and the 250-ton *Aid* reckoned as another £10,000 investment. Government ministers and officials (the Earls of Leicester and Shrewsbury, Lord Chancellor Sir Christopher Hatton, Sir Walter Raleigh and Sir John Hawkins) joined London merchants and leading sea rovers (Drake himself, Martin Frobisher, Christopher Carleill and Thomas Fenner) in providing another nineteen ships, eight pinnaces (besides ten 'carried in poop'), and the remaining £40,000 of the cost. In the fleet there went 2,300 mariners and soldiers, the soldiers (1,200 or 1,300 of them) in twelve companies, were volunteers or men 'volunteered' by their masters, for the most part raw recruits, not 'even so trained as to know but some part of their order.'[6]

With these forces Drake set sail from Plymouth on 14 September 1585. Obediently he began by demonstrating off Bayona and Vigo. There he was further delayed by bad weather, so that he could not leave until a day or two after (he learnt to his chagrin) the last of the year's treasure fleets arrived safely in San Lucas.[7] It may well have been hope of catching them, as much as fear of the Queen staying his voyage, that had caused him to leave Plymouth in great haste, tumbling his stores, etc. higgledy-piggledy aboard whichever ship was nearest to hand. To get things sorted out and to organise and exercise his raw soldiery, he moved on from Bayona to Santiago in the Cape Verde Islands. There he met no resistance but also found no plunder beyond a few cannon and some church bells.

---

[6] Corbett, ed. (1898), 42. Spanish opinion often was even lower: Wright, ed. (1951), 121–22.

[7] 'It escaped us but twelve hours the whole treasure which the King of Spain had out of the Indies this last year, the cause best known to God; we had that instant very foul weather': Drake to Burghley, 26 July 1586, in Corbett, ed. (1898), 84. That this refers to October 1585 is clear from Bravo's evidence: Wright, ed. (1951), 122.

After a ten-day rest at Dominica on the uninhabited St Kitts, necessitated by a fever epidemic among his soldiers, Drake set out against the first of his Caribbean targets, Santo Domingo in Hispaniola. A few ships that he sent ahead discovered the only practicable landing place on that surf-battered coast apart from the one directly under the guns of Santo Domingo's castle. It was ten miles from the city and a few Spaniards kept watch there at night. Drake, however, made contact with the native Maroons who duly dealt with the watch. So he was able to land Carleill with about 1,000 troops without alerting the city, towards which they marched through the night. Meanwhile Drake and the ships sailed round and at daybreak began to threaten a landing under the castle. The Spanish forces, horse and foot, came out to oppose it, but suddenly found Carleill falling upon them from the rear. Cut off from the city, they fled by boat across the harbour to the countryside, the castle garrison following them during the night. For the next month the English stayed in Santo Domingo, virtually undisturbed. They took a few ships in the harbour, captured 240 guns, 'set part of their castle on fire and burned all their images of wood, broke and destroyed all their fairest work within their churches. We had in this town much plate, money, and pearl hidden in walls and other places.'[8] But all that fell far short of the 500,000 ducats that Drake was said to have hoped to gain there in plunder and ransom![9] After destroying part of the city, he had to be content with 25,000 ducats (under £5,000) as ransom for the rest.

Thereupon, on 1 February 1586, he left Santo Domingo and sailed off southwards for the Spanish Main. Contrary winds forced him away to the west of his first targets there and brought him, after a brief look-in at Rio de la Hacha on 9 February, to Cartagena, the chief trade centre of those parts. It was from there that the *flota* of Tierra Firme, after collecting at Nombre de Dios the tribute of Peru and the rich output of the Potosí silver mines, sailed to join the Mexican *flota* at Havana in the spring for the long voyage back to Spain. Cartagena lay at the head of a large lagoon that formed its harbour. The main entrance was the deep-water, 1,400 yard-wide Boca Grande, about half a league westwards of the town. A league

---

[8] Corbett, ed. (1898), 18.
[9] Ibid., 71.

farther on was the narrower Boca Chica, with a deep channel between rocks and only 200 yards wide. It was through this that Drake piloted his ships into the outer harbour. He there turned back and anchored just inside the Boca Grande. There, as dusk fell, he landed Carleill with about six companies of troops on the narrow strip of land that led back to the town.

At midnight they began to feel their way slowly forward, in an assault that gives a very good idea of the texture of combined operations 'at the water's edge'. After three and a half miles covered in the face only of negligible resistance, they came to a narrow neck of land, barely fifty paces wide, between the sea and the inner harbour. Across this were a ditch and a stone wall with six demi-culverins and sakers[10] mounted on it. Just in front, along the inner harbour shore, 300 troops were stationed. Behind them were another eleven pieces of ordnance planted in two galleys aboard which were another 300 shot and pikes. These forces very effectively covered the pathway but Carleill marched his troops along the very edge of the water down on the seaward side where most of the enemy's fire passed harmlessly over their heads. Moreover, this brought them to the one weak spot in the defences, a gap between the end of the wall and the sea, left for horsemen and carts to go out and in. There the defenders crowded behind wine barrels filled with earth. The English shot gave a volley 'even at the enemy's nose' and then all rushed forward. 'Down went the butts of earth and pell-mell came our swords and pikes together . . . Our pikes were somewhat longer than theirs and our bodies better armed [i.e. armoured], for very few of them were armed',[11] and they fled back into the town, followed by the rest of the defenders of the wall. Earlier Frobisher, a mile and a half away to the south with some pinnaces, had heard the shooting at the encounter with the horsemen and had thereupon landed his feint attack upon the fort that guarded the landward side of the narrow, chained, entrance to the inner harbour. The Spaniards, who had been given very inflated reports of the English numbers, feared that this heralded another, larger, attack from their rear; although a few of them attempted to stand at street barricades, most fled 'to their wives whom they had carried into other places of the

---

[10] Guns firing shot of approximately 9 lb and 6 lb weight respectively.
[11] Hakluyt (1927), 7:95.

country before our coming',[12] leaving Carleill in full possession of the town. Next day the enemy ran the two galleys ashore and burned them and abandoned the fort.

From Cartagena Drake had hoped to move on to Nombre de Dios and from there to send the bulk of his troops into the hinterland: on small pinnaces and boats up the Chagres river and then overland by mule track the remaining five leagues to Panama. He had hoped at least to sack that city, perhaps with luck to capture the year's treasure and silver from Peru and the Potosí mines as they were gathered for transport onwards across the Isthmus to the *flota*. But the sickness contracted at Santiago had already reduced his soldiers to a bare 700 fit for duty. That, as his land captains agreed on 27 February, ruled out any further major enterprise. They believed they could hold Cartagena, provided the sea captains could guarantee them against the armada reported to be coming from Spain, but they advised accepting the £27,000 or £28,000 ransom the town was offering and then making for home. Once again it was a very disappointing sum. Before leaving England Drake had apparently hoped for a million ducats from Cartagena and a million from Panama. After capturing Cartagena he had demanded £100,000 for its ransom. Eventually after six weeks' bargaining and burning, all he obtained was 110,000 ducats, or £30,250 with another £300 for sparing a monastery outside the walls. With that, he set sail on 31 March, only to return for a week a few days later to unload a sinking prize and with the Spanish governor's trembling 'assent, to use the town's ovens before more biscuit for his fleet.'

Drake finally got away on 18 April and nine days later arrived off Cape San Antonio at the western tip of Cuba. There, before leaving for England he had hoped, as a crowning achievement, to capture the final assembly port of the *flotas*, Havana, possibly even to leave his troops to hold it. With his now sadly depleted forces he had to forego such hopes. He got past Havana and as far as Metanzas, where on 23 May (having been delayed by contrary winds—a constant problem for early-modern combined operations), he turned north to the coast of Florida. He kept the shore in sight, looking for St. Elena, a Spanish outpost lying between the settlement Raleigh

---

[12] Ibid.

and Granville were trying to establish at Roanoke and the *flotas* homeward route from Havana. He failed to find it, but did discover and destroy St. Augustine, a place of 250 houses guarded by a fort with a company of foot. He then moved on to Roanoke, the commander and garrison of which he took on board his ships, at their request. They all arrived safely back at Plymouth on 28 July 1586.

The expedition had thus failed to achieve any of its objectives. It had missed the treasure *flotas*. Far from establishing an outpost at Havana or elsewhere in the Spanish Indies, it had evacuated the Roanoke settlement, England's only foothold in the New World. It brought back only enough booty to repay its investors fifteen shillings in the pound.[13] The Queen, instead of the million ducats (£275,000) that Drake apparently had promised her,[14] got back her two ships (now valued at £8,000) and in addition £6,696 16s 4d worth of captured brass ordnance and £654 in pearls.[15] Nevertheless, the expedition had not been a failure. Indeed as Burghley wrote, 'truly Sir Frances Drake is a fearful man to the King of Spain.' The arrogant impunity of his behaviour off the Spanish mainland, off Bayona and Vigo, had given new heart to Spain's continental enemies, dejected by Parma's capture of Antwerp. He had also laid bare the weak defenceless condition of the Spanish Indies and made them weaker still by denuding them of so much of their artillery. Over the next few years, it is true, 'the Spaniards were able to repair and considerably strengthen those defences.' They were allowed to do so because Drake's 1585–86 expedition, coming on top of the despatch of Leicester and 7,000 English troops to aid the Dutch, at last convinced Philip II to build up his Atlantic sea power to settle finally with Elizabethan England.

To disrupt the preparations of that Armada was the primary purpose of Drake's next expedition, in 1587.[16] In this he again took ten companies of soldiers (1,000 men), but the troops took no part in 'singeing the king of Spain's beard'—the famous raid into Cadiz harbour on 19 April, in which Drake plundered '32 shippes of

---

[13] Corbett, ed. (1898), 85–96.
[14] Wright, ed. (1951).
[15] Corbett, ed. (1898), 94–95.
[16] Corbett (1898) 97–206; Hakluyt (1927) 4:281–85. The chief secondary accounts are in Corbett (1899), 2:60–107, and more especially Mattingley (1959), 86–122 and Andrews (1967), 110–24.

exceeding great burthen, laden, and to be laden, with provision' for the invasion of England. They also took no part in the final episode: the capture of the homeward-bound East India carrack, the *San Felipe*, with its £114,000 cargo, £40,000 of which went to the Queen. In the meantime, however, the troops had done an important service by securing the fleet a safe anchorage and watering place

Early on 5 May about a thousand men were landed near Lagos, but found the town too strongly fortified for them to capture. They were promptly withdrawn. Eight hundred of them were then landed again close to Avelera castle, whose small garrison fled to Cape Sagres castle. Sagres castle, whose guns commanded the anchorage, was guarded on three sides by 'a marvelous high upright cliff' and in front by a battlemented wall, forty feet high.[17] Drake, under cover of a hail of small shot, brought up faggots to set fire to the gate. After a couple of hours, the garrison surrendered. Next day the English troops moved westwards and captured another castle and also the fortified friary and castle of Cape St. Vincent. The capture and dismantling of those four castles secured Drake a safe anchorage, from which the fleet was able in two and a half weeks to intercept and destroy the flow of essential supplies coming up from the south and the Mediterranean to Lisbon, the main base of the slowly gathering Armada. The destruction, in particular, of a great quantity of pipe staves, necessary for making water barrels, was a vital blow against Philip II's invasion plans.

Drake might have stayed even longer had the lure of the rich homecoming carrack not distracted him. However, by abandoning his station at Cape Sagres and sailing off westwards in search of the carrack, he achieved even more. Philip II, fearing he had gone to intercept the treasure *flotas*, ordered Santa Cruz to sea in pursuit and Santa Cruz eventually sailed off with a substantial part of the Armada's fighting galleons. It was October before he got back to Lisbon with his ships and crews in no shape to set out again that year for England. The brief episode at Sagres in 1587 showed how effective even Elizabethan amphibious operations could be when limited strictly to precise strategic aims, and when naval and military elements were kept in appropriate balance.

---

[17] Corbett, ed. (1898), 136.

The great expedition of Norris and Drake to Portugal two years later manifested what disastrous results could follow when the private enterprise contributions heavily outbalanced those of the state and when the military element outweighed the naval.[18] The original plan for this 1589 expedition, as agreed with Norris and Drake on 20 September 1588, was to:

(1) attempt to burn the ships in Lisbon and Seville;
(2) take Lisbon;
(3) capture the Azores.

These were reasonable aims. Lisbon was as much the main, essential, base of Spain's Atlantic fleet as the Medway/Thames was of the English navy; Seville was the centre of Spanish traffic with America; and the Azores were a vital staging point for the treasure ships from America.

The forces envisaged for these operations were likewise appropriate. Six of Her Majesty's warships, the *Revenge* and *Nonpareil* (500 tons), *Dreadnought* (400), *Swiftsure* (360), *Foresight* (300), and *Aid* (240) with two pinnaces; with twenty of 150 tons and upward from London and other ports; and permission to freight others; transports for a military contingent of 8,000 English troops with a battery of six siege guns; and it was hoped, 4,000 Dutch with their own transports. The shipping should have been adequate to deal with the battered survivors of the Armada. The military contingent was certainly considerable, but 1587 had shown that it would be too dangerous for ships alone to try to force their way up the Tagus without the support of a land force strong enough to master the castles and batteries at Cascaes, St Julian, and Belorn, and possibly to occupy Lisbon itself.

The September discussions however, had also taken note of 'Mr. Cavendish offers for a trade into the Indias' [he had just returned from a voyage round the world], and of 'Articles of offers from the King Antonio' [the Portuguese pretender].[19] Both of these held a

---

[18] Most of the relevant English documents are printed in Wernham (1988); see also *CSP Span.*, *CSP Ven.* and Monson (1902), 1:177–225. The chief secondary works, besides the two introductions to Wernham (1988) and Monson (1902), are Wernham (1984) 1–130; Andrews (1967); Cheyney (1914), 153–89; Corbett (1899), 2: 286–333; and Hume, (1896), 2–72.

[19] Wernham, ed. (1988), 11.

strong appeal for some of the great London merchants who were investing in the expedition. Drake, too, had been dealing with Don Antonio since 1583. There was thus from the beginning the possibility of a serious divergence of aims between the government and the private investors, Drake among them. And indeed in the euphoria after the defeat of the 1588 Armada, an enormous outburst of popular enthusiasm for the expedition did dangerously increase the private enterprise element in its composition. The shipping rose to over 100 sail, though only a bare half dozen could compare with the Queen's six in tonnage and firepower. Similarly, by the time the expedition assembled at Plymouth, volunteers had poured in, in such numbers that the army had been 'almost double increased'—according to a list of April 8 from Norris and Drake, to 17,390 men.[20]

All this had driven the Queen's original promised contribution of £20,000 up by now to £37,609,[21] besides another £11,678 for the pay of English troops withdrawn from the Netherlands when the States proved unwilling to provide the hoped for Dutch troops. Also, of course, the enormous expansion of the private enterprise element in the expedition made it much harder for the Queen to keep it to its original strategic purpose—burning the ships and seizing the Azores. It was all the harder because the battered survivors of the Armada had been unable to make Lisbon and had been forced by westerly gales most of them to Santander, others to San Sebastian and elsewhere toward or deep in the corner of the Bay of Biscay. There they were well off the direct route to Lisbon and the Islands, little plunder was to be looked for, and the overgrown English expedition was an unwieldy instrument for operations so deep into the Bay.

Elizabeth did what she could to keep the expedition on course. Her instructions to Norris and Drake (23 February 1589) went straight to the point:

> Forasmuch as the dire and principal end of the setting forth of our army under your charge tendeth chiefly to two purposes, the one to distress the king of Spain's ships; the other to get the possession of some of the Islands of the Azores thereby to intercept the convoys of the treasure that doth yearly pass that way to and from the West and

---

[20] Ibid., 118, 340.
[21] Ibid., 323.

East Indies; we would have you direct the whole course of your proceedings in such sort as may best serve to accomplish and perform the said two ends and purposes.[22]

In later instructions she reiterated that

before you attempt anything either in Portugal or in the said Islands, our express pleasure and commandment is that you shall first distress the ships of war in Guipizcoa, Biscay, Galicia, and in any other places that appertain either to the King of Spain or his subjects.

Nor should they attempt anything in Portugal unless they found 'upon good ground' that Don Antonio had great and as well affected a party there 'as he pretendeth', and that no great Spanish forces were assembled there. And three months later she was to remind them that

you did at sundry times so far forth promise as with oaths to assure us and some of our Council that your first and principal action should be to take and distress the King of Spain's navy and ships in ports where they lay. Which if ye did not ye affirmed that ye were content to be reputed as traitors.[23]

Possibly it was as a further restraint that she failed to provide the six siege guns.

For it is clear that Norris and Drake, even before they sailed from Plymouth, had decided to ignore Santander, San Sebastian and make straight for Portugal. Sir Roger Williams, commissioned as land commander should Norris become incapacitated, must have known their intentions better than anyone. So it is significant that when the young Earl of Essex galloped away from court to join the expedition in defiance of the Queen's orders, and with Williams on the *Swiftsure*, shipped away from the fleet to avoid recall, they made straight for Portugal. Don Antonio's assurances of enthusiastic and widespread support in Portugal clearly had proved too tempting to the soldiers, especially with their number now so swollen. His promises of commercial privileges and of letting the English into Portuguese trade with the Orient proved equally seductive to many investing merchants. And Drake, the naval commander, with his high respect for

---

[22] Ibid., 82–88.
[23] Ibid., 165.

soldiers, his arrogant contempt for Spanish sea power, and his long connections with Don Antonio, was no less readily seduced.

It seems clear, therefore, that Norris and Drake, the two joint commanders, were determined even before they left England to ignore the Queen's orders about Santander and to sail directly to Portugal. But it does also look quite likely that they had different ideas of what to do when they got there. One of the Spanish spies in Don Antonio's household wrote in March that 'it is whispered the landing will take place' at Peniche, some forty-five miles north of Lisbon.[24] On the other hand there is among the English state papers a 'Project' for a landing eastward of Cascaes and a bold dash up the Tagus, with land and sea forces in close visual contact, to force a way past St Julian and the other forts and so straight into Lisbon.[25] Now it seems quite possible that Drake himself was the author of this 'Project.' It has all the directness and dash that he had shown in 1587 and he did later write that 'if we had not been commanded to the contrary, but had landed at Lisbon, all had been as we could have desired it.'[26]

In this Drake was blaming the expedition's failure in Portugal upon the initial two weeks spent in attacking Coruña, conveniently forgetting that they had gone to Coruña not by the Queen's orders, which were much more concerned with Santander, but because before they left Plymouth a report came in 'that there are arrived to the number of 200 sail of ships of divers nations at the Groyne [Coruña] and other parts of Galicia and Portugal with store of ammunition, masts, cables, and other provisions for the enemy.'[27] Coruña was an unlikely destination for 200 laden merchantmen. But it was on the direct way to Lisbon and worth a brief inspection to make sure. For to capture a large number of those merchantmen and their contraband cargoes might go far to satisfy the investors in the expedition, the Queen among them. However, when it arrived

---

[24] *CSP Span.*, 524.
[25] Wernham, ed. (1988), 105–6. In my introduction (ibid., xxxi, xxxvii, xlvii) and elsewhere (Wernham (1984), 105), I suggested Sir Roger Williams as the author of this 'Project.' On further consideration I am now inclined to agree with Corbett (1899), 2:309, 321–22, and Hume (1896), 45–46, that the most likely author was Drake himself.
[26] Wernham, ed. (1988), 130.
[27] Ibid., 141.

off Coruña on April 23 and entered the harbour next day, all it found was two ill-manned Armada survivors, a hulk, a ship laden with pikes and firearms and a couple of galleys.

These few were hardly worth bothering about, but the soldiers, anxious to stretch their legs and display their prowess, now took control. Within three hours Norris had landed 7,000 of them on the narrow isthmus joining Coruña to the mainland. Next day he got another 2,000 ashore, with two demi-culverins. On 26 April they took the lower town; her crew burned the galleon *San Juan*, and the other three ships were captured. In the lower town the considerable stores of victuals, clothing, etc. were thoroughly rifled. A good deal of it was rotting and infectious, and together with the effects of the well stocked wine cellars on beer drinking English soldiery, produced an epidemic comparable to that acquired by the 1585 expedition at Santiago.

By now the English had done all, and more than all, that was worth doing at Coruña. Norris, however, went on to attack the far more difficult clifftop upper town, while small parties of his troops raided for a dozen or more miles in the countryside to the east. He excused this further delay by saying that he heard there was much munition and victual in the upper town, and that the wind was contrary (though they sailed with it still contrary six days later). He brought ashore a couple of demi-cannon to supplement the two demi-culverins, but one broke its carriage after a single shot and the rest had to cease firing because nothing had been provided to protect the gunners against enemy small shot. Also, in an attempt to explode a mine under one of the towers 'the powder broke out backwards.'[28] Eventually the guns did make a breach in the wall and the mine brought half the tower down. But 'the English common soldier [was] not well acquainted with matters of breach.'[29] Those assaulting the tower fled in panic when its other half began to fall down on them. Those assaulting the wall rushed forward overeagerly and found the rubble giving way under their weight, leaving half the wall still standing. Then on 6 May, hearing that Spanish troops—15,000; then 10,000; finally 8,000—were gathered at Puerto de Burgos, four or five miles to the east, Norris marched out with

[28] Wernham, ed. (1988), 262.
[29] Ibid., 150.

7,000 English and speedily routed them. This success against raw ill-armed local levies convinced the English 'that an army of 10,000 men, good soldiers, may pass through the whole realm without great danger' and emboldened Norris not only to demand the promised siege train but also thirty other old companies from the Netherlands (all that were left there of the auxiliary companies) 'to continue the war here all this year.'[30]

On 8 May, the day that Norris wrote those demands, the troops were at last re-embarked, leaving the upper town untaken. Next day the expedition sailed off, not eastwards toward Santander—a group of expert shipmasters and sea captains conveniently advised strongly against that—but southwards for Portugal. Picking up the *Swiftsure* with Essex and Williams on the way, it arrived on 15 May off Cape la Roca, just around the corner from Cascaes and the mouth of the Tagus. But that 'idle vain siege' of Coruña had given the enemy in Portugal '20 days respite to arm and put themselves in order.'[31] The Spanish viceroy, Philip II's able nephew the Cardinal Archduke Albert, had also been given time to round up any who might conceivably have led a rising for Don Antonio, though it is hard to believe that there would ever have been a large scale uprising by the Catholic Portuguese for a pretender coming in the baggage train of a heretic army. However, the delay at Coruña had also allowed desertion and disease to reduce the English army to little more than 10,000 men. Presumably for these reasons a council of war now decided to go back and land the army at Peniche, the place which, it had been 'whispered' back in March, had originally been intended. It is not known whether Drake or anyone spoke up for a direct approach to Lisbon up the Tagus, as the 'Project' had suggested. But anyway, Drake, as one of the joint commanders, could hardly have ridden roughshod over a council led by his fellow commander Norris, a famous soldier and a peer's son, as he had overridden his fellow sailor William Borough in 1586.

To land at Peniche, however, was to reduce the land operations in Portugal to a mere reconnaissance in force, a reconnaissance to test the real strength of Don Antonio's 'pretended' support. And when Norris and Essex marched off from Peniche on 18 May with

---

[30] Ibid., 149, 153.
[31] Ibid., 220, 224.

about 6,000 troops, they soon found that support to be indeed only
pretended—in the modern sense of the word. Less than 200 Portuguese
soldiers—'and those the greatest cowards that ever I saw,' Williams
wrote—deserted to them; a few barefoot friars and 'other mean people' gave them a mild welcome, and one gentlewoman brought Don
Antonio a basketful of cherries and plums.[32] That was all that came
of the fulsome promises which Norris and Drake had never attempted
to verify—they admitted later that before landing at Peniche 'they
never received any advice out of the country.'[33] They had based
their whole conduct of the expedition upon the hollow untested assurances of a fugitive, desperate, bankrupt pretender.

The six days' dusty march from Peniche to Lisbon, under a blis-
tering sun and with seriously inadequate transport, also decimated
the English troops by fostering the diseases picked up in the storehouses and wine cellars of Coruña. So the Spanish forces, which
probably outnumbered the English, made no attempt to halt the
march, except for a pre-dawn camisado on 22 May, and Essex and
Norris eventually arrived before Lisbon on the evening of 23 May.[34]
Many of their troops, already an inadequate number, were sickly or
exhausted. They had spent most of such powder and match as they
had been able to carry with them. They had no artillery, not even
a couple of demi-cannon and culverins as at Coruña. And Norris
found the walls of Lisbon 'very high and strong, contrary to that
which was told him.'[35] There was thus no need for any serious opposition from the garrison of the city, which anyway outnumbered the
besiegers. There was some skirmishing in the suburbs during the
morning of 24 May. A sally at noon that day, while the English
were enjoying a siesta, was repulsed back to the gates of Lisbon,
upon which Essex knocked with his pike in vain.

That was indeed about all he and Norris could hope to do. Another
desperate promise by Don Antonio on May 25 that 3,000 Portuguese
would join him in arms next morning persuaded Norris to stay on
that one more night. On the morning of 26 May there was no sign
of the phantom 3,000, so the army marched off for Cascaes. Now

---

[32] Ibid., 177, 190, 238.
[33] Ibid., 293.
[34] For this date, see ibid., appendix III.
[35] Ibid., 184.

the full folly of the Peniche landing became apparent. Just then some sixty unsuspecting Hanseatic and French merchantmen— presumably the ghostly 200 not found at Coruña—laden with corn, cables, masts and copper, sailed in. Drake was busy rounding up these ships when on 25 May, for the first time since the 8th, he got news of Norris and the army, news that they were in the suburbs of Lisbon. He at once called together a council of war of captains and shipmasters. They strongly advised against any attempt by ships alone to force their way up the Tagus to Lisbon. Drake, however, boldly overruled them and began immediately to prepare 'two thirds part of the best ships of the navy and best manned' to sail up past St Julian as soon as the wind turned favourable, leaving the other third to guard Cascaes. The wind did not come favourable until the morning of 27 May. On the previous evening Norris and his troops had marched into Cascaes.[36]

For almost another fortnight fleet and army stayed virtually unmolested around Cascaes, 'thinking to make a second attempt upon the city [Lisbon] if by any means our wants could be supplied either by the King [Don Antonio] or out of England.'[37] But the military contingent was reduced to 5,735 serviceable men and 2,791 sick, and Don Antonio's promises had lost all credibility. So on 3 June it was decided to sail for the Azores. The troops were barely all reembarked when on 6 June letters from the Queen arrived, dashing all hope of reinforcements from home. Ten days of very strong winds then forced the fleet northwards towards the Isles of Bayona, where, on 20 June, 2,000 troops—'as many men as were able to fight'— were landed before Vigo.[38] The town, empty of inhabitants and all things except a great store of wine, was duly fired, and it was decided that the troops this time were to make their way with Norris back to England. Drake with the Queen's ships and a dozen or so others was to try again for the Azores, but that too was again frustrated by violent storms. By 3 July, practically all the expedition had straggled back to Plymouth and nearby ports, having accomplished virtually nothing. And by the end of that month sixty of the survivors from the 1588 Armada set sail from Santander for Lisbon. Spain had an Atlantic fleet in being once again.

---

[36] Ibid., 294.
[37] Ibid., 180.
[38] Ibid., 279.

This fleet was not yet ready to renew the attempt upon England, but it would soon be strong enough to escort home the American treasure ships. As an English intelligencer wrote from St Jean-de-Luz on 15 July:

> If Sir Francis had gone to Santander as he went to end the Groyne, he had done such a service as never subject had done. For with twelve sail of his ships he might have destroyed all the forces which the Spaniards has there, which was the whole strength of the country by sea. There they did lie, all unrigged and the ordnance on the shore and some 20 men only in a ship to keep them. It was far overseen that he had not gone hither first.[39]

That disastrous oversight did indeed allow a rebirth of Spain's Atlantic sea power. By 1594 it was threatening to acquire an advanced base at Brest. The only adequate deep water haven on the southern side of the English Channel, not only was it capable in its roads of sheltering '1,000 ships of greatest burden', but in addition, because the prevailing winds 'blew from between south and west', if those ships embarked for England they would have the weather-gauge over any defending English squadrons.[40] This threat was only prevented by the actions of troops under Sir John Norris, serving alongside the forces of Elizabeth's ally, Henry IV of France, and supported by a squadron commanded by Sir Martin Frobisher.

A small English army, commanded by Norris, had been operating in Brittany since 1591. Following Henry IV's conversion to Catholicism in July 1593, Spain's Breton allies, the Duke of Mercoeur and the Catholic Leaguers, had concluded truces and seemed on the way to deserting to the Royalists. So in late March 1594 the Spanish forces from Blavet marched into the Crozon peninsula. On its extreme north point, still named the Pointe des Espagnols, they built a fort commanding the narrow entrance to Brest Roads on the southern side, and it was reported that they meant to build another opposite on the north side about the Point de Portzie. That was a threat that England could not ignore.

The first reaction was to plan for a powerful expedition of 6,000 or 7,000 or more English troops and maybe twenty of the Queen's ships, commanded jointly by the Earl of Essex and Lord Admiral

---

[39] Ibid., 217.
[40] L&A, 196; Wernham (1961), 341; see also Stapleton, ch. 10, below, pp. 336–7.

Howard, to expel the Spaniards from Blavet and all Brittany.[41] Eventually, however, in late July a more modest operation with a more modest objective was decided on.[42] Sir John Norris was to continue in command of the land forces. He was to take over 2,000 men newly levied in England to bring the twenty-six companies of his army up to their full strength of 4,000. With seven companies, 1,000 men, recently brought over from the Netherlands, he would thus have an unusually high proportion of seasoned troops. He would also have 100 horse, fifty miners, and eighteen gunners with an extra six heavy cannon. The naval contingent, now under Sir Martin Frobisher, was also reduced to four Queen's ships—the *Vanguard* and *Rainbow*, and the rather smaller *Quittance* and *Crane*—with two other pinnaces, the *Charles* and *Moon*, six London armed merchantmen, and eight Dutch ships.[43] These naval forces were to be used *only* 'to such end as may necessarily and directly tend to the recovery of the fort [Crozon] and clearing the said haven' of Brest.[44]

Due to contrary winds, it was 1 September before Norris and his men landed at Paimpol. From there he hastened to join the other English troops and the Breton Royalist commander, Marshal Aumont, who were clearing the northern approaches to Brest by taking Morlaix. The castle there surrendered upon sight of Norris' cannon being landed and Norris was eager to press on against Fort Crozon, but Aumont took his time. It was therefore 2 October before Norris, with 1,000 of the English foot, leaving the rest to secure Quimper (and thus Brest's southern approaches), arrived before Fort Crozon, which Frobisher had been occasionally bombarding with his ships for the past month.[45]

---

[41] Wernham (1984), 321–36.

[42] The principal sources for this operation are in *L&A*, vol. 5; *CSP Dom. 1591–94*; *HMC Sal.*, vol. 4; Monson (1902), vol. 1; de Carné, ed. (1899); van Meteren (1602). For modern accounts see Cheyney (1914), 299–304 (somewhat cursory); Nolan (1995); and Wernham (1984), 521–54, which treats the French and Dutch diplomatic background rather more; see also below, Fissel, ch. 7, pp. 229–32.

[43] The *Swiftsure* and *Dreadnought* were at first included but apparently did not in the end go. Oppenheim, in Monson (1902), 1:304, from the Pipe Office Declared Account 223 l.

[44] *L&A*, 5, no. 334.

[45] Ibid., no. 340. Frobisher had also on 23 Sept. landed 400 sailors to support a small force of French horse that had been sent forward to close the approaches to the fort: ibid., no. 345; van Meteren (1602), 135.

Fort Crozon was built on a three-sided promontory. Two sides fell sheer to the sea; the third, a steep slope no more than 250 paces wide, was barred at the top by a ditch and a wall with flanking bastions at either end. The slope up provided hardly so much as a shrub to cover besiegers from the fort's guns and small arms, which indeed killed a senior English officer, Anthony Wingfield, and a dozen more on 8 October. The trenches therefore had to be dug almost half a mile back and, because in many places there was no more than a couple of feet of soil above the solid rock, trenches and artillery platforms often had to be fronted with curves and sandbags several feet high. Strong westerly winds and almost incessant rains made matters worse. The trenches were often deep in water and Frobisher's ships were forced several times to seek refuge in Brest Roads.

It is little wonder, therefore, that it was 23 October before the artillery could be mounted and the battery begun. Eventually fourteen pieces were mounted—two French culverins, two landed from the Dutch warships, the six cannon Norris had brought from England, two culverins from the *Vanguard*, and two demi-cannons from the *Rainbow*. The importance of heavy cannon landed from ships is once again revealed. The battery's first 300 shots, aimed at the wall, did little more than shake down bits of the turf and faggot covering. Another 800 shots, however, aimed at the parapet, did enough damage to encourage Norris to attempt a lodgement in the ditch, but this was repulsed with considerable loss. To make matters worse, ten barrels of English gunpowder were exploded by a careless gunner, burning about fifty men.[46] The besiegers' position was beginning to cause anxiety. The English had over 1,500 men sick or wounded of their original 4,603; until a reinforcement of 400 arrived on 7 November, the French were down to a mere 600 or 700, and every night Norris had to send them 300 of his Englishmen.[47] Together they were little if at all stronger than the 400 men of the Fort's garrison and the 3,000 Spaniards that were advancing slowly from Blavet to its relief. Moreover, it was getting late in the year for Frobisher's ships to stay in those stormy and rock-strewn waters.

---

[46] *L&A*, 5: no. 351; van Meteren (1602), 137–9.
[47] *L&A*, 5: nos. 298, 349.

Indeed, Aumont and his council of war now decided to abandon the siege, until Norris sharply told him that the English would continue it, whatever the French might do. Norris surely found it easier to reach this remarkably bold decision because of his expedition's focused objective; there was no plundering to be done, only a clear strategic end to be reached, however difficult in practice. Sir John's resolution persuaded the Marshal to change his mind and order a general assault on 7 November.[48] From eleven in the morning attack after attack was launched, with small success and considerable casualties. Finally just as the November sun was setting the attackers at last broke through and relentlessly slaughtered the garrison almost to a man. Sixty English and 400 French soldiers had lost their lives.[49] Frobisher, who had come ashore with a contingent of his sailors to reinforce the assault, was wounded and died of gangrene as he got back to Plymouth.

Although by February 1595 the remarkable improvement in Henry IV's general position and the terminal collapse of the Catholic League as a result of his conversion had allowed the withdrawal of the last English troops from France, the burden of the war upon England's limited resources showed little sign of diminishing. The military situation in Picardy and Brittany still gave increasing cause for anxiety; in Ireland O'Neill and O'Donnell were in open rebellion; and in Spain a new Armada was clearly preparing. All this required or threatened substantial increases in expenditure. Parliament had, it is true, in 1593 voted taxation worth around £400,000, but it had spread the collection over four years. Pressure on the Dutch to repay £100,000 of the Queen's past expenses in their behalf proved unavailing. A long series of naval and privateering operations had captured the rich East Indian carrack the *Madre de Dios* in 1592 but had totally failed to intercept any of Spain's treasure from the New World. It was therefore natural that thoughts turned once again to Drake's old idea of catching that treasure at its dispatching end: at Panama, Nombre de Dios, or Havana.

On 29 January 1595 Hawkins and Drake received the Queen's commission for just such an operation.[50] For various reasons it was

[48] Ibid., no. 351; van Meteren (1602), 139–40; Moreau (1960), 198–9, 202.

[49] *L&A*, 5: no. 355; van Meteren (1602), 140–1; Moreau (1960), 202–5.

[50] The sources are printed or listed in Andrews, ed. (1972); see also Hakluyt (1927), 7:183–212. For secondary accounts, see the editorial commentaries in Andrews,

late July before they had assembled a force of six Queen's warships, seven 200 to 330-ton Londoners and fourteen smaller vessels, with about 1,500 sailors and almost 1,000 soldiers. Then the alarms over Spanish naval preparations threatened to keep them in the eastern Atlantic. They only got away when they learned from prisoners from a captured Puerto Rico frigate that a treasure ship of the 1595 *flota*, the 350-ton *Begoña*, had been dismasted in a storm and forced to seek shelter in San Juan de Puerto Rico with two and a half million ducats aboard her. This persuaded the Queen to let them sail, on condition that they were home by May.

All this virtually ensured that the expedition lost its, admittedly extremely optimistic, strategic purpose and became yet another voyage for plunder. For, if once they got those two and a half million ducats in their holds, the temptation to run for home would be overpowering; and anyway, they could not hold Panama for long enough to significantly disrupt the flow of treasure if they were to be home by May 1596. From now on things went from bad to worse. Drake, not for the first time, had sailed with his logistics inadequate or in a muddle. To Hawkins' extreme annoyance, but with the support of Sir Thomas Baskerville (commander of the land forces) and his soldiers, Drake now insisted on a detour to the Grand Canary where 'much honour and good refreshment' might be had. The Spanish defences, however, frightened them off a landing at Las Palmas. The time spent also allowed five fast sailing Spanish frigates to get ahead of them. The frigates had just set sail from San Lucar to fetch home the *Begoña* treasure. Off Guadeloupe they captured the 35-ton *Francis* and, learning from their crew of Hawkins and Drake's approach, were able to give San Juan nine days' warning of its danger. The delay allowed San Juan's defenders to learn of the threat and prepare sufficiently for an amphibious attack. Their preparations included, vitally, landing the guns and gunners, the munitions, powder and match from the frigates and the *Begoña*—without these, the Spanish believed the island could not have been successfully defended.[51] On 22 November, Drake approached San

---

ed. (1972) and the penultimate chapter of Andrews (1967) 158–79; see also Corbett (1899), 2:375–400, Williamson (1927), 471–90, and Wernham (1994), 24–54.

[51] Andrews, ed. (1972), 151–2. See Map 9.

Juan Island from the east, and dropped anchor within cannon shot
of the Matadiabolo battery that protected the inlet of the Boqueron
lagoon, the entrance to the San Antonio Channel (guarded by San
Antonio fort) and the southern side of the islet. The Matadiabolo
guns fired 28 rounds, one of which burst into Drake's own cabin,
slaying two officers dining at his table. The following evening, 23
November, Drake approached from the west and struck more directly
at the harbor of San Juan, braving the formidable fortifications of
the El Morro fortress in a nocturnal assault led by shallow draught
boats that could evade the sunken hulks blocking the harbour mouth.
These raiding parties suffered significant losses and succeeded only
in damaging a couple of frigates, which induced Drake to sail off
empty-handed. But a key point was the increased defences, on all
points, which deterred Baskerville and his captains from a sustained
effort. In defence against amphibious attack, as in prosecuting combined operations, a balance between naval and military was important.

Hawkins had died within sight of San Juan and so Drake now
led the expedition for the Spanish Main. Presumably to allow time
for the silver of Peru to arrive at Panama, they dawdled along the
coasts of the Main, burning and plundering Rio de la Hacha,
Rancheria, and other small settlements, eventually reaching Nombre
de Dios on 27 December. There two days later Baskerville landed
with 600 or 700 'armed men, besides surgeons and . . . boys' to
march overland to Panama.[52] It would have been far easier to go,
as seems to have originally been intended, by boat up the Chagres
River as far as Casa de Guives and then march just the remaining
five leagues. But presumably the soldiers, weary of their long stay
aboard ship, preferred to march the whole day. It took them along
a mule track 'cut out of the woods and rocks, both very narrow and
full of mire and water', a march 'so sore as never Englishman
marched before.'[53] Sniped at by small parties of Spaniards lurking
in the woods, after three days they came up against a new defence
work at the Capira Pass, 'in a marvelous strait way upon the top
of a hill which we must needs pass.'[54] For three hours they battered
vainly against it. Men were falling, victuals were already short, and

---

[52] Hakluyt (1927), 7:193.
[53] Ibid.
[54] See Wernham (1994), 51–4.

powder and match damp. Moreover, it was reported (though falsely) that this was only the first of several such works on the way to Panama.

So, as at Las Palmas and San Juan, but with more justification, Baskerville for the third time turned tail. By 2 January 1596 he was back at Nombre de Dios. Less than a month later, he was left in sole command of both land and sea forces by Drake's death of the prevalent fever. How he fought his way at Cape San Antonio around Cuba into the Florida Channel and home against the eight royal galleons and thirteen armed merchantmen sent from Spain under Bernardino de Avellanedo, is part of purely naval history and involved no further combined operations. But it was clear evidence that the Caribbean was no longer the place of easy picking that Drake had always known, clear evidence too that to cut off the flow of treasure to Spain at its dispatching end by holding a base deep in the heart of Spanish America was now—as indeed it had probably always been—beyond the strength of Elizabethan England.

Even as the Drake–Hawkins expedition was arriving off San Juan de Puerto Rico, Lord Admiral Howard had been proposing a considerably more ambitious operation against mainland Spain. He secured Essex's enthusiastic support by offering him a share in the command. By May 1596 they had gathered in Plymouth eleven of the Queen's twenty-one first-line warships, two of her six second-line, her 150-ton *Tremonbana*, and three of her pinnaces, together with twelve Londoners and sixty transports and victuallers carrying some 6,480 troops (half of them experienced in the Low Country wars), and eighteen Dutch warships with almost 4,000 Dutch troops.[55]

The destination of these forces was kept a very close secret, even after they had put to sea, and it was only the day before they arrived off Cadiz on June 19 that news reached Cadiz and Seville that eighty of them had been sighted eastward bound off Lagos. Until then the Spaniards had been convinced that, if they came at all, it would

---

[55] The chief sources are Laughton, ed. (1902); Hakluyt (1927), 9: 249–76; Monson (1902), 1:344–95, 2:1–20; Vere (1657), 24–45; Usherwood (1983); Academia de la Historia (1860), 205–455; *CSPDom. 1595–97*; PRO, SP France 36, SP Holland, III, and SP Spain, V; Birch, ed. (1754); Devereux (1853), vol. 1; *HMC Sal.*, vol. 6; *CSP Ven.*, vol. 8; Edwards (1868), vol. 2. The chief secondary accounts are Corbett (1900), 1–133; Cheyney (1926), 42–91; Kenny (1970), 166–223; Wernham (1994), 55–123; Hammer (1999), 248–57.

again be against Lisbon as in 1589, for that was where the bulk of
Spain's naval forces were. It seems that Essex, too, would have preferred such a move, but as he wrote later 'from Lisbon I was barred
by name in my instructions.' He added (very unfairly, as we have
seen) that anyway, 'our seamen are made of the same stuff that Sir
Francis Drake and his company were when they lost the occasion
to take Lisbon for fear of passing by the castle of St Julian's.'[56] This,
together with the timing of the expedition and the size of the military component, strongly suggests that Howard's original idea was
to seize and hold Cadiz long enough to capture the shipping out-
ward bound for America with cargoes estimated to be worth
£3,500,000 and perhaps also to catch the even richer homeward-
bound *flota*, already known to have left Havana with some £4,000,000
aboard—to seize the king of Spain's treasure from the Indies at the
receiving rather than the dispatching end.

So here was another expedition with its joint commanders at cross-
purposes. Essex clearly had ideas well beyond Howard's plans or the
Queen's intentions. In a letter to the Council which he instructed
his secretary not to deliver until he himself was well on the way to
Spain,[57] he urged that they should leave, 'as it were, a thorn stick-
ing in his [the king of Spain's] foot' by establishing a base in a
Spanish port from which the English fleet might destroy Spain's
naval forces piecemeal and also blockade the Indies trade at the
receiving end.[58] But even more grandiose ambitions shone through
a letter he left for the Queen. In it he argued that whereas in France
and Flanders she was 'but a coadjutor after the fashion of Switzerland
or petty common states', in Spain she might 'make war like a mighty
prince, of yourself', for 'your troops shall possess ports unguarded
and if you please take towns unfortified and meet with nothing but
bosoms who will rather quit every place than fight.'[59] It is small wonder that the Queen's instructions had barred him from Lisbon or
that Howard assured Burghley that he had 'no meaning to con any
rash or unadvised course.'[60]

---

[56] Hulton MS, quoted in Wernham (1994), 125–6.
[57] Birch, ed. (1754), 2:20–1.
[58] PRO, SP Domestic 259, no. 12 (printed in Devereux (1853), 1:349–56).
[59] Birch, ed. (1754), 2:19–20.
[60] BL, Lansdowne MS 115, no. 13.

He was put to the test as soon as the fleet arrived off Cadiz on 20 June. The council of war, after several indecisive meetings, then decided to attack the town from the seaward side, in Sta Catalina bay, before attempting the shipping in the harbour. As had previously been ordered, a third of each regiment was embarked in the ships' boats, marshalled in ranks, no boat leaving its rank and one carrying a St George's permanent acting as guide and director. All were to set forward at a set pace to the beat of a drum and stop when the drum ceased beating.[61] The soldiers who framed these orders had, however, reckoned without the wind and the waves and soon after the troops had embarked a near gale began to roll in the Atlantic breakers, swamping several boats, drowning a number of men, and making a landing increasingly impracticable.

Yet Essex, the army commander, could not be persuaded to call off the attempt. He had gone into one of his accustomed sulks because he had wanted to attack the shipping first and make sure of a great profit for the expedition and the Queen. He had indeed, hung back, in his flagship, the *Due Repulse*, as they passed the harbour entrance, hoping to get others to follow him in. It was only when Raleigh's intervention persuaded Howard to agree to attack the shipping that the landing against the town was called off. But by the time the troops had been re-embarked and the fleet regrouped, 'the day was far spent' and the tide fast ebbing out of the harbour. So it was next morning before part of the fleet could force its way in. By then the Spaniards had withdrawn the richly laden merchant fleet, of more than thirty vessels, and three frigates into the inner harbour and stationed their six royal galleons across the narrow strait between the inner and outer harbours, between Puntales and Matagorda Point. By the time two of those galleons had been captured and the rest destroyed the tide was again on the ebb. The way into the inner harbour was becoming too shallow for the larger English warships to enter. But it was still not too late for some of the smaller flyboats and the warships' boats to go in and seize those virtually defenceless merchantmen.

Essex, however, was more concerned by now with securing Cadiz as a base for the larger operations he had outlined in those letters

---

[61] Laughton, ed. (1902), 1:61–2; Usherwood (1983), 135–7. According to Corbett, these are the earliest known orders for landing troops from ships in face of an enemy.

left for the Queen and Council. He collected about 2,000 troops from the ships nearest to land, embarked them in the ships' boats and to the beat of a drum as laid down in the recent orders, and landed them unopposed in a sandy bay on the Cadiz side of Puntales. Sir Conyers Clifford was despatched with half the troops southwards to hold the narrowest part of the isthmus against any attackers from the mainland. With the rest Essex and Sir Francis Vere advanced northwards toward Cadiz, looking for 'a convenient place to encamp till my Lord Admiral with the rest of the forces and the ordnance were landed.'[62] However, they found a considerable enemy force drawn up in battle order under the city wall, which they drew into combat and routed, presenting a golden opportunity. When most of the were Spanish troops were back inside the city, they slammed the gate shut leaving a number still outside. These got back into the city by clambering over the wall where a ditch had been dug and the earth piled against the wall to strengthen it against cannons. Some of the English scrambled in after them, with Essex close behind. While these forty or fifty pressed forward toward the market places, others found their way in by an ill-guarded sally port and eventually the main body broke in through the city gates. After some sharp street fighting, most of the Spaniards took refuge for the night in the castle and fort St Philip. So, by the time the Lord Admiral arrived with the main part of the land forces, Cadiz was already virtually in English hands. Next morning the occupation was completed. The Spaniards in the castle and fort surrendered and gave hostages for a ransom (never paid) of 120,000 ducats.

It was a remarkably fortunate outcome to a remarkably hazardous adventure. The danger in which Essex had placed himself and his 2,000 men had perforce totally preoccupied the Lord Admiral and the other leaders of the expedition. His astonishing success brought an immediate pell-mell rush by everyone, sailors and soldiers, officers and men, to plunder this, one of Spain's richest cities. The unfortunate consequences was that the anxiety to get Essex safely reinforced and then the greedy rush for plunder left neither men nor means to deal with those thirty-odd merchant-men in the inner harbour and the Spaniards were given time to set them on fire and destroy the lot.

---

[62] Vere (1657), 35.

For the next couple of weeks the expedition stayed in Cadiz, debating what to do next, and systematically sacking, and finally setting fire to the city. The council of war did on June 24 decide to keep Cadiz, but four days later they made this decision dependent upon enough victuals being found in the fleet and the city to maintain a garrison of 3,000 or 4,000 men for four months. The Lord Admiral Essex with their flagships, the *Ark Royal* and *Due Repulse*, and the weaker ships should then return to England to secure before the end of the four months adequate further supplies of men, munitions, and victuals from England, the Netherlands and Barbary. Meanwhile Lord Thomas Howard and Raleigh, with four of the best of the Queen's ships and a sufficient number of others should cruise to the Azores to intercept the homecoming *flota*.

Now, however, Essex intervened. 'He absolutely refused to give his consent that there should be any other governor left there then himself, pretending that his credit with Her Majesty would not be able to procure supplies in due time for any other; he did assure himself so much of Her Majesty's favour toward him as she would not suffer him to perish in that defence.'[63] This brought to an abrupt end all thought of holding Cadiz, for neither the Lord Admiral nor any of the others dared face the Queen's wrath if they left Essex behind. The survey of the victuals in the fleet, which purported to show that it was insufficient for even two months' supply, simply confirmed the inevitable, and on 4 July the expedition sailed away from Cadiz.

That was the end of the expedition's combined operations apart from five days spent landing at and sacking Faro and the villages around. The only significant fruit of that futile action was the acquisition of much of Bishop Osorius's library for Thomas Bodley's new library at Oxford. By the end of the first week in August the ships were all back in Plymouth. They had taken and sacked Cadiz, but they had missed the rich prizes in the inner harbour. They had also left untouched the main strength of Spain's armada, which lay in Lisbon and the Biscayan ports. A mere ten days after the expedition's return to Plymouth, the Indies *flota* with its £4,000,000 cargo sailed safely into San Lucar. And little more than two months later,

---

[63] Laughton, ed. (1902), 1:83–4.

with the bulk of the Queen's ships still in dockyard hands, the armada set sail for the channel. Luckily for England, on October 18 it was scattered by a severe gale, driven back into Coruña, Ferrol, and other Biscayan ports, with the loss of seven galleons, twenty-five merchant-men, many smaller craft, and 2,000 men. So little did England owe to Howard and Essex's ambitious expedition.

The Earl of Essex was himself no less disappointed than the Queen and Council with the achievements of the expedition. As early as August 2, while still at sea, he had begun writing a paper,[64] to prove two things:

> The one that it was not my fault that we did Her Majesty and those that sent us out no great service; the other that we should not be less forward in the like understandings hereafter, though the success of this hath not answered our expectations.

He spent the first quarter of this paper defending himself over the failure to secure the fleet bound for the Indies and for the failure to hold Cadiz; and blaming, a little more justly, the 'seamen', the Lord Admiral and Raleigh in particular, for rejecting his pleas for ships to be sent to the Islands to intercept the homeward-bound *flotas* and for action against enemy ships in other ports besides Cadiz.

Then, turning to the future, on the basis 'that it is better to make war offensive than defensive', he ruled out both 'incursions upon the land' by England's inexperienced and half-trained troops, and 'idle wanderings upon the sea' by fleets of sailing ships so much at the mercy of the weather. Instead he proposed using a force of 2,000 or 3,000 'well chosen' soldiers to seize and hold an Iberian port— Cadiz or Lisbon or both—as a secure base for an English fleet to destroy Spanish shipping piecemeal and in addition to establish a double blockade at the receiving end to cut off both the essential supplies of naval stores and corn from the Eastlands and also 'his golden Indian stream, whereby we shall cut his life veins and let out the vital spirits of his estate.'

This was undoubtedly the most complete, coherent, lucid, and persuasive strategy that anyone had so far suggested, a strategy with the most mature understanding of the proper use of the military as

---

[64] Hulton MS (formerly BL, Loan MS 23); Ungerer, ed. (1974), 445; Henry (1953), 363–93; Hammer (1999), 255–7, 260.

a subsidiary handmaid in the effective exercise of sea power. It is therefore particularly unfortunate that Essex was too occupied in the autumn of 1596 with the frantic defence preparations against the threatened armada, to complete the paper as he had intended by explaining 'how facile it is first to take and then to keep' either Cadiz or Lisbon. For that is the doubtful point of his argument, the point where we catch a strong whiff of armchair strategy. His capture of Cadiz in 1596 was, after all, something of a fluke. Would it be so easy to do again or as easy to do against Lisbon? Would 3,000 English troops, however 'well chosen', be able not only to take, but to hold, either of these places against the military might of Spain? Above all, could they be assured of essential stores and reinforcements being available to replace wastage, casualties, and disease? Could they be assured of those supplies and reinforcements, even if available, arriving in time across the stormy Bay of Biscay and the open Atlantic? In 1563 foul weather and southwesterly gales had prevented reinforcements and supplies reaching the besieged and plague-ridden English garrison in Le Havre in time to prevent its surrender. And Le Havre was a mere 100 miles across the Channel from Portsmouth.

Perhaps fortunately for England Essex was not given the opportunity to test these ideas in practice. He did persuade his fellow councillors, and eventually the Queen, that the best way of destroying the slowly recuperating Ferrol Armada was to back up a powerful fleet with a landing force of 5,000 'well chosen' troops. After the Spanish capture of Amiens (1 March 1597) and Dutch reluctance ruled out his plan of providing most of these 5,000 by withdrawing the 2,000 English from Picardy and another 2,000 from the Netherlands, he got the council to agree to draw 4,000 well-trained men from the southern, midland, and East Anglian counties, stiffened by 1,000 seasoned troops from the Netherlands, to form the landing force supporting a fleet of sixteen of the Queen's ships, eight armed marching men, ten Dutch warships, and forty-eight transports.[65]

---

[65] The chief sources for the 1597 plans and operations are: PRO, SP Domestic, vols. 262 to 264: SP Spain, vol. 5; *HMC Sal.*, vols. 6–7; *APC*, vol. 27; Monson (1902), vol. 2; Birch, ed. (1754), vol. 2; Collins, ed. (1746), vol. 2; Vere (1657); Purchas (1907; Devereux (1853), vol. 2; Edwards (1868), vol. 2; *CSP Ven.*, vol. 8. For the secondary accounts, see Corbett (1900); Cheyney (1926); Wernham (1994).

Essex clearly looked on these proposed Ferrol operations as a first step in implementing the wider and more ambitious 'double blockade' ideas he had earlier outlined. And his commission did indeed allow him to 'invade, enter, burn and spoil and to keep any place within the said King of Spain's dominions' until the Queen recall him.[66] His instructions, however, allowed him only two objectives: to destroy the Armada and then and only then to lie at the Azores for the treasure *flotas*.[67]

In the event, he failed even to do either of these two limited matters. When the fleet got to sea on 10 July, half was soon driven back by fierce storms. The other half, led by that old sea dog Lord Thomas Howard, rode out the storms and then waited off Coruña for the rest until recalled on July 28. The reunited expedition was then delayed again by adverse winds and when it eventually got to sea on 17 August, it did so with only the 1,000 troops from the Netherlands garrisons. The 4,000 'well chosen' men levied in England had been discharged on 11 August, partly because of the lateness of the season, partly because the July storms had left them short of transports for 775 men and made many so seasick that Lord Thomas Howard reckoned most would perish if taken to sea again.[68]

So the attack on the Ferrol Armada was back to where it had started, as a purely naval operation. Within a week even that was found to be impracticable and the fleet moved south to cruise off southern Portugal for the carracks and the *flotas*. On 30 August, however, Essex was informed by Raleigh, who heard it from a Southampton privateer, who had heard it from another privateer, who had been told it by a West Indian shipmaster whom he had captured, that the Ferrol Armada had sailed for the Azores on August 4. Without, it seems, attempting to verify this fourth hand report, Essex and the council of war decided at once to sail off in pursuit. Not finding the Armada there, they persuaded themselves that it must still be in Ferrol and in no condition to sail for many weeks. So they decided to wait at the Azores in hope of catching the Indies fleets. The likeliest way of catching them before they could reach safety in Angra, on Terciera, the Islands' one secure haven, would

---

[66] Printed in Collier, ed. (1860), 239–44, from PRO, Treaty Rolls 76/215.
[67] PRO, SP Domestic 263, no. 102.
[68] *HMC Sal.*, 7:346.

have been to cruise well to the westward, around Flores. But Essex allowed 'his flexible nature to be overruled' by false rumours and 'by divers gentlemen who, coming principally for land service, found themselves tired of the sea.'[69] With well under 1,000 troops now serviceable, he dared not attempt the well-defended Terciera. Instead he made landings on nearby Fayal, Pico, and Graciosa.[70] That at least kept the fleet a little to the westward of Angra, if only a little. But on 28 September he ordered all the ships eastward to St Michael's. The orders did not reach four of the Queen's ships and about midnight one of the four, Sir William Monson's *Rainbow*, found itself in company with eight royal galleons and numerous 'merchants of good force', part of the homeward bound *flota*. By morning, when the other three Queen's ships joined Monson, the *flota* was already almost in Angra. An attempt was made by ships' boats to burn or bring away the last arrivals, but that was repulsed by heavy enemy gunfire. When Essex and the rest of the fleet summoned from St Michael's by pinnace came back on 3 October, they found the Indies fleet even farther beyond their reach.

So it was back to St Michael's for water and to give the 'land gentlemen' and soldiers another chance to stretch their legs. The heavy Atlantic surf and 400 enemy shot entrenched beyond it forbade a landing at the principal town, Punta Delgada. The troops did eventually land farther eastward along the island, but after a skirmish or two they were re-embarked on October 10 and the whole expedition set sail for home. It had, after all, proved little more than another of those 'idle wanderings upon the sea' of which Essex had written so scornfully.

All, however, was not yet over. For on 9 October, the day when the expedition began to take leave of St Michael's, the Ferrol Armada also put to sea, sixty fighting ships, seventy-six others, with 8,600 troops. Its aim was to seize Falmouth and then to catch Essex's fleet as it straggled home on a converging course from the Azores. It got within ten or twenty leagues of the Lizard before, on 12–13 October, once again it was scattered by a fierce storm and driven back to Ferrol, Coruña, and elsewhere in Galicia. Less than two weeks later, on 25 October Lord Thomas Howard sailed into Plymouth with six

---

[69] Monson (1902), 2:28–9.
[70] Cf. figures 6–7. See Map 1.

of the Queen's ships and a number of others. Essex followed in next morning and the rest dribbled in over the next few days. So narrowly had the Armada missed its target.

The lesson was even sharper than in 1596 and it was duly learned. For the remainder of the war the Queen's ships, led by seamen such as Leveson, Monson, and Mansel, under Sir Robert Cecil's guidance, concentrated upon its true strategic objective, the enemy's fleet. After 1597 the only serious combined operation was a private enterprise, (though under royal commission), by the Earl of Cumberland and London merchant-privateers in 1598.[71] With 18 ships, eleven of them sizable privateers and including Cumberland's 600-ton *Malice Scourge*, and 1,000 troops, they aimed to seize San Juan de Puerto Rico and hold it as a base from which to prey upon the *flotas*. Cumberland did capture San Juan, succeeding where Drake had failed. But disease reduced his 1,700 soldiers and sailors to fewer than 1,000, many of them sick. So his attempt to intercept 'the King of Spain's treasure from the Indies' at the dispatching end also had to be abandoned. Yet again an 'English expedition lacked the resources to hold what [it] had taken.'[72]

The truth was that Elizabethan England had neither the resources nor the manpower to establish either a 'double blockade' of its enemy at the receiving end or a single blockade at the dispatching end. Commercially focused warfare might have the potential to disrupt the Spanish economy but in practice it proved disruptive of the English military operations aimed at carrying it out. The operation in Brittany in late 1594 and the brief few days at Sagres in 1587 were easily the most successful of all Elizabethan combined operations. This was so because in each case the privateering element was virtually non-existent, so that plunder was not the main goal; each expedition was a limited force with a limited objective, its purpose purely strategic and its operations government controlled; and because each had a composition appropriate to its purpose and with an appropriate balance between land and sea contingents.

The other amphibious forces sent forth to attack Spain's Atlantic ports, islands and colonies and the fleet which shielded them, failed or were only moderate successes because the crown was so often

---

[71] Cf. Williamson (1920), 174–218; Wernham (1994), 250–7.
[72] Fissel, ch. 7, below, pp. 224–5.

obliged to attempt to make a campaign pay for itself through plunder. Objectives could thus be dangerously diversified and hence unclear. In addition, many expeditionary forces had to be constituted of necessity from private resources; the composition (and hence the balance) of such forces could be largely or even wholly a matter of chance, while they were difficult for the crown's appointed commanders to control, even when they themselves had focused aims, because the profit imperative was so important for a high proportion of their forces. Until the English state itself possessed the finances, war fleet and standing army necessary to mount combined operations without the help of private enterprise and without itself regarding plunder as a highly desirably objective, divided purposes would further invite failure.

Bibliography

Archival Sources

BL   Lansdowne MSS
PRO   Pipe Office, Declared Accounts
        Treaty Rolls
        SP Domestic
        SP France
        SP Holland
        SP Spain

Printed Primary Sources

APC   *Acts of the Privy Council of England*, ed. J. R. Dasent *et al.*, new series, vol. 27 (London: 1903).
CSP Dom.   *Calendar of State Papers, Domestic, Elizabeth, 1591–94* and *1595–97*, ed. M. A. Everett Green (London: 1867, 1868).
CSP Span.   *Calendar of letters and state papers relating to English affairs, preserved principally in the archives of Simancas, Elizabeth, 1558–1603*, ed. M. A. S. Hume, vol. 4 (London: 1899)
CSP Ven.   *Calendar of State Papers and Manuscripts relating to English Affairs, existing in the Archives and Collections of Venice, and in other Libraries of Northern Italy*, vol. 8, 1581–1591, ed. H. F. Brown (London: 1894).
HMC Sal.   *Calendar of the Manuscripts of the Most Hon. the Marquis of Salisbury, preserved at Hatfield House, Hertfordshire*, vols. 4–7 (London: 1892–9).
L&A   vol. 5, *July 1593–December 1594* (London: 1989).

Academia de la Historia [Spain] (1860) *Coleccion de Documentos ineditos para la Historia de Espana* (Madrid: 113 vols, 1842–1895—volume published 1860).
Andrews, K.. ed. (1972) *The Last Voyage of Drake and Hawkins*, Hakluyt Society, 2nd series, 142 (Cambridge: 1972).
Birch, T., ed. (1754) *Memoirs of the Reign of Queen Elizabeth*, 2 vols (London: 1754).

Bruce, J., ed. (1844) *Correspondence of Robert Dudley, Earl of Leycester during his Government of the Low Countries, in the Years 1585 and 1586*, Camden Society, 1st series, 27 (London: 1844).

Carné, G. de, ed. (1899) *Documents sur la ligue en Bretagne. Correspondance du duc de Mercœur & des ligueurs bretons avec l'Espagne*, 2 vols, Archives de Bretagne 11, 12 (Vannes: 1899).

Castellanos, J. de (1921) *Discurso de el Captain Francisco Draque, que compuso Juan de Castellanos [. . .] 1586–7*, ed. A. Gonzalez (Madrid: 1921).

Collier, J. P., ed. (1860) *The Egerton Papers*, Camden Society, 1st series, 12 (London: 1860).

Collins, A., ed. (1746) *Letters and Memorials of State [. . .]*, vol. 2 (London: 1746).

Corbett, J. S., ed. (1898) *Papers Relating to the Navy During the Spanish Wars 1585–87*, Navy Records Society 11 (London: 1898).

Hakluyt, R. (1927) *The Principal Navigations, Voyages, Traffiques & Discoveries of the English Nation*, 10 vols (Dent edn; London & Toronto: 1927–8) vols 4, 7, 9.

Jameson, K. (1934) 'Some New Spanish Documents dealing with Drake', *English Historical Review* 49 (1934) 14–31.

Laughton, J. K., ed. (1902) *The Naval Miscellany*, vol. 1, Navy Records Society 20 (London: 1902).

Meteren, E. van (1602) *True Discourse Historical of the Succeeding Governors the Low Countries*, trans. T[homas] C[hurchyard] and Ric[hard] Ro[binson] (London: 1602).

Monson, W. (1902) *The Naval Tracts of Sir William Monson*, 2 vols, ed. M. Oppenheim, Navy Records Society 22–23 (London: 1902).

Moreau, J. (1960) *Mémoires sur les guerres de la Ligue en Bretagne*, ed. H. Waquet, Archives historiques de Bretagne, 1 (1960).

Purchas, S. (1907) *Hackluytus Posthumus or Purchas his Pilgrimes*, 20 vols, Haklutyt Society, extra series (Glasgow: 1905–7), vol. 20.

Ungerer, G., ed. (1974) *A Spaniard in Elizabethan England: The Correspondence of Antonio Perez*, Colección Támesis, serie A, Monografías 27, vol. 1 (London: 1974).

Usherwood, S. and E. (1983) *The Counter Armada of 1596: The Journall of the 'Mary Rose'*, ed. S. and E. Usherwood (London: 1983).

Vere, F. (1657) *The Commentaries of Sir Francis Vere*, ed. W. Dillingham (Cambridge: 1657).

Wernham, R. B., ed. (1988) *The Expedition of Sir John Norris and Sir Francis Drake to Spain and Portugal, 1589*, Navy Records Society 127 (London: 1986).

Wright, I., ed. (1951) *Further English Voyages to Spanish America 1583–1594*, Hakluyt Society, 2nd series 99 (London: 1951).

Secondary Sources

Andrews, K. (1967) *Drake's Voyages: A Re-Assessment of Their Place in Elizabethan Maritime Expansion* (London: 1967).

Cheyney, E. (1914) *A History of England from the Defeat of the Armada to the Death of Elizabeth*, vol. 1 (London: 1914).

——. (1926) *A History of England from the Defeat of the Armada to the Death of Elizabeth*, vol. 2 (London: 1926).

Corbett, J. S. (1899) *Drake and the Tudor Navy*, new edn, 2 vols (London: 1899).

——. (1900) *The Successors of Drake* (London: 1900).

Devereux, W. (1853) *Lives and Letters of the Devereux, Earls of Essex, in the Reigns of Elizabeth, James I and Charles I, 1540–1646*, 2 vols (London: 1853).

Edwards, E. (1868) *The life of Sir Walter Ralegh, based on Contemporary Documents*, 2 vols (London: 1868).

Hammer, P. E. J. (1999) *The Polarisation of Elizabethan Politics. The Political Career of Robert Devereux, 2nd Earl of Essex, 1585–1597* (Cambridge 1999).

Henry, L. W. (1953) 'The Earl of Essex as Strategist and Military Organizer', *English Historical Review* 68 (1953) 363–93.

Hume, M. (1896) *The Year After the Armada and Other Historical Studies* (London: 1896).

Kenny, R. (1970) *Elizabeth's Admiral: The Political Career of Charles Howard, Earl of Nottingham, 1536–1624* (Baltimore & London: 1970).

Mattingley, G. *The Defeat of the Spanish Armada* (London: 1959).

Nolan, J. (1995) 'English Operations around Brest 1594', *Mariner's Mirror* 81 (1995) 259–74.

Wernham, R. B. (1961) 'Elizabethan War Aims and Strategy', in *Elizabethan Government and Society: Essays Presented to Sir John Neale*, ed. S. T. Bindoff, J. Hurstfield and C. H. Williams (London: 1961) 340–69.

——. (1984) *After the Armada: Elizabethan England and the Struggle for Western Europe 1588–1595* (Oxford: 1984).

——. (1994) *The Return of the Armadas: The Last Years of the Elizabethan War against Spain 1595–1603* (Oxford: 1994).

Williamson, J. (1927) *Sir John Hawkins*, 2nd edn (Oxford: 1927).

——. (1938) *The Age of Drake* (London: 1938).

Williamson, G. (1920) *George, Third Earl of Cumberland (1558–1605)* (Cambridge: 1920).

ENGLISH AMPHIBIOUS WARFARE, 1587–1656:
GALLEONS, GALLEYS, LONGBOATS AND COTS[1]

Mark Charles Fissel

English collective memory focuses on the successful amphibious landings that altered the course of the history of the British Isles in 1066
and 1688. The prevention of amphibious attacks on England, for
example those attempted by Philip II, Napoleon and Hitler, reinforced in the English imagination the importance of defensive amphibious warfare. While English strategies were more defensive than
offensive, the island kingdom learned the techniques (and how to
surmount the logistical hurdles) of amphibious warfare, ultimately
imposing its will in lands beyond the Narrow Seas. Within the British
Isles themselves, amphibious operations often determined dominance
amongst the Irish, Scots, Welsh and English. The settlement of northeast Ireland encompassed incursions, raids and migration across the
country's numerous bays, rivers and lakes.[2] Medieval and early modern Scottish-Irish conflicts incorporated varieties of aquatic craft,
including fleets of galleys.[3] For example, in 1557 the Crown unleashed
an 'amphibious offensive' against western Scotland in order to prevent Scottish amphibious succour of O'Neill's rebellion in Ulster.[4]

This essay argues that English riverine and lacustrine warfare, conducted in and around the British Isles, were significant and consistently successful, but have been overshadowed by the more famous,

---

[1] The author thanks his co-editor, fellow contributors, as well as Wayne Mixon,
Simon Healy, Brad Gericke, John Nolan, Wendy Turner, Rob Bledsoe, Matthew
Jennings, Randle Berlin, Maureen Akins, Jenna Thomas-McKie, Adam Siegel, Mark
Danley, and David Ulbrich.
[2] For but one example, see Hill (1861), 130 particularly, and 123–4 for background; T. Bartlett and K. Jeffrey, eds (1996), 40–3, 54, 57, 62–8. Also, Lenman
(2001), 114.
[3] The term 'galley' must be used with care, of course, especially when drawing
directly from contemporary sources. See Bennell, (1974) 9–26 and 169–85. Perhaps
the strangest Hibernian amphibious craft of the sixteenth and seventeenth centuries
were the 'nevogs' the Irish fashioned by slaughtering their mounts and stretching
the horsehides around a sort of frame to make a boat: Stafford (1631), 364.
[4] Lenman (2001), 58.

but less effective, exploits of Elizabethan amphibious operations against Spain and in the Caribbean. In their Hibernian operations English arms distinguished themselves, especially in Ulster, immediately prior to and during the Irish Nine Years' War (1594–1603).[5] Amphibious warfare succeeded in Ireland at a time when English land forces there were suffering serious reverses.

First, large-scale amphibious enterprises were still relatively novel and immature in the late sixteenth century, and thus the state encountered difficulties in mounting and sustaining sizeable operations, in contrast with purely naval operations. Second, these operational deficiencies were compounded by the difficulty of perpetuating the techniques of amphibious warfare (as for example articulated below by Sir George Carew). Collective memory was impressionistic and mirrored the strategic ambivalence that characterised Elizabethan operations, and to a great extent, expeditions under Charles I. Generally speaking, English offensive strategy oscillated between striking into the enemy's homeland, and wreaking havoc upon the enemy's commerce upon the seas and in distant ports.

Third, as a result of the above, English governments (as well as Philip II of Spain) often possessed unrealistic and grandiose expectations of what amphibious warfare could deliver to the state (and, on occasion, to individuals). Fourth, given the obstacles (literally and figuratively) faced by amphibious forces on the offensive, defensive amphibious warfare held sway in most cases. For example, the English failed to penetrate Iberia or establish themselves in the Caribbean, just as the Spaniards failed to invade England. Notable exceptions, however, were the limited riverine and lacustrine operations of English forces in Ireland.

Fifth, English amphibious warfare in Ireland was remarkably and consistently successful in a theatre of operations where the English were failing in the prosecution of land warfare. For example, Sir Henry Docwra's amphibious offensive secured Lough Foyle, shifting Irish hopes to the rather similar Spanish landing at Kinsale.[6] English combined operations triumphed, however, and the amphibious tactics that had been perfected in Ulster provided a model for the

---

[5] On the 'Irish' (as opposed to 'European') Nine Years' War, see above, in ch. 1, p. 43; and Lenihan, ed. (2001b), 377.
[6] Morgan (2004c), 73–89.

reduction of Dunboy and ultimately all Ireland. Sixth, by keeping alive the English war effort during the period 1593–1601, amphibious operations made possible the subjugation of Ireland and thus paved the way for plantation under James I.

Seventh, amphibious warfare was practiced both on the large-scale and in more manageable Irish operations through firepower and mobility. However, where the sea-going galleons and frigates have been praised, the cots and longboats that plied loughs and rivers have been largely ignored. Eighth, and finally, large-scale English amphibious operations reached maturity during Admiral Robert Blake's service to the Commonwealth and Protectorate. The process of 'state-formation' engendered by Parliament's struggle to survive and win the civil war matured the state's institutions sufficiently to sustain offensive amphibious operations.

Elizabethan operations at Cadiz in 1587 and 1596 left an indelible impression on contemporary England, later generations, and historians. Largely forgotten were failed sea-going combined operations characterised by ambiguous strategies and operational incoherence. Elizabeth's 'grand strategy' (or lack of one) and the role of her navy remain controversial. A distinguished reviewer writes, 'Naval power was central to English military strategy and operations ... The Royal Navy was the only permanent military institution from 1511 to 1642. ... [L]and forces were auxiliaries in her naval struggle against Spain. The Navy protected her island state from the immense Spanish army in Flanders.'[7]

These views place the sixteenth century English military establishment in a context more appropriate to that of the post-1650 era. The Elizabethan contest with Spain was predominantly a land struggle, fought in the Low Countries, France and Ireland. Naval expeditions against Iberia and the Caribbean were sporadic and either failed outright, or could not hold the harbour they had taken. From 1572, with Elizabeth's intervention in the Netherlands, into the early Stuart period, England sustained a consistent and tenacious military presence on the Continent (in concert with Protestant allies). True, soldiers needed vessels for transportation. But the 'Royal Navy' was greatly augmented by privately owned ships. At the height of the war with Spain, 1598–1599, Elizabeth 'left the sea almost exclusively

---

[7] Wheeler (2002), 637.

to private enterprise.[8] Even in its infrequent expeditions, Elizabeth's navy could not operate without merchant vessel auxiliaries. The Queen kept in service only as many royal vessels as she could afford, and naval commanders complained bitterly about the precipitous disbandment of forces, lack of supplies and unpaid mariners. Elizabeth's navy fought no decisive battles, and even the dispersing of the Armada in 1588 owed as much to fireships and severe weather as it did to seadog gunnery. Nor was the miracle of 1588 decisive. It marked the beginning of a decade of desperation. More Catholic armadas gathered, and the religious and dynastic divisions of the Low Countries Wars spread to France and elsewhere. The most permanent military establishment was arguably the Ordnance Office, which had been created in the late medieval period more for land warfare than to supply a Royal Navy that had not yet been fully institutionalised.

The Mechanics of Amphibious Warfare

Success in ocean-going amphibious operations was, technically speaking, difficult to attain. In the words of R. B. Wernham, 'Sea power had never before been used as an independent arm operating over vast distances of ocean. Because it was so novel, its potentialities were too optimistically estimated and the difficulties of its employment very inadequately foreseen.'[9] Even the best ships of the line *circa* 1587–1640 had (comparatively speaking) difficulty sailing before the wind. When approaching continental targets, a westerly wind might run these 'leewardly sailers' aground.[10] The 'new-style' frigates[11] slipped into harbours and ports and commenced firing. In bringing to bear their guns, the vessels played a dangerous game, for English *bertoni*[12] had deep draughts, and the limitations of chart-making made detection of shoals and submerged objects an inexact science.

---

[8] Wernham (1994), 251. Paul Hammer has observed, 'Although naval developments have gained most of the attention (and plaudits) of modern scholars, the reformation of Elizabethan land forces was more significant at the time. . .': Hammer (2003), 256.

[9] Wernham (1961), 366.

[10] Usherwood (1983), 69. The author has profited from reading John Stapleton's unpublished remarks on the subject.

[11] A swift war-vessel, powered by sails, with 28–60 guns, high decks, known for firepower and manoeuverability—see Thrush (1991), 34–41.

[12] The popular Italian name for the English frigates interloping in the Mediterranean.

The mechanics of conveying ships in close to shore, whether to act as seaborne artillery platforms or to disembark troops, also remained risky through the seventeenth century. Getting soldiers to the beach, especially in the face of fire or with the enemy present, posed for commanders vision problems that complicated tactical deployment. From an anchorage 600 yards off shore, it is an optical impossibility to gauge how heavily the surf is running, for only the rear of the swell may be seen. Thus longboats might be launched even though pounding surf might make landing virtually impossible. En route to the shore, boats are pitched in the troughs between waves, obscuring signals from their ship and, excruciatingly, blocking from sight action on the beach itself.

The ambiguity between early-modern land warfare and naval warfare accounts for the difficult (and lengthy) transition from straightforward conveyance of land soldiers to foreign soil by troop transports, and the very different operational complexities of getting troops ashore in the midst of hostile action. Treatises generally failed to address the unique problems posed by amphibious assault:

> [T]he boates that shall land the troopes shall all be marshaled in Ranke according to such a front as the place of descent wyll permytt which order of march in Rowing or saling they shall precisely keepe, no boate thrusting out of a hinder ranke into a former, nor shrinking out of the former into a hinder, of which order such land men as command the troopes and such sea men as direct the boates shall give a strict accompt. Thatt all the boates in the hinder rankes shall have there ey on the boate that leadeth them, and all the boates in the first ranke shall observe the boate that is appointed to be their guyde and director, which boate shall carry eyther a st Georges flag or a white Pendent in the Prow and shall keepe in the heade of the the first ranke at the going of [off] from the shypes. Thatt when the Drom that beateth the first ranke shall beate a march they shall all row forward such a pace as the first leadeth who shall be appointed to row no faster than the slowest boate may conveniently keepe companie and if the leading boates stay and the Dromes cease beating then shall they all stay, or if the sayd leading boate lead backward, or torne her course som other way he shall do the lyke. The first boates being landed shalbe led to a fytt place to make a stand to secure the grownd of descent. . . .[13]

---

[13] Treatise by Sir George Carew, 1596, LPL, Codex 250, printed with commentary and annotation by Usherwood (1983), 69, 136–7.

While the author, Sir George Carew, advocates the securing of the
beachhead, the practicalities of getting the boats ashore is never
addressed in terms of navigating heavy surf or anticipating fire from
the shore. Rather, like the infantry treatises of the early-modern
period, he is obsessed with formation and order. Such an emphasis
did little to transmit expertise from one generation to its successors.
Nor was the treatise published. Like the second Earl of Essex's notes
on amphibious warfare, these limited observations remained relatively uncirculated.

Carew delineates the operational duties of the mariners from those
of 'landmen.' Naval vessels routinely accommodated land soldiers as
part of the crew. Marine assault was a capability upon which Drake
insisted. Off Cape St Vincent, during the 1587 expedition, Sir Francis
determined to launch an amphibious assault, initially against Sagres,
but ultimately (as events turned) against Lagos, largely because he
had amphibious capabilities and was loathe to return to England
without unleashing English 'marines' against the Portuguese or
Spaniards.[14] Drake articulated his faith in combined operations roughly
a year later, urging yet another amphibious pre-emptive strike as the
best strategy to defeat Phillip II's armada.[15]

Intermingling the 'services' oftentimes precipitated trouble, and the
reaction of the sailors was unpredictable. Sailors and 'landsmen' usually followed different chains of command, even aboard ship. Answering
to officers whose experiences differed and whose interests competed
complicated operations and guaranteed a quarrel when land soldiers
acting as 'marines' plundered a city, whilst the seamen were denied
the opportunity to come ashore and enrich themselves.[16] However,
Plymouth sailors recruited for Sir Francis Drake's 1587 voyage refused
to board ship because their duties included disembarking if necessary to fight on land. The sailors' attitude towards amphibious service depended upon the prospects for plunder (a sentiment they
shared with more than a few of their commanders). These operational limitations reflect the immaturity of amphibious warfare in the
sixteenth century.

---

[14] Kelsey (1998), 287–8, 294–5.
[15] PRO, SP 12/209/40, old ff. 77–77v/new ff. 58–58v, printed in facsimile in
Rodger, ed. (1988), 42–5. Above, Wernham, ch. 7, pp. 187–8.
[16] Hammer (1997a), 622–4.

Ambivalent Strategies

Drake's descent on Cadiz, described in the previous chapter, instilled inordinate confidence that English amphibious actions could deliver a crippling blow to an enemy, thus precluding the necessity of an expensive land mobilization or shifting the location of hostilities to the territory of the aggressor. These assumptions, though sometimes true, were also unrealistically optimistic. The 1587 raid did not prevent the arrival of a Spanish fleet in the Channel in 1588, an expedition that nearly brought England and Protestant Europe to their knees.[17] The stunning devastation and dispersal of the 1588 Armada, however, reinforced the English strategists' notion that amphibious assault could reap victory at a relatively small price.

As the Elizabethan theatre of operations broadened through the 1580s and 1590s, fiscal constraints limited viable strategies. Thus while amphibious operations allowed the state to project its power upon Iberia, or against Catholic armies in Europe, or to intercept the transport of Spanish supplies and wealth, not all these objectives could be met at once. The Portugal expedition pursued two contradictory strategies, of setting up an outpost in Iberia (a plan later reprised by the Earl of Essex) and raiding. Despite the firepower and mobility of piratical raids on the fringes of the Atlantic, Drake and his compatriots might temporarily disrupt the Spanish grand strategy but they could not defeat it.

English amphibious warfare was often undermined by a lack of strategic focus and operational consensus. Limited resources prevented the English from sustaining a major initiative, such as blockading the Iberian Atlantic ports. Instead, some thought English efforts should be channelled to Calais, Normandy, Brittany as Henry IV's had been. Drake and Hawkins advocated a Caribbean strategy. Lastly, Lord Admiral Howard and others at court preferred a direct strike against Spain itself. Sir Roger Williams, the accomplished Elizabethan commander of land forces, saw the choice as lying among a trio of stratagems. First, the Army of Flanders might be defeated in the Netherlands; second, Iberia, the enemy's homeland, could be assailed; or third, the treasure fleets might be plundered and thus Phillip's

---

[17] Parker (1976), 358–368.

paymasters confounded.[18] Elizabeth's strategy vacillated among these three theatres in reaction to Spanish deployments. But like the English, Spanish efforts were undermined by Phillip II's advisors' unwise policy of trying to pursue simultaneously a trio of strategies.[19] In amphibious warfare, such strategic ambivalence often led to tactical blunders and carelessness in operations.[20]

The reputation of English combined operations, tarnished by the failures of 1589 and 1595, was rehabilitated by the sacking of Cadiz in 1596.[21] Like the 1587 raid, this triumph, too, fired the imagination of subsequent generations. But, as Bruce Wernham has argued in this volume, the capture of Cadiz in 1596 'was a remarkably fortunate outcome to a remarkably hazardous adventure.'[22] Indeed, within four months, Spain launched another armada, casting as much doubt on the decisiveness of the 1596 attack as upon the 1587 raid. In both cases armadas were delayed but not destroyed. The dominant strategy shifted again: Caribbean operations were revived, as the seizure of treasure appeared more feasible than the occupation of the Iberian Atlantic ports.

In mid-June 1598 the Earl of Cumberland, like Drake, approached Puerto Rico from the east, determined on an immediate landing just west of Condado point, far from the guns of the El Morro fortress. Here again, the English commander underestimated the efficiency of the Matadiabolo battery.[23] A landing near Boquéron would have required braving the Matadiabolo cannon and stopping short of the beach in the face of stakes that bristled in the shallow water. The Earl's 1,700 men moved south and attempted to seize the San Antonio Bridge that linked the island of San Juan with the main island. Wading through the currents brought the English no success and

---

[18] PRO, SP 78/24/79, Williams to the Privy Council, 24 April 1591, quoted by Wernham (1961), 347–8.

[19] Parker (1998), 182–3.

[20] Early-modern English land warfare was often characterised by tactical ingenuity, in contrast with the relative immaturity of naval warfare in the period. Fissel (2001), 7–6, 13, 16, 21–23, 26, 28, 31–3, 47, 57, 117, 120, 127, 134, 137, 142, 144, 151, 164–5, 170–80, 216–17, 220, 223–35, 250, 252–3, 263–4, 266–7, 286, 293, 297.

[21] Hammer (1997a), 182–202 and (1997b), 621–42; above, Wernham, ch. 7, pp. 203–7.

[22] Ch. 7, above, p. 206. However, see Hammer (1997a), 182–202.

[23] Cf. Wernham, above, ch. 7, p. 202.

very nearly drowned an armour-clad Cumberland. A resolute Spanish defence, behind a withdrawn drawbridge guarded by ordnance and pikes, blocked the English advance on the town. Stalled, the attackers absorbed a punishing cannonade from Matadiabolo's five bronze artillery pieces positioned on the Boquerón peninsula.

The extent of Cumberland's foolishness in repeating Drake's tactical mistake was revealed when a one-hour bombardment from a single vessel put Boquerón out of action. This was accomplished in a combined operation wherein 200 'marines' established a second beachhead near Boquerón and attacked Matadiabolo from land whilst an expendable vessel fired upon the fortress and defensive positions from nearly point-blank range. Though the craft ultimately foundered upon the shore, the attack beat the Spaniards from Matadiabolo. The main body came ashore, effectively flanking the stalwart defence of the San Antonio Bridge and prompting the defenders to withdraw westward to the town.

The numerical superiority of the invaders allowed them to overcome their tactical blunders. On 18 June Cumberland found the remaining defenders had fled to El Morro. Cumberland's siege craft proved better than his direction of amphibious operations, and the citadel surrendered on 1 July 1598. But, ironically, as had been the case in Iberia, the English expedition lacked the resources to hold what it had taken. Despite overcoming their initial tactical mistakes, the English had overreached themselves. Cumberland's fleet abandoned San Juan and sailed homeward on 27 August.[24]

There were few genuinely successful offensive combined operations on the high seas and in the Atlantic ports, and even then strategic limitations prevented England from holding ground it had taken. Government and commanders quarrelled over strategic priorities in the Atlantic and Caribbean. The consequent oscillation of royal strategies bedevilled operational cohesion. Commanders made mistakes both strategic and tactical repeatedly. While marauding did slowly undermine Spanish trade, the strategy of plunder failed. 'The English never captured a treasure fleet, and thus never succeeded in paralyzing the Spanish war effort.'[25] But at reign's end, the spoils and

---

[24] Wernham (1994), 254–6; Monson (1902), 204–25; Spence (1995), 157–73; Corbett (1900), 228–52.
[25] Andrews (1966), 224.

glory of Elizabethan actions against Cadiz (limited in strategic value as they were) remained in the English collective memory, while the failures (such as those in Puerto Rico) and near-disasters (such as the combined operation against Portugal in 1589) were largely forgotten.[26]

Seaborne achievements were defensive and temporary, and simply delayed the amphibious threat against England in 1587 and again in 1596. These actions did not prevent the sailing of Spanish armadas in 1588, 1597 and 1599. When faced with the choice of burning the intended 1597 armada in the port of Ferrol or seeking the Spanish treasure fleet, the Earl of Essex and his comrades found the former operation too daunting and the latter too tempting.[27] As for the Queen, she neither could achieve nor desired the destruction of Spain, for the latter nation counterbalanced French ambitions. Safeguarding her realm and regime from Roman Catholic invasion remained Elizabeth's strategy, as ambiguous and ambivalent as it might be. What operational methods best served that strategy, however?

Offensive and pre-emptive amphibious operations might prevent enemy assault on the state's coastal defences but simultaneously could also provoke and justify those attacks. Therefore, the conduct of England's defensive strategy often mirrored its offensive strategic ambivalence. The Spaniards' arrival off the English coast in summer 1588 should have fit England's essentially defensive strategy. Guarding the beaches was a long-lived tradition, especially on the southern coast of the British Isles. As long ago as 56–55 B.C., when Caesar's legionaries met native resistance on the shoreline, and as recently as Winston Churchill's defiant 'we shall fight them on the beaches' speech, there persisted a substantial strategic (and tactical) conviction that confronting the aggressor at the water's edge, in other words disrupting the amphibious invasion at its most precarious stage, was Albion's best defence.

However, Elizabeth's advisors never could, in 1588 or after, reach consensus concerning the superiority of littoral defence as against gathering inland more substantial forces that could dislodge an invader from his beachhead.[28] Against the Armada of 1588 they compro-

---

[26] Hammer (1997b), 621–42.
[27] Wernham (1994), 165–9, 171–2; idem, above, ch. 7, pp. 210–11.
[28] BL, Harleian MSS 6798, ff. 25–41v, and 132, ff. 2–17v.

mised. They fielded forces totalling 27,000 infantry and 2,500 cavalry (although actual field strengths were doubtless less than this) along the southern shoreline with orders to engage immediately any landings in their vicinity. In theory this tactical deployment would impede and delay the invaders enough to allow other forces and inland militias to rush to the invasion site.

England's shires had long observed (with varying degrees of efficiency) the 'Auncient Order for Beacons.'[29] In Kent, the Armada's targeted disembarkation point, a network of unlit bonfires rested upon the various hilltops. Lookouts anticipated the invaders.[30] In land-locked counties as well, the beacon system was kept in readiness.

> In euerie place beacons be erected and persons dwellinge therbie be assigned to ouersee the watche therof, and at eurie beacon a keavill [lookout] is appoynted, by which the watchemen may certeynly discover the fieringe of that beacon frome whome they are to receyve their warninge.[31]

With a decentralised and regional system in place to repel enemy landings, or at least keep invaders at bay until an amalgamated force of trained band soldiers could be gathered, the Crown focused upon pre-emptive action against foreign ports from which vessels could be launched against England and Wales. Conversely, Philip II's Council of State was encouraged by the abundance of suitable ports and landing sites that dotted the English coastline, making virtually all regions of the realm vulnerable to amphibious incursion.[32] Spain's veteran army in the Low Countries needed only to cross the few but treacherous miles of the Channel The Duke of Parma, who

---

[29] J. Wake, ed. (1926), 7–8.
[30] See 'A Carde, of the Beacons, in Kent', printed in Lambard (1596), 70–1, and reprinted in numerous modern works. See also White (1934), 77–96.
[31] Goring and Wake (1975), 12, article 12. Even after the Elizabethan war years the beacons of the coastal defense system were tended to, for example in 1613–1619. The upkeep of the piles of flammable material and 'seagards' (the latter a service often performed by paid 'watchers') usually was enforced when the early Stuarts perceived a specific external threat, from the mobilizations surrounding the Cleves-Julich war to the arrival of a Spanish fleet in the Downs in 1639. Wake (1935), liv, lvi, lx; Quintrell (1993), 24, item 48; 30, item 61; 33, item 71; 43, item 109; 46, item 124; 47, item 125; 80–1, item 244; 84, item 253; 85, item 254; 87, item 261; 89, item 263; 119, item 322; 121, item 329; 132, item 354; 136, item 362, article 7 and cross reference to note 284 on 381; 192, item 480; 243, item 590; 321, item 700; 322, item 701; 324, item 702; 342, item 734.
[32] Loomie (1963), 288–300.

commanded the latter forces, assembled 17,000 soldiers in late July 1588. Since the men could not be deployed upon the coastline for fear of revealing the Armada's strategy they could only embark within thirty-six hours of the flotilla being sighted.

On 27 July 1588 the Armada appeared off Boulogne, prompting Sir Thomas Scott and Sir John Norris to muster thirty ensigns of infantry and three cornets of cavalry at the Downs.[33] On 30 July, the realm's beacons came into play when signal fires were ignited on the Lizard, at the tip of Cornwall, when spanish vessels came within view.[34] As formidable a sight as the Armada's entrance into the Channel presented, the Spanish failed to meet the challenges of a major amphibious operation. Despite Parma's Herculean triumph of amphibious logistical planning, the Armada commander Medina Sidonia's inability to fathom amphibious operations and understand the practical problems involved in linking up with the Duke's transports undermined the enterprise, and ultimately the campaign. Medina Sidonia unreasonably and repeatedly requested 40–50 flyboats from Parma. He also insisted that the Duke's 'marines' venture forth without sufficient convoy. The planned conjunction failed and the Army of Flanders never undertook the eight to twelve hour voyage to Margate.[35]

What should have been an amphibious conveyance became an indecisive running naval battle in the Channel from 30 July through 4 August 1588. Clearly English seamanship impressed their Spanish adversaries, as Lord Admiral Howard's vessels manoeuvred, took the wind, and inflicted cannonades so intense that Spanish veterans of Lepanto sailing with the Armada reckoned the English unleashed twenty times the firepower that they had seen in that earlier grand naval battle.[36] But for all the powder spent, only one Spanish galleon was sunk. More damaging were simple fireships,[37] sent among the anchored Armada off Calais Roads on 7 August, and reprised on

---

[33] McGurk (1970), 71, 79–89; Boynton (1967), 160.

[34] Nolan (1991), 401.

[35] Parker (1998), 229–50; Hammer (2003), 151. See also Guilmartin (2002), 180–1, pointing out that earlier communication between the Armada and Parma might have resulted in a successful rendezvous.

[36] Fernandez-Armesto (1988), 142–3, 151, 158–9.

[37] Vessels laden with explosives and/or flammable materials sent out to ignite enemy ships.

10 August, when the Spanish cut their cables, anchors and moorings in a panic. In late August and September, as the Armada circumnavigated Scotland and Ireland, storms sank the largest number of ships.

The Armada was indeed defeated, but English ordnance claimed only a solitary victim, and despite the devastation wrought upon Phillip's fleet by gales and storms during the homeward journey, the defeat of the Armada was not decisive, for more Spanish fleets would sail against England over the coming decade. There remained fear not only of Spanish galleons, but galleys as well, for 'galleys were universally regarded as being at their most formidable in their natural habitat, coastal waters. Wherever coastal defence was needed, Spanish officers always demanded, and English always feared, the presence of galleys'.[38]

Combined Operations in Brittany

Rethinking their strategy for the 'enterprise of England', some of Phillip's ministers recommended the Breton harbour of Brest as 'a perfect staging base for a new armada.'[39] A deep-water port more proximate to England than was Iberia could provide logistical support for a large-scale invasion of the British Isles. From Brest, galleys might be deployed and join with land-based forces to secure much of the Breton peninsula as well as to threaten England and English forces abroad.[40] Sir John Norris told the Queen that Spanish control of Breton ports would be as prejudicial to England as if the Spaniards occupied Ireland.[41] While the French governor of Brest exercised vigilance against a Spanish attempt on his city, a modest English garrison under Norris occupied Paimpol on 5 May 1591.[42]

In March 1593 Don Juan de Aguila, operating out of Blavet, swooped down on Brest Roads and fortified the point of the Crozon

---

[38] Rodger (1998), 92.

[39] Nolan (1995), 259–61; above, Wernham, ch. 7, pp. 197–200.

[40] For a comparison of the fighting capabilities of galleys and galleons, see Guilmartin (2002), 106–181, 206–213, Rodger (1996), 303–4, 306–8, 314, 317 and Rodger (1998), 82–3, 85–7, 91.

[41] L&A, 5: no. 320, 290 (F415).

[42] MacCaffrey (1992), 153; Nolan (1997), 183; idem (1995), 262.

peninsula. The harbour entrance to Brest now lay in Spanish hands. Norris and Sir Martin Frobisher gathered reinforcements and cannon from England to succour Sir Thomas Baskerville, who remained in Brittany with a depleted force. Baskerville countered Spanish movements through the spring and early summer of 1594 in concert with Marshal Aumont, leading local levies and regular French troops. The allies seized the port of Morlaix. Frobisher's flotilla arrived and unloaded indispensable siege artillery, reinforcements and supplies, intimidating a castle on an islet in the estuary into surrender in the process. Five days later Frobisher sailed to Brest Roads to commence the bombardment of Fort Crozon, dubbed 'El Leon' by its Spanish occupiers.

Norris planned to join with Baskerville in the port of Morlaix. Unfortunately, Morlaix harbour's passage proved hazardous for the troopships. Lacking local pilots, they diverted to Paimpol, Norris's old headquarters, which had no dockside accommodation for large ships. Norris's marines 'waded ashore and dragged their heavy equipment through shallow water.'[43] The problem was securing a safe haven capable of accommodating deep draught ships and possessing adequate dock facilities to unlade equipment and large numbers of men. The alternative was to use river barges, similar to those shown in figure 8, and troop transports, generally flat-bottomed, hard-to-manoeuvre, and vulnerable to enemy fire.

Norris had intended to exploit Morlaix's dockyards and port as a staging area in which to collect the recently delivered ordnance and embark his infantrymen. From there he would convey the English companies to Brest via barges. But England's dubious ally, Marshal Aumont, struck a bargain at the surrender of Morlaix that admitted only Roman Catholics into the town. Norris and his Protestant troops had to march to Brest. Frobisher wisely had already shipped Norris's siege train from Morlaix's port facilities to the burgeoning siege works around Fort Crozon.

Aguila's Spaniards, ensconced in the newly constructed fortress of El Leon, faced allied naval bombardment while Norris's English and Aumont's French besieged the landward side of El Leon, its impos-

---

[43] *L&A*, 5: no. 316, 287–8 (F397); no. 319, 289–90 (F404); no. 334, 298 (F527, F529, F530); no. 337, 300 (F538); no. 338, 300–301 (F541, F548); no. 339, 301 (F556, F557); no. 340, 302 (F566, F568); no. 342, 303 (F568); Nolan (1995), 262–7.

ing fortifications perched on a cliff top.[44] After a month's slogging, a French mine breached the defences; a desperate assault followed. Frobisher's sailors led the charge through the now-opened fortress gate and annihilated the garrison.[45]

The fall of El Leon had a tremendous if temporary impact on English coastal defence because the Spaniards had been denied a strategic port. Indeed, the armadas of 1597 and 1599 foundered in part because they lacked such a docking facility. The expulsion of the Spaniards from Brest Roads and the Crozon peninsula allowed Elizabeth to redeploy her forces in Brittany and the Low Countries to the increasingly insecure Irish theatre. However, while Spanish galleons could not operate out of the less functional Breton port of Blavet, galleys could. The loss of El Leon had stymied the 'galleon strategy'. Denied the advantage of sending galleons out of Brest, the Spanish now set about deploying galleys from Blavet.

The heavy ordnance mounted in a Spanish galley's bow might bombard coastal defences. Galleys' ability to manoeuvre inshore, powered by oars, made them the ideal vehicle to disgorge enemy infantry upon West Country beaches. Since the triumph of French galleys over Henry VIII's ships in 1513, English amphibious defences remained vulnerable to galleys, so much so that 'the galley was, for Englishmen, the modern naval weapon-system, the one they feared and envied above all.'[46]

The departure of English forces from Brittany between November 1594 and January 1595 gave Spanish vessels more room to manoeuvre in the Channel. In May 1595 a Spanish shallop[47] from Blavet penetrated Falmouth harbour and snared prisoners who might know about English naval preparations at Plymouth. The Lord Lieutenant of Cornwall, Sir Francis Godolphin, anticipated the interdiction of English vessels off the Scilly Isles and perhaps a massive Catholic invasion. Around 17 July 1595, Cornish militia repelled an incursion south of Padstow, at St Eval. Shortly after dawn on the 23rd,

---

[44] *L&A*, 5: no. 345, 304–305 (F576, F577, F595); above, Wernham, ch. 7, pp. 198–9; Nolan (1995), 267–9.

[45] *L&A*, 5: no. 350, 307–308 (F606, F610, F611); no. 351, 308–309 (F623, F632); no. 355, 310 (F633, F634, F641, F643); above, Wernham, ch. 7, p. 200; Hammer (2003), 180–2; Nolan (1995), 270.

[46] Rodger (1998), 82

[47] *Chaloupes* or sloops included a broad category of vessels that operated in shallow waters, powered by oars or sails, oftentimes a small two-master with lugsails.

the Spaniards disembarked around Mousehole two hundred infantry who burnt and plundered at will. Godolphin rallied the locality and summoned naval forces from Plymouth. The Spaniards next struck at Newlyn with their full raiding party of 400 pikemen and arquebusiers. Godolphin was powerless to stop the invaders from taking most of Penzance.

The Spanish galleys might have established a base at Scilly or launched attacks farther east had not Cornish forces positioned a pair of cannon in western Mounts Bay. Additional amphibious raids were launched, with less success than at Mousehole, Newlyn and Penzance, at Cawsand Bay and the Welsh western coast.[48] England's defences had been breached successfully by a significant force and towns damaged. Elizabeth's government redoubled its efforts to improve coastal defence.[49]

England's focus on littoral defence in the mid-1590s was prompted, too, by the geographic breadth of the wars of religion. The Queen's soldiers, many of whom had experience with estuarine and riverine operations, were redeployed with some regularity as the strategic situation changed. Ferried out of the Low Countries into Brittany and thence to Ireland, English soldiers carried their continental combat expertise in various forms of amphibious warfare to new theatres, with mixed results. Many had participated in combined operations against Iberia, and thus had expertise in ship-to-shore amphibious warfare, in addition to what they had learnt fighting on lakes, rivers and in estuaries.[50]

Elizabethan forces gained naval and amphibious experience in the French wars of religion as they had in the Dutch Wars. Fighting for the Protestant cause, they penetrated estuaries, navigated tidal basins and shallow rivers. On 7 October 1562, for example, the *Brigandine*, a 'moderately large oar/sail driven vessel' carrying somewhat fewer than 200 English soldiers, breached a river barricade erected by royalist forces besieging Rouen. The *Brigandine* and her sister vessel, firing bronze cannon and small iron guns, pierced the obstruction but were destroyed in the process. However, four smaller English

---

[48] Boynton (1967), 190–1.
[49] Rowse (1969), 403–6.
[50] BL, Lansdowne MS 1218, old ff. 125–152/new ff. 113–140v; Fissel (2001), 177–80.

boats got through in the wake of the pair of vessels' destruction and reached Rouen.[51] At Le Mans in 1590, English troops manufactured an amphibious craft by lashing together barrels and ladders.[52] Riverine operations in north-western France were evolving simultaneously with lacustrine and riverine operations in Ireland, and there was some cross-pollenisation when English companies were transferred.[53]

Ireland

All English soldiers arrived in Ireland by water, and it was a logical extension of a logistical necessity that transformed transport ships into combat vessels. Ireland's terrain and geography made the Irish Nine Years' War (1593–1601) a showcase of lacustrine and riverine joint operations. The 'vital centre' of the conflict was Ulster, where rivers, lakes and hills shaped the course of the war. The eastern coast had long been used to invasions from the Western Isles of Scotland and Britain's mainland. In the northwest, the emptying of the River Foyle into Lough Foyle provided an avenue for incursions, especially at the site of what would become Londonderry. In the southwestern region of Ulster, the River Erne and its associated loughs bounded Connaught, where the ford at Ballyshannon was of great strategic significance.[54] Directly south, routes snaked through Sligo and the eastern region of Lough Gill. Ballyshannon (between Donegal Bay and Lough Erne) sat along the river at a crucial point.

'Amphibious operations were clearly necessary to make any inroads in Ulster.'[55] River routes were essential for the subjection of Ulster because of the 'Drumlin belt' that stretched from County Down to Donegal Bay. This formidable topographical barrier presented obstacles to any army approaching from the south. The numerous hillocks, wooded corries and bogs, prone to frequent flooding, compelled

---

[51] Glasgow (1968), 285. The small iron pieces were deck-mounted swivel guns, known later as 'latankas.'

[52] Fissel (2001), 164.

[53] BL, Lansdowne MS 1218, old ff. 125–152/new ff. 113–140v, discussed at length in Fissel (2001), 177–9.

[54] Hayes-McCoy (1931–3), 141–59.

[55] McGurk (1997), 7.

armies to resort to river transportation, especially when they hauled artillery and wagons. An important crossing lay at Enniskillen, in county Fermanagh, a town squarely located on Lough Erne. Finally, in southeast Ulster, the River Blackwater and its celebrated fort provided the gateway to the rest of Ireland, especially to the Pale.[56]

Londonderry, on the west bank of the River Foyle, was surrounded by waterways and bogs in the early seventeenth century. At the turn of the century, the defences of the fort that would become the city of Londonderry incorporated six gun platforms, as is illustrated by a map of 'the Island and forte of the derry.'[57] The Foyle flowed into the lough, arcing around the 'island' of Londonderry. Forts were positioned at the river bends.

Sir Henry Docwra, commander of the Derry garrisons, possessed 'Certaine Shipps called Crompsters with other barks and bardges.'[58] Their two-fold mission was to provide tactical support for the penetration of Lough Foyle and its tributaries, and to act as a coast guard in the estuaries and coastal waters: 'gyve order to your Crompstres, barques and barges . . . to stop those Scottish gallies and boates as haue trade with the Rebbells . . . or . . . bring them . . . victuals powder or mvnitions.'[59] Victualling and water transport were thus inextricably linked with 'aquatic defences.' Commissary Robert Newcomen, for example, had cots (roughly hewn, dug-out boats) laden with barrels of beer towed up river to a thirsty garrison.[60] Command of the rivers facilitated victualling, which in turn secured the logistical base for domination of the region.

Actions were undertaken from sailing craft and oared vessels, with ordnance mounted in the bows of the latter. The well-armed *Grace of God* from Newcastle and the *Samaritan* of London patrolled the Foyle and its tributaries from May 1600.[61] A flotilla consisting of a

---

[56] Hayes-McCoy (1940–1), 263–8.
[57] PRO, SP 63/207 pt. 6/84 I, reproduced in McGurk (1997), 222, and in (2001), 90, 95–7, attributing the map to Joyes Everard (an engineer from the Netherlands) and Thomas Rookewood (deputy surveyor).
[58] LPL, Carew MS 632, f. 189, printed in O'Donovan, ed. (1849), 287–9. The editor assigns the date of March 1599, but they are most likely March 1599/1600.
[59] Ibid., 291; Morgan (2004c), 73–87.
[60] PRO, SP 63/173/8 III, f. 31.
[61] McGurk (1997), 221–2.

30 tonne barque, a pair of 20 tonne boats and a 14 tonne vessel made up a semi-permanent presence on Lough Erne used for tactical operations as well as transporting victuals.[62] The Governor of Connaught, Sir Oliver Lambert, obtained a vessel that could destroy the galleys of the Gaelic corsairs Flaherty and O'Malley and 'cleare the Coasts.' Lambert's new galley carried fifty mariners and 'roes with 15 oares on a side.'[63] He was seconded by the amphibious craft of Docwra that controlled the Foyle. Captain Hugh Clotworthy patrolled Lough Neagh, and a similar flotilla operated out of Ballyshannon and patrolled the tributaries of the Erne.[64] These miniature navies engaged enemy river craft as well as snipers who fired on royal vessels, and they also proved capable of assaulting castles.

Taking keeps and perfecting riverine amphibious assaults

In Ireland, water often assumed the function of fortification, as a 'natural moat' to protect a keep. Amphibious assault thus became a part of English siege craft. Customarily, the Irish erected keeps that stood on islands in the middle of loughs.[65] The Irish tendency to withdraw into these keeps prevented their engaging English amphibious raids when they were most vulnerable—during the process of disembarkation. For example, Sir Oliver Lambert crossed the River Moy en route to Sligo in early June 1602. The Irish occupied a pair of castles 'on the best ffordes', but offered no resistance during the two days and a night the English ferried across the Moy. Lambert observed that 'the enemy might have had a great advantage of us, if they had adventured to withstand our first landing.'[66] Given the Gaelic specialisation in mobile operations, it is astounding that such defenders preferred to await a siege rather than sallying forth to disrupt the attack.

---

[62] PRO, SP 63/211/38, new ff. 115–115v, 31 May 1602. The cost *per annum* (including sails, cables, anchors, cordage, and crews) should have been £2000, but the Irish establishment could only muster £700 annually, and needed the balance paid in England.

[63] PRO, SP 63/211/61C, old f. 137/new f. 68, 18 June 1602.

[64] McGurk (2001), 105; *CSP Ir.*, 9:280 etc.; *CSP Ir.*, 11:63–4, 396–7, etc.

[65] The strongholds were often referred to as *crannóga* and served as arms caches as well places of refuge: see McGurk, (2001), 105. Unique Gaelic fortifications included *bastles*, peel towers and tower houses: Ohlmeyer (1998), 129.

[66] PRO, SP 63/211/61C, old ff. 131–132/new ff. 165–165v; Carroll (2004), 224.

Operations at Clonoan Castle and Enniskillen Castle demonstrated that Irish fortifications were indeed vulnerable to amphibious assault, rendering ineffective the strategy of sheltering in a keep surrounded by water. When Sir Richard Bingham attempted Clonoan Castle, six miles northeast of Corofin (County Clare) with a hundred English soldiers and a few kearne, he 'wanne the Castell . . . and the warde within . . . without . . . any great Ordynaunce.' Bingham advanced to Castle Necallye (Hag's Castle, set upon a man-made islet in Lough Mask, Ballinrobe, County Mayo). 'The seidge was all by water in Boats, and coulde not [be] otherwyse'.[67]

In mid-January 1594, chieftain Hugh Maguire of Fermamagh sheltered in Enniskillen Castle on the island in the great Lough. Waters flowing from the Erne into the Lough were much wider then than now, and were swollen from heavy rains.[68] The Gaels had built sconces and planted stakes to impede English river traffic.[69] Captain John Dowdall (a pioneer in Hibernian amphibious warfare) operated out of Castle Enisce and harassed Maguire by capturing the rebels' food supply, namely 700 cows. Dowdall protected his cattle thievery with a 'troope of loose shott.' Maguire, spying his animals being herded away on the other side of the Lough, launched a boat to investigate. The English fired on the approaching cot, slew two men, and sent the survivors rowing back to the island. The English also over-ran a sconce that Maguire had built 'within a small lough' nearby and put the defenders to the sword. They burnt the structure. Six days later the English rooted out yet more sconces, stakes, and obstacles that had been placed along the waterside to impede river craft. This mid-winter siege and waterborne assault required close logistical support and erection of fortifications and camps for the besiegers.

By 25 January Captain Dowdall had entrenched within caliver shot of Enniskillen Castle. This artillery was of fairly modest calibre, three 'ffaukonets', which battered the castle walls.[70] On Saturday,

---

[67] BL, Harleian MS 357, printed in O'Donovan, ed. (1849), 194–5.

[68] PRO, SP 63/173/4, new f. 8, the Lord Deputy to the Privy Council; Falls (1950), 177.

[69] PRO, SP 63/173/17 IV, new f. 57.

[70] Ibid. and PRO, SP 63/173/16 I, new f. 49. The absence of heavier pieces, such as a 'culvering' [sic for culverin] available to the forces, was due to the difficulty of transporting artillery. See SP 63/173/4, new f. 8, on the 'culvering' and seasonal 'moisture.' On over-all strategy, see Lenman (2001), 111–12.

2 February 1594, Dowdall launched three boats across the Great Lough. In the lead was a 'greate boate',[71] sporting a mast and oars. Aboard were 67 assault troops, protected and hidden from view by 'hurdells and hides' stretched over the deck. Following closely were a pair of cots each with fifteen soldiers, scaling ladders positioned astern. In the bow of each cot were a pair of gunners aiming swivel guns at Enniskillen Castle. With a local guide's assistance, the great boat drew alongside the castle's barbican, where the English marines used 'Pyck-axes and other instruments' to breach the wall.[72] Maguire's thirty-six warders retreated to the castle keep, but ultimately surrendered. The English suffered only two wounded, injured by gunfire.[73] As Dowdall told the Lord Deputy, 'wee did assault the said Castle by boates, by Engins, and by Sapp [tunneling] and by Scaling.'[74]

Water sometimes supplemented obstacles erected to hinder advancing English land forces, especially at river crossings. In such circumstances, the land forces borrowed amphibious tactics. The Erne River flowed from Lough Erne past a point upon which Maguire's men built up modest earthworks and barricades, through a widening of the river called the 'Leape', and into a lough deep enough to accommodate English vessels, which were, however, too far distant to be able to help attack Maguire's fortifications. On 10 October 1593, Captain Lee and Captain Dowdall directly assaulted the defences by fording the River Erne. While flanking detachments of musketeers poured in a substantial fire that occupied the Irish, Dowdall and Lee's musketeers and sword-and-buckler men plunged into the River Erne and, waist-deep in the currents, returned fire against the sconce, before the defences were taken at sword point. Irish evacuation of the riverside allowed the English main army to cross and rout Maguire's gallowglasses.[75]

---

[71] Two English great boats (fifty feet in length, with a beam of eleven feet) were constructed in the 1589 building program, incorporating a kind of canopy (a 'companion') as well as 'a platform afore the shooting of two demi-culverins from either of them', indicating firepower would be applied from the bow (as a galley would fire) and perhaps the stern (depending if the 'companion' was a matching platform or in fact meant as a canopy). Bennell (1974), 176–7.

[72] PRO, MPF 1/80, formerly classified as SP 64/1/13. See also figures 10 and 11, illustrated below.

[73] BL, Cottonian MS Augustus I. ii, f. 39; PRO, SP 63/173/19 III, new f. 68.

[74] PRO, SP 63/173/19 I, new f. 64.

[75] BL, Cottonian MS Augustus I. ii, f. 38; Swift (1999), 43; Lenman (2001), 111. A gallowglass (*galloglaich*, or 'foreign warrior') was a professional, 'heavy' infantryman.

The tactic was reprised on 14 July 1597 when Lord Deputy Burgh assaulted the Irish-held Blackwater Fort. Five columns of English musketeers waded across the Blackwater and, possibly with axes, made a breach in the riverbank defences while the defenders returned fire with calivers, muskets and a trio of cannon. Burgh's daring frontal attack across a river proved decisive, despite the fact that the Irish had the advantage of firing from the security of a fortification.[76] Thus, firepower was exercised by infantry crossing rivers and marshes, as well as from small vessels. Moreover, it is striking that, when water was involved, the English won the engagement, whereas they lost many of the strictly land-based battles. Amphibious tactical expertise could thus have a more general application.

The climax of the Nine Years' War, however, occurred not in the vortex of the conflict, Ulster, with its loughs and rivers, but to the south, in Counties Cork, Kerry and Desmond. There, estuarine and riverside fortresses (especially those safeguarding ports) attracted the guns of seagoing vessels.[77]

Irish Littoral and Estuarine Operations

In taking Enniskillen Castle, the English had employed amphibious artillery against land-based defences. They did so again, at the siege of Kinsale, at the end of 1601, when a Spanish expedition garrisoned the town in support of the Irish rebellion. Commanding the Spanish garrison was none other than Don Juan Aguila, whose galleys had battled the English in Brittany and who had raided Cornwall.

As a harbour city, Kinsale possessed seaward and landward defences. The town was encircled by inlets and waterways (such as Oyster Haven) feeding from Millwater, Ballincurra Creek, and the Bandon River. Given this geography, the Elizabethan navy for the first and last time during the Nine Years' War was able to exploit seadog gunnery, ship-to-shore bombardment, and support of land forces by the transference of ordnance ashore. After first taking Rincorran

---

[76] Trinity College Dublin MS 1209/34. *CSP Ir.*, 5:165–8; Fissel (2001), 219.
[77] Loeber and Parker (1995), 67, 69.

Castle, situated on a peninsula that jutted into Kinsale harbour, the English navy then brought ashore the artillery needed for a siege.

Reacting to this English deployment on the coastline, Spanish ships diverted their 1,000 reinforcements to Castlehaven harbour, disembarking thirty miles from the beleaguered Kinsale garrison. The admiral of Elizabeth's Irish fleet, Sir Richard Leveson, whose flotilla had been anchored in Kinsale harbour, sailed to carry out an amphibious operation against these Spanish forces under the command of General Don Pedro de Zubiaur. The Spaniards had been busy securing beachheads in Munster as a prelude for a larger invasion. When Leveson's seven vessels penetrated Castlehaven harbour, they found their amphibious assault stymied by 500 Irish infantry defending the shore. Spanish vessels, however, could not engage the English ships due to contrary winds, and both sides contented themselves with firing salvoes. Leveson's cannonades forced the *Maria Francesca* to run aground, but Zubiaur riposted by evacuating the helpless vessel's ordnance and erecting a shore battery that pounded the English ships. The English cut their mooring cables and fled the harbour.[78]

More effective were the floating gun platforms used against Kinsale. Mountjoy told Carew, 'wee have now landed all our artillerye taken in Castell ne Parke [and] left a companye there and att Rincorin [castle]. This day the shipps doo land fower cullverins in the Iland to beate the towne. Wee have alreddie six peeces upon the raft.' The 'raft', capable of buoying half a dozen cannon, projected waterborne firepower without endangering English vessels. Presenting a low target, the 'rafts' fired with relative impunity. As Mountjoy put it, 'frome the raft wee doo great harme in the towne.'[79] The point here is that in Irish littoral and estuarine operations there were numerous imaginative applications of firepower, as had been the case in north-western France.

Dunboy (1602) constituted yet another example. In marching from Cork to Dunboy Castle during May and June 1602, a tedious but necessary exercise to eradicate enemies at his rear and to inspect strongholds, Sir George Carew was resupplied by sea. The terrain restricted his army's daily march to a mere three miles, 'and for 12

---

[78] McGurk (2004), 147–59; Silke (1970), 134–5 draws upon Spanish archival sources.

[79] LPL, Carew MS 615, f. 362v, 23 November 1601.

myles togeather the wayes are so straight [narrow] as in the best of it 3: men cannott marche in front, and in most places but in file.' Stretched out and unaccompanied by cavalry, the column proceeded in constant peril of an ambush, Carew asserting that 100 Irish could stymie 5,000 English upon this terrain.[80] When he came to Bantry Bay, Carew 'resolved to crosse the bay off [of] Bantrye by sea', bypassing the twenty-four mile land route with its formidable wooded hills and bogs. The 4,000 English managed to ferry themselves, without harassment from the Irish, to Bere Island, within sight of the small bay that lay before Dunboy Castle. Any amphibious approach would necessarily be piecemeal and time-consuming because the English 'had not Boats sufficient to transport all our Regiments at once.'[81] On the shore the Gaels had erected gabions and dug trenches. However, Carew spied an alternate landing site, unobservable to the entrenched defenders. He wafted a pair of regiments to the smaller island of Dinish; they fired on the Irish gabions as if in preparation for an amphibious landing. Two additional regiments now made for Dinish, as if the entire invasion force were mustering on that island. But rather than running ashore at Dinish, the vessels proceeded on and landed at the hidden beach. The Gaels responded tardily to this tactical manoeuvre, and the English secured the beachhead, repelling those Irish who came to dislodge them.[82]

Seaborne relief appeared for the beleaguered Dunboy defenders in the form of a Spanish ship which brought money, a 'Vicar Apostolic', assurances of Spanish intervention, and most useful, powder and shot. The Irish had at least a pair of cannon to defend the waterside castle. Carew countered by capturing Dursey Island and its garrison, which completed an aquatic circumvallation, with English ordnance firing across the estuary at numerous points. After the demolition of Dunboy's turret, a breach was made. The ensuing assault was characteristically brutal in its execution. The English had successfully stormed Dunboy castle by taking advantage of ordnance positioned upon peninsulas and the firepower of naval vessels dan-

---

[80] PRO, SP 63/211/37, old f. 95/new f. 111, 29 May; *Carew Calendar*, 235–6, no. 237, 13 May.

[81] Stafford (1633), 305, which extracts much from Carew's own account.

[82] Ibid., 304. The English possessed a pair of bronze falcons (light cannon that fired a six pound ball), which they apparently deployed smartly: 'our falcons made them hault'.

gerously skirting the shoreline.[83] The episode of the sack of Dunboy illustrated again the English facility in amphibious warfare, which successes included supplying Carew's column from the sea, aquatic transportation of troops, and estuarine combat.

Amphibious assault employing firepower enabled the English to subdue Irish localities, notably in Ulster and Munster. Once Irish strongholds were taken, English garrisons then held the regions in submission. This policy was not new in Anglo-Celtic relations. In 1547 the estuarine penetration of the Firth of Forth brought English galleys close to shore at the battle of Pinkie. The ensuing cannonades on the Scottish infantry determined the outcome of the contest. English garrisons, perhaps modelled upon the programme of Edward I, held the conquered territory. The Nine Years' War was both the best suited for small-scale amphibious operations and the most needful of large-scale garrisoning. From the outset, it was a 'garrison war.'

Maguire of Fermanagh had begun the Ulster War in May 1593 with incursions against the new settlements in Monaghan, first Sligo and Roscommon, and then against Monaghan's garrison.[84] The Gaelic superiority in mobility upon land had to be countered by English mobility and firepower on the seas, lakes, estuaries and rivers. In spring 1600 the new Lord Deputy, Charles Blount Earl of Mountjoy, and Sir Henry Docwra brought about through combined operations 'the accomplishment of the great venture, the planting of a garrison in Lough Foyle' and 'the most important single disposition of the war.'[85] While Docwra approached Londonderry, Mountjoy fought a diversionary action that culminated in the Battle of the Moyry Pass,[86] allowing Docwra to reach Culmore at the mouth of River Foyle. By the end of May 1600, the fort at Londonderry, unoccupied since the deputyship of Sir Henry Sidney, was being reconstructed.[87]

---

[83] Ibid., 306. The siege is illustrated between 310 and 311 and is depicted in this volume as fig. 16; Falls (1950), 320–323; Carroll (2004), 224.

[84] Hayes-McCoy (1990), 90; Ellis (1998), 336.

[85] Falls (1950), 262; Hayes-McCoy (1940–1), 269; McGurk (2001), 96; Morgan (2004c), 73–87.

[86] Hayes-McCoy (1990), 132–43.

[87] O'Donovan, ed. (1849), 236–9, 296–7; Falls (1950), 262–3.

Cemented by the amphibious disposition of 4,000 troops in the Londonderry area garrisons, Mountjoy's strategy in 1601–2 paralysed O'Neill and O'Donnell. The Spanish amphibious intervention (October–December 1601) succoured the Gaelic Irish but undermined a Catholic victory by concentrating Catholic forces at Kinsale, changing the nature of a war that arguably the Irish chieftains were winning.[88] Clearly, however, English amphibious operations exhibited success in loughs, rivers and estuaries, ranging from river-crossings to bloody sieges. These victories enabled the English to continue waging war until the Kinsale campaign turned the course of the conflict in their favour. Ireland's resulting pacification, which progressed into the 1630s, allowed the early Stuarts to intervene in continental struggles.

Amphibious operations on the Continent and against Scotland

With Gloriana's passing in 1603 and the achievement of a peace with Spain in 1604, England's need for offensive amphibious capability diminished through the reign of James I (1603–1625). The accession of Charles I, who pursued an aggressive foreign policy unseen since the campaigns of Henry VIII, precipitated war and a reprise of familiar designs such as plundering the Spanish plate fleet and attacking Cadiz.[89] While Caroline Britain did not exactly face the level of peril that threatened the Elizabethan regime, thanks to the divisions of the Thirty Years' War, nevertheless the strategic situation appeared to have parallels with the religious wars of the sixteenth century. Certainly that persistent English dilemma, strategic ambivalence, was reflected in Caroline combined operations. A descent upon Cadiz was almost predictable given Caroline historical conceptualisation. By including in the ranks descendants of men that had made that voyage in 1596, and invoking the spirit and reputation of the Elizabethan age, perhaps Charles hoped to harness collective memory and Elizabethan good fortunes in a similar victory.[90] But the 1625 expedition replicated and even exceeded that worst of

---

[88] See above, p. 218, 238; and Lenihan, ed. (2001b), 6–7; Morgan (2004c), 73–87.
[89] Fissel (2001), 255–61.
[90] Hammer (1997b), 641–2.

Elizabethan amphibious operations, the 1589 Portugal campaign, in terms of muddy strategy, poor execution, a wasteful march and an ineffectual siege.

The deliberations among the Iberian campaign's commander, Viscount Wimbledon, and his captains while they cruised off the coast of Spain in October 1625 occasioned one promising proposal that would not see fruition until the eighteenth century. Sir Henry Bruce, a veteran of continental service, spoke up for an amphibious assault on Gibraltar, a potential permanent naval base. Wimbledon's officers saw the past, not the future, and Cadiz was chosen over Gibraltar and other targets.[91] A 'low shoare' at Port St Mary, where the Guadalete River emptied into the Bay of Cadiz, was deemed 'more fitt for the landing of our men then any place about Saint Lucas' a dozen miles further distant.[92]

Despite having achieved the element of surprise, the plodding and disorganised landing on the shore below Fort Puntal led to numerous English casualties from gunfire. Tactical confusion regarding taking the town or repelling a relief force resulted in utter failure to secure their objective.[93] English expeditions, which still relied heavily on impressment and the incorporation of civilian crews, lacked sufficient specialised personnel to make amphibious landings go smoothly. At Cadiz, the royal navy's 'marriners [were supplemented with] unpractised and unskilfull roages of sailors and Thames watermen' who had no experience of, or inclination to engage in, combat. These recalcitrants also had great difficulty in managing sails in extreme weather and around hazards, which made them more of a threat to the vessels of the English flotilla than to the enemy ashore.[94] The expeditionary force was spared annihilation by a solitary tactical success, a spirited rear guard action led by Sir Edward Harwood, who would draw on that experience in penning a treatise for Charles I circa 1631–2.[95]

Despite an official investigation and a parliamentary debate over the conduct of the 1625 Cadiz expedition, little was learnt. Folklore

---

[91] Corbett (1904), 157–9. On Sir Henry Bruce, see Murdoch, ed. (2001), 3, 11, 64, 71, 110.
[92] Cecil (1626), 8.
[93] Fissel (2001), 259–60.
[94] BL, Additional MS 41616, f. 26.
[95] On Harwood, see below, pp. 250–1.

and confidence about amphibious warfare persisted but not techniques and practices. In 1627 an expedition to the Isle of Ré sought
a beachhead in the vicinity of La Rochelle from whence to gall
Louis XIII and spur on the local Protestant rebels. Again, as at
Cadiz, the disembarkation was bungled. 'All things were done in
confusion and tumult and there was no time to put the souldyers in
order.'[96] French defenders hid behind sand dunes, then charged while
the Duke of Buckingham's infantry were wading ashore. The French
cavalry came on quickly, outdistancing their foot and forcing the
English either to stand resolutely or be drowned in retreat.[97] Although
the English survived the onslaught and regrouped, momentum had
been lost. Buckingham's ensuing advance on Re's citadel and his
siege and storming of the fortifications were no more successful than
the initial landing.

Ré simply was the most recent in a series of large-scale sea-land
operations that had gone awry. Given these amphibious failures, it
seems odd that Charles I would risk his kingdoms in 1638–9 on a
strategy that depended heavily upon the execution of three interde-
pendent and virtually simultaneous amphibious descents. Facing a
rebellion in Scotland, the King planned to march his main army to
the Borders in spring 1639. A trio of trusted royal servants would
mount amphibious campaigns in support of their monarch: the
Marquis of Hamilton's amphibious landing in the east of Scotland
(preferably at Aberdeen), the Earl of Antrim's infiltration of the
Western Isles,[98] and Lord Deputy Sir Thomas Wentworth's Irish
army sent from Carrickfergus to Dumbarton, Ayr or Carlisle. Hamilton,
Antrim and Wentworth would collectively divide the Scottish Covenanters, diverting the rebels from confronting the royal expeditionary
force with their full strength.

Wentworth realised that marine expeditions were also within
Covenanter capability, and was thus understandably reluctant to
invest his limited and carefully managed military resources in Antrim's
expedition against Scotland. In October 1638, the Lord Deputy had

---

[96] Quoted by Stewart (1991), 113.
[97] Fissel (2001), 263–5 and sources on 356, note 38.
[98] Sir Henry Vane and the King regarded the coordinated amphibious operations of Antrim and Hamilton to be of 'soe greate importance'—NAS, GD 406/1/
1190, f. 1, 12 April 1639.

learned that the Covenanter Earl of Argyle had fortified the Western Isles with sixteen cannon and was busily drilling his tenants and friends. A rebel force in Scotland was now positioned three hours' sailing time from Ulster.[99] Sir Thomas's scepticism stemmed partially from his awareness that Argyle and much of the west of Scotland now was in rebellion. The Lord Deputy discovered a 'Plott layd by some Scotts and English seperatists to have taken the Castle of Knockfargus, and inviteing the Covenanters into this kingdome.' The malefactors were arrested but such occurrences determined Wentworth not to squander money, ships, and weapons on an unproven (and perhaps untrustworthy) commander.[100] Wentworth was that rarity among the Crown's servants, a man with strategic vision, and he perceived Antrim as impotent to engage Covenanter forces seriously.

On the other hand, the optimistic (and ambitious) Antrim characterised his MacDonnell adherents in western Scotland as beleaguered anti-Covenanters, implicitly suggesting relief from Ireland might secure this familial beachhead for the royal cause.[101] The Earl planned to rely heavily upon his kinsmen and their familiarity with traditional Irish longboats and galleys.

> ... it is high time for me to prepare longe botts or gallies against the springe for without 50 or 60 of them this service can not be performed.[102]

The Earl would bear the cost of the longboats. But he expected the King (via the Lord Deputy) to provide everything else, ranging from a dozen cannon to three infantry regiments. He asked Wentworth 'to gett wood leave [permission to cut timber in a royal forest] in his Majesties woods in the Countye of Londonderri for building of long boats with sixteene or twentye fower oares everi boate which must be don owt of hand and at least thirtye of them.'[103]

---

[99] OBL, Carte MS 66, f. 31, Wentworth to the King, 17 October 1638. For context, see Young (2001), 53–57.

[100] SCL, Wentworth-Wodehouse Papers 10b, f. 77.

[101] NAS, GD 406/1/1156, Antrim to Hamilton, 11 June 1638. 'This day I tooke my opportunitie to acquaint the Kinge that the smale remnant of my name in Scotland have refused to signe the covenent and thereupon I offered my one [own?] service. . . .'

[102] NAS, GD 406/1/652, f. 3, 14 Jan. 1638/9, Antrim to Hamilton.

[103] NAS, GD 406/1/1153, f. 2, second and sixth paragraphs, Antrim to Wentworth, 12 March 1638/9.

Although Antrim's military reputation has been somewhat rehabilitated by Professor Ohlmeyer, contemporaries expressed doubt
about his prospects for success. Amphibious enterprises required experienced 'marines', meticulous planning, and nearly flawless execution. Slyly concealing his scepticism about Antrim's ability, Wentworth
complimented the Earl for undertaking the enterprise. Then, as a
postscript, he pressed Antrim for details:

> I beseech your Lordship . . . to represe the number of your forces,
> how soone, and where, they will be ready to be imbarqued . . . to the
> intent shipping and all other Incidents for such an action may be
> thought of.[104]

Wentworth understood better than any of the King's servants how
complicated were amphibious operations. With several planned for
1639, and all parties short of resources, this was no time for an
amateur attempt at amphibious warfare by Antrim, who had neither
men nor arms nor money nor supervision from England. The Earl's
response was less than reassuring to Wentworth and Hamilton: 'All
I doe for the present is to provide bordes for makeing of long boates
or Gallyes'.[105] The sheer scale of Antrim's needs and demands, and
his timetable (he wanted two ships and a pair of pinnaces loaded
with arms and ammunition ready to sail by 5 April, less than a
month from the composition of his letter), made the Earl's hurried
amphibious endeavour appear dubious.[106]

The Irish Privy Council dispatched that veteran of the 1625 Cadiz
disaster, Sir Henry Bruce, along with one Captain Reade, to investigate Antrim's preparations.[107] The number of men and officers was
inadequate, they lacked equipment and training, and were no match
for the Covenanters ('good swordmen, and good bowemen, that will
give them fight assone [as soon] as they land.')[108] The Western Isles

---

[104] SCL, Wentworth-Wodehouse Papers 10a, f. 256, 22 Feb. 1638/9, from Dublin.
See comments of Aidan Clarke on this exchange, (1963), 111.
[105] SCL, Wentworth-Wodehouse Papers, vol. 10a, ff. 257–8, 26 Feb. 1638/9.
[106] NAS, GD 406/1/1152, Dillon to Antrim, 8 March 1638/9 and GD 406/1/1154,
Antrim to Hamilton, 17 March 1638/9.
[107] SCL, Wentworth-Wodehouse Papers, vol. 10a, f. 329, Wentworth to Antrim,
31 May 1639. On Bruce, see above, note 90.
[108] OBL, Carte MS 44, f. 344/260. Of course, the Council's objections were pri-

were deemed strategically inconsequential and indefensible. Better to 'lye uppon the entrance of Dunbarton-frith, as well to hinder the Scottish shipping which lye at Aire, and Urrin from trade, as to keepe them from makeing any attempt from thence, or landing any numbers of men in this kingdome, which they might very well doe if they found the Shipps soe far Northward as [the Isle of] Skye.'[109] This western blockade strategy mirrored Hamilton's actions in the Firth of Forth.[110] Bruce, the amphibious specialist, rendered his verdict and Wentworth shared it directly with King Charles. Antrim's party 'mean to beat, to bang, to conquer; but the Way how, the Means' were not apparent.[111]

Wentworth's opinion of Antrim's 'indeavour to have turned the sayler' is a timeless judgment on attempting to command amphibious operations without experience. According to the Lord Deputy, the Earl was 'little practised in what belongs [in] the good and orderly Conduct of such an Action . . . [F]ew men are borne Generalls, they have not that from their mothers but gaine it by tyme and practice.'[112] The early modern practice of interchanging land commanders and naval commanders explains in part why so very few seventeenth century military men had inherited a knowledge of amphibious warfare, Irish and otherwise. The fact that Lord Deputy Wentworth, Sir Henry Bruce and the Irish Council had to argue so vociferously against Antrim's proposal, in the face of Charles's endorsement of the expedition, suggests that the few practitioners of amphibious warfare available rarely frequented Charles's court or even had access to Whitehall, a particularly troubling state of affairs given the Crown's heavy dependence on combined operations in the strategy for the First Bishops' War.

---

marily political, and secondarily related to supply: see ff. 341/257–342/258 and Ohlmeyer (2001), 80–90.

[109] OBL, Carte MS 44, ff. 343/259–344v/260v.

[110] See Hamilton's comments regarding forces on the coast, and Argyle, in NAS, GD 406/1/1196, 29 May 1639.

[111] Knowler, ed. (1793), 355–6, 30 May 1639, in a letter which includes a superb assessment of the King's situation and good military advice on how to secure the North. Wentworth's grasp of strategy is impressive, especially considering he was writing from the other side of the Irish Sea. This is more evidence that Sir Thomas's judgment of Antrim's inability to wage amphibious warfare was sound.

[112] SCL, Wentworth-Wodehouse Papers, 10b, f. 76, 14 May 1639.

The Second Bishops' War, too, saw abortive amphibious expeditions. In the summer of 1640, the royal garrison at Dumbarton Castle (which was accessible from the Firth of Clyde), lay besieged by the Earl of Argyle. Wentworth (now Earl of Strafford) and the Earl of Ormonde strove to relieve and reinforce Dumbarton.[113] Antrim's schemes of 1639 were not entirely to have been in vain. A Captain Taverner suggested that 'boats are allready in Ireland either at Dublin or Coleraigne made by the Earl of Antrim' that could be used for an amphibious relief of Dumbarton Castle. Three or four galleys (with 'oars to row, if the wind should not serve them to sail') of 15 tons apiece, manned by crews of a dozen men per boat would suffice. After fitting out the vessels at Knockfergus, a royal navy convoy could escort these craft to the Isle of Bute, and farther if necessary.[114] Argyle possessed 'a ship of 16 piece of ordenance, 160 tunn built of one decke for saylinge', whose 'guns lie all alofte.' Against this Covenanter flagship, however, Charles could incite the recusant and dispossessed MacGregor clan ('Magrigories hilanders'), who operated '100 small boates which lie upon the passages [of the Firth of Clyde and the estuaries] and are maned [manned] with smale shotts, pistols, bowes and arroes.'[115]

In spring and summer of 1639, the previous year, Strafford had resided at Dublin Castle while coordinating his anticipated amphibious intervention into the British mainland. But in mid-August of 1640, Strafford was Lieutenant General of an English army of 12,000 foot and 3,000 horse marching through Yorkshire to the Borders. Embroiled in the command of a land army, Strafford had no choice but to marshal his amphibious forces in Ireland through his deputies. England's Lord General, the Earl of Northumberland, had fallen ill. Strafford, afflicted with gout and the stone, learned that 14,000

---

[113] OBL, Carte MS 1, f. 237, warrant from Strafford to Governor of HM Castle of Dumbarton, 24 Aug. 1640, sending 100 men and ten months' victuals. Unfortunately, the Castle garrison capitulated on 27 August; also Ohlmeyer (2001) 94.

[114] OBL, Carte MS 1, f. 335. The map of the approaches to the west coast of Scotland and the Firth of Clyde, drawn by a military engineer it seems, with explanatory notes in Ormonde's hand, is ff. 333v–334. I am grateful for discussion of this map with Michael Webb.

[115] OBL, Carte MS 1, ff. 333v–334; See also the captions and commentaries in Michael Webb's Bodleian exhibition, the published catalogue being Webb (1999), exhibit items 66, 30, 32; Kelly (1997), 45.

Covenanter infantry and 3,000 cavalry were within four miles of Berwick-upon-Tweed. With English troops still far from the Borders (the horsemen at Newcastle-upon-Tyne and the bulk of infantry were quartered at Selby-upon-Ouse), the opening of a 'second front' became imperative. The amphibious relief of Dumbarton Castle could divert Scottish forces to the West. To that end, Strafford ordered 'Two Flatt bottomed boates' put in service.[116] The Earl envisioned six to eight 'shallupes', powered by oarsmen, spearheading the relief effort.

> [A]t any time takinge the opportunity of the tyde approach the Castle not withstandinge the shallownese of the river, and admittinge, (as hath beene advertized) that a shipp be sunke in the Channell, the said Frigots drawinge but foure foote water, (more then which the said river heightens over all the flattes every tyde) there can be noe difficulty or meanes made to ympeach them nor will the Galleys or boates on the other party be able to make any considerable resistance or opposition. The said frigots beinge fitted with foure or sixe small drakes a peece, which beinge to encounter onley with open boates, is of sufficient advantage: to countenance which in their voyage thither, and retourne, it is held convenient, that twoe or three of his Majesties Pinaces accompany the said frigots and shallupes, to the mouth of the river of Clyde, to be theire safeguard from the attempte of any bigger shippes, and that they ride as high uppe in the said river as conveniently they may for draught of water, till the shallupes shall come of to them, having expedited theire designe.[117]

Strafford's plan drew upon the rich tradition of English amphibious warfare as it had been practised in Elizabethan Ireland. By stealth amphibious vessels would raid, and perhaps take, a stronghold bordered by water and defended by aquatic craft (the Covenanters' 'Galleys', boates', and 'bigger shipps'). In the end, this amphibious expedition was cancelled by the Scottish victory at Newburn and consequent end of the Second Bishops' War. Strafford's enterprises of 1639 and 1640 comprehended the practicalities of amphibious warfare, but the King's most able servant never had the opportunity to test his skills. Strafford's execution by parliamentary instigation on 12 May 1641 removed the one man who might have brought

---

[116] OBL, Carte MS 1, f. 235. Christopher Wandesford relayed from Dublin Strafford's dispatch, to Ormonde.

[117] Ibid., ff. 337–338v, 'A prop[o]sition for the relieving the Castle of Dunbarton. 1640'.

Charles victory over his enemies and who had certainly kept Ireland subjugated. Capitalising upon Strafford's demise, the Irish emulated the Scottish rebels.

The Wars of the Three Kingdoms (1641–1651) and the Subsequent Triumphs of Blake

Scotland's success was not lost on Irish Catholics, who revolted in November 1641. The Irish Rebellion resembled continental wars, with larger armies, land-based sieges, and quests for decisive battles. These conflicts contrasted with the smaller-scale Elizabethan actions of the Nine Years' War, with their amphibious operations in oared vessels and manoeuvrings for regional control.[118] Proven Irish tactics of harassment and skirmishing gave way to a more traditional art of war. In Pádraig Lenihan's words, 'After 1642 running battles [ambushes and skirmishes] became rarer as the Confederate armies developed along conventional lines'.[119]

When war came to England in 1642, the strategic nature of amphibious warfare also changed. The struggle between roundhead and cavalier was sometimes fought out in estuarine and littoral actions, usually in attempts to relieve a besieged town or garrison. But the old Elizabethan concern with continental incursions resurfaced as apprehension grew that foreign states (independently, or urged on by Charles I) might invade Britain and succour the King at the cost of imposing Catholicism. George Harwood, brother of the late Sir Edward Harwood, found amongst his deceased sibling's papers a treatise the Colonel had presented to Charles I during the French invasion scare of 1632. Harwood had campaigned in the Low Countries since the late 1590s, and led the rear guard action at Cadiz in 1625. He was fatally wounded at the siege of Maastricht in 1632.[120] Having served King, Country and the (international) Protestant Cause, the 'martyred' Harwood spoke with a credibility that transcended the deep political and religious divisions of 1642.

---

[118] The case for the rather sudden transformation of Irish warfare (though without background including Elizabethan lacustrine and riverine operations) is made in Lenihan (2001a), 221–9 and Loeber and Parker (1995), 66–88.
[119] Lenihan (1997), 123.
[120] Above, p. 243; Trim (2002), 384.

Colonel Harwood articulated the essentially defensive and amphibious nature of English strategy: 'arme at Sea, for that is the surest defence, for we can never be hurt by a forraigne enemy, by land, till we be first beaten at Sea.'[121] His formula for coastal defence reveals little that is original, as he advocates strengthening the navy, ensuring the availability of good mariners, promoting trade, and improving the militia. Harwood suggests that the trained bands should be comprised two-thirds of firearms but also argues for revival of the archery statutes and encourages the use of the longbow.[122] Harwood recycles traditional methods for combating traditional enemies. His was reassuring advice amid an unprecedented and unthinkable crisis.

In 1631–2, Colonel Harwood warned of French invasion designs; in 1642 his brother feared England's 'old Enemy the Spaniard.' George Harwood linked the crisis and anxiety of the civil war to coastal defence and the reputation of Elizabethan combined operations by appending to his brother's work a tract by the second Earl of Essex, the inclusion of which 'strengthen[ed] my brother's opinion for making Sea preparations'.[123] On the homeward leg of the 1596 voyage to Cadiz, the second Earl had penned a discourse on military strategy that '. . . embodied a fusion of ideas about the relative merits of land and sea power as instruments for waging war against Spain.' Essex's discourse treated amphibious warfare solely within the context of Anglo-Spanish actions, and he seemed oblivious to the contemporary successes of English amphibious warfare fought in the Hibernian theatre. The Earl's Irish campaigns of 1599, fought outside Ulster for the most part, failed to exploit the English advantage in amphibious operations.[124] By definition, defensive amphibious warfare focused upon defending the littoral boundaries of the realm from an external enemy. The irony was that in 1642 the threat came from within, a scenario that defied all of the ambiguous English strategies.

With the outbreak of the British Civil Wars, which many Englishmen regarded as linked with the Thirty Years' War, a hybrid of Colonel Harwood's views and those of the second Earl of Essex drew attention

---

[121] Harwood (1642), C3. The existence of this publication was pointed out to me by David Trim.
[122] Ibid., C3v.
[123] Ibid., A3v.
[124] Henry (1953), 363–93; Hammer (1999), 255–62; MacCaffrey (1992), 418–30.

to external threats at a time when internal division dominated the three kingdoms. The son of the victor of the 1596 expedition had emerged as a parliamentary leader and ultimately commanded the roundhead forces at Edgehill. However, Civil War amphibious operations bore little resemblance to sixteenth century paradigms.

During the English Civil Wars amphibious landings frequently shored up tottering civic defences, as Parliament used amphibious capabilities to reinforce key urban strongholds. The attempted betrayal of Kingston-upon-Hull was thwarted in June 1643 when forces from the parliamentary vessel *Hercules* landed and held the town until succour arrived by land. In October, Hull again owed its deliverance to an amphibious operation, when 650 infantry were brought in on a merchantman. In the aftermath, these 'marines' coordinated with the Hull garrison and local sailors to sally forth and storm the royalist siege works successfully. When royalists blockaded and besieged Plymouth in autumn and winter 1644–5, 300 roundhead mariners were brought in by water and stiffened resistance sufficiently to turn back the royalist assault. The cavalier threat against Wales, mostly in Pembrokeshire, was similarly contested in 1644. In those actions, amphibious operations went beyond relief of beleaguered garrisons and achieved tactical successes both defensive and offensive, in the latter case for example the parliamentary amphibious attacks against the Pill (a cavalier-held fort) and the town of Tenby.[125] Parliament had the means (namely a navy and a fiscal system) to prosecute amphibious warfare, for the most part an advantage denied to the royalists.

The efficacy of amphibious support in a siege was apparent to Admiral Robert Blake when he intervened at Lyme Regis in April– May 1644. He took part in directing the defence of the walls and coordinated with the parliamentary fleet to re-supply and reinforce the garrison. His first-hand experience as a defender benefited him later when he became the aggressor in the Channel and in continental waters.[126]

The English Civil Wars educated the army sent to re-conquer Ireland in 1649. Oliver Cromwell's Irish strategy differed from that of his Elizabethan predecessors in scale and intensity, and the old-

---

[125] Capp (1998), 162–6, 169–71.
[126] Baumber (1989), 33–9, 74–80.

style English amphibious warfare practiced in Eire was only occasionally employed. The Cromwellian conquest was fought on a continental scale to safeguard English plantation and to subjugate the entire island.[127] Amphibious operations, save for fording rivers by land armies, became increasingly the domain of the parliamentary navy and less so of land warfare. 'Naval transports played a decisive role aiding the land forces in attacks on Drogheda, Wexford, Limerick and Galway.'[128] Siege guns that would with difficulty have been transported by land arrived by sea before Drogheda, Carlingford and elsewhere. These actions were reinforced by blockades and interdictions.[129]

While besieging Ross Castle in County Kerry in 1652, the garrison of which was the last to hold out against Oliver Cromwell, Edmund Ludlow proposed an amphibious assault against the castle to be carried out by boats hauled by land to the Lakes of Killarney. The English 'Boats, each of which was capable of containing a hundred and twenty Men . . . rowed about the water [the lough] in order to find out the most convenient Place for landing'.[130] Ross Castle's garrison abruptly surrendered, probably because the cause was lost but perhaps also because folk memory reminded them that this type of English assault had succeeded in years past. There were parallels with earlier forms of English amphibious warfare, then, lacustrine and riverine as well as the transport of ordnance and estuarine interdictions. Renegade royalists had descended upon Carrickfergus in October 1651 rather in the style of Drake, disgorging landing parties, torching moored ships, and housebreaking.[131]

Strategically, the Commonwealth looked beyond Ireland. Admiral Blake secured the Channel and established a presence in the Atlantic and Mediterranean. Blake's amphibious landing to dislodge royalists on the Channel island of Tresco in April 1651, despite early blunders, wrested the Scilly Islands from the cavaliers. When an initial attack on the port of Old Grimsby faltered (due to navigational errors committed in the morning mists and the ensuing detection of the

---

[127] Wheeler (1999); Burke (2001), 257–77, 289–90; Wiggins (2000), 45–183, 225–43.
[128] Kerrigan (2001), 163.
[129] Ibid., 157–9, 161–2.
[130] Ludlow (1698), 416.
[131] Eames (1955), 45, quoting the *Tanner Letters*, 342.

landing forces), Blake made the necessary adjustments.[132] The second assault was spearheaded by mariners, who were less susceptible to seasickness and capable of 'sounding' their way to shore. Upon their disembarkation, the seamen were seconded by their soldier comrades, who managed to supply sufficient firepower and sturdy pikes to secure the beachhead. As a royalist lamented, 'they overpowered our men with multitudes and the strength of their pikes, having the help too of seamen, both to lead them on and to drive on their rear'.[133] Tresco and Bryher fell to the Commonwealth.[134]

Blake's nocturnal landing at St. Ouen's Bay in southwest Jersey in October 1651, hindered by rocks that studded the seafloor near the shoreline, again placed mariners in the boats of the vanguard. Smaller boats with shallow draughts avoided the submerged rocks. The mariners then guided the soldiers' landing craft through the darkness and extended bridge-like devices to haul in this second invasion wave. Caught off guard, the royalist commander failed to rally to the beach sufficient cavalry and militiamen to impede the disembarkation.[135]

Blake penetrated estuaries such as the Tagus. He blockaded where necessary and seized a coastal battery at Malaga in summer 1656. English firepower raked Malaga's defences, 'the frigates pouring their broadsides so fast upon them that [the defenders] ran away, the guns in which fort the Captain spiked, and after their intended execution done they came off again.'[136] At Tunis in April 1655, Blake demonstrated the maturity of English amphibious warfare. A council of war determined how the fleet would penetrate the harbour and engage the Turkish defenders. Enemy ships were broadsided, and boats dispatched smartly with minimal English casualties. The objectives of the assault, silencing the batteries and burning Turkish vessels, were paramount. Little time or energy was diverted to plunder and booty.

---

[132] Joseph Lereck's *A True Accompt of the late Reducement of the Isles of Scilly* and 'A Brief Relation' from *Perfect Diurnal*, both printed in Powell, ed. (1937), 119–122, 128–9.

[133] The Bishop of Down, an observer, to Secretary Nicholas, 13/23 May 1651, from *The Nicholas Papers* 1, 251, printed in Powell, ed. (1937), 113.

[134] Baumber (1989), 97–9.

[135] Kempton Hilliard's account, from *The Clarke Papers* 2 and *HMC Leyborne—Popham*, printed in Powell, ed. (1937), 136–40; Baumber (1989), 101–5.

[136] PRO, SP 18/129/76, printed in Powell, ed. (1937), 439, Robert Pointer to Commissioners of the Navy, 24 July/3 August 1656; Baumber (1989), 219–24.

The tactical goal was pursued steadfastly.[137] Operationally and conceptually, the 'old' amphibious warfare appended to land operations had passed into the orbit of an increasingly potent, specialised and professional Royal Navy. The attainment of a sustained capability for amphibious operations was a result of the maturation of an English state that now possessed the institutional and fiscal means to perpetuate an officer corps skilled in amphibious warfare and give them means to wage it.[138]

Blake, more so than his predecessors such as Drake, projected English state power. His combined operations benefited from the Commonwealth's systematic strategy that secured the British Isles, the Channel, extended into the Atlantic, the Mediterranean and even the Caribbean. These were not sporadic plundering raids and incursions, but rather the English state establishing itself as a global power.[139]

Conclusion

English monarchs and their governments held high expectations of amphibious warfare, as exemplified by Charles I's stubbornness in gambling the success of entire campaigns upon amphibious operations. Faith in marine fighting carried on into the era of the Commonwealth, wherein England, now making its presence felt in the Mediterranean, followed a more Clausewitzian paradigm by using amphibious (and naval) warfare as extensions of broadly conceptualised state policy. Only with the emergence of Admiral Robert Blake did large-scale seaborne amphibious warfare achieve the consistent successes that had been enjoyed by the longboats and cots of Anglo-Irish riverine and lacustrine warfare.

---

[137] *Perfect Diurnal*, a letter of 3/13 April 1655, printed in Powell, ed. (1937) with two others, 317–21; Baumber (1989), 204–5.

[138] Wheeler (1999b) in its entirety.

[139] One should not be misled by Blake's success in capturing the Brazilian *flota* in 1650, which brought political as well as fiscal benefits. Certainly in 1655 Lord Protector Cromwell eyed the alluring prospect of intercepting Spain's plate fleet as eagerly as had the Elizabethans. But the seizure of treasure ships was part of a broader economic and political program by which the Commonwealth, and then the Protectorate, sought to capture the carrying trade (i.e. the Navigation Act of 1651) and to project English power throughout the globe.

From the late Elizabethan period to the Restoration, the English state gradually projected its power through amphibious operations. Elizabethan raids, encompassing economic warfare against a Spanish empire via plunder, occasionally enriched individuals and constituted a continuation of commerce by means other than a strategic application of state force at the interface between land and sea.

Like the war with Spain, war in Ireland sought strategic security as well as private profits (and a remedy for royal debt). Simultaneous use of amphibious warfare tactics, especially in securing northern Ireland, furthered the long-range economic goal of plantation. Amphibious warfare proved crucial in subduing Gaelic resistance so that plantation could flourish in the Jacobean era. The nature of Ulster's topography was such that those who mastered its rivers and lakes reaped rich reward. English oared vessels in Ireland incorporated the three styles of amphibious warfare identified by Joe Guilmartin. At Dunboy they served as tactical infantry assault craft, at Lough Foyle as strategic raiding craft, and the actions at Enniskillen Castle exemplified heavily armed tactical attack transports.[140]

Ironically, it was in Ireland that the English most effectively transformed land warfare to amphibious operations. Certainly the Irish (prior to the battle of Kinsale in 1601) had in recent memory inflicted more defeats upon the English than had the Spanish, the French, or any other Roman Catholic power. However, although the Irish were less successful in resisting English coastal and inland combined operations, by the late 1590s they were winning the Nine Years' War on land with infantry. Amphibious operations gave the English a chance to wage war in a fashion different from that in which the Gaels were clearly prevailing. Oddly enough, the man who transformed the Nine Years' War into a traditional theatre of war was the very man who had proved that galleys could prevail against English coastal defences. Historians can only wonder what would have occurred had Don Juan Aguila intervened in Ulster immediately after his Cornish successes of 1595, rather than waiting until 1601 to arrive in Ireland, and then choosing to make a stand in the very different terrain of southernmost Ireland. What if Don Juan's expertise with oared vessels and amphibious operations had been

---

[140] Guilmartin (1974), 217–19. Professor Guilmartin published a revised edition of this classic work in February 2004.

utilised in Ulster, to counter Docwra's descent on Lough Foyle and the actions around Enniskillen Castle and Londonderry?

Over time, the English achieved success in several different types of amphibious warfare, defending their lengthy coastline, surmounting the formidable logistics of fighting aquatic actions (including sieges) upon a daunting Irish topography, and finally the specialisation of a 'marine' arm in naval engagements and landings. English success in raiding on the high seas had resulted in part from the proportional increase of firepower that was brought to bear. If the theory ran that strategy determined ship design, which in turn created tactical possibilities, and thus suggested appropriate armaments, then English amphibious warfare (especially in Ireland) should likewise be accorded the recognition given to naval warfare in general.[141] Firepower was not so devastating when unleashed from a cot or longboat, thus increasing the importance of formulating a wise strategy and conducting tactical operations nearly flawlessly. Although their crews and vessels were smaller than the grand English galleons (and cheaper as well), cots and longboats operated within an unpredictable terrain susceptible to ambush, and contended with the predictable supply problems inherent in fighting in a wilderness. Most impressive, longboats, cots and galleys proved effective in Gaelic siege warfare, and helped secure England's first colonial outpost.

In the transformation of England to 'Britain', it is clear that in terms of state formation and the beginning of a commercial empire, Irish amphibious operations (inland and littoral) were certainly of equal significance with three plundering raids on Cadiz followed by hasty returns home. True, exploits on the Spanish Main and in the Caribbean captured the imaginations of contemporary and subsequent generations. But the ambivalent strategies of Elizabeth and the early Stuarts, coupled with the immaturity of the English state and the practical complexities of combined operations (rarely dealt with in contemporary treatises), prevented amphibious warfare from reaching full potential. In the late sixteenth century, however, smaller scale operations in pursuit of the focused strategy of subjugating Ireland saw English oared vessels achieve the modest strategic and tactical successes that had eluded the Elizabethan seadogs in their sleek galleons.

---

[141] Parker (1996), 269–74, 286.

Sources and Bibliography

Archival Sources

BL   Additional MSS
      Cottonian MSS
      Harleian MSS
      Lansdowne MSS
OBL   Carte MSS
LPL   Lambeth Palace Library
      Carew MSS
NAS   National Archives of Scotland
      GD 406 Gifts and Deposits
      Hamilton MSS
PRO   SP 63 SP Ireland
      MPF   Map Collections
SCL   Sheffield City Library
      Wentworth-Wodehouse Papers
Trinity College Dublin MS 1209/34.

Printed Primary Sources

BND   *British Naval Documents 1240–1960*, ed. Hattendorf, Knight, Pearsall, Rodger,
      and Till, Navy Records Soc. 131 (Aldershot, Hants: 1993).
CSP   Ir. *Calendar of State Papers Relating to Ireland*, vols 5 (*October 1592–Jun. 1596*),
      9 (*March–October 1600*), 11 (*1603*) (repr., Nendeln, Liechtenstein: 1974).
L&A   vol. 5 (*July 1593–December 1594*) (London: 1989).

Camden Misc (1864) *Camden Miscellany volume the Fifth*, Camden Soc. 1st ser.: 87
      (London: 1864).
Carew Calendar (1870) J. Brewer and W. Bullen, eds, *Calendar of the Carew Papers in
      the Lambeth Library vol. 4 (1601–1603)* (London: 1870).
Cecil, E. (1626) Viscount Wimbledon. *A IOVRNALL, and Relation of the action . . . vpon
      the Coast of Spaine, 1625* (London: 1626).
Goring, J. and Wake, J., eds (1975) *Northamptonshire Lieutenancy Papers and Other
      Documents, 1580–1614* (Gateshead: 1975).
Harwood, E. (1642) *The advice of that worthy commander, Sir Edward Harwood, Collonel . . . Also
      a relation of his Life and Death. Whereunto is also annexed divers remarkable instructions,
      written by the late, and ever-famous Earle of Essex* (London: 1642).
Knowler W., ed. (1793) *The Earle of Strafforde's Letters and Dispatches*, vol. 2 (London:
      1793).
Lambard, W. (1596) *Perambulations of Kent* (second ed., London: 1596).
Ludlow, E. (1698) *Memoirs of Edmund Ludlow Esq; Lieutenant General of the Horse,
      Commander in Chief of the Forces in Ireland* (Vivay, Switzerland: 1698).
Monson, W. (1902) 'The Voyage of the Earl of Cumberland to the Island of Puerto
      Rico. . . .' in *The Naval Tracts of Sir William Monson* vol. 2, M. Oppenheim, ed.,
      Navy Records Soc. 23 (1902), 204–25.
O'Donovan, J., ed. (1849) 'A narration of the services done by the army ymployed
      to Lough-Foyle, vnder the leadinge of mee Sr Henry Dowcra. . . .', *Miscellany of
      the Celtic Society* (Dublin: 1849) 236–297.
Powell, J., ed., *The Letters of Robert Blake Together with Some Supplementary Documents*,
      Navy Record Soc. 76 (London: 1937).
Quintrell, B., ed., *The Maynard Lieutenancy Book, 1608–1639* (Chelmsford: 1993).
Rodger, N. A. M., ed., *The Armada in the Public Records* (London: 1988), pp. 42–5.

Stafford, T. *Pacata Hibernia. Ireland Appeased and Reduced* (London: 1631 and 1633).
Swift, M. *Historical Maps of Ireland* (Edison NJ: 1999).
Usherwood, S. and E. (1983) *The Counter-Armada 1596. The Journall of the 'Mary Rose'* (London: 1983).
Wake, J., ed. (1926) *A Copy of Papers relating to Musters, Beacons, Subsidies, Etc. in the County of Northampton A.D. 1586–1623* (Kettering: 1926).
——, ed., (1935) *The Montagu Musters Book A.D. 1602–1623* (Peterborough: 1935).
Webb, M. (1999) *Civil War. The Great Rebellion in Charles I's Three Kingdoms 1638–1653* (Oxford: 1999), Bodleian exhibition catalogue.
Wernham, R. B., ed. (1988) *The Expedition of Sir John Norris and Sir Francis Drake to Spain and Portugal, 1589*, Navy Record Soc. 127 (Aldershot: 1988).

Secondary Sources

Andrews, K. (1966) *Elizabethan Privateering. English Privateering during the Spanish War 1585–1603* (Cambridge: 1966).
Appleby, J. (1998) 'War, Politics, and Colonizations, 1558–1625', in *The Origins of Empire. British Overseas Enterprise to the Close of the Seventeenth Century* N. Canny, ed. (Oxford: 1998) 55–78.
Baumber, M. (1989) *General at Sea—Robert Blake and the Seventeenth-Century Revolution in Naval Warfare* (London: 1989).
Bartlett, T. and Jeffrey, K., eds (1996) *A Military History of Ireland* (Cambridge: 1996), 40–3, 54, 57, 62–8.
Bennell, J. (1974) 'English Oared Vessels of the Sixteenth Century', two parts, *The Mariner's Mirror* 60 (February and May 1974) 9–26 and 169–85.
Black, J. (1998) *War and the World. Military Power and the Fate of Continents* (New Haven, CT: 1998).
Boynton, L. (1967) *The Elizabethan Militia, 1558–1638* (London: 1967).
Burke, J. (2001) 'Siege Warfare in Seventeenth-Century Ireland' in Lenihan, ed. (2001b), 258–291.
Capp, B. (1998) 'Naval Operations', in J. Kenyon and J. Ohlmeyer, eds., *The Civil Wars. A Military History of England, Scotland and Ireland 1638–1660* (Oxford: 1998), 156–91.
Carroll, Clare (2004) 'From Defeat to Defiance: O'Sullivan Beare's Account of the Battle of Kinsale, the Campaign in West Cork and the Great March'; in Morgan (2004a), 217–28.
Clarke, A. (1963) 'The Earl of Antrim and the First Bishops' War', *Irish Sword* 6 (1963) 108–15.
Contamine P., ed. *War and Competition between States* (Oxford: 2000).
Corbett, J. (1904) *England in the Mediterranean*, vol. 1 (London: 1904).
——. (1900) *The Successors of Drake* (London: 1900).
Eames, A. (1955) 'Sea Power and Caernarvonshire, 1642–1660', *Transactions of the Caernarvonshire Historical Society* 16 (1955) 29–51.
Ellis, S. (1998) *Ireland in the Age of the Tudors: English Expansion and the End of Gaelic Rule* (London: 1998).
Falls, C. (1950) *Elizabeth's Irish Wars* (New York: 1950).
Fernandez-Armesto, F. (1988). *The Spanish Armada. The Experience of War in 1588* (Oxford 1988).
Fissel, M. (2001) *English Warfare 1511–1642* (London: 2001).
——, ed., (1991) *War and Government in Britain 1598–1650* (Manchester: 1991).
Glasgow, T. Jr. (1968) 'The Navy in the French Wars of Mary and Elizabeth I. Part II. The Navy in the Le Havre Expedition, 1562–1564', *The Mariner's Mirror* 54, (1968) 281–96.

Glete, J. (1993) *Navies and nations: Warships, Navies and State Building in Europe and America 1500–1862* 1 (Stockholm: 1993).

———. (2000) *Warfare at Sea, 1500–1650* (London: 2000).

Guilmartin, J. F. Jr, (2002) *Galleons and Galleys* (London: 2002).

———. *Gunpowder and Galleys. Changing Technology and Mediterranean Warfare at Sea in the Sixteenth Century* (Cambridge: 1974, revised Annapolis, Md.: 2004).

Hammer, P. J. (2003) *Elizabeth's Wars. War, Government and Society in Tudor England, 1544–1604* (Houndmills, Basingstoke: 2003).

———. (1997a) 'New Light on the Cadiz Expedition of 1596', *Historical Research* 70 (1997), 182–202.

———. (1997b) 'Myth-Making: Politics, Propaganda and the Capture of Cadiz in 1596', *Historical Journal* 40 (1997), 621–42.

———. (1999) *The Polarisation of Elizabethan Politics. The Political Career of Robert Devereux, 2nd Earl of Essex, 1585–1597* (Cambridge 1999).

Hayes-McCoy, G. (1931–3) 'Ballyshannon. Its Strategic Importance in the Wars in Connacht 1550–1602', *Journal of the Galway Archaeological and Historical Society* 15 (1931–3), 141–159.

———. (1990) *Irish Battles: A Military History of Ireland* (Belfast: 1990).

———. (1940–1) 'Strategy and Tactics in Irish Warfare, 1593–1601', *Irish Historical Studies* 2 (1940–1) 263–8.

Heath, I. and Sque, D. (1993) *The Irish Wars 1485–1603* (London: 1993).

Henry, L. (1953) 'The Earl of Essex as Strategist and Military Organizer, 1596–7', *English Historical Review* 68 (1953) 363–93.

Hewitt, G. (1964) 'Drake at San Juan de Puerto Rico', *The Mariner's Mirror* 50 (1964) 199–204.

Hill, G. (1861) 'Shane O'Neill's Expedition against the Antrim Scots, 1565', *Ulster Journal of Archaeology*, 1st ser. 9 (1861) 122–41.

Kelly, W. (1997) 'James Butler, Twelfth Earl of Ormond, the Irish Government, and the Bishops' Wars, 1638–40', in J. Young, ed., *Celtic Dimensions of the British Civil Wars* (Edinburgh 1997) 35–52.

Kelsey, H. (1998) *Sir Francis Drake. The Queen's Pirate* (London: 1998).

Kerrigan, P. (2001) 'Ireland in Naval Strategy 1641–1691', in Lenihan, ed. (2001b) 151–176.

Lenihan P. (1997) 'Celtic' Warfare in the 1640s', in John Young, *Celtic Dimensions of the British Civil Wars* (Edinburgh: 1997) 116–40.

———. (2001a) *Confederate Catholics at War 1641–9* (Cork: 2001).

———, ed., (2001b) *Conquest and Resistance. War in Seventeenth Century Ireland* (Leiden: 2001).

Lenman, B. (2001) *England's Colonial Wars 1550–1688* (Harlow, Essex: 2001).

Loeber, R. and Parker, G. (1995) 'The Military Revolution in Seventeenth Century Ireland', in J. Ohlmeyer, ed., *Ireland from Independence to Occupation 1641–1660* (Cambridge: 1995) 66–88.

Loomie, A. (1963) 'An Armada Pilot's Survey of the English Coastline, October 1597', *The Mariner's Mirror* 49 (1963), 288–300.

MacCaffrey, W. (1992) *Elizabeth I. War and Politics 1588–1603* (Princeton: 1992).

McGurk, J. (1970) 'Armada Preparations in Kent and Arrangements Made After the Defeat (1587–9)', *Archaeologia Cantiana* 85 (1970), 71–93.

———. (1997) *The Elizabethan Conquest of Ireland* (Manchester: 1997).

———. (2004) 'English Naval Operations at Kinsale' in Morgan (2004a) 147–60.

———. (2001) 'Terrain and Conquest, 1600–1603', in Lenihan, ed., (2001b) 87–114.

Morgan, H., ed. (2004a) *The Battle of Kinsale* (Bray, Wicklow: 2004).

———. (2004b) 'Disaster at Kinsale' in Morgan (2004a), 101–146.

———. (2004c) 'Missions Comparable? The Lough Foyle and Kinsale Landings of 1600 and 1601', in Morgan (2004a) 73–89.

Murdoch S., ed. (2001) *Scotland and the Thirty Years' War, 1618–1648* (Leiden: 2001).
Nolan, J. (1995) 'English Operations around Brest, 1594', *The Mariner's Mirror* 81 (1995) 259–74.
——. (1991) 'The Muster of 1588', *Albion* 23 (1991) 387–407.
——. (1997) *Sir John Norreys and the Elizabethan Military World* (Exeter: 1997).
Ohlmeyer, J. (2001) *Civil War and Restoration in Three Stuart Kingdoms. The Career of Randal MacDonnell, Marquis of Antrim* second ed. (Cambridge: 2001).
——. (1998) '"Civilizinge of those Rude Partes": Colonization within Britain and Ireland, 1580s–1640s' in N. Canny, ed., *The Origins of Empire. British Overseas Enterprise to the Close of the Seventeenth Century* (Oxford: 1998), 124–147.
Parker, G. (1996) 'The *Dreadnought* Revolution of Tudor England', *The Mariner's Mirror* 82: 3 (August 1996), 269–300.
——. (1998) *The Grand Strategy of Philip II* (London: 1998).
——. (1976) 'If the Armada had landed', *History* 61 (1976), 358–368.
Rodger, N.A.M. (1996) 'The Development of Broadside Gunnery, 1450–1650' in *The Mariners' Mirror* 82 (1996), 301–24.
——. (1998) 'Guns and sails in the first phase of English colonization, 1500–1650', in N. Canny, ed., *The Origins of Empire. British Overseas Enterprise to the Close of the Seventeenth Century* (Oxford: 1998), 79–98.
Rose, S. (2002) *Medieval Naval Warfare, 1000–1500* (London: 2002).
Rowse, A. L. (1969) *Tudor Cornwall* (New York: 1969).
Silke, J. (1970) *Kinsale. The Spanish Intervention in Ireland at the End of the Elizabethan Wars* (New York: 1970).
Spence, R. T. (1995), *The Privateering Earl: George Clifford, 3rd Earl of Cumberland, 1558–1605* (Stroud, Gloucestershire: 1995).
Stewart, R. (1991) 'Arms and expeditions: the Ordnance Office and the assaults on Cadiz (1625) and the Isle of Rhé (1627)', in Fissel ed. (1991) 112–32.
Thrush, A. (1991) 'In pursuit of the frigate, 1603–1640', *Historical Research* 64 (1991) 34–41
Trim, D. J. B. (2002) 'Fighting 'Jacob's Wars'. The Employment of English and Welsh Mercenaries in the European Wars of Religion: France and the Netherlands 1562–1610' (unpublished Ph.D. thesis, University of London, 2002).
Wernham, R. B. (1961) 'Elizabethan War Aims and Strategy', in Bindoff, Hurstfield, and Williams, eds, *Elizabethan Government and Society. Essays presented to Sir John Neale* (London: 1961).
——. (1994) *The Return of the Armadas The Last Years of the Elizabethan War Against Spain 1595–1603* (Oxford: 1994).
Wheeler, J. S. (1999a) *Cromwell in Ireland* (New York: 1999).
——. (1999b) *The Making of a World Power. War and the Military Revolution in seventeenth-century England* (Stroud, Gloucestershire: 1999).
——. (2000) review of Fissel (2001) in *Albion* 34 (2002) 637.
White, H. (1934) 'The Beacon System in Kent', *Archaeologia Cantiana* 46 (1934) 77–96.
Wiggins, K. *Anatomy of a Siege. King John's Castle, Limerick, 1642* (Rochester, NY: 2001).
Young, J., ed., (1997) *Celtic Dimensions of the British Civil Wars* (Edinburgh: 1997).
——. (2001) 'Invasions: Scotland and Ireland 1641–1691' in Lenihan, ed. (2001) 53–86.

THE KING'S TWO ARMS: FRENCH AMPHIBIOUS WARFARE IN THE MEDITERRANEAN UNDER LOUIS XIV, 1664 TO 1697*

Guy Rowlands

The second half of the seventeenth century and the first decades of the eighteenth saw a number of striking changes associated with the art of war: the creation of standing armies and fleets in being, the improvement and expansion of logistical infrastructures and an acceleration and intensification of fortress warfare. These fundamental and far-reaching changes had considerable knock-on effects both for the way amphibious warfare was conducted and the way it was organised. Yet thanks not least to Mahan's view that sea warfare after 1660 was geared essentially to driving the enemy's battlefleet and merchantmen from the sea, there has been a dearth of work on the equally important military sphere of coastal operations and amphibious warfare in this period.[1] The ground-breaking studies of British amphibious warfare in the mid-eighteenth century by Harding, Syrett and Tracy have not been matched by anything for the age of Louis XIV, regarding either Britain or France. In the francophone world, while Meyer and Corvisier have urged historians to relate naval history to military power on land, their conception of amphibious warfare has been somewhat restricted in scope and extremely limited in treatment.[2] This lacuna needs to be filled, for in the last quarter of the seventeenth century it was France which led the world in combined operations and amphibious warfare, as Louis XIV sought to project his power beyond French coastal waters and his land frontiers. Amphibious warfare was a major test of coordination for the

---

* I would like to thank my father Capt. Anthony Rowlands for his expert guidance on nautical matters and Dr Alistair Malcolm for his advice on Spanish comparisons. This article is dedicated to the staff of the Archives Nationales in Paris, whom I shamefully forgot to thank in the preface to my book.
[1] Harding (1999), 6; Guilmartin (1974), 17; Mahan (1965); Bamford (1973), 47.
[2] Harding (1991); Syrett (1970); Tracy (1995); Meyer (1989), 74–77; Corvisier (1995).

absolutist and dynastic state of the 'Sun King', and how the French navy coped with the realities of amphibious warfare and how it worked with the army in such matters will be the principal focus of this essay.[3]

Despite Mahan's focus on transoceanic war as generating the greatest appreciation of naval activity and its relationship to power politics, it was the Mediterranean where the great powers, and especially France, largely honed their techniques in amphibious warfare prior to the colonial wars of the 1740s and 1750s. Indeed, there were no strong French amphibious efforts in the eastern Atlantic, the North Sea or around the British Isles prior to 1689, if ever.[4] For France the Mediterranean theatres, by contrast, had an effect on the course and outcome of Louis XIV's wars disproportionate to the number of troops and ships committed to them. Up to 1700 Louis was particularly keen to wrestle the dominant position in the western Mediterranean from Spain, and there were plenty of towns and strategic plains on the coasts which needed to be controlled. In this he was following Richelieu, who had sought to force the Spanish into huge expenditure on protecting their empire and its communication lines. Between 1664 and 1690 the French Ministers of the Navy, Jean-Baptiste Colbert and his son the marquis de Seignelay, were explicitly set upon completing the task of achieving regional hegemony, while protecting French trade from North African corsairs.[5] Between 1672 and 1676 the French were able to drive down Dutch strategic capability and commitment in the Mediterranean, and by 1680 Spain was no longer in a position to resist the French navy. Between 1676 and 1694 France was not seriously challenged by an opposing fleet in the Mediterranean, and not until the 1700s did the regional balance of naval power tilt decisively against her.[6]

---

[3] Marine and galley troops will not receive treatment here, nor will the detail of opposed landings by French troops under fire from enemy shore positions be examined. I plan to consider these in another article.

[4] On early Caribbean amphibious warfare, see the extensive and illuminating Nerzic and Bouchet (2002) on the French descent upon Cartagena de Indias in 1697.

[5] Meyer (1981), 920; Meyer (1989), 80; Coutau-Bégarie (2000), 34; Dingli (1997), 166.

[6] Herrero Sanchéz (2000), 248–50; Meyer (1989), 80–81; Glete (1992), I, 197, 211; Ehrman (1953), 536, 544–48.

On land, by contrast, in the last quarter of the seventeenth century French domination was far from assured in the Mediterranean basin, so the assistance of the navy was vital for Louis XIV's war efforts.

The Mediterranean had, of course, been a traditional theatre, along with the Baltic, for European amphibious warfare, but between 1650 and 1700 the rules of the game were notably different from the previous two centuries, and this fifty-year era can in fact be seen as quite distinct for the nature of its naval warfare.[7] In the 1650s the heavily-armed sailing battlefleet emerged in north-west Europe and by the 1660s the line-of-battle had become firmly established in naval tactics, encouraging and requiring tighter discipline and order. Inextricably linked with the emergence of the battlefleet was a ratcheting-up of naval artillery power, used aggressively to try to sink enemy vessels.[8] In spite of a recognition by the mid-1670s that massive battlefleets fighting each other imposed excessive demands on their logistical infrastructures, it was not until 1695 that one great power, France, dramatically scaled back its use of such formations. In the meantime, battleships, deployed in smaller formations, were also used extensively not only for economic warfare but for the support of land campaigning too. Yet what makes this period distinctive from the eighteenth century is that states appreciated the value of mixing galleys and sailing ships to support land operations in the Mediterranean (and even the English Channel) until 1700.[9] By the early 1640s, a good decade before the emergence of battlefleets, galleys had already been reduced in status to auxiliary vessels.[10] They remained useful for dealing with coastal marauders and with enemy galleys which could often not be caught by sailing ships. And as coastal raiders themselves they were invaluable: the presence of French galley squadrons off the Spanish coast in the 1690s, conducting a number of diversionary descents, greatly worried Madrid.[11] But it was difficult to coordinate the movement of galleys with sailing fleets,

---

[7] An argument advanced most strongly in Palmer (1997).

[8] Harding (1999), 40, 59, 70–1, 85–92; Dessert (1996), 263; Palmer (1997), 125–26, 135, 143–44. On the battleship as a vessel, see Bérenger (1997), 10–19.

[9] Bamford (1973), 299.

[10] Roncière (1920), V, 87. The 1620s and 1630s were the crucial decades in exposing galley weaknesses.

[11] BNF Languedoc 96, fo. 73r: Estrées to maréchal de Noailles, 29 June 1691; AN Mar B²101, fo. 319r: Pontchartrain to maréchal de Noailles, 5 May 1694.

and it could take a long time for a galley squadron to make a voyage which sailing ships might accomplish far more quickly. Moreover, it was impractical to use them for mounting close blockades and they were but weakly armed compared to sailing broadside-armed warships.[12]

The 'personal rule' of Louis XIV also witnessed the culmination of fortress warfare. By the 1680s it was much more difficult for any state to assault fortresses than in the first half of the century, thanks to improved designs and a massive expansion in the number of heavy guns defending a place. Yet though historians have largely ignored fortresses when considering sea power, by the mid-seventeenth century amphibious warfare in the Mediterranean revolved around the possession, defence or capture of fortified coastal towns and cities, for two distinct reasons: if the territory under dispute were an island, then a port had to be secured and held; while on the continent fortresses dominated the overwhelming majority of great strategic points in coastal regions. To capture a coastal fortress in European waters would generally require a sizable land army, significant artillery capacity ashore, and command of the sea in the area of hostilities. The navy would act as supplier of troops, food and matériel, and as an observing force shadowing the siege to protect against enemy fleets.[13] Unsurprisingly, it was extremely difficult for the French to meet these conditions for success at any one time during the multi-front wars they fought in the 1670s and 1690s. Successful littoral warfare required effective planning, careful command distribution, and the maintenance of a firmly established logistical infrastructure for both the army and the navy so they could cooperate in the principal task of contemporary warfare: the control of territory through the control of fortresses.

---

[12] SHM Cartes SH49, no. 10: Instruction, 15 May 1697; no. 12: memorandum, 1 Jan. 1693; Nanteuil (1974), 9, 15–21; Laloy (1929), III, 352; AN Mar B¹12, fo.s 432r–36r, 439r: 'Galéres . . .', 1690; SHAT A¹1234, no. 163: maréchal de Noailles to Louis XIV, 17 June 1693.

[13] Only against weaker fortresses in the Caribbean and old-style fortifications in Europe were ships used as direct launchpads and siege platforms: on the failed attack on Tobago in 1677, see Hoste (1697), 397–98.

The Principal Operations

It took over two decades for Louis XIV's government to appreciate the realities of amphibious warfare, and in the early 1660s the French were starting from a wretchedly low base of infrastructure and experience in comparison with the Dutch and English. During the 1630s and 1640s, both France and Spain had pulled off some impressive successes in littoral warfare, interspersed with plenty of failures; but by 1652 neither power was able to mobilise significant naval forces in support of coastal sieges. In 1657–58, France relied entirely on Cromwell's navy for the maritime side of operations against Spain's Flanders strongholds, and was barely able to provide naval support for her own armies in the Mediterranean.[14] Reacting against this dismal state of affairs, Louis XIV himself was determined to make France self-sufficient in littoral warfare. Unfortunately, operations got off to a very poor start.

Keen to make use of his slowly-improving fleet, and to continue Mazarin's campaign against Islam,[15] Louis launched an expedition against north Africa in July 1664, only to see it go disastrously wrong. Disregarding expert advice, the imperious and impulsive duc de Beaufort, Grand Master of Navigation, settled on an attack against Djidjelli [figure 17], hoping to turn it into a major French fortress. But he and his advisers had, unknowingly, chosen an impoverished and open town with half-wrecked walls, served by poor landing sites. Moreover, the hopeless logistical arrangements and Beaufort's poor leadership of the expedition only compounded the situation.[16] In late October the French generals decided to evacuate Djidjelli but they had to fight their way out to the ships. Of 7000 troops who had left France and Malta, only 3000 returned.[17]

---

[14] Roncière (1920), V, 26–31, 38–50, 72–82, 85, 88–91, 104–7, 112–24, 140–44, 158, 160, 162, 167–68, 180, 196–98, 200–25; Firth (1909), II, 186–88; Harris (1912), I, 110–11; Bourelly (1886), 158.

[15] AN Mar B^{4}2, fos 293v–94r: Beaufort to Colbert, 30 June 1664.

[16] BNF Clair 880, fo.s 143r–45r: 'Relation . . .', 1665; AN Mar B^{4}2, fo.s 301v–5v, 308r: Beaufort to Colbert, 30 July 1664.

[17] AN Mar B^{4}2, fo.s 315r, 332r–33v: Beaufort to Colbert, 12 Sep., 7 Nov. 1664; fo.s 368r–69r: 'Relation . . .', 1664; fo.s 400r–2r: 'Response . . .', 1664; fo.s 405r–6v: Martel to Colbert, 22 Nov. 1664; BNF Clair 880, fo.s 150r–51r, 153v: 'Relation . . .', 1665.

Djidjelli was a textbook case in how not to conduct amphibious warfare, and after this episode Louis XIV did not try to capture any further towns in North Africa, instead resorting to bombardments from the sea. Painful lessons were learnt from the Djidjelli fiasco, but more were to come in 1669, this time in the face of the Ottoman state forces. After seventeen years of desultory efforts, in late 1666 the Ottomans stepped up their efforts to wrest Crete from Venice, moving in on the final Venetian stronghold of Candia. After an unofficial French expedition paid for privately in 1668, Louis XIV contributed 16 warships, 13 galleys, over 30 auxiliary vessels, and around 6000 troops in May 1669 to a relief armada sailing under the Papal banner.[18] This time, the French were much better prepared than at Djidjelli, taking a colossal amount of victuals with them, but they incurred severe casualties, including the loss of Beaufort, who was commanding the fleet but killed while fighting ashore. With Beaufort out of the way only days after arrival, there were no more disastrous setbacks or problems for the French part of the Christian contingent. More tellingly for the fateful outcome of the siege, the Venetians failed to provide sufficient backing either for French sorties to disrupt Turkish earthworks or for French coastal operations, precipitating unilateral French withdrawal at the end of August, which in turn forced the Venetians to capitulate.[19] From the Candia expedition, the French government learned a number of things. Although there was no supply breakdown, Candia's great distance from France had thrown the need for even better planning and logistical support into sharp relief in ways that not even the Djidjelli expedition had done. Secondly, the king should henceforth avoid putting senior nobles and princes of a feckless and excessively vainglorious character in charge of such expeditions. And finally, in amphibious warfare at least, France should avoid entanglements with allies who were not subordinates but upon whom they utterly depended.

The Candia expedition had at least given the French a chance to hone their skills in ship-to-shore delivery of supplies, defensive coastal

---

[18] Hanlon (1998), 149–63, the best English-language summary of the war; Nanteuil (1974), 11; Terlinden (1904), 191–92, 196–97, 201; Nouzille (1987), 126, 132–34; Rousset (1862–64), I, 260; BNF Fonds Italiens 385, fo.s 56r–57v: 'Estat', 1669.

[19] Terlinden (1904), 229–32, 276; Nouzille (1987), 137–47, 150; Rousset (1862–64), I, 262; Cordey (1910), 72, 127–28: Navailles to Vivonne, 24 July, 17 Aug. 1669; ibid., 87: Vivonne to Colbert, 28 July 1669; Nanteuil (1974), 29–30.

operations, army-navy liaison, and naval artillery support. During the following decade the maréchal de Vivonne, who had been present at both Djidjelli and Candia, drew on the lessons learned in order to sustain the revolt of Messina in north-eastern Sicily against the Spanish for three years after 1675. Vivonne was determined in particular not to be pinned down in Messina city itself. Strategically this was defensive amphibious warfare as at Candia; but the operations conducted around Sicily were repeatedly of an offensive nature. The entire expedition was better-managed and better-supported, if far from ideally so, and the amphibious operations which actually took place were both encouraging and effective.[20] What prevented spectacular success was the lack of crown commitment; the split between the Secretary of State for War, Louvois, and Colbert's son and deputy Seignelay over which politico-military strategy to pursue; and ultimately Louis XIV's reluctance to treat the revolt as anything more than a diversionary theatre.[21] Given the host of international and local problems that outright conquest of Sicily would have caused, the French government was probably correct to intervene with the purpose only of distracting Spain (even though they did not think through how best to keep her under pressure).[22] Considering the poor French track record in amphibious operations, Louis and Louvois were sensible in considering an assertive campaign in 1674–76 to be too ambitious, and it was only the surprising naval successes by Vivonne and Duquesne against the Spanish and Dutch off Stromboli, Agosta and Palermo in 1676 which led the king to increase his commitment to enable some further gains on the eastern coast to be made (to no great strategic effect). Nevertheless, for all the strategic problems of the Sicilian expedition, the actual amphibious operations conducted by Vivonne and his subordinates around the island demonstrated considerable improvements in French performance since Djidjelli.

After 1678 there were few attempts by France to use amphibious force to save a city or to use a city surrounded by hostile territory

---

[20] The Sicilian revolt has received detailed treatment from Emile Laloy (1929–31), but the sheer scale of this three-volume work makes the revolt impenetrable to all but the most determined reader.

[21] Rousset (1862–64), II, 374–82, 394–95, 399, 408, 436–37; Laloy (1929–31), I, 619–20; II, 294.

[22] Quincy (1726), I, 461; Laloy (1929–31), II, 47–50, 56–58, 586–87; III, 219–20, 236, 244–46; Rousset (1862–64), II, 445–53.

as an amphibious base. The beleaguered garrisons of Limerick in
1690–91, Gibraltar in 1704 and Minorca in 1708 were essentially
left to fend inadequately for themselves against British attacks. Instead
Louis XIV's government confined itself in the 1680s to amphibious
descents and in the 1690s to combined-arm sieges of enemy fortresses.
In both these fields French arms more than distinguished themselves,
but this owed much to a more realistic and wiser sense of the bounds
of the possible.[23] In 1684 the French navy showed what by now it
could deliver alone in the attack on Genoa [figure 19]. Relations
between Louis XIV and the republic were never good, perhaps unsurprising given Louis' emphatic claim that Genoese sovereignty
belonged to France, but matters deteriorated rapidly during the 1680s.
In mid-April 1684 a French fleet, consisting of 14 line-of-battleships,
20 galleys, 10 new bomb ketches and 37 auxiliary craft, arrived off
Genoa to intimidate the republic into a humiliating agreement. With
negotiations failing the defenders fired on the French, who replied
with a massive bombardment lasting two days causing colossal damage to the city. Persisting in a stubborn refusal to give in to French
demands only brought down on the Genoese a heavily-armed amphibious assault by 1800 ships' marines and 2000 galley troops who
destroyed the suburb of San Pier d'Arena before being evacuated,
all in less than a day. A further two-day bombardment ensued, and
after the bulk of the French fleet withdrew the republic quickly
capitulated in the presence of a blockading squadron.[24] Europe had
seen nothing like this kind of seaborne attack before. Four years
later, in late 1687 and throughout the summer of 1688, the French
government drew up plans for a similar amphibious descent upon
the Papal States to capture the port of Civita Vecchia at the nadir
of relations between Louis XIV and the Papacy.[25] Without question
this expedition would have succeeded had war against the Holy
Roman Empire not erupted in September, forcing its indefinite
postponement.

---

[23] In the early 1680s a planned amphibious assault on Algiers was considered,
after further reflection, to be infeasible with fewer than 20,000 men. See Peter
(1995), 97–98.

[24] Louis XIV (1970), 48; Saint-Hilaire (1903–16), II, 28; Quincy (1726), II, 86–87,
96; SHM Bib 386(–1), 87–97.

[25] Rousset (1862–64), IV, 64; AN Mar B²67, fo.s 194bis, 209r: Seignelay to
Vauvré, 21 and 23 Aug. 1688.

For the next five years French naval priorities switched to the English Channel and British Isles, yet in this theatre there were no serious amphibious operations thanks largely to insufficient crown commitment, but also because of the defeat of Vice-Admiral Tourville at La Hogue in June 1692 by the English navy.[26] However, elsewhere, for the first time since the 1650s littoral warfare in the Mediterranean combining large-scale naval support with land armies began to be conducted, and now it was far better organised. In 1674 the French did not use the navy to support and protect the land siege of Rosas on the Catalan coast, and they paid the price: when Tromp's Dutch fleet appeared and landed ships' marines, the French were left with no choice but to raise the siege. The Nine Years' War saw no such mistakes. During March and April 1691 the comte d'Estrées commanded a force of eight battleships and 20 galleys which transported and assisted with munitions and provisions, and also provided seaward cover, for the sieur de Catinat's siege of the Savoyard ports of Villefranche and Nice.[27] This campaign was to set the pattern for the rest of the war in the Mediterranean, but henceforth such combined operations would be on the Catalan coast and only from 1693 did the French government begin using the fleet as an instrument for improving their position in Iberia. That year, with the French army still apparently confined to the foothills of the Pyrenees, the Spanish were expecting an inland campaign accompanied by some irritating naval bombardments. It came as a shock to Madrid when news arrived that the formidable but neglected fortress-town of Rosas had been invested by sea on 27 April and by land the following day, surrendering less than two weeks later. As at Nice, the navy played a significant role in its capture, supplying

---

[26] Symcox (1974), 9–81, 96, 100–1; Symcox (1967), 150, 334–5, 346, 350, 358. Between 1689 and 1692 the French fleet acted in Irish waters as nothing more than a glorified transport service: see Simms (2000), 67–69, 101–3, 247–48. The only amphibious descent came in a raid on Teignmouth in August 1690: see AN Mar B⁴12, fo. 446v: 'Copie du memoire . . .', 15 July 1690; fo.s 437r–38r: 'Galéres . . .', 1690.

[27] Peter (1995), 103; Quincy (1726), II, 411, 414; AN Mar B⁴13, fo.s 299r–300r: 'Relation . . .', 20 Mar. 1691; fo.s 285r, 313r–v: Estrées to Pontchartrain, 4 Mar., 8 Apr. 1691; fo. 383v: Vauvré to Pontchartrain, 31 Mar. 1691; SHAT A¹1077, no. 6: Louvois to Catinat, 5 Jan. 1691; no.s 63, 88: memoranda, n.d. [end of Jan. 1691], 4 Feb. 1691; A¹1079, no.s 245, 258, 266, 290bisbis, 305: Catinat to Louvois, 15, 17, 21 and 23 Mar., 3 Apr. 1691.

3500 marine and galley troops, but in a measure of just how crucial the navy was to success in Catalonia, the withdrawal of the
naval forces (plus the transfer of some troops to south-east France)
prevented the maréchal de Noailles from following up his success
with another combined-arm attack on Palamos.[28]

The capture of Palamos had to wait until June the following year,
when Tourville's fleet of 50 battleships supplied the logistical support needed for the siege, landing additionally 3000 marine troops
and naval artillery officers and engineers, and providing significant
ship-to-shore bombardment of the place. A reluctant Tourville, worried that the use of battleships as transports made them vulnerable,
then transported further *matériel* for Noailles' successful inland siege
of Gerona later that month.[29] For all that, campaigning in Catalonia
now stalled, principally because the effort of mobilising resources that
year had now exhausted the army and navy's civilian contractors.
The oft-noted entry of Russell's English fleet into the Mediterranean
in August 1694 actually had no discernible effect on the course of
the war, and its withdrawal through the straits of Gibraltar just over
a year later was an unsurprising consequence of Britain still lacking
its own naval base in this sea.[30] Yet French logistical and strategic
weakness meant that the new commander in Catalonia, the duc de
Vendôme, could not contemplate besieging Barcelona until 1697,
after he had been reinforced with troops from the Italian theatre
following the Treaty of Vigevano in October 1696 ending the war
there.

Barcelona was considered unpropitious for a maritime siege; one
memorandum stated it had only 'a cove in a poor beach', while its

[28] SHAT A¹1234, no.s 57, 67, 71: Trobat to Barbezieux, 21 Apr., 2 and 8 May
1693; no. 103: maréchal de Noailles to Louis XIV, 29 May, 9 June 1693; AN Mar
B³80, fo.s 227r, 230v–31r: Trobat to Pontchartrain, 29 May, 9 June 1693; BNF
Languedoc 96, fo.s 99v–100r: 'Guerre de Catalogne', n.d.; SHM Bib 386(–1), 89;
Peter (1995), 107.
[29] Peter (1995), 107–8; BNF Clair 888, fo.s 344v–45r, 346v, 350v, 367r–v: Tourville
to Pontchartrain, 30 May, 3 and 14 June, 3 Aug. 1694; fo. 420r–v: Tourville to
Phélypeaux, 24 July 1695.
[30] SHAT A¹1336, fo. 220v: Ferrand to Barbezieux, 27 Aug. 1695; A¹1338, no.
144: Louis XIV to Vendôme, 30 Aug. 1695. Russell's overwintering in Cadiz during 1694–95 has been seen as a decisive moment when the English navy began to
claim control of the Mediterranean, but the poor state of Russell's fleet by the summer of 1695 reveals how vital it was for Britain still to secure its own naval base
in Mediterranean waters. Cf. Stapleton, ch. 10, below, pp. 347–8.

port was considered too shallow for anything but galleys to enter. Furthermore, during 1696 the Spanish had strengthened the port's seaward defences and the fort of Montjuïc covered the whole of the harbour from heights, so all in all an effective bombardment (as opposed to diversionary firing, which was indeed carried out) was out of the question.[31] Equally problematic, on land Vendôme was faced with the problem of having insufficient troops to complete a circumvallation even of the landward city walls. A fleet of, this time, nine battleships and 30 galleys was designated for the campaign. Indeed without the support of the fleet the siege would have been simply impossible, such was the threat of the Spanish both cutting the French land lines to Gerona and reinforcing the Barcelona garrison by sea. Vendôme insisted the navy bear the burden of transporting most of the *matériel*.[32] The siege began on 15 June and was to be long and bloody, lasting until 10 August. During that time Vendôme drew by fiat on the navy's human and material resources to supplement the land forces as necessity demanded. Without the assistance of the navy the siege would not have succeeded at all.[33] The fact that it did owed everything to extensive planning, massive logistical mobilisation, extensive (if not always perfect) cooperation between naval and military officers, and good leadership on both land and sea. It was a remarkable demonstration of what thirty years of military and naval reform was capable of producing if placed in the right hands. It remains an indication of what could have been achieved by France in the War of the Spanish Succession had Louis XIV been able to mobilise sufficient resources.

---

[31] SHM Cartes SH49, no. 21: 'Remarques...', n.d. [1697?]; AN Mar B⁴18, fo. 202v: [Herbault] to Pontchartrain, 5 Aug. 1697.

[32] SHAT A¹1338, no. 38: Vendôme to Louis XIV, 13 June 1695; A¹1378, no.s 42, 65, 83: Vendôme to Louis XIV, 2 and 22 June, 20 July 1696; A¹1417, no. 69: Vendôme to Louis XIV, 28 May 1697; no. 83: Lapara to Barbezieux, 10 June 1697; AN Mar B²128, fo.s 408v–13r: 'Instructions...', 15 May 1697; B³80, fo. 254r–v: Trobat to Pontchartrain, 4 Sep. 1693; B⁴18, fo.s 179v–81r: Estrées to Pontchartrain, 26 July 1697; SHM Bib386(–1), 91; Symcox (1974), 168. Serious planning for the siege began as far back as June 1695.

[33] SHAT A¹1417, no. 92: Vendôme to Louis XIV, 21 June 1697; A¹1418, no. 53: Vendôme to Louis XIV, 29 July 1697; no. 71: 'Capitulation de Barcelonne', 10 Aug. 1697; AN Mar B²121, fo. 321v: Phélypeaux to bailli de Noailles, 12 June 1697; fo. 488r: Pontchartrain to Vendôme, 5 June 1697; B⁴18, fo.s 170r–v, 201v: Estrées to Pontchartrain, 20 June, 5 Aug. 1697.

Military and Naval Administration, Logistics and Amphibious Warfare

Some brief consideration of the improvements in the army and navy under Louis XIV is now called for. Louis XIV was determined from as early as the Frondes (1648–54) to gain firm royal control over his armed forces, and in this he was aided by Michel Le Tellier and his son the marquis de Louvois as Secretaries of State for War, and Colbert and Seignelay as Secretaries of State for the Navy: the king set the parameters of policy and had the ultimate say-so on proposals, but the ministers and their advisors should be given the credit for analysing the problems and carrying through the decisions. Between 1660 and 1690 the armed forces underwent a renaissance, and for all the remaining deficiencies the results were visible in the huge expansion in the number of soldiers and sailors under arms, and the number of ships under royal control.

For the army, greater sustainability and larger size were gained through administrative reforms which not only disciplined the officers more effectively but also took into account their private interests. On top of this there was a recasting of the military treasury system (the *Extraordinaire des Guerres*), while last but not least, after 1672 the high command became far more tractable thanks to Louis XIV manipulating their private interests in the service of the Bourbon dynasty. The determination of not only the War Ministry but also the high command to instil firmer discipline and subordination in an age of mounting concern about personal conduct had borne sufficient fruit by 1690 that observers reflected on the *relative* professionalism of the French officer corps, at least in comparison with other European armies.[34]

The sailing navy was a more difficult, more complicated matter and had to be built up from a position of humiliating weakness in 1661, when it consisted of only ten battleships and twelve frigates.[35] Thanks to the impulsion of the Colberts, between 1665 and 1697 the crown built the navy up to 286 battleships, even if 149 of them were out of commission during the latter year. For all the decline in the number of operational ships from the mid-1680s, the navy

---

[34] See Rowlands (2002).
[35] On the weakness of the navy in the 1650s and early 1660s, see Roncière (1920), V, 180–223; Dessert (1996), 182; Dingli (1997), 100.

was at least able to put competitive fleets to sea until 1706. Back in
the 1660s neither king nor ministers had expected the navy to grow
to such a size.[36] The circumstances of the navy's funding —its heavy
dependence on semi-private fisco-financiers—made it difficult to put
to sea en masse,[37] and the navy was not nearly so effective nor so
easily deployable an instrument as the army throughout Louis XIV's
reign. For one thing, it was, for operational purposes at least, effectively
divided between the Levant fleet in the Mediterranean and the Ponant
fleet on the west coast and English Channel. But the organisational
changes which the officer corps and ports underwent were nevertheless far-reaching, and did make amphibious warfare considerably
more viable.

Colbert evolved a network of *intendants de la marine* and *commissaires*
who exercised considerable control over ports and arsenals, and all
the activities therein. They also looked after the chartering of merchant vessels when necessary.[38] The high command was given a
clearer structure, and though there were insufficient general officers
in the navy, they were at least promoted on merit, until promotions
became devalued rewards after 1706.[39] The more serious problem
was creating an officer corps. It was one thing expanding the number of royal officers from 246 in 1669 to 847 four years later, but
another to shape them into a disciplined, effective body. Despite
tighter royal political control and efforts to create a more socially
and culturally cohesive officer corps, achieving a satisfactory level of
reliability was not an easy task. When ships' captains displayed too
much independence, especially in the Levant fleet (where line-of-
battle tactics that had forced discipline in the Ponant had hardly
been employed), it threatened the cohesion of whole expeditions. As far
as the crown was concerned, subordination in the navy had in 1694

---

[36] Dessert (1996), 180–84, 198; Symcox (1974), 77; Meyer (1979), 166; AN Mar
G121, fo. 81r: memorandum, 5 Dec. 1694.

[37] Dessert (1996), 49, 54–57, 75, 279–82; Symcox (1974), 41. Note that the sailing fleet only supported one amphibious operation at full fleet strength, at Palamos
in 1694.

[38] Dessert (1996), 28, 40–46; Dingli (1997), 136–37; AN Mar B²128, fo. 415v:
Pontchartrain to Vendôme, 15 May 1697; B³99, fo. 219r: Vauvré to Pontchartrain,
28 July 1697; B⁴18, fo. 208r: [Herbault?] to Pontchartrain, 29 Aug. 1697.

[39] AN Mar G121, fo. 266r: 'Estat . . .', [post-1758]; fo. 88r: memorandum, 5
Feb. 1694; Dessert (1996), 109, 225–26, 237–38; Bamford (1973), 103; Laloy
(1929–31), III, 206.

still not reached the tolerable level it had attained in the army, even
if matters were considerably better than in Beaufort's day.[40] Nevertheless, managing the officer corps was relatively easy compared with
the administrative complexity of mobilising enough sailors to man
the royal fleets. Between 1668 and 1673 a series of edicts built one
on another set up the *inscription maritime* which divided seafarers into
three rotating *classes* for service. Despite serious difficulties in implementing this system (especially in the Mediterranean provinces), and
a growing administrative paralysis once war was under way in both
the 1670s and 1690s, the deficiencies were at least not so great as
to thwart any planned amphibious attacks entirely, and the *inscription maritime* was a considerable improvement (at least as far as the
king was concerned) on the previous absence of system.[41]

Alongside the sailing fleet, there were, of course, the galleys.
Inheriting only eight essentially private craft from Mazarin's regime,
after 1663 Louis XIV and Colbert made a determined effort over
the next three decades to bring the galleys under full royal control
and expand the numbers of craft: by the middle of the Dutch War
approximately 25 were available and in 1690 a peak of 50 was
reached. In 1697 there were 34 operating in the Mediterranean. The
French needed such a large galley fleet, which was manned without
too much difficulty by political prisoners and convicts, to ensure maximum flexibility in littoral operations, defensive and offensive. And
if in practice there were almost no galley encounters between the
two western Mediterranean powers in 1659–1700, the French still
felt they needed a powerful force to challenge and deter the Spanish
galley fleet, which remained substantial until the end of Habsburg

---

[40] Dessert (1996), 220–21, 232–33; Corvisier (1995), 132; Symcox (1974), 23–31;
Clément (1864), III(i), 192: Colbert to Martel, 25 Nov. 1669; 226–28: 'Instruction . . .',
[Apr. 1670]; Roncière (1920), V, 348, 350; Dingli (1997), 118, 132–35; AN Mar
B²128, fo. 506r: Pontchartrain to Estrées, 12 June 1697; Laloy (1929–31), II, 430,
524, 533–34, 698; III, 128, 374; AN Mar A¹9–10: various ordonnances; B⁴2, fo.
293r: Beaufort to Colbert, 30 June 1664; G121, fo.s 74v, 75v: memorandum, 1694;
fo.s 88v, 90v: memorandum, 5 Feb. 1694; B³78, fo. 29r: La Jonquière to Pontchartrain,
22 Jan. 1693; B³99, fo.s 434r–35v: Duclos to Pontchartrain, 24 July 1697.
[41] Corvisier (1995), 124; Dingli (1997), 109, 110–12, 115–16, ; Dessert (1996),
201–2, 211–18; AN Mar A¹13, no. 50: edict, Aug. 1673; no. 37: ordonnance, 18
July 1673; B²93, fo. 490r: Pontchartrain to Estrées, 10 June 1693; Laloy (1929–31),
II, 53, 414, 797–98, III, 141–4; Symcox (1974), 15–19; Bromley (1987), 122, 133;
Meyer (1981), 910–16.

rule.[42] As in the sailing fleet, officer indiscipline remained trouble-
some until severe measures were taken in the 1680s, and by the following decade detailed, uniform procedures were in use and the
galleys were deemed acceptably organised.[43] Of direct relevance for
amphibious warfare, though, there persisted an air of ill-disposition
between the galley and sailing officers throughout the reign, diminishing only gradually under crown pressure. The galley officers, claim-
ing precedence, had to be slapped down and their subordination to
battleship officers of the same rank reiterated three times by the
crown. Only with the Nine Years' War does the truculence of galley officers appear to have subsided. But such was the sense of griev-
ance felt by the galleys that Louis in 1677 and again 1693 ordered
them never to cruise with his sailing ships except in cases of real
necessity, and also to remain quite separate even when anchored in
the same ports and roads.[44]

Supply

A large and improved army and navy enabled Louis XIV to contemplate amphibious warfare as a tool of strategy in the Mediterranean,
but to breathe life into the armed forces required effective provi-
sioning of supplies, especially victuals or *vivres* as they were known,
and which came under the purview of the provincial intendants, and
those of the army and navy. The dreadful logistical arrangements
for the Candia and Sicily expeditions—based on thorough miscon-
ceptions of local economic circumstances—proved the need to use
the state and its machinery more effectively, and demonstrated the
futility of trying to live off the locality away from the French frontiers.[45] After the Dutch War the government seems to have absorbed

[42] Meyer (1981), 920; Glete (1992), I, 251; Roncière (1920), V, 330; Bamford (1973),
15, 22, 24, 29, 43, 45, 78, 99; ACC S2, fo. 169r: memorandum, 18 Feb. 1697.

[43] Bamford (1973), 69, 97–106, 301; Cordey (1910), 24: Louis XIV to Vivonne,
22 Apr. 1669.

[44] Bamford (1973), 53, 105; AN Mar A¹8, no. 51: ordre du roi, 14 Apr. 1668;
A¹17, no. 12: règlement, 31 Mar. 1677; B²93, fo. 515r: Pontchartrain to Estrées,
17 June 1693; B²94, fo. 694v: Louis XIV to bailli de Noailles, 7 Aug. 1693; fo.s
1098v–99r: Pontchartrain to La Jonquière, 2 Dec. 1693; B²128, fo. 409v: 'Instructions',
15 May 1697; Laloy (1929–31), III, 206.

[45] Cordey (1910), 10: 'Instructions', 30 Mar. 1669; Nanteuil (1974), 29; Laloy
(1929–31), I, 514; II, 23–24, 458, 572–73, 720, 808–9; III, 160–61, 317, 321;
Rousset (1862–64), II, 410–11, 440–41.

the alimentary lessons of Candia and Sicily, and came to rely on direct supply from France instead for its overseas operations. This naturally depended on the existence of effective means of creation and delivery.

For the army the system which was to see France through most of Louis XIV's reign had been essentially put in place by the 1650s, with entrepreneurs known as *munitionnaires* contracted by the royal council to supply bread to the field armies under the direct supervision of the War Ministry. After the War of Devolution (1667–68), there was a dramatic improvement in delivery, aided by Louvois' establishment of magazines and his untiring efforts to force *munitionnaires* to stock them in sufficient time for early entries on campaign.[46] Nevertheless, the improvements to magazines and the networks of *munitionnaires* were for the most part restricted to the northern half of France, resulting often in spasmodic delivery in the Mediterranean during the Dutch War.[47] Essentially, if government fiscal policies and harvest shortages caused trouble across the board, especially in 1692–94, at least the fundamentals of the *munitionnaire* system were more sound than in the first half of the century and larger armies could now be fed. A similar picture can be painted of the navy. In this arm, victualling remained truly chaotic and disruptive of expeditions until October 1669, when Colbert took control away from the ships' captains and vested it instead with crown officials and large-scale contractors.[48] These reforms should not be underrated and they did make it possible to plan operations with a stronger certainty that they could be sustained, but if miracles were expected then none materialised, and *munitionnaires* were too frequently stretched to the very limit of their resources.[49]

At the heart of the French state's ability to supply amphibious expeditions and littoral campaigning lay the port infrastructure, which for all its continued inadequacies was developed on a sufficient scale to facilitate major operations in the Mediterranean after 1670. The

---

[46] Iung (1983), 286, 299–306; Parrott (2001), 382–85; André (1906), 440–48; Rousset (1862–64), I, 248–50; Corvisier (1983), 191.

[47] Laloy (1929–31), II, 721, 796.

[48] Dingli (1997), 140–41; Mémain (1936), 5; AN Mar A^{1}9, no. 29: arrêt, 2 Oct. 1669; Cordey (1910), 204: Colbert to Infreville, 21 Sep. 1669.

[49] Laloy (1929–31), I, 513; II, 252, 408–10, 461–64, 564–66; Rousset (1862–64), II, 411; Dessert (1984), 77, 398.

improvements at Toulon, the only large deepwater port on the French Mediterranean coast, illustrate well how the course of port development both helped and impeded amphibious warfare.[50] Prior to its overhaul beginning in the 1670s, it was cramped, posing severe problems of security and shelter in the arsenal and a harbour both too small and too clogged with naval debris. By 1669, in the light of some ameliorations already undertaken in facilities, Colbert and his engineers were thinking of developing Toulon to cope with a fleet of up to 50 line-of-battleships using it as their main base. And the Dutch War revealed the desperate need to get on with this task, as supplying the Sicilian expedition had been plagued by delays at Toulon.[51] By 1691 the port could cope with a far larger number of vessels than before, and without such a radical overhaul the amphibious attacks against Nice and Barcelona would have been very difficult to mount. Yet the way the port was redesigned and reconstructed over the succeeding thirty years suggests a greater desire to fulfil Toulon's potential for ship-*building* and repair rather than to turn it into an effective launch-pad for decisive action. The premium was placed on the general expansion of facilities and not focussed sharply enough on the easing of actual fleet operations.[52]

Most neglected were the victualling quarters, and if facilities were such that sufficient food could be cobbled together for a standard naval squadron, it was a completely different matter when Toulon was being relied on as a depot and production and loading centre for a land army as well. The lack of magazines for the naval *munitionnaires* considerably delayed and inconvenienced the commissioning of ships during the early part of the Sicilian expedition, leading in 1676 to the construction of six new ovens to add to the existing six, plus two new grain warehouses. Intendant Arnoul, however, estimated that thirty ovens were needed, plus commensurate storage facilities. Unfortunately, no more than a couple of these were built,

[50] Peter (1994) provides a clear account of the development of Toulon, and much of the subsequent discussion is built on his work, but the commentary on how this relates to naval operations is largely my own.

[51] Dessert (1996), 119–21; AN Mar B⁴2, fo. 294v: Beaufort to Colbert, 30 June 1664; Peter (1994), 23, 25, 43, 46, 48–51

[52] Peter (1994), 195–96, 282; Clément (1864), III(i), 294–95: memorandum, 8 Oct. 1670; SHAT A¹1079, no. 130: Vauvré to Louvois, 14 Feb. 1691; no. 261: Catinat to Louvois, 18 Mar. 1691.

accordingly forcing the government to use the 15 bakeries of the city. Only in 1695, aware of the need to use Toulon for a future assault on Barcelona, did the king accept a new plan for the bakery which was supposed to double its monthly output. Fate then intervened in a conflagration the following year which destroyed the naval bakeries, and not until 1701 was production restored to its pre-fire levels. Moreover, until 1705 storage facilities for wheat and flour remained wholly inadequate. Throughout this period, then, *munitionnaires* had to make do with scattered and small, less secure buildings beyond the arsenal walls. All these deficiencies in victual supply impeded amphibious warfare: the brief Genoa expedition in 1684 exhausted the port, and food supply for the 1691 campaign against Nice suffered delays and had to be routed in part through Antibes.[53] More generally, the preparation of ships and the provision of supplies for both the army and navy for the Catalan campaign of 1697 were sluggish, delaying the investing of Barcelona and nearly forcing Vendôme to withdraw before he had even started. This was not entirely the fault of inadequacies at Toulon, but did reflect another difficulty this port posed as a launch-pad for amphibious operations—the city's location made it difficult to get large quantities of wheat and flour there in a short space of time, so much so that the army *munitionnaires* (and the artillery) in 1697 were ordered to distribute stocks to Agde, Arles, Marseille and smaller ports for loading. The scattering of supply bases the length of the Provence-Roussillon coast only further delayed the start of operations in Catalonia that year.[54]

Toulon therefore remained under-equipped to support major amphibious operations, and, with the possible exception of Marseille, the same can be said of those ports on which the galleys and lesser craft depended.[55] Galleys needed to be able to call at a number of stations if they were to be fully effective, yet the ports of Languedoc

[53] Clément (1864), III(i), 246: Colbert to Matharel, 5 July 1670; Peter (1994), 85, 221, 226–27, 288; SHAT A^{1}1077, no. 6: Louvois to Catinat, 5 Jan. 1691; no. 63: memorandum, n.d. [late Jan. 1691]; A^{1}1079, fo. 259: Vauvré to Louvois, 17 Mar. 1691.

[54] SHAT A^{1}1416, fo.s 105r–6v: Saint-Pouange to Barbezieux, 9 May 1697; fo. 114r: Comolet to Barbezieux, 10 May 1697; A^{1}1417, no. 69: Vendôme to Louis XIV, 28 May 1697; no. 79: Esgrigny to Barbezieux, 7 June 1697.

[55] Bamford (1973), 22, 53–64.

and Roussillon, which had so much potential for supporting amphibious warfare down the Spanish coast, were extremely difficult to use. Access from the sea was difficult in several case such as Sète, and the underdeveloped ports of Roussillon could not store *matériel* in any great quantity, nor provide adequate numbers of barges and boats. All this compounded the difficulties of assembling and carrying sufficient supplies, and slowed down the efficiency of the galleys in convoying them, for the Barcelona campaign of 1697.[56]

What the navy really needed, if France was to dominate the Mediterranean, was a forward base away from the homeland to sustain littoral operations, even if such places could never be more than dependents of the homeland.[57] On a limited scale both Rosas and Palamos were used, but only as supply depots, from 1693 and 1694 respectively; nor did they make the most of Minorca when it was at their disposal in 1700–08. Only at Messina in 1676–77 did the French, half-heartedly, attempt to go further and develop full port facilities.[58] The failure to exploit such bases when they were available made amphibious operations overseas worryingly reliant on the under-supplied southern French ports and upon convoys. With these too the state took a long time to appreciate how they could be best organised. It was difficult enough to assemble and despatch convoys according to plan, yet the government compounded the problem by preferring to use a few large convoys protected by slow, lumbering battleships rather than many small ones. The reason, of course, was fear of corsair activity, but in the Mediterranean large convoys made little sense: merchants preferred fast dashes in small groups supported by lighter protection vessels who could deal with, for example, the Dutch privateers who preyed upon French shipping between Provence and Sicily in the second half of 1677 and who were too fast for battleships to catch.[59] Quite simply, the French navy was not effectively deployed for long-distance or out-of-area protection of merchantmen acting as suppliers to amphibious operations.

---

[56] Ibid., 35, 38; SHM Cartes SH49, no. 12: memorandum, 1 Jan. 1693; SHAT A¹1416, fo. 200v: Barbezieux to Pontchartrain, 4 May 1697.

[57] Pointis urged Louis to establish a forward base in an Irish port to support James II in 1689–91, but the failure to do this meant only a token force of French ships could help the Jacobite cause: Symcox (1974), 85; idem. (1967), 251, 361.

[58] Laloy (1929–31), III, 137, 159, 308, 336.

[59] Ibid., II, 796; III, 108–9, 120, 148–54, 161, 295–96, 325.

This is not to say that the provision or delivery of supplies for amphibious warfare saw repeated failure during the 'personal rule' of Louis XIV, but it does underline the structural limitations on combined arm flexibility. Alongside these structural problems went concerns over demarcation of responsibilities which could impede operations. There was little inter-arm strife over the transporting of troops, although cavalry units were understandably reluctant to transport their mounts by sea.[60] In the matter of food supplies, by contrast, there were plenty of difficulties for many years between the two arms. The *vivres* for the army and navy were kept separate as far as possible, and though at first it might appear illogical to continue to use two different *munitionnaire* companies for army and navy during the Sicilian expedition, this did mean that both companies together could draw on a larger network of suppliers and contacts than a single, giant company would have managed. But sometimes separate arrangements could go too far: in the Sicily expedition the War Ministry had to charter its own ships to carry the army's pay which, for some reason, the navy would not accept. As Vivonne recognised, where the army and navy were operating together and mutual support was necessary, it needed the king himself to be tough in arbitrating between the different *munitionnaire* companies and to force ministers to direct suppliers, treasurers and even intendants into implementing orders they found unpalatable. These clashes diminished both in frequency and intensity, and, though tussles persisted between the two ministries about sharing the costs of sieges, the years 1691–94 saw visibly closer logistical cooperation between them.[61] And it was just as well, because the topography of Catalonia and southeastern France made land campaigning in these regions wearing and expensive, there was a chronic shortage of mules throughout the decade, and there was always a risk of losing cannon over precipices. When Catalonia exploded in revolt against the French occupiers in the winter of 1694–95, land transport became virtually impossible

---

[60] AN Mar B³80, fo. 249r: Trobat to Pontchartrain, 21 Aug. 1693; B²129, fo. 49r: Pontchartrain to Estrées, 14 July 1697; B⁴18, fo. 200r: [Herbault?] to Pontchartrain, 25 July 1697; Montbas (1926), 217–19.

[61] Cordey, 256: 'Journal . . .'; Laloy (1929–31), II, 24; III, 105, 135–36, 167, 171; SHAT A¹1417, no. 90: Trobat to Barbezieux, 19 June 1697; AN Mar B²129, fo. 194v: Pontchartrain to Estrées, 28 Aug. 1697; B³78, fo. 400r: Barbezieux to Pontchartrain, 15 Oct. 1693; B³100, fo. 28r–v: idem, 12 Oct. 1697.

without impractically heavy escorts for nearly another two years, and Spanish guerrillas continued to threaten land supply routes throughout 1697.[62]

The navy, using *flûtes*, *brigantins*, *tartanes* and even converted fireships,[63] consequently carried a large proportion of the munitions for just the short hop from Roussillon to Rosas in 1693, and again for the 1694 campaign, when Tourville carried all the flour and the whole siege train to Palamos by sea and the galleys were used to return the burst and buckled cannon back to Roussillon. In 1697 Vendôme equipped the army, which was setting out from Roussillon, with only twenty days of subsistence out of fear that too many carts would be an encumbrance should the Spanish have disputed the passes en route to Barcelona. The navy took up the principal burden. On board 12 battleships and frigates, 30 galleys and 150 transports was carried an unprecedented load: 316,000 cannonballs, 11,617 bombs, 29,000 grenades, 44 siege cannon, 18 mortars, just under 40,000 siege tools, 500,000 pounds of gunpowder, and 40,000 sacks of flour and oats. Even then, galleys and transports had to be despatched halfway through the siege to pick up yet more powder and shot.[64] On arrival, disembarkation had to be done as speedily as possible so sieges would not be disrupted, not least by enemy ships, but this proved easier in theory than in practice. Bad weather and the nature of the transport vessels, which were not designed for discharging their cargoes at sea especially in choppy waters, played their part; but sheer inexperience injected an element of chaos into the unloading process near Villefranche in 1691. Practice improved the navy's

---

[62] SHAT A¹1079, no. 259: Vauvré to Louvois, 17 Mar. 1691; A¹1234, no.s 86, 97, 100, 103: maréchal de Noailles to Louis XIV, 20, 24, 27, 29 May 1693; A¹1378, no.s 121, 124: Vendôme to Louis XIV, 13, 16 Sep. 1696; A¹1417, no. 4: Esgrigny to Barbezieux, 14 Jan. 1697; no. 88: Trobat to Barbezieux, 16 June 1697; A¹1416, fo. 198r: Barbezieux to Pageau, 2 Sep. 1697; A¹1418, no. 104: Vendôme to Louis XIV, 27 Aug. 1697.

[63] AN Mar B²94, fo. 530v: Pontchartrain to Estrées, 24 June 1693; fo. 693v: Pontchartrain to Noailles, 7 Aug. 1693; AN Mar B³80, fo. 248v: Trobat to Pontchartrain, 21 Aug. 1693.

[64] BNF Clair 888, fo.s 344v–45r, 367r–v: Tourville to Pontchartrain, 30 May, 3 Aug. 1694; fo.s 383r, 390r: 'Journal', 1694; SHAT A¹1417, no. 76: Esprit to Barbezieux, 6 June 1697; no. 78: Esgrigny to Barbezieux, 7 June 1697; A¹1416, fo.s 78v–79v: 'Estat', [23 Apr. 1697]; A¹1418, no. 57: Trobat to Barbezieux, 31 July 1697; AN Mar B⁴18, fo. 181r: Estrées to Pontchartrain, 26 July 1697; fo. 202r: [Herbault?] to Pontchartrain, 5 Aug. 1697.

performance, and galleys were being used systematically from this year on to tow cargo vessels and guide them into the shallows, with *tartanes* proving more manoeuvrable than the larger *flûtes*. The disembarkation of supplies for the Barcelona siege was considerably smoother, with a fixed rendezvous between army and fleet at Mattaro designated on the basis of real knowledge of coastal topography; but even with a high degree of coordination, the colossal amount of *matériel* to be landed still took a week to get ashore.[65] In all this, there remained the problem that the navy had to find and hire private vessels as cargo craft, and the contracts agreed were generally for a very short duration, which meant that some were being let go even when more supply movements were imperative.[66]

So much for the planned cooperation between army and navy over supplies. Unforeseen, ad hoc assistance was often required too, and similarly the record was one of truculence in the 1670s followed by willingness in the 1690s as Louis' ministers and commanders recognised that the king would not tolerate damage to his war effort caused by institutional rivalry. In spite of Seignelay's warning to marine troop officers in March 1677 not to allow land troops to share in their provisions, Vivonne and the *intendants* distributed food as they saw fit on the spot. Fortunately, Seignelay's jealousy was not the pattern of later wars: during the Nice campaign the galleys gave four days of food to 5000 land troops because their flour had not arrived. Only when the *munitionnaires* began mixing up the army's and navy's supplies in 1697 did Pontchartrain[67] raise objections, knowing full well this was a recipe for fraud.[68] This stronger sense

---

[65] AN Mar B²93, fo.s 411v, 489r: Pontchartrain to Estrées, 13 May, 10 June 1693; fo. 516r: Pontchartrain to Trobat, 17 June 1693; B⁴13, fo. 293v: memorandum, 20 Mar. 1691; fo.s 393r–v, 397r: chevalier de Noailles to Pontchartrain, 18, 29 Mar. 1691; SHAT A¹1234, no. 110: Trobat to Barbezieux, 31 May 1693; A¹1417, no.s 59, 85: Vendôme to Louis XIV, 22 May, 11 June 1697; no. 76: Esprit to Barbezieux, 6 June 1697.

[66] SHAT A¹1416, fo. 77v: Barbezieux to Dandigné, 23 Apr. 1697; AN Mar B³99, fo. 218v: Vauvré to Pontchartrain, 28 July 1697.

[67] Louis de Phélypeaux, comte de Pontchartrain, Secretary of State for the Navy, 1690–99, succeeded by his son Jérôme, comte de Maurepas.

[68] Laloy (1929–31), II, 672; III, 155; AN Mar B⁴13, fo. 393r–v: chevalier de Noailles to Pontchartrain, 18 Mar. 1691; B²93, fo. 515v: Pontchartrain to maréchal de Noailles, 17 June 1693; B²101, fo. 410r: idem., 5 June 1694; B²94, fo. 694v: Louis XIV to bailli de Noailles, 7 Aug. 1693; B²129, fo. 323r: Pontchartrain to Vendôme, 9 Oct. 1697.

of goodwill was also reflected in the army helping to tide the fleet over with supplies on a smaller scale.[69] It was now all being done with remarkably good grace, if sometimes for money as well.

The Navy Inshore: Ships and Shot

On the back of a more coordinated logistical infrastructure and the improvement of military and naval organisation, the French state was able to wage more effective amphibious warfare than ever before in the Mediterranean and outside Europe. We must now turn to the combat operations on the ground, and look at the parameters of the possible in a number of areas, most notably inshore ship manoeuvres, and combined-arm artillery and siegework performance.

The Mediterranean may have enjoyed a favourable tidal pattern for landings and anchoring, but effective amphibious warfare in this period required a deepening knowledge of hydrography and cartography, and a willingness to use it.[70] As late as 1670 Colbert was acutely aware that half this sea was unknown to French pilots, and existing portolan maps were inferior replicas of much older ones originating in the fourteenth century. Most of the pilots of the French Levant were entirely experience-taught, illiterate and had no knowledge of hydrography. With a large expansion of the navy underway it was clear that such amateurism could not persist. The following year Colbert accordingly set up the Service Hydrographique de la Marine, whose remit was to provide the crown with maps of all coasts and to institutionalise seamanship. From the middle of the decade Seignelay kept up the pressure for mapping the Mediterranean, with the Spanish coasts surveyed between 1683 and 1687. Accompanying this, a series of chairs in hydrography were founded in 1671, 1677, 1683 and 1686 at a number of French maritime universities,

---

[69] AN Mar B²93, fo. 515v: Pontchartrain to maréchal de Noailles, 17 June 1693; B³80, fo. 237v: Trobat to Pontchartrain, 14 June 1693; SHAT A¹1234, no. 161: maréchal de Noailles to Louis XIV, 14 June 1693; AN Mar B⁴18, fo. 185r: Estrées to Pontchartrain, 6 Aug. 1697; fo.s 193r, 204r: [Herbault?] to Pontchartrain, 10 July, 11 Aug. 1697. The army had to help the marine troops considerably more than the fleet.

[70] In 1664 the French had some information at their disposal regarding Djidjelli's waters but Beaufort ignored it: BNF Clair 880, fo. 144r: 'Relation . . .', 1665.

while the ordinance of October 1683 established a system for training and licensing pilots based upon their accumulation of experience
and knowledge of theory.[71] Naturally matters did not improve overnight.
Tourville in 1684 complained that naval officers evaded hydrographic
training or tried to cheat in exams, and knowledge was still limited
during the Nine Years' War. In preparation for a descent on the
Papal States, Seignelay ordered an urgent accumulation of information on the Italian coast from Elba to the mouth of the River Tiber
in August 1688, and it seems clear that the French were still surprisingly ignorant of the waters around Villefranche and Nice three
years later. Just after the end of the war the bailli de Noailles' galleys spent two months cruising off the Italian coast spying out putative landing sites.[72]

The need for a more systematic knowledge of coastal waters was
vital because of the obstacles to navigating vessels inshore, whether
for amphibious warfare or not. It was upon the line-of-battleships,
the men of war, that the French navy came to rely for major coastal
operations under Louis XIV, but they were particularly difficult to
manoeuvre. First, until the 1720s French ships had tillers rather than
more responsive steering wheels. More problematic, though, was the
shape of a battleship, particularly in the case of first and second-
raters. Such vessels in the mid-seventeenth century still had high
freeboards, rising steeply in the stern half, that caused grave problems in high beam winds, while the French in particular constructed
heavy vessels, the depth of whose keels prevented sailing in very
shallow waters. From 1673 the navy reduced embellishments to
improve sailing qualities in an apparent realisation that its ships were
not efficiently shaped, but this produced relatively marginal improvements. Only gradually after 1702 did French ships became proportionally wider above the waterline, tapering far less amidships, and
it was not until the 1720s and 1730s that the bow deck came to be
reduced in prominence, while the spritsail topmast disappeared alto-

---

[71] Roncière (1920), V, 413–17; Clément (1864), III(i), 230: 'Instruction', [Apr.
1670]; III(i), 294–95: memorandum, 8 Oct. 1670; Dingli (1997), 126–28; Harding
(1999), 145.
[72] AN Mar B⁴9, fo. 396r–v: Tourville to Seignelay, 16 Dec. 1684; B²67, fo. 209r:
Seignelay to Vauvré, 23 Aug. 1688; B⁴13, fo. 295r: memorandum, 20 Mar. 1691;
SHM Cartes SH49, no. 11: 'Instruction', 9 July 1698.

gether leaving just a bowsprit.[73] Manoeuvring was taxing, but through-out the seventeenth and eighteenth centuries French battleships also found it particularly difficult to take up a fixed station. Following the rule that one should anchor directly into the wind, early modern ships generally needed to anchor beam-on to the shore, and even with two anchors at bow and stern a ship would be vulnerable to a lee shore, especially if she possessed a high freeboard. There were, of course, fewer lee shores in the Mediterranean than the Ponant, but currents could still be treacherous and cause dangerous drifting. On top of this ships had to be anchored in such a way that they could meet the enemy at very short notice in formation. Furthermore, given these anchoring imperatives, shore bombardments were made especially problematic by the distribution of guns on board the ships, pointing overwhelmingly to starboard and port rather than ahead or astern.[74] It is therefore unsurprising that ship-to-shore bombardments from a static position were relatively rare.

To get round these problems, in 1681–82 French naval officers came up with a revolutionary new weapon of war, a hitherto unseen vessel called the *galiote à bombes*, by converting a small transport ship of two to three hundred tons to mount two mortars, fixed to its deck by a bronze sheet, and installing six light guns either side of the stern for skirmishing [figures 20, 27]. It was crewed by up to 60 men. Using these *galiotes* the navy could now bombard shorelines and cities from the sea, raining immense destruction down on Algiers in 1682 and 1683, Genoa and Tripoli in 1684, and Algiers again in 1688. Getting the *galiotes* into place was as complicated in its own way as manoeuvring battleships. A long boat would carry an anchor towards the target, dropping it approximately 800 metres off shore, and then take back and attach the warping cable, of a typical length of 3000 metres, to the *galiote*. The *galiote* would then also be tied to the anchors of a battleship to stabilise it, using equally long ropes. Sometimes with the battleships following, it could then be hauled in from about 3 kilometres offshore to between 1600 metres (daylight) and 800 metres (night), and then commence bombardment. This was

---

[73] Dessert (1996), 268, 279; Glete (1992), I, 247; Acerra (1995), 6–7. See also the wooden models in the Musée de la Marine, Paris.

[74] Hoste (1697), 332, 335; Dessalles (1847), II, 6: maréchal d'Estrées to Colbert, 27 Dec. 1677.

all very well in theory, but the anchoring system, especially where several *galiotes* were involved, was like a spider's web which could easily result in anchor cables lying across each other; *galiotes* could be stationed too closely together, thereby confusing each other's cables; and the longboats did not always accurately judge the distance to the shore for the anchor dropping point. Inexperience caused precisely these problems in Algiers in 1682, though the French learned swiftly from their errors that year.[75]

Galleys still had the advantage that they were flexible and dependable, and though severe and contrary winds could handicap inshore manoeuvres, galleys could still be of immense help in French amphibious operations.[76] Their deployment inshore at the 1693 siege of Rosas prevented the Spanish infiltrating reinforcements into the garrison by sea, which an absence of French galleys would have allowed. At Genoa in 1684 they were split into two formations on either end of the lines of *galiotes* and battleships, supporting the *galiotes* and preventing any enemy vessel leaving the port.[77] With the difficulties other vessels faced inshore, they (and longboats) could be used as tugs. Furthermore, the ability of galleys to use their oars to stabilise their position could be employed for the benefit of other craft: for the French bombardment of Turkish positions at Candia on 24 July 1669 Vivonne, aware of the nautical dangers battleships faced in shallows, interspersed them with and lashed them to his galleys. In spite of a battleship exploding and damaging a number of galleys, it proved an edifying lesson in how good cooperation could overcome inshore sailing adversity. However, arranging and stabilizing vessels for a bombardment remained a lengthy process: as late as 1697 it could take six hours.[78]

---

[75] Harding (1999), 111; Glete (1992), I, 249–50; Molyneux (1759), II, 92; Peter (1995), 11, 77, 81–82; Pointis (1740), 19; Quincy (1726), II, 9–19, 23–24, 95; BNF Estampes Coll. Hennin 5368.

[76] Bamford (1973), 15, 34.

[77] BNF Languedoc 96, fo. 99r: 'Guerre de Catalogne'; AN Mar B⁴14, fo. 543r: memorandum, 1693; SHAT A¹1234, no. 135: Trobat to Barbezieux, 7 June 1693; Quincy (1726), II, 87.

[78] AN Mar B⁴12, fo. 437r: 'Galéres avec Tourville á Tignmouth', 1690; Pointis (1740), 12–13, 25–26; Cordey, 60: Instructions, [July 1669]; ibid., 88: Vivonne to Colbert, 28 July 1669; AN Mar B⁴3, fo.s 235v, 237v: Martel to Colbert, 3 July, 9 Aug. 1669; B⁴18, fo. 173v: Estrées to Pontchartrain, 7 July 1697.

One should not imagine that being brisk and efficient during coastal operations was unimportant for the navy. Apart from the danger vessels faced from the coast and the enemy upon it, fleets also had to take account of enemy naval activity. Between 1664 and 1697 the real worry for the French fleet was an enemy naval force disrupting supply chains, breaking blockades, or defeating French naval forces in combat. Ideally this would be avoided by France remaining the dominant maritime power in the western Mediterranean, as was the case in 1676–93. At the very least, though, local naval superiority was crucial, and when from 1694 this became increasingly hard to sustain it provoked considerable anxiety among French commanders. In 1697 the French belief that an Allied fleet would at some point enter the Mediterranean forced Vendôme into directing the main attack on Barcelona against the strongest part of its walls using brute force, rather than employing more gentle, roundabout but slower techniques. In fact, as the siege began to drag on unexpectedly the prospect of an Allied fleet entering the Mediterranean and forcing the French squadron away from the city caused Pontchartrain to fret at Versailles. This year, the French Levant fleet at sea, for all its power off Barcelona, would have been hard put to deter the English Royal Navy from intervening in the siege had it arrived in time.[79]

Naval Artillery

The navy's role was in part that of securing the local waters so the engineers and artillery could wear down a maritime fortress. But the navy was also expected to contribute actively to a siege using its own technical staff and guns. There is insufficient space to examine in any detail the developing capacity of the French technical corps during Louis XIV's reign, but some things must be said about the capacity of both land and naval engineers for sieges. Essentially, French war engineering was handicapped by the fragmented nature

---

[79] Cordey, 67: Vivonne to Navailles, [19 July 1669]; AN Mar B²121, fo. 320v: Phélypeaux to Estrées, 12 June 1697; B²129, fo. 28v: Pontchartrain to Vendôme, 10 July 1697; SHAT A¹1416, fo. 141v: Louis XIV to Vendôme, 15 June 1697; A¹1418, no. 46: Esgrigny to Barbezieux, 27 July 1697.

of the personnel, who were isolated in small groups and organised
by province. From 1674 Vauban did what he could to develop a
structure, and there was a massive expansion in engineer numbers
from less than thirty in 1661 to 276 by mid-1691. But only after
1690 was greater cohesion developed through a unified Directorate-
General of Fortifications.[80] Unfortunately there was little success in
blending the construction and siege engineers, and the overwhelmingly majority of engineers remained stuck in the subaltern ranks of
the army and navy on poverty pay. At least there were sufficient
land engineers about who knew how to conduct sieges. By contrast,
naval expertise in siege warfare was thin on the ground: naval engineers were used in 1691 at Nice and Villefranche and in 1694 at
Palamos, but in 1697 the Cartagena de Indias expedition was forced
to use volunteer soldiers and officer cadets as its engineer brigade,
with a fireship captain at their head.[81] Engineers were central to
sieges, but so too was artillery, and in littoral warfare there was in
this respect a more even balance of contributions between army and
navy. The land artillery, under the jurisdiction of the Grand Master
of Artillery, suffered from a yawning gulf between the huge quantity of heavy guns available by the 1680s (around 6,000) and their
poor quality. As with the engineers, the internal hierarchy of the
artillery officer corps and the feeble career structures for these men
produced a disorganised, under-trained and demoralised service.[82]
Below the officer level it was even worse. Again, as with the engi-

[80] Blanchard (1979), 60–66, 69, 76, 82, 102–13; Vauban (1910), II, 133: Vauban
to Louvois, 6 Nov. 1675; II, 148: Louvois to Vauban, 14 June 1677; II, 169: Louvois
to Vauban, 27 June 1678; II, 379–80: Vauban to Le Peletier de Souzy, 17 Feb.
1693; André (1906), 530–31, 534; Corvisier (1983), 359, 371; Rousset (1862–64),
I, 242–45.
[81] Blanchard (1979), 72, 77–81, 85, 116–19, 125, 137; Vauban (1910), II, 328,
474, 481: Barbezieux to Vauban, 22 July 1691, 6 July 1698, Oct. 1699; II, 498–99:
Vauban to Souzy, 7 Jan. 1701; Peter (1995), 103, 107, 111; Pointis (1740), 20, 48.
[82] BNF Fonds Français 4560, fo.s 32v–55v: artillery états, 1666; AA 1w21(3), no.
7: memorandum, [winter 1694–95]; AA 1w6, n.p.: Faultrier to Louvois, 14 Dec.
1678; n.p.: Louvois to Faultrier, 26 Dec. 1678; no. 1: memorandum, 1694; no. 3:
memorandum, [Jan. 1711]; n.p.: memorandum by Boisriché, Nov. 1695; no. 5:
memorandum, 'vers 1712'; SHAT A¹1224, fo. 135r: Catinat to Louis XIV, 24 Oct.
1693; A¹1378, no. 35: Trobat to Barbezieux, 25 May 1696; AN FA G⁷1789, no.
275: état, [c.1684–96]; no. 165: memorandum, [c. 1701–2]; Vauban (1910), II, 500:
Chamillart to Vauban, 26 Jan. 1701; Daniel (1721), II, 545; Sautai (1901), 142;
Saint-Rémy (1697), I, preface; Le Bouyer (1819), I, 305–7: Vauban to Louvois, 17
Oct. 1688; Belhomme (1895), 123.

neers, there were too few subordinate specialist troops; and both the engineers and the artillery had to borrow reluctant men from the infantry on short-term loan for technical tasks in siege warfare. Unsurprisingly, they were poorly trained, maladroit, disobedient and did not understand the principles of fortification.[83]

At first, in the 1660s, the contrast between the land and naval artillery was not that great in terms of quality, though the navy possessed far fewer guns; yet by 1700 the navy had massively outstripped the army in what it could offer and this was evident from the occasions on which the two arms collaborated. The navy's gunpowder was less reliable than that manufactured for the army, but when it came to the cannon, the navy acquired vastly more per head than the army, and they were of no worse quality. Furthermore, the Colbert almost totally abandoned the use on sailing ships of cannon with a calibre of less than 10 pounds, concentrating on 18- and 24-pounders. One begins to get a sense of just how much firepower Tourville therefore had at his disposal at Beachy Head in 1690 when his fleet contained 4,600 guns. Land armies simply could not match this.[84] What counted, of course, was what one did with this firepower, and as early as 1670 Colbert set out his hopes for the French navy to surpass the English in the quality of their gunnery.[85] There was a slow start to fulfilling this ambition, for there was no artillery corps in the navy until 1682, and not until 1692 did the baron de Pointis, *commissaire général de l'artillerie* for the Ponant, persuade the king to expand this service, to give the officers a wider remit than merely the *galiotes*, and also to subordinate the cannoneers to the *commissaires généraux* who now took full responsibility for improving naval gunnery in general. For the rest of that decade any operations in which naval guns were involved vis-à-vis the shore were placed under

---

[83] AA 1w6, n.p.: Faultrier to Louvois, 14 Dec. 1678; n.p.: Louvois to Faultrier, 26 Dec. 1678; no. 3: memorandum, [Jan. 1711]; Belhomme (1895), 64–65, 126; Saint-Rémy (1697), I, 24, 36; Vauban (1910), I, 306: 'De l'Artillerie', 1691–92; II, 313: Vauban to Louvois, 20 Sep. 1689; II, 399–400: Vauban to Souzy, 13 Oct. 1693; Daniel (1721), II, 542; Saint-Hilaire (1903–16), III, 308–9: Saint-Hilaire to Louvois, 8 July 1690; SHAT A¹1239, no. 83: Vigny to Louvois, 7 July 1691.

[84] Taillemite (1970), 26, 31; Laloy (1929–31), II, 432–33, 446, 537–40; SHM Bib 386(-1), 24; Dingli (1997), 155; Peter (1995), 20–23; SHM Bib 386(-5), 6; Dessert (1996), 264–65. French galleys were relatively lightly armed, by comparison, with only one 'chaser' of over 24 pounds and a handful of much smaller cannon.

[85] Clément (1864), III(i), 294–95: memorandum, 8 Oct. 1670.

the command of one of the two *commissaires généraux*, who now had the status of a line-of-battleship captain. It remained frustratingly hard to persuade naval officers to become artillerymen, but at least ordinary sea officers were becoming more exposed to training in the use of their shipboard artillery.[86]

So too were ordinary sailors. There was limited artillery training available from mid-1664, but only in 1676 were proper, ordered gunnery schools set up to provide eight months training for the *apprentis-canonniers*, including on board ship, and it was not until October 1691 that the marine troop companies in each port were ordered to detach one hundred men in turn for three-month training courses with cannon.[87] Certainly there were limitations to the effectiveness of this system, and senior officers thought there were still, by the 1690s, too few trained gunners for their needs, forcing them to give very basic instruction to other sailors and ships' marines once embarked on board the fleet. Firing discipline and accuracy still left a lot to be desired, not least in excessive use of powder which wore away the guns too quickly.[88] And the crewing of *galiotes* still left a lot to be desired. For ten years after their introduction in 1682 the bombardier corps was fairly loosely organised with only 200 fully-trained men in Toulon, but firmer shape was provided in April 1689, followed by a full reorganisation of this service at Pointis' instigation three years later. For all that, there were too few bombardiers for the navy's needs. Absolute numbers increased in the mid-1690s, but the total number in the Levant, precisely where they were needed for offensive operations, was reduced in order to establish a company at Brest for *defensive* purposes.[89] Yet, despite the disappointment that remained, the situation by the Nine Years' War was nevertheless considerably better than it had been in the 1660s, and comparatively speaking French gunnery and bombardment had become highly effective.

---

[86] AN Mar C³75: 'Mémoire sur l'Artillerie de la Marine', 7 Oct. 1694; 'Mémoire' from Grandpré, 30 Aug. 1716; 'Mémoire concernant le Corps d'Officiers d'Artillerie de la marine', 1750; 'Mémoire de ce qui reste a faire sur l'artillerie de la marine', 29 Dec. 1694; Peter (1995), 1–2, 5, 7–8, 27–29, 31–34, 47.

[87] AN Mar B⁴2, fo. 294v: Beaufort to Colbert, 30 June 1664; SHM Bib 386(-5), 3, 8, 11; Peter (1995), 53–54, 69; Laloy (1929–31), II, 432–33.

[88] Peter (1995), 47–51, 55, 70–71

[89] Idem., 7, 57–67; AN Mar C³75: 'Mémoire' by Grandpré, 30 Aug. 1716; D'Orves to Maurepas, 23 Mar. 1749; SHM Bib 386(-5), 8: ordonnance, 16 Apr. 1689; BL King's Ms. 40, fo. 81; Nerzic and Bouchet (2002), 92–93.

The navy's guns could be used in amphibious warfare in two distinct ways: either bombardment of the shore from the sea, or through the landing of naval guns, and each will be considered in turn. In the 1660s it was still far from clear just how effective the massed guns of a fleet could be against shore positions, and a great deal of trial and error lay ahead. It was self-evident that artillery firing from ships was less accurate than artillery firing from fixed positions on land, and that bombardments depended upon suitably calm conditions afloat. It was also quite apparent that bombarding an attacking force (i.e. with the fleet acting to support a fortress under siege) was easier than bombarding a defending garrison and fortress. This did not mean that the results were decisive, for such a bombardment of the Turkish lines at Candia on 27th July 1669, in which between twelve and fifteen thousand shots were expended, had little effect on the siege—the Turks had an extensive trench system in which they sheltered and the French as yet had no means of firing explosive mortar bombs to shore which could churn up earthworks.[90]

Faced with bombarding a fortress, a fleet was up against even more problems. First, coastal fortifications could fire back, and stone walls were more solid than the wooden variety possessed by ships. It is certainly true that in the last third of the seventeenth century it was a lot more dangerous for a fleet to bombard fortresses in European waters than it had been one hundred years earlier, as the targets now possessed more gun embrasures and cannon to fill them. Effective breaching of *trace italienne* fortifications required the stationing of cannon in batteries at 100 yards or less distance from the walls; but heavy guns could do extensive damage, especially to wooden vessels, at up to 500 yards. An effective siege required prolonged bombardment of fortress walls, and while a ship could survive mutual cannonading for a few hours, it could not (unlike land artillery) withstand such exchanges for the days on end required to breach the enemy walls. Galleys, with their relatively light armament and construction, were particularly vulnerable after the mid-seventeenth century. All this has led historians to dismiss naval bombardments as largely ineffectual, and it does appear that planners in the 1690s felt that a fleet could make little headway against a town with a

---

[90] Nouzille (1987), 140, 142; Nanteuil (1974), 26; Cordey, 63: 'Instructions', [c.10 July 1669].

bombardment unless a land force had already made considerable progress in reducing its walls.[91] Furthermore, there was the unavoidable, geographical fact that cliffs, beaches and channels meant that ships, delivering broadside gunnery, often could not easily align themselves with a target. But it would be a mistake to write off altogether the potential of battleships in sieges. Although it was foolhardy for a ship to take on a fortress alone, Molyneux, writing in 1759, suggested that it was possible for a ship to come within range of a fortress and sustain little damage, for fortresses were stronger in some directions than others and it all depended on the angle of approach (which, admittedly, depended upon hydrographic knowledge and good pilotage skills).[92] Furthermore, naval bombardments could work against relatively poor coastal fortifications that were under-gunned, as at Villefranche in 1691; and if there were a sufficient number of ships to spread the enemy's attention, providing enough bombardment to keep the defenders' heads down, then a sea bombardment could take place. This had been the hope at Rosas in 1693, where the fortress, situated on the edge of a deep gulf, was assaulted by land from the seaward side—unfortunately bad weather prevented the battleships from carrying through the plan, and the land force had to shoulder the entire burden of breaching the walls. These tactics were considerably more successful at Cartagena de Indias in 1697.[93]

There was more to heavy weapon activity than breaching walls, of course, for shipboard artillery could be used for diversions, covering fire and indiscriminate destruction. At Barcelona Vendôme was unable to use the cannon of the fleet directly against the main bastion of attack because it was over 500 yards from the shore and at an oblique angle to the coast. He did, however, have the galleys cannonade other parts of the city in diversions on two occasions, in one case forcing the Allied commander to call off a major cavalry attack on the French siegeworks, so allowing Vendôme to mount a successful attack on the covered way. The same year Pointis simi-

---

[91] Dessert (1996), 265; SHAT A¹1234, no. 161: Noailles to Louis XIV, 14 June 1693; Guilmartin (1974), 79; Harding (1999), 108; Molyneux (1759), I, 75.

[92] Molyneux (1759), II, 112–13.

[93] Pointis (1740), 46, 56; SHM Cartes SH249, fo. 67r: 'Rélation du siege de Carthagene . . .', 1697; Crouse (1943), 227, 230.

larly used his battleships to distract the attention of parts of the Cartagena garrison.[94] Artillery afloat was also used to support the landing of troops and marines, as it had been in the sixteenth century. For example, at Genoa in 1684 ten galleys laid down a forward bombardment just ahead of the landing force of 2,800 men in the suburb of San Pier d'Arena. The longboats ferrying them ashore were mounted with one-pound 'pierrier' cannon for covering fire. Ten years later experiments were underway in Marseille to create small mortars capable of throwing grenades forward from longboats, and at Cartagena Pointis mounted a gun and a mortar on four *traversiers* (single-masted, single-decked craft), using them for covering landings and activity ashore equally.[95] With battleships, though, the shoreline could be fairly thoroughly scoured to clear the way for a landing force, as evidence from the Caribbean shows at Tobago in 1677 and Cartagena twenty years on.[96]

With *galiotes à bombes* at his disposal, a commander had far greater flexibility in sieges, not least because these craft could withstand an enormous degree of punishment thanks to their large crews and low, massively reinforced freeboards. As well as being employed in the expeditions of the 1680s, they were used in smaller numbers during the Nine Years' War: three served at the sieges of Nice, two at Rosas and Palamos, one at Cartagena, and two plus a converted frigate at Barcelona.[97] The effectiveness of such mortars naturally depended upon their distance from the target, so that bombardments by day would be less sure than those carried out at night from perhaps half the distance. At Barcelona the mortars were considered to have made a significant contribution in demoralising the defenders and spreading fire in several quarters of the city during the first weeks of the siege. If excessive use of powder and shoddy casting had not within a few short days led the *galiote* mortars to seize up and become

---

[94] AN Mar B⁴18, fo. 173v, 179v: Estrées to Pontchartrain, 7 and 26 July 1697; Pointis (1740), 27; SHM Cartes SH249, fo. 66v: 'Rélation du siege de Carthagene . . .', 1697.

[95] Quincy (1726), II, 91–92; BNF Clair 888, fo. 353r: Vauvré to Pontchartrain, 14 June 1694; Pointis (1740), 19.

[96] Crouse (1943), 114, 202, 221.

[97] BL King's MS 40, fo. 134; Pointis (1740), 42; AN Mar B⁴13, fo. 292r: memorandum, 20 Mar. 1691; B²93, fo. 530v: Pontchartrain to Estrées, 17 June 1693; B²128, fo. 411v: 'Instructions', 15 May 1697.

potentially lethal to their handlers, considerably greater damage would have been done to the Catalan capital bringing an earlier end to the siege.[98]

The navy could have a much more devastating impact when it actually put its guns ashore. With purely seaborne attacks, unsupported by land-based forces, getting guns ashore was vital, especially if the enemy was likely to possess cavalry. Even when the navy was working with a separate field army, setting up cannon and mortars on land also made a lot of sense, and extensive use of naval artillery on land indicates that carriage adaptation was by no means an insurmountable problem. Louvois even refused to send an artillery train to Sicily because he felt the navy could provide the necessary gunners, weaponry and equipment. In 1694 cannon and mortars were landed for the Palamos siege, while twelve naval artillery officers were present either on board the fleet or ashore for its duration; and in 1697 the navy provided Vendôme with an extra six 24-pounders and two mortars for the land batteries at Barcelona.[99] The physical process of transferring the artillery from ship to shore involved a considerable amount of ingenuity on a scale not seen before the mid-seventeenth century, and in this regard naval officers demonstrated engineering skills that amazed their army colleagues. At Nice two *chaloupes carcassières*—decked launches—drawn from the Toulon arsenal and requiring a crew of about six men, were used to ferry heavy weapons to the beach. Catinat, the commander-in-chief, confessed to having little idea of how naval artillery could be landed or set up, and he was astonished that a combination of ropes and muscle power could raise cannon, including 12-pounders, onto precarious ridges around the city.[100]

---

[98] SHM SH249, fo. 52r: 'Journal', 1697; AM B⁴18, fo. 170r–v: Estrées to Pontchartrain, 20 June 1697; fo. 191r: [Herbault?] to Pontchartrain, 27 June 1697; B³99, fo.s 208r–9r, 225r, 229v: Vauvré to Pontchartrain, 14 and 28 July, 4 Aug. 1697.

[99] SHM Bib 386(-5), 6; Laloy (1929–31), II, 226, 248, 795; III, 351; Peter (1995), 107–8; SHAT A¹1418, no. 6: Dandigné to Barbezieux, 6 July 1697; no. 19: Esgrigny to Barbezieux, 14 July 1697; AN Mar B⁴18, fo. 193r: [Herbault?] to Pontchartrain, 10 July 1697.

[100] SHAT A¹1079, no. 261: Catinat to Louvois, 18 Mar. 1691; AN Mar B⁴13, fo.s 292r, 295r–v: memorandum, 20 Mar. 1691; fo.s 308v, 319r–v: Estrées to Pontchartrain, 4 and 14 Apr. 1691; fo.s 380r–82v: Vauvré to Pontchartrain, 31 Mar. 1691.

Not only was the navy highly skilled at transferring guns ashore: man-for-man it also outperformed the land artillery corps, and this was particularly the case with the officers. Pointis and Deschiens de Ressons, the two *Commissaires généraux d'Artillerie* of the navy, were crucial to the capture of Nice, and acquired such high reputations that land commanders were able to secure their services in 1693 and 1697. In a somewhat embarrassed tone, Ressons in May 1693 actually had to ask Pontchartrain if he could be withdrawn from the command of the maréchal de Noailles in Catalonia, not because of any friction between him and the general but simply 'because I would rather be under your sailcloth'. Four years later Estrées seconded three officers and 30 bombardiers to the land forces before Barcelona, and then met a second and a third request for further personnel assistance, relieving them every two days. Vendôme sweetened his demands with a promise to allow the navy to run its own ten-gun battery over which the land artillery would have no jurisdiction.[101] Land commanders were not disappointed by their performance, for naval personnel were considerably more adept at handling guns than the reluctant ordinary soldiers whom land artillery officers were forced to borrow from infantry regiments. The navy's mortars stationed ashore destroyed the morale of the Nice garrison, and it was a *galiote* lieutenant, Clavel, who landed a mortar bomb slap bang on top of the citadel's magazine, causing a catastrophic explosion which dramatically shortened the siege.[102]

The Command and Control of Amphibious Operations

French combined operations against fortresses therefore relied heavily for their success upon the technical and firepower support of the navy for a besieging army. But even with a more sophisticated,

---

[101] AN Mar B⁴13, fo. 380r: Vauvré to Pontchartrain, 31 Mar. 1691; B⁴14, fo. 508v: Ressons to Pontchartrain, 23 May 1693; B²129, fo. 8r: Pontchartrain to Estrées, 3 July 1697; B⁴14, fo.s 188r, 190v, 195r: [Herbault?] to Pontchartrain, 19 and 27 June, 15 July 1697.

[102] AN Mar B⁴13, fo. 313r–v: Estrées to Pontchartrain, 8 Apr. 1691; fo. 385r: Vauvré to Pontchartrain, 31 Mar. 1691; B³80, fo. 228v: Trobat to Pontchartrain, 5 June 1693; B⁴14, fo. 508v: Ressons to Pontchartrain, 23 May 1693; B⁴18, fo. 197r: [Herbault?] to Pontchartrain, 21 July 1697; Peter (1995), 17.

extensive infrastructure backing amphibious warfare, with a greater
degree of technical know-how, and all-round improvements in the
armed forces since the days of Richelieu and Mazarin, operations
still depended upon effective command and control. Coordination
from the centre was critical, but the impact and scope of this should
not be exaggerated. The 'stratégie de cabinet', by which Louis XIV
is understood to have tried to micromanage military campaigning
after 1675, has been overstated as an argument for understanding
the conduct of this king's wars. It was more a system of coordination than of domination.[103] The extent to which Louis and his ministers interfered in combined operations depended, as with simple
land operations, on where the campaigning was taking place, and
for the Mediterranean, owing to difficulties in communication and
self-confessed ignorance of the regions, Louis was prepared to dele-
gate decisions much more to his commanders on the ground. Of
course, because Louis prized his ability to allocate resources, personnel and matériel, his decisions at court did prove important for
amphibious warfare. Occasionally, owing to vanity in the first half
of the 'personal rule', his deployment of enormous and impractical
battleships could be counter-productive,[104] but on the whole, given
his more hands-off approach in the Mediterranean, and the fact that
different ministries were involved, the king's decisions usually reflected
a wide range of factors.

In the first instance, bringing together the land and naval forces
was the responsibility of the secretaries of state, under the immediate direction of the king who had to arbitrate between the competing interests of the War and Navy Ministries. The triangular relationship
between ministries and forces on the ground was not always sufficiently
cordial to promote success. Indeed, in Sicily the two ministries were
pushing for very different strategic approaches during the first two
years of the expedition. Louis XIV consequently insisted that Vivonne's
despatches be broken into two separate letters, one on land affairs
which would be transmitted via Louvois, the other on maritime affairs
via Colbert and Seignelay. Outgoing despatches from the court would
be divided by area of competence in the same way. This had also
been the pattern for the Djidjelli and Candia expeditions, as minis-

---

[103] See Rowlands (2001).
[104] Laloy (1929–31), III, 121–22.

ters, anxious lest the forces for which they had responsibility slipped from their grasp, wrung such concessions out of the king.[105] Keen to reduce the potential for a similar divergence of attitudes and interests over French involvement in Ireland in 1689, Louis XIV handed responsibility solely to Seignelay.

Arguably no one way of allocating ministerial responsibilities in amphibious operations was better than another, and sometimes commanders worked against the interests of their own ministers as much as against the rival ministry. What mattered more was that the king coordinated directives from the centre, while the commanders brought their forces together in harmony out in the field and at sea. The first test facing the senior operational commanders was to ensure the army and navy arrived at the same place at agreed times, communications being conducted by small, fast vessels such as feluccas carrying instructions for rendezvous. Considering that each force was usually setting out from a different location this was easier said than done: Estrées' premature arrival off Rosas in 1693 alerted the Spaniards that this was the probable target, in spite of his hasty withdrawal to put them off the scent.[106] Communications remained fairly rudimentary throughout this period, even when both sets of forces had arrived on site and sometimes even when the ships were within shouting distance of the shore. Land commanders would go aboard ship to dine and confer, while fleet officers would come ashore for short periods to be party to more detailed planning of a siege. Such personal contact between land and sea commanders remained central because signalling was still in its infancy. Thanks to Tourville, by 1689 the French had made considerable strides in developing a flag and blank-shot system for use between ships, but signalling between ship and shore was still very primitive, with ad hoc and unstandardised (if increasingly complex) significations laid down by commanders on the spot.[107]

---

[105] Primi Visconti (1988), 98–99; Laloy (1929–31), II, 44; AN Mar B⁴2, fo. 289r: Beaufort to Colbert, 10 June 1664; Louis XIV (1806), V, 447, 549.

[106] AN Mar B²93, fo. 458r: Pontchartrain to Noailles, 27 May 1693; SHAT A¹1417, no. 64: Vendôme to Louis XIV, 24 May 1697; A¹1234, no.s 80, 86: Noailles to Louis XIV, 17 and 20 May 1693; no.s 81, 83: Du Breuil to Barbezieux, 18 and 19 May 1693.

[107] AN FA B²93, fo. 413r: Pontchartrain to Estrées, 13 May 1693; B⁴18, fo. 173v: Estrées to Pontchartrain, 7 July 1697; BNF Clair 888, fo. 352r: Vauvré to

Co-ordinating the army and navy on campaign was not just a matter of communications, however. It also required smooth relations between the army and fleet at the level of theatre command. Traditionally historians have argued that in the seventeenth and eighteenth centuries amphibious operations had to be under the control of both an admiral and a general, each supreme in his own sphere, and they have advanced a variety of propositions to support this view: navies had become too specialised, while the army jealously maintained a sense of social superiority; there were no commanders available equally well-versed in land warfare and seamanship at an adequate level; speed of deployment (arising from a single chain of command) was unimportant until the twentieth century; and limited 'professionalism' meant amphibious warfare until the mid-eighteenth century was relatively ineffective.[108] This argument does not, however, stand up to scrutiny for the reign of Louis XIV, especially if sieges are considered the essence of amphibious warfare in this era. French success in 1697 against Cartagena de Indias came precisely through speed of landing and deployment, vis-à-vis the relative sluggishness of defending forces. In European waters forces or matériel had to be landed swiftly before an enemy fleet arrived (as at Bantry Bay in 1689).

Furthermore, particularly in the French case, a fluid, opaque, immature military hierarchy really required a single individual capable of holding an entire operation together. The political culture of *ancien régime* France was characterised by a particularly acute form of aristocratic rivalry based on competition for status and position, and coloured by loosely-defined, if heartfelt, notions of honour. In the army it remained extremely strong throughout the seventeenth and eighteenth centuries, and even within Colbert's navy a more diluted form of this spirit existed. In both cases, this *Zeitgeist* had the potential to disrupt military operations by cutting across the hierarchy—it was notably problematic before the mid-1680s, and still visible, if reduced in intensity, thereafter. Sensitivities were further aggravated when the two arms were supposed to be collaborating,

---

Pontchartrain, 14 June 1694; Palmer (1997), 140–41; Hoste (1697), 418–24; Tunstall (1990), 8–9, 48–50; Molyneux (1759), II, 196; Cordey (1910), 61, 63, 221; Nanteuil (1974), 24; Anderson (1971), 246; Nerzic and Buchet (2002), 121, 132–33.
    [108] Creswell (1952), 5; Nanteuil (1974), 14; Harding (1989), 41.

thanks to natural (and perennial) rivalry between them and the ignorance on the part of many army officers of the constraints under
which their naval colleagues were always working. The greatest obstacle to the execution of orders throughout the armed forces was a
deep-rooted cultural assumption that superiors could only make
demands of their subordinates if they were specifically authorised by
the crown to do so—holding a nominally superior military rank was
not always enough if the individuals concerned were not part of the
same unit. This was a particular headache when army and navy
officers were serving alongside each other, and though the king did
develop a series of regulations on shore service in the final years of
the seventeenth century, the ageing maréchal d'Estrées warned the
government in 1697 that the king still needed to elaborate an explanation of subordination that cut across both arms-of-service.[109] The
potential for inter-service fractiousness was also enhanced by the
nature of the political system, which tied the officers of each arm
to their government minister. A unifying figure with sufficient moral
and political authority to maximise collaboration between army and
navy was consequently highly desirable as supreme commander of
an operation.

Decisions were nevertheless complicated by Louis XIV's dynastic
policies which affected his choices of commanders. On the one hand
determined to maintain a balance of interests within the upper ech-
elons of the nobility, Louis was also perennially manipulating those
interests in the cause of safeguarding the future for both his legitimate successors and illegitimate progeny. He demonstrated a consistent (though not exclusive) desire to appoint princes and senior
nobles selectively in so far as this would strengthen his own and his
dynasty's political position, and as long as the war effort, he hoped,
would thereby be advanced. Occasionally though, he felt he had
no choice but to work through men he was ill-inclined to favour
but whose talents could not be ignored.[110] If so he could always con-
sole himself with one crucial consideration: the weak nature of the

---

[109] BNF Clair 888, fo. 347v: Tourville to Pontchartrain, 3 June 1694; AN Mar
C³75: 'Mémoire' by Grandpré, 30 Aug. 1716; Rousset (1862–64), II, 400–2; AN
Mar B³100, fo.s 81v–82r, 96r: maréchal d'Estrées to Pontchartrain, 31 May, 28
June 1697; B²129, fo. 439r–v: ordonnance, 10 Nov. 1697.
[110] See Rowlands (2002), pp. 312–17, 326–35.

military and naval hierarchy basically necessitated the appointment
to supreme command of a man whose social status was exalted, and
who would therefore be able the more easily to iron out problems
as they arose on campaign. In addition to easing relations between
the two arms-of-service, a grandee as commander-in-chief—whether
a favourite of the king or not—would also be more likely to secure
the respect of non-French authorities with whom he might have to
deal: the Venetians in 1669, the Sicilians in 1675–78 and the Catalans
in 1693–97.

Ideally, any grandee placed in overall charge of combined operations would be both competent and emollient. Even more ideally,
a commander-in-chief would understand both land and sea warfare,
and where this was not the case (and even where it was) operations
would be handicapped. France was actually fortunate that the rapid
development of its navy between 1664 and 1690 meant there were
plenty of naval officers who had served ashore extensively earlier in
their careers, such as Vivonne and Victor-Marie, comte d'Estrées.[111]
For all this, though, the personal amphibious skills of the naval commanders did not on the whole produce their elevation to supreme
command. Tourville's expertise in amphibious warfare, acquired
between 1669 and 1684, was unparalleled; but his limited knowledge of land campaigning prevented his appointment to full command over any combined operations. In 1694, he was effectively
subordinated to Noailles, though both were *maréchaux de France*.[112] The
besieging of maritime fortresses on the European continent was put
under the control of the commander-in-chief of the land army, even
if consultation with the naval generals was deemed necessary by the
king. Only if an expedition required the overseas transport of all
forces and the continuous use of maritime power in an isolated theatre did the naval commanders assume a more dominant role.

So who commanded the major combined operations in the Mediterranean in this period? As Grand Master of Navigation, François
de Bourbon-Vendôme, duc de Beaufort, had absolute and prior claim
to lead French forces in the 1660s; he was well-versed in naval and

---

[111] Dessert (1996), 231, 242, 258; Cordey (1910), 80.
[112] Cordey (1910), 81; 'Liste', [July 1669]; Dessert (1996), 253; Peter (1995),
72–79, 82, 84, 89–91; AN Mar B²101, fo.s 319r, 453r: Pontchartrain to Noailles,
5 May, 16 June 1694.

military administration; and as a grandson of Henri IV through his
bastard father, César, duc de Vendôme, he should have been able
to provide a degree of leadership second to none. It was not to be,
for Beaufort shared character traits—Louis XIV saw them as flaws—
all too common in men of his station during the mid-seventeenth
century: he was impulsive, reckless, suicidally courageous and obsti-
nate, and the combination of such attributes wrecked the Djidjelli
expedition.[113] This setback seems to have pushed the king into exert-
ing tighter control over the navy, but for political reasons he still
did not feel able to discard Beaufort. For as long as the deeply unreliable Beaufort was living and active, no combined operation could
therefore be placed in the hands of *any* one man. Fortunately, in
1669 the Papal admiral, Vincenzo Rospigliosi, was in overall command of the Christian forces sent to aid the Venetians, allowing
Louis an excuse to split authority over the French contingent. Beaufort
was nominal commander-in-chief and channelled communications
back to France, but Vivonne was commander of the galleys and only
had to obey Beaufort when the two arms of the navy were united
(which he sought to avoid), while the duc de Navailles was set up
as the real counterweight to Beaufort. Navailles was to weigh up the
situation of Candia on arrival, and make the final decision about
whether the French contingent would go ashore and if so, where
they would be landed. He was to command the expedition on land,
was given a veto on the departure of ships from the Candia vicinity, and would be present in all naval councils of war.[114] Between
the three principal commanders there was actually a surprising degree
of cooperation, and Beaufort's complete disregard of the king's orders
in participating in a sortie from the city brought about his own death
only six days after his arrival, an event which, for all its tragedy,
undoubtedly had beneficial effects on French naval and amphibious
warfare. At a time when people still did not fully respect royal wishes
if they conflicted with loosely-defined hierarchical principles, Beaufort's status as a prince and his excessive egotism made him a liability in combat and a perennial threat to French amphibious cohesion.
After Beaufort's demise Vivonne assumed command of the sailing

---

[113] BNF Clair 880, fo.s 144v, 147v, 150v: 'Relation . . .', 1665.
[114] Terlinden (1904), 198–99; Cordey (1910), 10, 15: Instructions, 30 Mar. 1669;
ibid., 29: Louis XIV to Beaufort, 17 May 1669; Nouzille (1987), 128, 136.

and galley fleets combined, while Navailles now had untrammelled authority ashore, and a certain degree of harmony ensued.[115] Nevertheless, Navailles had ruled himself out of future command of combined-arm operations: leaving aside the king's anger over his tactless withdrawal of French forces in late August, Navailles had been the one pushing for the absurdly premature and ill-planned sortie in which Beaufort was killed. Like Beaufort, his judgment could not be trusted, but unlike Beaufort his services could be dispensed with while he remained alive.

So splitting command at Candia had proved no more successful than having a supreme commander at Djidjelli, for success required talent, judgment and restraint on the part of the leaders. In this respect, the Dutch War was a turning point. At least after 1675, Louis XIV used commanders-in-chief in the Mediterranean whose authority he knew would be respected but also whom he thought he could trust to get on with the job. The commander-in-chief of the Sicily expedition, Louis de Rochechouart, maréchal-duc de Vivonne, was the first of these men, and oversaw France's transition to effective littoral campaigning and amphibious warfare in extremely difficult circumstances. Between 1663 and 1666 Vivonne gained extensive experience of galley manoeuvres and sailing fleet action; he was at the head of the régiment de Picardie when it landed at Djidjelli; and in March 1669 he was named as General of the Galleys, giving him a key role as a patronage broker and wide-ranging powers over galley administration. Vivonne's importance and skill have been downplayed by contemporaries and historians alike, often without justice and partly owing to the double adultery of the king with his sister, the marquise de Montespan. Tourville was probably fair in his criticism of Vivonne's excessively lengthy preparations, and intendant Arnoul back in Provence thought he deteriorated as an administrator after going to Sicily—Vivonne was certainly no great logistician. But he showed immense tact, real tactical skill and an ability to coordinate operations around Sicily that would have defeated most of his fellow commanders. As a duke he had the requisite status to be not only a credible military leader,

---

[115] Nouzille (1987), 137, 139; Terlinden (1904), 95–96, 221–22; Cordey (1910), 192: Maulevrier to Colbert, 30 June 1669; ibid., 51–52: Martel to Vivonne, 2 July 1669.

but also viceroy of Sicily to which he was named by Louis in January 1675 before his arrival in Messina. His elevation to the dignity of *maréchal de France* in August 1675 quietened the malcontents in his command and, now he felt more secure, led him to inform the court more regularly of developments in his theatre. His character, moreover, was ideally suited to the era and the episode: he was affable and accommodating, and rarely for a *grand* he was modest and emollient. Undersupplied by the government with troops and matériel, he was acutely aware of the need to maintain the goodwill of the eastern rim of Sicily, leading him to restrain his intendants who were inclined to harsh, undiplomatic behaviour in matters of commerce and the private interests of the local elites. For the entire time he was in Sicily Vivonne had no aides-de-camp, no salary either as naval or as land commander, merely his ordinary income from his personal revenues and state offices. Yet he had vast expenses and went heavily into debt to support the expedition. And he became increasingly angry in mid-1676 with Louvois' deliberate cultivation of other general officers in his command. Lacking logistical support and political commitment from France, it was astonishing that he maintained the expedition and the Messina revolt as long as he did.

The success of the Genoa operation in 1684 owed much to the energising presence of Secretary of the Navy Seignelay in person, working with Tourville, his favourite amongst the naval generals. But the naval character of this operation, from which the land army was excluded, made it unusual. At the next major combined operation in the Mediterranean, against the County of Nice in 1691, difficulties resurfaced. Nicolas Catinat, lieutenant-general in charge of the army of Italy, was ignorant of maritime matters. He was given carte blanche to use the navy as he saw fit to capture Nice and Villefranche, but unfortunately he had little idea how to handle it, and as a consequence of his inexperience the *intendant de la marine* Vauvré—a civilian administrator—came to dominate the conduct of the siege to the irritation of the naval commanders.[116] To the mounting frustration of the comte d'Estrées, commanding the fleet, Catinat ignored his wishes and advice, influenced by the shore-based Vauvré who

---

[116] AN Mar B⁴13, fo. 285r: Estrées to Pontchartrain, 4 Mar. 1691; fo.s 291r, 293r: memorandum, 20 Mar. 1691; SHAT A¹1077, no. 88: memorandum, 4 Feb. 1691.

sought to acquire all the credit for the naval contribution to the campaign in an attempt to worm his way into Louvois' good books. It was not mere pique that induced Estrées' protests: Vauvré took insufficient precautions in landing supplies and matériel, and had even ordered naval officers and vessels to leave the fleet without consulting Estrées. This was no way to ensure orderly conduct of operations.[117]

On the Catalan coast matters were easier, especially because the Noailles family was amphibious itself. The maréchal de Noailles' uncle Adrien de Wignacourt became Grand Master of the Order of Saint John of Jerusalem, the Knights of Malta, in mid-1690; while the *maréchal*'s brother, the bailli de Noailles, was Lieutenant-General of the Galleys throughout the 1690s and commanded them in all major operations. It is striking that in 1693 the galleys manoeuvred at the discretion of the maréchal de Noailles but the sailing fleet could remain at the siege of Rosas or depart as the comte d'Estrées saw fit.[118] The *maréchal* himself was not especially good at anticipating and understanding the needs and capacity of the navy, nor at realistic planning ahead; but he remained on cordial terms with the sailing fleet commanders, and as a favourite of the king enjoyed greater authority than that provided even by his status as a duke and peer. His governorship of Roussillon throughout this period, and of Languedoc as *locum tenens* for the young duc du Maine until the mid-1690s, facilitated the mobilisation of transportation resources for littoral warfare.[119]

The most successful and powerful of all those commanders put in charge of amphibious operations by Louis XIV was Louis-Joseph de Bourbon, duc de Vendôme, who succeeded Noailles as commander-in-chief of the army of Catalonia in June 1695. Like Vivonne, Vendôme was General of the Galleys (since September 1694), but

---

[117] SHAT A¹1079, no. 300: Vauvré to Louvois, 31 Mar. 1691; AN Mar B⁴13, fo.s 288r–v, 302r, 303r: Estrées to Pontchartrain, 11 and 22 Mar. 1691; fo.s 304v–5r: memorandum by Estrées, 22 Mar. 1691.

[118] BNF Clair 888, fo.s 346v–48r: Tourville to Pontchartrain, 3 June 1694; fo. 355r: Vauvré to Pontchartrain, 17 June 1694.

[119] BNF Languedoc 96, fo. 69r: Cardinal de Janson to Noailles, 5 Sep. 1690; AN Mar B²93, fo. 434v: Pontchartrain to Estrées, 20 May 1693; B²94, fo. 589r: Pontchartrain to Noailles, 8 July 1693; fo. 694r–v: Louis XIV to bailli de Noailles, 7 Aug. 1693.

unlike him he never went to sea. As early as July 1694, two months before his installation in office, he was already wielding extensive and competent authority over the galleys and their officers (including in some very technical matters). In part this was because he had been governor of Provence, albeit a distant one until 1693, for twenty-five years. Moreover, he was the grandson of Henri IV's bastard César, duc de Vendôme, and consequently not only a *prince légitimé* but also nephew to the late duc de Beaufort. His own brother Philippe, Grand Prieur de France of the Order of Malta, had been present at Candia as a youth, and though he enjoyed a land-based military career Philippe was a powerful focus for French *chevaliers de Malte* serving in Louis XIV's forces. In addition, between 1693 and 1695 Vendôme acquired some appreciation of littoral warfare as commander of the land corps defending the Côte d'Azur. It also helped that he was on good terms with Pontchartrain and his son Phélypeaux.[120] During the final year of the Nine Years' War, Vendôme was not just running the land operations in Catalonia, but also the entire war effort in the Mediterranean. Naturally he assumed direct control over galley activities, and Versailles deferred entirely to his decisions. He was also given full control to organise and deploy the naval troops who would serve ashore. More unusually, in 1697 the sailing fleet under the comte d'Estrées was, in *all* matters, placed entirely at Vendôme's disposal not just for the Barcelona siege but, it was anticipated, for the subsequent winter as well.[121]

Vendôme enjoyed such massive authority—unparalleled under Louis XIV—because he was a favourite of his second cousin the Grand Dauphin, he enjoyed excellent relations with the king, and, like Vivonne earlier, he was emollient, open-minded and reasonable,

---

[120] BNF Clair 888, fo. 364v: Tourville to Pontchartrain, 15 July 1694; ACC S1, fo.s 188r–89r: 'Dispositions . . .', 1694; fo.s 192r–93r: 'Rapport . . .', 18 Mar. 1695; fo. 215v: Pontchartrain to Vendôme, 25 May 1695; fo. 230r: Phélypeaux to Capistron, 9 June 1695; S2, fo. 81r, 112v: Ponchartrain to Vendôme, 30 May, 28 Aug. 1696; fo. 126r–v: Phélypeaux to Vendôme, 5 Sep. 1696; SHAT A¹1377: Louis XIV to Vendôme, 8 Oct. 1696; AN Mar B²122, fo. 108r: Phélypeaux to Vendôme, 31 July 1697.

[121] AN Mar B²128, fo. 410r: 'Instructions', 15 May 1697; fo. 505v: Pontchartrain to Estrées, 12 June 1697; fo. 531v: Pontchartrain to Vendôme, 19 June 1697; B²121, fo. 273r: Phélypeaux to bailli de Noailles, 29 May 1697; B²129, fo. 10r: Pontchartrain to La Jonquière, 3 July 1697; fo.s 141r–v, 186r: Pontchartrain to Vendôme, 14 and 26 Aug. 1697.

determined to get the best out of his subordinates. He was careful
to listen to the advice of both army and navy officers and was never
so arrogant as to think he alone had the answers. He was also fortunate that he secured exactly the senior officers he wished for his
command, and he then helped his clients both in the navy and the
army.[122] Vendôme's control over the sailing fleet owed much to the
appointment of the comte d'Estrées as commander, which he had
specifically requested in spite of the fact that the Estrées family held
the Vice-Admiralship of the Ponant.[123] From spring 1695 Vendôme
sought to reduce the influence of Tourville, Vice-Admiral of the
Levant, but the king would not permit Estrées to exercise power in
the Provence ports, only over the Levant fleet. That he was prepared to disrupt the vice-admiralty arrangements to this degree to
humour Vendôme says much for his appreciation of the duke. But
why did the duke want Estrées so much, and did it matter? The
answer is that Estrées was Vendôme's second cousin once removed,
and the two families worked closely on political matters throughout
the seventeenth century, though this did not prevent Estrées inform-
ing Pontchartrain of the progress at Barcelona in a somewhat independent spirit. His claim on command was backed by his experience
in Mediterranean littoral warfare and by the extensive thinking and
advice provided from the 1670s by his father Jean, maréchal d'Estrées,
to the king to engage in amphibious warfare against the Spanish
and Dutch in Europe and the Americas. Louis XIV knew that the
presence of the comte d'Estrées would give Vendôme both excellent
support and the necessary authority over the navy as well as the
army in what was likely to prove a very tough siege, as indeed it
was. As it turned out, Estrées and the navy performed admirably,
within the constraints of poor intelligence on the Allied fleets.[124]
The utter absence of conflict between army and navy testifies, in the
context of earlier, less successful or less happy campaigns, to the
crucial roles of social relations and personal chemistry in French

---

[122] AN Mar B²129, fo. 193v: Pontchartrain to Vendôme, 28 Aug. 1697.

[123] See Dessert (1996), pp. 237, 249–51 on Jean and Victor-Marie d'Estrées as
naval commanders.

[124] ACC, S1, fo. 215r: Pontchartrain to Vendôme, 25 May 1695; AN Mar B²122,
fo. 59v: Phélypeaux to Estrées, 18 July 1697; B²129, fo. 162v: Pontchartrain to
Estrées, 21 Aug. 1697; SHAT A¹1418, no. 76: Vendôme to Louis XIV, 15 Aug.
1697.

amphibious warfare in this period; and to the need for a grandee of competence to take overall command of combined operations whenever this was possible.

Conclusion

For amphibious warfare to be successful under Louis XIV two great, separate war machines now had to be brought together for purposes neither was exactly set up to fulfil. Forty-four years after the Sun King's death, Thomas Molyneux asserted:

> In War, and in no Sort, more than the littoral, it is all Calculation, of Distances, of Time, and the comparing together of Forces that are ever in motion, in order to bring themselves in a Situation capable of acting with the most Advantage one against the other.[125]

Human skill was, of course, central to bringing off successful operations, while the coordination of ships and land forces was obviously vital. But what Molyneux did not capture in this declamation, which this essay has sought to do, is the importance of logistical, technological and administrative infrastructures behind amphibious warfare. The sheer scale of the French standing army and navy, both the largest in the world by the 1690s, gave Louis XIV advantages over his enemies in amphibious warfare, *if he chose to exploit their potential*. In the last quarter of the seventeenth century, the capacity of the Maritime Powers for amphibious warfare was no greater than that of the French, and their ability to mount combined operations involving both army and navy was, if anything, less developed. Moreover, France could reach into all theatres of war involving the western European powers: for all its deficiencies, the naval infrastructure of the late seventeenth century at least had the merit of projecting French power into both the north-eastern Atlantic region (where it was not used effectively for amphibious warfare) and the Mediterranean (where to a certain extent it was).

Nevertheless, one should not look at the army and navy through a bureaucratic lens, for in France, as elsewhere, private interest moulded institutions and affected their performance. At the apex of

---

[125] Molyneux (1759), II, 98.

this private-public world stood the king, and with combined operations he had to confront the fact that the socio-political problems
which already caused repeated difficulties just within each arm-
of-service now had to be contained on a cross-arm basis. Through
personality, determination, careful selection and handling of his
commanders after 1672, and a better appreciation of the interests
of his army and navy officers, Louis XIV was on the whole able to
enforce a degree of good order in combined operations. When combined with French advances in military and naval technology, particularly gunnery, hydrography and *galiotes à bombes*, this was a recipe
for effective and fairly regular use of amphibious operations. Alas,
what Louis did not provide was sufficient commitment and strategic interest. There were already hints of difficulties ahead from 1694,
but there was nothing fundamentally wrong with French amphibious capabilities that could not be eased by greater mobilisation of
financial resources and a strong determination to maintain the western Mediterranean as *mare nostrum*. After 1697 neither of these vital
factors were forthcoming, for reasons by no means entirely the king's
fault.

Consequently, in the War of the Spanish Succession the French
lost their grip in amphibious warfare in European waters. They
mounted formidable combined expeditions to capture Nice and try
to take Barcelona in 1705–6, only for the effort finally to exhaust
the logistical and financial capacities of the southern French ports.
The mounting British challenge in the Mediterranean could now no
longer be met. After 1692 the British already had sufficient command of the English Channel, but the capture of Gibraltar in 1704,
followed by Minorca four years later, also gave them domination of
the Mediterranean. In both this sea and in the Caribbean they developed major forward bases which allowed for the projection of naval
and amphibious force, something the French, presumably from
financial constraints, had never seriously tried to do. This did not
make the British intrinsically better at amphibious warfare, as Molyneux
and Richard Harding have shown, and if the French could establish local naval superiority or found themselves up against a weak
British commander (as at Minorca in 1756) then they could still
achieve successes.[126] But from 1694 the British were pulling ahead

---

[126] Molyneux (1759), II, 8–9; Harding (1991).

in the crucial matter of ship numbers; they maintained on the whole a careful balance between naval and army expenditure; and they were coming to develop a fiscal-military state that was better able to weather the demands of eighteenth-century warfare. The last real chance the French had to contain them—the effort to recapture Gibraltar for the Bourbons over the winter of 1704–5—ended in destruction at the hands of a superior British fleet thanks to weak resource allocation. For all the development of the French navy, refined amphibious techniques and the successes in combined operations these brought between 1675 and 1697, it must be remembered that there was no serious challenge from other powers in the Mediterranean during this era. Ultimately when there was a real, sustained threat, Louis XIV's failure to provide sufficient support for amphibious warfare condemned the French to a subordinate status in this sea and allowed the British to rule its waves for the next two-and-a-half centuries.

Sources and Bibliography

Archival Sources

AA   Archives de l'Artillerie, SHAT Vincennes, France.
ACC   Archives Condé, Château de Chantilly, France.
AN   Archives Nationales, Paris, France.
    FA   Fonds Anciens
    Mar.   Fonds de la Marine
BNF
    Collection Languedoc
    Clair   Collection Clairambault
BL
    King's MSS
SHAT   Service Historique de l'Armée de Terre, Vincennes, France.
SHM   Service Historique de la Marine, Vincennes, France.
    Cartes   Dépôt des Cartes et Plans
    Bib.   Bibliothèque de la Marine

Printed Primary Sources

Clément, P. (1864) *Lettres, instructions et mémoires de Colbert*, vol. 3, part 1, ed. P. Clément (Paris: 1864).

Cordey, J. (1910) *Correspondance du Maréchal de Vivonne relative à l'expédition de Candie (1669)*, ed. J. Cordey (Paris: 1910).

Hoste, P. (1697) *L'Art des Armées Navales ou Traité des Evolutions Navales* (Lyon: 1697).

Le Bouyer, P. (1819) *Mémoires et correspondance du maréchal de Catinat*, 3 vols, ed. P. Le Bouyer de Saint-Gervais (Paris: 1819).

Louis XIV (1806) *Oeuvres de Louis XIV*, 6 vols, ed. P. A. Grouvelle and P. H. de Grimouard (Paris: 1806).

———. (1970) *Mémoires for the Instruction of the Dauphin*, ed. P. Sonnino (London: 1970).

Molyneux, T. More (1759) *Conjunct Expeditions: or Expeditions that have been carried on jointly by the fleet and army, with a Commentary on a Littoral War*, 2 parts (London: 1759).

Pointis, J.-B. de Saint-Jean, baron de (1740) *Monsieur de Pointi's Account of the Expedition to Carthagena, in the Year, 1697* in *A Genuine and Particular Account of the Taking of Carthagena by the French and Buccaniers, in the Year 1697* (London: 1740).

Primi Visconti, G. B. (1988) *Mémoires sur la cour de Louis XIV, 1673–1681*, ed. J.-F. Solnon (Paris: 1988).

Saint-Hilaire (1903–16) *Mémoires de Saint-Hilaire*, 6 vols, ed. L. Lecestre (Paris: 1903–16).

Saint-Rémy, P. Surirey de (1697) *Mémoires d'Artillerie*, 2 vols (Paris, 1697).

Vauban (1910) *Vauban: sa famille et ses écrits, ses oisivetés et sa correspondance*, 2 vols, ed. E. de Rochas d'Aiglun (Paris: 1910).

Secondary Sources

Acerra, M. (1995) 'Les projets d'arsenaux de Pierre Puget 1671 et 1676' in *Etat, marine et société. Hommage à Jean Meyer*, ed.s M. Acerra, J.-P. Poussou, M. Vergé-Franceschi and A. Zysberg (Paris: 1995), 1–13.

Anderson, R. (1971) 'The Sicilian War of 1674–78', *Mariner's Mirror*, no. 57 (1971), 239–65.

André, L. (1906) *Michel Le Tellier et l'organisation de l'armée monarchique* (Paris: 1906).

Bamford, P. (1973) *Fighting Ships and Prisons. The Mediterranean Galleys of France in the Age of Louis XIV* (London: 1973).

Belhomme, V. (1895) *L'Armée française en 1690* (Paris: 1895).

Bérenger, J. (1997) 'Le vaisseau de ligne' in *Les européens et les espaces océaniques au XVIIIᵉ siècle. Actes du colloque de l'Association des Historiens Modernistes des Universités*, 22 (1997), 7–23.

Blanchard, A. (1979) *Les 'ingénieurs du roy' de Louis XIV à Louis XVI. Etude du corps des fortifications* (Montpellier: 1979).

Bourelly, J. (1886) *Cromwell et Mazarin. Deux campagnes de Turenne en Flandre* (Paris: 1886).

Bromley, J. (1987) 'Quelques réflexions sur le fonctionnement des classes maritimes en France, 1689–1713' in *Corsairs and Navies 1660–1760* (London: 1987), 269–80.

Corvisier, A. (1983) *Louvois* (Paris: 1983).

———. (1995) 'Quelques réflexions sur les relations entre armée et marine sous l'Ancien Régime' in *Etat, marine et société. Hommage à Jean Meyer*, ed.s M. Acerra, J.-P. Poussou, M. Vergé-Franceschi and A. Zysberg (Paris: 1995), 123–34.

Coutau-Bégarie, H. (2000) 'Seapower in the Mediterranean from the Seventeenth to the Nineteenth Century', in *Naval Policy and Strategy in the Mediterranean. Past, Present and Future*, ed. J. Hattendorf (London: 2000).

Creswell, J. (1952) *Generals and Admirals. The Story of Amphibious Command* (London: 1952).

Crouse, N. (1943) *The French Struggle for the West Indies 1665–1713* (New York: 1943).

Daniel, G. (1721) *Histoire de la milice françoise*, 2 vols. (Paris: 1721).

Dessalles, A. (1847) *Histoire générale des Antilles*, 2 vols. (Paris: 1847).

Dessert, D. (1984) *Argent, pouvoir et société au Grand Siècle* (Paris: 1984).

———. (1996) *La Royale. Vaisseaux et marins du Roi-Soleil* (Paris: 1996).

Dingli, L. (1997) *Colbert, marquis de Seignelay. Le fils flamboyant* (Paris: 1997).

Ehrman, J. (1953) *The Navy in the War of William III, 1689–1697. Its State and Direction* (Cambridge: 1953).

Firth, C. (1909) *The Last Years of the Protectorate, 1656–1658*, 2 vols. (London: 1909).

Glete, J. (1992) *Navies and Nations. Warships, Navies and State Building in Europe and America, 1500–1860*, 2 vols (Stockholm, 1992).

Guilmartin, J. (1974) *Gunpowder and Galleys. Changing Technology and Mediterranean Warfare at Sea in the Sixteenth Century* (Cambridge: 1974).

Hanlon, G. (1998) *The Twilight of a Military Tradition. Italian Aristocrats and European Conflicts, 1560–1800* (London: 1998).

Harding, R. (1989) 'Sailors and Gentlemen of Parade: some Professional and Technical Problems concerning the Conduct of Combined Operations in the Eighteenth Century', *Historical Journal*, 32 (1989), 35–55.

——. (1991) *Amphibious Warfare in the Eighteenth Century: the British Expedition to the West Indies, 1740–1742* (London: 1991).

——. (1999) *Seapower and Naval Warfare 1650–1830* (London: 1999).

Harris, F. (1912) *The Life of Edward Mountagu, K.G., first Earl of Sandwich (1625–1672)*, 2 vols. (London: 1912).

Herrero Sanchéz, M. (2000) *El acercamiento hispano-neerlandés (1648–1678)* (Madrid: 2000).

Iung, J.-E. (1983) 'Service des vivres et munitionnaires sous l'ancien régime: la fourniture du pain de munition aux troupes de Flandre et Allemagne de 1701 à 1710', 2 vols., unpublished dissertation for the *diplôme d'archiviste-paléographe* (Ecole Nationale des Chartes, Paris: 1983).

Laloy, E. (1929–31) *La Révolte de Messine. L'expédition de Sicile et la politique française en Italie (1674–1678)*, 3 vols. (Paris: 1929–31).

Mahan, A. (1965) *The influence of sea power upon history, 1660–1783* (repr. London: 1965)

Mémain, R. (1936) *Les équipages de la Marine de Guerre au XVIIe siècle. Matelots et soldats des vaisseaux du roi. Les levées d'hommes sur la côte du Centre-Ouest de la France au temps de Colbert et de Seignelay (1661–1690)* (Paris: 1936).

Meyer, J. (1979) 'Louis XIV et les puissances maritimes', *XVIIe siècle*, no. 123 (1979), 155–72.

——. (1981) 'Gens de mer en Mediterranée au XVIIe siècle: la France et l'Espagne, essai de comparaison' in *Le genti del mare Mediterraneo*, ed. R. Ragosta, 2 vols. (Naples: 1981), 2: 905–36.

——. (1989) 'Stratégies navales et terrestres: domaines complémentaires ou indépendants? Le cas de l'Ancien Régime', in *Mélanges André Corvisier. Le soldat, la stratégie, la mort*, ed. P. Chaunu (Paris: 1989).

Nanteuil, H. de (1974) 'Le duc de Vivonne et ses galères à l'expédition de Candie 1669', *Revue historique des armées*, no. 1 (1974), 7–31.

Nerzic, J.-Y. and C. Bouchet (2002) *Marins et flibustiers du Roi-Soleil. Carthagène 1697* (Aspet: 2002).

Nouzille, J. (1987) 'Une intervention extérieure au XVIIe siècle: l'expédition française de Candie (1669)', *Revue internationale d'histoire militaire*, no. 68 (1987), 114–56.

Ozanam, D. (1989) 'Jean Orry: munitionnaire du Roi, 1690–1698', *Histoire Economique et Financière de la France: Etudes et Documents*, 1 (1989), 61–97.

Palmer, M. (1997) 'The "Military Revolution" Afloat: the Era of the Anglo-Dutch Wars and the Transition to Modern Warfare at Sea', *War in History*, no. 4 (1997), 123–49.

Parrott, D. (2001) *Richelieu's Army. War, Government and Society in France, 1624–1642* (Cambridge: 2001).

Peter, J. (1994) *Vauban et Toulon. Histoire de la construction d'un port-arsenal sous Louis XIV* (Paris: 1994).

——. (1995) *Les artilleurs de la marine sous Louis XIV* (Paris: 1995).

Quincy, C. de Sévin, marquis de (1726) *Histoire militaire du règne de Louis le Grand*, 7 vols. (Paris: 1726).

Roncière, C. de La (1920), *Histoire de la marine française*, vol. 5 (Paris: 1920)

Rousset, C. (1862–64) *Histoire de Louvois et de son administration politique et militaire*, 4 vols. (Paris: 1862–64).

Rowlands, G. (2000) 'Louis XIV, Vittorio Amedeo II and French Military Failure in Italy, 1689–96', *English Historical Review*, no. 115 (2000), 534–69.

——. (2001) 'Louis XIV et la stratégie de cabinet: mythe et réalité', *Revue historique des armées*, no. 222 (2001), 25–34.

——. (2002) *The Dynastic State and the Army under Louis XIV. Royal Service and Private Interest, 1661–1701* (Cambridge: 2002).

Sautai, M. (1901) *Les Frézeau de La Frézelière* (Lille: 1901).

Simms, J. G. (2000) *Jacobite Ireland, 1685–91* (Dublin: 2000).

Symcox, G. (1967) 'Louis XIV and the War in Ireland, 1689–1691. A Study of His Strategic Thinking and Decision-Making', unpublished PhD thesis (UCLA: 1967).

——. (1974) *The Crisis of French Seapower 1688–1697. From the* Guerre d'escadre *to the* Guerre de course (The Hague: 1974).

Syrett, D. (1970) *The Siege and Capture of Havana, 1762* (London: 1970).

Taillemite, E. (1970) 'Les problèmes de la Marine de Guerre au XVIIe siècle', *XVIIe siècle*, 86–87 (1970), 21–37.

Terlinden, C. (1904) *Le Pape Clément IX et la guerre de Candie (1667–1669)* (Louvain/Paris: 1904).

Tracy, N. (1995) *Manila Ransomed. The British Assault on Manila in the Seven Years War* (Exeter: 1995).

Tunstall, B. (1990) *Naval Warfare in the Age of Sail. The Evolution of Fighting Tactics 1650–1815* (London: 1990).

THE BLUE-WATER DIMENSION OF KING WILLIAM'S WAR: AMPHIBIOUS OPERATIONS AND ALLIED STRATEGY DURING THE NINE YEARS' WAR, 1688–1697*

John M. Stapleton, Jr

Introduction

Amphibious operations are among the most important and least studied aspects of warfare in the latter seventeenth century. When Stadholder William III, Prince of Orange, entered London on 18 December 1688[1] at the head of an army landed by sea just one month before, he demonstrated amphibious operations' military potential.[2] The Stadholder-King's successful campaign[3] made possible a diplomatic revolution that dramatically influenced the histories of not only England and the Dutch Republic but of Europe as a whole. The success of the 'Dutch Armada' led allied officials, particularly in London, to be seduced by the promise of amphibious warfare.[4] Indeed, one English pamphleteer writing at the height of the Nine Years' War (1689–1697) maintained that all that was needed to bring the allies victory was to land an army on the French coast, march it through the country, and challenge the enemy to fight. Then, he concluded, 'if they have success, the French king must subscribe to any terms.'[5]

---

* I thank Jaap Bruijn, Mark Charles Fissel, Jamel Ostwald, and Geoffrey Parker for their comments on earlier drafts of this essay.

[1] All dates in this essay are in the New Style, unless noted OS (Old Style).

[2] On the Glorious Revolution, see esp. Israel, ed. (1991A); Israel (1991B); Parker & Israel (1991); and Haley (1992), 21–34. On William' expedition, see Carswell (1969) for the English perspective and van der Kuijl (1988) for the Dutch perspective.

[3] Although some might argue that it was not a true military campaign, Dutch participants in the operation such as Colonel Willem van Wassenaer-Duvenvoirde, referred to their march through England as a 'Campagne': ARA RAZH, Huisarchief der Familie van Wassenaer, 4: 'Journal van de Campagne van Engelandt 1688', unfoliated.

[4] Childs (1987), 215–17.

[5] PRO, SP 8/15, ff. 102: 'Reasons for a Descent into France'; also in *CSPDom.*, 4:452.

Most amphibious operations were neither so simple nor so decisive, however. While William's invasion might have appeared to be just a matter of putting troops ashore and challenging the English Army to fight, the ease with which James was toppled obscured the amount of preparation and care that William and the Dutch government had poured into the operation. Careful planning and luck were the secrets of its success, factors that at least a few contemporaries seem to have overlooked.[6] The Dutch Armada's success, however, contrasts sharply with amphibious operations conducted by the Maritime Powers—England[7] and the Dutch Republic—during the European Nine Years' War.[8] While both states had had considerable experience in amphibious warfare prior to 1688, as allies their operations were only marginally successful. Successful operations in Ireland during the war's first years were followed by a series of failures, from the abortive descent on the Normandy coast in 1692, to the bloody repulse of allied raiders at Brest in 1694, to the failed attempts on the privateering haven of Dunkirk. The only successful amphibious operations after Ireland were the bombardments of French coastal towns during the last four years of the war, and their military utility is open to debate. When considering the dominant position the allies enjoyed at sea, particularly following their victory at La Hogue in 1692, their lack of success in amphibious warfare is all the more striking.

In many ways, the Nine Years' War—sometimes called King William's War—was a watershed in the history of amphibious warfare. With William and Mary's accession to the throne, England and the United Provinces became allies in the war against Louis XIV,

---

[6] Although most evidence suggests that actual planning began only in the spring of 1688, the possibility of invading England was likely discussed seriously as early as 1686. See King (1914), 9; Carswell (1969), 79–80; Baxter (1966); and Israel (1991B), 114–15.

[7] In 1688, the English Crown commanded the military establishments of England, Scotland, and Ireland. Although the Act of Union which combined the kingdoms of England and Scotland was not enacted until 1707 (and 1801 for Ireland), for simplicity's sake, the term 'British Army' is used to refer to the three military establishments together, while reference to England, Ireland, or Scotland refers to the aforementioned establishments individually. Since there was only one naval establishment, it is referred to in this essay simply as the English or Royal Navy.

[8] For the characterization of this conflict as the *European* Nine Years' War, see above, p. 43.

and partners in the naval war. Although maritime interests were of vital importance to the allies, William determined that the main Anglo-Dutch war effort would be on the continent rather than at sea. The defeat of the French navy at La Hogue coupled with the growing cost of the land war, however, led Louis XIV to concede control of the Atlantic Ocean and the English Channel to the allies.[9] William looked for ways to utilize the Maritime Powers' superiority at sea in pursuit of his Continental Strategy. A combined Anglo-Dutch fleet was called upon to mount amphibious operations in support of a continental war. Its mixed results reflect not only a certain failure on the part of naval and military commanders to grasp the limitations of the tools at their disposal, but also highlight shortcomings common in seventeenth century operational planning as well. Only through trial and error would the allied commanders begin to grasp both the limitations and the potential of such operations. Amphibious failures demonstrated that such operations did not hold the key to victory as many English naval and military commanders had supposed. Nevertheless, allied amphibious operations show the emergence of a fledgling but bold maritime strategy. During the War of the Spanish Succession (1701–1714), Anglo-Dutch amphibious operations would be more successful, a clear indication of the Nine Years' War's impact on the evolution of amphibious warfare and Anglo-Dutch naval strategy.

Amphibious Warfare in the Latter Seventeenth Century

Amphibious warfare has always been difficult to define. What constitutes an amphibious operation and what differentiates it from either land or naval warfare? In the most basic terms, amphibious warfare is the projection of a state's *seapower* inland. Although land forces generally play an important role in amphibious warfare, such forces are always tied to the fleet and the sea. It is this dependence on the fleet that differentiates amphibious forces from land forces.[10] Thus, while amphibious warfare's conduct has evolved with time, its basic nature has not changed since the first soldiers landed from the sea

---

[9] See Symcox (1974), 1–11 *et passim*.
[10] See Harding (1991), 1–2.

on a hostile shore; and while it occupies a very specific place in the taxonomy of war, it is more closely tied to war at sea than war on land.

In their study of twentieth-century military affairs, Allan Millett and Williamson Murray identify four levels of military activity, levels as relevant in the latter seventeenth century as they are today: the political, strategic, operational, and tactical levels.[11] Millett and Murray define military affairs at the political level, or *policy*, as 'a government's position, statement, or plan of action designed to influence and determine future decisions and actions in the polity's interest.'[12] In wartime, policy encompasses the government's war aims. Those aims are influenced by the state's understanding of the war's causes, its conduct, conclusion, as well as its consequences. The 'strategic level' on the other hand, concerns the deployment of the state's military resources to achieve those ends. *Strategy*, in general terms, is the plan for the employment of military assets to achieve a particular war aim. At the strategic level, amphibious warfare is an element of *naval strategy* since amphibious forces were most often part of a naval force's capabilities.[13]

If strategy is the plan for the employment of forces toward a particular goal, *operations* are actions taken in pursuit of those objectives. *Amphibious operations* are operations mounted by naval and/or military forces against coastal targets, whether the capture of an enemy port, the destruction of enemy military or naval assets, or the establishment of a beachhead for future operations. As the name implies, amphibious operations pursued specific goals as part of a larger strategy. In the seventeenth century, just as today, such operations usually included soldiers or marines landing from the sea, though sometimes they might only entail the use of naval firepower to attack coastal targets.

Tactics are the methods used by military forces to achieve their operational objectives. Historians almost never refer to the actions taken by amphibious forces as 'amphibious tactics,' however. Yet, to refer to the *methods* of amphibious warfare as 'amphibious operations' technically is incorrect, since tactics refer to various ways of employing amphibious forces in pursuit of specific operational goals, while

---

[11] This taxonomy of war is based on the discussion in Watman (1989) 1–30. For a more recent description of this taxonomy, see Murray & Millett (2000), 583–9.

[12] Murray & Millett (2000), 583–9.

[13] Watman (1989), 3.

amphibious operations pertain to their larger strategic aims. Based on this definition, the methods that comprised such operations really should be referred to as *amphibious tactics*. In the latter seventeenth century, there were three: landings, raids, and bombardments.

A *landing* was the riskiest option available to commanders of amphibious forces. As the name implies, landings required transporting military forces from the sea to an enemy shore with the purpose of satisfying a particular objective, whether it was the capture of a key town or installation, the defeat of an enemy force, or the conquest of territory. It demanded the most resources—both military and naval—for its success, and could yield the attacker the greatest gains if successful, or the greatest losses if it failed. Landings are the most 'amphibious' of amphibious tactics but were also the most difficult to execute. They required careful planning to insure success, an element that was often lacking in allied operations during the Nine Years' War. For these reasons, they were less common than other tactical forms during this period. The most notable landings during the latter 17th century were William's invasion of England in 1688, Schomberg's expedition to Ireland in 1689, and the Duke of Marlborough's landing in Munster in 1690.

Like landings, *raids* required landing soldiers or marines with the goal of hitting coastal targets. The principal difference between landings and raids were the latter's more limited duration and scope. A precursor to the modern-day commando raid, raids in the early modern period were also intended to strike quickly at a hard to hit target of some strategic importance. The forces involved were generally smaller than those desired for seaborne landings, usually a few battalions, but sometimes a force of several thousand might be involved. In the latter seventeenth century, raids usually targeted objectives of *maritime* importance that could not be neutralized by using conventional naval forces. Like landings, raids too were risky, but if properly executed could yield fantastic results far outweighing the forces committed to them. The Dutch raid on Chatham and Sheerness, the English naval bases on the Medway, during the Second Anglo-Dutch War is the best—and most famous—example of a successful raid during this period. It is also notable for the first large-scale employment of marines.[14] Nevertheless, raids were risky and the

---

[14] In a well-coordinated operation, Dutch naval forces sailed up the Medway and

dangers involved coupled with the specialized nature of such operations limited their utility. During the Nine Years' War, the allies conducted only one raid—on the French anchorage at Brest in 1694—which ended in catastrophe for the assault force.

The *bombardment* of enemy coastal targets by shipboard artillery was the last type of tactic employed by amphibious forces. In some ways the early modern equivalent of an aerial bombing raid, bombardments tended to be more punitive than strategic. During the Nine Years' War, bombardments were conducted against French harbours, especially those that housed corsair fleets. The employment of the bomb-ketch made seaborne attacks more devastating than ever before. Armed with one or two heavy mortars capable of lofting their bombs hundreds of meters, the bomb ketch was the first specialized assault vessel. Developed by the French as the *galiote à bombes*, the bomb ketch was first employed against the Barbary corsairs in 1682.[15] Their most successful employment prior to the Nine Years' War, however, was the bombardment of Genoa in 1684 when French bomb vessels rained some 13,300 bombs on the city, destroying more than two-thirds of it [figure 19].[16] Ironically, France suffered the most from its own invention. During the Nine Years' War, the allies conducted no less than nine bombardments against French coastal towns, mostly on the Channel coast. Although bombardments included a relatively small number of what one would consider 'land forces' in their conduct, they were by far the most common amphibious tactic employed by the allies during the Nine Years' War.

Of the tactics open to commanders of amphibious forces, bombardments evolved the most during the course of the war. Bomb-ketches, by their very nature, were difficult to employ. Mortars required a stable platform to be fired accurately, something difficult to find in a ship rocked by the motion of the waves. To improve the accuracy of their salvoes, bomb vessels were anchored in place. Yet even while anchored, heavy wave action would render their fire

---

Thames Rivers to attack ships while parties of marines silenced shore batteries and captured key facilities. When it was over, they had destroyed six capital ships and nine lesser vessels, while the 80-gun *Royal Charles* was taken. See Rogers (1970); Dorren (1948), 11–15; Hainsworth & Churches (1998), 157–67; Jones (1996), 175–8.

[15] On the dimensions and armament of these first bomb vessels see Ware (1994), 9–10; Rowlands, ch. 9, above, pp. 287–8, 295; and figures 20 and 27.

[16] Lynn (1999), 173–4; Rowlands, ch. 9, above, pp. 270, 287, 295.

inaccurate. Consequently, bombardments required almost perfect weather conditions for the vessels to hit their targets. The ships' modest size coupled with their voracious consumption of ammunition, furthermore, required that ammunition tenders accompany them at all times. Not surprisingly, the bomb ships and their support vessels made attractive targets for shore batteries. In order to offset this, bombardment vessels were always accompanied by warships whose job it was to suppress the fire of the shore batteries. Unlike contemporary drawings of such operations like the bombardment of Dieppe for example [figure 25], warships often interposed themselves between the bomb-vessels and the shore batteries, the bomb-ships lofting their shells over their protectors. Given the number and type of vessels involved, bombardments were very tricky operations.[17] Under good conditions, a flotilla of bomb ketches could inflict serious damage to coastal targets, as the allies demonstrated in 1694 when the combined fleet destroyed much of Dieppe. Under poor conditions, however, bombardments were inaccurate and ineffective.[18] Nevertheless, the bomb ketch was arguably the first purpose built weapon specifically intended for use in amphibious operations, and thus was an important step in creating true amphibious capability in early modern navies.

At the same time, both the Dutch and English navies had begun experimenting with specialist amphibious troops. Marines date their inception to the 1660s, the English and Dutch raising their first regiments of marines in 1664 and 1665 respectively. Up to that time, European navies had relied upon regular infantry formations in lieu of specialized amphibious forces. The poor showing of these *ad hoc* marine formations during the First Anglo-Dutch War, however, prompted the Dutch Council of State to propose raising regiment of true marines as early as 1657.[19] It took the eruption of the Second Anglo-Dutch War in 1665, however, to breathe new life into that proposal. In December 1665, Willem Jozef Baron von Gent, garrison commander of Hellevoetsluis, raised the first regiment of marines in Dutch service. The four-thousand-man regiment was organized in companies of 120 men, each commanded by a captain. England's

---

[17] Ware (1994), 87–93.
[18] Ibid.
[19] See Ten Raa & de Bas (1921), 144–6; and Dorren (1948), 1–3.

first regiment of marines had been raised a little over a year earlier.[20] Because the marines were expected to serve as musketeers both
on land and at sea, both Dutch and English marines were equipped
with the new flintlock musket instead of the older matchlock, a much
more reliable weapon given the damp conditions aboard ship. At
sea, marines were expected to take part in the ship's daily work routine when not tasked with specific 'amphibious' duties.[21]

In spite of their value in times of war, marine regiments were
usually among the first units disbanded in peacetime. During the
Second Anglo-Dutch War, marines demonstrated their value when
they took part in some of the most successful amphibious operations
of the latter seventeenth century. Although the English conducted
successful amphibious operations, most notably the devastating raid
on Dutch shipping at Vlieland and Terschelling, it was the crucial
role of marines in the successful Dutch raid on the Royal Navy facilities on the Medway that truly illustrated what might be accomplished by well-trained specialist troops.[22] During the war with France
(1672–78), Dutch marines continued to demonstrate their ability as
specialist troops both at sea and on land. Nevertheless, upon the
conclusion of hostilities the Dutch Republic disbanded its marines
and did not raise new regiments until after the conclusion of the
Nine Years' War.[23] England, on the other hand, retained its marines
only to see them disbanded in the wake of the Glorious Revolution.
Thus, when the Nine Years' War erupted in 1689, neither the Dutch
Republic nor England had any marine regiments on their military
establishments.

Amphibious operations continued to be quite rudimentary. Because
they fell between the cracks, or rather, between the services, the
intricacies of amphibious combat escaped the grasp of most officers,
naval and military alike. There were no manuals to guide them on
the use of marines, and the few proponents who did advocate rais-

---

[20] Dalton (1960), 142: and Brooks (2002), 10–11.

[21] Ten Raa & de Bas (1921), 146–7, 472; and Dorren (1948), 3–7.

[22] Although in terms of ships taken or destroyed the Chatham raid paled in comparison to the English raids on Vlieland and Terschelling, in terms of effect Chatham
was decisive and helped the Dutch negotiate a favorable end to the war. See the
works cited in fn. 14 above.

[23] Ten Raa (1950), 291–2.

ing these specialist troops could not agree on what their duties should be. Should marines be infantrymen or sailors? Which branch did they serve? Indeed, more than forty years after the conclusion of the Nine Years' War, there was still no clear definition of the term 'marine.'[24] It was only on the eve of the War of Austrian Succession that British officials began to formulate a concept of what marines ought to be. During the 1739 debates surrounding the formation of marine regiments (yet again!), Parliament concluded that marines ought to understand the duties of both soldiers and sailors. They decided that '[t]he marines service should be *amphibious*; they must know how to behave by sea as well as land.'[25] With the Royal Navy only coming to grips with marines' duties in the late 1730s, it is not surprising that the Maritime Powers' degree of amphibious expertise in the last decade of the seventeenth century was still primitive.

Amphibious Operations and the War in Ireland, 1689–91

In January 1689, the Maritime Powers lacked a coherent naval strategy. Rather than finding England's armed forces prepared for war, William found them in disarray as a result of the Glorious Revolution. With the Dutch Republic already at war, William moved quickly to coordinate the actions of the Dutch and English militaries. While he tried to prepare the shattered English Army for war on the continent, he also took steps to establish cooperation between the Dutch and English navies. On 20 December 1688, only days after arriving in London, William sent for representatives from the Dutch Republic to negotiate the conditions of Anglo-Dutch maritime cooperation. One month later, those deputies met with their English counterparts and began the process of hammering out a program of naval cooperation, negotiations begun a month before he and Mary were crowned King and Queen of England.[26]

---

[24] The first English 'marine' regiments were, in fact, not officially termed marines until 1690 when they were raised again following the Glorious Revolution; prior to 1690, marine regiments in English service were officially referred to as 'Maritime' or 'Admiral's' regiments: Marini (1983), 39–45.

[25] Ibid. (italics mine).

[26] See Clark (1923), 8–43, esp. 15–40; Hattendorf (2002), 181–3; Warnsinck (1934), 9–24; and Ehrman (1953), 250–3.

The chief product of the negotiations was the Treaty on Combined Fleets. Concluded on 29 April 1689, the agreement in part established the parameters of William's naval strategy and set the tone for the Anglo-Dutch maritime relationship for the next fourteen years. Using the existing Westminster Treaty as a starting point, the new agreement revised the proportion of ships to be contributed by the English and Dutch from 3:2 to 5:3.[27] The initial Dutch proposal asked for a quota of fifty English warships to be joined by thirty Dutch men-of-war. The Combined Fleet in turn was divided into two squadrons: a Channel and Irish Sea squadron comprising fifty ships, and a Mediterranean squadron of thirty. An additional force of ten frigates would protect commerce between England and the United Provinces. The new treaty's provisions would enable the allies to meet the French fleet on equal terms.[28]

The allied command structure set the tone for the Anglo-Dutch maritime relationship. In the original Dutch proposal, command of the Combined Fleet would go to the captain of the force first attacked by the enemy. The English refused this proposal and instead demanded command of the allied fleet at all times. Despite the Dutch delegates' alarm at the possibility that an English junior officer, through unforeseen circumstances, might find himself in command of a larger Dutch force commanded by a flag-officer, they eventually conceded: according to the final agreement, the highest-ranking officer of the English forces present would exercise control of the Combined Fleet, regardless of the number of Dutch ships present and the senior Dutch commander's rank.[29] Ultimately, English admirals would formulate allied maritime strategy, with William's approval. On land the opposite was true: William and his allied generals would direct the war in the Spanish Netherlands. The military relationship that would see Britain and the Dutch Republic through the War of the Spanish Succession had been established.

The Treaty on Combined Fleets also suggested the role William had envisioned for coalition naval power. As a Dutchman and a soldier, William viewed seapower both as a military and as a diplo-

---

[27] Hattendorf (2002), 178–86.
[28] Ehrman (1953), 251; De Jonge (1839), pt. 1, 163–8; and Bruijn (1989), 118–21.
[29] Ehrman (1949), 252–3; Clark (1923), 39–40; and Bruijn (1998), 122–3.

matic instrument. For him, the crucial theatre of war would be the Spanish Netherlands, a natural buffer between France and the Dutch Republic. It was here where he intended to deploy the weight of British and Dutch military resources, and it was here where he believed the war would be won or lost. For the fleet to have an impact on the war in the Spanish Netherlands, however, it had to effect a diversion of French resources away from that theatre. William saw the dispatch of a sizable squadron to the Mediterranean Sea as just such a diversion. Not only would it buttress Spain, Savoy, and Habsburg Austria in the Mediterranean but might make these peripheral theatres real threats to France, and thus directly affect the deployment of French military resources.[30] William's view of the fleet's role as an instrument of a continental strategy was in sharp contrast to the way most Englishmen viewed naval strategy. Historically the Royal Navy, not the army, was England's first line of defence and the central instrument in its military arsenal. England's traditional role was maritime and many Englishmen opposed a large-scale continental commitment as contrary to the nation's natural interests. England, many believed, could better employ its armed forces against French commerce, its colonies, and on the periphery through amphibious attacks on the French coast rather than in a costly continental war.[31] This difference between William's view of the escalating war with France and that of his critics would be decided, in large part, by the Maritime Powers' ability to use their amphibious resources to good effect.

James II's landing in Ireland in March 1689 postponed this debate, however. With his eyes on the Low Countries, William had hoped to settle the rebellion in Ireland peacefully, however his negotiations with James' Lord Lieutenant of Ireland ended in failure.[32] With the French king now actively supporting James II, the war in Ireland became a threat to the revolution settlement in Britain, and thus suddenly became William's top priority. Almost immediately, he dispatched several regiments to bolster the few Protestant strongholds

---

[30] For the origin of William's Mediterranean strategy, see especially Ehrman (1949) 269–92; Ehrman (1953), 495–9.

[31] For good examinations of the contemporary debate on what constituted England's 'proper' strategy see especially Childs (1987), 210–11; and Rose (1999), 117–18, 124–30.

[32] Baxter (1966), 253.

in the north until an expedition could be assembled. The only solace he could find in the eruption of hostilities was that it helped spur Parliament to declare war on France and bring England into the allied coalition.[33]

Amphibious operations would be crucial to Ireland's recapture. With little of the logistical infrastructure and resources—population, roads and canals—found in northwest Europe, Ireland could not adequately support continental-style armies. Consequently, allied armies were forced to bring most of what they needed with them, particularly food, dry fodder, and ammunition. The fact that Ireland lacked an adequate road network meant that the army's train, by necessity, remained small. Likewise, the absence of an established, friendly supply network meant that virtually everything the army consumed had to be shipped in by sea until magazines were established. Under these circumstances, it is not surprising that amphibious operations played such a pivotal role in the war in Ireland.

Schomberg's Ulster Expedition

Control of the seas, particularly the Irish Sea between England and Ireland, was crucial for any invasion of Ireland. Allied weakness at sea had allowed not only James II not only to return to Ireland, but French reinforcements to reach him there. In late April, Admiral Château-Renault succeeded in disembarking 1,500 French troops along with much needed money, arms, and equipment at Bantry Bay in spite of the English fleet's intervention.[34] Although William's supporters continued to resist James' forces in Londonderry and Enniskillen, it was August before an expeditionary force was ready to sail. Commanding the force was the Duke of Schomberg.[35] Although an excellent officer earlier in his career, the septuagenarian Schomberg was a less vigorous commander in 1689. He was also beset with problems beyond his control. Indeed, when he was given command of the expedition in July, preparations should have been long underway. When he arrived in Chester, however, he found them far from complete and, in spite of his best efforts, was plagued by delays.[36]

---

[33] Horwitz (1977), 27; and Rose (1999), 106.
[34] Ehrman (1953), 260–66; Simms (1969), 66–9.
[35] Hora-Siccama (1915), 626–7.
[36] Dalton (1960), 3: 1–9; Simms (1986A), 91–104 and (1969), 62, 121–2.

By the time his forces embarked for Ireland in late August, only two-thirds of his force was prepared to sail. Approximately 15,000 men had been assembled, but the remaining 8,000 troops were still forming and would not be ready until September.[37]

Schomberg's original campaign plan was straightforward. Escorted by the Irish squadron, his force would sail from Hoylake to Belfast Lough in Ulster. After landing he would march to Derry, lift the siege, and establish a foothold for future operations. If he was fortunate, the main Jacobite army might be brought to battle and defeated before the end of the campaign season. But when the Jacobites lifted the siege on 10 August, the expedition's objectives suddenly changed. With Derry now secure and Schomberg's force still assembling, the defeat of the Jacobite army became the operation's goal. Logistical difficulties hampered his plans and caused still further delay. A lack of sufficient transport ships meant that only half of the force could be shipped to Ireland in one go, forcing Schomberg to divide his force into two waves. The first, comprising twelve regiments of infantry and much of his artillery, would establish the beachhead in Bangor Bay. The second wave, which comprised his remaining infantry, all of his cavalry, and much of his transport, would join him there as soon as it was complete. Only then would he begin his march on Dublin.

The logistical difficulties that hampered the expedition from the start were at least in part the fault of Schomberg's commissary-general, John Shales. Shales had served under James II, though he had never been on campaign. At the time, he was regarded as the best qualified to make the expedition's logistical preparations.[38] Schomberg's incessant complaints demonstrate his frustration with the inadequacy of the operation's planning, and suggest that Shales was out of his depth.[39] The inexperience of Schomberg's troops compounded the difficulties. Hendrik Trajectinus, Count von Solms-Braunfels—one of William's most trusted and experienced Dutch generals—assisted him as second-in-command, but neither he nor Schomberg had much

---

[37] Simms (1969), 121 and (1986A), 91–104; Childs (1996), 193–195.

[38] Under Shales' care English troops had suffered from similar logistical difficulties at Hounslow Heath in 1688: Childs (1980), 98.

[39] For Schomberg's logistical difficulties, see especially Walton (1894), 69–77; and Simms (1986A), 92–6.

faith in the expedition's English officers.[40] The army's inexperience on so many levels was a recipe for disaster.

Nevertheless, the expedition began well enough. On 23 August 1689, Schomberg's first contingent of infantry, approximately 9,000 men, landed in Bangor Bay—observed, but unopposed.[41] After consolidating the beachhead, he captured Belfast without loss on 27 August. Next he turned his attention to Carrickfergus. Determined to hold out as long as possible, the castle's small but tenacious garrison held up Schomberg for a week, but in the end the weight of Schomberg's artillery proved more than a match for the castle's ancient defences. With the walls breached in several places, the garrison surrendered, eliminating Jacobite resistance near the beachhead.[42]

Establishing a foothold proved easier than keeping his army supplied, however. When the force sailed for Ireland, the bulk of its supplies had not yet been assembled. This did not prove an immediate problem since the fleet carried some provisions with it. But when the balance of the force arrived in early September, the army's logistical difficulties grew in proportion to the number of men ashore. On 12 September, Schomberg advanced from Carrickfergus south to Dundalk both to threaten the Jacobite army moving up to oppose him and to help ease his increasingly tenuous supply situation. Schomberg hoped to sustain his army by foraging until he reached the Dundalk campsite, where he expected to be re-supplied by the fleet, but the Jacobites dashed any hope of that when they put Newry, a town midway between Carrickfergus and Dundalk, to the torch.[43] When Schomberg finally arrived at the Dundalk campsite on 17 September 1689, he found neither provisions nor transport awaiting him as promised. He now had close to 20,000 men ashore but almost no supplies to sustain them.[44] Schomberg's offensive ground to a halt. James II's army had advanced north to Ardee, a short march from Schomberg's position at Dundalk. Recognizing the position's

---

[40] Most regiments seem to have suffered from either bad colonels or junior officers, and sometimes both: Dalton (1960), 3:105–23. For Solms' military career, see Hora-Siccama (1915), 653.

[41] See Simms (1969), 122.

[42] *CSPDom, 1689–90*, 231; Simms (1986A), 92–3; and Doherty (1998), 88–90.

[43] *CSPDom. 1689–90*, 251–2; and Simms (1986A), 93–4.

[44] Simms (1986A), 94–5; and Walton (1894), 77–8.

strength, James was content to wait for the Huguenot general to make the next move.

Schomberg was in no position to attack, however. The Dundalk camp might have been defensively formidable, but it was an unfortunate campsite. Anchored on the left by the sea and covered in front by a stream, the campsite was low-lying and damp. Rainy weather only added to the misery. Lacking not only food, but also adequate clothing and shoes, the troops grew weak from dysentery and other illnesses. The raw English levies were particularly vulnerable. Unused to campaigning, they did not know to build huts or dig latrines. While the veteran Dutch and Huguenot battalions lost few men to illness, the inexperienced English formations were decimated.[45] The situation continued to deteriorate. Although Shales had managed to establish a magazine in Belfast, most of the train's wagons and horses had still not arrived and without adequate transport the provisions could not reach the troops. Between 17 September and 15 November, close to 7,000 of Schomberg's troops died in the Dundalk Camp: between a third and a half of his entire force depending upon the source consulted. In the end, the fallen soldiers were as much victims of poor planning and logistics as of inexperience and inclement weather.[46]

As an operation, Schomberg's expedition was a failure. Its goal had been to defeat James' forces in one campaign season. Instead, inadequate planning and poor logistics led to the loss of the army entrusted with that task. Now, not only would the war in Ireland continue into 1690, but the army's decimated regiments would have to be filled by new drafts, as well. Even more importantly, an effective commissariat would have to be established to replace the one headed by the incompetent Shales. To restore the army's logistic administration, William turned to the Dutch Army's veteran purveyors. Meanwhile, he augmented Schomberg's inexperienced English troops with seasoned foreign regiments. By the time William arrived to take command in June 1690, the army in Ireland bore a closer resemblance to the allied army in the Low Countries than to the English one that set sail for Ireland the previous August.[47]

---

[45] Doherty (1998), 90–92; Simms (1986A), 95–104; and Walton (1894), 69–77.
[46] Doherty (1998), 90–92; Simms (1986A), 94–101; and Walton (1894), 77.
[47] Childs (1991), 51–4; and Simms (1969), 136–7.

Although a failure, Schomberg's expedition did establish a solid foothold for the reconquest of Ireland. The 1690 campaign, culminating in William's victory at the Boyne, proved to be the turning point. With the establishment of a large allied army in Ireland and control of the Irish Sea assured, defeat of the Jacobites was only a matter of time. Events elsewhere, however, were to have an important influence on the remainder of the 1690 campaign. While William's forces were engaged at the Boyne, the Anglo-Dutch fleet was defeated by the French at Beachy Head, giving the Louis XIV temporary control of the Channel and threatening the King's communications with England. With the remnants of James' army at Limerick, William was suddenly faced with the dilemma of either besieging Limerick that season and risk being cut off from England by French seapower, or of leaving the subjection of Ireland to his subordinates and returning to England at once with the knowledge that the war would continue into 1691. Although William chose the former, the Jacobites would not be defeated on his timetable. Patrick Sarsfield's ambush of the allied siege train deprived William's forces of precious siege guns and powder, and made an effective siege of Limerick impossible.[48] In spite of determined, bloody attacks, William's forces were unable to capture the town and were forced to withdraw. The war in Ireland was destined to continue into 1691.

Marlborough's Munster Expedition

The 1690 campaign season would not end in failure for the allies, however. During the summer of 1690, at the height of the invasion scare, Sir John Churchill, 1st Earl of Marlborough—the commander in England in William's absence—proposed leading an amphibious expedition to capture the towns of Cork and Kinsale in Munster. Marlborough's plan was a bold one. With 5,000 men from his army in England, he would land near Cork, link up with a detachment of roughly the same size from the main allied army, and besiege Cork and Kinsale supported by the fleet. Not only would their capture eliminate Jacobite resistance in southern Ireland, but it would deprive them of their most important seaborne link with France as

---

[48] See Simms (1969), 166–8.

well.[49] When he proposed the audacious plan to the Queen's council in August 1690, he met strong opposition from virtually everybody save the Earl of Nottingham and Admiral Russell, both of whom supported the plan.[50] When the Queen referred it to William, the King immediately recognized its potential, writing to Marlborough:

> I strongly approve of your plan to embark with 4,000 infantry and the marines, which together make 4,900 men, and is a sufficient force to capture Cork and Kinsale. You will have to take enough munitions with you, and use the ship's guns, for we can send you none from here. But for cavalry I will send enough, and will take good care that the (enemy) army shall not be a burden upon you. It is only time which must be saved, and you must hasten as quickly as you can....[51]

To ensure that the main Jacobite army did not interfere with the expedition, William ordered his second-in-command in Ireland, General Goddard van Reede-Ginkel, to keep the Jacobite army away from Cork and Kinsale. He emphasized that if the enemy approached, he was to be attacked if the ground would allow it.[52]

The force Ginkel detached to assist Marlborough was under the Duke of Württemberg.[53] Also a lieutenant general, Württemberg had 3,500 allied infantry and 1,500 horse under his command, roughly the same number of men as Marlborough. Given their rank and the comparable sizes of their commands, Württemberg's participation could have posed real command problems for the operation, particularly since he had seniority over Marlborough. Fortunately, the two men were able to work together with little friction.[54]

---

[49] Kinsale was the westernmost port in the British Isles and one of the few strategically placed to intercept French ships sailing to the English Channel from Brest. For its strategic importance see Ehrman (1953), 370, 413–15.

[50] Daniel Finch, 2nd Earl of Nottingham, was Secretary of State for the northern department from 1689 to 1692 and briefly for the southern department in 1693–94. A Tory, Nottingham was well-liked by William and very influential in naval affairs for the first half of the war. Edward Russell, 1st Earl of Orford, was the most important figure in the war at sea. During much of William's reign, he served as both Commander-in-Chief of the fleet and senior Lord of the Admiralty. For details, see Ehrman (1953), 270–4, 306–8.

[51] Quoted in Chandler (1984), 36. Ehrman (1953), 369n. notes that Nottingham took credit for giving Marlborough the idea.

[52] *CSPDom. 1690–91*, 111–12; and *Europische Mercurius* (1690), 3:184–5.

[53] Ferdinand Wilhelm, Duke of Württemberg-Neustadt, commanded the Danish corps in English pay: see Danaher & Simms (1962), 141–2; and Ringoir (1981), 2.

[54] Chandler (1995), 39–40.

After a delay of more than two weeks due to adverse winds, the expeditionary force, escorted by the main Anglo-Dutch fleet, set sail on 27 September from Portsmouth and arrived off the entrance to Cork harbour on 1 October. After a minor skirmish with a Jacobite battery covering the harbour mouth, the fleet proceeded to Passage West, seven miles from Cork, and began disembarking men and supplies. On 4 October, facing little resistance, Marlborough was able to establish outposts on the edge of town and position some of his heavy guns in preparation for the siege. The next day, Württemberg's cavalry effected a link-up with Marlborough's troops. The first phase of the operation had been completed without incident.

Jacobite dispositions in Munster assisted the allies' efforts. Cork and Kinsale posed two very different defensive problems for Jacobite commanders [figures 21–23]. Cork's commander, Colonel Roger MacElligott led a fairly-strong garrison of 4,500 men, but Cork's medieval stone walls and the dominant surrounding hills made it difficult to defend. Its one modern defensive work, the sixteenth-century Elizabeth Fort on the town's south side, was dominated by the same surrounding heights that rendered the rest of the city vulnerable.[55] Without command of the heights, Cork was indefensible. Kinsale's defences, on the other hand, comprised two relatively modern forts, but with a smaller garrison of about 2,000 men under Sir Edward Scott. Commanding the city and harbour was the James's Fort, situated east of town on an island-like peninsula that covers the harbour's entrance; and the Charles Fort, built on the opposite side of the harbour mouth. Kinsale was stronger than Cork but required a larger garrison for its effective defence. Unfortunately for the Jacobites, MacElligott determined to make his stand at Cork.[56]

The sieges of Cork and Kinsale were relatively brief by the standards of the day. When Marlborough's troops arrived before Cork's walls on 4 October, his pickets managed to drive off the defenders in the incomplete works on the southern heights. With the heights to south of the city in allied hands, the city walls were immediately

---

[55] During the siege, musketeers positioned in the Red Abbey's steeple were able to target defenders of the Elizabeth Fort. One eyewitness noted that these musketeers 'did good service in galling the Irish': see Chandler (1984), 38–9; Simms (1969), 177–80 and (1986B), 120–22.

[56] Doherty (1998), 143–4.

vulnerable to allied artillery fire. By 6 October, batteries on both sides of the town were smashing breaches in the town's walls. After a day of bombardment, MacElligott opened negotiations. Realising his position was desperate, he hoped to gain favourable terms, but Marlborough was unwilling to grant them and MacElligott continued his hopeless defence. The next morning the allies resumed their bombardment, expanding the breach in the eastern wall of the town. Early that afternoon they launched a general assault on the breach, the English from the south side of the river and Württemberg's Danish and Dutch troops from the north. They were supported by fire from the bomb ketch *Salamander* and other vessels that had sailed up river at high tide, as well as the batteries established on the heights. The storming parties had to wade across the river in water up to their armpits, but the ferocity of the attack induced MacElligott to capitulate. That evening the garrison of the Elizabeth Fort also surrendered.[57]

Even before the last shots were fired at Cork, elements of the allied army had set off for Kinsale to begin operations there. Arriving on 10 October, the commanders of the allied advanced party hoped to capture the town without a fight, but Scott refused their summons to surrender. After attempting to fire the town to deny it to the allies, Scott withdrew his men into Charles Fort where he posted the bulk of his garrison, leaving 450 men in James Fort.[58] Realizing that they would have to wait for their siege train before they could attack Charles Fort, Marlborough and Württemberg tried a surprise attack on James Fort, since it was the weaker of the two and deserters informed them it contained a much smaller garrison. Just after dark on the same day, a party of grenadiers in assault boats crossed the Bandon River and managed to surprise the garrison. In the fierce fighting that followed, half of the defenders and their commander were killed, and the old fort fell.[59]

Now the allies focused their attentions on the Charles Fort. Unfortunately for them, bad weather complicated siege preparations. Unable to ship the artillery to Kinsale, the allies had to drag their

---

[57] *Europische Mercurius* (1690), 4: 16–18; *CSPDom. 1690–91*, 131–2; Chandler (1984), 37–41; and Simms (1986B), 123–126.

[58] Chandler (1984), 41–2; Danaher & Simms (1962), 86.

[59] Danaher & Simms (1962), 86–9; Simms (1969), 182–3.

heavy guns overland using teams improvised from cavalry mounts. The delay cost them ten days. Not until 22 October was the first battery ready; the rest of the artillery was only in position two days later. Once the batteries opened fire, it took only two days for them to breach in the walls and Scott promptly parleyed for terms. On 27 October 1690, only eighteen days after the allies had first arrived before the town, it was in their hands.[60]

Although the capture of Cork and Kinsale marked the end of the 1690 campaign in Ireland, the Irish war would continue for another year. Their capture, however, reinforced French opinion that their position in Ireland could no longer be sustained. In fact, Louis had already decided to abandon Ireland well before Marlborough embarked upon his Munster expedition. His decision to do so drew criticism both at home and in Ireland, especially in the wake of the French victory over the Anglo-Dutch fleet at Beachy Head and the Jacobites' successful defence of Limerick. However, like William, Louis did not want to divert energy and resources to what he felt was a sideshow. Ireland and the Irish would continue to serve his purposes well enough by drawing off Anglo-Dutch men and resources from the Low Countries. Allied naval resources, necessary for sustaining the Irish campaign, continued to shuttle supplies and equipment to Ireland, but William would send no more land forces there. By the time Ginkel captured Limerick in the fall of 1691 to end the war in Ireland, the focal point of allied naval operations, and the amphibious operations that accompanied them, had shifted to the seas surrounding France.

A Strategy of Descents? Amphibious Operations, Politics, and Strategy, 1691–1694

The end of the war in Ireland was an important turning point both in terms of England's war effort and for Anglo-Dutch amphibious operations. Its conclusion fuelled discussion over England's military role within the Grand Alliance and the direction of its military commitment. When William—with the backing of the States-General—

---

[60] *Europische Mercurius* (1690), 4:18–21; Simms (1969), 182–4; and Chandler (1984), 41–2.

intervened in English affairs in 1688, however, it was with the implicit understanding that English troops would be sent to the continent in support of the Republic.[61] Initially, England's commitment to the alliance remained small. In 1689 William ordered 10,000 men to the Low Countries but by 1690, that force had withered to fewer than 5,000. In 1691 with more than 35,000 British troops still in Ireland, only 12,000 (or 17 per cent of the army's total strength) were serving their king in the Low Countries.[62] In contrast, the Republic had committed over 60,000 troops (more than 85 per cent of its total strength) to the Spanish Netherlands.[63]

French victories in the Low Countries underscored the need for more troops in the theatre. After the allied victory at Walcourt in 1689, coalition forces suffered defeat after defeat at the hands of the French. In 1690, with William in Ireland, the allies were decisively defeated at Fleurus, opening much of the Spanish Netherlands to French raids. The next year William took command of the army, but could not prevent the loss of Mons, a key fortress. After three campaign seasons, it was clear to William and his generals that more men were needed to offset French strength in the Low Countries. Additionally, the growing inability of the Spanish government in Brussels to defend its territories threatened the Dutch Republic's own security and made it evident that the States-General would have to shoulder an even greater share of the allied war effort there.[64] William thus eagerly anticipated the release of English troops from Ireland to buttress his hard-pressed Dutch forces in the Low Countries.[65]

Likewise, the naval war was equally gloomy for the allies. The French victory at Beachy Head in 1690 highlighted allied maritime weaknesses and England's vulnerability to attack from the sea. The

---

[61] Israel (1991B), 120; Haley (1992), 30–1.

[62] See PRO, SP 8/5, f. 12, SP 8/8, f. 121; BL, Add. MS 15897, ff. 89–90; Luttrell (1692–93), 28–9.

[63] ARA, StG 8107: 'Ordinaries Staten van Oorlog, 1691'; StG 8108: 'Extraordinaris Staten van Oorlog, 1691'; Müller (1873), 2:227–30.

[64] See de Schrijver (1965), 80–98.

[65] William increased the scale of the British Army's commitment to the coalition from just over 17% of its forces in 1691 to close to 60% of them in 1692: see Heinsius (1874), 2:46–7: William III to Heinsius, 17/27 Nov. 1691; PRO SP 8/13, ff. 12f.: 'The Disposition of all their Majesty's Land Forces' and 'List of Their Majesties' British Forces in Flanders in 1692'.

Combined Fleet's inability to beat the French to sea placed it at a strategic disadvantage. Although administrative inefficiency both in England and the Dutch Republic was part of the problem, geography played a crucial role as well. The English navy's most recent wartime experience had been fighting the Dutch in the narrow seas. Its most important naval yards were well suited to that purpose, being close to the principal Dutch bases and well positioned to take advantage of weather conditions in the Channel. They were poorly situated for a war with France.

France's most important naval base in a war with England was Brest, at the tip of the Breton peninsula. Further west than any of England's bases, it enjoyed the advantage of the Atlantic's prevailing westerly winds. Its capacious harbour, known to the English as the Brest Water, was well protected both from the weather and enemy attacks. Although an easterly breeze was required for the fleet to leave the Brest Water, once on the open sea westerly winds could swiftly carry it to the Channel mouth. Allied ships sailing from bases in the Thames estuary (and from Rotterdam in the case of the Dutch), on the other hand, usually had to fight contrary winds all the way to the Atlantic. Consequently, it cost the allies more sailing time than it did the French to reach the same piece of ocean.[66] When combined with the problem of coordinating the allied fleets, Admiral Russell and his subordinates found it virtually impossible to intercept the fleet before it put to sea or worse still, before the Toulon fleet joined it. In spite of the admiralty's efforts at improving more westward bases at Portsmouth and Plymouth, the strategic advantage enjoyed by the French forced William and his admirals to look for ways to frustrate the Brest fleet, just as the same strategic considerations had driven the English government to help the French king (then its ally) to recapture Brest from Spain in the 1590s.[67]

William recognized Brest's strategic importance. In 1674, the Dutch Navy had landed troops on Belle Île in an effort to neutralize the Brest fleet, an operation that ultimately ended in failure.[68] When ships sailing from Brest managed to deliver supplies to the besieged Jacobite garrison at Limerick, William's determination to destroy that

---

[66] Wernham (1961), 341–2; Ryan (1968), 50–2.
[67] Ehrman (1953), 416–29; Wernham, ch. 7, above, p. 197.
[68] Lynn (1999), 123–4.

dangerous base was renewed. In April 1691, he ordered Russell to sail for Brest and attack the fleet there if practicable. But when Russell arrived at the end of June the French fleet had already sailed, so the attack was postponed. Russell and many of his officers felt an attack on Brest extremely hazardous in any case. Not only was the port well defended, but the entrance to the harbour was difficult to navigate as well. The bay leading to the Brest Water, the Iroise Channel, was only 20 miles across, dangerously narrow for the lee-wardly sailing warships of the day.[69] Unable to attack the anchor-age with seapower alone, William and his naval commanders began to explore the possibility of an amphibious assault.[70]

In general, William had little faith in descents as a strategy for waging war. Although militarily useful, amphibious assaults had to have solid objectives, whether it was the destruction of an impor-tant base, the conquest of territory, or the diversion of enemy resources. His subjects viewed the war differently from their Dutch king, how-ever. England was an island nation and a maritime power first. While his supporters at court might have believed war on the continent was necessary, most MPs viewed the navy, rather than the army, as England's principal weapon. Many believed a maritime or 'Blue-Water' war aimed at strangling French trade would better serve England than would a costly commitment on the continent.[71] Not surprisingly, in 1691 with the war in Ireland winding down, the rul-ing Tories as well as Country MPs began to criticize the continen-tal direction of William's strategy. Opposed to a large standing army and the tax burden that came with it, they believed direct military involvement in Europe was against the nation's interests. 'Our part is little more than defensive,' one pamphleteer noted. Instead of send-ing troops, England should isolate France from its colonies by attack-ing its maritime assets some maintained. 'Scour the coast and you secure the island and the trade, which is the life of it.' War on the continent could only hurt England's economy and do little else. Another critic lamented that the king's strategy was 'exhausting the Wealth, the Stock of the Nation, in the vast Sums drawn out from

---

[69] Ryan (1968), 52–4.
[70] HMC (1913), x.
[71] For a discussion of the origins of Britain's blue-water policy, see Baugh (1988), 33–58, especially 37–40; and French (1990), 1–31.

thence, for the Use of Foreign Countries, and the numerous Troops paid to those Countries.'[72]

The alternative was a 'Blue-Water Strategy', focused on attacking French trade and amphibious descents on the coast. The strategic rationale behind such a strategy is colourfully summed up in a 1693 treatise:

> By a descent of a royal army you may come to a fair battle. 18,000 or 20,000 English horse and 30,000 or 50,000 foot may force the French King to a fair battle, and that, being as many as can come to a fight, there is good ground to hope for success both on the good-ness of the cause (which is to deliver ourselves and the rest of Europe from slavery) and from the English courage which was ever reckoned superior to the French when they could come to a fair battle.[73]

The author notes that if an English army were landed in France, it was not to 'spend their time to take towns,' an obvious reference to (and criticism of) the war in the Low Countries, 'but to march through the country till they force a fight, wherein, if they have suc-cess, the French king must subscribe to any terms.'[74] The author's ignorance of military matters and amphibious warfare is only sur-passed by his naiveté. He never explains how this hypothetical force is to sustain itself in France. Even the operation's duration seems to have been ignored. With such fantasies being proposed, especially in the wake of the fiasco at Dundalk, it is not surprising that William was a little suspicious of his subjects' perception of the strategic real-ities facing England and the allied coalition.

Not all proponents of descents were ignorant of the strategic pic-ture, however. Jacob Surendonck was one of the most important Dutch proponents of a strategy of descents. Convinced that landings on the French coast might break the stalemate in Flanders, Surendonck advocated using amphibious operations as a form of diversionary attack. Later to become one of Grand Pensionary Anthonie Heinsius' military advisors during the War of the Spanish Succession, Surendonck had begun drafting plans for a landing on the French coast in 1692 and continued to present them to William's associates and advisors throughout the war.[75] Most of his plans envisaged landing a sizable

---

[72] Both quoted in Rose (1999), 117.
[73] PRO SP 8/15, no. 102: 'Reasons for a Descent into France.'
[74] Ibid.
[75] ARA, RAZH, *Inventaris Archief Jacob Surendonck*, iii–ix; ARA RAZH, AJS B-1.a, no. 27 (unfoliated): 'Consideratien op dese conjuncturen van tyden, en saken, om

military force in France—preferably Normandy—to force the French
into fighting a battle on allied terms away from the Low Countries
and its belts of fortifications. This, he believed, would force Louis
to weaken his forces there to deal with the new threat, which in
turn would break the stalemate.[76] Although his plans appear never
to have been implemented, they do resonate somewhat with William's
maritime strategy. Both in the planning of the abortive descent on
Normandy in 1692–93 and, after the failure of the Brest operation
in 1694, the implementation of a bombardment strategy, Surendonck's
plans seem at least to have been consulted.[77]

If not an advocate of a descents strategy, William did believe they
could be useful. Indeed it was William himself who proposed mounting the amphibious assault on Brest, maintaining it was the only way
of defeating the Brest fleet short of fleet action. But he also believed
descents could be useful in other ways. William was keenly aware
of the growing opposition in Parliament to his continental strategy.
He must have been also aware of the MPs' predilection for descents.
With the war on the continent likely to require a greater English
commitment, the promise of a landing in France was certain to
soothe some of William's opponents while at the same time allowing him to send more troops to the Low Countries. When he made
known his intention to conduct a descent into France in 1691 during the fall parliamentary session, its members 'broke thro' the rules
and formes of Parliament to add 12,000 men to the army'.[78] William
had surely proposed the descent as a way both to continue his war
on the continent while at the same time attacking an important and
dangerous maritime threat.[79] Not only would such an operation satisfy Parliament's 'blue-water' proponents but it would serve the strategic end of eliminating France's most dangerous naval base, a base
deemed impossible to attack solely with conventional naval forces.

Vrankrijk tot heden te brengen, en het verlies van Namen te repareeren . . ., 9 July
1692'; no. 28 (unfoliated).

  [76] ARA RAZH, AJS B-1.a, nos. 28, 30.

  [77] ARA RAZH, AJS B-1.a, no. 38: 'Remarques op de tegenwoordige Campagne
te Water en te Lande de 4 July 1694'.

  [78] HMC (1913), xiii.

  [79] For an analysis of William's role, see Ryan (1968), 51–7.

La Hogue, Brest, and St. Malo

The first plan for a descent was formulated in the winter of 1691–92. Although it met with opposition when first proposed to the Cabinet Council, in the end William's plan was accepted, at least tentatively. It called for an attack against both Brest and St. Malo since they were 'the places which were most dangerous, the one to trade, and the other to the safety of the nation.'[80] It was intended that troops released from Ireland would provide the manpower for the operation, thus maintaining allied troop strength in Flanders. The attack was to be carried out by twenty infantry battalions, two regiments of horse, and one of dragoons—18,000 men all told, under the command of the Duke of Leinster (Schomberg's youngest son), supported by the main allied fleet under Admiral Russell. Ships were assembled at Kinsale and in the Thames, camps were established nearby to facilitate the rapid embarkation of troops and, to sustain them once in France, three months provisions were ordered. By the end of April, most of the required men and ships had been assembled and were waiting for the word to go.

News that the Sun King was planning a descent of his own meant that William's invasion had to be put on hold until the threat subsided. The allied victory at La Hogue on 29–31 May ended the invasion scare; it also changed the strategic situation dramatically. With the bulk of the tattered French fleet recovering in Brest and St. Malo, an amphibious attack on either port would complete the victory. Unfortunately for the allies, delays caused by a combination of indecision, circumstance, and bad luck impeded the operation. The requisite transport ships had been assembled in April, but the crews were promptly pressed into service to fill the fleet's depleted ranks, leaving the transports unmanned. It would take months to reassemble the scattered crews. At the same time, the French siege of Namur threatened to unhinge the allied position in the Low Countries. With the situation in the theatre deteriorating, William refused to release the troops originally earmarked for the descent on the grounds that horse and dragoons were not needed for a raid against a hostile port.[81] Assured that an attack would be just as successful without them, William urged Nottingham to proceed.

---

[80] Quoted in Ryan (1968), 57.
[81] Japikse, ed. (1928), 2: 32–3; De Jonge (1839), pt. 1, 371–2; Aubrey (1979), 133; Ehrman (1953), 399–401; and Ryan (1968), 56–7.

With fewer troops available, the expedition's architects suddenly began to have second thoughts. Leinster protested that without cavalry the descent could not succeed. Nottingham agreed. Writing to the Earl of Portland, William's chief advisor, on 24 June 1692, he complained:

> The King expects the horse to be sent to Flanders, and that we must not expect any foot from thence this summer. This breaks all our measures here, and yet I should acquiesce in his Majesties pleasure if I did not think this resolution would be of fatall consequence to his Majesties affairs and government.

Nottingham believed a descent on the Normandy coast was the best way of prosecuting the war, rather than wasting troops in Flanders where a few thousand men would not be missed. He believed weakening the assault force would have dire consequences:

> Considering that the French have sent and are still sending great numbers from Flanders, is it possible for the king to attempt a siege with the army as it is? Or will it become impossible for want of 7,000 foot if he should send them hither? I hope the answers to all these questions will not be such as I do not wish: but suppose them to be so, and I know the consequence will be very mischevious: yet surely good success in what I propose, and the prospect of it as fair as we could wish, will abundantly compensate for any of those misfortunes, for whether a town more or less be won or lost in Flanders, certainly the advantage or disadvantage is not comparable to the destruction of their fleet, which leaves all France open to an invasion and will encourage Parliament to pursue it with utmost vigour and resolution.

At the heart of Nottingham's argument was the very direction of the Anglo-Dutch war effort itself. Only a descent with the destruction of the French fleet as its objective, he maintained, could 'open France to an invasion' and thus result in allied victory. Failure to act would lead the king's critics to accuse him of pursuing a strategy aimed at Dutch goals, a strategy that was sure to end in failure.[82]

Nottingham's letter to Portland highlights the difference between William's Continental strategy and the Blue-Water strategy favoured by Nottingham and the Tories. For Nottingham and his supporters, an amphibious assault on St. Malo and the French fleet anchored there would open France to future amphibious attacks. For William,

---

[82] HMC (1913) 231–3: Nottingham to Portland, 14 June 1692 [OS].

a man better acquainted with amphibious operations than either Nottingham or Russell, descents alone could never result in victory. The only way to defeat France was through Flanders. Nottingham would not get his 7,000 men.[83]

With William's mind made up, Nottingham and Russell were faced with conducting the operation with 12,000 instead of 18,000 men. Soon, however, other factors intervened, overshadowing the lack of forces. The prevailing westerly wind outside the harbour made anchoring dangerous, and the arrival of additional French shore batteries at St. Malo only compounded it. And Leinster continued to complain that without cavalry, the assault would fail. A council-of-war aboard HMS *Breda* finally decided the operation was simply too difficult and unlikely to succeed. William was not surprised when he received the news. Indeed, even before Russell and the other officers made their decision, he had issued orders for a descent on Dunkirk in the event that the attack on St. Malo was found impracticable.[84] After months of preparation and vast expense, the force sailed around and did nothing. William showed his dissatisfaction with the whole affair by sacking Nottingham, though the seemingly indispensable Russell was kept on.[85] Dunkirk too was found to be too heavily defended for an actual attack. In the end, the allies conducted their descent on the friendly port of Ostend and 12,000 men were added to William's army in Flanders.[86]

The abortive descent in 1692 illustrates the difficulty inherent in amphibious operations in the latter seventeenth century. None of the commanders, save William, seem to have recognized the significance of La Hogue and the necessity to use the forces at hand quickly. Instead, indecision, inflexibility, and inter-service rivalry frustrated a promising opportunity. Clearly, the operation had to be practicable, well designed, and conducted with unity of purpose. The 1692 operation enjoyed none of these preconditions. William's correspondence shows that while he continued to push for the operation, its archi-

---

[83] Ibid.; Ryan (1968), 58.

[84] Philip Aubrey, *The Defeat of James Stuart's Armada*, 142–144; *Ehrman* (1953), 400–407; and Ryan, 'William III and the Brest Fleet,' 57–59.

[85] Nottingham lost control of the Navy, though William kept him in the government: Ehrman (1953), 408–13; Horwitz (1977), 103–14; and Ryan (1968), 63.

[86] D'Auvergne (1693), 57–65.

tects found numerous reasons to abandon it, a clear indication of how William's view of descents clashed with the views of the plan's architects. A council of war made up of both naval and military officers each with their own perceptions of what was and what was not possible in an amphibious operation led to inaction. Leinster's letter to Nottingham vividly illustrates the problem such operations faced when left to a council of war:

> It is the opinion of the Flagg officers of the fleet that its not practicable to attempt any thing against the enemy's shipps at St. Maloe with any shipps of the fleet, till the town itself be [so] farr reduced by our land forces as that the said shipps which shall be sent in may receive noe great annoyance from the enemy gunns in the attempt; and the generall and feild officers of the army are of the opinion that they are not capable to doe any service at that place without the assistance of the fleet.[87]

Both the army and navy had their own separate concerns, and neither seems to have consulted the other while the operation was on the drawing board. It was only when the force reached the Normandy coast that its architects suddenly found their plan wanting. But it was not just the plan that was weak. By leaving the operation to a council of war, William inadvertently contributed to its failure. When it came time to decide whether to proceed or not, the admirals refused to risk their fleet and the generals their troops. Ironically, each blamed the other for their own force's shortcomings, a 'catch-22' that might not have occurred had the operation been made the responsibility of a single commander rather than a committee.

The End of Descents: the Brest Disaster

The failure of the 1692 operation did not quiet Parliament's demand for additional descents, however. Although St. Malo had been found too difficult to attack in 1692, the French attack on the Smyrna fleet the following summer led leaders in the Admiralty—and even William himself—to reconsider an amphibious assault on the formidable naval base at Brest. William's Cabinet Council actually proposed an assault on Brest in 1693, but abandoned the project for the same reasons

---

[87] HMC (1913), 344–5: Leinster to Nottingham, 28 July 1692 [OS].

that it was scrapped in favour of St. Malo in 1692.[88] The destruction of the Smyrna fleet changed the political climate in England, which in turn forced a reassessment of the Brest operation. Admiral Russell was now First Lord of the Admiralty; Nottingham and the Tories had been abandoned in favour of the Whigs. The change in government was accompanied by a change in naval policy. Although traditionally the Tories had been the strongest proponents of a blue-water strategy, the Whigs, with their merchant interests, now demanded action against the fleet that had done so much harm.[89] William, however, was more determined than ever to send the main fleet the Mediterranean, where he believed it could better protect allied commerce from French attacks and support the operations of his Spanish allies in that theatre.[90] At the same time, he too believed something should be attempted. A raid on the Brest fleet at anchor would satisfy the Whigs on whose financial support he depended for prosecuting his war in the Low Countries. Just like the descent on St. Malo, the raid on Brest was a compromise. Politics put Russell in the unenviable position of having to conduct an operation that he had deemed too difficult in 1692 with twice the resources. As the newly appointed Lord High Admiral, he was hardly in a position to obstruct a plan supported by his own political party, particularly in the wake of the botched St. Malo operation and the Smyrna fleet disaster. With the navy's honour on the line, he had no choice but to swallow hard and soldier on despite his own misgivings.[91]

The problems associated with an attack on Brest had not changed since 1692—if anything they had become more acute. First, there would be fewer forces available: 7,000 men as opposed to the 12,000 available in 1692. Although the whole Combined Fleet would sail to Brest, only Lord Berkeley's squadron would make the actual assault

---

[88] Childs (1987), 220–221; and Ryan (1968), 62–63.

[89] William abandoned the Tories in the autumn of 1693 because the Whigs were willing to support the war on the continent. His decision to attack Brest seems, in part, to have been in response to the Whigs' desire to see something done following the devastating French attack on the Smyrna fleet. Indeed most MPs and military officers who supported the operation were Whigs. For details, see Childs (1987), 220–22; and Horwitz (1977), 116–18, 123–139.

[90] William had begun actively pursuing sending a fleet to the Mediterranean following the allied victory at La Hogue in 1692: Ehrman (1949), 272–5.

[91] Ehrman (1953), 513–15.

on the port. Berkeley had thirty-six ships of the line, nine bomb vessels and fireships, seven frigates, and a number of transports and support craft at his disposal. Although the stated goal of the operation was to destroy the French fleet, no one really seems to have believed they would catch it in port. If Brest was found empty, Berkeley would be left behind to conduct the assault regardless, while Russell proceeded to the Mediterranean with the Combined Fleet. The assault force, under Lieutenant General Thomas Talmash, was to capture the Roscanvel Peninsula, which dominated Brest's inner harbour, by amphibious assault. What he was to do once ashore is difficult to know for sure. His orders were extremely vague: to destroy ships, installations, and otherwise pin-down French forces in the area. And yet if the ships were gone, how could a force of just 7,000 men attack a modern fortress and its harbour installations successfully when operations against similar fortresses in the Low Countries required 20,000 to 30,000 men at least? Perhaps the vagueness of Talmash's orders could be ascribed to operational flexibility. Still, it seems strange that after years of planning for an amphibious assault on Brest, it should have no specific and—most importantly—no truly *attainable* military goal in mind.[92]

As predicted, when the force arrived in Camaret Bay on 16 June 1694, Berkeley discovered that the fleet had sailed. Worse yet, the French seemed to already know the allies' plans and had prepared for just such an attack.[93] Although the British did not know it then, the great military engineer Vauban himself had supervised the construction of new forts, earthworks, batteries, and casemates to guard against amphibious assault [figure 24]. The entrance to the harbour and all the possible landing beaches were covered by hundreds of guns and mortars, while between 8,000 and 9,000 regulars were stationed in the city and its outer defences to repel any seaborne invader. The Roscanvel Peninsula, where Talmash's force was to land, was particularly well defended. Given the nature of late seventeenth century amphibious forces, an assault against such defences required a miracle to succeed.[94]

---

[92] See Childs (1987), 230–231, 344, 355.

[93] Marlborough's role in leaking information to the French is well known and still open to speculation: Childs (1987), 224–5.

[94] The description of the Brest operation is based on: PRO, SP 8/15, ff. 66–8:

As soon as the fleet arrived heavy mortars opened fire, forcing
Berkeley to move his heavier ships out of range. With the element
of surprise clearly gone, it is surprising that he and Talmash considered going on with the plan. Still determined to make an attempt,
on 18 June 1694 Talmash led his force to the beach. Escorted by
frigates, the first wave of boats paddled towards the shore under
heavy fire. As their escorts engaged the shore batteries at close range,
the first longboats reached the beach only to find entrenched enemy
troops there. Fired on by shore batteries and dug-in musketeers,
Talmash's troops stood little chance. Although he tried to form up
his men to attack the French earthworks, heavy fire and the appearance of enemy cavalry on the beach made this impossible. With further attacks fruitless, Talmash ordered the survivors back to the boats
only to find that the tide had gone out, stranding many of them.
Some of his troops surrendered, unable to escape. Talmash, and a
handful of survivors managed to float several boats and return to
the fleet.

During the operation, the assault forces and supporting ships
suffered 2,000 casualties, including 300 dead—one of them Talmash
himself, mortally wounded in the final retreat. Of the seven frigates
assigned to provide supporting fire for the assault forces, one was
sunk and the rest damaged, one severely.[95]

The Limits of Seapower: Amphibious Operations and Continental War, 1694–1697

The failure of the Brest raid discredited the strategy of descents and
demonstrated the limits of seapower and amphibious warfare. Like
the attempt on St. Malo in 1692, the Brest operation demonstrated
that attacks on fortified harbours were impossible given the technology of the day. The failures at St. Malo and Brest also silenced

---

'The Relation of Capt. Nathaniell Green, Volonteer with Lt. Gen. Talmash in the
Expedition to Brest, given the 13th of June 1694'; ARA RAZH, Archief van Anthonie
Heinsius, 317 (unfoliated): 'Memoire en Relaas van t' rescontre in Cameresbay,
ontrent de haven van Brest'; *Europische Mercurius* (1694), 1:291–297; and Childs
(1987), 226–35.
[95] For casualties see ARA RAZH, *loc. cit.*; *Europische Mercurius* (1694), 1:297; Childs
(1987), 234; and Ehrman (1953), 515.

those who maintained that a purely maritime strategy was the most effective way for England to wage war against France. For the remainder of the Nine Years' War, Parliament gave William more leeway in employing Britain's military resources. By 1695, Britain's armed forces had expanded to over 100,000 men, the largest army in its history to date, with over 60,000 of its troops deployed in the Low Countries.[96] For the last three years of the war, there would be little opposition to William's continental strategy.

A Shift in Strategy: the Combined Fleet in the Mediterranean

The Brest operation coincided with an important shift in the strategic direction of the allied war effort at sea and, consequently, the conduct of amphibious operations. William had always intended to send a squadron of ships to the Mediterranean. Indeed, the Treaty on Combined Fleets stipulated sending a sizable coalition naval force to the region, but France's intervention in Ireland in 1689 and their defeat of the allies at Beachy Head in 1690 made it impossible to realize. Only small squadrons were sent to the Mediterranean in 1690 and 1691, before the allied victory at La Hogue established allied control of the Channel, a prerequisite for sending the Combined Fleet to the Mediterranean.[97] The presence of such allied squadrons in the Mediterranean failed to prevent the French attack on the Smyrna Fleet and the crippling economic losses that ensued, however. William realized that since Louis XIV seemed unwilling to risk the Brest fleet in the Channel, and since allied amphibious operations were incapable of yielding the kind of decisive results their advocates had promised, the most effective way to utilize allied superiority at sea was to send the weight of the Combined Fleet to the Mediterranean where it might prove more useful for allied war effort.[98]

Most naval historians recognize the allied 1694 campaign in the Mediterranean as a watershed in maritime strategy. William's plan for 1694 was to send the Combined Fleet—some sixty-three men-

---

[96] These figures include all three military establishments. See Stapleton (2003), 113–28, 211–19.
[97] Ehrman (1949), esp. 272–3.
[98] Ibid.

of-war excluding Berkeley's squadron assaulting Brest—under Russell
to the Mediterranean while Berkeley's squadron of 36 men-of-war
plus auxiliaries would cover the English Channel. Almost immediately, Russell's made his presence felt. The Combined Fleet halted
the French advance down the Catalonian coast, saving Barcelona
for the time being, and forcing the French fleet under Tourville to
retire to Toulon. The Anglo-Dutch presence in the Mediterranean
had produced the effect William had hoped for. Next, despite Russell's
vigorous opposition, William took the momentous step of ordering
the Combined Fleet to winter in the region.[99] The logistical challenges of refitting the fleet in Spain were great, but the presence of
the fleet continued to have a positive influence on the allied war
effort in the theatre. In early 1695, Russell was reinforced by four
battalions of infantry, thus giving the Anglo-Dutch fleet a modest
amphibious capability.[100] For much of 1695, Russell supported his
Spanish allies, transporting troops from Italy to Spain and providing naval artillery support where needed. Although he did not conduct any large-scale amphibious assaults in the Mediterranean, his
ships' guns, bomb vessels, and marines aided the Spanish attempt
to recapture Palamos. The timely arrival of Tourville's Toulon fleet,
however, forced the allies to give up the siege.[101] Nevertheless, the
presence of the Anglo-Dutch fleet in the Mediterranean in 1695
proved a success. Its presence not only helped bolster the Spanish
defence of Catalonia, thus demonstrating the importance of naval
power in the land campaigns there, but it also proved that William's
strategic vision was correct. Although a permanent Anglo-Dutch presence in Mediterranean would not come until the Spanish Succession
War, William's decision to send the Combined Fleet to the Mediterranean showed his appreciation for the strategic potential Anglo-
Dutch naval power possessed to influence events in that important
theatre of war.

A Campaign of Bombardments

Meanwhile, the failure of the Brest raid led William to look for other
ways to utilize allied naval assets in the absence of a direct French

---

[99] Lynn (1999), 243–244.
[100] See Childs (1995), 76–7.
[101] Ibid., 79–80.

challenge. With no French fleet to fight following La Hogue, the Combined Fleet had to do something to justify the money spent to keep it afloat. Unable to curb the activities of French privateers through fleet action, William and his admirals looked to bombardments as a means of striking at France's effective privateers. In the fall of 1693, the allied fleet bombarded St. Malo, an attack that served as a model for later bombardments. For four days, bomb-ketches lobbed shells into the city while ships-of-the-line traded shots with the city's shore batteries.[102] The climax of the attack came when the allies sailed a fireship or 'infernal machine' into the harbour itself. Although the explosion of the ship caused 'part of the town to go up in flames,' it failed in its design to destroy the harbour because it exploded prematurely.[103] Half the town had been burnt but the harbour—the principal target of the attack on the town—remained intact.

In spite of these mixed results, bombardments seemed a safer option than descents against well-defended enemy ports. In the summer of 1694, following the attack on Brest, Berkeley shifted the emphasis of his operations to the bombardment of coastal cities with the intention of giving 'the enemy as much trouble and do them as much injury as we can'.[104] William hoped the appearance of Berkeley's squadron would cause alarm and draw French troops to the coast. On 22 July, after waiting five days for the weather to improve, allied bomb-ketches began hurling their shells into Dieppe [figure 25]. The first day alone, the allies fired 1,100 bombs into the unfortunate city; after two days, the mortars stopped firing and the fleet moved further down the Normandy coast, leaving two-thirds of the town a charred ruin, a harbinger of things to come.[105] Two days later, Berkeley struck again, this time at Le Havre [figure 26]. Unlike at Dieppe, French counter-battery fire was effective and managed to sink one of the allies' bomb ships. The onset of rough seas, furthermore, cut short the allied attack and demonstrated the necessity for near-perfect conditions for bombardments to be effective. Nevertheless, the bomb-ships succeeded in destroying nearly one-

[102] *Europische Mercurius* (1693), 2:320–326.
[103] Ibid., 2:325.
[104] Quoted in Ryan (1968), 65.
[105] *Europische Mercurius* (1694), 2:90–94; and De Jonge (1839), pt. 1, 470–5.

third of the town. In the early autumn, Berkeley struck both Calais and Dunkirk. Although terrifying for towns' inhabitants, these bombardments proved comparatively ineffective, the result of poor conditions and, in the case of Dunkirk, very formidable defences [figure 28].[106]

William's decision to bombard French coastal cities was in part a reaction to the Combined Fleet's inability to mount effective amphibious assaults, but the new strategy still served his ultimate aims. Rather than expending valuable ground forces in apparently futile seaborne attacks, William would use the fleet's firepower—particularly its bomb-vessels—to inflict damage on havens for French privateers. Largely punitive in nature, the bombardment of French ports was, however, a less than perfect solution to the privateering menace. In 1695 and 1696, ships continued to bomb French cities that harboured corsairs. But allied bombardments against their principal base at Dunkirk ended in failure despite the use of another 'infernal machine'.[107] Stout defences, shallows and wind, coupled with the difficulty in coordinating such operations, demonstrated the impossibility of effectively attacking Dunkirk with ships alone. In spite of failures at Dunkirk, other allied bombardments did prove somewhat successful. By the end of the war, allied bomb vessels had conducted no fewer than nine bombardments of six different coastal towns. Though it is clear that these attacks did not seriously affect French commerce raiding, they did cause damage, a legitimate goal in any war of attrition.

Conclusion

The Nine Years' War was a turning point for the evolution of allied maritime strategy and the conduct of amphibious operations. On the surface, allied amphibious operations were less than impressive. In spite of their preponderance of naval assets, the Maritime Powers found it difficult to employ their amphibious forces effectively. During the war's course, England and the Dutch Republic together con-

---

[106] See especially *Europische Mercurius* (1694), 2:94–6, 165–7; and De Jonge (1839), pt. 1, 474–9, 510–16.

[107] See *Europische Mercurius* (1695), 2:99–116; de Jonge (1839), pt. 2, 18–31; Ehrman (1953), 572–4; and Roorda (1984), esp. 166–9.

ducted or planned fourteen separate amphibious operations including the bombardment campaigns. With their victory at La Hogue in 1692, the Combined Fleet gained control of the English Channel and the seas surrounding northern France. Nevertheless, they found it difficult to bring their naval assets to bear. Conflicting strategies, political pressure, and the lack of a strong naval leader contributed to the Maritime Powers' difficulties at sea. Although rudimentary, the tools of amphibious warfare were adequate enough. The Dutch invasion of England in 1688 demonstrated what might be accomplished under the right circumstances. In spite of this success, however, the Maritime Powers were never able to replicate an amphibious operation on a similar scale against France.

Parliament's obsession with descents and the conviction in England that amphibious assaults alone could win the war conflicted sharply with William's European perspective and his determination to commit English resources to the continent. The provincialism of England's blue-water advocates clashed with military realities that their Dutch king understood much better. The war in Ireland obscured these differences at first. Schomberg's Ulster expedition showed both the complexities and the difficulties inherent in large-scale amphibious operations. While it was relatively easy to land on an unopposed shore, sustaining an invasion force from the sea required careful planning and logistical expertise. In Schomberg's expedition both were lacking, with predictable results. Marlborough's assaults on Cork and Kinsale, on the other hand, illustrated the potential of well-planned amphibious operations. Marlborough played to the strength of amphibious forces—their speed and mobility—while downplaying their weaknesses. By linking up with land forces, the operation did not have to be sustained entirely from the sea. While not flawless, Marlborough's Munster expedition showed that successful amphibious operations were possible under the right circumstances.

For much of the war, Parliament, William, and his admirals quarrelled over what those right circumstances were. Motivated more by military necessity than political expediency, William believed amphibious operations should have specific strategic objectives. His rudimentary knowledge of naval affairs, however, forced him to rely on his admirals' expertise, men who were often too concerned with striking the right political chord than finding viable military solutions. Russell's opposition to William's proposed attack on Brest in 1692 contrasts strangely with his support for a similar, but even more dangerous assault on the port in 1694. In 1692, Russell deemed the operation too risky based on Brest's geography and defences; in 1694, he supported it not because the military circumstances had changed but because his Whig supporters demanded it. Driven by political concerns on the one hand and operational ones on the other, Anglo-Dutch amphibious operations were often hamstrung by divergent goals. In spite of its strategic potential, the descent on St. Malo was abandoned because its architects recognized neither its potential nor the changed strategic situation. In spite of the potential for success, none its planners were willing to risk the political embarrassment of failure. Consequently, they allowed a council of war to decide the operation was not feasible instead of finding a solution. The same political considerations plagued the failed Brest raid. The council of war's indecision at St. Malo led planners of the 1694 Brest operation to remove operational flexibility; only if the attack failed were Berkeley and Talmash permitted to try something else. Ironically, it took an amphibious disaster to silence those critical of the king's continental strategy.

In the end, William's decision to send the fleet to the Mediterranean and the implementation of the bombardment campaign against French Channel ports signalled the beginning of a more effective maritime strategy in support of William's continental objectives. The Combined Fleet's cruise in the Mediterranean not only served the allied coalition well by supporting its Spanish and Savoyard allies, but also demonstrated a more effective use of seapower against France. Instead of attempting a direct attack on the French coast, the Anglo-Dutch fleet shifted its main force south where naval power not only played a more pivotal role in land operations but where the Maritime Powers could show their support for their allies. Russell's opposition to William's Mediterranean strategy demonstrates the divide between his more traditional view of British seapower and William's European perspective. In spite of the fleet's limited cruise, it showed that it could be more useful in the Mediterranean, where amphibious operations held more promise, than in the Channel, where the fleet could do little except show the flag and shell unfortunate coastal towns.

William's strategy was realized during the War of the Spanish Succession. Lacking a foreign king to criticize, Parliament was forced to accept responsibility for formulating its own strategy. Ironically, the ruling Whigs adopted William's continental strategy as their own. No longer would Parliament demand fruitless descents on the French coast. Brest had taught them—just as Dieppe would do for another coalition almost 250 years later—that assaults on well-defended ports were suicide for amphibious forces. Just as William intended, the Mediterranean became the focus of the Maritime Powers' naval strategy. Anglo-Dutch amphibious operations complemented the coalition's Mediterranean strategy. Parliament learned that amphibious operations were not likely to deliver decisive results. But as successful assaults on Gibraltar and Minorca would later demonstrate, amphibious attacks still had a vital role to play as part of a well-formulated naval strategy.

Sources and Bibliography

Archival Sources

ARA
  StG   Archief Staten Generaal (1.01.05)
  RAZH   Rijksarchief in Zuid Holland, Den Haag
             Archief van Anthonie Heinsius (3.01.19)
         AJS Archief van Jacob van Surendonck (3.20.57)
             Huisarchief der Familie van Wassenaer (3.20.63)
BL   Add.   Additional MSS
PRO SP 8   King William's Chest 1670–1698

Printed Primary Sources

CSPDom.   Calendar of State Papers, Domestic Series, of the Reign of William and Mary, ed. W. J. Hardy, vol. 2, *May 1690–October* 1691, vol. 3, *November 1691–December 1692* and vol. 4, *1693* (London: 1898–1904).

Bland, H. (1727) *A Treatise of Military Discipline* (London: 1727).

d'Auvergne, Edward (1693) *A Relation of the Most Remarkable Transactions of the Last Campagne in the Confederate Army, Under the Command of His Majesty of Great Britain; and After, of the Elector of Bavaria, in the Spanish Netherlands, Anno Dom. 1692* (London: 1693).

Dalton, C., ed. (1960) *English Army Lists and Commission Registers, 1661–1714*, 6 vols (London: 1892–1904), vol. 1, *1661–1685*, vol. 2, *1685–1689*, vol. 3, *1689–1694* (repr., London: 1960).

Europische Mercurius (1690, 1693, 1694, 1695) *Europische Mercurius, Behelzende Al het voornaamste 't geen, zo omtrent de zaaken van Staat als Oorlog, in alle de Koningryken en Landen van Europe, en ook zelfs in verscheidenen Gewesten van d' andere Deelen der Wereld, is voorgevellen, 1690*, each in 4 parts (Amsterdam: 1690, 1693, 1694, 1695).

Heinsius, A. (1874) *Het Archief van den Raadpensionaris Antonie Heinsius*, ed. H. J. van der Hiem, vols 1–3 (The Hague: 1874).

HMC (1913) Royal Commission on Historical Manuscripts, *Report on the Manuscripts of Allan George Finch, Esq., of Burley-on-the-Hill, Rutland*, vol. 4, *The Correspondence of Sir Daniel Finch, Earl of Winchilsea and Nottingham*, ed. F. Bickley, HMC 71 (London: 1913).

Japikse, N., ed. (1928) *Correspondentie van Willem III en van Hans Willem Bentinck, Eersten Graaf van Portland: Eerste Gedeelte (I): Het Archief van Welbeck Abbey* ('s-Gravenhage: 1928).

Luttrell N. (1692–93) *The Parliamentary Diary of Narcissus Luttrell, 1692–1693*, ed. H. Horwitz (Oxford: 1972).

Secondary Sources

Aubrey, P. (1979) *The Defeat of James Stuart's Armada, 1692* (Leicester: 1979).
Baugh, D. (1988) 'Great Britain's 'Blue-Water' Policy, 1689–1815', *The International History Review* 10:1 (Feb. 1988) 33–58.
Baxter, S. (1966) *William III and the Defense of European Liberty, 1650–1702* (New York: 1966).
Brooks, R. (2002) *The Royal Marines: 1664 to the present* (Annapolis, Md.: 2002).
Bruijn, J. (1989) 'William III and his Two Navies', *Notes of the Navy Records Society* 43 (1989) 117–132.
——. (1998) *Varend Verleden: De Nederlandse oorlogsvloot in de zeventiende en achttiende eeuw* (Amsterdam: 1998).
Carswell, J. (1969) *The Descent on England: A Study of the English Revolution of 1688 and its European Background* (London: 1969).
Chandler, D. (1984) *Marlborough as Military Commander* (Staplehurst, Kent: 1984).
——. (1995) *Marlborough as Military Commander* (Staplehurst, Kent: 1995).
Childs, J. (1980) *The Army, James II, and the Glorious Revolution* (Manchester: 1980).
——. (1987) *The British Army of William III, 1689–1702* (Manchester: 1987).
——. (1991) *The Nine Years' War and the British Army, 1688–97: The Operations in the Low Countries* (Manchester: 1991).
——. (1995) 'Secondary Operations of the British Army During the Nine Years' War, 1688–1697', in *The Journal of Army Historical Research* 73 (1995) 69–98.
——. (1996) 'The Williamite War in Ireland', in *A Military History of Ireland*, ed. T. Bartlett and K. Jeffery (Cambridge: 1996) 188–210.
Clark, G. N. (1923) *The Dutch Alliance and the War Against French Trade, 1688–1697* (Manchester: 1923).
Danaher, K. and Simms, J. (1962) *The Danish Force in Ireland, 1690–1691* (Dublin: 1962).
Dorren, C. (1948) *De Geschiedenis van het Nederlandsche Korps Mariniers van 1665–1945* (The Hague: 1948).
De Jonge, J. (1839) *Geschiedenis van het Nederlandshe Zeewezen*, deel 4, *Tweede Oorlog Met Frankrijk*, 2 parts ('s-Gravenhage: 1839).
Doherty, R. (1998) *The Williamite War in Ireland, 1688–1691* (Dublin: 1998).
Ehrman, J. (1949) 'William III and the Emergence of a Mediterranean Naval Policy, 1692–4', *Cambridge Historical Journal* 9 (1949) 269–92.
——. (1953) *The Navy in the War of William III, 1689–1697: Its State and Direction* (Cambridge: 1953).
French, D. (1990) *The British Way in Warfare, 1688–2000* (London: 1990).
Hainsworth, R. and Churches, C. (1998) *The Anglo-Dutch Naval Wars, 1652–1674* (Gloucester: 1998).
Haley, K. D. H. (1992) 'The Dutch, the Invasion of England, and the Alliance of 1689', in *The Revolution of 1688–1689: Changing Perspectives*, ed. L. G. Schwoerer (Cambridge: 1992) 21–34.
Harding, R. (1991) *Amphibious Warfare in the Eighteenth Century: The British Expedition to the West Indies, 1740–1742* (Woodbridge, Suffolk: 1991).
Hattendorf, J. (2002) '"To Aid and Assist the Other": Anglo-Dutch Cooperation in Coalition Warfare at Sea, 1689–1714', in *Anthonie Heinsius and the Dutch Republic, 1688–1720: Politics, War, and Finance*, ed. A. de Jongste and A. Veenendaal, Jr (The Hague: 2002) 177–98.
Hayton, D. and O'Brien, G., eds (1986) *War and Politics in Ireland, 1649–1730* (London: 1986).

Hora-Siccama, J. (1915) *Aantekeningen en Verbeteringen op het in 1906 door het Historische Genootschap uitgegeven Register op de Journalen van Constantijn Huygens den Zoon* (Amsterdam: 1915).

Horwitz, H. (1977) *Parliament, Policy and Politics in the Reign of William III* (Manchester: 1977).

Israel, J., ed. (1991A) *The Anglo-Dutch Moment: Essays on the Glorious Revolution and its World Impact* (Cambridge: 1991).

Israel, J. I. (1991B) 'The Dutch Role in the Glorious Revolution', in Israel (1991A) 105–162.

Jones, J. R. (1996) *The Anglo-Dutch Wars of the Seventeenth Century* (New York: 1996).

King, H. L. (1914) 'Brandenburg and the English Revolution' (Ph.D. diss., University of Freiburg [published Oberlin, Ohio]: 1914).

van der Kuijl, A. (1988) *De glorieuze overtocht. De expeditie van Willem III naar Engeland in 1688* (Amsterdam: 1988).

Lynn, J. (1999) *The Wars of Louis XIV* (New York: 1999).

Marini, A. J. (1983) 'Parliament and the Marine Regiments, 1739', in *Assault From the Sea: Essays on the History of Amphibious Warfare*, ed. M. L. Bartlett (Annapolis, Md.: 1983).

Müller, P. L. (1873) *Wilhelm von Oranien und Georg Friedrich von Waldeck: Ein Beitrag zur Geschichte des Kampfes um das Europäsche Gleichgewicht*, 2 vols. (The Hague: 1873).

Murray, W. and Millett, A. (2000) *A War to be Won: Fighting the Second World War* (Cambridge, Mass.: 2000).

Parker, G. and Israel, J. (1991) 'Of Providence and Protestant Winds: the Spanish Armada of 1588 and the Dutch Armada of 1688', Israel, ed. (1991A) 335–363.

Ringoir, H. (1981) *Nederlandse Generaals van 1568 tot 1940* (The Hague: 1981).

Roorda, D. J. (1984) 'De loopbaan van Willem Meester', in idem, *Rond Prins en Patriciaat: Verspreide opstellen door D. J. Roorda* (Weesp, 1984) 156–171.

Rose, C. (1999) *England in the 1690s: Revolution, Religion, and War* (Oxford: 1999).

Ryan, A. (1968) 'William III and the Brest Fleet', in *William III and Louis XIV: Essays 1680–1720 by and for Mark A. Thomson*, ed. R. Hatton and J. Bromley (Liverpool: 1968).

Simms, J. (1969) *Jacobite Ireland, 1685–91* (London: 1969).

——. (1986A) 'Schomberg at Dunkalk, 1689', in Hayton & O'Brien, eds (1986) 91–104.

——. (1986B) 'Marlborough's Siege of Cork', in Hayton & O'Brien, eds (1986) 105 ff.

Stapleton, J. M. (2003) 'Forging A Coalition Army: William III, The Grand Alliance, and the Confederate Army in the Spanish Netherlands, 1688–1697' (Ph.D diss., The Ohio State University, 2003).

Symcox, G. (1974) *The Crisis of French Seapower 1688–1697: From the guerre d'escadre to the guerre de course* (The Hague: 1974).

Rogers, P. (1970) *The Dutch in the Medway* (Oxford: 1970).

Ten Raa, F. and de Bas, F. (1921) *Het Staatsche Leger, 1568–1795*, deel 5 *Van het sluiten van den vreede te Munster tot de verheffing van Prins Willem III van Oranje tot kapitein-en admiraal-generaal der Vereenigde Nederlanden (1648–1672)* (Breda: 1921).

Ten Raa, F. (1950) *Het Staatsche Leger, 1568–1795*, deel 7 *Van de verheffing van Prins Willem III en zijn gemalin tot Koning van Groot-Brittannië tot het overlijden van den Koning-Stadhouder (1688–1702)* (The Hague: 1950).

de Schrijver, R. (1965) *Jan van Brouchoven Graaf van Bergeyck 1644–1725: een halve eeuw staatkunde in de Spaanse Nederlanden en in Europa* (Brussels: 1965).

Walton, C. (1894) *History of the British Standing Army AD 1660 to 1700* (London: 1894).

Ware, C. (1994) *The Bomb Vessel: Shore Bombardment Ships of the Age of Sail* (Annapolis, Md.: 1994).

Warnsinck, J. (1934) *De vloot van den Koning-Stadhouder 1689–1690* (Amsterdam: 1934).

Watman, K. (1989) 'The Effectiveness of Military Organizations', in, *Military Effectiveness*, vol. 1, *The First World War*, ed. A. Millett and W. Murray (Boston: 1989) 1–30.

Wernham, R. B. (1961) 'Elizabethan War Aims and Strategy', in *Elizabethan Government and Society: Essays Presented to Sir John Neale*, ed. S. T. Bindoff, J. Hurstfield and C. H. Williams (London: 1961) 340–69.

MEDIEVAL AND EARLY-MODERN INSHORE, ESTUARINE, RIVERINE AND LACUSTRINE WARFARE*

D. J. B. Trim

Amphibious operations are not necessarily either ship-to-shore operations or the projection of oceanic power onto land: they also take other forms. This essay is a study of the conduct of inland and inshore amphibious warfare. What 'inland amphibious warfare' entails may seem obvious, but to be precise, it entails warfare on rivers, lakes, canals and marshes. 'Inshore amphibious warfare' is more indistinct; in considering it, I examine amphibious operations that, while carried out on the seaward side of the ocean-continent divide, take place 'near or close to the shore'[1]—especially those that take place in the waters of harbours and anchorages.[2] Of course, all amphibious operations carried out at the land-sea interface will at some point involve action in such waters; however, many operations simply *cross* the inshore stretch en route from sea to land. The operations examined here are *located* on inshore waters: that is, they involve consistent actions thereon, rather than only landings (whether raids or invasions) or defences against them. In practice, many inshore waters are the estuaries of rivers, or lagoons; though seas and rivers (like ocean and land) are distinct, there is, between high sea, inshore waterway and inland waterway, no clear distinction—they merge into each other and so, therefore, can operations on them, both physically and conceptually. Thus, this essay is not a study of two distinct types of amphibious operation, but rather of one broad category, in which waterborne forces that do more than merely transport are integral, but always operate in close, or very close, proximity to the shore or bank.

---

* I am grateful to Mark Fissel, Paul Van Dyke, Matthew Bennett and Malyn Newitt for criticism of early drafts and to Mark Fissel, Guy Rowlands and Winifred Trim for suggestions, and encouragement. Research in Paris was made possible by grants from the British Academy and the Huguenot Society of Great Britain and Ireland.
[1] OED (1989), *s.v.* 'inshore, in-shore', definition 'B'.
[2] See ibid.; *Oxford Military Dictionary* (2001), *s.v.* 'inshore patrol'.

Because, however, amphibious warfare on estuaries, rivers, lagoons and lakes has certain characteristics, dictated by geographical factors, this essay is also a study of the influence of geography on warfare, in which I attempt to apply, albeit in limited fashion, the approach of Fernand Braudel, in his classic history of *The Mediterranean and the Mediterranean World*, to military operations.[3] In this essay, as with Braudel, geography and topography are not ends in themselves, but rather are 'means to an end'.[4] I explore the factors that shaped medieval and early-modern commerce and urban development (specifically in port towns and cities) in such a way as to shape, in turn, those operations undertaken against, or in defence of, cities or towns lying on a coast or on important inland waterways.

The relative freedom over terrain attained by military commanders after the industrial revolution often blinds us to the very real constraints that governed military operations in the past. Military historians tend to remember that good roads are a relatively recent development, but to forget that operational choices were circumscribed by far more than the absence or presence of highways.[5] We are so accustomed to our modern mastery over our environment that we often lose sight of the limits placed on military operations by a wide range of geographical factors; however, warfare—and perhaps especially amphibious warfare—was shaped by physical realities moulded over millennia (such as the fluvial drainage patterns of a region), which were in turn shaped by geological factors, and only gradually by human engineering projects. In order 'to rediscover the slow unfolding of' these structural and geohistorical realties and assess their impact on estuarine, riverine and lacustrine amphibious warfare from 1000–1700, like Braudel, I 'make full use of evidence . . . and landscapes' from across the period and across a range of environments. Much of the evidence comes from Europe (broadly defined) in the early-modern period, but it is contextualised by material from all the

---

[3] Braudel (1972). Braudel did examine 'The Forms of War' (ch. vii, in vol. 2) but only in a limited and not entirely satisfactory way. McGurk (2001) examines the influence of terrain on operations in late-Tudor Ireland. Stephenson, ed. (2003) examines the impact of geography on a series of battles, but is disappointing in the lack of comparative analysis. Meyer (2000) more successfully integrates geography into early-modern military history.

[4] Braudel (1972), 1: 23.

[5] E.g., Keegan (1993) has an index entry for 'roads and railways', but none for rivers.

continents (save Australia) and all of the seven centuries covered by this volume; I combine all the evidence 'across time and space' in order to detect permanent traits or characteristics.[6] Similar geographic conditions can be found globally and so inshore and inland amphibious operations followed similar patterns across the world.

Analysis of the geographical factors that influenced warfare in this period provides the basis for analysing the conduct of inland and inshore amphibious warfare in the period 1000–1700. I attempt to explain why it took place where it did and in the manner it did, drawing on evidence from Europe, in particular, but also more generally from across the period and the continents, inasmuch as what is of interest is not a particular conflict, campaign or operation, but rather the characteristics of war fought in particular types of land/waterscape.[7] Amphibious operations within or on the fringes of the continents have been an important part of warfare and deserve to be both better known and better understood. As will be seen, warfare in such terrain takes characteristic forms.

Rivers, lakes and canals appear infrequently in naval histories; though common enough in military histories, they normally feature, like estuaries or inlets of the sea, merely as obstacles to be negotiated, often in the face of an active defence.[8] It is important, therefore, to stress that waterways in the period in question were more significant as conduits than as barriers. In consequence, medieval and early-modern inland and inshore amphibious warfare was largely focused on gaining, exploiting or denying the capability to transport goods, *matériel* and troops on inland or coastal waterways. Operations to enable or prevent the crossing of rivers or other bodies of water by armies, and to capture or defend lacustrine or marshland strongholds are two types of inland and inshore amphibious operation, but more important were operations to interdict riverine traffic, or coastal traffic; to take or hold key control points along riverways or inlets; and most important were operations aimed at seaports.

---

[6] Braudel (1972), 23. Braudel uses the term 'structural realities', but Kinser (1981) shows that the more appropriate term, for much of Braudel's work and certainly for what I examine here, is 'geohistorical'; cf. Cheng (2000), 67.

[7] That is, my concern is 'not just [with] specifying particular human actions, collective or individual, but [more with] ascertaining the continuity or discontinuity among them' (Kinser [1981], 64). It is because there is continuity that it is possible to speak of characteristic forms of inland amphibious warfare.

[8] E.g., Stephenson, ed. (2003), 51–70.

Operations against seaports were particularly important, both because of the nature of maritime transportation and because so many great ports owed their significance to the river networks they accessed. Only during the seventeenth century did European naval forces begin regularly to remain outside close proximity of the shore for prolonged periods. Before then, although mariners no longer followed the ancient practice of beaching at night, ships and squadrons generally sailed along coasts as far as possible, while remaining as close to them as possible. Coasts lacking havens were thus of little interest to sailors and of course naval fleets developed from the merchantmen that sailed from ports. The shipping and expertise in its use required by amphibious operations was thus to be found 'only in regions where the sea provide[d] opportunities for harbourage, or in lands . . . washed by large and navigable rivers.'[9] When harbourages were combined with large and navigable rivers, ports resulted.

The nature of medieval and early-modern geography and topography was such, however, that only rarely could seaports be secured by pure sea-land operations. In order to capture or control a coastal port it was frequently necessary to dominate a complex of coastal and estuarine waters. Operations against ports were thus often campaigns to secure a particular coastal region. In addition, seaports were often actually situated well inland, connected to the sea by rivers and/or lagoons. Amphibious campaigns against such ports therefore often involved inland, rather than inshore, operations. Thus, efforts to take or blockade seaports are frequently difficult to distinguish from campaigns to capture or control riverports or other key points on rivers and such operations naturally share many similar characteristics.

It is necessary, then, initially to consider the place of rivers, lakes, coastal waterways and the ports they supported in the broader scheme of things and examine how they related to each other; I necessarily borrow theories and terminology from geography and urban studies.[10] Understanding the influence of geographical and topographical factors is necessary to understand why inshore and inland amphibious operations were carried out where there were (including some of the operations considered in earlier chapters) and helps to

---

[9] Chakravarti (1930), 651.
[10] See Dyer (2000), 103.

explain why they were conducted as they were. Having explored those factors, I then briefly consider the different types of inshore and inland amphibious operation and how they were conducted. I necessarily draw on a limited range of examples, sufficient to illustrate important themes, before finally drawing conclusions.

Geography

Lakes and lagoons, firths and fjords, bays, bogs, and rivers all could and did obstruct communication in the medieval and early-modern world.[11] But they did not obstruct the movement of military forces as much as might be supposed because, as we will see, pre-industrial armies were very good at crossing such watery obstacles. In any case, these quasi-maritime and fluvial features also facilitated communication. Where riverine transport was possible, it was preferred to terrestrial transport because across the world roads were rare (or non-existent) and poor in quality where they existed (China was only a limited exception). In any case, the capacity of land transport was more limited: wheeled traffic was rare in many parts of Europe and Africa (and non-existent in Central and South America) into the late sixteenth century (or beyond). Boats could carry more than mules or llamas and carry it both more cost-effectively and more expeditiously.[12] Rivers were the arteries of the medieval and early-modern world, their networks amplified by the lakes through which rivers flow and which are their sources, by parts of some wetlands, and (towards the end of this period) by canals. All these together comprise a fluvial system.

Inland waterways, however, were in turn important to a great extent because they connected to that greater corridor of commerce and communication—the sea. That connection was fundamental. Lacustrine transport might be important in and of itself on large lakes; and of course some commerce on rivers and canals took place solely between riverine ports, especially well inland. However, in practice it is rare to find riverine traffic that occurred with no

---

[11] E.g., Parker (1977), 22–3.
[12] Braudel (1972), 1: 190, 282–85; Roberts (1995), 461, 467; Parker (1977), 22; Cunliffe (2001), 39–40, 43–53, 331–6, 542–3; Leonard (1968), 10, 64, 83, 86, 119.

reference to seaports, for the influence of seaports spread far inland
through transshipment. The structures of waterborne trade in river
basins generally reflected the fact that goods, wealth and people could
ultimately have egress from that basin onto the sea. It in turn provided another, although admittedly more dangerous, means of communication. Sea voyages were more subject to delay by bad weather
than most riverine voyages or land journeys, but maritime travel was
potentially much faster than terrestrial or riverine transport and certainly could carry much greater cargoes, while it was also comparatively cheap.[13] With good reason, then, were harbourages called
roads in English (a usage that has only become uncommon in the
twentieth century). The sea was the highway of the pre-industrial
world, even though commerce clung to its coastal fringes.

Armies and their associated paraphernalia, too, were transported
more efficiently and expeditiously by water than by road, especially
'siege ordnance and supplies'.[14] Inland and inshore amphibious warfare was both more common and important in this period than it
has been since because technological innovations in the eighteenth
century and after reduced the importance of waterborne transport.
With the rise of more effective states, in Europe roads were constructed more widely and to a higher-quality standard throughout
the course of the eighteenth century; greater construction of bridges,
draining of marshes and, eventually, drawing-off of river water to
supply fresh water to urban populations, meant natural obstacles
impeded roads less; also, the reforms in artillery during the last forty
years of that century—usually associated with Jean-Baptise de
Gribeauval (1715–1789)—made artillery lighter and more easily trans-
portable and technological evolution also made wagons more manageable, durable and reliable. Hence, for a variety of reasons, armies
could move across country more quickly and efficiently. These trends
accelerated in the nineteenth century and spread across the globe
with European empires; railways and the internal combustion engine
confirmed the supremacy of terrestrial transport. But in the Middle
Ages and right up to the early eighteenth century, supply and artillery

---

[13] E.g., Braudel (1972), 1: 356–61, 576–9; Roberts (1995), 161–2, 368; Cunliffe
(2001), *passim*, esp. ch. 12.
[14] Duffy (1985), 39. And see e.g. Braudel (1972), 1: 304, 480; Duffy (1985), 29,
49; idem (1979), 161; above, pp. 125, 234, 333–4; below, 401.

trains were most efficiently shipped by water, and waterborne traffic was still a key element in the economies of most of the world's societies (outside arid zones).

The chief issues at stake in inland and inshore amphibious operations, then, were protecting friendly and disrupting hostile commercial and/or military traffic along riverine, lacustrine and coastal waterways. Very often, however, the point, or at least an integral part, of controlling such fluvial communication was controlling seaports, which were in turn also frequently the targets of military operations because of the access they provided to networks of inland waterways. This is a point to which we will return, but it is important to stress that very often ports were part, indeed economically the most important part, of fluvial systems; they were geographically and economically intertwined not only with the sea, but with rivers.

Rivers

What were the socio-economic (and thus military) implications) of 'fluvial drainage'?[15] It is of course large rivers—rivers that penetrate far inland and are consistently wide and deep—that attract the most traffic and are therefore the centres of the greatest economic activity. The Danube, Rhine, Vistula, Elbe, Seine, Loire, Garonne, Tagus and Po in Europe; the Nile and Tigris-Euphrates in the Middle East; the Volga, Don and Dnepr in western Eurasia; the Indus, Brahmaputra, Ganges, Irrawaddy, Salween, Mekong, Yellow (Huang He) and Yangtze-Kiang (Chang Jiang) in southern and eastern Asia; the St Lawrence and Mississippi in North America; the Amazon in South America—all have been corridors of commerce since ancient times, often the sites on which civilisations developed. But it is not a river's size alone that matters: the Zambezi, for example, in southern Africa, which David Livingstone hoped would open the region up to trade and settlement, is too encumbered with waterfalls, rapids and shallows for great commercial exploitation. Rivers which are not navigable from the sea can be important for regional commerce, while if they are tributaries of a larger river they can become extensions of its commercial network. Thus, the dimensions and suitability for

---

[15] Carr (1992), 17 *et passim.*

traffic of the entire fluvial system is as important as the size or navigability of its core river alone. The Nile was an avenue of trade in
ancient times, but chiefly contributed to the development of Egyptian
civilization as a source of irrigation, rather than as a conduit for
trade with the interior of Africa. Rivers smaller than the Nile are
more important than it as avenues of communication and trade
because their tributary networks are more substantial.

The riverine components of the fluvial system are both route networks and lines of force. The system's nodal points are where transshipment or portage take place, and where waterways intersect; these
points are thus critically important in strategy, logistics and operational art.[16]

That they are important reflects the interconnection between rivers
and the sea. As already suggested, it is not only because rivers unite
the interiors of continents that they have been so important in human
history; it is also because they combine continental space with maritime space. And all the contributory parts of a fluvial system are,
or can be, effectively arms of the sea, through transshipment, or
portage. They allow maritime space to extend into the bowels of the
continents.

Points at which transshipment occurs are key in riverine and associated amphibious operations. Where ships from the sea can no
longer navigate upstream, maritime commerce could come to an
end. It does not because, around that point, ports spring up at which
goods can be transferred from ocean-going ships to riverine vessels,
capable of penetrating further upstream, which may, in turn, trans-
ship goods to smaller craft again. It is only at the point that boats
cannot make progress up a river that it finally ceases to be an arm
of the sea, but the reach of the sea is mediated through the transshipment points. The precise point at which a river ceases to be
navigable from the sea can change over time: silting and shingling
drastically affect the navigability of a river, especially near its mouth;
and as sea-going ships become larger and of deeper draught, their
inland riverine range becomes more limited. In any case, the presence of gorges, swamps or other physical conditions that can impede
construction of wharfs and quays, not to mention urban develop-

---

[16] Cf. Braudel (1972), 1: 277.

ment, also affect the siting of ports, as do social and political factors. As a result, the location of transshipment ports is not crudely determined simply by the depth of a river. But the basic facts remain—that geography dictates that maritime and riverine trade can only be extended via transshipment points, which thus attract commercial and hence economic and political development and in turn become important military targets.

Where transshipment is not possible, the extension of maritime and riverine space may still be possible, through portage. Where rivers are interrupted by cataracts or rapids, making progress by boat impossible, or where the terrain produces too many bends and twists, or a river splits into too many channels or bayous (often associated with swamps), making progress difficult or slow, such obstacles may be circumvented. Where the landscape permits, vessels of certain size may be not only drawn out of the water (a common practice for maritime and riverine traffic in this period) but also hauled across land to the next clear patch of stream. Isthmuses, too, were crossed by such means from ancient times, linking inshore waterways. By portage, famously, the Vikings penetrated from Sweden, via the great rivers of western Eurasia, into the Black Sea and Mediterranean; and as we will see, by portage, too, the Cossacks and Muscovites were able to extend trade and raids into the Sea of Azov and Black Sea. However, although Corinth is an excellent example of exploitation of an isthmian portage site, riverine portage sites have rarely been subject to commercial and urban development in the same way as transshipment points.

Geography also produces other important military points on rivers, and inlets (whether of the sea or lakes). Locations at which tributaries intersect with larger streams, or where rivers join or leave lakes, are natural sites of commercial development, as the intersection of different fluvial routes is potentially also the conjunction of different regions. At narrows and shallows waterways can be forded, and bridges (whether permanent or pontoons) more easily constructed. Such sites were often contested, because both landscape and waterscape naturally funnel conflict to them.

Seaports and Estuaries

In addition, however, these sites were also often the sites of seaports, which brings us back to the sea-land interface. The zone in which riverine and maritime are conjoined is the *estuary* and estuarine ports were the most significant outlets of fluvial systems.

The very fact that critical *riverine* sites could coincide with *sea*ports reflects the fact that, '[h]istorically, most of the great ports have been *interior* ports', that is, ports 'away from the open ocean', rather than *exterior* ports, 'directly on the coast':

> Sailing vessels needed protection from the weather and a few days' difference in travel time was not important. Moreover, ships were small, and estuaries were deep enough to be no hindrance to ocean traffic. Most important, before the building of railroads and adequate roads land transport was difficult and slow, so that a seaport located as far inland as possible was at the same time a regional capital that not only provided maritime and land transport but possibly performed political, economic, and social functions as well.[17]

With the growth in ships' size (and thus their draught) and their seaworthiness in the last quarter of a millennium, the benefits of the protection from weather afforded by an interior port are now outweighed by the difficulties of access and restrictions imposed by tides.[18] But in the pre-industrial world, significant ports tended not to be sited directly on the sea.

There are exceptions. Few Mediterranean ports lie at the mouths of rivers, both because these are even more dangerous to shipping there than elsewhere, carrying, as they do, 'alluvial deposits into a sea with no tides, and because there are fewer large or navigable rivers giving access to interiors, due to 'the mountain barrier lying directly behind the Mediterranean coastline' and to the arid conditions of most of northern Africa.[19] There is thus a relative paucity of ports in general, as well as of estuarine ports; this may help to explain the relative lack of interest of historical major Near Eastern inland empires in the coastal littorals.[20]

Even 'interior ports' were not always on estuaries. The fjords on which lie Trondheim (the medieval capital of Norway), Christiania (as Oslo was known from 1624–1877), Bergen and Stavanger are deep inlets of the sea, rather than estuaries; the magnificent 'Rade

---

[17] Weigend (1958), 186.
[18] Ibid.; Weigend (1955), 242–3.
[19] Braudel (1972), 1: 317.
[20] See Revere (1957), 38–9, 41–3.

de Brest' (known as the Brest Water to early-modern Englishmen)[21] is not the product of a river estuary and the same is true of Portsmouth Harbour; similarly the inlet of the Zuider Zee on which Amsterdam lay was not really the estuary of the small River Amstel. Moulmein, a port much fought-over down the centuries, lies at the mouth of the River Salween, but is still an interior port, as it is shielded from the Bay of Bengal by Bilyugan Island. Cartagena in South America and Venice lay on lagoons.

Generally, however, ports were situated on rivers and while some exterior ports were literally at a river's mouth, most lay inland. River-based seaports fall into a further two categories.[22] First are estuarine ports, within a day's ride of the sea. Such ports, close to the rivermouths are nevertheless deliberately interior rather than exterior ports, chiefly because of the advantage of protection from the elements (noted above) or because some estuaries, as they approach the sea, form excellent anchorages in which the boundary between river and sea is frequently difficult to draw. Such estuarine ports were Bayonne, Belfast, Bristol, Cork, Dartmouth, Falmouth, Gdansk, Kingston-upon-Hull, Lisbon, Liverpool, Lorient, Lübeck, Plymouth, Rochefort, Rotterdam, Southampton, Truro and Waterford in the Old World; and New Amsterdam/New York, New Orleans, the important Mayan entrepôt of Bacalar (near the Bay of Chetumal), and the complex of ports around the Gulf of Xicalango in the New World. The greatest ports on the Arabian Sea are exterior, but early-modern Goa lay on the estuary of the River Mandavi (an important point in understanding the Portuguese attacks on it, as Malyn Newitt showed earlier in this volume).[23] All this is without counting towns that are no longer ports (and sometimes no longer even harbours) but which used to be: among them Barnstaple, Brouage, Bruges, Carmarthen, Exeter, Gloucester, Haarlem, Harfleur, Morlaix, Rye, Sandwich, Wareham and Winchelsea in France, England and the Low Countries; and Masulipatnam in India. Or Dover, which was in pre-Roman and up to early medieval times a harbour on the estuary of the river Dour, although the shape of the landscape has

---

[21] Above, ch. 10, 336.

[22] Most of the ports that follow can be found on maps 1, 2, 4 6, 8–11.

[23] Ch. 4, above, pp. 112, 118; and see Ames (1997), 401; Encyclopædia Britannica (2003), *s.v.* 'Goa'.

since changed. If it owes its enduring importance to its ideal location on the shortest routes across the Channel and between London and the great Continental cities, nevertheless it became a port in the first place because it was a protected, estuarine haven.[24]

Other river-based seaports, however, lay much farther upstream and their locations often reflected riverine geography. Glasgow is 20 miles from the Firth of the Clyde (but at least 40 from the open sea); Dordrecht is well over 30 miles from the North Sea on the Maas. London on the Thames and Nantes on the Loire are both about 35 miles from the sea. Bassein and Yangôn (Rangoon) are the two great deep-water ports of Burma, the former about 25, the latter 60 miles upstream, on the easternmost and westernmost branches of the delta of the Irrawaddy. Bremen, Antwerp and Hamburg are respectively 43, about 55 and about 65 miles from the North Sea, on the Weser, Scheldt and Elbe Rivers. Limerick and Rouen lie over 50 miles from the mouths of the Shannon and the Seine; Bordeaux lies at the end of the Gironde, the estuary of the Garonne River, 60 miles inland. Mrauk-U, chief city of the sixteenth-century Burmese kingdom of the same name, was located on the Kaladan River about 60 miles inland. Cuttack and Calcutta (Kolkata) each lie well inland on river deltas: Cuttack also some 60 miles upstream at the apex of the Mahanadi River delta; Kolkata about 96 miles upstream on the Hugli (Hooghly) River, which is in fact one of the mouths of the great Ganges River. Guangzhou (Canton) lies near the head of the Pearl River estuary (Chu Chiang K'ou), more than 90 miles inland from the South China Sea. Topping all these, Buenos Aires, on the Río de la Plata (River Plate), lies 150 miles from the Atlantic, while Quebec lies well over three hundred miles from the open sea. Most of these ports have been the subjects of military action and most have been subject of amphibious operations at least once. In every case, the access to (and egress from) fluvial systems which they provide is a big part of the reason why.

There were often smaller ports at the mouths of the rivers on which inland-seaports were located. Today, these exterior riverine ports have often (though by no means always) surpassed the inland ports but, in the period 1000–1700, Bremerhaven, Cuxhaven, Exmouth, La Pointe, Le Havre, St-Nazaire and Travemünde, to take just a

---

[24] Muddle (1934), 504–5.

few examples, were all secondary to, if not actually satellites of, Bremen, Hamburg, Exeter, Bayonne, Rouen, Nantes and Lübeck. If these were not always what geographers term outports for the ports lying upriver,[25] their capture or quarantine was still essential when the inland port was a military objective.

The location of these ports far inland sometimes reflected, again, that estuaries could create magnificent anchorages far from the open sea—the Clyde, the Elbe, the (medieval and early-modern) Scheldt in Europe and the St Lawrence and Plate in North and South America spring to mind. But some are on a river proper rather than an estuary; and often the location of such inland seaports reflected fluvial geography: riverine intersections; narrows, that can be readily bridged; and transshipment points. For example, Quebec lies at the confluence of the St. Lawrence and Saint-Charles rivers; Hamburg at the point the Elbe intersects with two of its tributaries. Medieval Dordrecht was on an island, where several channels of the Meuse intersected. Nantes is situated at the head of the estuary of the Loire River, where it is joined by the Erdre and the Sèvre rivers; but Nantes, in addition, was sited in a spot 'where the river was still easily navigable' from the sea 'and where a bridge could be constructed.' Rouen, too, 'lies in an optimal position where deep-water ships can penetrate and where the [Seine] can easily be bridged'. Rouen still received seagoing vessels into the 1930s, so probably early-modern ships could navigate the Seine above Rouen, but in practice it was the point at which transshipment occurred. Kidwelly Castle (a key English fortress in medieval West Wales) and Bordeaux were similar, save that Kidwelly's position combined the *lowest* crossing point on the River Gwendraeth *and* the farthest point it was navigable from the sea (to allow for amphibious relief of sieges). Bordeaux grew up 'at the lowest point at which the [Garonne] could be bridged', but also 'was an excellent base for navigation both to the ocean and upstream into the interior'. So it, too, like Nantes, Rouen and Kidwelly, was a transshipment point as well as a bridgeable locale.[26]

---

[25] Vigarie (1979), 472, asserts (*pace* Konvitz, 18), that 'Le Havre has never been Rouen's outport'. This may be the case, but as we will see Le Havre was nevertheless a target because it was the gateway to Rouen.

[26] Encyclopædia Britannica (2003), *s.v.* 'Quebec', 'Hamburg', 'Meuse River',

The medieval port of Sluys was the transshipment port for the cities of Bruges and Ghent. In late medieval Yucatán, the interior port-town of Chetumal enjoyed a flourishing trade, but Bacalar, which lay inland another twenty miles as the boat sails, also profited from 'a thriving commerce' because it lay on a lake where goods could be transferred from seagoing vessels (including large canoes) to the boats and smaller canoes that could go further into the hinterland.[27] Although Gloucester is not a seaport today, the city is situated at the head of the Severn Estuary, at the point where the river ceases to be tidal, and so was a point of exchange between river boats and, in antiquity and probably into the seventeenth century, by medium-sized sea-going vessels. When Calcutta was founded, in the late seventeenth century, its position was deliberately chosen partly because it was at the transshipment point on the Ganges (and partly because local water features made it easily defensible).[28] Even when their location was not determined by a transshipment zone, deep-inland ports nevertheless naturally tended to become major transshipment sites.

The tendency of seaports to be estuarine sites is very significant because it meant that amphibious operations mounted against such ports necessitated inshore operations instead of quick movements from ocean to continent; furthermore, they often had to include from the start, or very quickly embraced or even became, inland operations.

Thus far we have considered the geography of fluvial systems and how this influences the location of seaports. Fluvial geography does more, however, than affect where seaports are sited—as already suggested, in addition it greatly influences which ports become economic and political centres and thus helps to determine strategic and operational objectives. In these processes, both human and physical geography is important. The existence of riverine hinterlands whose resources could be tapped and the nature of the physical environment in and around estuaries were crucial factors in the success and failure of ports and also affected the conduct of amphibious operations near those ports or rivers.

'Nantes'; Cunliffe (2001), 52–3, 58, 50–1; Avent (1991); Kenyon (2002); Weigend (1955), 217.

[27] Harding (1995), 158. Chapman (1957), 130–1, 135; Clendinnen (1987), xii.

[28] Evans (1993), 238. Encyclopædia Britannica (2003), *s.v.* 'Calcutta'.

Hinterlands

The majority of significant ports were culmination points of significant inland waterway systems. The interchange of oceanic and riverine was the *raison d'être* for most medieval and early-modern ports on the shores of the Atlantic and Indian Oceans and the North, Baltic and China Seas: they were the route nodes where maritime and fluvial networks interlocked. Through them, maritime space was extended virtually, via fluvial systems, into continental space; and their wealth derived from their central role in mediating commercial exchange between what geographers call *organised* oceanic or maritime space, on the one hand and what might be termed organised riverine space on the other.[29] This 'organised riverine space' (*i.e.* the socio-economic system based on a fluvial system) was a port's hinterland.[30]

That is not to say that a port could *only* be successful if it accessed a hinterland worth trading with, whether economic or natural hinterland. The geography of the Mediterranean (as noted above) made it generally an exception. The 'classical port cities of Asia'—Aden, Hurmuz, Calicut, Banda Aceh, Malacca and Makassar—tended to be 'redistribution centres', rather than to 'have access to hinterlands';

---

[29] See Braudel (1972), 1:317; Cunliffe (2001), 32–33, 45; Brioist (1997), 10; Broeze (1997), 2–3; Weigend (1958), 190; and see also ibid., 185, 193; Weigend (1956), 3; and Weigend (1968), 178–9.

[30] 'Hinterland' has a variety of meanings. Whereas today it means 'the area serving and being served' by any urban area, it originally was strictly applied to ports. It retains a specific application 'in the field of port geography', but is still usually defined in terms of economic activity, especially of the types of vessels that use a port and the type of commodities shipped on them from it (which though relevant for pre-industrial ports is most applicable to 20th-cent. ports). Originally, however, 'hinterland' was often defined 'in terms of the valley of the river on which the port was located or . . . of the drainage basin of the river'—for which the term 'natural hinterland' later came to be used. Because I am using the term as a tool in analysing *ports*, in the medieval and early-modern epoch, in this essay I use 'hinterland' for a port's zone of 'economic and cultural activity' or influence within the region drained by the river(s) on which a port lies, or in its tide-water zone. See *Dictionary of Geography* (2004), *s.v.* 'hinterland'; Weigend (1956), 1–3 (at 1); van Cleef (1941), 308–9 (at 308); Eiden and Irsigler (2000), 44; Weigend (1958), 192, 194; Elliott (1969), 154, 157–60, 153; Dyer (2000), 103. To summarise (in the terms of a formulation of the geographer G. G. Weigend), a hinterland is an 'organized and developed land space which is connected [to] a port by' a fluvial system, 'and which receives ships or goods through that port': Weigend (1958), 193. Where I contrast hinterlands in this sense with hinterlands in the more standard sense, I refer to natural or economic hinterlands.

but Cairo and Alexandria had unique access to a phenomenally rich, if very long-range, economic hinterland.[31] Moreover, 'much of the ... development [of] Bombay, Colombo, and Bangkok ... was based on ... "hinterland promotional" policies in which the development of harbour facilities, inland transport and selective commodity production for export ... went hand-in-hand.' Aden, too, grew as a port because it was a good harbour close to a region with unique goods to trade, even though there were only relatively poor communications with that region, and none by water; Diu in north-eastern India, drew 'on the great contiguous, and politically common, production area of Gujarat'; and Masulipatnam briefly assumed international importance in the seventeenth and eighteenth centuries not because of its geographic or physical attributes, but rather because it was part of a wider political economy and regional economic structures; the decline of these doomed the port-city.[32] In all these cases, the hinterlands were purely socio-economic, rather than natural.

Far more often, however, ports owed their economic and political importance to the fact that they could exploit natural hinterlands. This was true globally, as a few examples will indicate.

In the first three centuries of our period (roughly 1000–1300) Palembang, at the opposite end of Sumatra to Banda Aceh, utilised the resources of a river-basin hinterland (that of the Musi River), while Guangzhou, 'the most important port of the [medieval Chinese] empire', accessed the hinterland of the Pearl River.[33] In England, Gloucester was, as noted above, a port of reasonable significance during this period and was (as we will see) to assume considerable importance in the Civil Wars of the 1640s, precisely because it 'lay at the heart of a converging web of river systems'.[34] Bristol and Hull likewise developed not only because of their intrinsic qualities as havens, but also because of their extensive hinterlands. Devon, in the south-west of England and one of that country's most famous sea-faring regions, is also worth considering. For example, despite the medieval importance of the county's northern ports (Barnstaple,

---

[31] Pearson (1991), 70.
[32] Broeze (1997), 10; Saleh Shihab (1997), 20–22; Pearson (1991), 72, and 99; Subrahmanyam (1997A), 35, 59.
[33] Manguin (2000), abstract; Andaya (1993); Clark (1995), 52.
[34] Evans (1993), 242.

Bideford and Ilfracombe) they never became as well established and important as the southern Devon ports (of which Plymouth, Dartmouth, Brixham, Teignmouth, Exmouth and Exeter were only the most prominent). A number of factors were responsible, but importantly the southern ports, especially Exeter, Dartmouth and Plymouth accessed larger, more populous and agriculturally richer hinterlands than did the northern ports—Exeter, among the largest cities in England in this period, owed its prosperity and administrative importance to its hinterland; but in consequence it was the target of William the Conqueror's campaign in 1070, of the Western Rebellion in 1549, and contested again in the English Civil War.[35]

In France, Bordeaux was from ancient times not only a base for sea-going ships but also for 'navigation . . . upstream into the interior.' Its natural hinterland is the lands washed by two significant rivers, the Garonne and the Dordogne, and drains the rich lands of the Aquitaine basin, of which it was the main port. Toulouse and Languedoc lay in the economic hinterland of Marseilles as well the natural hinterland of Bordeaux, but certainly contributed to the latter's commerce. Thus, Bordeaux's great medieval prosperity was based to a great extent on its rich riverine hinterland.[36] This also attracted hostile military action from ancient times.[37] So extensive was the hinterland of the Seine that medieval and early-modern Rouen was an outport of Paris and thus capitalised on the capital's wealth, as well as the general resources of the Seine basin.[38]

In the Americas, Xicalango, on the Gulf of Mexico, had access inland via a range of inshore and riverine routes, west, south, and northeast—and in consequence was the centre of 'five major groups of ports' that collectively constituted perhaps the most significant area for Aztec long distance trade. Only one of the ports actually lay on the sea, however and the most powerful ports lay 'inland from the coast'; they 'controlled vital trade routes' into the hinterland thanks

---

[35] Childs (1997), 286; Carr (1992), 21–2; Kowaleski (1992), 64, and 66, tables 7.1, 7.2; Youings (1992), 101. On Exeter's hinterland see below, p. 381 and n. 62.

[36] Weigend (1955), 217–19, 229, 241; Cunliffe (2001), 50–1, 515, 524; Brioist (1997), 77–8. (NB: a hinterland can be in the zones of influence of more than one port: cf. Weigend (1956), 15; Weigend (1958), 193–4; *Dictionary of Geography* (2004), s.v. 'hinterland'.)

[37] Weigend (1955), 219.

[38] Cunliffe (2001), 543; Benedict (1981), ch. 1.

to their situation on 'the great rivers which flowed down from the highlands'.[39] The Bay of Chetumal region in the Yucatán was, before *c.* 1500, a commercial centre for that whole peninsula, as the 'point of embarkation for overseas trading and for receiving goods from the hinterland', acquired via an extensive canoe-borne trade through 'bays, lagoons, rivers, lakes and marshes'.[40]

The Chetumal/Balacar hinterland thus was linked partly by coastal waters, while it must also be noted that the River Dordogne actually flows into the Gironde downstream of Bordeaux. Thus inshore waters sometimes linked different fluvial systems into one hinterland. Indeed, on a grander scale, along the French coast from the Gironde to Quiberon Bay are many shoals but sufficient stretches of sheltered waters to connect the separate Loire, Charente and Garonne/Dordogne fluvial systems. To term this a hinterland is misleading but collectively they formed, even in pre-industrial times, a discrete organised space—part riverine, part maritime.[41]

Physical Umlands

Access to hinterlands was crucial, then, for a plurality—perhaps the majority—of the world's significant ports. The examples of Bordeaux and Chetumal point, however, to the fact that access to wider fluvial systems, however, was commonly not straightforward because the approaches to great river-based seaports were often very complicated and consisted of zones of interlinked inshore and inland waters.

Geographers use the term 'umland' for an area 'contiguous to a city', which it serves, but which also is served by it, comprising a single economic and cultural unit. But an umland is also defined as 'a sphere of influence, catchment area, tributary area, or urban field.' If we use these terms in the sense of physical, rather than human, geography and bear in mind that an umland and its town have a fundamental unity, then 'physical umland' provides a good term to define these zones, within or overlapping with a port's hinterland,

---

[39] Ibid., 135–40, at 136, 138; Clendinnen (1987), 147.

[40] Chapman (1957), 130–3 at 131, 134–35.

[41] Cunliffe (2001), 51–4. For early-modern recognition of how La Rochelle, towards the southern end of this space, drew on Quiberon, at its far north, see BN, MS Fr. 3193, f. 70r: advice of Sieur de Tavanne, [1572]; Bibliothèque Mazarine, MS 259, n.f.: 'articles concernant le Comte de Montgomery', Jan. 1574.

control of which is essential if meaningful control of the port (much less its hinterland) is to be secured, and that is the term used elsewhere in this essay.[42] They are zones in which amphibious operations often occur.

Such physical umlands were typical of estuarine ports across the world. For example, state formation in medieval southern Sumatra led to the creation of a Malay polity centred on the prosperous port of Palembang, on the Musi River. But because it is almost 50 miles from the sea, at the apex of the Musi delta, control of the port of Palembang meant little without control also of the complex deltaic system through which the Musi reaches the sea, and of the vast marshy foreland through which it flows.[43] The trade of the great medieval port-cities of what today is southern France (Narbonne, Montpellier, Marseilles and Perpignan, though only in the fourteenth century or after were the last three brought under the rule of the French crown) relied on a wide range of trade goods, including products of the cities in question and fish from grounds elsewhere in the Mediterranean. However, commodities from Languedoc and Provence more generally were a pivotal part of their exports: their trade indeed relied 'upon the surrounding countryside'. Also important was salt, extracted from 'their marshy coasts' and coral, likewise derived from inshore waters. These cities' prosperity was thus, if not wholly, at least largely dependent on controlling the coastal fringe, both onshore and immediately offshore, as well as riverine access to the interior; control of the local out-ports, which were an integral part of the larger port-cities' economic base, was also essential—as it would be to any aggressor seeking to disrupt the cities' commerce or annex it for his own.[44] We have already seen that the pre-Colombian prosperity of both the Bay of Chetumal and the Gulf of Xicalango groups of ports derived from extensive hinterlands, but while the trade of the Xicalango ports took place on 'great rivers' flowing from the interior, the port-towns themselves were sited amid 'a network of rivers, lagoons, swamps and bogs'; similarly, the Chetumal region was one 'of bays, lagoons, rivers, lakes and marshes, all of which

---

[42] *Dictionary of Geography* (2004), *s.v.* 'umland'; Spelt (1958), 362, 364–5; and see van Cleef (1941), 308, 310–11; Dyer (2000), 103; Eiden and Irsigler (2000), 43–4.
[43] Andaya (1993).
[44] Abulafia (1988), 185, 198–99, 202; Abulafia (1987), 189, 191, 196.

made for extensive canoe travel'.[45] So to control the commerce of
either region an aggressor had first to come to grips with the respective fluvial systems, encompassing not only rivers and lakes but also
inshore waters.

For sixteenth-century Mrauk-U, access to the coast 'was mediated
by a complex web of deep creeks and streams' and canals; the
Kaladan fluvial system composed its physical umland.[46] Cartagena,
by the end of the sixteenth century 'one of the most important cities
in Spanish America', lies on a bay, so masked by islands that there
are only two entrances, with the city itself on a smaller bay or lagoon,
further protected by a peninsula; São Salvador da Bahía, the capital of Brazil in the seventeenth century, lay on the vast Baía de
Todos os Santos, fed by several rivers. To capture either entrepôt,
it was necessary to control the shore of the bay and its associated
waters. Similarly, Cadiz lay on a promontory at the mouth of the
River Guadalete, but its harbour—which made it significant—was a
bay formed by the river's estuary but it split into several channels
and lagoons. Taking Cadiz thus involved more than a straight sea-
land assault, and the English experiences in 1596 and 1625 reflected
this.[47]

Where the Seine finally merges into the sea, its mouth is over five
miles wide. From there to Rouen (75 miles as the river winds) constitutes one great estuarine umland, with multiple channels, islands
and shallows, all of which, as we will see complicated operations
against Rouen in 1562 and 1592. One of the most extensive umlands
was that of La Rochelle, which ranged from the ile d'Oléron in the
south to the long ile de Ré and the estuary of the Sèvre in the
north, a stretch of over 30 miles, much of it protected from Atlantic
by Oléron and Ré, encompassing the important ports of Brouage
and Rochefort (on the estuary of the Charente River) in the south
as well as La Rochelle, towards the north, united by inshore waters.
La Rochelle had a significant maritime commerce, but its shipping
in addition ranged the inland waters of the Loire basin and of the
Gironde and its hinterland (which led to conflict with the Dukes of

---

[45] Above, p. 374; Chapman (1957), 131, 136, 138.
[46] Subrahmanyam (1997B), 202–3.
[47] Grahn (1991), 169–70 (at 169), 190; Teensma, ed. (1999); Russell-Wood (1990),
208; Cunliffe (2001), 46–7; Wernham (1994), 92ff.; and see idem, above, ch. 7, pp.
205–6; Fissel, ch. 8, above, p. 243.

Aquitaine in the twelfth century and the Kings of England in the fourteenth—the rulers of Bordeaux). In particular it drew on the Charente system, which was as much La Rochelle's hinterland as Rochefort's; Rochellais mastery of the river was the springboard for Huguenot occupation of much of the Charente basin early in the third war of religion (1568–70).[48] The whole of this umland was to be contested during successive royal offensives against La Rochelle from 1570.

Finally, Antwerp throughout the early sixteenth century was the greatest port in the world, with 2,500 ships a week anchoring there or in its outports. Its status 'as the greatest commercial and financial center of the age' resulted partly from its central location in the Hapsburg composite monarchy, and partly from its geographic centrality, 'lying at the confluence of overland and maritime routes'. Antwerp's trade also, however, resulted from its export of goods and produce of the Low Countries. Some of these came from the southern provinces (what today is Belgium), accessed via the Scheldt; however, many also came from the north—accessible through the cramped inshore and inland waterways of Zealand and southern Holland. The ports of Zealand controlled Antwerp's trade. He who controlled Flushing, Middelburg, Ter Veere, and Arnemuiden (all on the island of Walcheren), Bergen op Zoom and Ter Goes could control the waters of the Scheldt and interdict most of the intra-Netherlands traffic to Antwerp from the north; even more crucially, control of just Flushing and Arnemuiden could potentially give control of the access/egress point between Antwerp and the sea. For this reason, the Italian geographer Ludovico Guicciardini considered the harbour of Arnemuiden the central point of Europe, measuring all distances to the chief ports of Christendom from it.[49] As the Eighty Years' War was to prove, to blockade Antwerp, or to lift such a blockade, fighting around the city itself was less important than fighting on the estuary of the Scheldt and the islands in it.[50]

---

[48] Cunliffe (2001), 51–2, 105, 526, 530; Mollat de Jourdin (1992), 162–3; Barbot (1889), 324; BN, CCC 24, f. 361: de Blandin to Catherine d'Médicis, 8 Sept. 1568.
[49] Parker (1977), 26; Duplessis (1997), 93; Sicking (2001), 555–6, 558, 568.
[50] See below, pp. 385–7, 389–90.

Physical Environment

The complicated approaches to ports and/or their hinterlands highlights the physical factors that shaped amphibious operations in
inshore and inland waters. Because ports owe their existence to their
location at the land-sea interface, they are significantly affected by
the physical conditions of that interface, which in turn usually affect
military, naval or combined operations against them. Ideally, ports
should have an 'easy entrance, deep water [and] a small tidal range'.
Great ports usually enjoyed all these conditions; where they were
wholly absent, ports might not be founded, while if they were, their
survival and prosperity was uncertain.[51] The absence of ports did
not necessarily mean that the commerce of the riverine system would
have no outlet: in West Africa for example, maritime and riverine
space did interlink despite the absence of good ports;[52] but in general a lack of ports was certainly a limiting factor. Thus, the environment at the land-sea (and maritime-riverine) interface was one of
the most important factors influencing port development.

Issues arising from the terrestrial side were geological and geomorphological. Geology was important because port facilities needed
open space, so that cliffs or high ground could prevent a harbour
developing into a port, while the rocky shores associated with such
geological formations might make a haven unattractive. Harbours
needed deep, sheltered waters but also easy access and where a port's
harbour declined, it was likely to follow the same fate. Whether this
happened reflected the geomorphological evolution of rivers: in particular the extent to which sediment is carried downstream to estuaries and forms into shingle, banks and bars.

Where there were poor physical conditions, ports usually did not
emerge and hinterlands did not develop, at least not in this period.
Newcastle became an important port only in the nineteenth century—although the Tyne was a major river, the region's geology
'impeded port development' at both the rivermouth and the inland
riverine sites where important ports later developed, after Victorian
engineering could construct a great industrial port to exploit the

---

[51] Weigend (1958), 185–6 (at 186); and see Russell-Wood (1990), 198.
[52] See below, pp. 395, 405.

Tyne hinterland's mineral resources.[53] Alternatively, ports might develop for economic or political reasons, but if so then political changes could doom them. Masulipatnam, the first British trading settlement (1611) on the Bay of Bengal and in the mid-seventeenth century one of the dozen largest 'urban settlements in South Asia' (and the subject of several amphibious assaults, as a prize of war in the struggles between France, Britain and the Netherlands), lay 'about half a league up river'. The rivermouth was a harbour of poor quality so that ships had to stand off while goods were transshipped to small boats. Only particular conditions in the regional political economy allowed the emergence of Masulipatnam as a first rank entrepôt and when these changed its inherent geophysical qualities were not good enough for it to survive as a port.[54] Dover was similar, albeit with a different outcome. In the early Middle Ages it suffered from both the silting up of its river, and the accumulation of a shingle bar, caused by debris falling from eroding cliffs. But if Dover had not existed, kings and cross-Channel traders and travellers would have had to invent it: it was a vital base for the control of the 'narowe see'; it was the gateway to a very rich prosperous and resource-rich economic (rather than natural) hinterland; and was on the most direct route across the Channel. Thus, sufficient work was carried out to ensure its survival—but it took a combination of unique commercial, political and economic factors to overcome nature's negatives (and today's harbour is mostly artificial).[55]

In most cases, accumulation of silt or shingle, reducing the draught of ships that could ride in a haven, and creating sandbanks, shoals and bars, was a death-knell to a port and could lead to a rival port supplanting it. The large volumes of sediment washed down the Seine never blocked Rouen, but caused problems further downstream in the estuary. The medieval ports of Harfleur and Honfleur (major ports and venues for several fifteenth-century English expeditionary forces) were replaced by Havre-de-grâce—a deliberate sixteenth-century creation to get round the silt problem; Harfleur was ultimately left inland, while Le Havre (as it is known today) required substantial works in the nineteenth century to keep it open. Like Harfleur,

[53] Elliott (1969), 154–5.
[54] Subrahmanyam (1997A), 34, 38, 59, and (1997B), 208.
[55] Anon. (1436), 2; Muddle (1934), esp. 505.

Wareham, Rye and Winchelsea, three of early-medieval England's greatest ports, all today lie some miles *inland* because the estuaries on which they lie have completely filled in with silt and shingle; the same felt befell Brouage, near La Rochelle, an important port as late as the sixteenth century.[56]

Gloucester never rivalled nearby Bristol because, before Gloucester could be reached from the sea, 'currents, shallows [and] ever changing sand banks of the upper estuary' all had to be safely navigated, as did tidal shifts, whereas Bristol had only the latter to deter ships from sea.[57] Carmarthen, on the Tywi, became the chief Anglo-Norman military and political centre in west Wales partly because it was navigable from the sea—so too were the important garrisons of Kidwelly and Laugharne, on the Gwendraeth and Taf, both of which flow into the Twyi estuary; Kidwelly was in addition a medium-sized port into the sixteenth century. But the silting of the Gwendraeth and of the Twyi estuary more generally reduced Kidwelly to insignificance and greatly reduced Carmarthen's importance.[58] Similarly, the Indian city of Khambhat (Cambay), on the estuary of the Mahi River, was a thriving port in late thirteenth century, when it caught Marco Polo's attention; it was still of some importance in the early sixteenth century, when the Portuguese seized it and used it as a base; but silting eventually made it insignificant as a port.[59] Bayonne, likewise, in the thirteenth century was an important source of ships for English navies, but its maritime trade began to wane in the fourteenth century—partly due to wider political and economic factors but its decline was exacerbated in the fifteenth century 'when the harbour approaches began to be obstructed by sandbars and silting.'[60] The silting of the Dee estuary in the sixteenth century caused the decline of Chester as a port; Liverpool replaced it as England's most important north-western port. Seville was the premier Spanish port of the sixteenth century, but longshore drift gradually accumulated into a bar that closed off the estuary of the Guadalquivir River;

---

[56] See Curry & Hughes, eds (1994), 39, 67, 170. 188; Encyclopædia Britannica (2003), *s.v.* 'Le Havre'; Cunliffe (2001), 26, 58; Brioist (1997), 57; Broughton (1978), chs 1, 4; van Rolleghem (1969).
[57] Evans (1993), 235–36, 238.
[58] Kenyon (2002), 3; Avent (1991).
[59] Above, p. 109; Encyclopædia Britannica (2003), *s.v.* 'Gujarat'.
[60] Rose (2000), 144–5; Cunliffe (2001), 536.

by the end of the seventeenth century Seville 'had lost its economic might' and been supplanted by Cadiz. The Charente, in the Middle Ages and sixteenth century a commercially important fluvial system, linked by coastal waters with La Rochelle and the Loire estuary, today is 'a miserable stream so badly silted that it is barely fit for canoeing.' The gradual encumberment of the southern shore of the wester Scheldt eventually cut off the maritime access of Sluys (which had become the out-port of Bruges after it lost its maritime access).[61]

To consider Devon again, although Teignmouth enjoyed considerable maritime prosperity in the early fourteenth century it never achieved enduring importance because of the bar at the mouth of the Teign; its merchant fleet became limited to smaller vessels engaged in local commerce. Totnes on the Dart was so sizeable a port in medieval times that the twelfth-century 'historian' Geoffrey of Monmouth identified it as the entry port of Brutus (the mythical Trojan founder and eponym of Britain), of the invading armies of the Roman generals-cum-emperors Vespasian and Constantine, and the legendary kings Ambrosius, Uther and Arthur. Silting prevented access by seagoing ships to Totnes from the seventeenth century on, but Dartmouth, closer to the mouth, was untroubled in this period by sandbanks and it throve. At the mouth of the river Exe lies the port of Exmouth, but in medieval and early-modern times Exeter, ten miles upstream, was the chief port of the Exe, the hinterland of which Exeter dominated. Although it was no longer navigable from the sea from the fourteenth century on, maritime access was restored by the construction of a canal in the 1560s and in the sixteenth century Exeter had 'massive wharfs', but the canal was inadequate for modern shipping.[62]

Teignmouth's decline was also due to complex currents and eddies in the approaches to the port, which highlights the fact that the action of the sea, as well as the condition of the estuary or harbour, also affected ports and estuarine approaches. Reefs, shoals and tidal conditions were often crucial: for example, another important reason why southern Devon ports outdid their northern counterparts

---

[61] Palliser (1992), 3. Brioist (1997), 9–10, 62; Cunliffe (2001), 46–7; Konvitz (1978), 18, 105.
[62] Carr (1992), 20; Kowaleski (1992), 62, 66–7; Childs (1997), 286–8, table 3; Gidlow (2004), 210; Grant (1992), 130; Youings (1992), 99–100.

was the county's 'relatively inhospitable north coast', with reefs and
tide rips and overfalls common along the northern (Bristol Channel)
coast, whereas along the southern (English Channel) coast, the estuaries were broader and gentler, tidal races, rips and overfalls were
less of a problem and reefs uncommon. The Eddystone Rocks, a
(notorious) exception, are sufficiently distant from the Tamar estuary and Plymouth not to damage that port's status.[63] Dangerously
strong surf is another strong negative for a would-be port, especially
when combined with a bar; this was to prove an important factor
for Europeans trying to establish trade, often by force, in Africa,
where established ports were fewer.[64]

All these terrestrial, maritime and riverine physical factors influenced
port and consequently hinterland development but they were of
course also potentially limiting factors for military commanders, especially tactically and logistically. It is essential, then, for studies of
amphibious operations to take into account the environment in physical umlands, and inshore and inland waterways more generally.

Geography: Conclusions

Rivers provided the primary means of conducting commerce within
all but desertous regions. Furthermore, because they also ultimately
connect to the sea, they could become extensions of maritime space,
further extending the economic potential of fluvial systems. As a
result, maritime amphibious operations could also extend into inland
amphibious operations. Because fluvial systems were routes, operations were more likely to be aimed at controlling access to the potential for trade and transportation they offered, than at simply seizing
a crossing point over them. The locations from which they could be
controlled were river narrows; the intersections of tributaries with
core rivers, or rivers with lakes; transshipment and portage zones;
and of course ports—both internal (solely riverine or lacustrine) ports
and seaports.

Seaports are key nodal points on maritime routes but because, in
this period, most large ports were riverine they were also the points
through which maritime space extends inland. Because estuaries allow

---

[63] Carr (1992), 21–4 at 23; also Kowaleski (1992), 64 and Youings (1992), 101.
[64] E.g., Hair (1997), 8.

access to hinterlands, amphibious forces attacking a coast could attempt to take advantage of the riverine system to which estuaries give access. Likewise, an estuary forms a point of egress *from* the hinterland and may thus provide bases for military and naval forces; this may, again, make the estuary a target for hostile action, as well as necessitating its defence against such action. Equally, because ports were not just harbours, but also often sites of industry and political power, and controlled geographic choke points and riverine (and terrestrial) trade routes, ports were bound to be targets for assault; however assaults in such cases frequently would be obliged to take place in (not just across) inshore waters and in inland—estuarine—waters.

Economically and socially it is difficult to distinguish clearly between the maritime space on which the port lies, and the inland riverine space (with associated lakes and canals) in which the port culminates (or begins). As we have seen, very often the reason for a port's location, even its very existence, is that it accesses *both* oceanic space *and* continental space, and allows the former to incorporate the latter, at least in hinterlands. Geographically, too, as we have seen, oceanic space gives way to continental space gradually and commonly through an interim zone, because very often access to hinterlands is not through one great waterway but rather through a network of waterways—not by one great riverine artery but a network of veins, as it were: the physical umland. All this means that, in order to control the commercial potential of a port (whether one is seeking to blockade it or not), or to acquire it by conquest, an aggressor typically had to engage with the complex of coastal land- and water-formations of which ports typically were a part—and not infrequently had to engage, furthermore, with the fluvial systems that comprised a port's commercial network.

Inshore, Estuarine and Riverine Operations against Seaports

Because ports were situated where amphibious operations were geographically more likely to take place, those operations frequently focused on ports. But those operations were commonly inshore and/or inland amphibious operations, as opposed to the classic 'land-sea interface' amphibious operation.

In modern warfare, amphibious landings aimed at capturing a port have been either undertaken close to the objective, whose capture

(as in the Operation Torch landings in North Africa in 1942) therefore becomes an integral part of the assault landing process; or at
some distance from the objective, whose capture becomes immediately the objective for a land campaign conducted by ground forces,
with perhaps some support from naval bombardment (as in the
Cotentin Peninsula in 1944 and the Falklands in 1982, aimed at
Cherbourg and Port Stanley respectively). In medieval and early-
modern warfare, however, ports were usually captured only after
prolonged efforts, but efforts made by *combined*, rather than ground,
forces, and requiring substantial interweaving of waterborne and land-
based elements. Thus medieval and early-modern practice falls between
modern practices.

   This reflects various geographic and technological developments.
Dredging and draining has often greatly simplified the sea- and landscape around ports, and modern ports are more often exterior than
in the past, so that direct assault has been more feasible in the last
hundred years. Urban sprawl means that many ports which once
occupied only part of the shore of a haven, now occupy most or all
of it (so that what today might be a direct assault would in the past
have been a landing removed from the objective). Then, too, direct
assault on a city was a desperate business for medieval and early-
modern amphibious forces, lacking the bombardment capacity of
their twentieth-century successors. In any case, as we have seen, ports
were often located well inland and/or might be accessible only
through a complex physical umland.

   Medieval or early-modern armies generally had to be landed on
shores of havens, for only thus could their necessary supplies be
landed; and although naturally they tended to be landed in the road-
steads—or near the mouths of the rivers—on which lay the ports
they were intended to capture, nevertheless they needed to control
the whole of that haven, or estuary, along with the associated waterways, in order to effect that capture. Achieving this control required
sometimes lengthy and always complicated operations in physical
umlands. Because 'land' and 'sea' literally blurred into each other
(with shallow and shoaled waters close to shore, lagoons, tidal creeks,
fens that might or might not flood in wet years, other marshlands,
and so forth to take into account), distinctions between 'military' and
'naval' operations blurred as well in such campaigns, which were
intrinsically combined operations.

Operations on the Seaward Side of Estuaries and Umlands

Initial control of rivermouths was essential and this led to operations against ports at rivermouths—sometimes exterior ports despite their estuarine location—but often the aim of such operations was not really the rivermouth itself. Rather, it was the great port that lay upstream (and, implicitly, the hinterland on which it drew). For example, Travemünde was attacked by Christian III in 1536 not because of its own economic importance but because capturing it obstructed Lübeck's access to the sea.[65] Fighting in 1562–63, between the French crown and its rebellious Protestant subjects (the Huguenots) aided by an English continent, revolved around Le Havre—not because of its importance as a seaport *per se*, though the French were concerned that it might become a potential debouchment point for future English invasions, as Boulogne and Calais (neither of them interior ports) had been; but the main point about controlling Le Havre was that it was the outlet for the Seine. It thus could block the entire trade of Paris. Indeed, while Rouen was an objective because of its importance as a centre of production and regional administration and because it was a great commercial city, it was also important because it was an outport of Paris.[66] Sluys was the target of a famous, prolonged siege by the Duke of Parma in 1587, chiefly because its capture would extend Spanish control of the south bank of the Scheldt estuary (the physical umland of Antwerp), but also because Sluys gave, by canals, egress to the commerce of Bruges and Ghent; the Dutch and their English allies were jubilant over its recapture in 1603 because it restored their control over both shores of the Scheldt.[67]

Indeed, Antwerp's access to the sea is so complex that, in the early part of the Eighty Years' War, controlling its physical umland was perhaps the major issue at stake in campaigns. Antwerp itself, the greatest port-entrepôt in the Atlantic world, did not join the *opstand* against Spain in 1572, but Flushing had been one of the first towns to join the uprising. The prolonged to-and-fro fighting that followed on Walcheren and South Beveland, with the rebels and

---

[65] Sicking, ch. 3, above, p. 85.
[66] Below, p. 389.
[67] See Williams (1590), 49; below, p. 393; Israel (1995), 260; Maland (1980), 32.

their English and Huguenot allies taking Ter Veere and twice attempting and failing to capture Ter Goes has received much attention from historians of the early-modern English art of war, partly because it is fully and memorably described (in English) by two of the participants in the fighting.[68] Rebel control of all the northern shore of the west Scheldt and of Antwerp's access to the east Scheldt was postponed by a decisive Spanish counter-attack, across lands inundated by the sea, which secured (for the moment) Ter Goes, but the Dutch retained control of the Wester Scheldt and thus still stymied Antwerp's maritime trade. In 1573 the Spanish tried to open access to Antwerp, but desperate combat on the confined and shallow waters between Middleburg, Beveland and the Flanders shore ended in a Dutch victory.[69] The control thus secured over the west mouth of the Scheldt was never lost, but that was not simply due to this one victory. The Scheldt umland more generally was still up for grabs and this shaped the Dutch Revolt in the next three years. The successful siege of Middelburg (to the north of Flushing) by the Prince of Orange's forces in 1574 was undertaken with Antwerp (to the south-east) in mind: taking Middelburg gave them uncontested control over Walcheren and it was this that was the key to their control over the Scheldt, which was preserved through the capture of Middelburg and a concurrent second victory between riverine forces in the estuary. Meanwhile, Zierikzee dominated the eastern Scheldt as Flushing did the west; it consequently became the focus of the main Spanish campaign of the summer of 1575 and Zierikzee's eventual capitulation in July 1576 was thought at the time to be a decisive blow in the war.[70]

The mutiny of almost the entire Spanish army changed the nature of the war; Antwerp joined the rebellion and for the next seven years the focus of operations was mostly in the southern Low Countries, but the steady northward advance of Spanish forces brought Antwerp under siege in 1584–85. Operating from the landward side of the umland (which was in Dutch hands), they only needed to cut Antwerp's

---

[68] See Williams (1618); and ASC MS 129, ff. 13–14: narrative of Walter Morgan, also in Caldecott-Baird, ed. (1976), 90–4.

[69] BN, MS Fr. 16127, f. 114r: Mondoucet to Charles IX, 25 Sept. 1572. ASC MS 129, ff. 23–4: Morgan's narrative; Caldecott-Baird, ed. (1976), 122–6.

[70] Caldecott-Baird (1976), 161–6; van Vliet (1997), 166–7; van Loo (1997), 177; Parker (1977), 164, 167–8.

access to it, not to the sea (see below). Having reconquered Antwerp, however, they gained only in prestige, not trade, because total Dutch control of the Scheldt still blockaded the once-mighty entrepôt entirely. The siege of Sluys in 1587 (noted above) was the first Spanish step towards regaining control of Antwerp's physical umland. In the Armada year, 1588, Parma was occupied by the siege of Bergen op Zoom. Its fall would clear parts of the northern and eastern shores of the Scheldt estuary, a necessary preliminary for the attacks on Beveland and Walcheren that would reopen the Scheldt. However, Bergen held out and this was the high-water mark of the Spanish war effort, both in the Scheldt and in the Netherlands more generally.[71]

Only in 1584–85 was Antwerp actually besieged, yet throughout 1572–76 and 1584–88 it was the real subject of many of the operations carried out by Dutch and Spanish forces. In all of them, waterborne military capacity was an essential supplement to ground forces.

Similarly, in 1570, 1572–73, 1577 and 1626–28 operations by the French crown against the Protestant stronghold of La Rochelle and counter-operations by the Huguenots and their English allies were not directed simply against the fortifications of La Rochelle itself, but rather ranged over the whole of its extensive physical umland.[72] For La Rochelle to be contained or captured, it had to be cut off from its umland and the several fluvial systems to which that gave access. In 1570, the royalists sent a squadron of galleys to capture Brouage and capture German ships carrying munitions to the Protestant army, but an English and Huguenot force drove it off. It then attempted to blockade the Charente, but was defeated again.[73] In 1572–73, when La Rochelle successfully resisted one of the greatest sieges of the sixteenth century, the royal generals were well aware of the need to occupy the small islands around La Rochelle and the île de Ré and especially the easternmost tip of Ré itself (connected with the mainland at low tide by a thin spit of land)—enabling them to command the narrow waters through which any relief fleet from

---

[71] Wernham (1984), ch. 2.
[72] Described on p. 376.
[73] Barbot (1889), 372–3; d'Augbigné (1618), 326; BSHPF, MS 371, f. 64: 16th-cent. life of the Baron de La Garde; see Wedgwood (1962), 51.

England would have to travel.[74] However, although they repelled an attempt by an Anglo-Huguenot fleet to break through to La Rochelle, they were unable to prevent single ships from England and Holland frequently slipping through to replenish the city and the royal siege ended in disaster.

In 1577, the Catholic forces (starting from a weaker position) were unable to besiege La Rochelle directly, but took steps to strengthen the crown's position *vis-à-vis* the city. A concentrated effort resulted in the capture of Brouage, but English intervention from the sea helped to ensure that an expedition sent against the ile de Ré was defeated.[75] This meant that when, in 1627–28 the Huguenot stronghold was attacked again, this time successfully, the crown's forces had to engage in sustained fighting on Ré before it was finally occupied. Even then, only after Cardinal Richelieu had a huge dike built across La Rochelle's harbour mouth did the city fall; but this celebrated engineering work in La Rochelle's immediate vicinity could be constructed only because of royal control of the islands and coasts of its physical umland.[76]

Only in 1573 and 1628 was the city of La Rochelle itself besieged. Operations had first to be mounted against the outer ports, islands, estuaries of its umland; only, that is, after working from the exterior of the umland in, cutting La Rochelle off from its means of access to maritime and riverine space, could the city itself be besieged.

Other Estuarine and Umland Operations

When an inland seaport is attacked from its landward side then operations can target it directly. Yet though operations of this sort may less frequently centre on a port-city's rivermouth outliers or physical umland, they will still often need to be combined operations. To be sure, Exeter was the subject of famous sieges in 1070, 1549 and 1645, while Exmouth was normally left relatively quiet; but this reflected the besieging forces' ability to cut Exeter's narrow link to

---

[74] BN, MS Fr. 3193, f. 70v: de Tavannes treatise; MS Fr. 3324, ff. 64, 74: Sr. de Losses to *Amiral* de Villars, 20 Mar. 1573 and duc de Montpensier to Villars, 24 Apr. 1573.
[75] See van Rolleghem (1969), 9; Trim (2002), 138.
[76] Wedgwood (1962), 52–3; and see Fissel, above, ch. 8, p. 244.

the sea. In contrast, large rivers, especially in estuarine zones, might support relief convoys; in such cases, if friendly forces occupied a port downstream from an inland seaport, then, even after hostile troops had notionally occupied all the land around it, it could still receive reinforcements and supplies. Amphibious operations then focused on maintaining, or cutting, the fragile fluvial lifeline.

At Rouen in 1562, for example, after the city was cut off by Catholic troops in September, the English and Huguenot forces in Le Havre determined to send reinforcements. This was a large force, of about a thousand English and Huguenot soldiers, carried in six vessels. Between Le Havre and Rouen, however, there were many narrows and shallows, and the Catholic forces had deliberately been disposed to prevent any riverine relief. At Caudebec, about 25 miles (as the crow flies) inland from Le Havre, where there were significant sand banks, the Seine 'had been greatly impeded by the placement of obstacles and there were strong land defences as well' and here the relief force was ambushed. One of the ships 'stroke on the sands' and there were significant casualties on the other craft. About half the relief force got through to Rouen, but it was not enough to save the city, which fell 17 days later.[77] The Protestant commanders had concluded that 'the passage betwixt Newe Haven [Le Havre] and Roan [was] so garded at Cauldebeck and other places & the navigation of the ryver so dystroyed' that no troops could 'come from Newhaven to Roan onlesse they be strong ynough to marche by lande.' The Catholic thus achieved their aim, though the fact that a Huguenot galley escaped the city's fall and made it past Caudebec showed that perhaps, had things been better managed, more troops could have been pushed through to Rouen.[78]

When the Duke of Parma besieged Antwerp in 1584–85, the dispositions of his troops included several strong defensive positions on the Scheldt River; these did some damage to the regular convoys sent from the north, but not enough to stop them. For example, on 7 October 1584, as a member of Antwerp's garrison reported, 'about two hundred vessels came hither from Holland and Zealand, laden

---

[77] PRO, SP 70/43, f. 53r: Smith to Throckmorton, 17 Oct. 1562; Birch (1840); Trim (1999B), 79–80, 82–6 (at 83).

[78] PRO, SP 70/43, f. 186v: Throckmorton to Elizabeth I, 30 Oct. 1563; SP 70/43, f. 196r: Warwick to Privy Council, 30/31 Oct. 1562.

with victuals', unscathed save for one ship damaged by the Spanish artillery. The next month, a company of English troops made it from Flushing despite being told 'that passage to Antwerp was stopped'; one soldier reported how at one point 'twenty cannons on each side the water played upon us, but hurt none of the ships', save one damaged.[79]

Eventually Parma increased the size and number of batteries and obstacles on the Scheldt, to considerable effect. Ultimately the river was barred entirely by dikes and the famous siege-bridge (which had piles 75 feet long and may have been the model for Richelieu's dike at La Rochelle). Kouwensteyn Dike was the scene of fierce battles between the Dutch and Spanish in late April and early May 1585. The Dutch coordinated attacks by both troops and ships, both from the estuary and from the city. But the Spanish defences of the dike and bridge were ultimately too strong and too much in depth: several times Dutch forces seized some Spanish positions, but the Spanish were always able to bring up more troops from reserve positions, resulting in multiple defeats for the increasingly desperate Dutch forces.[80] The successful maintenance of the Kouwensteyn dike and the siege-bridge ultimately doomed Antwerp.

In 1644, during the English Civil War, the main Parliamentary army under the Earl of Essex occupied the ports of Lostwithiel and Fowey after being outmanoeuvred by Charles I. Essex hoped to be supplied by the Parliamentary fleet, which had mastery of the sea. The fleet had shortly before played a crucial role in the successful defence of Lyme Regis. But it was an exterior port. The estuary of the Fowey River was small and could be easily commanded by the Cavalier army's artillery, while Fowey's harbour was in any case probably too small for the volume of shipping necessary to supply the army. Essex and his army were forced to capitulate to the king.[81]

Alternatively, a seaport that is estuarine but not deep inland may be attacked fairly directly from the sea, even directly by naval units, although because such an operation still involves estuarine combat, it is inherently likely to be amphibious, because the confined nature of the waters will likely produce a conjuncture of naval and mili-

---

[79] *CSPF 1584–85*, 87, 151: Bizarri to Walsingham, 12 Oct., and Morys to same, 23 Nov., 1584.

[80] E.g., ibid., 436–9, 470, 477–81: reports from Antwerp; Parker (1990), 82n; Trim (2002), 159–60.

[81] Wedgwood (1958), 359–61; and see ch. 8, above, p. 252.

tary force. In 1667, for example, the Dutch attacked the English ports of Chatham and Sheerness, on the Medway Estuary, to strike at the Royal Navy's bases there. There was a boom and a fort covering the mouth of the Medway at Sheerness, but the fort lacked its full complement of guns and was quickly destroyed. An English squadron had meanwhile advanced to the mouth of the Medway and anchored, covering the boom, as did batteries of artillery set up on shore. Their combined weight of fire sank five ships and the Dutch (like their forebears at Kouwensteyn) were halted. But overnight they found an alternative deep-water channel and used this to get close enough to the shore batteries to put them out of action, which enabled them to break through the boom. They then advanced on Chatham; while the line-of-battleships anchored and engaged artillery on shore, marines were landed, who burned naval stores, and fireships were sent into the anchorage with devastating effect. On the ebb tide the Dutch sailed away having recorded a famous victory.[82]

Interior ports that were not inland ports can lie near the seaward side of their physical umland. Even they, however, very often would not fall to a sea-land amphibious assault alone. Operations against such ports frequently still needed to encompass the umland, for otherwise the port could still receive supplies from its hinterland, which might also provide a base for a force that could break the siege of a port. The capture of such a port might thus require an inshore/inland amphibious operation. The Dutch expedition mounted for an attack in 1624 on São Salvador da Bahía, the capital of Brazil (Portuguese, but Portugal and its empire was under Spanish rule from the late-sixteenth to the mid-seventeenth centuries) consisted of between 25 and 35 ships, carrying 1,700 soldiers. The campaign that followed (and which resulted in the capture of São Salvador) involved both combats at sea between Dutch and Spanish ships, assault landings on the fortifications around the Baía de Todos os Santos (on which the city lies), manoeuvres and combats on land between the disembarked Dutch soldiers and their Iberian counterparts and finally a threatened assault on Salvador's landward defences.[83] Two separate fleets were sent to recover Salvador da Bahía in 1625, one Spanish,

---

[82] Smith (1928), 36–8; Stapleton, ch. 10, above, pp. 319, 322.
[83] Teensma, ed. (1999), 1:42–60: anon. Portuguese narrative (c. 1625) of the loss of Salvador.

of almost 40 ships and one Portuguese of 23 ships, but carrying three and regiments of infantry respectively. The Iberians recaptured São Salvador, using bombardment both from the fleet and from siege works constructed by the disembarked troops.[84] Even when an operation against a port of this kind was carried out successfully straight from the sea, it might be a preliminary to riverine exploitation. Sir Francis Drake's successful attack on Cartagena in 1586, described in chapter seven, was partly to capture the treasure gathered there prior to despatch on the *flota* via Havana back to Spain. However, the *flota* could have been attacked elsewhere; Cartagena was also attacked in order to give access to its hinterland.[85]

Tactical and Operational Lessons

Early-modern battleships could stand up to (and even beat) shore batteries, *if* they were close. The success of shore batteries must not be taken for granted; they need to be well sited and sufficient weight of shot deployed to deal with ships that may, depending on the size of the waterway, be large enough to deploy considerable guns themselves, especially if, as on the second day at the Medway, the ships come in close. This highlights the need for waterborne forces to work closely with ground forces which may mean coming literally close to shore. Coordinated bombardment by land-based artillery and by naval artillery was an important factor in the successful siege of Honfleur, on the estuary of the Seine, by Henri IV's forces in 1590. If the ships had not come well into the estuary of the Seine, in order to get close enough for the bombardment, the port may well not have fallen.[86] In contrast, though, after the Duke of Parma relieved Henri's siege of Rouen in April 1592, he marched on Caudebec, to attempt to reopen the river to Le Havre. Caudebec was only weakly fortified by Protestant forces, but it had the support of a flotilla of Dutch ships on the river. These suffered badly, however, from the fire of Parma's artillery and eventually withdrew further downstream.[87] This failure of waterborne artillery is in con-

---

[84] *Ed. cit.*, 1: 94–101: anon. Portuguese narrative (*c.* 1625) of the recapture of Salvador.
[85] Above, p. 186.
[86] BSHPF, MS 753, n.f.: Philippe DuPlessis-Mornay to Henri IV, 6 Feb. 1590.
[87] Lloyd, (1973), 184.

trast to events at Caudebec and the Medway, but compares to initial Spanish failures downstream from Antwerp. In this case, it may have been because, whereas sea-going ships could deploy guns that were larger and thus longer-ranged, enabling them to stand off out of range of shore-based artillery, riverine craft mounted smaller guns and so could were close enough to suffer from Parma's land-based artillery. Similar conditions may have obtained at Fowey. The optimum weight of land-based artillery will therefore vary from situation to situation, depending on what type of enemy vessels might be able to engage them. In addition, riverine obstacles do not in and of themselves block rivers, especially to forces that are both land-based and water-based. They must be stoutly defended, as Caudebec and Kouwensteyn were in 1562 and 1585 and as the Medway boom was not in 1667.

Defensive, as well as offensive, operations can be amphibious. Sluys held out against the concentrated power of the Spanish army of Flanders as long as it did partly because its defence (like that of Malta in 1565) involved a conjunction of force, even the use of almost literal amphibians: infantrymen turned swimmers (a skill rare among early-modern people).[88] Equally, however, the Spanish defence against Anglo-Dutch relief attempts was also amphibious, effectively combining ground and waterborne forces on Sluys's link to the Scheldt estuary as a guard against relief.[89]

Finally, it seems clear that estuary ports are particularly vulnerable to combined operations. This chimes in with contemporaries' views: for example, 1583–84, the veterans of amphibious operations who were making detailed plans for the Spanish Armada identified London as 'the only sensible target for a Spanish invasion', both because it was the capital and because it *was easily accessible from the sea*'.[90] The nature of estuaries is such that, even today, it is better not to attack them with naval forces only; or, if attacking estuarine ports from the land, with ground forces only. The amphibious dimension brings a better chance of success.

---

[88] Williams (1590), 48–9; Guilmartin, ch. 6, above, pp. 150, 173.
[89] Digges (1590), 2.
[90] Martin & Parker (1988), 109, emphasis mine.

Port Operations: Conclusions

Operations against seaports were very likely to involve operations on estuaries and other inshore waters, and on coastal lagoons, lakes and marshy areas, in which close cooperation between land-based and waterborne forces was essential and the distinctions between them blurred. Of course, blockade could effectively exert control over a port, but blockade from the sea was only realistically possible from the eighteenth century on, after advances in maritime technology produced ships capable of maintaining station for weeks (or months) on end—and after, too, the intellectual and cultural shift had been made in thinking to allow navies to maintain such blockades.[91] In the period 1000–1700, blockade from the sea was not a realistic option. Thus, aggressors had to occupy rivermouths, which in the case of large rivers meant occupying both shores of an estuary. This, again, still often required inshore and riverine operations, while, unlike purely maritime blockade, it also allowed for a military or amphibious response—which, in turn, would produce fighting in the constrained, shoal-ridden, shallow waters and soft lands of estuaries, deltas, rivers and coastal lakes and swamps.

Campaigns of this type are less frequent in modern amphibious warfare, but are not extinct. In 1944, the Allied capture of Antwerp, with its port facilities intact did not make its capacity available to the desperately troubled Allied logistical effort—that only became possible after the lengthy campaign to clear Antwerp's riverine access, which necessitated inshore and estuarine operations of a different character to the assault landings that characterized most combined operations of World War II and after.[92] Had Allied commanders, at several levels, been less focused on ports and assault landings and been more historically aware they would have realized that the capture of many major ports is only complete when most or all the associated waterways are under control—and that to achieve this requires a certain type of cooperative operation. Coalition operations in southern Iraq in 2003 necessitated not merely the seizure of Al-Faw (effectively achieved by assault from the sea on the first day of the campaign) but also control of the Shatt al-Arab, Lake Al-Hammar,

---

[91] Cf. pp. 428, 449, below.
[92] See sources cited in n. 53, on p. 18, above.

and the Tigris-Euphrates marshes. On this occasion there was, it seems, a greater realization that amphibious warfare is not simply a matter of ship to shore assaults—power must often be projected not only from sea to land, but on the waterways that flow inland as well. The study of inshore, riverine and estuarine warfare is thus of both historical interest and practical importance for current practitioners of amphibious warfare.

Other Inshore and Inland Operations Launched from the Sea

Amphibious operations were sometimes launched from the sea into river networks without being aimed at capturing a seaport. Louis IX crusaded in the Nile delta in the mid-thirteenth century because 'control of Egypt' had been identified as 'crucial to the recovery and protection of the Holy Land'; but control of Egypt necessitated control of Cairo (a riverport), which could only be reached by moving up the Nile so that, in turn, Cairo could only be taken if the Nile delta were controlled—hence the amphibious operation described in chapter two.[93] Early European expeditions to West Africa (in the mid- to late sixteenth century) found that imposing themselves by force on the coastlines of Guinea and the Cameroons availed little, because commerce was controlled by the native tribes that controlled the canoe-based navigation on the region's rivers. As a result, initial European assaults to break this control were not just coastal raids in the literal sense—coastal trading venues were often mere landing places and, even when more than that, were not important political centres and therefore raids tended to be attempted penetrations of the riverine systems on which the desired land-sea trade depended, rather than attacks on the actual littoral.[94]

In a military campaign undertaken as part of an amphibious strategy or grand strategy, waged along a littoral, with inland campaigning only incursions, never really far from the sea, control of the inlets and inshore waters was vital. It was not enough simply to leave garrisons, as on land—their purpose may be simply to *hold* places,

---

[93] Bennett, ch. 2, above, pp. 62–3ff.
[94] See Hakluyt (1958), 32–3; Austen and Derrick (1999) ch. 2; Hair (1997), 7–9; Austen (1983), 3–6.

whereas often the aim with guarding waterways is to prevent enemy traffic on them so the guarding force is in a dynamic situation, unlike (some) stationary garrisons. Equally, the movement of supplies (or troops; or even ships) 'at sea' very often meant through inshore waters, sometimes straying onto lagoons and rivers. This meant that when waging a 'coastal' campaign, or even mounting a campaign from a port, it was necessary to identify, capture and hold crucial points on coasts that control the waterways on which they are sited.

At the strategic level, Dover's significance as a control point for the 'narowe sea' (*i.e.*, the English Channel) was recognised in the first half of the fifteenth century and the significance of the Scilly Isles for the western approaches to England before its end.[95] Hurmuz, Banda Aceh and Malacca all similarly lay 'on or near choke points'—the 'strategic nodal points [of early-modern] Asia's maritime space'.[96] Copenhagen's importance (and status as a military target) derived from its location on The Sound, the narrow waterway linking the Baltic and North Seas.

At the operational and tactical level, key points were often insular. For example, during Henry III's war in France in the 1240s he used his fleet mostly in essentially naval or maritime activities, such as simple transport of troops, or sweeps to protect his sea lines of communication from French naval attack. But in addition he ordered the Warden of the Channel Islands to capture Mont St Michel (a celebrated island-fortress, west of Avranches) if possible, because control of it would provide greater security in the inshore waters around the Breton and Norman coast. He also had English troops occupy the isles of Ré and Oléron.[97] Carisbrooke Castle had a permanent garrison, even in the sixteenth and seventeenth centuries, when the permanent English military establishment was very small, because it dominated the Isle of Wight. The potential of islands to control inshore waterways motivated the English defence of Ré in 1577 and unsuccessful attempt to capture it in 1627; and the occupation of the islands in the Firth of Forth by the Marquess of Hamilton in 1639 (during the Bishops' Wars): the strategic vision was sound, but

---

[95] ASC MS 103: anon. treatise; Anon. (1436); AAE, Mémoires et Documents Angleterre 98, f. 5: Henry VII to Charles VIII, 3 Mar. 1486.

[96] Pearson (1991), 70; Saleh Shihab (1997), 17.

[97] Weir (1972), esp. 85–89; cf. Rose (2000), 143.

the administration was wretched and the operation came to naught.[98] Islands could also be valuable bases, inasmuch as they were more readily defensible than terrestrial bases. Thus, at an early stage of Sir John Norreys's 1591 campaign in Brittany, he captured the island of St Brieuc, which provided the base for an advance inland.[99]

Of course, it was not only islands that were valuable 'control points'. In the late fifteenth and early sixteenth centuries, the Venetians garrisoned and heavily fortified Negropont, Modon and Lepanto, in Greece, and deployed strong amphibious forces to relieve Turkish sieges of them, because each was located at a vital choke point on an important coastal route.[100] During Norreys's 1594 campaign in Brittany (aimed at securing Brest and its harbour from the Spanish), even after he had concluded operations at Morlaix and Quimper securing his flanks for the final operation against Brest, he still kept a watch on St-Malo and Conquet in order that the inshore traffic along the north coast (part of his army's line of supply) be maintained.[101] Penzance, Falmouth, Portland and Hurst Castle were also sites of permanent garrisons in the sixteenth and seventeenth centuries, partly to protect the regions but also to ensure that the sheltered waters they commanded were not used by privateers and pirates.[102]

Sometimes interdiction of coastal traffic could not be done conveniently from one point and had to be undertaken against a zone. The Catholic effort against La Rochelle in 1572–73 included attempts to block coastal traffic from Brouage (within the city's physical umland) and the Loire hinterland, to the north but still linked by inshore waters.[103] Alternatively, control of inshore waterways was not only to prevent the movement of hostile forces, or attacks on coastal lines of communication; it could also facilitate movement of friendly forces. In 1600, when the Dutch Republic launched its greatest offensive in 32 years of war, against the North Sea coast of Flanders, there were

---

[98] Young & Lawford (1970), appendix; Fissel, above, ch. 8, pp. 244, 247.
[99] Hammer, ed. (2003), 241: Robert Cecil to Hatton, 31 Aug. 1591; PRO, SP 78/25, ff. 318r–21r: Norreys to Burghley, 16 Sept. 1591.
[100] Pepper (1993).
[101] OBL, MS St Amand 6, f. 15r: Henri IV of France to Norreys, 26 Oct. 1594.
[102] Young & Lawford (1970), appendix.
[103] BN, MS Fr. 3193, f. 70r: Sieur de Tavannes, treatise, [1572]; MS Fr. 4765, f. 27v: duc de Nevers, journal, 2 Apr. 1573.

no operational reasons (such as achieving tactical surprise or outflanking a line of defences) to ferry the Dutch army to Flanders, rather than marching it south—but it was much easier and quicker to move it by water than land [figure 13].[104]

Inland Operations

On the whole, riverine amphibious operations were intended to exploit or control rivers as conduits. There obviously was some use of rivers (and inlets, lakes and bogs) for defensive purposes, but on the whole they were more important for communication. Much defensive use was actually a form of control, to prevent the passage on these important arteries of men, munitions, goods and gold; but there were also many attempts to ensure that movement was smooth, or to regulate that flow. This involved maintaining and using specialist fleets, but also the identification of key points at which rivers could be crossed, or otherwise controlled.

Riverine and Lacustrine Fleets

The fleets maintained on fluvial systems were sometimes simple extensions of navies, but more often they were specialist forces, both in construction and in personnel. These fleets could very easily operate on inshore waters as well, sometimes even on the high seas, but it was their ability to operate on rivers which distinguished them, and so all such fleets are considered here. The predominant type of vessel in such riverine fleets, from Central America, to West Africa, Latin Christendom, the Eurasian steppes, and southern Asia, was small, shallow-draught and oar-driven: examples ranged from galleys to canoes; across the globe, such craft were ideally suited to operating in the cramped, shallow waters of rivers, lakes, lagoons, canals and swamps. Such fleets were best crewed by specialists—neither the ships nor the personnel of high seas fleets could be simply transferred to inland waters and have good prospects of success. Moreover, inland fleets always operated in close proximity to shore, to which the omnipresent rowers could easily debark to fight, and they gen-

---

[104] See Orlers (1610), 148–53.

erally cooperated with ground forces. These fleets, then, were intrinsically amphibious, not naval, forces.

Traditionally, any military campaigns in regions dominated by large rivers and/or lakes (or even marshland) were assumed to require not only troops but also vessels. An ancient Indian text characterises a navy as one of the integral elements 'of a complete army' while one Indian king 'laid it down that boats should be utilised for military purposes when the theatre of hostilities abounded in water' and in 1071 William the Conqueror used a fleet on the Fens (a network of marshland and rivers, sometimes inundated by the nearby North Sea) to capture Ely from rebels.[105] 'Sizeable fleets' were regularly used on 'Italian rivers and lakes in conjunction with armies' in the fourteenth and fifteenth centuries; so integral were these riverine and lacustrine squadrons that the leading historian of medieval Italian warfare calls them an 'essential feature of land warfare'—but 'one which has been almost entirely ignored by military historians.'[106] Similarly the fifteenth-century Hungarian King Matthias Corvinus maintained a river fleet whose vessels, armed with early cannon, provided support of ground forces; this fleet 'played an important role' in his military successes.[107]

The French navy maintained a small squadron of galleys on the Seine, based at Rouen; one of the first actions of the Huguenot insurgents in May 1562 was to seize these galleys.[108] When planning the (doomed) relief of Rouen, the first point a senior English officer made was that transports alone would not work, they had to be escorted by galleys or shallow-draft sailing ships (or preferably both).[109] Fleets of galleys, sailing vessels and combinations thereof were integral parts of the Spanish and Dutch forces in the Eighty Years' War; they were important throughout the war, but especially in Holland and Zealand in the 1570s. These fleets ranged from large sea-going vessels, to much smaller oared craft, right down to large rowing boats and barges (the latter used simply for transport) [figures 8, 13, 14] and operated in a variety of conditions: from the relatively open waters of the Zuider Zee and Scheldt, to the lakes of north Holland,

---

[105] Chakravarti (1930), 647. Bennett, ch. 2, above, p. 53.
[106] Mallett (1974), 172.
[107] Rázsó (1982), 135.
[108] *CSPF 1562*, 45: Saull to [Clough], 23 May 1562.
[109] Ibid., 335: Killigrew to William Cecil, 1 Oct. 1562.

to the waters (part lake, part estuary, part swamp) around Dordrecht and South Beveland, moving between them along rivers and canals. In the campaigns around Haarlem and Alkmaar in 1572–3 and Leiden in 1574, both sides used combined forces: the Spanish to besiege the cities, the Dutch to pass through supplies and reinforcements to them and attempt to defeat the Spanish, while the Spanish countered. On the face of it land campaigns, these in fact were quintessentially amphibious. A more-or-less straight naval battle on the Haarlemmermeer in 1573 (almost the only Spanish victory on inland waterways in all the Eighty Years' War) was the decisive event in the long drawn out siege of Haarlem; freebooters from Zeeland, who had come via inshore and inland waterways, were an important part of the 'fleet of about 150 flat-bottomed vessels' that rescued Leiden in 1574; but more generally the distinctions between ground and waterborne forces broke down almost entirely. Rivers, bogs, canals and lakes were integral parts of the terrain and therefore riverboats were essential, troops had to be able to take to the water, and the crews of vessels had frequently to fight on shore—then, during the winter, when the fluvial features froze, Dutch arquebusiers on skates became the ultimate military amphibians.[110] That the Dutch Revolt survived immense Spanish pressure in its early years was in no small part due to the 'the rebels being crafts masters of [the] arte' of handling small craft in the waters between land and sea 'thorowe lone tyme spente in the experience therof' and their ability to integrate this mastery of inshore and inland waters into their land campaigns.[111]

In Japan, fleets mostly operated on coastal waters, however, in the 1570s, Japanese pirate-lords challenged the 'land-based regional hegemonies', using the *atakebune*, which pioneered vessel-based firearms and ironclad hull defences (flame-proof, rather than shot-proof); these pirate fleets also operated occasionally on lakes and estuaries, includ-

---

[110] See ASC MS 129, ff. 21–2, 27–8, 33–4: narrative of Walter Morgan; BN, CCC 337, pp. 9–10: de Mondoucet to Henri III, 11 Mar. 1573; BN, MS Fr. 16127, f. 131r: idem, 5 Sept. 1573; GAL CR 10, Magistrates of Leiden to the Governor, Nov. 1573; GAL CR 51: 'Instructie eñ Eeds voorde vrijbuijters in Leijdens', 5 June 1574; van Vliet (1997), 166; and also ibid., 153, 155–6, 162, 166–7; Caldecott-Baird (1976), 114–21, 133–8; van Loo (1997), 176–7; and *CSPF 1585–86*, 328–9.

[111] ASC MS 129, f. 37r: narrative of Walter Morgan. And see BN MS Fr. 16127, f. 131r: Mondoucet to Henri III, 5 Sept. 1573.

ing a famous battle in the mouth of the Kitsu River.[112] Meanwhile, throughout the sixteenth and seventeenth centuries the Ottoman Turks regularly preferred river transport, whenever possible, to move both artillery and associated ammunition, and the vast amounts of wheat, flour and barley necessary to support their unusually large (and cavalry-heavy) armies. Hence, they directed their campaigns up river valleys where possible. The importance of river transport in the Ottoman conduct of operations is reflected in the Turks' maintaining a fleet on the Danube which in the late seventeenth century totalled fifty-two ships, manned by a total of over four thousand crew and soldiers.[113] Eventually, however, their opponents beat them at their own game. 'The conquest of Turkish Hungary from 1683 to 1700 was only achieved thanks to a flotilla of river galleys and the intensive use of boats for transport.'[114]

Shallow-draught oar-driven vessels were commonly used on the great steppes and around the Black and Azov Seas. The Cossacks of the Don and Dnepr River basins used rowing boats that could be portaged around rapids and shoals—vessels with flat bottoms and no keels that could operate in shallower waters than Ottoman galleys. Their use of such vessels frustrated a Turkish campaign against them in 1614–15, and was, indeed, such an irritant to the soldiers and officials of the Sublime Porte that in 1620, when a large Cossack raiding party was captured, the men were burned alive in their boats. The use by the Turks of vessels basically copied from the Cossacks was a factor in the reassertion of Ottoman power around Azov in the 1630s. Muscovy, too, deployed special shallow-draught flotillas on the Don, against the Turks in Azov, and against the Khanate of the Crimea from the 1640s on.[115]

Many parts of Africa and southern Asia were dominated by thick forest in which no roads existed, so that transportation of goods, or of course of armies, could only take place on rivers, or along the coast, utilising the shallow, relatively protected inshore waters. In an invasion of such regions, it was a necessity to have a fleet of some

---

[112] See Shapinsky (2005) (I am obliged to Mark Fissel for this reference).
[113] Murphey (1999), 72, 100, 235; Duffy (1979), 199–200. And see also Murphey (1999) 70, 85–89, 93–99, 230–31.
[114] Meyer (2000), 100.
[115] Black (2002), 194, 172; Finkel (1992), 466; Braudel (1972), 1: 191–2.

kind to operate in conjunction with ground forces (if, indeed, a clear
distinction existed between such riverine forces and ground troops).
But such a fleet did not have to include ocean-going ships—it might
be better off without.[116]

Europeans were to find themselves constantly on the back foot
when dealing with the riverine, lacustrine and inshore fleets of India,
Southeast Asia and West Africa, even though riverine fleets were
common back in Europe. Perhaps it was because when they accessed
the rivers that flowed into the Indian Ocean and Bay of Bengal they
did so on large ships, capable of making the long voyage from
Portugal, the Netherlands and England. Perhaps, too, the success the
Portuguese, Dutch and English enjoyed against Asian exterior ports
with the great *naus* and galleons of Europe inculcated a mind set
that *these* were the decisive weapon in conflicts with Asian (and
African) peoples. But, as Jeremy Black argues, the large big-gun carrying warships 'had only limited value in the important inshore, estuarine, deltaic and riverine waters of the world', especially when
fighting local forces well adapted to those conditions.[117]

Riverine and inshore fleets were well established in Asia. When
an early sixteenth-century ruler of Bengal invaded Assam, which
could only be penetrated along its great rivers, his army's operations
were based around the manoeuvres of his fleet; he was opposed, in
turn, by Assamese forces that also operated in both elements.[118] The
kingdom of Mrauk-U, in what today is the Arakan region of Burma,
derived much of its wealth from trading the goods of the Kaladan
hinterland to the principalities of what today are India and Malaysia.
However, it also derived much wealth from raiding for slaves along
the coastal waters to its east and thence into Assam and Bengal,
along the region's great rivers.[119] Bengal suffered particularly badly
at the hands of these raiders, who, as a European traveller described,
'in light galleys ... entered the numerous arms and branches of the
Ganges, [and] ravaged ... Lower Bengal ... often penetrating forty
or fifty leagues up the country'.[120] To counter this the Nawab of

---

[116] This was the case in the Baltic, where Sweden had a high seas navy distinct
from its inshore fleet, which was intended to cooperate with the army in landings,
and estuarine and riverine operations: see ch. 5, above.
[117] Black (2002), 172.
[118] Chakravarti (1930), 654–5.
[119] Subrahmanyam (1997B), 208, 210–11, 216, 226, 246–7.
[120] Ibid., 213, 232.

Bengal put together a fleet of armed galleys intended for river combat, in which the early medieval Bengali principalities had traditionally been accomplished as part of their conflicts.[121] The Arakanese did have some deep-water ships, which they used for raids directly across the Bay of Bengal, but shallow-draught craft made up the bulk of the waterborne forces of the kings of Mrauk-U, because their power depended on 'control of [the Kaladan] river system and its resources'.[122] The same was true of the kings of Palembang.[123]

The capture of Malacca by the Portuguese in 1511, which owed much to their fleets of powerful *naus*, discussed by Malyn Newitt, did not end the resistance of the Sultan of Malacca. This was, as Black points out, because the 'heavily gunned Portuguese warships, with their deep draught and reliance on sails, were vulnerable to shallower draught oared boats' in certain areas along the African, Indian and Indonesian coasts. The Sultan of Malacca was able to exploit this to continue hostilities.[124] The Portuguese practice of amphibious warfare revolved around use of heavily-armed warships and therefore almost always took place only at the land-sea interface, or at the maritime edge of estuaries. Their attempts to expand into Mrauk-U in 1518 failed because their ships were unable to access the capital from the sea; a standard Portuguese account of the lands to the east of India even declared that Burma 'does not have any sea-port', though, as we have seen, this was not the case. After Arakanese raiders carried out destructive raids on Portuguese settlements in the 1610s, the expedition sent against Mrauk-U in 1615 ended in disaster. Further raids in 1643 simply had to be suffered.[125] What the indigenous forces did well was to mix medium-sized sailing ships, still capable of navigating into the hinterland, with swarms (literally hundreds) of small, oared craft, often equipped with firearms.[126] Portuguese attempts to access the Musi River hinterland in Sumatra also failed, after their attack on Palembang was defeated by a mix of landward fortifications and riverine forces.[127] Similarly,

---

[121] Chakravarti (1930), 654.
[122] Subrahmanyam (1997B), 252 and see 216, 220, 227–8, 236, 239.
[123] See ibid., 252; Andaya (1993).
[124] Black (2002), 64, 171–2 (at 171).
[125] Newitt, ch. 4, above, pp. 116–18, 121; Subrahmanyam (1997B), 205–6, 210, 227–8.
[126] Subrahmanyam (1997B), 220, 239.
[127] Andaya (1993), 69.

Portuguese attempts to expand inland from the Indian Ocean littoral of eastern Africa persistently failed, even when advances were
made along the rivers. Portuguese mastery of the littoral, itself stem-
ming from mastery of oceanic-based amphibious warfare, did not
translate into mastery of inland waterways, or even of the inshore
waters in parts of East Africa.[128] This was partly because of a lack
of vessels that could deal with specific riverine circumstances in the
backcountry. They knew how to construct such craft, having, in the
very early days of Indian conquest, constructed oared boats specifically
to be used on rivers, to disrupt the Calicut pepper trade.[129] But this
was an exception. Perhaps success in projecting power from the high
seas onto the coasts had been so extraordinary, it limited operational
understanding of what was required to project power inland.
Contrariwise, the fact that the Portuguese were so utterly reliant on
sea-based amphibious warfare meant that when they were mastered
at sea (by the Dutch in the 1620s), it was disastrous.[130] They lacked
a capacity to defy the Dutch as indigenous peoples defied them,
from inland waterways.

However, the Dutch did only a little better in Malaya and Sumatra
after taking Malacca from the Portuguese in 1641 and Palembang
from its inhabitants in 1659. In the 1630s their ships had successfully been able to negotiate the Kaladan as far as Mrauk-U itself,
despite the presence of the Arakanese river fleet. But in Sumatra
Dutch attempts to penetrate from the eastern coast inland on the
great rivers met with failure: 'European weaponry . . . had little effect
on the success or failure of campaigns in the interior. The cannonades and blockades that had been fairly effective in besieging downstream settlements were useless, for boats were always vulnerable to
hidden enemy attack from the jungle curtain and it was not easy to
engage the enemy in battle on land [in the] thick rain forest'.[131]

Meanwhile, just as the Portuguese were stymied in Malaya and
Burma in the 1510s, so the Spanish conquest of the Aztec kingdom
in the 1520s did not lead immediately to the invasion of the Yucatán,
and its final conquest was delayed, partly because of the Mayans'
ferocity in battle but partly because Spanish ships, with their bat-

---

[128] Newitt (1998); idem, ch. 4, above, p. 118; and see Pearson (1998), ch. 3.
[129] Albuquerque (1990), 117 (I owe this reference to Malyn Newitt).
[130] Newitt, ch. 4, above, pp. 117–21; Disney (1986), 87.
[131] Subrahmanyam (1997B), 211, 219–20 (at 220), 239; Andaya (1993), 68–9,
133–4 (at 134).

teries of cannon, were of limited value in the shallow waters, reefs and treacherous currents typical of Yucatán's coasts, or in its complicated swampy riverine systems. Mayan canoes could be large enough to be a threat to smaller Spanish ships, yet remain more manoeuvrable, and able to access shallower waters. Parties of warriors roamed the inshore and inland waters of Central America on canoes, raiding enemy outposts, even carrying out long-range raids on other Spanish colonies, all in defiance of Spanish strength at sea.[132]

The Duala people of the Cameroons controlled the riverine trade of their part of West Africa up to the late nineteenth century because the Wouri, Kwa Kwa and other rivers were navigable from the sea 'for only about 150 kilometres . . . in a territory of almost 500,000 square kilometres.' Even in this area, riverine conditions were more suitable for the Duala's fleets of canoes than European ocean-going ships; the latter's prima facie superiority was not so great in practice as to provide a decisive advantage and so the Europeans did not 'push their zones of contact' even 'to the limits of riverine navigability', much less beyond.[133]

However, what has too often been overlooked is that Western Europeans, who after all were used to conducting riverine operations in their own countries, did adapt abroad and waged amphibious warfare to great effect. If the Mayans defied the Spanish from canoes, the Aztecs' story was rather different. They probably regarded the lake which surrounded their capital city of Tenochtitlán (modern-day Mexico City) as a safeguard—as Cortés noted, the 'great city' lay 'a distance of two leagues, from any side from which you enter'.[134] But Cortés realized that the lake permitted movement, as well as preventing it, and he deployed ships and boats to attack the Aztecs successfully. He had vessels constructed modelled on the *bergantine*, a Mediterranean smaller derivative of the war galley, a vessel with ten to twelve banks of oars rowed with two men to an oar and four to a bench, and deployed these on Lake Texcoco.[135] As Mark

[132] Chapman (1957), 131, 135; Clendinnen (1987), 5–7, 11–12, 15–18, 23.
[133] Above, p. 395; Austen (1983), 3, 7.
[134] Quoted in Chapman (1957), 119.
[135] Leonard (1968), 140, 142, 145–6 (I am indebted to John Guilmartin for the observation that Cortés's vessels were not brigantines, but *bergantines* and a description of them).

Fissel showed in chapter eight, the English made a virtue out of
necessity in Ireland, using rivers not only to transport men and *matériel*
but also as the basis for offensive actions against Irish fortified positions that defied ground forces alone. This mastery of riverine and
lacustrine logistics and tactics was an important element in the successful English colonisation of Ireland. It also led to specialised flotillas
of riverine and lacustrine vessels for use in cooperation with the
army. Fissel highlights the emphasis placed on 'cots' and galleys. To
some extent, the English in Ireland were drawing on the existing
pattern of many vessels in the Highlands, the Isles and northern
Ireland. But this ability to adapt to local conditions won the English
their first empire: in the Celtic west and north of the British Isles.[136]
Meanwhile, English privateers took 'small oared pre-fabricated raiding vessels with them to assist with operations in the inshore waters
of the Caribbean'. Such vessels did not appear in lists of ships sent
on expeditions, because these focus on what were later to become
known as line-of-battleships, but they were there and essential for
operating in a region where reefs are common.[137] As we have seen,
the Dutch may have endured reverses, but did take Palembang and
reach Mrauk-U, which had been beyond the Portuguese, while the
Muscovites successfully adapted Cossack vessels to project power into
the Sea of Azov and Black Sea littorals.

Crossings[138]

River lines were, of course, sometimes used as defensive barriers.
The Counts of Flanders used the Scheldt thus in their wars with the
Holy Roman Emperor over Valenciennes in 1006–7 and 1054; Philip
VI attempted to hold the Somme against Edward III in 1346 but
was thwarted by the English assault crossing at the ford of Blanche-
taque.[139] Edward I of England held the line of the Severn in 1265,
as part of an overall offensive strategy: by holding Gloucester, he

---

[136] In ch. 8, above, *passim*. Black (2002), 172. For the Celtic parts of the British
Isles as England's first colony see, e.g., Ohlmeyer (1998).

[137] Black (2002), 172.

[138] See Brummett (2001) for a sustained (and unorthodox) reflection on military
river crossings.

[139] Verbruggen (1997), 324. Nicolle (2000).

prevented Simon de Montfort and his army from crossing the Severn. In Wales, they suffered from inadequate supplies and were isolated from de Montfort's allies, allowing Edward to defeat the rebel armies in detail, ending the Barons' Revolt.[140]

Rivers, however, were crossed more readily than some might imagine and therefore were not great barriers. True, the Rhine was a border in Caesar's time—but not during the Roman Empire, or for that matter the early Holy Roman Empire. Charlemagne's empire spanned it. The Netherlands always spanned it and still does. Even in ancient times, well-organised armies, like the Assyrians', had been able to cross rivers with relative ease (even having pontoon trains as part of their armies).[141] Not only rivers could be crossed by armies: the Menai Straits, between Wales and Anglesey, was bridged by a bridge of boats constructed by Edward I in 1282, as part of his campaign that year in northern Wales.[142]

That achievement, though it speaks volumes for medieval capabilities, was probably something of a rarity. However, from the beginning of the sixteenth century great rivers were regularly crossed by even large armies. Spanish armies during the Eighty Years' and Thirty Years' Wars were accustomed to both building and removing bridges 'inexpensively and quickly', usually (though not always) bridges of boats.[143] From the early seventeenth century, European armies incorporated pontoon trains as a matter of course, along with artillery trains, and regularly crossed rivers. The Evangelical Union's army that campaigned against Jülich in 1610 had such a train and thereby campaigned across a series of rivers.[144] The main Parliamentary army under the Earl of Essex during the English Civil War 'possessed a large and well equipped' pontoon train.[145] Operational exigency led to it being stationed from 1642 to 1644 at Gloucester, at the head of the Severn estuary. Sir William Waller moved it a short

---

[140] Verbruggen (1997), 337; Encyclopædia Britannica (2003), s.v. 'Montfort, Simon de, Earl of Leicester'.
[141] Keegan (1993), 169–71.
[142] Verbruggen (1997), 343.
[143] Parker (1990), 82.
[144] See BN, MS Fr. 654, ff. 39v–43v: Simon Stevin, treatise, [1611?]; Trim (1999A), 348n.
[145] Evans (1993), 232.

distance downstream in March 1643, using the bridge of boats to make 'one of the most boldly implemented encircling manoeuvres . . . in the whole Civil War', destroying a Welsh Royalist army in the battle of Higham. The Royalists, too, had pontoon trains, and Waller, a month after Higham, deliberately launched a combined operation, from land and river, to capture Tewkesbury, in order not only to capture its bridge across the Avon, but also to capture Prince Maurice's bridge of boats deployed there to cross the Severn; the captured boats were redeployed downstream to Gloucester. But that autumn the Parliamentary pontoon train was transferred upstream from Gloucester, to form a new bridge of boats at Tewkesbury as part of Essex's successful relief of besieged Gloucester—one of the turning-points of the war. Cromwell in 1651 won the last battle of the civil wars, at Worcester, by outflanking Charles II's army using two pontoon bridges.[146] The Ottoman Turks had to cope with a great number of 'major rivers and their tributary systems' whenever campaigning in Hungary or across its western and northern borders but fording or bridging rivers and streams generally only delayed progress, rather than halting it, because the Ottomans were masters of such crossings, not least with pontoon trains, which also formed an integral part of their armies.[147]

But to be able to cross waterways it was necessary to have control of the waterway. Henry III in 1242 was attempting to recapture lands he believed to be his on the other side of the River Charente, which was the then current border of his lands with those of the King of France. He had to secure a crossing of the Charente, which a contemporary chronicler described as 'deep and unfordable'; only two bridges crossed it, and it was essential that Henry secure these before his campaign could proceed, and to this end he used his naval forces, sending a number of galleys, strongly manned with soldiers (mostly crossbowmen), deep upriver, to defend one of these key bridges.[148]

---

[146] Ibid., 240–2.
[147] Murphey (1999), xv, 24, 67–9 (at 69), 73.
[148] Weir (1972), 91–2.

Riverine Control Points

This need for control of a river highlights the fact that, just as traffic in inshore waters could be facilitated or prevented from key control or choke points, so too on fluvial systems. Of course, inshore and inland waterways were not only used by military traffic. They were also used by regular commercial traffic—and in this period armies regularly relied on such trade, so normal commercial traffic often had a direct relevance to military supply, even beyond the more modern concern of attacking an enemy economy. Even when armies did not arrange for the passage of supplies, river ports could often supply sufficient victuals for a sizeable force, simply from what was there. In consequence, access to and control of deltaic, riverine and canaline systems absolutely underpinned operational art and strategy, in a way true of railways for late nineteenth- and early twentieth-century generals but perhaps nothing else.

Thus, Cortés, on his march to Tenochtitlan in 1519 was following a map of the province of Acalan, which was interwoven by a network of rivers. On approaching the powerful river-port of Itzamkanac, 'hungry and destitute on the march', his army received a wealth of foodstuffs, drawn from the Acalans and transported thither by canoes. Largely because of the experiences of Cortés, the Spanish commander Montejo planned in 1529 to use the region as his base for an offensive on the Yucatán; however because Acalan's trade, based on the interconnection of riverine and coastal traffic, had collapsed under Spanish rule, Itzamkanac was judged no longer able adequately to supply military operations.[149] The nature of the terrain of early-modern Ulster, 'compelled [the English] armies to resort to river transportation, especially when they hauled artillery and wagons.'[150] Frederick Hendrik of Nassau's great breakthrough against the Spanish in 1632, during the Thirty Years' War, was directed along the Maas River valley, not least because it allowed for easier supply of the army.[151]

Again, however, to use waterways for commerce, or for supply, or for movement of troops, necessitated having control. Control of

---

[149] Chapman (1957), 143–4.
[150] Fissel, ch. 8, above, p. 234.
[151] Israel (1980), 486.

castles or other strong points along a river, or inlet, was typically vital not for bridging purposes, but to prevent (or to impose!) interdiction of lines of communication. In the eleventh century, after Muslim conquerors inflicted defeats on the Jats, of north-western India, the Jats retreated to islands in the Indus and its tributaries. But the Muslims would not allow them to retain possession of such a crucial spot; a fleet of 1400 boats was built in Multan, which dealt the Jats a heavy defeat.[152] Hernán Cortés on his march to Honduras in 1524 took pains to carry out a series of executions in Iztamkanac, hoping to overawe the locals and so to avoid insurrection on his lines of communication.[153] The rivers, canals, and lakes of the northern Netherlands carried a flourishing trade in the late sixteenth and the seventeenth centuries, a trade that extended into north-west Germany and of course the southern Netherlands, which from the 1570s on were under Spanish control, whereas the north had become the Dutch Republic. 'So substantial was [the] transfer of foodstuffs along the inland waterways of the Low Countries and Westphalia, that from an early stage in the Dutch revolt' these waterways were of crucial strategic significance. From very early on in the Eighty Years' War they faced repeated closure. The Prince of Orange and the States of Holland closed all waterborne traffic between rebel towns and loyalist towns in the early 1570s. In the 1580s, the States General then in Brussels 'endeavoured intermittently to halt trade by river, canal and overland with the Walloon towns.'[154] After the loss of Antwerp, not only was the Scheldt permanently blockaded, but also all trade on the great rivers was embargoed beyond certain points. The effect was to cause Parma's troops 'considerable hardship'. Other Protestant princes also interdicted Spanish trade where possible: in 1585, for example, the Duke of Bouillon, whose castle at Sedan was on the Meuse, refused to allow a convoy carrying 'a great preparation of grayn and other victell . . . to be sent down the ryver . . . for the Prince of Parma's army'. In the 1590s and first years of the seventeenth century, the States General resorted again several times to closing the rivers, but only for short times, 'so as to inconvenience the Spanish forces' during particular campaigns.[155]

---

[152] Chakravarti (1930), 657.
[153] Chapman (1957), 143.
[154] Israel (1980), 461–2.
[155] Bruce, ed. (1844), 53–4: Burgley to Leicester, 16 Jan. 1585/6; Israel (1980), 462, 463.

Dutch concern about control of the Roer River (and the Rhine) was the major cause of the campaign against Jülich in 1610, even though an armistice with Spain (for twelve years) had only just agreed the year before.[156]

After the end of the Twelve Years' truce in 1621, there was for a further fifteen years more regular resort to closure of the inland waterways to the 'passage of foodstuffs and certain materials beyond Dutch territory', in order, again, to impede 'Spanish or imperial armies in the field'.[157] In pursuance of the Dutch Republic's policy of closing the rivers to trade with the Spanish Netherlands and Germany, a garrison was maintained at Zutphen, and on several occasions forces were deployed to the Ems and Weser; of course, all the while the Scheldt was blockaded not only by the fleet hovering at Flushing but also by fortifications both there and at Middleburg, Ter Veere, Bergen op Zoom and Zierikzee.[158] Their Habsburg enemies, for their part, developed Kaiserswerth (on the Rhine between Düsseldorf and Duisberg) into a major fortress, because from it the Dutch Rhine trade could be cut; and in 1634 the Spanish 'sought to cut off the Dutch garrison at Maastricht by establishing fortifications blocking the Maas in and around Stevensweert'.[159] In 1614, they had refused to yield up the recently taken German city of Wesel, as the Dutch were demanding, because (as one English observer rightly noted), 'The Spaniards gain great benefit by command of the rivers Rhine and Lippe.'[160]

The Ottomans likewise deliberately sited major fortresses to guard the junction of major rivers, along which their lines of supply flowed.[161] A river did not have to have a port to be capable of being exploited by waterborne forces, and so although there were, for example, no important ports in this period on or near the mouth of the River Tyne in northern England (as noted earlier), nevertheless it was the site of one of the few permanent garrisons in seventeenth-century England.[162] Reading, west of London, during the English Civil War was fought over both because it controlled passage across a river (it

---

[156] Trim (1999A), 337–8, 348n.
[157] Israel (1980), 461, 464–90.
[158] Ibid., 470, 482–3.
[159] Trim (1999A), 351; Israel (1980), 486.
[160] HL, MS EL 1599: 'Whether it bee probable [. . .] that the Spaniards will render the towne of Wesell', 1614.
[161] Murphey (1999), 100.
[162] Young & Lawford (1970), appendix; Elliott (1969), 154.

had a bridge, and was an important road junction) and passage along
a river, for it was also a point of transshipment between different
types of riverine carrier.[163]

Final Thoughts

Inland and inshore amphibious warfare was more important between
1000 and 1700 than ever since. Geographical considerations affected
strategy and operational art, as well as the tactical management of
combat. The very location of many campaigns was determined by
factors that had little do with military skill, or indeed human
influence—by where rivers flowed and whether they intersected with
advantageous anchorages. One does not with to be too determinis-
tic about this, for we have seen that human as well as physical factors influence whether a port grows and becomes prosperous or not—
economy and society may be as influential as geography in this
respect. However, the tendency in all pre-industrial societies was for
trade to follow rivers, so that patterns of communications (and therefore of settlement more generally) to a great extent were determined,
in this period, by factors over which humans had only limited
influence. And of course most ports were located at geographically
advantageous sites. Thus, the influence of geography, especially on
amphibious warfare, must not be underestimated. When Christian
III attacked Travemünde in 1535 and when European traders fought
river battles on the Musi in Sumatra they were, as they probably
felt, acting for strategic, political or economic reasons—but at a
fundamental level, the location of these campaigns was decided by
geography.

Operational studies must give detailed consideration to patterns of
fluvial drainage. This is true in general, but is particularly true when
considering pre-industrial warfare, for the reasons already noted. In
the period covered by this volume the positions of canals, lakes, bogs
and rivers affected the movement of troops and supplies—affected
even the very places supplies could be obtained, or the types of supplies that might be obtained at them. Nor was it only location that

---

[163] See Griffin (1996).

mattered; the conditions of these water features were also important. Thus, in assessing past campaigns it is necessary to be aware not only of where lagoons, lakes, bayous, channels, rivers, canals and swamps were located, but also of how their dimensions differed at different times of the year and in different climatic conditions. Also of importance was how these component parts of fluvial systems interlocked with towns, roads and diverse crop-yielding and manufacturing regions. Even when medieval or early-modern commanders were not directly impelled in operational decision-making by terrain, they were indirectly affected and usually to a very great extent. Historians, then, no less than the great captains of the past, must be, if not geographers, at least geographically competent, in order to understand the conduct of warfare—this is even more true of historians of amphibious warfare, because of the way it combines distinct physical media.[164]

Warfare on inshore and inland waterways is quintessentially amphibious because, in such waters, earth and water are always in close proximity, so that military operations benefit from, if not necessitate, cooperation of ground and waterborne forces. Where coastal waters and rivers come together, ports are most often found, and so operations against ports, even when mounted from their landward side, also benefit from contributions by both ground and waterborne forces, used cooperatively. Geographical factors shape military operations as much as organisation, technological developments, tactical systems, or the decision-making of 'great captains'. This is true of all military operations, but perhaps especially of combined ones, because these necessarily involve a conjuncture of landscape with seascape; and it is certainly true of amphibious operations waged on the fringes and internal arteries of the continents.

Sources and Bibliography

Archival Sources

AAE   Archives des Affaires Étrangères, Mémoires et Documents Angleterre
ASC   All Souls College Oxford, Codrington Library, MSS

---

[164] Guilmartin, above, ch. 6, p. 150.

Bibliothèque Mazarine, MSS
BNF   CCC   Cinq Cents de Colbert
         MS Fr. Manuscrits Français
BSHPF Bibliothèque de la Société de l'Histoire de Protestantisme Français, MSS
GAL   Gemeetearchief Leiden
         CR   Collectie Ramazotti
HL   EL   Ellesmere and Bridgewater MSS
OBL   St Amand MSS
PRO   SP 70   SP Foreign, Elizabeth I
                   SP 78   SP France

Published Primary Sources

CSPF 1862, 1584–85, 1585–86
         Calendar of State Papers, Foreign Series, of the Reign of Elizabeth I, 23 vols, ed.
         J. Stevenson, S. C. Lomas et al. (1863–1950) vols 5, 19, 20.
Albuquerque A. de (1990) *Albuquerque: Cæsar of the East. Selected Texts by Afonso de
    Albuquerque and His Son*, ed. and trans. T. F. Earle and J. Villiers (Warminster: 1990).
Anon. (1436) *'The Libelle of Englyshe Polycye.' A Poem on the Use of Sea-Power 1436*, ed.
    Sir George Warner (Oxford: 1926).
d'Aubigné A. (1618) *L'Histoire universelle*, vol. 2 (Maille: 1618).
Barbot A. (1889) *Histoire de La Rochelle depuis l'An 1199 jusques en 1575*, ed. D. d'Aussy,
    3 vols, *1534–1571*, *Archives historiques de La Saintonge et de L'Aunis* 17 (Montreuil:
    1889).
Caldecott-Baird D., ed. (1976) *The Expedition in Holland 1572–1574. The Revolt of the
    Netherlands: The Early Struggle for Independence from the Manuscript of Walter Morgan*
    (London: 1976).
Digges T. (1590) [nominally anonymous] *A Breife and True Report of the Proceedings of
    the Earle of Leycester for the Reliefe of the Town of Sluce, from his arriuall at Vlishing, about
    the end of June 1587, vntill the surrendrie thereof 6 Iulij nexxt ensuing* (London: 1590).
Evans J. X., ed. (1972) *The Works of Sir Roger Williams* (Oxford: 1972).
Hakluyt R. (1958) *Voyages and Documents* [1598–1600], selections and intro. J. Hampden,
    World's Classics 562 (London: 1958).
Hammer P. E. J., ed. (2003) 'Letters from Sir Robert Cecil to Sir Christopher
    Hatton, 1590–1591', in *Religion, Politics and Society in Sixteenth-Century England*, ed.
    Ian W. Archer et al., Camden Soc. 5th ser. 22 (2003) 197–267.
Orlers J. J. (1610) *Den Nassauschen Lauren-crans: Beschrijvinge ende af-beeldinge van alle de
    Victorien, so te Water als te Lande, die Godt Almachtich de [. . .] Staten der Vereenichde
    Neder-landen verleent hefte [. . .]* (Leyden: 1610).
Teensma B., ed. (1999) *Dutch-Brazil, 1, Two Unpublished Manuscripts about the Dutch
    Conquest (1624) and the Iberian Recovery (1625) of Salvador da Bahia in Brazil* (Rio de
    Janeiro: 1999).
Williams R. (1590) *A Briefe discourse of Warre*, in Evans, ed. (1972).
———. (1618) *The Actions of the Lowe Countries*, in Evans, ed. (1972).

Published Secondary Sources

Abulafia D. (1987) 'Narbonne, the Lands of the Crown of Aragon and the Levant
    Trade 1187–1400', in *Montpellier, la Couronne d'Aragon et les pays de Langue d'Oc
    (1204–1349)*, Mémoires de la Société archéologique de Montpellier 15 (Montpellier:
    1987); in Abulafia (1993), as pt. XIV.
———. (1988) 'The Levant Trade of the Minor Cities in the Thirteenth and Fourteenth
    Centuries: Strengths and Weaknesses', in *The Medieval Levant: Studies in Memory of
    Eliyahu Ashtor (1914–1984)*, ed. B. Z. Kedar and A. L. Udovitch, Asian and
    African Studies 22 (1988); in Abulafia (1993), as pt. XI.

——. (1993) *Commerce and Conquest in the Mediterranean, 1100–1500*, Variorum Collected Studies 410 (Aldershot and Brookfield, Vt.: 1993).

Ames G. J. (1997) 'The Straits of Hurmuz Fleets: Omani-Portuguese Naval Rivalry and Encounters, c. 1660–1680', *The Mariner's Mirror* 83 (1997) 389–409.

Andaya B. W. (1993) *To Live As Brothers: Southeast Sumatra in the Seventeenth and Eighteenth Centuries* (Honolulu: 1993).

Austen R. A. (1983) 'The Metamorphoses of Middlemen: The Duala, Europeans, and the Cameroon Hinterland, ca. 1800–ca. 1960', *International Journal of African Historical Studies* 16 (1983) 1–24.

Austen R. A. and Derrick J. (1999) *Middlemen of the Cameroons Rivers: The Duala and their Hinterland c. 1600–c. 1960*, Cambridge African Studies, 96 (Cambridge: 1999)

Avent R. (1991) 'The Early Development of Three Coastal Castles', in *Sir Gâr: Studies in Carmarthenshire History*, ed. H. James (Carmarthen: 1991) 167–88.

Benedict P. (1981) *Rouen during the Wars of Religion* (Cambridge: 1981).

Black J. (2002) *European Warfare, 1494–1660* (London & New York: 2000).

Braudel F. (1972) *The Mediterranean and the Mediterranean World in the Age of Philip II*, 2 vols, trans. S. Reynolds (New York, Evanston, San Francisco and London: 1972)

Brioist P. (1997) *Espaces maritimes au XVIIIe siècle* (Paris: 1997).

Broeze F. (1997) 'Introduction', to Broeze, ed. (1997) 2–16.

Broeze F., ed. (1997) *Gateways of Asia: Port Cities of Asia in the 12th–20th Centuries*, Comparative Asian Studies Series 2 (London & New York: 1997).

Broughton H. (1978) *Wareham: Its Interesting History, Ancient and Modern* (Wareham/ Swanage, Dorset: [1978]).

Bruce J., ed. (1844) *Correspondence of Robert Dudley, Earl of Leycester, during his Government of the Low Countries, in the Years 1585 and 1586*, Camden Society [1st ser.] 27 (London: 1844).

Brummett P. (2001) 'The River Crossing: Breaking Points (Metaphorical and "Real") in Ottoman Mutiny', in *Rebellion, Repression, Reinvention: Mutiny in Comparative Perspective*, ed. J. Hathaway (Westport, Conn. and London: 2001) 215–31.

Carr A. P. (1992) 'The Environmental Background', in Duffy *et al.*, eds (1992) 17–24.

Chakravarti P. C. (1930) 'Naval Warfare in Ancient India', *Indian Historical Quarterly* 4 (1930) 645–64.

Chapman A. C. (1957) 'Port of Trade Enclaves in Aztec and Maya Civilization,' in Polyani *et al.*, eds (1957) 114–53.

Cheng-Chung Lai (2000) 'Braudel's Concepts and Methodology Reconsidered', *The European Legacy* 5 (2000) 65–86.

Childs W. (1997) 'The Commercial Shipping of South-Western England in the Later Fifteenth Century', *The Mariner's Mirror* 83 (1997) 272–92.

Clark H. R. (1995) 'Muslims and Hindus in the Culture and Morphology of Quanzhou from the Tenth to the Thirteenth Century', *Journal of World History* 6 (1995) 49–74.

Clendinnen I. (1987) *Ambivalent Conquests: Maya and Spaniard in Yucatan, 1517–1570*, Cambridge Latin American Studies 61 (Cambridge: 1987).

Curry A. and Hughes M., eds (1994) A*rms, Armies and Fortifications in the Hundred Years* [sic] *War* (Woodbridge, Suffolk: 1994; paperback repr., 1999).

Dictionary of Geography (2004) *A Dictionary of Geography*, ed. Susan Mayhew, 3rd edn (Oxford: 2004).

Disney A. (1986) 'Goa in the Seventeenth Century', in *The First Portuguese Colonial Empire*, ed. M. Newitt, Exeter Studies in History 11 (Exeter: 1986) 85–98.

Duffy M. *et al.*, eds (1992) *The New Maritime History of Devon, 1, From Early Times to the Late Eighteenth Century* (London & Exeter: 1992).

Duffy C. *Siege Warfare: The Fortress in the Early Modern World 1494–1660* (London and Henley: 1979).

——. (1985) *Siege Warfare, 2, The Fortress in the Age of Vauban and Frederick the Great 1660–1789* (London, Boston, Melbourne and Henley: 1985).

Dyer C. (2000) 'Trade, Urban Hinterlands and Market Integration, c. 1300–1600: A Summing Up', in Galloway, ed. (2000) 103–9.

Duplessis R. S. (1997) *Transitions to Capitalism in Early Modern Europe* (Cambridge: 1997).

Eiden H. and Irsigler F. (2000) 'Environs and Hinterland: Cologne and Nuremberg in the Later Middle Ages', in Galloway, ed. (2000) 43–57.

Elliott N. R. (1969) 'Hinterland and Foreland as Illustrated by the Port of the Tyne', *Transactions of the Institute of British Geographers* (1969) 153–70.

Encyclopædia Britannica (2003) *Encyclopædia Britannica* Standard Edition 2004 CD-ROM. Copyright © 1994–2003 Encyclopædia Britannica, Inc. May 30, 2003.

Evans D. S. (1993) 'The Bridge of Boats at Gloucester 1642–44', *Journal of the Society for Army Historical Research* 71 (1993): 232–42.

Finkel, C. F. (1992) 'French Mercenaries in the Habsburg-Ottoman War of 1593–1606', *Bulletin of the School of Oriental and African Studies, University of London* 55 (1992) 451–471.

Galloway J. A., ed. (2000) *Trade, Urban Hinterlands and Market Integration, c.1300–1600*, Centre for Metropolitan history Working Papers 3 (London: 2000).

Gidlow C. (2004) *The Reign of Arthur: From History to Legend* (Stroud: 2004).

Grahn L. R. (1991) 'Cartagena and its Hinterland in the Eighteenth Century', in Knight & Liss, eds (1991) 168–95

Grant A. (1992) 'Devon Shipping, Trade, and Ports, 1600–1689', in Duffy *et al.*, eds (1992) 130–38.

Griffin S. (1996) *The Siege of Redding: April 1643* (Bristol: 1996).

Hair P. E. H. (1997) 'The Experience of the Sixteenth-Century English voyages to Guinea', *The Mariner's Mirror* 83 (1997) 3–13.

Harding V. (1995) 'Cross-channel Trade and Cultural Contacts: London and the Low Countries in the Later Fourteenth Century', in *England and the Low Countries in the Late Middle Ages*, ed. C. Barron and N. Saul (Stroud: 1995; paperback edn, 1998) 153–68.

Hoeven M. van der, ed. (1997) *Exercise of Arms: Warfare in the Netherlands (1568–1648)* History of Warfare 1 (Leiden: 1997).

Israel J. I. (1980) 'The States-General and the Strategic Regulation of the Dutch River Trade, 1621–1636', *Bijdragen an mededelingen betreffende de geschiedenis der Nederlanden* 95 (1980) 461–91.

——. (1995) *The Dutch Republic: Its Rise, Greatness and Fall 1477–1806* (Oxford: 1995).

Keegan J. (1993) *A History of Warfare* (London: 1993).

Kenyon J. R. (2002) *Kidwelly Castle* (3rd edn; Cardiff: 2002).

Kinser S. (1981) 'Annaliste Paradigm? The Geohistorical Structuralism of Fernand Braudel', *American Historical Review* 86 (1981) 63–105.

Knight F. W. and Liss P. K., eds (1991) *Atlantic Port Cities: Economy, Culture, and Society in the Atlantic World, 1650–1850* (Knoxville, Tenn., 1991).

Konvitz J. W. (1978) *Cities and the Sea: Port City Planning in Early Modern Europe* (Baltimore and London: 1978).

Kowaleski M. (1992) 'The Port Towns of Fourteenth-Century Devon', in Duffy *et al.*, eds (1992) 62–72.

Leonard J. N. (1968) *Ancient America* (N.p. [Time-Life]: 1968).

Lloyd H. A. (1973) *The Rouen Campaign, 1590–1592* (Oxford: 1973).

Loo I. van (1997) 'For Freedom and Fortune. The Rise of Dutch Privateering in the First Half of the Dutch Revolt, 1568–1609', in van der Hoeven, ed. (1997) 173–95.

McGurk, J. (2001) 'Terrain and Conquest 1600–1603', in *Conquest and Resistance: War in Seventeenth-Century Ireland*, ed. P. Lenihan, History of Warfare 3 (Leiden: 2001) 87–114.

Maland D. (1980) *Europe at War 1600–1650* (London: 1980).

Mallet M. E. (1974) *Mercenaries and their Masters: Warfare in Renaissance Italy* (London: 1974).

Manguin P. Y. (2000) 'Les cités-états de l'Asie du Sud-Est côtière de l'ancienneté et de la permanence des formes urbaines', *Bulletin de l'École française d'Extrême-Orient* 87 (2000) 151–82.

Martin C. and Parker G. (1988) *The Spanish Armada* (London: 1988).

Meyer J. (2000) 'States, Roads, War, and the Organization of Space, in *War and Competition between States*, ed. P. Contamine (Oxford: 2000) 99–127.

Mollat de Jourdin M. (1992) 'Les enjeux maritimes de la guerre de Cent ans', in *Histoire militaire de la France*, 1, *Des origines à 1715*, ed. P. Contamine (Paris: 1992) ch. 8.

Muddle I. E. (1934) 'The Suitability of the Port of Dover as an Outlet for Its Developing Hinterland', *The Geographical Journal* 83 (1934) 503–12.

Murphey R. (1999) *Ottoman Warfare 1500–1700* (London: 1999).

Nicolle D. (2000) *Crécy 1346: Triumph of the Longbow*, Osprey Campaign 71 (Oxford: 2000).

OED (1989) The Oxford English Dictionary (2nd edn, 1989).

Ohlmeyer J. (1998) '"Civilizinge of those Rude Partes": Colonization within Britain and Ireland, 1580s–1640s', in *The Oxford History of the British Empire*, 1, *The Origins of Empire*, ed. N. Canny (Oxford and New York: 1998) 124–47.

Oxford Military Dictionary (2001) *The Oxford Essential Dictionary of the U.S. Military* (New York: 2001).

Palliser D. M. (1992) *The Age of Elizabeth: England under the later Tudors 1547–1603* (2nd edn; London: 1992).

Parker G. (1977) *The Dutch Revolt* (London: 1977).

——. (1990) *The Army of Flanders and the Spanish Road* (Cambridge: 1972; corrected edn, 1990).

Pearson M. N. *Port Cities and Intruders: The Swahili Coast, India and Portugal in the Early Modern Era* (Baltimore: 1998).

Pearson M. N. (1991) 'Merchants and States', in *The Political Economy of Merchant Empires*, ed. J. D. Tracy, Studies in Comparative Early Modern History 2 (Cambridge and New York: 1991) 41–116.

Pepper S. (1993) 'Fortress and Fleet: The Defence of Venice's Mainland Greek Colonies in the Late Fifteenth Century', in *War, Culture and Society in Renaissance Venice: Essays in Honour of John Hale*, ed. D. S. Chambers, C. H. Clough and M. E. Mallett (London: 1993) 29–56.

Polyani K. *et al.*, eds (1957) *Trade and Market in Early Empires: Economies in History and Theory*, ed. K. Polyani, C. M. Arensberg and H. W. Pearson (Glencoe, Ill.: 1957).

Rázsó G. (1982) 'The Mercenary Army of King Matthias Corvinus', in *War and Society in Eastern Central Europe*, 3, *From Hunyadi to Rákóczi: War and Society in Late Medieval and Early Modern Hungary*, ed. J. M. Bak and B. K. Király, Brooklyn College Studies on Society in Change 12, Social Science Monographs–Eastern European Monographs 104 (New York: 1982) 125–40.

Revere R. (1957) '"No Man's Coast": Ports of Trade in the Eastern Mediterranean', in Polyani *et al.*, eds (1957) 38–63.

Roberts J. M. (1995) *The Penguin History of the World* (London: 1990; revd pb. edn, 1995).

Rolleghem J. van (1969) 'Le port de Brouage: jadis rival de La Rochelle', *Revue historique de l'armée*, new ser. 25: 2 (1969) 7–17.

Rose S. (2000) 'Bayonne and the King's Ships, 1204–1420', *The Mariner's Mirror* 86 (2000) 140–7.

Russell-Wood A. J. R. (1990) 'Ports of Colonial Brazil', in Knight and Liss, eds (1990) 196–239.

Saleh Shihab H. (1997) 'Aden in Pre-Turkish Times (1232–1538): The Arabian Entrepot of the Western Asiatic Seas', in Broeze, ed. (1997) 17–32.

Sicking L. (2001) 'Charles V: Master of the Sea?' in *Carlos V, Europeísmo y universalidad*, ed. J. Castellano and F. González, v2, *La organizacíon del poder* (Madrid: [2001]) 553–73.

Smith F. F. (1928) *A History of Rochester* (London: 1928).

Spelt J. (1958) 'Towns and Umlands: A Review Article', *Economic Geography* 34 (1958) 362–369.

Stephenson M., ed. (2003) *Battlegrounds: Geography and the History of Warfare* (Washington, D.C.: [2003]).

Subrahmanyam S. (1997A) 'Masulipatnam Revisited, 1550–1750: A Survey and Some Speculations', in Broeze, ed. (1997) 33–65.

——. (1997B) 'Slaves and Tyrants: Dutch Tribulations in Seventeenth-Century Mrauk-U', *Journal of Early Modern History* 1 (1997) 201–53.

Trim D. J. B. (1999A) 'Sir Horace Vere in Holland and the Rhineland, 1610–1612', *Historical Research* 72 (1999) 334–51.

——. (1999B) 'The "Foundation-Stone of the British Army"? The Normandy Campaign of 1562', *Journal of the Society for Army Historical Research* 77 (1999): 71–87.

Van Cleef E. (1941) 'Hinterland and Umland', *Geographical Review* 31 (1941) 308–11.

Verbruggen J. F. (1997) *The Art of Warfare in Western Europe during the Middle Ages*, trans. S. Willard and Mrs R. W. Southern (2nd edn; Woodbridge, Suffolk: 1997).

Vigarie A. (1964) *Les grands ports de commerce de la Seine au Rhin: leur evolution devant l'industrialisation des arriere-pays* (Paris: 1964).

——. (1979) Review of Konvitz (1978) in *The Geographical Journal* 145 (1979) 471–2.

Vliet A. P. van (1997) 'Foundation, Organization and Effects of the Dutch Navy', in van der Hoeven, ed. (1997) 153–72.

Wedgwood, C. V. (1958) *The King's War, 1641–1647* (London: 1958).

——. (1962) *Richelieu and the French Monarchy* (New York: 1962).

Weigend G. G. (1955) 'Bordeaux: An Example of Changing Port Functions', *Geographical Review* 45 (1955) 217–43.

——. (1956) 'The Problem of Hinterland and Foreland as Illustrated by the Port of Hamburg', *Economic Geography* 32 (1956) 1–16.

——. (1958) 'Some Elements in the Study of Port Geography', *Geographical Review* 48 (1958) 185–200.

——. (1968) Review of Vigarie (1964), in *Economic Geography* 44 (1968) 178–9.

Weir M. 'English Naval Activities, 1242–1243', *The Mariner's Mirror* 58 (1972) 85–92.

Wernham R. B. (1988) *After the Armada: Elizabethan England and the Struggle for Western Europe 1588–1595* (Oxford: 1984).

——. (1994) *The Return of the Armadas: The Last Years of the Elizabethan War against Spain 1595–1603* (Oxford: 1994).

Youings J. (1992) with Cornford P. 'Seafaring and Maritime Trade in Sixteenth-Century Devon', in Duffy *et al.*, eds (1992) 98–107.

Young P. and Lawford J. (1970) *History of the British Army* (London: 1970).

Unpublished Secondary Sources

Newitt M. (1998) 'Portuguese Warfare in Africa in the Sixteenth and Seventeenth Centuries: A Failure for the Military Revolution' (Paper read at the Medieval and Early Modern Warfare Seminar, Department of War Studies, King's College London, 11 Nov. 1998).

Shapinksy P. D. (2005) 'Lords of the Sea: Pirates, Violence, and Exchange in Late Medieval Japan' (Ph.D. dissertation, University of Michigan).

Trim D. J. B. (2002) 'Fighting 'Jacob's Wars'. The Employment of English and
    Welsh Mercenaries in the European Wars of Religion: France and the Netherlands
    1562–1610' (unpublished Ph.D. thesis, University of London, 2002).

ILLUSTRATIONS

1. Christian III's attack on Copenhagen, 1536. Woodcut from Hermann Hamelmann *Oldenburgisch Chronicon, das ist, Beschreibung der löblichen vhralten Grafen zu Oldenburg vnd Delmenhorst* (Oldenburg: 1599).

2. The fleet of Pedro Álvares Cabral, 1500. From *Memória das Armadas* (*c.*1568) (Academia das Ciências de Lisboa).

3. Portuguese ships entering the Bab El-Mandeb (the straits between Yemen and Djibouti, west of Aden). From the *Roteiro… do Mar Roxo*, by Dom João de Castro (MS in University of Coimbra Library).

4. A Portuguese *nau do alto bordo* (carrack), arguably the finest contemporary depiction (*c.*1555) of such a vessel. From Pieter Brueghel, 'The Fall of Icarus', Musées Royaux des Beaux-Arts de Belgique, Brussels.

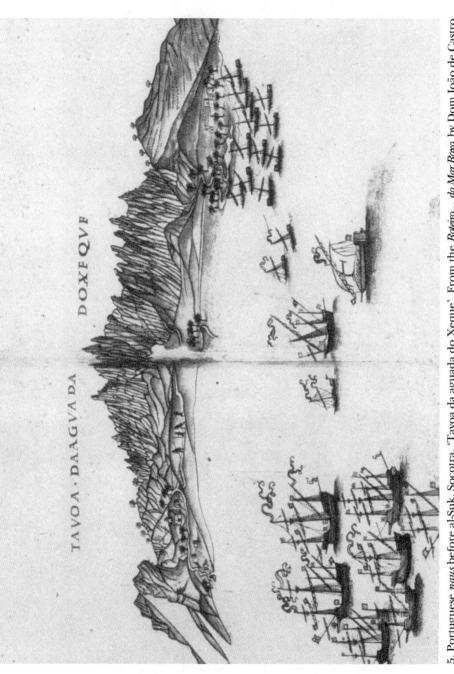

TAVOA·DAAGVADA   DOXFQVF

5. Portuguese *naus* before al-Suk, Socotra. 'Tavoa da aguada do Xeque'. From the *Roteiro... do Mar Roxo*, by Dom João de Castro (MS in British Library, reproduced by its permission).

6. A panoramic view of the Spanish landing in the Azores, 1583. Fresco painting from the *Sala de batallas*, El Escorial Palace near Madrid (photograph courtesy of the Patrimonio Nacional and reproduced by its permission).

7. Spanish landing in the Azores, 1583: detail of a landing craft. As previous, detail.

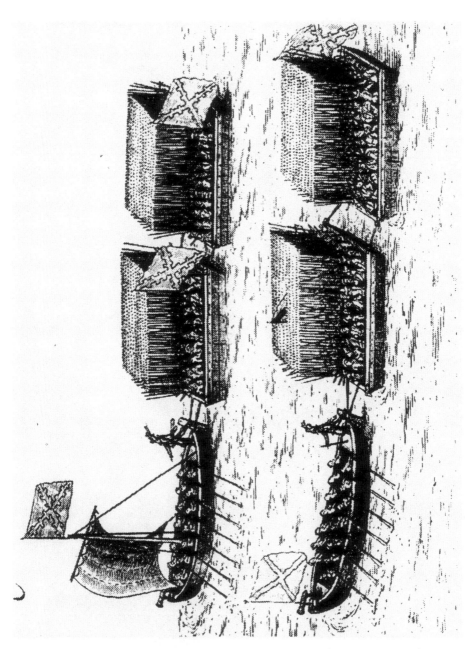

8. Spanish troop-barges towed by longboats on a river in the Low Countries, c. 1580s. Biblioteca Nacional, Madrid, MS Res 210/272 (photography by the author; reproduced by permission).

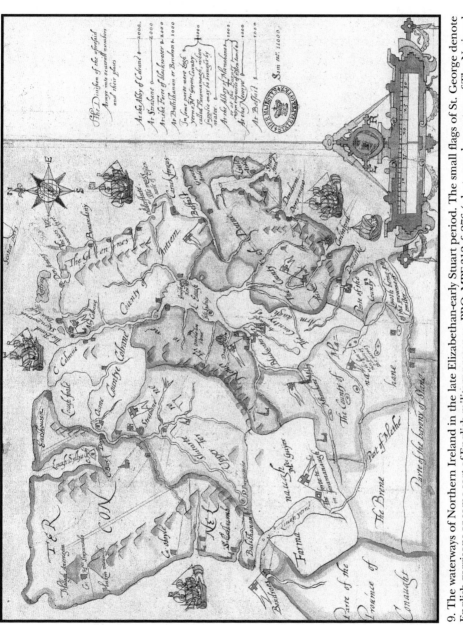

9. The waterways of Northern Ireland in the late Elizabethan-early Stuart period. The small flags of St. George denote English garrisons or some sort of English military presence. PRO, MPF 312, f. 276 (photograph courtesy of The National Archives and reproduced by its permission).

A samon were
Musketeres plast behinde a rock
Dudly Loftus
Captaine Lea
Captaine John Dowdall
Our leading battle
Sr Patrick Barnewell
Musketeres plast to flanck

10. English troops cross the River Erne, 10 October 1592. English sword-and-buckler men ford the River Erne in a frontal assault on a fortified Irish position whilst English musketeers provide flanking fire across the riverbend. BL, Cottonian MS Augustus I/ii, f. 38 (photograph courtesy of the British Library, reproduced by permission).

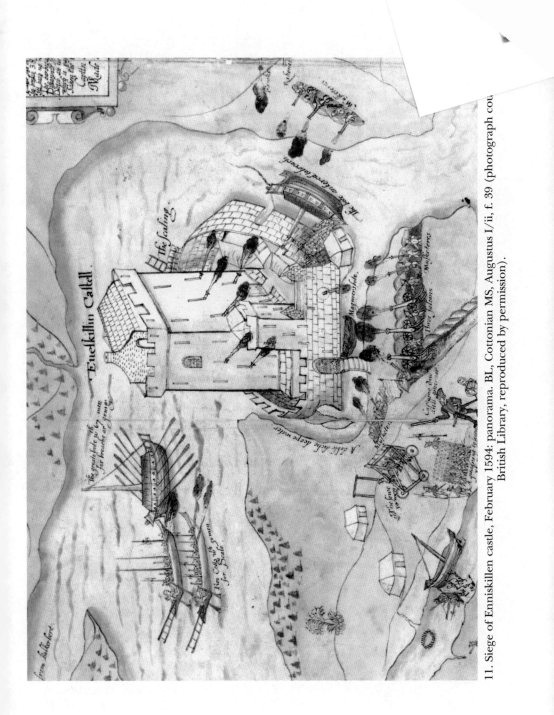

11. Siege of Enniskillen castle, February 1594: panorama. BL, Cottonian MS, Augustus I/ii, f. 39 (photograph cou[rtesy of the] British Library, reproduced by permission).

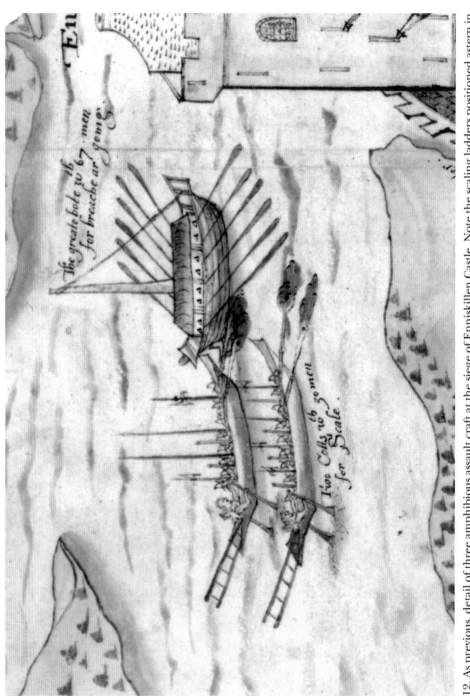

The greate bote w 67 men
for breache ar going.

Two Cotts w 30 men
for Scale.

En[...]

12. As previous, detail of three amphibious assault craft at the siege of Enniskillen Castle. Note the scaling ladders positioned astern in the two cotts.

13. Partial view of the passage of the Dutch army across the mouth of the Scheldt and its landing in Flanders, 21 June 1600. From a plate in Jan Janszoon Orlers, *Den Nassauschen Lauren-crans: Beschrijvinge ende af-beeldinge van alle de Victorien, so te Water als te Lande, die Godt Almachtich de [...] Staten der Vereenichde Neder-landen verleent hefte [...]* (Leyden: 1610), between pp. 148–9.

14. As previous: detail of a transport craft.

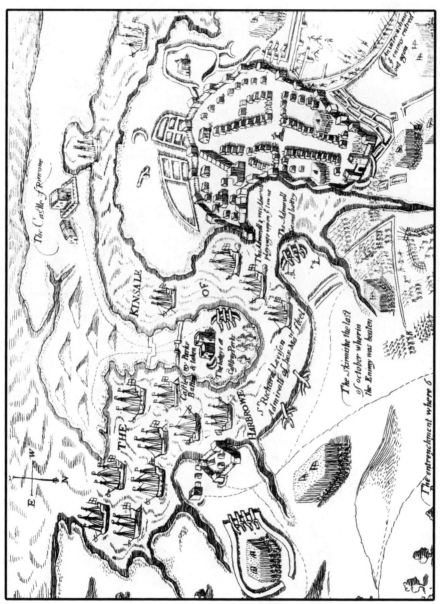

15. Broad panorama of the siege and battle of Kinsale, October 1601–January 1602, inclusive of ship-to-shore action. Contemporary print, Hargrett Rare Books and Manuscript Library, University of Georgia Libraries (reproduced by permission).

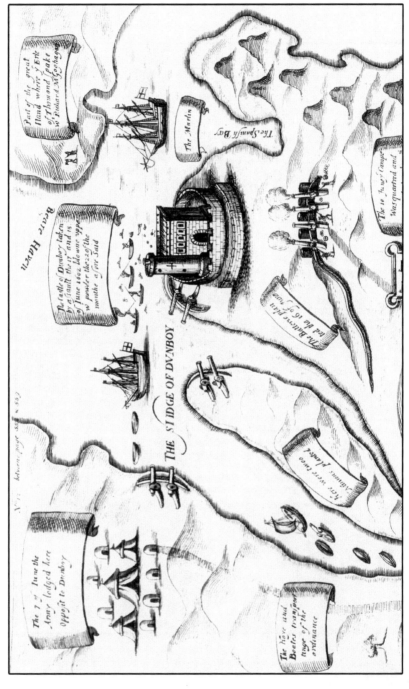

16. The Siege of Dunboy, 1602. Note the shallow-draught vessels that have ferried the siege artillery to an inlet. From Thomas Stafford, *Paceta Hibernia* (1631), Hargrett Rare Books and Manuscript Library, University of Georgia Libraries.

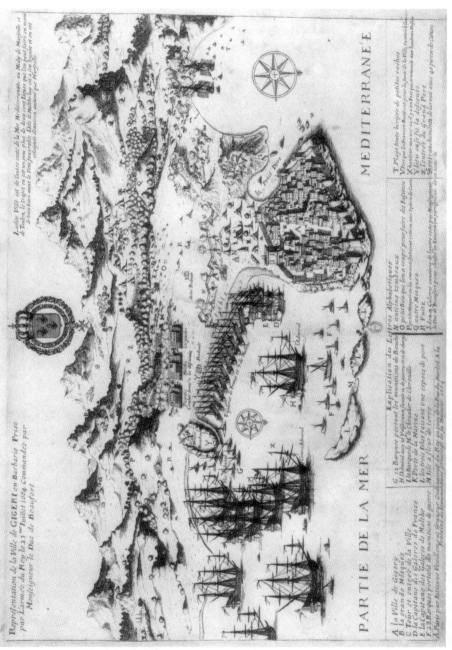

Reproduction de la Ville de GIGERI en Barbarie Prise par l'armée du Roy le 23.me Juillet 1664 Commandée par Monseigneur le Duc de Beaufort

Ladite Ville est de l'autre costé de la Mer Mediterranée, au Midy de Marseille et de Toulon, le trajet en est un peu plus d'Aux cent Lieues que l'on peut faire en moins de trois Iours avec le Vent favorable. Elle est Maistre luy est a son Egard et en ont obligent donnant autour par Marseille

PARTIE DE LA MER

MEDITERRANE'E

A   la Ville de Gigery
B   la grand Mosquée
C   Tour et entrée de la ville
D   la Capitane des Galeres de France
E   la Capitane des Galeres de Malthe
F   18 Barques portant les munition de guerre.
λ Paris par Estienne Vouillemont Graveur Ordinaire du Roy en son Ilse Rue de la Rue du Marest A la Nation 1664

Explication des Lettres Alphabetiques
G   12 Barques portant les munitions de Bouche
H   Redoubt aux 12 Vaisseaux tenans a la pointe est d'aban
I   La Barquade M.re le Chevalier de Clereuille
K   Porte de la Marine
L   Les trois Islets faisant une espace de port
M Islet a fleur de terre

N   anciens tombeaux
O   petit Bois que l'on a coupé pour faire des Fassines
P   Petit Mosquée de communication sur spece de...
Q   quatre Mosquee
R   Puits
S   les 9 Galeres ennemies de l'autre costé par Monseigneur
Z   le Duc de Beaufort par dessus les Barricades aux 40 pierres du château

T   Plage haute herisée de petites roches
V   Vorque de François Barricants pour la fonde de la Ville, tumultée
X   Tambour au sec ou il y a en Porque arrennant sur l'endroict
Y   Islets où fut la deffente
z   l'entrée du grand Port
& trouvant les hommes de l'armée avec 40 pieces de canon.

17. Contemporary print of the French assault on Djidjelli, 1664. BNF, Cabinet des Estampes (reproduced by permission of the Bibliothèque Nationale de France).

18. Detail of the Danish landing at Råå, 29 June 1676. Rigsarkivet, Copenhagen: Landetaten, Krigscancelliet, Map til Christian 5.s Krigshistorie (from a photograph supplied by Det Kongelige Bibliotek Fotografisk Atelier, and reproduced with its permission).

19. The bombardment and descent on Genoa by the French fleet, 1684 (contemporary French print). BNF, Cabinet des Estampes (reproduced by permission of the Bibliothèque Nationale de France).

20. A French *galiote à bombes,* section cut away to reveal mortars, 1685. BL, King's MS 40, f. 93v (photograph courtesy of the British Library; reproduced by permission).

21. Dutch depiction of the siege of Cork, 1690. Plate in *Hollandsche Mercurius, behelzende het ghedenckweerdighste in Christenrijck voorghevallen, binnen 't gantsche jaer,* 41 (1690), 245 (photograph courtesy Universiteitsbibliotheek Leiden, reproduced by permission).

22. Dutch depiction of the sieges of Kinsale, 1690. Plate in *Hollandtsche Mercurius, behelzende het ghedenckweerdighste in Christenrijck voor-ghevallen, binnen 't gantsche jaer*, 41 (1690), 245 (photograph courtesy Universiteitsbibliotheek Leiden, reproduced by permission).

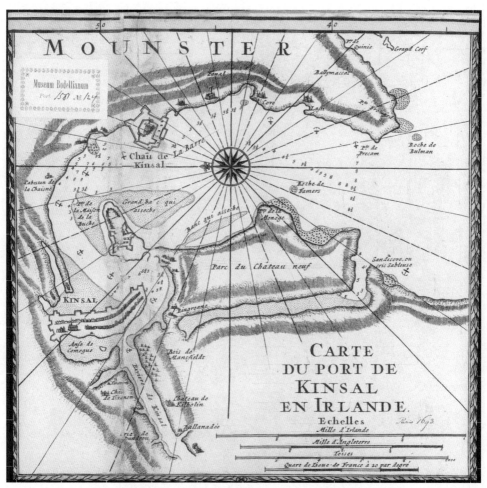

23. Contemporary plan of Kinsale (1693), showing the new waterside fortifications. Universiteitsbibliotheek Leiden, Collectie Bodel Nijenhuis, P.150.N.1261 (reproduced by permission).

24. Brest *c.*1694. Universiteitsbibliotheek Leiden (reproduced by permission).

25. The Anglo-Dutch bombardment of Dieppe, 1694. Plate in *Europsche Mercurius behelzende al het voornaamste 't geen in Europa is voorgevallen* (Amsterdam: 1694), between pp. 88-9 (photograph courtesy of Universiteitsbibliotheek Leiden, reproduced by permission).

Tab. 933.

HAVRE DE GRACE
Gebombardeert
en Geruineert Door
de Engelse en
Hollanders

A: 't Kasteel. B: de Haven. C: 't Magazyn. D: Galioten met geschut. E: Bombardeer Schepen. F: Engelsche en Hollagsche Vloot. G: de Stad in Brand. H: Schepen die of en aankomen

Petru: Bergh: fecit.

26. The Anglo-Dutch bombardment of Havre de Grace [Le Havre], 1694. Plate in *Europische Mercurius behelzende al het voornaamste 't geen in Europa is voorgevallen* (Amsterdam: 1694), between pp. 92–3 (photography courtesy of Universiteitsbibliotheek Leiden, reproduced by permission).

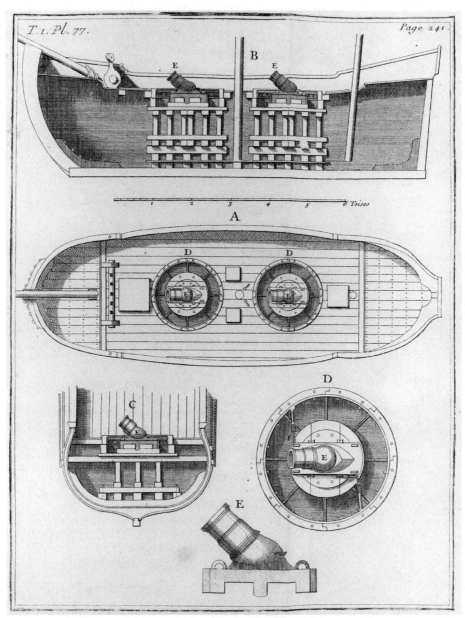

27. British Royal Navy bomb ketch, 1694, depicting mortars. Pierre Surirey de Saint-Remy, *Mémoires d'Artillerie* (2 vols, Paris 1697) vol. 1, plate 77 (reproduced by permission of the Syndics of the Cambridge University Library).

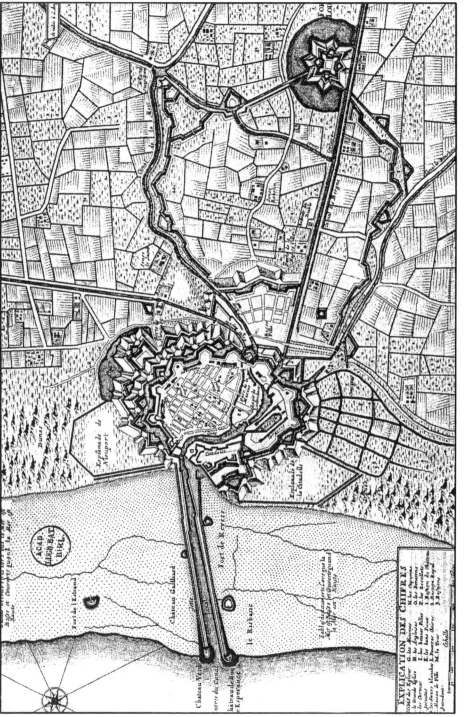

28. Contemporary plan of the city and citadel of Dunkirk, c.1700. Universiteitsbibliotheek Leiden (reproduced by permission).

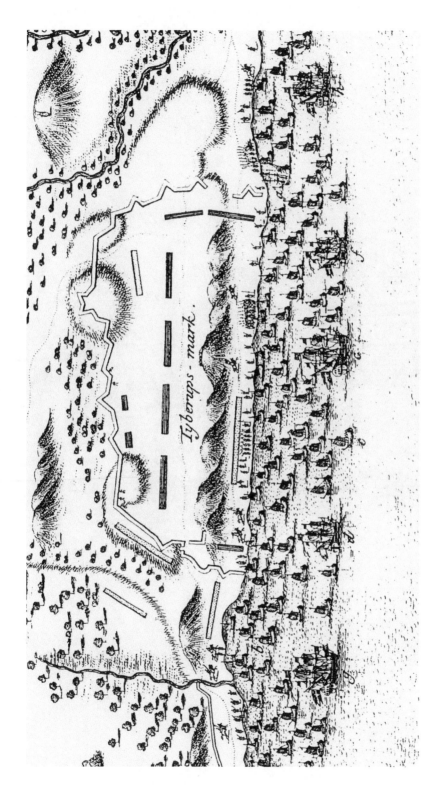

29. Swedish landing at Humlebaek, 4 August 1700: panorama. Krigsarkivet, Stockholm, Sweden: Historiska planscher 1700:19.

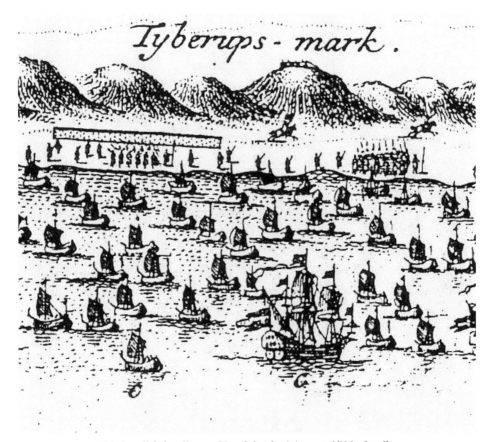

30. Swedish landing at Humlebaek, 4 August 1700: detail.

CONCLUSION

D. J. B. Trim and Mark Charles Fissel

What, then, have the essays in this volume revealed about amphibious warfare in the eleventh through seventeenth centuries? And what do they indicate about wider trends and developments in those seven hundred years?

We draw five types of conclusion: first, fundamental ones, relating to the purpose and function of amphibious warfare, especially in terms of commerce, state formation and European expansion. Second, conclusions about the operational and strategical levels of amphibious warfare. Here we argue that amphibious warfare is the most complex form of warfare and summarise the implications this had for its conduct during this period. We stress the flexibility and manoeuvrability of amphibious warfare, even in the era of sail and muscle power, but we also draw attention to the frequency with which medieval and early-modern statesmen and generals used amphibious warfare without clear strategic direction. Third, we draw conclusions about the tactical level of amphibious warfare, including where that overlaps with the operational level. Naval bombardment was often crucial in this period and this needs to be more widely recognised. The role of amphibious operations and tactics in defensive warfare is also stressed. Fourth, we summarise what the essays reveal about preparation for and organisation of amphibious warfare. We highlight the importance of developments in technology and scientific knowledge—such technical knowledge was, in this period, as since, an essential part of amphibious warfare; and we also consider the implications of the growth of professional structures. However, here, as elsewhere, we show that 'modernisation', whether in technology, or scientific or professional knowledge or structures was not a simple determinant of military success. Finally, we summarise what we see as the most important characteristics of amphibious warfare.

Amphibious Warfare: Fundamentals

Commerce, Entrepreneurship and State Formation

Mao Zedong asserted that war could not 'for a single minute be separate from politics'. He was probably adapting the celebrated dictum of Karl von Clausewitz that war is both a political act and a political instrument—'a continuation of political relations [and] carrying out of the same by other means'.[1] What is apparent, however, is that war also is (or can be) the continuation of commerce by other means.

Throughout the period covered by this volume, warfare in general (and amphibious warfare in particular) had strong economic aspects. Of course, this is true of other periods as well, but because amphibious warfare was complex and needed both land and sea components there was an even greater role for entrepreneurs in amphibious, than in specifically land or sea, warfare. This meant, however, that the aims of amphibious warfare were very often overtly commercial and/or economic and in several ways.

First, amphibious operations were frequently in aid of colonisation. The Portuguese were quintessential colonisers and, as Malyn Newitt shows, the successful practice of amphibious warfare was the foundation of their colonies. Amphibious operations helped Spain to acquire its American empire; R. B. Wernham describes a pan-oceanic economic struggle that revolved around Spain's overseas possessions. The economic context of Mark Fissel's essay is that amphibious successes helped pave the way for England's first colony.[2]

But as well as being a means to enriching the nation at large, combined operations often had to pay their own way. Thus, they were commercial or economic at the micro- as well as macro-level. This meant that sometimes plunder became an end, rather than just a means: this was the case with the sixteenth-century Portuguese operations in the Indian Ocean and the English attacks on Portugal and Spain in the 1580s and 1590s. Alternatively, the overall aims of warfare could be to disrupt rival economies—indeed, when that was the aim, combined operations were inherently likely to be the

---

[1] Bartlett (1992), 393:3, 686:14.
[2] Chs. 4, 11, 7, 8.

best method (given that commerce tended to be maritime, but therefore needing ports). In short, amphibious warfare was far more economic or commercial, and cultural, than political—Clausewitz's and Mao's view of war did not yet apply.

This was true of many societies, not just Europeans. Even in pre-Columbian Mexico, although the Aztecs' conquests were driven by their own internal dynamics, the most geographically isolated province brought into the Aztec empire was conquered by the *pochteca*—merchants who carried on trading relations exclusively with peoples beyond the borders of the Aztec empire and for whom the difficulties contingent upon distance were apparently outweighed by commercial factors.[3] Moreover when the *teucunenenque*—the royal trade officials responsible for regulating commerce within the empire and selling goods for the sovereign—were insulted and rejected in one province, King Moctezuma the younger was quick to declare war and reduce the towns in question by conquest.[4] The importance of commerce, both in its perceived role as a potential enricher of the nation generally, and, more particularly, as an immediate source of revenue for the sovereign, is striking.

The pursuit of warfare to achieve commercial and financial goals is, however, particularly characteristic of European warfare. This was true in the earliest part of our period, when Venice was able to divert the Fourth Crusade from attacking the Turks, the enemies of Christendom, in order to save the Holy Land, to attacking Constantinople and the Christian Byzantine emperor, in order to save Venetian trade. It was true in the fourteenth century, too: the great victory of the Hanseatic League and its allies over Denmark and Norway in the second war of Valdemar (1368–70) was really a triumph for war as a continuation of commerce over war as the projection of princely power. 'The Hansa only resorted to military expeditions if all else had failed', and when it did go to war, as against Valdemar, military operations were designed to realize the merchants' business interests.[5] Denmark was not partitioned amongst rival states and it was when the Hanseatic cities used amphibious warfare to obtain clear, limited, *commercial* ends, rather than in pursuit of overblown indefinite territorial aims that they were successful.

---

[3] Chapman (1957), 120–2, 142.
[4] Ibid., 123–4.
[5] Above, ch. 2, pp. 59–61 and ch. 3, p. 80.

But when amphibious warfare began to be used outside Europe it was a particularly valuable mode of warfare, because the same ships that carried trade goods could also transport soldiers. It was also a source not only of enriching the national economy but also of direct revenue for the sovereign.

In the New World the Spanish were usually concerned initially with the prospect of plunder almost to the exclusion of all else, so that they showed little interest in native trading networks; and by contrast with the conquest of areas for gold, the Mayan regions of Mexico were not definitively conquered until 1546–7, a quarter of a century after the conquest of the Aztec lands, to a great extent because the Yucatan had little gold—the 'lure of richer plunder from . . . regions of the Aztec Empire' drew the Spaniards elsewhere![6] Once areas had been brought into the empire, however, they were quickly tied into the transoceanic trading network that served primarily to enrich the Habsburg monarchy. The Portuguese and Dutch in Asia particularly blurred the distinctions between conflict and commerce. The former were discussed in chapter four. No chapter specifically explores Dutch action in the East and West Indies, but Professor Newitt's essay provides the template: essentially, what the Portuguese had done to Arab, Indian and Malayan rulers across the Indian Ocean in the sixteenth century, a hundred years later the Dutch did—both to the indigenous rulers, but also to their European predecessors' 'Estado da India', which was attacked across the Indian Ocean; the Dutch also attacked Spanish outposts in the Philippines. When the Dutch West India Company turned its attention to the New World, the same was true. The Dutch not only attacked commerce or blockaded ports—their expeditions sought to capture territory and succeeded, capturing the Brazilian cities of Salvador de Bahía in 1624 and Pernambuco in 1630.[7] Although Dutch campaigns against Spaniards (as well as indigenes) were often essentially naval, still, the relentless pursuit of war for a commercial end meant the amphibious potential of naval warfare was always stressed. For

---

[6] E.g., Chapman (1957), 130, 133. Although Mayan ability to wage inland and inshore amphibious warfare was also a factor: above, pp. 404–5.

[7] See ch. 4, above; Boxer (1965) and (1991); Van Dyke (1997); Trim, ch. 11, above, pp. 391–2.

example, a fleet of eight ships sent from Holland to the East Indies under the command of Arent Gijsels in 1629, tasked with conducting operations against the Dutch East India Company's European rivals in Asia, carried over 'two thousand soldiers on board besides the crew'.[8]

The problems, from the point of view of sovereigns and states, were twofold. First, it was often individual nobles, corporations or entrepreneurs who profited from amphibious operations, so that success in the latter did not necessarily strengthen a dynasty or state. Hanseatic successes enriched the individual cities of the Hansa and so helped to keep them apart, rather than unite them. Portuguese practice of amphibious warfare, though expert, was so commercially driven, and so limited to the littoral, that ultimately it did not greatly strengthen the Portuguese state. The Lusophone trans-oceanic empire was never as strong as it superficially seemed, and it enriched the kings of Portugal far less than their subjects. By 1570, the Portuguese monarchy was near bankrupt and obliged to resort to desperate schemes to recoup its position, which ultimately ended in disaster.[9] The Habsburgs learned from the experience of their Portuguese cousins and retained control over the import of treasure back into Europe, while the Dutch Republic had a degree of control over the Dutch East and West India Companies so that they did enrich the Netherlandish state as well as individual Netherlanders. Yet ultimately the Spanish struggle to maintain empire drained the mother country and enriched the colonies; Dutch and English merchants in the East Indies rejected state guidance and their bitter disputes disrupted relations between their parent nations.

The second problem was that, as Professor Wernham shows, though '[c]ommercially focused warfare might have the potential to disrupt [a hostile] economy . . . in practice it proved disruptive of the . . . military operations aimed at carrying it out.'[10] Some Dutch military operations of the Eighty Years' War were disrupted by the involvement of 'freebooters'—private forces fighting for profit and so not as subject to discipline as the paid forces of the States-General.

---

[8] Teensma, ed. (1999), 2:18: Correia de Sá to Philip IV of Spain, 17 Sept. 1630 (summarizing reports of interrogation of Dutch prisoners).

[9] Trim (1997), 8, 23–4.

[10] Above ch. 7, p. 212.

English operations throughout Elizabeth's reign and on into the seventeenth century were often at the mercy of entrepreneurs who bankrolled a large part of the forces involved. Amphibious operations were thus a double-edged sword for a sovereign or state using them primarily as economic or commercial weapons. All this was the consequence of the plunder imperative.

All this said, amphibious warfare was undoubtedly an excellent means for power projection.[11] This made it an instrument of European expansion, but in aiding the territorial and commercial expansion of European states overseas it sometimes also helped them expand at home. It was thus an important element in state formation. Despite the negative aspects already outlined, the Habsburg experience in the sixteenth century, and the English and, to an extent, Dutch experience in the sixteenth and seventeenth centuries was that the greater wealth and power that accrued from mastery of amphibious operations and consequent acquisition of colonies and/or disruption of rivals' commerce benefited the respective nation-states. Then, too, the ability to mount increasingly complex and ambitious amphibious operations was an important ingredient in the success of the Vasa and Bourbon dynastic states.[12] Amphibious warfare also played a role in state formation because it provided an incentive to create the hierarchies and other structures of control that allowed the state to take over from entrepreneurs.

However, in considering state formation in this period, it must be remembered that the commercial revolution (and we are reaching back to its origins in the late fifteenth century) generated public revenues through taxation and stimulation of the economy. Further, private entrepreneurs maintained vessels on a long-term basis, and these could be important supplements to a force planning amphibious operations. Therefore, private capital (not a ubiquitous state bureaucracy) and entrepreneurship might sustain a state's ability to engage in land-sea operations. Indeed, the confluence of private capital and entrepreneurship with fledgling (or temporary) state-sponsored naval expeditions seemed entirely natural to the medieval and early-modern European mind and remained common until the end of this period. As late as the 1650s, Robert Blake, whose abilities Mark

---

[11] This is discussed in more detail below, pp. 427–9.
[12] See chs. 5 and 9 in particular.

Fissel rightly highlights in chapter eight, 'still had as his ideal a fleet in which the proportion of hired merchantmen could be reduced to two-fifths.'[13] Privateering remained a vast industry in Britain, France, the Spanish Netherlands and Britain's North American colonies until well into the eighteenth century.

The essays in this volume highlight a number of issues about the interrelationship of amphibious warfare and commerce that are still unclear. How expensive were amphibious operations, compared to naval and military ones? To what extent was it possible to wage amphibious warfare successfully on the cheap? Did the entrepreneurial element allow it to be conducted without too much cost to the state? Did it need a major central investment if it was to be effective, as in the eighteenth century? What percentage of amphibious expeditions from say *c.* 1500–1800 had essentially economic targets? To what extent were the forces in expeditions sent against ports drawn from rival ports? Hopefully this volume will stimulate further research on these questions.

Power Projection and Culture

Amphibious warfare was the best means for European power projection into the liminal- and then non-European worlds, not least because it allowed the use of heavy guns that could never have been deployed solely on land. It could also be waged very effectively from a narrow base. If a large port-city was captured then mastery of only a very narrow hinterland was needed to maintain it, and from it a disproportionate amount of damage could be done to rival economic and power infrastructures. Thus, an amphibious force could, from a small geographical base, harass and even dominate a very large area, as the Portuguese and Dutch did in East Africa, India and Southeast Asia.[14] Only amphibious operations could penetrate shallow waters, rivers, and lakes, as Trim illustrates in his essay. Thus amphibious operations were regarded, despite the problems associated with them, as sometimes the only way to make inroads into territory (especially in an age before railways and expressways). This utility, along with the prospect of dominating regions through

---

[13] Anderson (1988), 27.
[14] Boxer (1991); Newitt, ch. 4, above; Van Dyke (1997).

'brown water' vessels (as in Ireland, the Low Countries and south-east Asia) literally opened new pathways to conquest. There was therefore a strong incentive to use amphibious warfare despite the problems inherent to it that made it difficult to get right;[15] or at least to get right from the point of view of the state as opposed to the private enterprisers who might supply many ships and/or troops.

The essays reveal that the evolution of European amphibious was not necessarily linear, or predetermined by the West's material culture, nor even inevitable. Jeremy Black has drawn attention to diversity in warfare over the years.[16] In terms of geography, riverine and lacustrine warfare presented different challenges than those encountered fighting on the high seas. For example, in his discussion of the drawing of the 1594 siege of Enniskillen (reproduced in figures 11 and 12) Geoffrey Parker remarks that the techniques being used 'explain why the English took nine years to suppress Tyrone's rebellion'.[17] As we have seen, however, the Enniskillen siege was a significant victory. The apparently esoteric blend of 'military revolution'-type technology (comparatively large siege guns) and medieval warfare (scaling ladders and axes) emphasises the eclecticism of the English art of war.[18] Thus, as Black argues, there was no single paradigm. The capture of Enniskillen Castle and its environs was a remarkable example of power projection (or force projection) at a time when traditional warfare was simply not doing the job in Ireland. Power projection was not simply a matter of resources; rather it was how resources were used. How they were used was determined by military, naval and amphibious thinking, in short the combatant's martial culture.

It is clear that success in amphibious warfare partly depended on how cultures conceptualised and then subsequently actualised warfare. The English in the sixteenth and seventeenth centuries had the resources (within reason) and ability to wage amphibious warfare, but they were held back by the concept of what the state could and could not do, and that dovetailed with their view of the individual/private sector in English society. In Sweden and Denmark, the

---

[15] Discussed below, p. 432.
[16] E.g., Black (2003), 7–8 (and in a number of works).
[17] Parker (1988), 30.
[18] Fissel (2001), xi–xii, 282–94.

kings embraced amphibious warfare and this helped to ensure that, when it was put into practice, it was with support from across military and naval institutions. It is also striking that in France, Sweden and Denmark, absolutist states, amphibious operations throughout the seventeenth century were conducted to further overall strategy and war aims, rather than simply to plunder. The Portuguese example, too, shows that a state's tenacity might project their power to the ends of the earth, but could be limited by conceptualisation: for example, the Portuguese reluctance to penetrate beyond the foreign littoral and into the hinterland.

Certainly the likelihood of successful amphibious warfare (like victory in warfare in general) was greatly augmented by the administrative structure of a centralised state. War demanded taxation (as the justification for the early English parliaments for example, and the Florentine *catasto*). The peril engendered by armed conflict justified to a population the state's need to gather revenue for the public defence, and the state's obligation to manage human resources as well as material resources.[19] What should be kept in mind regarding amphibious warfare was that once resources had been secured, the state had to formulate (consciously) viable strategies. And strategies are useless without proper coordination (organisation), tools of warfare (technology) and the intellectual flexibility to use them.

Ports

Ports played a pivotal role in medieval and early-modern amphibious warfare. This may seem obvious, but in the last century it has not been the case. From Gallipoli, to Dieppe, Operations Torch and Husky, Anzio, Normandy, Leyte and the Pacific island battles, to Inchon, and San Carlos, landings were made onto open beaches. In contrast, as the essays in this volume bring out, medieval and early-modern amphibious warfare typically focused on blocking or capturing ports, partly because they are safe harbours, but even more because they were potential sources of wealth. Ports represented the conjuncture not only of maritime and continental space, as Trim points out, but also of war and commerce.

---

[19] Lindegren (2000).

In twentieth-century amphibious warfare, technological advances made it possible both to land and then, to an extent, to maintain armies away from ports. The creation of artificial ports for the D-Day landings (the Mulberry harbours) is probably a red herring in this respect; the real key has been the increase in endurance of ships, owing to stronger construction and the introduction of oil-powered engines, and the consequent innovation of fleet refuelling and replenishing (aided by communication advances), so that in the Pacific in World War II, or in the South Atlantic in the Falklands War, a fleet could be a floating base. This is why the most likely sites for amphibious landings in the last century or so have been open beaches. Of course, often they are beaches close to good harbours and port-cities, whose logistical and transportation facilities make them desirable; but only often—not always. Still, even in World War II, the importance of ports affected the shape of campaigns and dictated the targets of amphibious operations. The Torch landings in 1942 were all in the near vicinity of ports, as was the Salerno operation in 1943, while access to Antwerp and use of its port facilities necessitated amphibious operations. In earlier centuries, such considerations shaped war even more and thus it is vital *not* to conceptualize amphibious operations as only or even essentially beach landings. Amphibious warfare in the period 1000–1700 (and indeed in ancient and later early-modern times) was focused on ports.

This partly reflected resulted from operational and strategic imperatives. Safe harbourages and dock facilities were indispensable for naval warfare, but of course the same amenities were what drew large-scale commerce and allowed armies, too, to be supplied. Ports could also control vital choke points on both maritime and inland waterways. Thus, they could attract military campaigns and were of course prime targets during attempted conquests.[20] In addition, strategic defence might engender amphibious raids on them to prevent them being used as bases for invasions or expeditions. For strategic and logistical reasons, then, strategy in a war might (as in the sixteenth-century Mediterranean) revolve around 'the attack, relief and defense of fortified ports'.[21]

---

[20] E.g., see Trim, ch. 11, above, pp. 384–94, 397; Jones (1942), 460–2.
[21] Guilmartin (1974), 107.

It is not only because ports could be logistical bases for future military and naval operations, however, that they were the focus of amphibious warfare. There were deeper economical, social and cultural factors at work.

Ports were important in the pre-industrial world because there were no urban industrial centers for the generation of wealth. Money was concentrated where commercial routes intersected, rarely elsewhere. Historically, entrepôts—the locales that serve as meeting-places and points of exchange for international or inter-regional traders—were typically sited on coastal or riverine sites. Because of this positioning, such port cities typically have been centres both 'of commerce and . . . of political and military power, the latter being deployed to maintain the pre-eminence of the entrepôt'. The tendency for amphibious operations in this period to be undertaken for specifically commercial or economic purposes made ports even more of a target, in and of themselves, regardless of their extra value as bases for further military operations, or for commanding seas or straits. In addition, however, ports were often also located at crucial liminal points between zones—if only on the vital point at which seagoing traffic could go no further up estuaries or rivers so that goods had to be trans-shipped to smaller carriers. Riverine and canaline systems were the veins of commerce and such transshipment locales were its nodal points.[22] Control of them was, again, an obvious strategic objective—and not simply to allow better supply to armies, but also for the future control of trade and even of cultural interaction between nations, peoples and regions.

Finally, ports were also foci for campaigns because of the medieval and early-modern culture of honour, which emphasised personal reputation and glory, so that the capture of a great port would greatly enhance the reputation of the prince who could capture it (or have it taken for him by his commanders). The capture of the French port of Boulogne by the English King Henry VIII's in 1544 seemed of great importance to his subjects, even though, as modern historians have pointed out, it could only ever yield but limited strategic fruit. The loss of Rouen in 1562 seemed far worse to the Huguenots than it might to us today, given that they and their English allies

---

[22] Chapman (1957), 115–16. Wake (1997), 74; Broeze (1997) 4; Trim, ch. 11, above, pp. 364–5, 369–70.

still held Le Havre, and thus blocked the Seine. The capture of
Antwerp by the Spanish seemed more disastrous in 1585 than it
would today, especially since, even in 1585, it was clear from the
recent history of the Dutch Revolt (much less from our knowledge
of events in 1944) that, because the Dutch held much of the shores
of the Scheldt, they would be able to blockade the city quite effectively,
so that its restoration to Spanish rule would not also restore the
wealth derived from its trade to Habsburg coffers.[23] But all three
cities were great prizes in and of themselves and the reputation
gained by taking such places was a reward in and of itself. Likewise
the loss of a port or port-fortress could be so dishonourable that
avoiding the loss of honour was in itself a motivation for an active
defence, in addition to any strategic or logistic considerations.[24]
Whether as attacker or defender, the issue of honour (which is similar to but not the same as prestige) again helped to focus medieval
and early modern operations on port cities and fortresses.

Thus, in considering medieval and early-modern amphibious warfare, modern conceptions have to be put aside. Open coastlines were
of little interest and no value to pre-industrial statesmen and commanders: operations involving maritime capacity, which of course all
amphibious operations do, were possible only in regions where there
were good anchorages, or in lands drained by large and navigable
rivers.[25]

Operational and Strategical Conclusions

The Most Complex Form of Warfare

Amphibious operations, because they *are* combined operations, are
inherently very complex and therefore very difficult. This has been
true throughout history; as one Royal Marine theorist of amphibious operations observed in 1940: 'A combined operation requires
the most careful planning and preparation, and during its execution
presents great problems in co-operation and coordination.' And he

---

[23] Trim (1999), 246–7; idem, ch. 11, above, pp. 385–7, 389–90.
[24] E.g., PRO, SP 70/43, f. 193r: Throckmorton to Cecil, 30 Oct. 1562.
[25] See Trim, ch. 11, above, p. 360.

perceptively noted that 'co-ordination of the three services' was the greatest problem. Indeed, as one narrative of the Normandy campaign observes, an amphibious assault 'requires more precise planning and organisation than any other military operation'.[26] But it is worth stressing that it was not only true in the modern era of industrialised warfare and 'triphibious' operations. In the eighteenth century, too, 'An amphibious assault [was] one of the most difficult of military operations.'[27] Nor was this the result only of developments during the eighteenth century. As many of our contributors show, in the period 1000–1700, too, amphibious operations 'were among the most difficult and most risky' endeavours that might be undertaken in war, because 'amphibious warfare is inherently more complex, more prone to uncertainty and ambiguity and more difficult to understand than warfare on land, at sea, or in the air.'[28]

Although amphibious operations of this period lacked the size and complexity of those in the twentieth century, command and control mechanisms were also far more limited (conceptually *and* technologically), so that the problem inherent to combined operations of all ages—how to co-ordinate forces on both land and water, drawn from different organisations with distinct (and often incompatible) hierarchies—was no less difficult to solve. Indeed, it was often more difficult: assembling a medieval or early-modern amphibious expedition required combining not only navies and armies, or different allied nationalities, but also a range of different types of force, with different organisations and institutional allegiances, reflecting the diversity of society in an era when centralized states did not yet exist or were still in their formative stage.

In addition, both the technologies *and* tactical modes used in medieval and early-modern combined operations frequently were new and not yet fully tried; and the inchoate nature of many medieval and early-modern military institutions meant that knowledge gained by experience was not always transmitted, accurately or at all, whether to contemporaries or the next generation. The technologies were, moreover, still evolving and the medieval and early-modern world-

---

[26] Quoted in Bittner (1991), 359. McKee (1964), 10.
[27] Syrett (1973), 269; see also Burne (1939), 103; and Harding (1991), 198.
[28] Sicking, ch. 3, above, p. 92; Guilmartin, ch. 6, above, p. 150; and see also chs. 5, 8, above, pp. 123, 218.

view was not well adapted to taking on board radical change. The mindset was static rather than progressive in the modern sense. So not only were the technologies new and not fully tried, they were difficult to grasp and (especially) to apply.

The complexity of amphibious warfare in this period is an important point, for even while the great potential of amphibious operations for the projection of power was encouraging early-modern European powers to use amphibious warfare, its problematic nature was a constraint on its use. Thus, whereas the fourteenth-century Hanseatic League waged amphibious war because this was the only way to safeguard trade, the sixteenth-century States of Holland rejected it as too expensive, because of the risks inherent in it.

A fundamental obstacle to the successful conduct of amphibious operations is that it is necessary to resolve difficulties in both land and water. John Guilmartin draws attention to 'the inherently greater complexity of movement along the boundary separating two distinct mediums or performance regimes than within a uniform medium or regime'.[29] Arguably the progression of difficulty when operations have to be undertaken in a second physical element is geometrical, rather than arithmetical: they square, rather than double. This problem affects all combined operations.

Other difficulties, too, are inherent to amphibious operations, regardless of period. Transferring troops from ships to shore in a state ready to do combat effectively is innately difficult, requiring exhaustive planning before, and no little skill during, the operation. Men, equipment and victuals (and often animals) need to be embarked with forethought first for conditions on the voyage but second and above all for their landing, while appropriate measures need to be taken for their maintenance and discipline while afloat; in the absence of all these, their efficiency after landing is likely to be grossly impaired. Then, too, unusual command and control mechanisms need to be developed—and then implemented—to ensure that troops and ships are properly prepared for a landing and then carry out that landing effectively.[30] Many of these remarks apply, too, but in reverse, to the evacuation of troops from a combat situation.

---

[29] Above, ch. 6, p. 150.
[30] Syrett (1973), 269–70; Aston (1920), 26–8; cf. Mackesy (1970), printing PRO, WO 1/411, 331–8: regulations for Russian troops when embarked, 1799.

Because of the complexity of combined operations, the coordination of land and sea forces is vital for success—yet is remarkably difficult to achieve. When in the course of amphibious operations naval and land elements have become disaggregated, failure has usually resulted. It is perhaps not surprising that British defence planners in the 1920s–'30s, with the Gallipoli campaign very much in mind, took the view that, for amphibious assaults to avoid disaster, they had to be very small in size and aims, involving only a few ships and less than a battalion of troops.[31] The Allies went on to show in World War II that this was not so, but suffered problems along the way and the difficulty in actually combining the different forces and elements in combined operations is evident from the declaration, in US combined service doctrine of the 1960s, that an amphibious operation '*is* characterized by closely integrated efforts of forces trained, organized, and equipped for different combatant functions'[32]—an excellent example of an organization attempting by categorical statement in theory to achieve an actual state of affairs which is in fact unlikely to exist.

However, while failure to coordinate properly land and sea aspects, with consequent failure for the mission more generally, has been a *leitmotif* of amphibious warfare at least up to the Second World War, in the period up to *c.* 1700 coordination was even more difficult than in following centuries. Princes and their ministers increasingly recognised that amphibious warfare provided an excellent means of projecting power, and this in step with enhanced ambitions. Yet because amphibious operations were so complex, early-modern states lacked the financial and logistical means to mount them from their own resources. The rulers of early-modern states, with their counsellors, might think as grandly as their modern descendants, but lacked their institutional infrastructure: they could conceive of expeditions larger than they could actually set forth—strategically they had eyes bigger than their stomachs.

In consequence, amphibious operations could only be prepared in cooperation with and after negotiation with a range of non-state actors: cities, provincial estates, guilds and companies, and individual merchants and nobles. And while this affected military and naval

---

[31] MacGregor (1992), 607–8.
[32] Quoted in O'Connor (1974), 97, emphasis supplied.

establishments in the early-modern period more generally, because amphibious forces had to be drawn from *both* land *and* sea forces, in amphibious operations there were typically *two* sets of local, regional, mercantile and noble prejudices and lobbies whose reservations had to be overcome, or whose own preferences and imperatives had to be accommodated.

To mount an amphibious expedition thus stretched the resources of the early-modern state even more than fielding an army or a fleet; and such expeditions inevitably revealed the signs of strain. Troops and ships often came, as we have seen, from 'private', not state resources, or from a variety of state resources, which meant sometimes the resultant force was multi-institutional in origins; sometimes (as in the case of Crusading armies, early-modern Habsburg forces, Christian forces fighting the Ottoman Turks, Anglo-Scots forces in Ireland, and Anglo-Dutch forces in the Nine Years' War) multi-ethnic, if not multi-national; or multi-faith. And in this period multi-institutional rivalries could almost rival those between different nations and tongues, if not of different faiths.

Alternatively, an expedition might only be possible by alliance with other princes or states—from the Crusades, through the Hanseatic League's conflicts, to the Christian defence of the Mediterranean, to King William's wars, amphibious warfare in this period was often coalition warfare. As a result of the commonplace multiplicity of sources for troops and ships, raised from different areas, under different authorities, different paymasters and so forth, spheres of command and authority were frequently blurred. Obstructionism rarely went as far as that of the States of Holland which in 1536, in the face of a centralising Habsburg Admiralty, actually prevented a planned amphibious operation from taking place. But the failure of the Hanseatic League's allies to appear in the proper strength caused the Hansa's defeat in the first war of Valdemar in 1361–2.[33] And such dramatic breaches of promise were not the only danger inherent to operations which combined nationalities as well as types of forces—hostility between different ethnicities, or simple misunderstandings due to different languages or customs, whether among land or sea forces or both, were almost as potent a threat to the

---

[33] Ch. 3, above.

success of an operation. Even the most straightforward and most successful Elizabethan amphibious operation, that in Brittany in 1594, succeeded despite serious difficulties caused by differences between the English and French allies. Differences between English and Dutch helped to disrupt the attempted relief of Sluys in 1587 and the planned offensive against the Spanish in the East Indies and China Sea in the mid 1620s, and were a factor in operations during the European Nine Years' War.[34] Command of amphibious operations was never straightforward in this period, even when control of armies and navies by states was increasing.

Furthermore, as a result of the frequently blurred command structures, professional hierarchies were more difficult to establish, and hence systematization and perpetuation of expertise was inhibited, so that the lessons of experience in combined operations were not necessarily learned. Finally and crucially, obtaining plunder was frequently either a desire of or a necessity for the commanders of expeditions sent forth to wage amphibious warfare, whether to repay private investors, recoup state expenses, or often both. In consequence, the objectives of expeditions not only often shifted until they differed from the original concept, but also frequently became multiple and blurred, rather than focused. A prince or republic might decide to set forth an amphibious expedition for a specific purpose, but very often to mount the expedition it was necessary to take steps that necessitated changing its aims.

All too often, then, an amphibious expedition's doom was inherent in its constitution. To coordinate forces in medieval and early-modern amphibious warfare was certainly an art, not a science, not least because it involved coordination not only of army, navy and marine corps units (which nineteenth- and twentieth-century militaries have found difficult enough), but also of a variety of almost private armies and navies—all with barely a handful of staff officers! Thus, if things often went wrong, in medieval and early-modern amphibious warfare, we ought not be surprised; rather, combined operations in the period 1000–1700 worked very effectively surprisingly often. This was partly because medieval and early-modern commanders were used to having to negotiate with subalterns and keep

---

[34] Above, pp. 198, 200, 324–5, 337–9, 351, 393; Van Dyke (1997).

different ethnicities apart—but it was also because a number of commanders of expeditions prioritised overcoming the huge obstacles to
effective combination and coordination of different forces and, perhaps because they were used to a balancing act, were successful to
an impressive degree.

When medieval and early-modern combined operations succeeded,
good leadership was an important ingredient—as it has been in
amphibious warfare in all periods. What made good leadership difficult
was that command was very often divided. This was to be an endemic
failing. For example, from the immediate aftermath of Gallipoli right
up to the start of World War II, even after the Japanese landings
at Tientsin in 1937 had helped to spark the institution by the UK
Chiefs of Staff of an Inter-Service Training and Development Centre,
dedicated to the development of effective combined operations, the
British army and navy were unwilling to face up to the complications of integrating operations and still refused even to accept the
basic necessity of subordinating a combined operation to a single
supreme commander, ultimately with a joint staff.[35] In riverine operations in Vietnam, the US Army and Navy (and Marines and Coast
Guard!) never worked out satisfactory command and control for their
'brown water' squadrons. Unity of command is a lesson that should
not have needed relearning, but did, and probably still does.

One way to master the complexities of amphibious warfare, whether
technical, operational, logistical or administrative, is to study previous amphibious campaigns in order to identify the problems that
must be solved. In a sense, this volume of essays is but the last in
a long line of historical analysis of amphibious warfare, dating back
at least to the late 1580s. The original commander-in-chief appointed
for the Spanish Armada was the Duke of Santa Cruz, who had commanded the successful Spanish amphibious invasion of the Azores
in 1583 and, as part of his preparations for the invasion of England,
he had his staff closely study 'past amphibious operations, from the
successful landings of the Romans and Saxons in Kent to those of
the Lancastrians in the fifteenth century. . . . The more recent attempts
of the French (in 1545, against the Isle of Wight) and the Papal
adventurers (at Smerwick) were also noted', and so, no doubt, was

---

[35] Harding (2000); Maund (1949), 5–6; Bittner (1991), 357.

the recent operation in the Azores [figures 6–7]. We do not know whether the Duke of Medina Sidonia (who succeeded to command on Santa Cruz's death from natural causes) studied the papers prepared by Santa Cruz's staff based on their research; it seems doubtful.[36] But it may not have mattered, for the Armada's problem in 1588 was that it never got the chance to carry out an amphibious operation—the English fleet and North Sea weather kept it away from the English coasts and left it as a naval, rather than amphibious operation. It is, however, clear that Elizabeth I's senior commanders drew on each other's experience in the war with Spain, as English tactics at La Coruña in 1589 and Cadiz in 1596 clearly reveal the benefit of experience.[37] The great improvement in French practice of amphibious operations in the later part of the seventeenth century also, as Guy Rowlands shows, was due to a conscious determination to learn the lessons of earlier failures.[38]

Flexibility

Amphibious warfare offers great operational flexibility, because it can be so mobile. This was particularly true in the period 1000–1700, where land communications were no faster than the speed of a horse, and armies could not proceed faster than a man might walk. Seagoing operations still owned the monopoly on speed, and speed gave amphibious raiders a marked advantage, particular in tactical operations. The slowness of medieval and early-modern communications proportionally increased the value of manoeuvrability and tactical flexibility. Amphibious operations could exploit a change in situation in an era where tactical options, especially in combat situations, were minimal compared to modern operations. Traditional forces are more static and thus inert in many tactical situations, which amphibious operations could exploit in a substantial fashion.[39]

This flexibility and manoeuvrability were among the factors adduced by Liddell Hart in support of the superiority of a grand strategy based on expeditionary warfare. It was present in pre-industrial amphibious warfare too. The mobility of Portuguese maritime forces

---

[36] Martin & Parker (1988), 109. Fissel, ch. 8, above, p. 228.
[37] Ch. 7, above, pp. 193, 206.
[38] Ch. 9, above.
[39] Meyer (2000), 100–8.

was disconcerting and destructive to their enemies in the Indian Ocean.[40] Considering the threat posed by the Spanish Armada in 1588, Sir Walter Ralegh observed that the enemy fleet 'may be seen at sunset . . . at the Lizard, yet by the next morning they may [be off] Portland; whereas an army on foot shall not be able to march it in six dayes.' Seventeen years later, an unknown English strategic theorist gloomily commented on the danger inherent in the Spanish ability to make 'landings where they please'.[41] The sophisticated ability to deploy and shift forces as needed was, as Jan Glete shows, a key element in early-modern Sweden's ability to punch above its weight in the Baltic and northern Germany. Mark Fissel in chapter eight draws attention to the English use of 'firepower and mobility' in Ireland.[42]

Strategy

To exploit amphibious warfare's flexibility clear strategic goals were essential. That is, the aims and objectives of an amphibious operation, as well as its chain of command, plan of attack, logistics, etc, needed to be clear, or else utter failure was all too possible. Of course, such clarity is desirable in all actions of war, but purely military or naval operations are more likely to achieve at least operational success than amphibious operations due to the latter's complexity.

One of the chief dangers of amphibious warfare is that combined operations will be launched simply because they can be, rather than to secure strategic goals. Too many eighteenth- and nineteenth-century British amphibious 'descents' were motivated not so much by what most aided national war aims, but by what could be done, and where it could be done most easily.[43] This was also a failing of the Allies in the Second World War. Admiral Cunningham, Field Marshall Alexander and Admiral Ramsay, reflecting on their experience of the landings in North Africa, Sicily, Italy, and other proposed amphibious assaults, stressed the need for amphibious operations to be conducted not just because landing craft were available, naval

---

[40] Newitt, ch. 4, above.
[41] Ralegh, quoted in Gatchel (1996), 5–6; cf. Map 4. Anon. (1605), art. 7.
[42] Above, ch. 5, p. 146 et passim; ch. 8, p. 219.
[43] Burne (1939), 104–5.

strength permitted landings, or coastal places *could* be captured; but rather to execute, facilitate or support realistic military strategies. Ramsay, too, emphasised that the operational plan must be based wholly on the strategic objective.[44]

Some amphibious operations, however, arguably result from *no* strategy. Certainly many amphibious operations in the period 1000–1700 were *not* undertaken to further strategic visions; rather, they were undertaken for specific operations, such as plundering and the capture or relief of specific ports, for economic, logistical or prestige reasons. This could have unhappy consequences: examples include the Hansa's expedition to Denmark in 1362, the Spanish Armada in 1588, the Elizabethan expeditions to Lisbon in 1589 and the Azores in 1597, and arguably the 1694 expedition to Brest (mounted to meet political enthusiasm for a strategy of 'descents').[45]

Tactical and Operational Conclusions

The importance of bombardment

The role of naval bombardments in early-modern warfare is under-researched.[46] The provision of 'naval gunfire support' might be assumed to be a modern phenomenon, dependent on the increase in weight, range and, even more, accuracy of artillery fire since the industrial revolution. Certainly, in modern combined operations, naval gunfire support has been critical. Planning for the greatest amphibious operation of all, the D-Day landings, Admiral Ramsay stressed the role of 'naval supporting fire and Field Marshal Montgomery wrote that the Allied forces 'must blast our way on shore'. As a result of the failure to apply the lessons of the Pacific, where initial bombardments were crucial to the success of the US Navy and Marines' island-hopping campaign against the Japanese, the Allied preliminary bombardment on D-Day was not as heavy as it should have been—and in some places, the price was paid in lives. But

---

[44] Cunningham, quoted in Barnett (1991), 632; Reid (1992), 121; Ramsay (1944), rubric 'The Assault Plan'; and see Barnett (1991), 680.

[45] See above, pp. 73–5, 188, 228–9, 189–97, 336–7, 339, 344–6.

[46] Lynn (2005).

naval gunfire support was also important *after* landings, in protecting the lodgements—the fire of a range of battleships, cruisers and
destroyers (even the latter mounted a gun heavier than used by most
land-based artillery) was vital in the aftermath of the Salerno, Anzio
and Normandy landings, breaking up German counter-attacks by the
sheer weight of fire.[47]

Naval artillery fire was also important in the sixteenth and seventeenth centuries. Of course, range and accuracy did not compare
to modern standards, obliging ships either to bombard from ineffective
ranges or come so close to defences that they were themselves endangered by return fire.[48] The effects on fortifications did not always
match those achieved by nineteenth-century European fleets in the
era of 'gunboat diplomacy', as noted in chapter one. Thus, as Malyn
Newitt notes, Vasco da Gama on his first visit to Mozambique Island
in 1498 'bombarded the palisades which had been erected in front
of a village on the mainland for three hours and only succeeded in
killing two people'. In April 1669 another Portuguese fleet bombarded Muscat for several days without decisive effect.[49] The latter
case may have reflected the proliferation of sophisticated military
defences throughout the world, which increasingly safeguarded places
from fleets' gunfire alone—a Portuguese squadron had bombarded
Muscat two years earlier 'to some effect'. Even if the city had not
acquired *trace italienne*-style fortifications in the interim, the fact is
that, as the period went on, successful bombardment of *defended* locales
became more difficult. The sheer weight of fire from shore forts
(which could mount as many guns as ships, even if they did not
have the most up-to-date defences) alone might deter fleets.[50]

In contrast, earlier in the period, ship-borne mobile heavy artillery
was potentially 'more dangerous for medieval fortifications highly
vulnerable to gunfire than were heavy and immobile guns used from
land against ships'; even in the late seventeenth century there were
still some cities and fortresses—perhaps with no, or ill maintained
trace italienne fortifications, or lacking coastal defence batteries—that

---

[47] Ramsay (1944), rubric 'Naval Supporting Fire'; Montgomery, quoted in Carver
(1992), 159; Murry & Millett (2000), 380, 419.
[48] See Guilmartin (1974), 162–4; Trim, ch. 10, above, pp. 392–93.
[49] Above, p. 113; Ames (1997), 402.
[50] Harding (1991), 198; Ames (1997), 401; Guilmartin (1974), 76–7, 80; Ramsay
(1944), *loc. cit.*; Rowlands, ch. 9, above, p. 293.

fleets alone could bombard effectively.[51] In addition, in the late seventeenth century technological evolution produced specialist bombardment vessels which helped to even the balance between shore defences and naval artillery. These *galiotes à bombe* or bomb ketches [figures 20, 27] could take great punishment but lacked good sea-handling capability—their sole purpose was to project heavy firepower onto shore. Using them was a difficult art, but when handled properly they could inflict formidable destruction [figures 19–20, 25–7].[52]

However, while purely naval bombardments can form part of an amphibious strategy, bombardment in this period seems to have worked best when deployed in coordination with land-based forces or an assault from the sea—in other words, as part of a combined operation. Even *galiotes à bombes* were often used in conjunction with landings.[53]

Bombardment from sea or river could be decisive against fortifications: famously in the successful Turkish siege of Constantinople in 1453, but also, as we have seen, in the siege of Honfleur in 1590, and in the frequent English attacks on small strongholds in Ireland and Scotland in the sixteenth and seventeenth centuries and in the Mediterranean under Louis XIV.[54] In all these cases, it was not naval bombardment alone that brought results, but rather the application of ship-based artillery fire in support of action by ground forces. The weight of bombardment could also smooth the progress of landings. In 1494, for example, during Charles VIII's invasion of Italy, usually remembered for the French use of (relatively) mobile field artillery, at Rapallo, near Genoa, the French fleet made perhaps history's first assault landing covered by cannon fire, which succeeded partly because of the weight of fire concentrated against the shore by naval artillery. In 1598, English use of a coordinated naval bombardment and assault landing neutralised the Spanish forts defending San Juan de Puerto Rico where purely maritime and terrestrial actions had failed. In 1684 the combination of bombardment and landings by the French brought the Republic of Genoa to its knees in a week.[55]

---

[51] Above, pp. 71, 268–71, 287, 293–94, 332–4, 339; see also Guilmartin (1974), 80.
[52] Above, pp. 270, 287–8, 292, 295–6, 320–1, 345–6, 349–50.
[53] E.g., above, ch. 9. p. 270; ch. 10, p. 333.
[54] Above, ch. 11, p. 392; ch. 8, *passim*; ch. 9, pp. 270–2.
[55] Le Roy Ladurie (1994), 83; Fissel, ch. 8, above, p. 225; Rowlands, ch. 9 above, p. 270.

Bombardment could also have a powerful effect when in support of ground troops conducting what would have been, without the naval gunfire support, straight military operations. An English fleet accompanied the army that invaded Scotland in 1547 and bombarded the Scottish army during the Battle of Pinkie; an English fleet bombarded the French army at the Battle of Gravelines (1557); an Anglo-Dutch fleet came close inshore to bombard the Spanish army during the Battle of Nieuwpoort (1600) and an English fleet did likewise to help the Anglo-French army against the Spanish at the Battle of The Dunes (1657). In the cases of Pinkie and Gravelines contemporaries declared that the fleets' action made an important contribution to victory: the bombardment at Pinkie is explicitly said to have disrupted the Scottish pike formations, an important tactical factor, and at Gravelines it is said to have killed many men (though this may well be exaggeration) while a contemporary illustration of Nieuwpoort shows the Spanish formations fighting nearest to the sea as having suffered casualties.[56]

Given the range limitations on early-modern artillery, the effects may have been more moral than fatal. But this could be said about the effects of firepower for much of the six centuries of their use in warfare. As in twentieth-century amphibious campaigns, ship-board cannon were heavier than any land-based field pieces and many siege guns, so that the weight of fire must be considered. The English warship *Prince Royal*, constructed in 1610, carried more guns and probably greater 'total weight of artillery' than all fifty-two galleys in the Ottoman fleet of the infamous Barbarossa, in 1534, put together; the *Sovereign of the Seas*, launched in 1637, carried a hundred heavy guns, whereas a few years later during the English Civil War, twenty was a lavish allocation for the main armies. The French fleet at the battle of Beachy Head in 1690 mounted 4,600 cannon, when field armies might have a hundredth of that.[57] The effects of such a massive weight of fire (and the associated noise, smoke and so forth) on troops' morale must have been horrible.

---

[56] Churchyard (1579), sig. L4; anon. (1597), 36; Orlers (1610), plate 33 (between pp. 152–3); and see Caldwell (1991), 79–80, 84, 87–8; Fegan (1999), 47–50.

[57] Guilmartin (1974), 40; Young (1973), 30–1; Rowlands, ch. 9, below, p. 291.

Defensive Amphibious Operations and Tactics

Amphibious offensive operations are often best met by an amphibious defence. Defence against a purely military threat could normally
be solely land-based; defence against a naval operation might require
a combined defence, but an amphibious operation would require a
greater degree of combined defence than a naval attack alone. Shore
batteries and forts on islands in harbours were standard defensive
works for the protection of coastal towns, whether naval bases or
not, but while these might, as we have seen, suffice to deter a purely,
or even predominantly naval threat, they would not suffice if the
force afloat had any significant ability to deploy ashore. Thus, it was
essential to defend by land and by sea and to do so cooperatively.
Thus, in 1536, one of the planners of the Habsburg and allied attack
on Copenhagen observed that an amphibious expedition could
approach the city 'without problems if [it] were only' defended by
land.[58] A major underlying factor in the loss of Quebec in 1759 was
the failure of the French commander, the Marquis de Montcalm,
'to hold strategic points which commanded the waters adjacent to
Quebec, and allowed the British to seize them'.[59] In other words,
he failed to mount an amphibious defence against what was indu-
bitably an amphibious threat, and paid the penalty. Sixteen years
later, an army from the rebellious American colonies besieged Quebec;
amongst many factors in the successful defence of the city in 1775–76,
as opposed to its fall in 1759, was the fact that the British garrison
had the support of ships and maintained maritime communications,
whereas the rebel force, other than canoes and small boats, was
essentially land-based. Earlier, Dutch mastery of integrating ground
troops with 'brown water' fleets was an important factor in the successful defence of Alkmaar, Leiden and prolonged the defence of
Haarlem and Sluys.[60] The Germans and Italians were unable to
mount a combined army-navy defence in Sicily in 1943, because of
Allied sea-power, which was then used three times to carry out from
the sea flanking attacks impossible or difficult on land alone, to break
German communications.[61]

---

[58] Sicking, ch. 3, above, p. 88.
[59] Keyes (1943), 17.
[60] Trim, ch. 11, above.
[61] Whitehouse (1964), 69–76. Keyes (1943), 101–2.

Islands, in particular, are often defended better by amphibious than by purely naval or military defensive systems. Because the sea surrounds them, they invite landings from the sea, even in support of fleet actions (or of a land campaign), in a way not as true of the coastlines of continents (or very large islands) where the opportunity to launch attacks from all sides, or at least several directions, does not exist. Territories drained by great rivers may become almost equivalent to islands in this regard: thus, the British fleet in 1759 threatened, 'by amphibious strokes', French communications with Quebec, over thirty miles away from the city.[62] Peninsular, as well as insular targets, invite amphibious assault, whether as a main operation, or in support of land campaigns. The British in 1799 attempted to use their command of the North Sea and Zuider Zee to outflank their Franco-Dutch opponents in North Holland; the British and French landings at Suvla Bay attempted to outflank the enemy position on the Gallipoli peninsula in 1915. In these two campaigns, the amphibious turning movement in fact came to nothing, even without an amphibious defence, but arguably in both cases insufficient use was made of the manoeuvrability inherent in amphibious operations.[63] In contrast, Allied forces made great strides in the Arakan peninsula (in Burma) in 1944–5 by use of a series of landings, jumping down the peninsula sequentially; but then the Arakan was also part of a complex thicket of islands and river estuaries and the amphibious strategy adopted there exploited, as in Sicily the previous year, the particular vulnerability of islands to sea assault.[64]

To guard against this type of vulnerability, the multinational defenders of Malta in 1565, the Spanish defenders of San Juan de Puerto Rico in 1595, and even the brief British administration in Hawaii in 1843, in planning to protect islands against the threat of a truly amphibious operation—as opposed to the threat solely of raiding ships—all had both military *and* naval components in their defensive plan; and did so because it was necessary.[65] Their successful defences are in marked contrast to that of the Sultanate of Paté in 1678 in the face of Portuguese amphibious assault. Lacking the naval strength

[62] Keyes (1943), 17.
[63] Burne (1939), 113, 117; Aston (1920), xii.
[64] Lyman (2004), 72 *et seq.*; Murray & Millett (2000), 491, 302–3.
[65] Above, ch. 6, *passim*; ch. 7, pp. 201–2; and Bliss (2003), 25.

to withstand a powerful Portuguese squadron, the Sultan's troops fought on the beaches and were defeated there, dooming the city of Paté (which lies on an island) to a long siege, which it lacked the resources to withstand. The city was sacked twice and its ruler and his allies executed.[66] A more balanced defence might have avoided this fate, as in the case of Malta in 1565.[67]

Insular targets are also, however, vulnerable to amphibious counter-offensive. For example, the Hanseatic besiegers of Helsingborg in 1362 and the Turkish besiegers of Malta in 1565 were both caught out by assaults that raised both sieges; the Turks withdrew in moderately good order, whereas the Hansa defeat ended the First War of Valdemar.[68] In contrast, the Turkish forces in Crete in 1669 were strong enough and capably handled enough both to maintain the siege of Candia and to hold off the Papal-French would-be relief force, though here the Christians were troubled by a lack of coordination that did not affect the Spanish in 1565.[69]

In defending against amphibious assault more generally, coastal terrain features are very important. Where objectives lie on or near peninsulas or capes, it is essential to control the isthmus or similar necks of land. The Spanish defenders of Cartagena in 1586 had the right idea, seizing the narrow neck of land between the sea and inner harbour, but they were driven off by Christopher Carleill's bold attack; the English under Sir John Norreys and the Earl of Essex respectively made sure they seized the isthmus joining La Coruña to the mainland in 1589 and the isthmus near Cadiz in 1596, isolating both cities, which then fell.[70] Of course, sometimes it is essential to control a peninsula or isthmus because it commands important bays or other land features. Hence the Spanish governor of Malta's determination to hold Fort St Elmo at all costs in 1565 and the fortification of the Crozon peninsula near Brest by the Spanish in 1594.[71] The Spanish governor of seventeenth-century Rio

---

[66] Ames (1997), 405–6. The Portuguese soon after fell foul of an Omani fleet and were driven away, but not before the city's sack and sultan's execution. For Paté, see map 7.

[67] See ch. 6, above.

[68] Above, ch. 3, p. 74 and ch. 6, pp. 176–7.

[69] Above, ch. 9, p. 268.

[70] Above, ch. 7, pp. 185, 193, 206.

[71] Above, ch. 6, pp. 171–2 and ch. 7, pp. 197–9; maps 10, 12.

de Janeiro province who 'with great diligence looked after the vigilance and guard of Cabo Frio' also acted wisely, for his action was
instrumental in thwarting a Dutch expedition in 1630.[72]

When a landing has taken place, it is important for the defenders to attempt to ensure that the means of egress from the landing
zone is blocked. This was what the Spanish defenders tried to do
at Cartagena in 1586, but failed. The German defenders at Anzio
in 1944 provide perhaps the best-known example of accomplishing
it successfully.[73]

Preparation and Organisation

Technology and Scientific Knowledge

Technology took off in the eighteenth century in a number of ways,
and made naval warfare, in particular, more potent; this had a knock-
on effect on amphibious warfare: it became even more extensively
used and (generally) successful. The preceding essays have examined
the earlier, formative, period, but technological innovation was still
important, whether it be the development of horse transports in the
early Middle Ages, or the development of larger, more powerful cannon, and ships that can act as storehouses and/or heavy gun platforms in the sixteenth century.[74]

Technological innovation had knock-on effects. The evolution of
warships in the sixteenth and seventeenth centuries produced vessels
with deeper draughts—potentially very dangerous given that amphibious operations inherently involve vessels in action close to shore.
Transports were frequently shallow-draught or even flat-bottomed (of
the sort depicted in figures 7, 8, 12 and 14), but they had only a
short-range because of their poor sailing properties, so that, while
they might be used to transport troops from a fleet to shore, the
troops still had to travel in the fleet which had to come reasonably
close to shore. Furthermore, the ideal was of course that the line-

---

[72] Teensma, ed. (1999), 2: 17: Correia de Sá to Philip IV, 17 Sept. 1630.
[73] Wernham, ch. 7, above, p. 185. Merglen (1968), 145–51; Murray & Millett
(2000), 382.
[74] See chs. 2, 3, 4, 6, 9, 10.

of-battleships would support landings with their broadsides, but the ranges of artillery in this period meant that for such support to be effective often necessarily entailed entering the shallows. For all these reasons, as naval technology evolved in the sixteenth century and took off in the seventeenth century, the danger posed by shoals, reefs and shallows grew ever greater—and so, in consequence, did the need for reliable charts.[75]

The response was to acquire greater knowledge and the foundation of modern hydrography. For example, 'superior naval cartographic knowledge and expertise' was a chief foundation for the 'stunning victory' gained by the French expeditionary force in recovering St Andrews Castle in Scotland from the English in 1547. This reflected the knowledge and enthusiasm of particular individuals, but in the later seventeenth century the French state fostered cartography and hydrography at the institutional level. James Cook's meticulous survey and mapping of the St Lawrence River, the necessary preliminary to Wolfe's capture of Quebec in 1759, and the painstaking, long-term Allied investigations of the Normandy coast, including sampling the seafloor, confirm the importance of developing auxiliary sciences in support of amphibious operations.[76]

Part of the difficulty in conceptualising how to wage amphibious warfare was that the European concepts of distance and frontiers remained inchoate until the eighteenth century.[77] The sea enabled forces to move rapidly, and with heavy loads of equipment and victuals, but how then to translate these resources (and project their inherent power) back to land-based operations? Memory and experience, coupled with ability to use technology, could only come with professionalism and permanence. A cadre of specialists had to develop, and inherit suitable state institutions that were malleable enough to reckon with the fluidity of the science of amphibious warfare.

Amphibious operations have to take into account not only maritime, fluvial and terrestrial geology, hydrology, cartography and statistics, but also meteorological conditions, both on land *and* water.

---

[75] See Fissel, ch. 8, above, pp. 220–1, 230; Newitt, ch. 4, above, pp. 118–19; Guilmartin (1974), 59, 79, 81; Rowlands, ch. 9, above, pp. 286–9; Stapleton, ch. 10, above, pp. 332–3, 350.

[76] Bonner (1996), esp. 578–80 at 578; Rowlands, ch. 9, above, pp. 285–6; Syrett (1972), 270.

[77] Meyer (2000), 99–104, 106–7, 113–22, 124–7.

Before the twentieth century, there was little that could be done about weather but its effects must be stressed. It is reasonably well known that superior weather forecasting was an important part of Allied success at D-Day, allowing them to re-schedule the landings, postponed by storms, for a short break in the bad weather predicted by Allied, but not by German, meteorologists. In contrast, the English assault landing at Cadiz in June 1596 had to be postponed after the ships' boats had already been lowered and the troops transferred to them, when a near gale sprang up.[78] The effects were felt at the strategic and operational levels as well. William the Conqueror and his army kicked their heels on the east coast of the English Channel for three months before favourable winds finally allowed them passage; Charles V lost an entire fleet and entire army with it in an autumn gale off Algiers in 1541; and while Charles had pushed his luck with the late sailing of this expedition, storms 'unusual in their seasonality and severity' helped to finish off Spain's planned amphibious invasion of England in 1588 (the Armada), summer storms did likewise to the English amphibious counteroffensive against Lisbon the following year, and had an impact on the English expedition to the Azores in 1597; and unpredictable storms first harmed then ultimately helped William of Orange's expedition to England in 1688.[79] It is worth emphasising to modern readers that medieval and early-modern amphibious operations were not only liable to disruption by bad weather (the same is true today) but the fact that this same weather could only be guessed at, even within 24-hour periods, with even medium-range forecasting of any accuracy unimaginable.

Military and Naval Interchangeability

Only when permanent fleets and naval administrative bodies emerged in the mid- to late-seventeenth century did there emerge a separate naval profession and 'a distinct naval art' (necessary to deal with the technologically more advanced ships and more sophisticated navigational techniques that had emerged by this period), in contrast to

---

[78] Murray & Millett (200), 421; Wernham, ch. 7, above, p. 205.
[79] Corvisier (1995), 73; Parry (1958), 531; Anderson (1983), esp. 16–19; above, chs 7, 10, pp. 196, 210, 315.

'the essentially part-time seagoing military activities of previous years'.[80] Only then was command at land and sea irrevocably split. This development was aided by the coincidental emergence of a distinct *military* profession in the mid- to late-seventeenth century; the mastery of distinct bodies of knowledge that went with professionalisation ensured that, thereafter, the naval officer's realm was the sea, and the army officer's the land. Prior to that, however, there was little or no sense among officers that sea and land service was distinct.[81]

A distinct conception of a *sailor* existed and 'sailors' might refuse to take part in land actions—but sailors were labourers. The presumption that military command was the natural vocation of the noble (or gentle) man meant that it was widely presumed, in turn, that military officers could command ships as well as companies, with no fall-off in performance. It was not uncommon for officers with no previous maritime experience to be placed in command of ships.[82] As late as the 1650s, the English Republic logically termed its naval commanders 'Generals at Sea'. For many soldiers, war was war, regardless whether fought on earth or water.

This is one reason why an amphibious operation cannot be defined simply in terms of the combination of army and navy, as already noted.[83] The lack of clear naval and military professions certainly sometimes had a negative effect on the conduct of amphibious operations, because very often men with little experience would be given key commands. However, it may also have had a positive effect, for often officers had experience of what today would be termed naval *and* military commands, which was exactly what was needed in amphibious warfare. The interchangeability of officers may thus have provided some unity between land and sea forces that otherwise would have been lacking and helped to overcome the absence or limitations of central command and control structures. In sum, it was not automatically a liability; it may even have sometimes been a

---

[80] Barnett (2000), 697; above, p. 23.

[81] Trim (2003); Roy (1987), 188; Guilmartin (1974), 107.

[82] E.g., the captains of English ships in the fleet that fought the Armada in 1588, in the several fleets sent to the West Indies, and in those sent to attack Lisbon in 1589, Cadiz in 1596 and the Azores in 1597 included many military officers, including some whose first (or only) naval commands were ships in these fleets: e.g., Ellis, ed. (1852), 296–7, 301–5, 307, 415, 322–3.

[83] Ch. 1, above, p. 22.

factor in success. This once again warns against assuming that military change in Latin Christendom in this period necessarily produced improvements: often they did, but sometimes they did not; the 'rise of the state', much less of 'the West' was thus not an inevitable result determined by technological or organisational change.

Wider Conclusions

Many readers will, understandably, expect a book about pre-modern warfare, state formation and European expansion to illumine the military revolution debate. The editors believe that amphibious warfare has been overshadowed and sometimes ignored in that scholarly debate, and thus we deliberately have focused on the characteristics of amphibious operations rather than to divert attention to the labyrinthine literature on 'military revolutions' or 'revolutions in military affairs' (RMAs). However, it is important to set out the degree to which the conclusions of these essays resonate with the military revolution paradigm(s).

Historians have been encouraged to 'approach the subject of military revolution and its increasingly complex ramifications from a synthetic perspective, seeking to cross intellectual fault lines'.[84] The military revolution debate is not necessarily a clash of mutually exclusive theories; all the rival claimants to the military revolution/RMAs mantle together, synthesised, may give us the most accurate representation. Although the editors perceive a period of truly revolutionary change in the early sixteenth century, certainly the development of amphibious warfare, as depicted collectively by our contributors, seems more evolutionary (spread over centuries); and we would agree with Professor Showalter that multi-levelled evolutionary processes were an important part of the great changes in the art and science of war that occurred in early-modern times.[85] But evolutionary processes are often seen as progressive and inevitable and the essays herein do not convey any sense of pre-determinism. The narrative sequences suggest that military conflict is a close run thing and can also lie in the balance. No mono-causal theory is advocated in any

---

[84] Showalter (2003), 10.
[85] Ibid., 9.

of the essays, and no homage is paid to historical inevitability (including the 'rise of the West').

The essays support Jeremy Black's recent emphasis on the diversity of military practice (rather than lumping the multifarious examples within the infamous 'dominant paradigm')[86] and the dangers of pre-determinism in military history (or economic history for that matter). They also, however, provide evidence clearly supporting Geoffrey Parker's view that scientific knowledge and military technology facilitated the 'rise of the West' (albeit by no means making that 'rise' inevitable). Characteristic of their empirical approach to problems, Europeans conceptualised and institutionalised war, including amphibious warfare, over time, and created conditions that were propitious for capitalism, industrialisation and (above all) imperialism.

One aspect of the phenomenon of late medieval and early-modern military change that has not received much attention in the military revolution debate is that phenomenon's relationship to the commercial revolution. Although institutionalization and state-formation are dramatic through the period 1000–1700 (perhaps because of the nature of the records Europeans kept and the ubiquity of politics in European society), commerce seems to have possessed a dynamic of its own. As the examples of the Italian Renaissance city-states and the Portuguese and Dutch empires demonstrate, the strength and utility of the state were proportional to the revenues that could be drawn from the economy as a whole. Power projection, on both land and sea, rests on resources generated by commerce and the means of production.

Finally, it is clear that the ability to marry ground forces with sea- or river- or lake-borne forces afforded great benefits to a state's war-making capability. The ability to wage effective amphibious warfare enabled Portugal, a tiny state, to dominate the entire Indian Ocean; it was essential in the defence of the Spanish empire; it helped Sweden to dominate the Baltic and surpass, for a time, the larger states of Russia, Poland-Lithuania and Brandenburg-Prussia; it was crucial in England's subjugation of Ireland and assimilation of Scotland; it helped the northern provinces of the Netherlands to attain and maintain independence from the Spanish Monarchy; and was an

---

[86] Black (2003), 7–8.

important (and overlooked) factor in the attainment of European primacy (albeit short-lived) by Louis XIV's France. But mastery of amphibious warfare was not a once-and-for-all achievement; for it to confer a lasting advantage on a state, its commanders and statesmen had not only themselves to master the tactical, operational, organisational and logistical complexities of amphibious warfare, but also to develop institutional structures able to transmit amphibious proficiency to succeeding generations—and able, too, to accommodate and integrate technological developments into amphibious praxis. Where such institutions were lacking or lacked flexibility, and/or where, for whatever reasons, rival states or empires developed either an amphibious capability or the ability to use it effectively, then powers that had formerly exploited amphibious warfare to their advantage could find themselves undermined by it—whether in relative terms, as rivals proved better able to exploit opportunities, or in absolute terms, suffering amphibious attacks themselves. In the period covered by this volume this happened to the Ottoman Turks and Portugal; as the eighteenth century dawned it was happening to Spain and Sweden; and in due course it would happen, too, to the Netherlands and France.

If three points above all emerge about amphibious warfare from this volume they are its *utility* for commercial, political (and, in the twenty-first century, humanitarian) power projection, but also its multifaceted *complexity*. These lead to the final point. Amphibious capability can be almost endlessly reconfigured to meet different physical, political and strategical environments—but because mastery has to be relearned by each generation, and adapted to changing technology, organisational culture and strategic exigencies, ongoing comparative historical analysis is essential for the scholar and practitioner alike. The history of amphibious warfare will always repay further study.

Works Cited

Ames G. J. (1997) 'The Straits of Hurmuz Fleets: Omani-Portuguese Naval Rivalry and Encounters, c. 1660–1680', *The Mariner's Mirror* 83 (1997) 389–409.

Anderson J. L. (1983) 'Climatic Change, Sea-Power and Historical Discontinuity: the Spanish Armada and the Glorious Revolution of 1688', *Great Circle* 5 (1983) 13–23.

Anderson M. S. (1988) *War and Society in Europe of the Old Regime* (London: 1988).

Anon. (1597) *The Mutable and wavering estate of France, from the yeare of our Lord 1460, untill the yeare 1595* (London: 1597).

Anon. (1605) 'Considerations upon the likelihoode of the Spaniardes Resoluccon to breake their peace with the state of England on the first advantage or opportunitie meete to be laid hold upon', [1605]. HL, Ellesmere MS 1600.

Aston G. (1920) *Letters on Amphibious Wars* (2nd edn, London: 1920).

Barker T. M. (2000) 'A Debacle of the Peninsular War: The British-Led Amphibious Assault against Fort Fuengirola 14–15 October 1810', *Journal of Military History* 64 (2000) 9–52.

Barnett C. (2000) *Engage the Enemy More Closely: The Royal Navy in the Second World War* (London: 1991; paperback edn, London: 2000).

Bartlett J. (1992) *Bartlett's Familiar Quotations*, gen. ed. J. Kaplan (16th edn; Boston, Toronto and London: 1992).

Bittner D. F. (1991) 'Britannia's Sheathed Sword: The Royal Marines and Amphibious Warfare in the Interwar Years—A Passive Response', *Journal of Military History* 55 (1991) 345–364.

Black J. (2003) 'On Diversity and Military History', in 'Military Revolutions: A Forum', *Historically Speaking* 4:4 (April 2003) 7–9.

Bliss B. (2003) 'The Paulet Affair of 1843: A Turning Point in the Use of Coercive Force in Anglo-Hawaiian Relations during the Years 1825–1854?' (MA diss., King's College London, 2003).

Bonner E. (1996) 'The Recovery of St Andrews Castle in 1547: French Naval Policy and Diplomacy in the British Isles', *English Historical Review* 111 (1996) 578–98.

Boxer C. R. (1965) *The Dutch Seaborne Empire 1600–1800* (London: 1965; 1973).

——. (1991) *The Portuguese Seaborne Empire, 1415–1825* (2nd edn; London: 1991)

Broeze F. (1997) 'Introduction' to Broeze, ed. (1997) 2–16.

Broeze F., ed. (1997) *Gateways of Asia: Port Cities of Asia in the 12th–20th Centuries*, Comparative Asian Studies Series 2 (London & New York: 1997).

Burne A. H. (1939) 'An Amphibious Campaign—North Holland, 1799', *Army Quarterly* 39 (1939–40) no. 1 103–23.

Caldwell D. H. (1991) 'The Battle of Pinkie', in *Scotland and War AD 79–1918*, ed. N. MacDougall (Edinburgh: 1991) 61–94.

Carver M. (1991) 'Montgomery: Field Marshal Viscount Montgomery' in Keegan, ed. (1992) 148–65.

Chapman A. C. (1957) 'Port of Trade Enclaves in Aztec and Maya Civilization,' in *Trade and Market in Early Empires: Economies in History and Theory*, ed. K. Polyani, C. M. Arensberg and H. W. Pearson (Glencoe, Ill.: 1957) 114–53.

Churchyard T. (1579) *A generall rehearsall of warres, called Churchyard's choise* (London: 1579).

Contamine P., ed. (2000) *War and Competition between States* (Oxford: 2000).

Ellis H., ed. (1852) 'Naval Expeditions 1588–1603', *Archæologia* 34 (1852) 296–349.

Fegan T. (1999) '"The Flandric Shore": Cromwellian Dunkirk', *Cromwelliana* (1999) 43–58.

Fissel M. (2001) *English Warfare 1511–1642* (London: 2001).

Gatchel T. L. (1996) *At the Water's Edge: Defending against the Modern Amphibious Assault* (Anapolis, Md.: 1996).

Guilmartin J. F. Jr (1974) *Gunpowder and Galleys: Changing Technology and Mediterranean Warfare at Sea in the Sixteenth Century* (Cambridge: 1974).

Harding R. (1991) *Amphibious Warfare in the Eighteenth Century. The British Expedition to the West Indies 1740–1742*, Royal Historical Society Studies in History 62 (Woodbridge, Suffolk and Rochester, N.Y.: 1991).

——. (2000) 'Learning from the War: The Development of British Amphibious Capability, 1919–29', *The Mariner's Mirror* 86 (2000) 173–85.

Jones H. M. (1942) 'Origins of the Colonial Idea in England', *Proceedings of the American Philosophical Society* 85 (1942) 448–65.

Keegan J., ed. (1992), *Churchill's Generals* (London: 1991; paperback edn, s.l.: 1992).

Keyes R., Lord (1943) *Amphibious Warfare and Combined Operations; The Lees Knowles Lectures, 1943* (2nd edn, Cambridge: 1943).

Le Roy Ladurie E. (1994) *The Royal French State 1400–1600*, trans. J. Vale (Oxford: 1994; orig. *L'État Royal 1460–1610*, Paris: 1987).

Lindegren J. (2000) "Men, Money, and Means", in Contamine, ed. (2000) 129–62.

Lyman R. (2004) *Slim, Master of War* (London: 2004).

Lynn J. (2005) 'Comment', as part of the panel 'Aspects of Amphibious Warfare in the Early Modern World' (Society for Military History Conference, Charleston, S.C., Feb. 2005).

MacGregor, D. (1992) 'The Use, Misuse, and Non-Use of History: The Royal Navy and the Operational Lessons of the First World War', *Journal of Military History* 56 (1992) 603–16.

McKee A. (1964) *Caen: Anvil of Victory* (London: 1964; 1984).

Mackesy P. (1970) 'Regulations in Troopships: Hume Popham and the Russian Expedition of 1799', *The Mariner's Mirror* 56 (1970) 229–30.

Martin C. and Parker G. (1988) *The Spanish Armada* (London: 1988).

Maund L. E. H. (1949) *Assault from the Sea* (London: 1949).

Merglen A. (1968), trans. K. Morgan. *Surprise Warfare: Subversive, Airborne and Amphibious Operations* (London: 1968; published as *La guerre de l'inattendu*, Paris: 1966).

Meyer J. (2000) 'States, Roads, War, and the Organization of Space', in Contamine, ed. (2000) 99–127.

Murray W. and Millett A. R. (2000) *A War to be Won: Fighting the Second World War* (Cambridge, Mass. and London: 2000).

O'Connor R. G. (1974) 'The U.S. Marines in the 20th Century: Amphibious Warfare and Doctrinal Debates', *Military Affairs* 38:3 (Oct. 1974) 97–103.

Orlers J. J. (1610) *Den Nassauschen Lauren-crans: Beschrijvinge ende af-beeldinge van alle de Victorien, so te Water als te Lande, die Godt Almachtich De Edele Hooch-mogende Heeren Staten der Vereenichde Neder-landen verleent heft, Duer het wijs ende clouck belegt des Hooch-ghebooren Fursts Maurits van Nassau, uyt gegeven tot een eewige memorie* (Leyden: 1610).

Parker G. (1988) *The Military Revolution: Military Innovation and the Rise of the West, 1500–1800* (Cambridge: 1988).

Parry V. J. (1958) 'The Ottoman Empire, 1520–66', *New Cambridge Modern History*, 2, *The Reformation 1520–1559*, ed. G. R. Elton (Cambridge: 1958) 510–33.

Ramsay B. (1944) 'Combined Operations' (Lecture, [1944]; CAC, MS RMSY 8/22).

Reid B. H. (1991) 'Alexander: Field Marshal Earl Alexander', in Keegan, ed. (1992) 104–29.

Roy I. (1987) 'The Profession of Arms', in *The Professions in Early Modern England*, ed. W. Prest (London: 1987) 181–219.

Showalter D. (2003) 'Thinking about Military Revolution', in 'Military Revolutions: A Forum', *Historically Speaking* 4:4 (April 2003) 9–10.

Syrett D. (1973) 'The Methodology of British Amphibious Operations during the Seven Years' and American Wars', *The Mariner's Mirror* 58 (1973) 269–80.

Teensma B., ed. (1999) *Dutch-Brazil*, 2, *A Forgotten Letter Written by Martim Correia de Sá, Governor of Rio de Janeiro, 1630* (Rio de Janeiro: 1999).

Trim D. J. B. (1997) 'Early-Modern Colonial Warfare and the Battle of Alcazarquivir, 1578', *Small Wars and Insurgencies* 8:1 (1997) 1–34.

——. (2003) 'Introduction' to *The Chivalric Ethos and the Development of Military Professionalism*, ed. idem, History of Warfare 11 (Leiden: 2003) 1–38.

Van Dyke P. (1997) 'Maritime Rivalry in Early Modern Trade: The Anglo-Dutch Fleet of Defence, 1620–1622' (Paper read at Harris Manchester College, Oxford, June 1997).

Wake C. (1997) 'Banten Around the Turn of the Sixteenth Century: Trade and Society in an Indonesian Port City', in Broeze, ed. (1997) 66–108.

Whitehouse A. (1964) *Amphibious Operations* (2nd edn, London: 1964).

Young P. (1973) *The English Civil War Armies* (London: 1973).

GENERAL INDEX

and economic warfare, 43; Bourbon
dynastic state, 426; bourgeoisie
encroach on princely power, 80;
bureaucratic organisation, 23;
centralisation, 429; early-modern, 13,
23, 90, 435; English, 218, 257;
English state: matures, 255,
establishes itself as a global power,
255, gradually projects its power,
256; fiscal-military states, 137, 311;
finances: 43, 213; finances: of
Elizabethan government, 181;
Swedish-Polish wars, 136; financial
capacities: of southern French ports,
310; financial institutions, 1;
financial power, 2; financial
resources, 2; of Louis XIV, 310;
financing of amphibious warfare, 41;
fiscal: maturity of English state, 255;
fiscal constraints, 223; fiscal policies:
of French government, 278; English
government, 218; infrastructure for
French amphibious operations, 267;
institutional, 435; institutional
structures, 38, 44; in Sumatra, 375;
maturity of English state, 255;
military and naval establishments,
44–5, 316, 322, 396; military
expenditure: by the British, 311;
nation-states, 1–4, 422; Ordnance
establishments, 23; organisational
developments and resources
available, 436; permanent army and
a permanent navy: created by Vasa
monarchy in 1520s, 126; permanent
establishments, 23; Portuguese
monarchy: need for revenue, 425;
Portuguese state, 42; professional
structures, 421; Russian, 129;
standing armies, 38, 263; state
institutions, 449; state policy, 255;
state power, 43; state-building, 6;
the case of Britain, 453; war
finance, 73; war finance: of the
Habsburg monarchy, 181
States of Holland, 81, 86, 87, 89, 90,
91, 92, 94, 434, 436
States-General: Dutch, 334, 335, 410,
425
stratégie de cabinet, 298
strategies, 37; ambiguous, 219;
ambivalent, 218, 257; contradictory,
223; grand, 38, 45. See also
amphibious grand strategy,

blue-water strategy, maritime
strategy, and continental strategy.
strategy, 4, 6, 8, 16, 27–30, 33–4,
36–8, 41, 44–5, 65, 124, 327, 421,
432; against Armada of 1588, 222;
ambivalent, 242, 351, 352;
amphibious, 28, 33, See also
amphibious strategy; and amphibious
warfare, 250, 277; and control
points such as Dover, 396; and
evironment, 454; and fiscal
considerations, 223; and French
weakness, 272; and geography, 264,
412; and infrastructure, 435; and
limitations of firepower, 257; and
location of Kinsale, 331; and Lord
Deputy Wentworth, 245, 247; and
Louis XIV, 310; and Low Countries
waterways, 410; and military
activity, 318; and Ministries of War
and the Navy, 298; and ports, 430;
and Portuguese bases, 109; and
potential of Anglo-Dutch navy, 348;
and Prussian towns, 134; and
riverine control points, 409; and
ship design, 257; and 'small wars',
92; and the application of the
power of the state, 256; and the
Atlantic economy, 43; and the goals
of amphibious operations, 440; and
the Puerto Rico expedition, 201;
and the Sicilian expedition, 269; and
the state, 429; and the Swedish
navy, 133; and the Western Isles,
247; and Ulster geography, 233;
and victory at La Hogue, 340;
and weather forecasting, 450;
Anglo-Dutch, 317; available to
English in 1594, 200; Caribbean,
223; combined fleet in the
Mediterranean, 347; conceived by
Essex, 209; continental. See also
continental strategy; Danish, 142;
defined, 318; divergence of English
aims, 190; Dutch, 89; Elizabethan,
181, 208, 210, 212–13, 219, 224–6;
English, 217–18, 226, 243, 251;
English debate over, 325; English
military, 219; foci of Malta's
defenders, 178; French, 269; French
advantage 1690–1, 336; grand, 29,
30, 33, 35, 37, 439; Habsburg, 162;
holding of river lines, 406; in 1639,
247; in coastal areas, 395; in

INDEX OF PEOPLE AND PLACES

OPERATIONS INDEX